FEDERAL RULES OF EVIDENCE MANUAL

SIXTH EDITION

By

Stephen A. Saltzburg

*Howrey Professor of Trial Advocacy, Litigation
and Professional Responsibility
George Washington University
National Law Center*

Michael M. Martin

*Professor of Law
Fordham University
School of Law*

Daniel J. Capra

*Professor of Law
Fordham University
School of Law*

**A Complete Guide to the
Federal Rules of Evidence**

Volume One

THE MICHIE COMPANY
Law Publishers
CHARLOTTESVILLE, VIRGINIA

SUMMARY TABLE OF CONTENTS

VOLUME ONE

VOLUME TWO

Article V. Privileges

Article VI. Witnesses

Article VII. Opinions and Expert Testimony

VOLUME THREE

Article VIII. Hearsay

Article IX. Authentication and Identification

Article X. Contents of Writings, Recordings, and Photographs

Article XI. Miscellaneous Rules

PART THREE

RULES APPROVED BY SUPREME COURT BUT REJECTED BY CONGRESS

TABLE OF CONTENTS

Article II. Judicial Notice

Article III. Presumptions in Civil
Actions and Proceedings

Article IV. Relevancy and Its Limits

AN INTRODUCTION TO ORGANIZATION:
HOW TO USE THE BOOK

In an effort to provide all the information concerning the Federal Rules of Evidence in the simplest and clearest way, we have divided this edition into three parts. It is our hope that each Part will add a dimension to the understanding of the reader.

Part One traces the history of the movement to codify rules of evidence generally before focusing on the particular events that gave rise to the specific Federal Rules of Evidence that are the subject of this enquiry. Although this history may not aid in the understanding of each individual Rule, those who have not followed the debate over the utility of codification and over what to codify may find this brief background to be of general interest. Some insight into the creation of Rules may also help in interpreting several of them.

Part Two is the heart of the book. Each Rule is individually analyzed. The analysis takes the following illustrative form.

RULE 1. A RULE OF EVIDENCE

A. *Official Text of the Rule.*

The exact text of the particular Rule signed into law by President Ford on January 2, 1975, as part of Public Law 93-595, 88 Stat. 1926 et seq., and subsequent additions, all as amended to date, begin the analysis.

B. *Editorial Explanatory Comment.*

Following the official text of each Rule is a concise explanation of the Rule, the way it operates, and a discussion of important questions that have arisen under the Rule. When problems with a Rule are apparent, we attempt to highlight some of the difficulties that Bench and Bar have experienced and to anticipate some developing problems. No contention is made here that all potential problems are exhaustively covered. Such a task would be impossible. Where, however, a problem is both obvious and significant, we believe it is important to attempt to solve it. Our answers are concededly debatable. At times we have no ready answer. Still, we attempt to pose the important questions and to suggest possible solutions that Judges and lawyers may want to consider.

C. *Annotated Cases.*

Important Federal cases construing the Rule are either cited or discussed. At times we repeat our discussion of a case under several Rules for the convenience of the reader.

Despite the fact that we have included numerous cases, we have not offered a mechanical compendium of all decided cases. Rather, we have screened every decided case, assessed its importance, and summarized the important ones in this Manual. The cases are arranged first by topic. The topics represent various sections of the Rule or classes of cases decided under it. Within these topics the cases are arranged by circuit. See, e.g., Rule 103. We hope this organization will maximize the usefulness of the Manual.

D. *Legislative History.*
Relevant portions of legislative history are provided. These include:

Advisory Committee's Note.
Set forth in this section is the Advisory Committee's Note accompanying each Rule approved by the Supreme Court on November 20, 1972 (with the exception, in most instances, of Rules deleted by Congress). Even though many of these Rules were modified by the Congress and differ in form in the official text contained in Section A, the Note is still important. It contains a wealth of authority to which Judges and lawyers may wish to refer to understand the Rule or to do further research about the Rule or general area of the law with which they are concerned. Moreover, it is the beginning of a "legislative" history that is important in understanding how the final draft came into being. If a Rule has been amended, subsequent Advisory Committee's Notes have been included also. In the end, however, it must be remembered that where the words of the Rule are clear, the "plain meaning" of the Rule will control over any contrary indication in the Advisory Committee Note.

House Subcommittee on Criminal Justice Notes.
The first Congressional body to examine the draft of the Rules approved by the Supreme Court was the House Subcommittee on Criminal Justice, a subcommittee of the House Committee on the Judiciary. This Subcommittee made important changes in the Rules, and we include, where pertinent, the Subcommittee Notes explaining why the changes were made. It should be noted that the Subcommittee developed one draft of the Rules and tentatively approved it on June 28, 1973. After receiving comments and criticisms, the Subcommittee amended its draft on October 10, 1973, and sent its proposed final draft to the full House Judiciary Committee. This section of the book contains the Subcommittee Notes in the later draft, i.e., the October 10, 1973 draft. However, whenever the Subcommittee made a major change between the first and second drafts, the Notes explaining both drafts are included. Whenever only one Note appears, the reader can safely assume that it is from the October 10, 1973 draft, and that this Note is not appreciably different from the one found in the earlier draft. We have used the word "Notes" in our heading as a reminder that there are two separate sets of Notes, even though most often it is only necessary to present the later Note.

Report of the House Committee on the Judiciary.

Some of the changes recommended by the House Subcommittee on Criminal Justice were accepted by the full Committee on the Judiciary, while others were rejected. H.R. 5463, a bill sent to the floor of the House by the full Committee, was subjected to only a few amendments on the House floor. The bill is an important step in the legislative history of the Federal Rules of Evidence. Report No. 93-650 accompanied the bill. Whenever the Report makes reference to any significant change in the Rules drafted by the Advisory Committee, that portion of the report is included in this section. Although we have not included every single reference in the Report, it is our hope that we erred on the side of including anything that anyone might find to be relevant in understanding a particular Rule. The separate views of the members of Congress found in the Report are also included in this section. The House bill was approved with several amendments by the House of Representatives on February 6, 1974. House Reports relating to later amendments are specially noted.

Report of the Senate Committee on the Judiciary.

The Senate Committee recommended several major changes in H.R. 5463. These changes are discussed in Report No. 93-1277. Following the same procedure outlined in the previous section, whenever the Senate Report makes reference to a change in the House draft, or to its interpretation of a Rule, we have attempted to include it in this section. Once again we have left out references that do not provide any insight into why a change was made or into the intent of the Congress in choosing certain language, but we have attempted to include all relevant material. The Senate passed its version of the bill on November 22, 1974. Senate Reports relating to later amendments are specially noted.

Report of the House and Senate Conferees.

This Report (House No. 93-1597) accompanied the bill actually approved by both Houses of Congress.

Citations to Hearings and Debates.

Several days of hearings on the proposed Rules of Evidence were held before the Subcommittee on Criminal Justice. In addition to the testimony of numerous witnesses, the Subcommittee had before it many documents and letters submitted in opposition to or in support of the proposed Rules. Hearings were also held before the Senate Committee on the Judiciary.

Whenever material found in the Hearings is helpful in understanding the way in which a Rule developed, we have endeavored to include a citation to it. Similarly, whenever the debate on the floor of either the House or Senate on the Rules casts light on particular provisions, we have included a reference to the debate. It is our hope that this information may provide some guidance, especially to Judges, when a difficult problem of interpreting a particular Rule is encountered.

In Part Three of this Book, we include those Rules originally proposed by the Advisory Committee that were rejected by Congress. The Advisory Committee's Notes to these Rules have also been included.

PART ONE

Background of Codification Generally
and the Federal Rules Specifically

1. *The Push to Codify*

The background of the codification movement in the United States is a curious one; there appears to have been and still to be a fairly constant demand among some lawyers for evidentiary codes. But, until relatively recently, it was exceedingly difficult to build up sufficient momentum to enact codes into law. "Ambivalent" is probably the best word to describe the longtime attitude of many lawyers towards legislation in the evidentiary domain.

There is apparently some appreciation of the benefits of uniformity and ease of ascertainment of the rules when a statute is enacted. At the same time, there is some fear that legislation produces wooden rules, and some concern that case-by-case adjudication is a superior means of doing justice. Lurking in the background also is a sense, for most lawyers, that some evidentiary rules are of questionable value and that some may even approach the realm of the absurd. But the problem has been to find the appropriate means to change the rules without impairing the functioning of those that are justifiable and that are working well.

Legislation, at first glance, offers a nice clean solution. One swing of the legislative (or rulemaking) axe and the umbilical cord tying present to past is cut, and legislation emerges that solves the problems of the past and serves the needs of the future. But when it is remembered that not all lawyers agree on which are silly rules and which are wise, that too radical a departure from tradition makes it difficult to enact legislation, that the problem of too much rigidity is a real one, and that there are many possible solutions, not simply one, the difficulties of enacting legislation become readily apparent.

Common-law courts, on the other hand, can examine the facts of particular cases and seek to mold rules to fit those facts. They are also somewhat free to modify past rules to meet present needs. However, the mere mention of the term *stare decisis* should serve to explain one of the "problems" of common-law courts, i.e., precedent is important and resistant to change. Moreover, while molding rules to fit particular facts may do justice in individual cases, it makes practicing law much more difficult because the lawyer has difficulty predicting precisely what a Court will say about the rules of evidence in any given case. Finally, there is the feeling on the part of many Judges that once a rule has stood over time, even if it is of questionable value, legislative intervention is a more appropriate response than judicial overruling.

More could be said on the relative advantages and disadvantages of legislation and adjudication. It is sufficient for the purposes of this brief background, however, to note that the demand for codification has never come unanimously from the lips of the members of the bar. Codification has had its opponents as well as its adherents. It is, in fact, difficult to review the history of the last fifty years and to derive any firm conclusion as to whether feelings about codification of evidentiary rules differ greatly from the feelings of most lawyers about the relative merits of legislation versus adjudication generally.

2. *The Path to the Supreme Court*

Not surprisingly, much of the impetus toward legislation arose from enactment of the Federal Rules of Civil Procedure in the late 1930s. When the original Advisory Committee on Civil Rules issued its report in 1937, it suggested that evidentiary rules be largely excluded, since at that time there was no ready reference for codification and there was apparently insufficient time for the task. It is also likely that inclusion of evidentiary rules with the Rules of Civil Procedure would have provoked much of the same controversy that surrounded the 1970s attempt at codification and thus would have diverted attention from the much needed Rules of Civil Procedure. The Chairman of the Advisory Committee, Attorney-General William D. Mitchell, said:

> There was tremendous pressure brought on the advisory committee by those familiar with the subject of evidence insisting that there was a need for reform which we did not meet, and some advisory committee should tackle the task of revising the rules of evidence and composing them into a new set of rules to be promulgated by the Supreme Court.

In 1939, the American Law Institute turned to the subject of evidence, and with Professor Edmund Morgan of Harvard as its Reporter, promulgated the Model Code of Evidence in 1942. Despite the "tremendous pressure" of which the Advisory Committee Chairman had spoken, no jurisdiction ever adopted the Model Code of Evidence.

While unadopted, the Model Code was not entirely disregarded. In 1943, the American Bar Association took action. Its House of Delegates directed a study of uniform evidentiary rules and, the following year, specifically provided that the Model Code should serve as the basis of the study.

In the interim, the Advisory Committee had an opportunity once again to consider whether it should undertake to compile rules of evidence. It concluded: "While consideration of a comprehensive and detailed set of rules of evidence seems very desirable, it has not been feasible for the Committee so far to undertake this important task."

Since the American Bar Association recognized that the Model Code as drafted would not receive support from the various states, it enlisted the National Conference of Commissioners on Uniform State Laws in a program of revision in the hope that acceptable rules could be promulgated.

The actual drafting by the Commissioners began in 1950 and culminated in the Uniform Rules of Evidence, in 1953. Only a handful of jurisdictions (e.g., California, Kansas, New Jersey, Utah, and the Virgin Islands) have adopted comprehensive evidence codes based upon the Uniform Rules. Like the Model Code, the Uniform Rules were not the stimulus to reform that some had hoped they would be. In 1958, the House of Delegates of the American Bar Association urged the Judicial Conference of the United States to appoint a special committee to adapt the Uniform Rules for use in Federal

Courts in order to clarify and to improve the evidentiary rules and to provide a means of uniformity and conformity.

In March 1961, in special session, the Judicial Conference of the United States approved a proposal of the Standing Committee on Rules of Practice and Procedure that called for a project devoted to Federal Rules of Evidence. The Chief Justice implemented the proposal by naming a Special Committee under the chairmanship of the distinguished Yale Professor James William Moore. The Committee's mandate was to inquire into the feasibility and advisability of Federal Rules of Evidence. During 1961, its report (A Preliminary Report on the Advisability and Feasibility of Developing Uniform Rules of Evidence for the United States District Courts) was written. This report concluded that uniform Rules of Evidence were both advisable and feasible. On February 12, 1962, the report was circulated to members of the bar and to Judges. After considering their comments, the Standing Committee and the Judicial Conference confirmed the recommendation of the Special Committee. On March 8, 1965, Chief Justice Warren appointed an Advisory Committee on Rules of Evidence.

The Advisory Committee transmitted to the Standing Committee a "Preliminary Draft of Proposed Rules of Evidence for the United States District Courts and Magistrates" on January 30, 1969. On March 31, 1969, the Standing Committee circulated the preliminary draft to the Bar and Bench for consideration. It was not until October 1970 that the Standing Committee presented to the Judicial Conference its revised draft of evidentiary rules, which substantially modified the preliminary draft. The revised draft was approved by the Judicial Conference and referred to the Supreme Court. The Court concluded that the revised draft should be submitted for comments to lawyers and Judges in the same manner as the preliminary draft. This was done in March 1971.

Many comments and criticisms were made with respect to both drafts, and revisions were made in the revised draft, just as they had been made in the previous draft. After the Advisory Committee had reworked its product, it submitted it to the Standing Committee, which made some revisions before approving the draft and submitting it to the Judicial Conference. The Judicial Conference also approved the draft and then forwarded it to the Supreme Court in October 1971. Although the Court did not promulgate this revision of the revised draft, it did receive further comments and suggestions, including some from the Department of Justice. Upon receipt of these comments, the Court requested the Advisory Committee and the Standing Committee to evaluate them. Early in 1972, the Advisory Committee and the Standing Committee met again and made further modifications. This procedure, which did not allow for public comment on the final draft, was severely criticized. See, e.g., Testimony of George Halpern and George Frampton, Hearings on Proposed Rules of Evidence Before the Subcommittee on Criminal Justice of the House Committee on the Judiciary, 93rd Congress, First Session, at 158-92 (1973). In any event, on November 20, 1972, the Supreme Court approved a final draft.

3. *The Legislative Response*

Had the same procedure that was used in adopting the Federal Rules of Civil Procedure and the Federal Rules of Criminal Procedure been used with respect to the evidentiary Rules (a procedure that would also have applied absent any contrary Congressional action), the Supreme Court draft would have become effective automatically after the passage of ninety days. It would have taken objections by both Houses of Congress to stop the Rules. Because Congress recognized the importance of the evidentiary Rules and because the label "substantive" was persistently applied to several of the Rules, Congress enacted in early 1973 Public Law 93-12, which provided that the Rules should not be effective until expressly approved by the Congress.

Two days after receiving the proposed Rules from Chief Justice Burger on February 5, 1973, the Subcommittee on Criminal Justice of the Committee on the Judiciary of the House of Representatives (formerly designated as Special Subcommittee on Reform of Federal Criminal Laws) opened hearings on the desirability of the uniform code of evidence and the merits of the Rules approved by the Supreme Court. After six days of hearings, and receipt of numerous written communications, the Subcommittee circulated a draft on June 28, 1973. Following extensive comments from the public, the Subcommittee revised its draft and on October 10, 1973, reported its revised draft to the full Judiciary Committee. On October 16 and 18, and on November 6, 1973, the full Committee debated the bill and amended it in several respects before reporting it to the full House. Several additional amendments were made by the full House before the Rules were passed on February 6, 1974. A Senate version of the Rules was passed on November 22, 1974, following hearings on July 4 and 5, 1974, before the full Senate Committee on the Judiciary. As a result of compromises by House and Senate conferees, the final bill was approved by the House on December 16, and by the Senate on December 18. It was sent to President Ford, who approved it on January 2, 1975, whereupon it became Public Law 93-595, 88 Stat. 1926 et seq.

4. *The Future of the Rules*

After almost twenty years under the Rules, it is fair to state that the goals of codification — increased certainty as to what the rules are, predictability, efficiency, and uniformity of result — have been met in part, but not completely. There is still some disuniformity and unpredictability. Part of the reason for disparate results is that several of the most important Rules (such as Rule 403 and the residual exceptions to the hearsay rule) call for an ad hoc judgment on the part of the Trial Judge that will necessarily vary from case to case. As to other Rules, the disuniformity is largely due to vague or misguided statutory language. See Becker & Orenstein, *The Federal Rules of Evidence After Sixteen Years — The Effect of "Plain Meaning" Jurisprudence, the Need for an Advisory Committee on the Rules of Evidence, and Suggestions for Selective Revision of the Rules,* 60 GEO. WASH. L. REV. 857 (1992) (presenting a catalog and summary of some problems that have arisen under the Rules, including "circuit splits, gaps and inconsistencies in the Rules, debates over fundamental policy, and innovative suggestions").

There is no question that some of the Rules are poorly drafted, and this has often led the Courts to reach results which they believe to be correct and just, even though such results are not mandated (and are even arguably prohibited) by the Rule. See Jonakait, *The Supreme Court, Plain Meaning, and the Changed Rules of Evidence,* 66 TEX. L.

REV. 745 (1990) (noting the reluctance on the part of many Courts to apply certain Federal Rules as they are written when to do so would lead to an unfair result).

Finally, some commentators have complained that under the Rules, Judges have lost the common-law power to promulgate new exclusionary rules of evidence, and that Judges are forced to admit evidence in certain circumstances even where they have legitimate doubts about its reliability or where exclusion would serve public policy. See Imwinkelreid, *The Meaning of Probative Value and Prejudice in Federal Rule of Evidence 403: Can Rule 403 Be Used to Resurrect the Common Law of Evidence?*, 41 VAND. L. REV. 879 (1988).

Still, on balance, the Federal Rules of Evidence have been a success. See Becker and Orenstein, *supra,* at 858 ("By most accounts, the Rules have been a great success."). Litigators and Judges undoubtedly have found it easier to master the Rules than a morass of common-law precedent; and many of the Rules have been uncontroversial and have led to uniform and just results in the Federal Courts.

One important question that has arisen is whether the codification of rules of evidence has totally supplanted the common-law previously developed in the Federal Courts. The Supreme Court has visited this question on three occasions, and a unifying principle can be derived from these cases. In *United States v. Abel,* 469 U.S. 45 (1984), the Court quoted with approval the statement that as a matter of principle, "under the Federal Rules no common law of evidence remains." Yet the Court in *Abel* analyzed and applied the evidentiary doctrine of impeachment for bias, even though there is nothing specifically concerning impeachment for bias in the Federal Rules. Given the widespread use of impeachment for bias at the time the Federal Rules were being drafted and adopted, the *Abel* Court found it unlikely that the drafters "intended to scuttle entirely the evidentiary availability of cross-examination for bias."

This would suggest that widespread common-law practice would still be relevant in the absence of a Federal Rule. When there is an explicit Federal Rule, however, a practice that was widespread under the common law will nonetheless be supplanted by the Rules. Thus, in *Bourjaily v. United States,* 483 U.S. 171 (1987), the Court rejected the common-law practice which required the prosecution to establish independent evidence of conspiracy by a preponderance of the evidence before a coconspirator's hearsay statement could be admitted. The *Bourjaily* Court found no support for this practice in the language of the Federal Rules, and stated that under the explicit terms of Rule 104, the coconspirator's hearsay statement itself could be used by the Judge in determining whether a conspiracy existed. Most recently, in *Daubert v. Merrell Dow Pharmaceuticals,* 113 S. Ct. 2786 (1993), the Court rejected the well-known common law *Frye* test for assessing scientific expert testimony, holding that it was superseded by Federal Rule 702.[1] The Court explained that common-law principles could serve as an "aid" to the application of the Federal Rules, but that they are superseded insofar as they are inconsistent with "a specific Rule that speaks to the contested issue."

The distinction, therefore, is between common law that is supplemental to and consistent with the Federal Rules, and common law that is inconsistent with a specific

---

1. See the Editorial Explanatory Comment to Rule 702 for a discussion of the difference between *Frye* and the reliability standard mandated by Rule 702 after *Daubert.*

Rule. Thus, the common law as to bias was not in conflict with any Federal Rule in *Abel* — in fact, it was consistent with the general principles of relevance and prejudice set forth in Rule 403 — whereas the common law was found to be in conflict with a specific Rule in both *Bourjaily* and *Daubert*. Of course, the determination of whether a particular Rule is specific enough to supersede common law is not self-evident. Legitimate arguments were raised in both *Bourjaily* and *Daubert* that the Federal Rules at issue therein were not necessarily in conflict with accepted common-law principles.

Finally, it must be remembered that, in one area at least, a common-law approach is mandated by the Federal Rule itself. Federal Rule 501 provides that the law of privileges in the Federal Courts shall be determined by principles of Federal common law, as developed in light of "reason and experience."

5. *Amendments to the Rules*

From time to time, certain Rules have been amended, some of the amendments originating in Congress and some generated by the Judicial Conference. The amendments have generally fallen into three categories: (1) technical amendments, such as those designed to make the Rules gender-neutral; (2) amendments responding to particular developments, such as the amendment to Rule 704(b), which resulted from Congress' dissatisfaction with proof of the insanity defense in the trial of John Hinckley; and (3) amendments that have sought to clarify problematic language, such as the amendment to Rule 609, concerning impeachment of witnesses with prior convictions — which, as originally written, created anomalous results when used in a civil trial.

The original Advisory Committee on the Federal Rules of Evidence was dissolved shortly after the Rules were enacted. For many years thereafter, there was no advisory committee specifically and exclusively assigned to the Federal Rules of Evidence; amendments were few and far between, especially compared with the amendments promulgated to the Federal Rules of Civil Procedure over the corresponding time period. See Becker & Orenstein, *The Federal Rules of Evidence After Sixteen Years — The Effect of "Plain Meaning" Jurisprudence, the Need for an Advisory Committee on the Rules of Evidence, and Suggestions for Selective Revision of the Rules,* 60 GEO. WASH. L. REV. 857 (1992) (noting six substantive amendments to the Federal Rules of Evidence during the first seventeen years — three initiated by Congress — compared with over one hundred substantive amendments to the Federal Rules of Civil Procedure during that time period).

In 1993, the Judicial Conference, responding to calls from Judges, scholars and practitioners, appointed a new Advisory Committee on the Federal Rules of Evidence. This committee meets regularly to consider proposed changes in the Rules, and it is possible that the pace of amendments to the Rules will pick up in the near future.

The presence of an advisory committee has not deterred Congress from promulgating amendments of it own. Thus, in the Violent Crime Control and Enforcement Act of 1994, Congress promulgated new Rules 413-415, without input from the Advisory Committee. The new Rules do, however, give the Judicial Conference 150 days to make recommendations; they are subject to reconsideration by Congress if the recommendations are negative.

PART TWO

The Rules Themselves

PREAMBLE

A. OFFICIAL TEXT

AN ACT

To Establish Rules of Evidence for Certain Courts and Proceedings.

Be it enacted by the Senate and House of Representatives of the United States of America in Congress assembled, That the following rules shall take effect on the one hundred and eightieth day beginning after the date of the enactment of this Act. These rules apply to actions, cases, and proceedings brought after the rules take effect. These rules also apply to further procedure in actions, cases, and proceedings then pending, except to the extent that application of the rules would not be feasible, or would work injustice, in which event former evidentiary principles apply.

B. EDITORIAL EXPLANATORY COMMENT

The preamble to the Act is straightforward. It provides that the Rules were to take effect on the one hundred and eightieth day after their enactment (i.e., July 1, 1975). Thus, any action brought after the date the Rules became effective is governed by them. With respect to actions tried between the date of enactment and the one hundred and eightieth day thereafter, the Rules did not apply, irrespective of when the action was filed. As for actions brought before or during the one-hundred-eighty-day-period and pending when the Rules actually took effect, the Rules applied unless the court found that it would be unfair for them to be so applied.

The preamble was important in the early years after the Rules took effect. Its importance declined, however, as cases filed before the Rules took effect were decided.

ARTICLE I. GENERAL PROVISIONS

RULE 101

A. OFFICIAL TEXT

Rule 101. Scope

These rules govern proceedings in the courts of the United States and before United States bankruptcy judges and United States magistrate judges, to the extent and with the exceptions stated in rule 1101.

B. EDITORIAL EXPLANATORY COMMENT

This Rule simply states that the Rules of Evidence are generally applicable in the Federal Courts whether a case is before a Judge, a Bankruptcy Judge, or a Magistrate Judge. Express reference is made, however, to Rule 1101, which more specifically identifies the proceedings in which the Rules are applicable and those in which they are not. Thus, the Rules are applicable in all civil and criminal cases and generally in cases in which Courts review agency actions *de novo*. They are also applicable in bankruptcy cases. They are inapplicable: (1) when a Judge is deciding a preliminary question of fact — preliminary, that is, to a decision on whether or not to admit evidence; (2) in grand jury proceedings and in preliminary examinations (such as suppression hearings) in criminal cases; (3) in probation and sentencing proceedings; (4) when a warrant is sought; (5) in bail proceedings; and (6) in any other proceedings in which Congress has explicitly stated that the Federal Rules are inapplicable — for example, Congress has provided that in pretrial hearings concerning criminal forfeiture of assets, the District Court "may receive and consider ... evidence and information that would be inadmissible under the Federal Rules of Evidence.'' 21 U.S.C. § 853(e)(3) (1988). See *United States v. Monsanto,* discussed in the annotations to this Rule.

It is not clear from the face of the Rules whether a Special Master appointed pursuant to Federal Rule of Civil Procedure 53 is limited to the Federal Rules in deciding evidentiary matters. The Rules could be read either way. At times, Rule 1101 appears to set forth a presumption that the Rules are applicable at all stages in all proceedings unless an exception applies. But beginning with part (d) of the Rule, the opposite reading might apply. It could also be argued that part (b) disposes of the matter and requires a Special Master to utilize the evidentiary rules, but part (b) may be confined to Judges. The matter is specifically addressed in Federal Rule of Civil Procedure 53, as amended by the Supreme Court in 1983. Subdivision (c) of the Rule reads in relevant part as follows:[1]

> Subject to the specifications and limitations stated in the order [of reference], the master has and shall exercise the power to regulate all proceedings in every hearing before the master and to do all acts and take all measures necessary or proper for the efficient performance of the master's duties under the order. The master may require the production before the master of evidence upon all matters embraced in the reference, including the production of all books, papers, vouchers, documents and writings applicable thereto. The master may rule upon the admissibility of evidence unless otherwise directed by the order of reference and has the authority to put witnesses on oath and may examine them and may call the parties to the action and examine them upon oath. When a party so requests, the master shall make a record of the evidence offered and excluded in the same manner and subject to the same limitations as provided in the Federal Rules of Evidence for a court sitting without a jury.

Enactment of Public Law 94-577 on October 21, 1976, to amend 28 U.S.C. § 636(b), and enactment of Public Law 96-82, October 10, 1979, to amend 28 U.S.C. § 636(c), means that Magistrate Judges now may perform more functions than in previous years. For example, Magistrate Judges may conduct evidentiary hearings, propose findings of fact for ultimate review by Federal Judges and, with the parties' consent, try all civil and misdemeanor criminal cases. The amended statute provides that a ''judge may designate a Magistrate Judge to serve as a special master,'' in which case Federal Rule of Civil Procedure 53 would be applicable.

Rule 101 is essentially a reference point to the more precise delineation of applicability of the Rules set forth in Rule 1101. For a more detailed exploration on the Rules' applicability, see the Editorial Explanatory Comment to Rule 1101, which covers, among other things, evidence rules in Tax Court and other specialized Courts, sentencing proceedings under the Federal Sentencing Guidelines, and the use of the Rules by Administrative Judges.

---

1. The quoted text reflects gender-neutralizing amendments in 1987.

C. ANNOTATED CASES

Daigle v. Maine Med. Center, Inc., 14 F.3d 684 (1st Cir. 1994): The Trial Court in a diversity medical malpractice action ordered that the plaintiff present her case to a prelitigation screening panel as required by state law, and when the panel unanimously found no acts of negligence, followed the state law by admitting the findings into evidence without providing an opportunity for impeachment. Affirming a judgment for the defendant, the Court held that the federal evidence rules governing hearsay and impeachment do not seek to displace the state's substantive policy implemented by the screening panel procedure.

United States v. Monsanto, 924 F.2d 1186 (2d Cir.) (en banc), *cert. denied,* 112 S. Ct. 382 (1991): In holding that continuation of an *ex parte* restraint of assets subject to forfeiture in the event of conviction requires a postrestraint, pretrial adversary hearing as to probable cause that the defendant committed the crimes providing a basis for forfeiture, the Court held that the Federal Rules of Evidence do not apply in the hearing.

United States v. Chase, 18 F.3d 1166 (4th Cir. 1994): The Court reversed a murder conviction, concluding that the rule that a defendant cannot be convicted of murder if the victim's death occurred more than a year and a day after the defendant's attack was a substantive rule unchanged by adoption of the Evidence Rules.

In re Oil Spill by Amoco Cadiz, 954 F.2d 1279 (7th Cir. 1992): In a nonjury damages trial arising from an oil spill in the English Channel, the Trial Court admitted considerable evidence it characterized as hearsay, thinking it would be too cumbersome to apply the rule. The Court noted that the hearsay rule applies in all trials — jury and bench, big and small — but after considering available exceptions, found no reason to upset the damages award on evidentiary grounds.

D. LEGISLATIVE HISTORY

Advisory Committee's Note

Rule 1101 specifies in detail the courts, proceedings, questions, and stages of proceedings to which the rules apply in whole or in part.

October 1987 Amendment

The entire Advisory Committee Note accompanying the amendment that became effective October 1, 1987, is as follows: "United States bankruptcy judges are added to conform this rule with Rule 1101(b) and Bankruptcy Rule 9017."

November 1988 Amendment

[Following the 1987 amendment to Rule 101, the Supreme Court sent to Congress a technical amendment correcting capitalization, effective November 1, 1988.]

December 1993 Amendment

On December 1, 1993, Rule 101 was amended to refer to "magistrate judges" as opposed to "magistrates." The Committee note to the revision states: "This revision is made to conform the rule to changes made by the Judicial Improvements Act of 1990."

RULE 102

A. OFFICIAL TEXT

Rule 102. Purpose and Construction

These rules shall be construed to secure fairness in administration, elimination of unjustifiable expense and delay, and promotion of growth and development of the law of evidence to the end that the truth may be ascertained and proceedings justly determined.

B. EDITORIAL EXPLANATORY COMMENT

The goals

This provision sets forth the goals of the Rules, which are to provide speedy, inexpensive, and fair trials designed to reach the truth. Although the Rule states that the Federal Rules should be construed to promote "growth and development of the law of evidence," Congress has perhaps made it more difficult than ever before for the law of evidence to grow, since changes in these Rules ordinarily cannot come by adjudication, but must come by amendments of the Rules. Enacted together with the Rules was 28 U.S.C. § 2076, which, as the Editorial Explanatory Comment accompanying Rule 1102 discusses in detail, changes the working relationship between the Supreme Court and the Congress with respect to Rules of Evidence. This obviously makes it more difficult for the Supreme Court to speed an amendment past the Congress. Congress thus may have impeded the growth and development of the law of evidence. While such an impediment may exist for good reason, its existence should nevertheless be noted.

Presumption of admissibility?

When Rule 102 states that the Federal Rule shall be construed so that the truth may be ascertained and proceedings justly determined, does this signify that the Judge who is doubtful of whether to admit or exclude evidence should always err on the side of admission in order to aid the search for truth?

The answer must be NO for several reasons. First, the Fourth Article of the Federal Rules makes it clear that certain evidence must be excluded even though it is relevant, because it is too prejudicial or possibly too confusing. In such instances, the search for truth would not be aided by admitting the evidence. When Trial Judges have doubts about the admissibility of evidence, they must always remember to balance the possible prejudicial effect of the evidence against its probative value. Only then can they be sure to assist the search for truth. Second, the Rules also recognize that there are other policies served by rules of evidence aside from reaching accurate decisions as to what happened in a particular case. In dealing with offers to compromise, evidence of insurance, subsequent remedial measures, and privileges, for example, the Trial Judge must consider factors other than accurate reconstruction of historical facts. Finally, Rule 102 itself notes that the Rules must be construed to eliminate unjustifiable expense and delay. In short, there are other factors to be weighed against the probative value of evidence.

Professor (now Judge) Posner has suggested that the basic goals of a judicial system are ascertaining the truth (i.e., determining historical facts accurately), but keeping the costs of litigation as low as is reasonably feasible. See generally *An Economic Approach to Legal Procedure and Judicial Administration*, 2 J. Legal Stud. 399 (1973). Other goals may also be established: protecting the sanctity of the individual (e.g., the Fifth Amendment); providing disincentives for governmental abuses (e.g., Fourth Amendment exclusionary rule); promoting safety (Federal Rule of Evidence 407); and encouraging other socially useful activity, such as payment of medical expenses (Federal Rule 409), or settlement of claims (Federal Rule 408). It should also be noted that the principle of ascertaining truth necessarily mandates certain rules of exclusion as well as rules of inclusion. Thus, a system concerned with the search for truth must protect against the possibility of biased and unbalanced decisionmaking (Federal Rule 403); and it must ensure that the evidence considered by the factfinder meets at least some minimal standard of reliability (Federal Rules 702-703 and 801-805). Judges are often called upon to balance the impact of a decision on "the search for truth," the burdens on the competing litigants, and the promotion of highly regarded social values. Ensuring that "proceedings [are] justly determined" as this Rule states is by no means a simple task.

Relationship to specific rules

Rule 102 gives the Trial Judge authority to fashion evidentiary procedures to deal with situations not specifically covered by the Rules.[1] In a few instances, however, Federal Courts, both Trial and Appellate, have used Rule 102 to disregard more specific Rules.[2] Rule 102 is not an invitation to Judges to treat other specific Rules as if they were nonexistent. As Rule 102 is used, it is important for Courts to differentiate when Congress has spoken and finally determined an issue and when Congress has left room

---

1. See, e.g., United States v. Bibbs, 564 F.2d 1165 (5th Cir. 1977), *cert. denied,* 435 U.S. 1007 (1978) (evidentiary procedure fashioned to deal with inconsistent statements); Benna v. Reeder Flying Serv., 578 F.2d 269 (9th Cir. 1978) (permitting defendant to offer surrebuttal evidence). See also United States v. Pantone, 609 F.2d 675 (3d Cir. 1979) (barring the government from opening the door to collateral matters).

2. See, e.g., United States v. American Cyanamid Co., 427 F. Supp. 859 (S.D.N.Y. 1977) (letter admitted over hearsay objection under Rules 803(24) and 102 on basis of need to do justice and elimination of expense and delay); United States v. Batts, 558 F.2d 513 (9th Cir.), *opinion withdrawn,* 573 F.2d 599 (1977), *cert. denied,* 439 U.S. 859 (1978) (balancing test read into "no extrinsic evidence" rule found in Rule 608 on basis of Rule 102; admission of rebuttal evidence held subject to sound discretion of Trial Court). See also McConnell v. Nooner, 547 F.2d 54 (8th Cir. 1976) (citing Rule 102, the Court held it proper for the Trial Judge to prohibit cross-examination as to a witness' prior conviction, where the Judge found that the witness had been rehabilitated, even though the witness had not received a formal pardon, annulment, or certificate of rehabilitation as required by Rule 609(c)).

for judicial interpretation.[3] Drawing lines between permissible and impermissible constructions of rules requires an understanding of congressional intent and a fair reading of statutory language. Of course, even where the intent of Congress might point in one direction for the general run of cases, the fact that Congress chose to avoid most constitutional decisions in drafting the Rules signifies that Judges must have some freedom to interpret rules to avoid constitutional difficulties in particular cases. Our general view is that Rule 102 is not a basis in any case for disregarding a more specific Rule. Otherwise, the entire notion of a uniform set of federal evidence rules is threatened.

Plain meaning

Rule 102 establishes a principle of flexibility in the application of the Federal Rules of Evidence. But the Supreme Court has made it clear that judicial flexibility has no place when the "plain meaning" of a Federal Rule of Evidence mandates a certain result. The two most recent examples of the Supreme Court's plain meaning approach are *United States v. Salerno,* 112 S. Ct. 2503 (1992), and *Daubert v. Merrell Dow Pharmaceuticals Corp.,* 113 S. Ct. 2786 (1993).

In *Salerno,* the prosecution immunized grand jury witnesses, who then unexpectedly gave testimony that was exculpatory to the defendants. The Court held that this grand jury testimony could not be admitted against the government at trial under Rule 804(b)(1), the prior testimony exception to the hearsay rule, unless it could be shown that the government had a "similar motive" to develop the testimony at the grand jury as it would have had at trial. The Court of Appeals had found it unnecessary for the defendants to establish a similar motive; it had reasoned that it would be unfair to allow the government to immunize witnesses in the hope of obtaining damaging testimony, and then to hide behind the hearsay rule if the testimony actually exculpated the defendant. But this concern, that the government could develop evidence in a one-sided manner, was found irrelevant by the Supreme Court in the face of a clear requirement in the Rule that a similar motive must be established. The Court contended that it had no authority to override the plain meaning of the rule by applying notions of adversarial fairness. Justice Thomas, writing for the Court, noted that the hearsay exceptions contained in the Federal Rules are both numerous and detailed. From this, he concluded that Congress "presumably made a careful judgment as to what hearsay may come into evidence and what may not," and that to respect Congress' determination, "we must enforce the words that it enacted." In essence, the Court held that it did not matter if the government had acted unfairly and had developed the evidence in a one-sided manner: The plain meaning of the Rule prohibited the Court from considering this unfairness.

---

3. See, e.g., United States v. Pellulo, 964 F.2d 193 (3d Cir. 1992) (admission without foundation of business records was reversible error, even though the documents were trustworthy; despite the general purposes of the Rules as stated in Rule 102, the express admissibility requirements in the Rules must be met; Rule 803(6) sets forth specific admissibility requirements for business records, and while the Rules "are to be liberally construed in favor of admissibility, this does not mean that we may ignore requirements of specific provisions merely because we view the proffered evidence as trustworthy.").

In *Daubert,* the Court held that the common-law test for assessing the admissibility of scientific expert testimony — the "general acceptance" or *Frye* test — was inapplicable in Federal trials. The Court reasoned that there was nothing in the plain language of Rule 702 that would support a standard as rigorous as that of "general acceptance."

The Court's reliance on the plain meaning rule has been criticized by several commentators. One of the most helpful critiques is provided by Judge Becker and Professor Orenstein, in *The Federal Rules of Evidence After Sixteen Years — The Effect of "Plain Meaning" Jurisprudence, the Need for an Advisory Committee on the Rules of Evidence, and Suggestions for Selective Revision of the Rules,* 60 Geo. Wash. L. Rev. 857, 867-68 (1992):

> Significant scholarly attention has been devoted to theories of statutory interpretation, particularly in light of the Court's recent trend toward plain meaning. In particular, there is a growing recognition that generalized, global theories of statutory interpretation are less helpful than approaches tailored to individual statutes. The Federal Rules present a fascinating, if peculiar, case study for plain meaning.
>
> The Rules govern an area of judicial activity where judges have firm opinions, strong interest, and perhaps some unique wisdom. The Rules are generally clear and well-written. Thus, a plain meaning approach does not trigger noticeable angst about our ability to understand and agree upon meaning. Many of the Rules, however, although "clear" and "plain," are purposely flexible. For example, whether information will "assist" [see Rule 702] or "confuse" [see Rule 403] the trier of fact is a quintessential judicial judgment call. Where Congress purposely left a point open or vague, attempts to justify various interpretations by resort to plain meaning are disingenuous.
>
> ...
>
> Many of the so-called plain meaning debates pose questions of how to resolve discrepancies between the plain text of the Federal Rules and the generally shared interpretation of the Rules deriving from preexisting common law traditions. Under the new theory of plain meaning, the language of the Federal Rules controls, even in light of a strong and persuasive common law tradition to the contrary. Obviously, where the Rules consciously and clearly depart from preexisting common law, that departure supplants the pre-Rules approach. Plain meaning is troubling, however, when there is no indication that Congress intended to deviate from the prior common law consensus, yet courts still use such "plain" interpretations to overrule the underlying common law that at least informed, and perhaps determined, congressional understanding and expectation.

Becker and Orenstein focus on an important problem, that the plain meaning approach threatens to repudiate the shared understanding of the Courts, derived from the common law, as to how a traditional rule of evidence should be applied. Another problem with the plain meaning approach is discussed by Professor Jonakait in *The Supreme Court, Plain*

Plain meaning (cont'd)

Meaning, and the Changed Rules of Evidence, 68 Tex. L. Rev. 745 (1990).[4] Professor Jonakait addresses several situations in which a plain meaning approach will reach a result that is simply wrong on the merits, either because it is unfair or not fully thought out by Congress. He notes that the Lower Courts have often rebelled against the plain meaning approach in these instances. The following are some (nonexclusive) examples in which many of the Lower Courts have opted for fairness and flexibility and have rejected a rigid adherence to the plain meaning doctrine:[5]

(1) The hearsay exception for declarations against penal interest, Federal Rule 804(b)(3), provides that if the hearsay statement is offered to exculpate an accused, it is not admissible "unless corroborating circumstances clearly indicate the trustworthiness of the statement." On its face, the Rule does not require corroboration for statements offered by the government that *inculpate* the accused. Yet many Lower Courts have required the government to establish corroboration for inculpatory statements offered under Rule 804(b)(3).[6] These Courts essentially reason that "adversarial fairness" prohibits them from imposing an admissibility requirement on the defendant that is not imposed on the government for the same category of statements. These cases, which are eminently reasonable both in terms of result and in their underlying assumption that Congress was not immune from error when it promulgated the Federal Rules, are, unfortunately, suspect under the Court's adherence to the plain meaning rule.[7]

(2) Rule 803(3) provides a hearsay exception for statements offered to prove a declarant's state of mind. Criminal defendants have often invoked this exception for their own out-of-court statements, offered to prove an innocent state of mind. For example, a defendant may offer a statement of anger at being "set up" by a friend when drugs are found in his luggage during a customs search. Many Courts have excluded these statements if they are self-serving and made under suspect circumstances (such as where the defendant would have had a motive to falsify concerning an innocent state of mind).[8]

---

4. As Professor Jonakait notes, the Supreme Court had, well before *Salerno,* employed the plain meaning rule in most of its cases concerning the Federal Rules of Evidence. See 68 Tex. L. Rev. at 745-55 (1990) (discussing Bourjaily v. United States, 483 U.S. 171 (1987); Huddleston v. United States, 485 U.S. 681 (1988); United States v. Owens, 484 U.S. 554 (1988); and United States v. Zolin, 491 U.S. 554 (1989)).

5. The cases supporting the propositions set forth in the text are analyzed in detail in the annotations to the particular Rules discussed.

6. See, e.g., United States v. Alvarez, 584 F.2d 694 (5th Cir. 1978). For further discussion of this point, see the Editorial Explanatory Comment to Rule 804.

7. In light of the Supreme Court's plain meaning approach to the Rules, some Courts have bowed to the plain meaning of Rule 804(b)(3). See United States v. Bakhtiar, 994 F.2d 970 (2d Cir. 1993) (inculpatory declaration against interest need not be corroborated). The Supreme Court, in Williamson v. United States, 114 S. Ct. 2431 (1994), considered the admissibility of a statement offered against the accused under Rule 804(b)(3). However, the Court did not find it necessary to consider whether corroboration was required, since it held that the Lower Court had used a faulty analysis to determine whether the statement was sufficiently disserving to qualify as a declaration against interest.

8. See, e.g., United States v. Faust, 850 F.2d 575 (9th Cir. 1988) (exculpatory letter written by the defendant is not admissible under Rule 803(3) since the defendant had time to reflect in drafting the letter, and thus any evidence of state of mind provided by the letter was unreliable).

These Courts have imposed a requirement that statements reflecting a state of mind must be "spontaneous" to be admissible; otherwise, these Courts contend, the statements are not reliable enough to be admitted. Yet there is no spontaneity requirement contained in the plain language of Rule 803(3).[9] So, after *Salerno* and *Daubert,* a Court should presumably set aside its legitimate concern over the reliability of these self-generated exculpatory statements.

(3) Rule 803(8)(B), the hearsay exception for public records, excludes reports setting forth "matters observed by police officers and other law enforcement personnel" if such reports are offered "in criminal cases." Read literally, the Rule would exclude a forensic report prepared by the police that indicated that the defendant was innocent. Such a report would be offered by the defendant, but the exclusion covers all police reports offered in criminal cases. Yet Lower Courts have refused to be bound by the plain meaning of the Rule, reasoning that Congress intended to regulate only those police reports that unfairly inculpate a criminal defendant, and finding little danger that police reports will unfairly exculpate the defendant.[10] This eminently sound reasoning is questionable under the plain meaning approach.

(4) Rules 803(8)(B) and 803(8)(C) both contain language that appears to provide a categorical exclusion of public records prepared by law enforcement personnel, when such records are offered against a criminal defendant. Read literally, these provisions would prevent the government from introducing simple tabulations of nonadversarial information. For example, the Rules literally exclude a routine printout from the Customs Service recording license plates of cars that crossed the border on a certain day. Courts have refused to apply the plain exclusionary language of these Rules in such a draconian fashion, however.[11] They reason that the language could not have been intended to exclude reports which are ministerial in nature and made under nonadversarial circumstances — even though the exclusionary language clearly applies to all law enforcement reports. Again, this eminently sound reasoning, designed to guarantee adversarial fairness for the *government,* is brought into question by a rigid adherence to the plain meaning doctrine.

(5) Rule 607 of the Federal Rules provides that "the credibility of a witness may be attacked by any party, including the party calling the witness." On its face, the Rule allows the government to call a witness favorable to the defendant for the sole purpose of "impeaching" the witness with a prior inconsistent statement that would not otherwise be admissible. Thus, the Rule by its terms permits the prosecutor to subvert the hearsay rule by proffering prior inconsistent statements, not made under oath (and therefore not

---

9. See United States v. Lawal, 736 F.2d 5 (2d Cir. 1984) (admitting exculpatory statement by the defendant, despite its likely untrustworthiness, on the ground that there is no spontaneity or trustworthiness requirement in Rule 803(3)).

10. See, e.g., United States v. Smith, 521 F.2d 957 (D.C. Cir. 1975) (despite its exclusionary language, Rule 803(8)(B) should be read in accordance with Congress' intent to exclude only public reports offered against a criminal defendant, and not a report offered in his favor).

11. See, e.g., United States v. Grady, 544 F.2d 598 (2d Cir. 1976) (reports concerning firearms' serial numbers were admissible because they were records of routine factual matters prepared in a nonadversarial setting); United States v. Orozco, 590 F.2d 789 (9th Cir. 1979) (customs records of border crossings are admissible under Rule 803(8) because they are ministerial and not prepared under adversarial circumstances).

Plain meaning (cont'd)

admissible for their truth under Rule 801(d)(1)(A)) in the guise of impeachment, knowing full well that the jury, despite a limiting instruction, will consider the statement for its truth. Yet despite the clear and permissive language of the Rule, Lower Courts have uniformly held that a prosecutor cannot call a witness solely to impeach him, because to allow this practice would be unfair and would undermine the hearsay rule.[12]

Despite the general criticism of the plain meaning approach, the fact is, as Becker and Orenstein state, that "it has arrived as a theory of choice in interpreting the Federal Rules." It is, therefore, an opportune time for the newly-constituted Advisory Committee on the Rules of Evidence to undertake a comprehensive review of the Rules to determine whether each Rule says what it means, and whether each Rule leads to a just and efficient result on its face.

It should be noted, however, that the plain meaning approach has its limits even as applied by the Supreme Court. The Court has recognized that if a Rule on its face would lead to an "absurd" result, then it cannot be read literally. In *Green v. Bock Laundry Machine Co.,* 490 U.S. 504 (1989), the Court encountered an anomaly in former Federal Rule 609, and concluded that Congress could not possibly have meant what it said. Former Rule 609 provided that a prior felony conviction, not based on dishonesty or false statement, was admissible to impeach a witness so long as the probative value outweighed its prejudicial effect "to the defendant." How should this Rule apply in civil cases? Read literally, it would mean that prior felony convictions would be automatically admissible against the civil plaintiff and his witnesses, yet they would not be admissible against the civil defendant and his witnesses unless the probative value outweighed the prejudice to the defendant. Thus, the plain meaning of the Rule granted a benefit — possible exclusion of convictions offered for impeachment — to the civil defendant that it did not grant to the civil plaintiff.

The Court in *Green* refused to construe Rule 609 in accordance with its plain meaning, concluding that "no matter how plain the text of the Rule may be, we cannot accept an interpretation that would deny a civil plaintiff the same right to impeach an adversary's testimony that it grants to a civil defendant." Yet the *Green* exception to the plain meaning doctrine is not itself so "plain." Reasonable minds can certainly differ as to whether a result is sufficiently "absurd" to trigger the exception to the plain meaning rule. And if the objection to former Rule 609 is that it merely led to an "unfair" result in civil cases, then it is difficult to justify the Court's adherence to plain meaning in *Salerno,* where the Court found itself unable to override an arguably unfair result in criminal cases. After *Salerno,* it is probably not fruitful to rely upon *Green* to try to overcome the plain meaning of one of the Federal Rules of Evidence.

---

12. See, e.g., United States v. Morlang, 531 F.2d 183 (4th Cir. 1975) (conviction reversed on the ground that the government should not have been permitted to call a witness for no other purpose than to impeach him); United States v. Hogan, 763 F.2d 697 (5th Cir. 1985) (convictions reversed because the government "called a witness for the primary purpose of impeaching him with otherwise inadmissible hearsay evidence"). The Court in *Hogan* reasoned that the danger of such a practice is that "the jury will hear the impeachment evidence, which is not otherwise admissible and is not substantive proof of guilt, but is likely to be received as such proof."

Judge or jury cases, civil or criminal cases

Despite the Supreme Court's adherence to a strict plain meaning approach, it is obvious that Trial Judges are allowed a high degree of flexibility in handling most admissibility issues. This is because the Rules mandate an ad hoc, balancing approach for many evidentiary questions — most importantly under Rule 403 of the Federal Rules. For these more flexible applications, Rule 102 can be cited as authority for a differentiated approach to admissibility questions, depending on whether the case is tried to a jury or to a Judge, and depending on whether the case is civil or criminal. It is true that the Rules are equally applicable to civil and criminal cases, and equally applicable to jury and bench trials. Yet a civil case tried to a Judge should not necessarily require the same evidentiary formalities as a criminal case tried to a jury.

For example, under Rule 403, a Trial Judge is authorized to exclude evidence where it is unduly prejudicial or confusing. But surely these considerations are mainly applicable to jury trials. We must presume — and the Trial Judge will certainly presume — that she will not be unduly confused or prejudiced by the proffered evidence. In this situation, Rule 102 can be used as authority for a flexible approach depending on the case, since the language of Rule 403 is not so plain as to mandate a single result.

It must be remembered that, without regard to Rule 102, certain Rules explicitly require different treatment for civil and criminal trials. So, for example, Rule 609 applies a heightened exclusionary test for criminal-defendant-witnesses — a test not applicable to other witnesses; and Rule 803(8)(C) prohibits the use of certain public reports against a criminal defendant, but there is no similar prohibition as to other litigants. Finally, the criminal defendant has constitutional rights to confrontation and compulsory process; these rights obviously supersede any interest in flexibility set forth in Rule 102.

C. ANNOTATED CASES

No significant decisions.

D. LEGISLATIVE HISTORY

Advisory Committee's Note

For similar provisions see Rule 2 of the Federal Rules of Criminal Procedure, Rule 1 of the Federal Rules of Civil Procedure, California Evidence Code § 2, and New Jersey Evidence Rule 5.

Citations to Hearings and Debates

Letter from Edward W. Cleary to Herbert E. Hoffman, March 22, 1973, in Supp. to Hearings on Proposed Rules of Evidence Before the Subcomm. on Criminal Justice of the House Comm. on the Judiciary, 93rd Cong., 1st Sess., at 3-4 (1973).

RULE 103

A. OFFICIAL TEXT

Rule 103. Rulings on Evidence

(a) *Effect of erroneous ruling.* — Error may not be predicated upon a ruling which admits or excludes evidence unless a substantial right of the party is affected, and

(1) Objection. — In case the ruling is one admitting evidence, a timely objection or motion to strike appears of record, stating the specific ground of objection, if the specific ground was not apparent from the context; or

(2) Offer of proof. — In case the ruling is one excluding evidence, the substance of the evidence was made known to the court by offer or was apparent from the context within which questions were asked.

(b) *Record of offer and ruling.* — The court may add any other or further statement which shows the character of the evidence, the form in which it was offered, the objection made, and the ruling thereon. It may direct the making of an offer in question and answer form.

(c) *Hearing of jury.* — In jury cases, proceedings shall be conducted, to the extent practicable, so as to prevent inadmissible evidence from being suggested to the jury by any means, such as making statements or offers of proof or asking questions in the hearing of the jury.

(d) *Plain error.* — Nothing in this rule precludes taking notice of plain errors affecting substantial rights although they were not brought to the attention of the court.

B. EDITORIAL EXPLANATORY COMMENT

Objections and offers of proof; general requirement

This Rule is a codification of the basic rules of offering evidence and objecting to admission of evidence. In order to preserve an objection for appeal, ordinarily a party must make a specific, as opposed to a general, objection. If, however, a specific ground is apparent, no absolute requirement of specification will be imposed.[1] Once an objection

---

1. See, e.g., Morrow v. Greyhound Lines, Inc., 541 F.2d 713 (8th Cir. 1976) (refusal to consider admissibility of expert testimony because of failure to object to testimony at trial or to question testimony in motion for new trial). But see United States v. Rivera, 513 F.2d 519 (2d Cir.), *cert. denied,* 423 U.S. 943

is made, if the Trial Judge excludes evidence, the party offering the evidence must make an offer of proof.[2] The Rule sensibly states that Trial Judges should attempt to conduct proceedings for the determination of the admissibility of evidence outside of the presence of the jury.[3]

The requirement of a timely and specific objection is not a mere formality. Objections are required so that the Court is notified of a possible error, thus providing the Court an opportunity to correct an error and obviating the need for appeal. Specific objections are also required, in fairness, to allow the opponent an opportunity for timely argument on the question. Finally, Courts are concerned that, without a requirement of timely objection, a party could remain silent at trial in the hope of a favorable trial outcome, with the insurance policy of an appeal should that hope not become reality.[4]

Harmless error, prejudicial error, plain error

The text of the Rule specifically mentions only plain error. In application, however, the Rule concerns three types of Trial Court error, each of which has been well-recognized by the Courts both before and after the passage of the Federal Rules. The three types of error are: (1) harmless error, which is error objected to at trial, but found on appeal not to affect substantial rights; (2) prejudicial error, also called reversible error, which is that raised at trial and found on appeal to affect substantial rights; and (3) plain error, which is error not raised at trial, but which is nevertheless so egregious that

---

(1975) (objection may still be considered on appeal if not raised because counsel has good reason to believe that prior decisions rendered objection futile).

On the specificity required in objecting to evidence, see United States v. Gomez-Norena, 908 F.2d 497 (9th Cir. 1990) (objection on Rule 404(b) and hearsay grounds does not preserve objection under Rule 403); United States v. Hutcher, 622 F.2d 1083 (2d Cir.), *cert. denied,* 449 U.S. 875 (1980) (objection to rebuttal evidence in the form "I will object to that" insufficient to preserve claim for appeal). See also United States v. Fendley, 522 F.2d 181 (5th Cir. 1975) (expression of concern for trustworthiness of business record was insufficient to preserve an objection that record was not made in ordinary course of business); Collins v. Wayne Corp., 621 F.2d 777 (5th Cir. 1980) (motion *in limine* to preclude particular line of questioning not sufficient to preserve claim of error as to specific questions).

It is, of course, essential to make a record of objections. See, e.g., United States v. Johnson, 542 F.2d 230 (5th Cir. 1976) (objection in chambers without court reporter present may not be sufficient to preserve evidentiary question for appeal).

2. See, e.g., Polys v. Trans-Colorado Airlines, 941 F.2d 1404 (10th Cir. 1991) (error not preserved where plaintiffs made no formal offer of proof after exclusion of expert deposition testimony); United States v. Winkle, 587 F.2d 705 (5th Cir.), *cert. denied,* 444 U.S. 827 (1979) (refusal to find error in exclusion of inconsistent statements as hearsay, even though statements were offered for impeachment purposes, because of failure to make offer of proof); United States v. Brady, 579 F.2d 1121 (9th Cir. 1978), *cert. denied,* 439 U.S. 1074 (1979) (refusal to consider admissibility of excited utterances).

3. See, e.g., Posttape Assocs. v. Eastman Kodak Co., 537 F.2d 751 (3d Cir. 1976) (testimony regarding insurance).

In United States v. Ledesma, 632 F.2d 670 (7th Cir.), *cert. denied,* 449 U.S. 998 (1980), the Court of Appeals criticized the Trial Judge's no sidebar conference rule, but found no prejudice from the argument of evidence issues within the hearing of the jury.

4. See, e.g., United States v. Bamberger, 456 F.2d 1119 (3d Cir. 1972) (party may not "sit by silently, take his chances on a verdict, and, if it is adverse, then complain of a matter which, if error, could have been eradicated during the trial").

it is considered and rectified on appeal.[5] Thus, the distinction between harmless and prejudicial error is dependent on whether substantial rights have been adversely affected by a mistake. The distinction between prejudicial error and plain error is dependent on whether the error is so grave as to excuse the party's failure to preserve it at trial.

The Circuit Courts have adopted conflicting standards of harmless error. Some Circuits have differentiated between civil and criminal cases, and have held that the standard for harmless error in a civil case is whether substantial rights were "more probably than not" untainted by the error.[6] Some Circuits have applied this same more-probable-than-not standard to criminal cases as well.[7] Other Circuits have held that errors are not harmless unless it is "highly probable" that they did not affect a party's substantial rights. This standard results in more reversals, but is hardly a wholesale ticket to reversal. Some Circuits hold that this "highly probable" standard is limited to criminal cases (applying the more-probable-than-not standard to civil cases), while some hold that it is equally applicable to civil and criminal cases.[8] Other Circuits have held that in criminal cases, the standard for harmlessness is whether the evidentiary error was harmless beyond a reasonable doubt.[9]

If the error is one of constitutional dimension, rather than merely evidentiary, the test of harmlessness on direct review is whether the prosecution can prove that the error was harmless beyond a reasonable doubt.[10] On habeas corpus review, constitutional error is considered by the more permissive standard of whether the error had a "substantial and injurious effect or influence in determining the jury's verdict."[11]

All these various standards are probably not as important as the judgment that is applied in determining the effect of an error on the verdict.[12] If the Appellate Court is left with a definite and firm conviction that the error was substantial enough to effect the fairness of the proceedings, then it will probably reverse regardless of the standard employed.

---

5. See, e.g., United States v. Restivo, 8 F.3d 274 (5th Cir. 1993) ("Plain error is error so obvious and substantial that failure to notice it would affect the fairness, integrity, or public reputation of the judicial proceedings and would result in manifest injustice.").

6. See, e.g., Haddad v. Lockheed Cal. Corp., 720 F.2d 1454 (9th Cir. 1983); Smith v. Chesapeake & Ohio Ry., 778 F.2d 384 (7th Cir. 1985).

7. See, e.g., United States v. Guerrero, 756 F.2d 1342 (9th Cir. 1984).

8. See, e.g., McQueeney v. Wilmington Trust Co., 779 F.2d 916 (3d Cir. 1985) (applying the "highly probable" no effect rule to both civil and criminal cases). On the conflict in the cases, see Becker & Orenstein, *The Federal Rules of Evidence After Sixteen Years — The Effect of "Plain Meaning" Jurisprudence, the Need for an Advisory Committee on the Rules of Evidence, and Suggestions for Selective Revision of the Rules,* 60 GEO. WASH. L. REV. 857, 892 (1992). For an argument that different harmless error standards should apply to different types of cases, see Saltzburg, *The Harm of Harmless Error,* 59 VA. L. REV. 988 (1973).

9. See, e.g., United States v. Lehder-Rivas, 955 F.2d 1510 (11th Cir. 1992).

10. Chapman v. California, 386 U.S. 18 (1966). Some constitutional errors can never be harmless. See S. SALTZBURG & D. CAPRA, AMERICAN CRIMINAL PROCEDURE 1286-89 (4th ed. 1992).

11. Brecht v. Abrahamson, 113 S. Ct. 1710 (1993).

12. *Id.* (Stevens, J., concurring) (noting that "the way we phrase the governing standard is far less important than the quality of the judgment with which it is applied.").

Some of the factors that are relevant to the harmless error inquiry include: (1) whether erroneously admitted or excluded evidence was "cumulative" on a point or, conversely, whether it was the only evidence in support of the point; (2) whether the Trial Court gave timely and effective curative instructions; (3) whether erroneously admitted evidence was relied upon by counsel in argument; (4) whether the error was discrete or pervasive; and (5) whether the error was made in a lengthy or short trial. Of course, if more than one error was made, the Appellate Court must assess the cumulative effect of the errors on the verdict. However, Appellate Courts have taken the view that no trial can be error-free, and the longer the trial, the less likely it is that a few discrete errors will have had an impact on the verdict. For further application of these principles, see the annotated cases under this Rule.

Difference between harmless error and plain error

The failure to preserve an objection does not mean that an Appellate Court is precluded from considering the evidentiary issue. It does mean, however, that the question is reviewed under the more stringent plain error standard of review.[13] The plain error test is more rigorous for the party seeking reversal than is the abuse of discretion standard, which is applied to most evidentiary rulings; and the abuse of discretion standard is itself so Trial Court-friendly as to make most evidentiary rulings reversal-proof.

In *United States v. Olano,* 113 S. Ct. 1770 (1993), the Supreme Court interpreted the plain error provision of Federal Rule of Criminal Procedure 52(b), which is substantially identical to the plain error provision of Federal Rule of Evidence 103(d); both Rules permit an Appellate Court to take notice of plain errors "affecting substantial rights although they were not brought to the attention of the court." Indeed, Rule 103(d) was patterned after Federal Rule of Criminal Procedure 52(b).[14] Consequently, the Court's interpretation of "plain error" in *Olano* is instructive on the application of the plain error standard of Rule 103.

The *Olano* Court identified three limitations on a Court's power to reverse because of errors that were not properly preserved for review in the Trial Court. First, there must be an error. Second, the error must be plain, which means it must be clear or obvious. Thus, even more deference is given to the Trial Court than under the deferential abuse of discretion standard of review. Finally, the plain error must affect substantial rights, which means in most cases that it must have been prejudicial in the sense of affecting the outcome of the case.

Most importantly, the *Olano* Court stated that the language of the plain error rule (unlike that of the harmless error rule) is permissive, not mandatory. The Court recognized that "the Court of Appeals should correct a plain forfeited error affecting

---

13. See, e.g., Government of the Virgin Islands v. Mujahid, 990 F.2d 111 (3d Cir. 1993) (admission of coconspirator's guilty plea was a serious error, but did not rise to the level of plain error; Court defines plain errors as those "particularly egregious errors that seriously affect the fairness, integrity, or public reputation of judicial proceedings").

14. See Advisory Committee Note to Rule 103(d), *infra.*

substantial rights if the error seriously affects the fairness, integrity or public reputation of judicial proceedings." However, a "plain error affecting substantial rights does not, without more" mandate reversal, because otherwise the discretion afforded by Rule 52 (and by Federal Rule of Evidence 103) "would be rendered illusory." The Court also made it clear that the burden of showing plain error and its effect on the verdict is on the appellant.[15] It follows that reversal for plain error is extremely rare and in the discretion of the Appellate Court. For example, the Court in *Olano* found no plain error even though alternate jurors were permitted to sit in on jury deliberations, in clear violation of Federal Rule of Criminal Procedure 24(c).[16] For applications of the plain error standard, see the annotated cases under this Rule.

Deferential standards of review

Whatever the standard of prejudicial or plain error, it is clear from the cases that it is difficult to meet. But most appellants do not even get the opportunity to test the harmfulness of error. This is because the deferential standard of review ordinarily employed makes it extremely difficult to prove error on an evidentiary question in the first place. While pure issues of Rule construction are reviewed *de novo,* there are very few such issues that arise in practice.[17] The same is true with mixed questions of law and fact, which are generally reviewed *de novo* but which are, again, relatively infrequent.[18] The vast majority of evidentiary rulings are reviewed under an abuse of discretion standard.[19] This has prompted one Court to state that appellants who challenge evidentiary rulings of the Trial Court "are like rich men who wish to enter the Kingdom; their prospects compare with those of camels who wish to pass through the eye of a needle."[20] Then, once passing through the eye of the needle, the appellant may still be without a remedy; the Appellate Court is more than likely to find that the error was

---

15. See also Angelo v. Armstrong World Indus., 11 F.3d 957 (10th Cir. 1993) (appellants "bear the burden of proving plain error and that it almost surely affected the outcome of the case").

16. For a notably more generous treatment of the plain error standard, see United States v. Copelin, 996 F.2d 379 (D.C. Cir. 1993) (declaring that there is a "huge presumption" of plain error when a Trial Judge omits a cautionary instruction when admitting impeachment evidence to which a jury could give substantive effect against a criminal defendant).

17. One example of a pure Rules construction would be whether an offer of compromise is excluded under Rule 408 when it is introduced by the party who made the offer; this is a question of whether the language of the Rule provides a per se exclusion or not. See the discussion of Rule 408, *infra.*

18. See Sandberg v. Virginia Bankshares, Inc., 979 F.2d 332 (4th Cir. 1992) (the admissibility of evidence purportedly covered by the attorney-client privilege is a mixed question of law and fact necessitating *de novo* review).

19. See, e.g., Horne v. Owens-Corning Fiberglass Corp., 4 F.3d 276 (4th Cir. 1993) (admission of evidence under prior testimony exception to the hearsay rule is reviewed for abuse of discretion); United States v. Duran, 4 F.3d 800 (4th Cir. 1993) (questions involving authentication of documents and reliability of in-court identification testimony are reviewed for abuse of discretion); United States v. Whalen, 940 F.2d 1027 (7th Cir. 1991) (admissibility of expert testimony reviewed for abuse of discretion).

20. United States v. Glecier, 923 F.2d 496 (7th Cir. 1991) (abuse of discretion standard applied to ruling under Rule 403).

harmless. All in all, reversal on the ground of an evidentiary error presents a daunting prospect.[21]

Affirmance on a different theory

Suppose that the prosecution in a murder trial offers a hearsay statement from the victim that implicates the defendant. The statement is offered and admitted as a dying declaration. On appeal, the Court holds that the Trial Court erred in finding that the victim, at the time of the statement, had given up all hope of recovery. The government argues, however, that the conviction should be affirmed anyway, since the victim made the statement while under the influence of a startling event and thus the statement could have been admitted as an excited utterance. Defendant responds that the excited utterance argument should be rejected since it is being made for the first time on appeal. How should the Appellate Court rule?

The general rule is that an Appellate Court may uphold the admission of evidence on any theory that finds support in the record.[22] This is a corollary of the principle of harmless error: Admitting the evidence on an incorrect ground does not prejudice the appellant where an alternative theory was available on which to admit the evidence.[23]

Despite the general rule, there are many cases in which Appellate Courts have refused to uphold an evidentiary ruling on grounds different from those used in the Trial Court. The leading case refusing affirmance on a different ground is *United States v. Shepard,* 290 U.S. 96 (1933). Shepard was on trial for murdering his wife. He called witnesses who testified that Mrs. Shepard had been planning to commit suicide. He was convicted largely upon his wife's statement to her maid that "Dr. Shepard has poisoned me." The statement was offered over objection and admitted at trial as a dying declaration. The prosecutor used the statement as proof of the assertions therein, and argued to the jury on that basis.

On appeal, the Supreme Court held that the statement was not admissibile as a dying declaration, because it was not made under a belief of impending death. The government argued that the statement could nonetheless have been admitted as circumstantial proof of Mrs. Shepard's state of mind as being inconsistent with suicide. But Justice Cardozo, writing for the Court, refused to consider this theory of admissibility since it had not been used at trial:

---

21. For a rare case of appellate success, see Government of the Virgin Islands v. Archibald, 987 F.2d 180 (3rd Cir. 1993) (in a rape case, there was no probative value in admitting the defendant's uncharged sexual relationship with a minor; reversal required where the defendant suffered severe prejudice in a close case resting on the credibility of the victim).

22. See, e.g., United States v. Lieberman, 637 F.2d 95 (2d Cir. 1980) (statement incorrectly admitted as a coconspirator declaration was nonetheless properly admitted since it fit the requirements of a declaration against interest: "We note that this basis for admission was not argued either at trial or on appeal. We may, however, uphold the admission on any theory which finds support in the record, regardless of the ground relied upon by the trial court.").

23. See United States v. Maher, 645 F.2d 780 (9th Cir. 1981) (error in allowing DEA agent to testify to his lay opinion about the modus operandi of drug dealers was harmless, where agent was qualified to give an expert opinion on that subject).

Affirmance on a different theory (cont'd)

> Here the course of the trial put the defendant off his guard. The testimony was received by the trial judge and offered by the government with the plain understanding that it was to be used for an illegitimate purpose, gravely prejudicial [i.e. to prove that Dr. Shepard had in fact poisoned his wife]. A trial becomes unfair if testimony thus accepted may be used in an appellate court although admitted for a different purpose, unavowed and unsuspected.[24]

How can *Shepard* be squared with the general principle that the Trial Court's ruling, though incorrect, should be affirmed where an alternative theory could have been used to admit the evidence? The answer lies in whether the appellant was prejudiced by the use of the evidence on an incorrect theory, in a way that would not have occurred if the evidence had been used correctly. Thus, in *Shepard,* the defendant would have been entitled to a limiting instruction if the evidence had been used for the purpose later proposed on appeal. The Court would have had to instruct the jury that Mrs. Shepard's statement could not have been used to prove that Dr. Shepard actually poisoned her, but only to prove that Mrs. Shepard believed it to be so, and thus may have had a state of mind inconsistent with suicide. But as the evidence was actually used at trial, there was no limiting instruction, since the statement was treated as a dying declaration, admitted for the truth of the facts asserted.

It follows that the *Shepard* exception will not apply when the evidentiary ground asserted on appeal serves the same purpose and would lead to the same use and consequences as the theory actually used at trial. The unfairness and prejudice in *Shepard,* where the government advanced on appeal a theory wholly unlike and different in effect from the one presented to the Trial Court, is not present where different theories serve the same purpose. For example, there would be no unfairness where records incorrectly admitted as business records could have been admitted as admissions: Both theories of admissibility serve the same purpose and would lead to the same consequences — proof of the truth of the matters asserted in the records.[25]

Nor can the appellant complain if the theory used at trial is less prejudicial than the theory that could have been used. For instance, if the government in a criminal trial offers bad acts as "other crimes" evidence, when in fact the crimes are encompassed by

---

24. See also United States v. Check, 582 F.2d 668 (2d Cir. 1978) (out-of-court statement offered at trial for its truth cannot be considered on appeal as "background" evidence: "it would be unfair to consider the admissibility of the evidence for any narrower purpose than that upon which the testimony was unquestionably offered and received at trial").

25. See, e.g., United States v. Williams, 837 F.2d 1009 (11th Cir. 1988) (records incorrectly admitted as business records could have been admitted as admissions; harmless error since "both evidentiary rules serve the same purpose — to permit the introduction of evidence proving the truth of the matter asserted"); United States v. Pedroza, 750 F.2d 187 (2d Cir. 1984) (error in admitting defendant's own statement under coconspirator exception was "immaterial" since it could have been admitted as a personal admission; both theories serve the same purpose of allowing statements to be considered for the truth of the matters asserted therein). See also United States v. Gallo, 782 F.2d 1191 (4th Cir. 1986) (other crimes evidence "is deemed admissible on appeal if it is admissible under Rule 404(b) on any theory").

the indictment, the error, if any, is harmless, since "the limiting instruction was more favorable than the defendant deserved."[26]

Even where the new theory of admissibility serves the same purpose as the one used at trial — such as substituting one hearsay exception for another — the fact remains that each theory of admissibility has its own unique proof requirements. The party who proffers the evidence must show by a preponderance that the applicable admissibility requirements are met.[27] It follows that a new theory of admissibility cannot be upheld on appeal unless the admissibility requirements supporting that theory were proved at trial. And given the fact that such theory was not pursued at trial, it will only be by happenstance that the necessary proof requirements would be met. It is uncertain, for example, whether the record will indicate that a statement could have been admitted as a dying declaration, when in fact it was admitted at trial as an excited utterance.

Even if there is proof in the record that would show that the Trial Court could have admitted the evidence under a different theory than the one actually used, an Appellate Court should be cautious before concluding that the appellee has proved that the admissibility requirements were met. This is because whatever proof was elicited below was asserted in another context, and the nonoffering party never had a chance to meet the proof in the context in which it is argued on appeal. For reasons similar to those given in *Shepard*, the nonoffering party can be prejudiced by being denied an opportunity to meet the evidence on a theory that was not argued at trial.[28]

On the other hand, the appellee can make a strong argument for affirmance where the theory of admissibility argued on appeal has requirements that will almost inevitably (though inadvertently) have been proved below. Thus, if the new theory of admissibility is that a statement could have been admitted as a party admission, the only proof requirements are that the statement was made by the party and is relevant to the case; these facts would have been shown below as a matter of course.[29] In contrast, an argument that a hearsay statement could have been admitted under the residual exception is usually precluded on appeal, since that exception requires advance notice to be given

---

26. See United States v. Mancari, 875 F.2d 103 (7th Cir. 1989) ("Mancari could hardly complain that the jury was permitted to consider the April 23 and May 2 transactions for a limited purpose when the jury should have been permitted to consider them without limitation because the indictment encompassed them after all.").

27. Bourjaily v. United States, 483 U.S. 171 (1987).

28. See, e.g., United States v. Ordonez, 737 F.2d 793 (9th Cir. 1984). At trial, the government did not suggest that it had laid a proper foundation to admit a drug ledger as coconspirator statements, and the reviewing Court would not sustain admissibility on this theory:

> For us to sustain a theory of admissibility not presented below, would unfairly rob appellants of the opportunity to argue the weight, sufficiency and trustworthiness of the evidence to establish a proper foundation before the trial judge, or to offer proof to controvert the facts now relied upon by the government.

29. See, e.g., Onujiogu v. United States, 817 F.2d 3 (1st Cir. 1987) (statement erroneously admitted as a statement pertinent to treatment could have been admitted as a party admission under Federal Rule 801(d)(2)(A)).

Affirmance on a different theory (cont'd)

to the nonoffering party; and advance notice is unlikely to have been given if the statement was not offered at trial as residual hearsay.[30]

Offers of proof

The Rule provides that an objection will ordinarily not be preserved unless the party makes an offer of proof. The offer of proof has an important function at both the trial and appellate level. At trial, the offer of proof informs the Judge what the proponent expected to prove by the evidence, thereby enabling the Judge to determine whether the evidence would be admissible for any purpose. On appeal, the offer of proof ensures that the record will provide enough detail with which to determine whether the Trial Court committed reversible error by excluding the evidence.[31]

The Rule does not specify what form the offer of proof should take. It seems that the fairest reading of the Rule is that counsel has the obligation only of representing to the Judge what the evidence would be if allowed to present it.[32] This does not mean that an offer of proof can be routinely dispensed with, however.[33] Of course, the more specific the representation, the more helpful it will be to both the Trial and Appellate Court. If the Trial Judge has doubts about counsel's ability to produce, or wishes to know more about the evidence, counsel may be required to offer a witness to give testimony so the record will be complete. Obviously, the more complete the record, the less likely it is that a new trial will be required. A Judge will have to weigh the costs of a full trial record — i.e., delay, expense, and even possible confusion — against the potential benefits of added insurance against the necessity for retrial.

---

30. See, e.g., United States v. Pelullo, 964 F.2d 193 (3rd Cir. 1992) (records erroneously admitted as business records at trial cannot be retroactively held admissible on appeal as residual hearsay; the defendant never received notice in accordance with Rule 803(24), and the Trial Court never made the predicate findings required by that Rule). Compare United States v. Nivica, 887 F.2d 1110 (1st Cir. 1989) (statement can be retroactively justified as residual hearsay, where it *was* proffered as residual hearsay at the trial, but admitted — erroneously — by the Trial Court as a business record; under the circumstances, the defendant was properly notified under Rule 803(24)). See generally Saltzburg, *Another Ground for Decision — Harmless Trial Court Errors,* 47 TEMP. L.Q. 193 (1974).

31. See United States v. Rayco, Inc., 616 F.2d 462 (10th Cir. 1980) (objection to exclusion of exhibit was not preserved, where exhibit was not made part of the record and the Court of Appeals was "unable to determine that the contents of the exhibit were so central to Rayco's case that its exclusion prevented examination of the real issues.").

32. See Fox v. Dannenberg, 906 F.2d 1253 (8th Cir. 1990) (counsel's statement as to witness' anticipated testimony is a sufficient offer of proof; it is not required that the proffered witness take the stand).

33. See Polys v. Trans-Colorado Airlines, 941 F.2d 1404 (10th Cir. 1991) (error not preserved where defendants made no offer of proof following exclusion of their expert's deposition testimony). One Court has upheld the practice of requiring an offer of proof of expert testimony to be made in the form of a written witness statement, rather than by question and answer. See Fidelity Sav. & Loan Assoc. v. Aetna Life & Cas. Co., 647 F.2d 933 (9th Cir. 1981) (noting that the "form of offers of proof is left to the discretion of the trial court").

The Rule states that an offer of proof is unnecessary where the substance of the evidence "was apparent from the context within which questions were asked." One example of this exception is where testimony is received and subsequently stricken. It is clear in these circumstances that an offer of proof is unnecessary, since the substance of the evidence is apparent. Another possible application of this exception arises with witness testimony, where it is clear from the question what the answer would be. Obviously, though, no such assurance is justified if the witness is hostile to the party who asked the question.

Timeliness of objections

Nothing in this Rule specifically states when an objection is timely, and when a motion to strike is sufficient. Generally, the rule has been that an objection to an improper question is waived if not made before the answer, since counsel is not allowed to gamble that there will be some benefit if it is answered. Federal Courts have shown much flexibility, however, in permitting objections or motions to strike following an improper question that is answered where counsel reacts swiftly, but not quite quickly enough. Of course, where the answer is objectionable but the question is not, a motion to strike is appropriate following the answer. Where demonstrative or documentary evidence is offered, the grounds for objection are ordinarily apparent at that time. Therefore, an objection should be made when the evidence is offered.

It should be noted that sometimes a ground for objection or for a motion to strike is not immediately apparent. As soon as the ground appears, it may be raised.

Rules 30(c) and 32(d) of the Federal Rules of Civil Procedure provide that objection must be made during a deposition to errors or irregularities in the form of the questions or answers, to the administering or taking of the oath, or to anything that might be corrected. Objections to the competency of a witness or to the materiality or relevance of evidence may be made at trial. Similarly, a 1993 amendment to Federal Rule of Civil Procedure 26(a)(3) provides that parties have fourteen days from the date of production to disclose any objections they have to deposition testimony or documentary evidence. All objections other than those under Rules 402 and 403 are waived if not made within the time period, unless good cause is shown. Rule 15(f) of the Federal Rules of Criminal Procedure is not as specific, but is interpreted to impose requirements similar to the Civil Rules.

Importance of specificity

A quick reading of Rule 103 might lead one to conclude that its principal purpose is to announce standards to be used for appellate review of Trial Court actions. It should be apparent, however, that the real thrust of the Rule is directed to action in the Trial Court. Whether or not an appeal is ever taken in a case, trial lawyers should utilize, and Trial Judges should require, specific objections and particularized offers of proof if evidentiary claims are to be adequately resolved during the course of litigation.[34] It is our view that Trial Judges, who bear with increasing frequency the burden of justifying their rulings on the basis of reasons articulated for the record, owe it to themselves to compel counsel to state precise grounds for opposing or supporting a point at trial. If the Trial Judge is alerted to the specific intentions of the parties, a ruling is likely to be better than if only general arguments are made.

It is axiomatic that a specific objection made on one ground will not preserve an objection to the same evidence on different grounds.[35] This rule is more than a formality. Courts recognize that a litigant will often choose a specific ground of objection, and reject another ground, for tactical reasons. There is no reason in these circumstances to allow reconsideration of this strategic choice on appeal. Moreover, where an objection is made on one ground, neither the Trial Court nor the opposing party has been properly notified on any other objection on different grounds.

Objections to details

Counsel must take care that an objection to proffered evidence is not so detailed and specific as to miss the forest for the trees. For example, an objection to specific language in a document is not an objection to the document itself. Likewise, an objection to the details of a prior conviction is not an objection to the conviction itself.[36] Generally, an objection as to details should be used only as a fallback argument once the more all-encompassing objection has failed.

Continuing objections

Often, a particular line of testimony or other evidence will present the same evidentiary objection that the nonoffering party has previously and unsuccessfully argued to the Court. In these circumstances, neither the Court nor counsel may find it productive to reiterate continuous objections at each point down the line, as if the issue had not been raised before. On the other hand, counsel must be concerned that a failure to renew an objection down the line could be deemed a waiver. Therefore, counsel should make clear that she has a continuing objection, on grounds previously stated, to the entire line of testimony or evidence; nothing in the Rule prevents the use of a continuing objection, and

---

34. See, e.g., Angelo v. Armstrong World Indus., 11 F.3d 957 (10th Cir. 1993) (objection that testimony on redirect was "beyond the scope" would reasonably be taken to mean that the testimony addressed issues not raised in cross-examination; therefore, the objection that the redirect testimony violated pretrial protocols set for expert testimony was not properly preserved for appeal: "The objecting party must make its objection clear; the trial judge need not imagine all the possible grounds for an objection.").

35. See, e.g., Bryant v. Consolidated Rail Corp., 672 F.2d 217 (1st Cir. 1982) (objection on relevance grounds does not preserve objection under Rule 404); United States v. Wilson, 966 F.2d 243 (7th Cir. 1992) (objection on relevance grounds does not preserve objection that the evidence is unduly prejudicial under Rule 403).

36. See United States v. Reed, 977 F.2d 14 (1st Cir. 1992) (motion *in limine* arguing that details of a prior conviction should be excluded, and requesting that prosecution be limited to questions about the fact of conviction and the nature of the defense, waived objection to the use of the conviction itself).

the procedure has been upheld by the Courts.[37] Of course, a continuing objection is only as good as the original one; as such, it only preserves the ground of review initially stated by counsel.[38]

Objections in multiparty cases

Suppose that two codefendants share a common defense but they are represented by separate counsel. If only one codefendant objects to proffered evidence, does this preserve the right to appeal for both parties or only one? Looking to the purposes of Rule 103, a strong argument can be made that the objection of one party should apply to both, assuming that the ground for objection was specific, and was equally applicable to both parties. Despite the inaction of one of the parties, the purpose of the Rule has been served: Both the Trial Court and the offering party have been properly informed of the nature of the objection. Nor can it usually be said that the inactive party has been negligent or has slept on his or her rights; a party in these circumstances can reasonably assume that it would be unnecessary to join in a proper and specific objection that is clearly applicable to both the objecting and the inactive party. There is little to be gained by "piling on." Consequently, Courts have held that a nonobjecting party may appeal an evidentiary ruling on grounds specified at trial by an objecting party in the same situation.[39]

The prudent course, however, is to join in an objection made by another party. Otherwise, it may later be found that the interests of the parties are not sufficiently aligned for the objection of one to be deemed the objection of the other.

In limine rulings

A party who foresees the use of prejudicial and arguably inadmissible evidence by the adversary may find it useful to make a pretrial motion *in limine* to exclude the evidence from trial. The most frequent use of a motion *in limine* occurs when a criminal defendant with prior convictions proposes to testify at trial. The motion *in limine* is particularly useful in this situation since otherwise the defendant would have to take the stand and gamble that his convictions would be excluded.

---

37. See United States v. Marshall, 762 F.2d 419 (5th Cir. 1985) (defendant had a continuing objection that need not have been repeated as to subsequent evidence admitted within the scope of the initial ruling).

38. See United States v. Gomez-Norena, 908 F.2d 497 (9th Cir. 1990) (continuing objection merely avoids "repeated objections to evidence admitted within the scope of the court's specific evidentiary ruling"; where continuing objection was made on character and hearsay grounds, an objection that the evidence was unfairly prejudicial under Rule 403 was not preserved).

39. See, e.g., United States v. Church, 970 F.2d 401 (7th Cir. 1992) (objection by counsel for one defendant held applicable to the other two); Howard v. Gonzales, 658 F.2d 352 (5th Cir. 1981) ("Unless the identity of the objector somehow affects the admissibility of the evidence, no reason appears why a party should be required to join in the objection or offer of another litigant aligned with him, in order to raise the issue on appeal.").

It is important to note, however, that an *in limine* ruling is not written in stone. The Judge is free to revisit the evidentiary question presented *in limine* when it arises in the context of the trial.[40] A new look at the issue may be necessary because often the decision to admit evidence must be made by balancing probative value and prejudicial effect. Ordinarily, such a balancing process cannot be conducted with certainty until the evidence is proffered at trial. As one Court put it, it is usually "too great a handicap to bind a trial judge to a ruling on a subtle evidentiary question, requiring the most delicate balancing, outside a precise factual context."[41]

A Trial Judge has discretion to rule *in limine* or to await developments at trial before ruling. The decision whether to rule in advance often will turn on the Judge's confidence or uncertainty concerning the relationship of particular evidence to a case as a whole. Rarely will Trial Judges be reversed for declining to rule *in limine*.[42]

Some Appellate Courts have even recommended that Judges delay ruling on the scope of impeachment until a witness testifies, since the exact nature of the testimony might be important in determining the scope of impeachment.[43] The one situation in which an *in limine* ruling may be mandated is prior to a second trial when the Trial Judge knows the evidence and the issues raised by the parties as a result of the first trial.[44]

Taking the stand to preserve an in limine objection

In *Luce v. United States,* 469 U.S. 38 (1984), a unanimous Court concluded that "to raise and preserve for review the claim of improper impeachment with a prior conviction, a defendant must testify."[45] The Court was justifiably concerned that a contrary rule would allow the defendant a windfall — he could argue on appeal that the Trial Court's erroneous pretrial ruling kept him off the stand, when in fact he might never have had an intention of taking the stand. The Court was also concerned that the harmless error determination, and indeed the determination of whether the Court was even in error, would be unduly speculative in the absence of the defendant's testimony at trial. While the Court in *Luce* had justifiable concerns and reached a reasonable conclusion, it must be recognized that *Luce* leaves a defendant with prior convictions in a difficult situation — in order to preserve an objection as to the convictions, he must take the stand and face a much higher probability of a guilty verdict once the jury hears about his past.

---

40. See Luce v. United States, 469 U.S. 38 (1984) ("Even if nothing unexpected happens at trial, the district judge is free, in the exercise of sound judicial discretion, to alter a previous *in limine* ruling.").

41. United States v. Griffin, 818 F.2d 97 (1st Cir. 1987).

42. See United States v. Browne, 829 F.2d 760 (9th Cir. 1987) (defendant had no right to definitive *in limine* determination; Trial Court was uncertain as to how it would rule at trial).

43. See United States v. Hickey, 596 F.2d 1082 (1st Cir. 1979).

44. See, e.g., United States v. Barletta, 644 F.2d 50 (1st Cir. 1981).

45. For a discussion of the advantages and disadvantages of permitting appellate review where the defendant complains about an impeachment ruling made *in limine* even though he did not testify, see Saltzburg, *Tactics of the Motion in Limine,* 9 LITIG., No. 4, at 17 (1983).

The Lower Courts have extended the *Luce* principle to other forms of impeachment, such as impeachment with bad acts under Rule 608.[46]

Renewing an in limine objection at trial

Because *in limine* rulings are provisional, a litigant ordinarily must renew an objection at trial in order to preserve it for appeal. Yet there will be some limited situations in which a motion *in limine* alone will preserve an objection. The Lower Courts have set forth three requirements for this exception to the contemporaneous objection rule: (1) The issue must be fairly presented to the Trial Court at the time of the pretrial hearing; (2) the issue must be of the type that can be finally decided in a pretrial hearing; and (3) the Judge must make an unequivocal ruling on the issue.[47]

As a policy matter, it makes sense to dispense with a contemporaneous objection requirement under these limited circumstances. Where the Trial Judge has already made a definitive ruling, on a matter that can be fairly determined before trial, a contemporary objection requirement imposes a needless formality. It must be remembered that Rule 46 of the Federal Rules of Civil Procedure, and Rule 51 of the Federal Rules of Criminal Procedure, both state that formal exceptions are unnecessary. If a formal exception were required in the limited circumstances set forth above, it would cause an unwarranted interruption of the trial. It would also result in a needless provocation of the Trial Judge, and in extreme cases it could subject the objecting attorney to sanctions. For example, in *United States v. Lui,* 941 F.2d 844 (9th Cir. 1991), the defendant moved *in limine* to exclude drug courier profile testimony. The Trial Judge found the motion frivolous and threatened to impose sanctions. Obviously, defense counsel in *Lui* should not have been required to risk sanctions by renewing his objection at trial; the Trial Judge made painfully clear how he would rule on such an objection. The Court of Appeals held that under these circumstances, the defendant had sufficiently preserved his objection to the profile evidence by moving to exclude the evidence *in limine.*

Other examples of rulings as to which a motion *in limine* has been held to preserve an objection include: (1) an *in limine* ruling that a prior conviction was automatically

---

46. See, e.g., United States v. Sanderson, 966 F.2d 184 (6th Cir. 1992) ("an appeal of a Rule 608(b) ruling is precluded where the defendant did not testify at trial"); United States v. Weichert, 783 F.2d 23 (2d Cir. 1986) ("there is no reason to distinguish Rule 608(b) cases from Rule 609 cases"); United States v. DiMatteo, 759 F.2d 831 (11th Cir. 1985):

> We now hold under *Luce* that a defendant's decision not to present a witness whose credibility would have formed the basis of an evidentiary objection under Rule 608(b) forecloses our ability to review the claim that the district court might have erroneously allowed extrinsic evidence to impeach that witness in violation of Rule 608(b).

47. See Cook v. Hoppin, 783 F.2d 684 (7th Cir. 1986); Greger v. International Jensen, Inc., 820 F.2d 937 (8th Cir. 1987); Palmerin v. City of Riverside, 794 F.2d 1409 (9th Cir. 1986).

admissible under Rule 609(a)(2);[48] (2) a ruling on the admissibility of posthypnotic recollection — the reliability of such evidence is an admissibility question independent of the context of the trial;[49] (3) a ruling on the admissibility of medical records as business records under Rule 803(6);[50] and (4) a ruling that a hearsay statement did not violate the defendant's right to confrontation.[51] For further examples, consult the annotated cases under this Rule.

Though there are some limited circumstances in which a party is entitled to rely on an adverse *in limine* ruling, the more prudent practice is to renew objections at trial, even if it may not always be necessary. Counsel can never be certain that the three requirements for preserving an objection *in limine*, set forth above, will be met in any particular case. As one Court put it, the three-part test "carries with it the inherent risk that the Appellate Court might find the objection was of the type that must be renewed and that the party, by relying on the motion *in limine*, has waived the objection."[52] Most evidentiary objections are based on trial context and will be waived if not renewed at trial. Thus, it makes sense to forgo an objection only in those limited cases where the Judge has made it clear that he or she will be annoyed (or more) by renewed objection on the point.[53] Should counsel believe that the Court has foreclosed an issue, obtaining a statement from the Court to that effect is prudent practice, and such a statement from the Court should be sufficient to ensure that the issue is preserved for appeal.

---

48. United States v. Mejia-Alarcon, 995 F.2d 982 (10th Cir. 1993), *cert. denied*, 114 S. Ct. 334 (1993) (noting that the Rule 609(a)(2) question is essentially a question of law — either a crime involves dishonesty or false statement, and hence is automatically admissible, or it does not; no judicial balancing is required at trial). The Court in *Mejia* contrasted other evidentiary questions which are "very fact-bound determinations dependent upon the character of the evidence produced at trial." For example, if the pretrial objection is made under Rule 403, it is extremely unlikely that the ruling will be definitive enough to dispense with an objection at trial. This is because Rule 403 requires a careful balancing of probative value and prejudicial effect that is ordinarily dependent on trial context. See Freeman v. Package Mach. Co., 865 F.2d 1331 (1st Cir. 1988) ("The importance of a contemporaneous objection is at its zenith in a situation such as this, where defendant's *in limine* motion invoked Fed. R. Evid. 403."). Similarly, if the defendant's conviction in *Mejia* had been held admissible for impeachment under Rule 609(a)(1) (rather than under the automatic admissibility standard of Rule 609(a)(2)), the defendant would have been required to renew his objection at trial in order to preserve it. This is because, as the Court in *Mejia* recognized, "any final determination as to admissibility under Rule 609(a)(1) rests on a balancing of the probative value and prejudicial effect of the conviction — a balancing that could only properly be performed after an assessment of the evidence that had come in up to the point of its admission."

49. Sprynczynatyk v. General Motors Corp., 771 F.2d 1112 (8th Cir. 1985).

50. Cook v. Hoppin, 783 F.2d 684 (7th Cir. 1986).

51. United States v. Szabo, 789 F.2d 1484 (10th Cir. 1986).

52. United States v. Mejia-Alarcon, 995 F.2d 982 (10th Cir. 1993).

53. See United States v. Haddad, 10 F.3d 1252 (7th Cir. 1993) (defendant should have renewed objection where it was clear that Trial Judge's *in limine* ruling was provisional: "he had not closed the door on this issue").

C. ANNOTATED CASES

RULE 103(a) — EFFECT OF ERRONEOUS RULING

Affirmance on a different theory

United States v. Williams, 837 F.2d 1009 (11th Cir.), *cert. denied*, 109 S. Ct. 490 (1988): The Court held that "yellow sheets" were properly admitted against a defendant charged with filing a false tax return, where the defendant's initials were identified at the bottom of several sheets. The government had not relied on the admissions exemption at trial, but the Court found no unfairness in permitting the exemption to be relied upon on appeal.

Harmless error — civil cases

Lataille v. Ponte, 754 F.2d 33 (1st Cir. 1985): The Court determined that the erroneous admission of an inmate's disciplinary record required reversal of a judgment for prison guards in an action alleging that the guards beat the inmate. In deciding that the error was prejudicial, the Court focused on "[t]he centrality of the evidence, its prejudicial effect, whether it is cumulative, the use of the evidence by counsel, and the closeness of the case."

Habecker v. Copperloy Corp., 893 F.2d 49 (3d Cir. 1990): The Court reversed a judgment for the defendants in a product liability action arising out of a forklift accident, holding that error in excluding testimony by the plaintiff's proposed expert was not harmless because it could not be said to be "highly probable" that the error did not affect a party's rights. In *McQueeny v. Wilmington Trust Co.*, 779 F.2d 916 (3d Cir. 1985), the Court reversed a judgment for a seaman in a Jones Act case, finding that the Trial Judge erred in excluding evidence from which it could have been inferred that the seaman had suborned perjury of a proffered witness. It determined that the error was prejudicial, and it held that the same standard should be used for assessing the harmless or prejudicial nature of errors in civil and criminal cases. Thus, it relied upon its prior decision in *Government of Virgin Islands v. Toto*, 529 F.2d 278 (3d Cir. 1976) (*infra*). In *Salas v. Wang*, 846 F.2d 897 (3d Cir. 1988), a medical malpractice case brought on behalf of a child who suffered severe brain damage, the Court applied its *McQueeny* harmless error rule and held that inappropriate remarks made by the plaintiff's counsel during closing argument did not require reversal of a judgment for the plaintiff.

Munn v. Algee, 924 F.2d 568 (5th Cir.), *cert. denied*, 112 S. Ct. 277 (1991): An automobile accident victim, following the tenets of her Jehovah's Witnesses faith, refused blood transfusions and died of her injuries. On trial of the ensuing wrongful death and survival action, her husband was asked about, *inter alia*, the Jehovah's Witnesses' refusal to "do service to their country" and to salute the flag. One Judge concluded that admission of the evidence was an abuse of discretion under the Rule primarily because it was utterly irrelevant to how sincerely the victim and her husband adhered to the faith. However, the Judge believed, because no prejudice was reflected in the verdict, that the error did not affect the plaintiff's substantial rights; the award of $10,000 for eight hours of pain and suffering was not so small as to arouse suspicion, and denial of any wrongful death damages might have reflected a belief that the victim would have lived had she taken blood transfusions. The concurring Judge disagreed that the evidence was irrelevant and said nothing about its prejudicial effect. The dissenting Judge considered that the calculated inflammatory effect of cross-examination regarding the views of other members of the faith had a prejudicial effect far beyond the probative value of the examination on the personal beliefs of the plaintiff-witness. In his view, there was no way a reviewing court could be sure the appeal to religious prejudice and nationalism "had but slight effect" on the verdict.

Haddad v. Lockheed Corp., 720 F.2d 1454 (9th Cir. 1983): Although it was error in an employment discrimination suit to admit testimony of the plaintiff's ex-wife that revealed marital communications, the Court found that the error was harmless and affirmed a judgment for the defendant. The Court held that "when an appellate court ponders the probable effect of an error on a civil trial, it need only find that the jury's verdict is more probably than not untainted by the error."

Aetna Cas. & Sur. Co. v. Gosdin, 803 F.2d 1153 (11th Cir. 1986): In a dispute between an insurer and its insured concerning the cause of a fire, the Court observed that the Circuits are divided on whether different harmless error standards should be used in civil and criminal cases. It did not offer an opinion on the question, since it found that certain evidence was improperly admitted and prejudicial under any standard.

Harmless error — criminal cases

United States v. Logan, 998 F.2d 1025 (D.C. Cir.), *cert. denied,* 114 S. Ct. 569 (1993): A defense witness in a drug prosecution was impeached with convictions for misdemeanor offenses of taking property without a right and distributing marijuana and PCP. The Court held the error was harmless because it was a witness rather than a defendant who was impeached, the prosecution did not emphasize the convictions, a proper limiting instruction was promptly given, the witness' story was confirmed in part by another witness, and the other evidence against the defendant was strong. The dissenting Judge observed that when a defendant does not testify and presents his case through others, improper impeachment (particularly of the defendant's chief witness) is likely to be prejudicial and not harmless.

United States v. Lamberty, 778 F.2d 59 (1st Cir. 1985): The Court reversed a postmaster's conviction for opening another's package, because the government wrongly elicited testimony that investigators suspected the postmaster of thefts. It stated that "[w]hen faced in a criminal case with a clearly prejudicial error, unless it is certain that the error is harmless beyond a reasonable doubt, a court should not be forced to gamble with a defendant's liberty." See also *United States v. Ferreira,* 821 F.2d 1 (1st Cir. 1987) (reversing bank robbery conviction for admission of evidence concerning weapons seized from the defendant upon his arrest; not a harmless error, using "beyond a reasonable doubt" standard).

United States v. Musacchia, 900 F.2d 493 (2d Cir. 1990), *cert. denied,* 111 S. Ct. 2887 (1991): The Court, reviewing a tax evasion case, held that error in permitting three prosecution witnesses to testify on direct about "truth-telling" provisions in their cooperation agreements was harmless, as elicitation of the testimony was not an intentional violation, the defense conceded the truthfulness of testimony by two of the witnesses, the third's testimony was peripheral, and the Judge gave a clear curative instruction not to consider the bolstering evidence.

United States v. Dowling, 855 F.2d 114 (3d Cir. 1988), *aff'd,* 493 U.S. 342 (1990): The Court applied its harmless error test for nonconstitutional errors in this case and found that error in the introduction of prior act evidence was harmless. The Court reached the same result in *United States v. Echeverri,* 854 F.2d 638 (3d Cir. 1988). In *Government of Virgin Islands v. Joseph,* 685 F.2d 857 (3d Cir. 1982), the Court, using the "beyond a reasonable doubt" test of harmless error (which it usually reserves for constitutional errors), reversed convictions for assault, robbery, and rape because two documents not admitted into evidence were submitted to the jury. In *United States v. Zarintash,* 736 F.2d 66 (3d Cir. 1984), the Court again seemed to equate its test for judging the effect of nonconstitutional error with the test used for constitutional errors. In *Government of Virgin Islands v. Toto,* 529 F.2d 278 (3d Cir. 1976), the Court had indicated that it would reverse criminal convictions because of error unless it could say that it is highly probable that the error did not contribute to the judgment of conviction. It reiterated this test in *United States v. Cook,* 538 F.2d 1000 (3d Cir. 1976).

United States v. Urbanik, 801 F.2d 692 (4th Cir. 1986): The Court reversed a defendant's marijuana convictions because coconspirator statements were improperly admitted. It stated that a nonconstitutional error could be harmless only where it is highly probable that the error did not affect the judgment.

United States v. Valdez, 722 F.2d 1196 (5th Cir. 1984): The Court reversed a conviction for extortion, finding that the use of hypnosis on an identifying witness presented dangers of undue suggestiveness and that the resulting evidence was more prejudicial than probative. It found that the admission of the evidence was prejudicial, not harmless, error. The opinion recognized that in some prior cases, the Court had appeared to test nonconstitutional errors by the demanding test of harmlessness required for constitutional errors. The Court stated that those prior expressions were inadvertent and that nonconstitutional errors are not as likely to require reversal as constitutional ones.

United States v. McFayden-Snider, 552 F.2d 1178 (6th Cir. 1977), *cert. denied,* 435 U.S. 995 (1978): Using the "beyond a reasonable doubt" test, the Court reversed convictions in a bank fraud case, holding that the prosecutor improperly attempted to impeach the defendant with proof of her sexual conduct and that evidence of bad checks she wrote was improperly admitted because "it directly imputed to her other bad acts that were not necessary to prove the prosecution's case." Furthermore, the Trial Judge failed to give complete limiting instructions. See also *United States v. Shepard,* 538 F.2d 107 (6th Cir. 1976); *United States v. Rowan,* 518 F.2d 685 (6th Cir.), *cert. denied,* 423 U.S. 949 (1975).

United States v. Dominguez, 992 F.2d 678 (7th Cir.), *cert. denied,* 114 S. Ct. 250 (1993): In a cocaine distribution prosecution, an agent testified that she had learned from Guatemalan police that tests of the delivered packages had revealed cocaine. The Court held it was harmless error to admit the testimony, as there was strong evidence of the defendant's participation in a conspiracy and no proof of the identity of a controlled substance is required. A dissenting Judge argued that all the evidence was consistent with an intent to engage in a sham transaction rather than a drug deal, so it was impossible to conclude that the hearsay evidence did not have a substantial influence on the jury's verdict.

United States v. Hitt, 981 F.2d 422 (9th Cir. 1992): Reversing a defendant's conviction for possessing a machine gun, the Court held it was reversible error to admit a photograph that showed a dozen weapons in addition to the one charged. The Court observed a conflict in the Circuit as to whether the harmless error test permits affirmance only if the Court can say with "fair assurance" that an error was harmless or whether affirmance is required if it is more probable than not that an error was harmless. The Court found that the error was prejudicial under either test and thus did not resolve the conflict. In *United States v. Dixon,* 562 F.2d 1138 (9th Cir. 1977), *cert. denied,* 435 U.S. 927 (1979), the Court said that plain error requires reversal only when it is *"highly probable* that the error materially affected the jury's verdict," whereas nonconstitutional error properly raised in the Trial Court requires reversal unless "it is more *probable* than not that the error did not materially affect the verdict" (emphasis in original). See also *United States v. Soulard,* 730 F.2d 1292 (9th Cir. 1984) (reiterating that nonconstitutional errors would not require reversal unless it is more probable than not that they affected verdict). In *United States v. Englin,* 571 F.2d 1069 (9th Cir. 1977), *cert. denied,* 435 U.S. 906 (1978), the Court indicated that, before deciding on the appropriate test for harmless error, it was appropriate to decide whether it was dealing with a violation of the hearsay rules only or with a confrontation problem. See also *United States v. Ragghianti,* 560 F.2d 1376 (9th Cir. 1977) (error for failing to give limiting instruction must be harmless beyond a reasonable doubt); *United States v. Tebha,* 770 F.2d 1454 (9th Cir. 1985) (constitutional standard used when exhibit not in evidence reaches jury).

United States v. Polsinelli, 649 F.2d 793 (10th Cir. 1981): The Court used the "beyond a reasonable doubt" standard in finding a mistake in the prosecutor's cross-examination of character witnesses to have been prejudicial error.

United States v. Lehder-Rivas, 955 F.2d 1510 (11th Cir.), *cert. denied,* 113 S. Ct. 347 (1992): The Court held that it was harmless error when the government suggested that the defendant in a cocaine importation conspiracy engaged in frequent "partying" and fathered an illegitimate child. A concurring Judge believed that the majority opinion improperly blended the "harmless beyond a reasonable doubt" standard applicable to errors of constitutional magnitude and the "harmless error" standard of Federal Rule of Criminal Procedure 52(a). In the majority's view, to the extent there is any difference in the standards, the Circuit has employed the constitutional standard for nonconstitutional evidentiary errors; in any event, the error in this case was harmless by either standard.

In limine rulings admitting impeachment
evidence — appealability

United States v. Griffin, 818 F.2d 97 (1st Cir.), *cert. denied,* 108 S. Ct. 137 (1987): The Court affirmed marijuana convictions, holding that the defendant failed to preserve for appeal an objection to an *in limine* ruling that the government could elicit from a witness the fact that he had been threatened by a third party if the defense impeached the witness with evidence that he withheld information from investigators for more than a year. Since the defense never attacked the witness, the threat evidence was not offered. The defendant could not appeal from the tentative ruling, since "it is too great a handicap to bind a trial judge to a ruling on a subtle evidentiary question, requiring the most delicate balancing, outside a precise factual context."

United States v. Weichert, 783 F.2d 23 (2d Cir.), *cert. denied*, 107 S. Ct. 117 (1986): The Court relied upon *Luce v. United States* (see Editorial Explanatory Comment) to hold that defendants in a fraud case could not challenge an *in limine* ruling permitting the government to ask an attorney-witness about his disbarment if he testified, since the defendants never called him as a witness. In *United States v. DiPaolo*, 804 F.2d 225 (2d Cir. 1986), the Court affirmed convictions for intimidating witnesses, holding that a defendant could not appeal an *in limine* ruling that denied his motion to preclude impeaching a witness with a prior criminal conviction, since the witness never testified.

Rojas v. Richardson, 713 F.2d 116 (5th Cir. 1983): The Court held in an employee's personal injury action that a motion *in limine* to preclude testimony about the plaintiff's status as an illegal alien did not preserve his claim of error, where his counsel mentioned the status during jury selection and made no objection to references by the defense.

United States v. Sanderson, 966 F.2d 184 (6th Cir. 1992): In a prosecution for theft of government property, the Trial Judge ruled that evidence of prior thefts by the defendant was not admissible on the government's direct case but would be admissible under Rule 608(b) to impeach the defendant if he took the stand. The Court held that the defendant was precluded from appealing that ruling because he did not testify at trial.

Jones v. Collier, 762 F.2d 71 (8th Cir. 1985): The Court ruled that a plaintiff in a civil rights action waived any objection to impeachment with a prior conviction by presenting evidence of the conviction on direct examination following an unsuccessful motion *in limine*. But see *United States v. Key*, 717 F.2d 1206 (8th Cir. 1983) (defendant permitted to appeal *in limine* ruling admitting prior convictions for impeachment even though he introduced them on direct).

United States v. Williams, 939 F.2d 721 (9th Cir. 1991): The Court held that a defendant convicted for possession of cocaine had waived the right to appeal from an adverse *in limine* ruling by bringing out the fact of his prior conviction during direct examination. By the defendant's strategic choice at trial, the Trial Judge and the government were deprived of a last chance to reverse their prestated positions.

United States v. Mejia-Alarcon, 995 F.2d 982 (10th Cir.), *cert. denied*, 114 S. Ct. 334 (1993): Although the Court affirmed a defendant's drug and firearms convictions, it held that he had preserved the right to appeal the Trial Judge's *in limine* ruling that a prior conviction for a food stamp offense could be admitted as a "dishonesty" crime for impeachment if he testified. Defense counsel made no objection to the introduction of the conviction during trial and in fact elicited testimony about it on direct examination of the defendant. While ruling that an *in limine* ruling could be appealed if (1) the issue had been adequately presented to the Trial Judge, (2) the issue had been of a type that can be finally decided in a pretrial hearing, and (3) the ruling was definitive, the Court stressed that "[p]rudent counsel will renew objections at trial" rather than take the risk that an appellate court would find one of the requirements unsatisfied.

United States v. DiMatteo, 759 F.2d 831 (11th Cir. 1985), *rev'g on remand* 716 F.2d 1361 (1983), *cert. denied,* 474 U.S. 860 (1985): The Court held, affirming a conviction for a marijuana importation conspiracy, that the failure to present a defense witness barred appellate review of an *in limine* ruling regarding permissible cross-examination and rebuttal of the witness.

In limine rulings admitting other evidence — appealability

Clausen v. Sea-3, Inc., 21 F.3d 1181 (1st Cir. 1994): The Court held in an employee's personal injury action that a defendant's objection to evidence of subsequent remedial measures was not preserved when it failed to renew the objection at trial after its *in limine* motion to exclude had been denied. In *United States v. Nivica,* 887 F.2d 1110 (1st Cir. 1989), the defendant sought an *in limine* ruling limiting the scope of cross-examination if he took the stand, but the Judge said he would be subject to cross-examination on all matters relevant to the issue at hand. The Court held that the defendant had not preserved the issue for appeal, as he did not testify. One Judge concurred because Circuit precedent did not limit *Luce* to Rule 609(a) issues. In *Freeman v. Package Machinery Co.,* 865 F.2d 1331 (1st Cir. 1988), the Court held that an employer waived any objection to a plaintiff's statistical proof in an age discrimination case by failing to object to an expert's testimony during trial. The Trial Judge had ruled *in limine* that the expert could testify if the employee laid a proper foundation, and the defendant failed to object after the foundation evidence was offered. Although the Court recognized that a ruling on an *in limine* motion may be definitive enough to excuse omission of an objection at trial, it stated that it was unclear in this case whether the defendant continued to object to statistical evidence and on what grounds. The Court added that "the importance of a contemporaneous objection is at its zenith in a situation such as this, where defendant's *in limine* motion invoked Fed. R. Evid. 403."

United States v. Ortiz, 857 F.2d 900 (2d Cir. 1988), *cert. denied,* 109 S. Ct. 1352 (1989): In a drug prosecution in which the defendant disputed identity, the Court cited earlier cases (discussed under Rule 404(b), *infra*) for the proposition that other act evidence may not be used to prove intent when the defendant denies altogether doing the act charged. In the instant case, the Court found that defense counsel appeared inclined to argue both mistaken identity and intent. Defense counsel did not challenge the Trial Judge's ruling that a prior conviction could be used to rebut the intent argument if it were raised, and thus waived any complaint about the ruling.

Government of Virgin Islands v. Joseph, 964 F.2d 1380 (3d Cir. 1992): The Court held that the defendant's failure to object at trial to hearsay evidence did not constitute waiver where the issue had been raised by a pretrial motion with supporting memorandum, had been considered at a hearing during the trial at which both counsel were given a chance to advocate their positions, and had been the subject of a definitive ruling made with no suggestion that it would be reconsidered at trial. In *American Home Assur. Co. v. Sunshine Supermarket,* 753 F.2d 321 (3d Cir. 1985), an action on a fire insurance policy, the insurance company had moved *in limine* to exclude evidence that the insured was not prosecuted for arson, but the Trial Judge had ruled that the evidence could be admitted if the company relied on opinions by local officials that the insured was responsible for the fire. Holding that the company preserved for appeal its claim that admission of the evidence was error, the Court reasoned that if an evidence issue is fully briefed and the Judge is able and willing to make a definitive pretrial ruling, there is no necessity for a litigant to repeat during the trial an objection to evidence that the Judge has indicated will be admitted.

United States v. Fortenberry, 919 F.2d 923, *denying reh'g en banc to* 914 F.2d 671 (5th Cir. 1990), *cert. denied,* 111 S. Ct. 1333 (1991): The defendant, charged with conspiracy to commit arson and other offenses, moved *in limine* to exclude evidence of uncharged crimes; at a hearing on the motion, the Trial Judge permitted defense counsel to enter a continuing objection to the testimony and instructed that objecting further at trial was unnecessary. The Court held that the continuing objection preserved error for appeal under the Rule, but noted its displeasure at the procedure, which precludes a reevaluation of admissibility in context. In *United States Aviation Underwriters, Inc. v. Olympia Wings, Inc.,* 896 F.2d 949 (5th Cir. 1990), the Court held that the insurer, in its declaratory judgment action to determine whether coverage applied to an accident involving its insured's aircraft, did not preserve objections to two witness' testimony regarding a settlement by objecting when another witness was asked about the settlement, even though introduction of the evidence violated an *in limine* ruling. See also *Marcel v. Placid Oil Co.,* 11 F.3d 563 (5th Cir. 1994) (denial of motion *in limine* to exclude expert's testimony not preserved when no objection made at trial); *Wilson v. Waggener,* 837 F.2d 220 (5th Cir. 1988) (*in limine* request to exclude parol evidence in contract action insufficient, without objection at trial, to preserve appeal; no plain error found).

United States v. York, 933 F.2d 1343 (7th Cir.), *cert. denied,* 112 S. Ct. 321 (1991): Because the defendant in a mail fraud and arson case did not renew at trial hearsay objections asserted *in limine* and overruled, the Court held that review was under a plain error standard. See also *United States v. Haddad,* 10 F.3d 1252 (7th Cir. 1993) (conditional *in limine* ruling admitting defendant's state court guilty plea not preserved when no objection made at trial). In *Cook v. Hoppin,* 783 F.2d 684 (7th Cir. 1986), the Court reversed a judgment for a landlord in a suit by a tenant's visitor who sustained injuries in a fall from an exterior stairway. It found that the Trial Judge erroneously admitted statements in medical records indicating that the plaintiff had been injured in a shoving or wrestling match. The plaintiff offered the records after the Trial Judge ruled *in limine* that they were admissible. The Court concluded that once the ruling was made, the plaintiff could treat it as the law of the case and rely upon it without waiving his objection to the records.

Hale v. Firestone Tire & Rubber Co., 756 F.2d 1322 (8th Cir. 1985): In a product liability action brought against manufacturers of a tire rim that separated and struck one of the plaintiffs as he attempted to inflate a truck tire, the Court found that a motion *in limine* to prevent the plaintiffs from using derogatory terms to refer to the rim was insufficient to preserve claims of error with respect to references made during trial by plaintiffs' counsel. The Court indicated that the defendants should have objected when the references were made during trial.

United States v. Palmer, 3 F.3d 300 (9th Cir. 1993), *cert. denied,* 114 S. Ct. 1120 (1994): Affirming a conviction for manufacturing marijuana plants, the Court held it was error (but harmless) to admit the defendant's postarraignment statement to law enforcement officials. Although the defendant had objected prior to trial to admission of the statement, he did not renew the objection at trial. The Court held, 2-1, that "requiring a contemporaneous objection immediately after the district court has denied a pretrial objection and motion on the same grounds would have the perverse result of making form the master of substance." In *United States v. Cuozzo,* 962 F.2d 945 (9th Cir.), *cert. denied,* 113 S. Ct. 475 (1992), the government represented at a hearing on the defendant's Rule 404(b) objection that it could show the defendant, who was charged with fraud, had previously participated in a similar scheme. The Court held that the evidence produced at trial was insufficient to allow a jury to find she had previously acted with fraudulent intent, but because she did not move to strike the evidence when the government failed to satisfy its burden of proof, the issue was reviewable only for plain error, and the Court found none. In *United States v. Lui,* 941 F.2d 844 (9th Cir. 1991), a defendant charged with importation and possession of heroin filed a motion *in limine* to exclude drug courier profile testimony; the motion was denied, and he did not object when the testimony was offered at trial. The Court reviewed admission of the testimony for abuse of discretion rather than plain error, because when the motion was denied as frivolous and sanctions were threatened, the defendant should not be penalized for failure to raise the objection again. See also *Palmerin v. Riverside,* 794 F.2d 1409 (9th Cir. 1986) (where Judge makes explicit and definitive ruling on *in limine* motion, an objection need not be renewed). In *Coursen v. A.H. Robins Co.,* 764 F.2d 1329 (9th Cir. 1985), a suit for Dalkon Shield injuries, two of the plaintiffs took involuntary dismissals with prejudice following an *in limine* ruling that evidence of their sexual history would be admitted. The Court held that a litigant cannot make a nonfinal order appealable by taking a voluntary nonsuit. It vacated the judgment of dismissal, however, and remanded the case because it was possible that the Judge as well as the litigants assumed that the dismissals were proper vehicles for obtaining review of the *in limine* ruling.

McEwen v. City of Norman, Okla., 926 F.2d 1539 (10th Cir. 1991): The Court held in a civil rights action that the plaintiff, whose motion *in limine* to exclude an expert's testimony had been denied but who made no objection when the expert testified at trial, had not preserved the issue for appeal. Only by specific, timely trial objection can the Judge entertain reconsideration of the grounds for the motion in light of the actual trial testimony and the surrounding circumstances developed at trial.

In limine rulings excluding evidence — appealability

Fusco v. General Motors Corp., 11 F.3d 259 (1st Cir. 1993): In a product liability action, the Trial Court granted the plaintiff's *in limine* motion to exclude a videotape in which the defendant purportedly demonstrated what would have happened had the product failed in the manner contended by the plaintiff. The Court held that the defendant had preserved its appeal without seeking to offer the tape at trial. Unlike renewing an objection after an *in limine* motion to exclude has been denied, which is "child's play," requiring renewal of an offer of proof would be wasteful and inconvenient where the pretrial proffer is adequate and the evidence has been excluded unconditionally.

McQuaig v. McCoy, 806 F.2d 1298 (5th Cir. 1987): In a false arrest and imprisonment action, the plaintiffs moved at a pretrial conference for admission of the entire internal affairs investigation report. The Trial Judge ruled that the report could be used for a limited purpose only, and the plaintiffs twice objected to the ruling during trial. Although the plaintiffs made no formal offer of proof, the Court, holding they had preserved the issue for appeal, stated that

> [i]n a situation such as the present case where the party has gone into such detail (six pages in the record) as to the substance of the evidence and why it should be admitted and where the actual investigation report was later filed as part of the record, we believe the issue has been properly preserved for appeal.

In *Garner v. Santoro,* 865 F.2d 629 (5th Cir. 1989), the Court held that a manufacturer was not required to make an offer of proof at trial on a government contractor defense, since the Trial Judge had precluded the defense well in advance of trial.

In limine rulings — requirement of record

United States v. Mitchell, 954 F.2d 663 (11th Cir. 1992): In a Hobbs Act prosecution of police officers for fixing drunk driving tickets, the Trial Judge granted the defendants' *in limine* motion to exclude on grounds of Rules 702 and 403 the testimony of a government expert on alcoholism and highway safety. There was no record of the arguments by counsel, the proffer of the expert's testimony made *in camera,* or the Judge's oral ruling; it was, therefore, impossible to conclude that the precluded testimony could under no circumstances have been admissible, so the Court vacated the order and remanded with instructions to conduct an adequate hearing. The Court also noted its doubts about the appropriateness of a pretrial ruling on the question, as relevancy issues depend on the exact state of the record at the time the evidence is offered.

In limine rulings — summary judgment

Zenith Radio Corp. v. Matsushita Elec. Indus. Co., 723 F.2d 238 (3d Cir. 1983), *rev'd on other grounds,* 475 U.S. 574 (1986): In a massive antitrust case against Japanese television manufacturers, the Court reversed most of the summary judgment for the defendants but expressed its approval of the District Court's substantial use of *in limine* hearings on evidence questions "not only because the court's *in limine* consideration was far more efficient than if the rulings were deferred until the trial, with consequent interruptions, but also because the *in limine* procedure permitted more thorough briefing and argument than would have been likely had the rulings been deferred." Although the Court noted that there are "countervailing considerations, especially with respect to relevancy rulings under Rule 403 which may be made pretrial without the benefit of the flavor of the record developed at trial," it found that the Trial Judge has discretion to make those rulings prior to trial and that the discretion was properly exercised in this case.

Objections — acquiescence in ruling

United States v. Rogers, 918 F.2d 207 (D.C. Cir. 1990): The defendant in a crack possession case objected on grounds of Rules 404(b) and 403 to other crimes evidence, but the Trial Judge admitted the evidence. During a conference on limiting instructions after the defendant rested, the prosecutor represented that the defendant was no longer objecting on Rule 404(b) grounds and defense counsel did not protest, nor did he request any limiting instruction. Affirming the conviction, the Court held that the Rule 404(b) objection had been waived by acquiescence, but the Rule 403 objection to the evidence was preserved, as the prosecutor had not mentioned it, and the defense lawyer, by making the strategic choice not to ask for a limiting instruction, did not thereby waive his remaining objection to admission of the evidence in the first instance.

Objections — failure to object

United States v. Lopez, 709 F.2d 742 (1st Cir.), *cert. denied,* 104 S. Ct. 187 (1983): Because no objection was made to conspirators' statements, the Court said that the Trial Judge was not required to make a finding that a conspiracy existed and that the declarants and the defendant were part of it before admitting the statements.

United States v. Sandini, 803 F.2d 123 (3d Cir. 1986), *cert. denied,* 107 S. Ct. 1306 (1987): In a marijuana conspiracy case, the Court held that a defendant could not argue on appeal that evidence should have been excluded under Rules 403 and 404(b), since neither of these Rules was relied upon in the Trial Court.

United States v. Mejia, 844 F.2d 209 (5th Cir. 1988): The Court declined to consider on appeal an objection to a document describing a company's business, since no hearsay objection was raised below. In *United States v. Vesich,* 724 F.2d 451 (5th Cir. 1984), the Court held that the failure to object to other act evidence barred review on appeal.

Helminiski v. Ayerst Labs., 766 F.2d 208 (6th Cir.), *cert. denied,* 474 U.S. 981 (1985): Affirming a judgment for a manufacturer in a product liability action, the Court rejected an argument that a failure to object to comments by the Trial Judge and opposing counsel should be excused because the plaintiff's counsel did not want to call attention to the comments by objecting. The Court reasoned that "[w]hile under limited circumstances an objection might only exacerbate an error in admission of testimony, ... counsel is generally not excused from bringing an objection to the court's attention," since "[a]ny other general rule would eviscerate Fed. R. Evid. 103(a)(1)." See also *United States v. Brady,* 595 F.2d 359 (6th Cir.), *cert. denied,* 444 U.S. 862 (1979) (failure to object to scientific evidence).

United States v. Pallais, 921 F.2d 684 (7th Cir. 1990), *cert. denied,* 112 S. Ct. 134 (1991): In a drug conspiracy prosecution, a witness was asked whether he had been told who would be flying a plane, the Trial Judge overruled a hearsay objection, and the witness then volunteered the names without objection. The government argued that the prosecutor should not be blamed because a witness blurts out an answer to a question that has not been asked, but the Court rejected the argument as shallow casuistry. Since it was clear to the witness and the defense counsel that the identity of the pilots was sought, the hearsay objection was timely and preserved the point for appeal. Error in admitting the evidence was harmless, however.

Owen v. Patton, 925 F.2d 1111 (8th Cir. 1991): During the trial of a personal injury action against a tavern owner whose employee allegedly committed a battery, defense counsel repeatedly brought out that the plaintiff's companions were now incarcerated, despite instructions to end the line of inquiry. Because the plaintiff's counsel did not object, move to strike, request special instructions, or move for a mistrial, however, the Trial Judge was not called upon to make a ruling that could result in error for failure to accommodate the request. Although the Court did not grant a new trial, it did exercise its discretionary authority to deny costs to the prevailing party. In *United States v. Michaels,* 726 F.2d 1307 (8th Cir.), *cert. denied,* 105 S. Ct. 92 (1984), the Court affirmed a conviction for conspiracy to bomb an automobile, declining to consider "foundation" objections to a magazine that was found to contain the appellant's fingerprint and a map resembling the neighborhood surrounding the bomb scene. The defendant failed to raise the objections at trial, and the Court indicated that admission of an exhibit on the basis of a general, not a specific, foundation is sufficient when no request is made for greater specificity. In *Terrell v. Poland,* 744 F.2d 637 (8th Cir. 1984), the Court affirmed a judgment for an insurance company, which proved arson in a suit on a fire insurance policy. The Court found that, by failing to object when it was offered, the plaintiffs waived their hearsay objection to a written statement of a person who stated that she saw the plaintiffs move furniture from their nightclub two weeks before the fire. A motion to strike at the close of the evidence came too late.

Esco Corp. v. United States, 750 F.2d 1466 (9th Cir. 1985): The Court held that a taxpayer who failed to object to the admission of letters as settlement negotiations could not raise the objection for the first time on appeal.

Objections — general relevancy objections

Bonilla v. Yamaha Motors Corp., 955 F.2d 150 (1st Cir. 1992): Reversing a judgment for the defendant in a product liability action arising out of a motorcycle accident, the Court held that an objection stated to be on grounds of Rules 402, irrelevancy, and 403, prejudice, was sufficient to preserve error in admission of evidence that the plaintiff had been convicted of speeding. The plaintiff specifically raised Rule 404(b) in a later request for an instruction to the jury; given the close relation between Rules 404(b) and 403, under the circumstances, the objections were sufficiently timely and specific. In *Bryant v. Consolidated Rail Corp.,* 672 F.2d 217 (1st Cir. 1982), an FELA action, the Court held that a relevance objection to a medical report admitted during cross-examination of the plaintiff was insufficient to preserve an objection that the report was improperly used as character evidence in violation of Rule 404.

United States v. Ashman, 979 F.2d 469 (7th Cir. 1992), *cert. denied,* 114 S. Ct. 62 (1993): Where a defendant commodities trader charged with fraud and RICO offenses had objected only to relevancy and materiality of evidence of other transactions but asserted inadmissibility under Rule 404(b) on appeal, the Court held that it would review the evidentiary ruling only for plain error. In *United States v. Wilson,* 966 F.2d 243 (7th Cir. 1992), the defendant objected on grounds of relevance to introduction of a gun at a trial for a cocaine distribution conspiracy. Affirming, the Court held that the defendant's argument on appeal that the prejudicial effect of the gun substantially outweighed its probative value had not been preserved by the objection, which alerted the Trial Judge only to problems under Rules 401 and 402, not Rule 403. See also *United States v. Field*, 875 F.2d 130 (7th Cir. 1989) (objection on grounds of relevancy and remoteness does not preserve Rule 404(b) objection).

Objections — incorrect specific objection

Brookover v. Mary Hitchcock Mem. Hosp., 893 F.2d 411 (1st Cir. 1990): In a medical malpractice action, the plaintiff introduced evidence that after the patient's fall the nurses in the defendant hospital said that he should have been restrained. The Court held that the evidence should not have been admitted as an agent's admission because there was no proof the nurses were employees of the hospital, but that the defendant had waived the objection by asserting only the declarants' lack of personal knowledge of the circumstances. See also *United States v. Barrett*, 766 F.2d 609 (1st Cir.), *cert. denied*, 474 U.S. 923 (1985) (changing grounds for objection from Rule 403 to Rule 608(b) not permitted on appeal).

United States v. Mennuti, 679 F.2d 1032 (2d Cir. 1982): In a prosecution for conspiracy to destroy residences in order to obtain insurance money, the Court found that a defendant could not complain that the Trial Judge's ruling — that if the defendant testified, he could be asked on cross-examination about another act — should have been barred by Rule 608 where his only objection at trial was based on Rule 403.

United States v. Johnson, 722 F.2d 407 (8th Cir. 1983): A defendant convicted as a felon possessing a firearm had objected on relevance grounds to admission of a BATF form that indicated that the gun had been shipped interstate. The Court ruled that a hearsay objection had been waived and rejected a claim that receipt of the form was plain error.

United States v. Gomez-Norena, 908 F.2d 497 (9th Cir.), *cert. denied*, 111 S. Ct. 363 (1990): In reviewing the admission of drug courier profile testimony, the Court noted that the defendant had not preserved the Rule 403 objection being asserted on appeal by his trial objections on Rule 404(b) and hearsay grounds.

Objections — specific grounds

Bonilla v. Yamaha Motors Corp., 955 F.2d 150 (1st Cir. 1992): Reversing a judgment for the defendant in a product liability action arising out of a motorcycle accident, the Court held that an objection stated to be on grounds of Rules 402, irrelevancy, and 403, prejudice, was sufficient to preserve error in admission of evidence that the plaintiff had been convicted of speeding. The plaintiff specifically raised Rule 404(b) in a later request for an instruction to the jury; given the close relation between Rules 404(b) and 403, under the circumstances, the objections were sufficiently timely and specific.

United States v. Musacchia, 900 F.2d 493 (2d Cir. 1990), *cert. denied*, 111 S. Ct. 2887 (1991): The Court held, in reviewing a tax evasion case, that the defendants' objection, without stating grounds, to prosecution witnesses' testimony on direct about "truth-telling" provisions in their cooperation agreements was sufficiently preserved because the ground of objection was apparent from the context.

United States v. Long, 574 F.2d 761 (3d Cir.), *cert. denied,* 439 U.S. 985 (1978): Other crimes evidence was admitted against appellant without a proper specific objection being raised. On appeal, the Court concluded that when no objection under Rule 403 is raised, the Court does not have to deal with the Rule. It added that "[w]here an objection does invoke Rule 403, the trial judge should record his balancing analysis to the extent that his exercise of discretion may be fairly reviewed on appeal. However, where Rule 403 is not invoked, the trial judge's balancing will be subsumed in his ruling."

Dixon v. International Harvester Co., 754 F.2d 573 (5th Cir. 1985): The Court overturned a judgment n.o.v. for the defendant in a personal injury action against the manufacturer of a crawler tractor. The Court found that, in the light of a motion *in limine,* the defendant's objections at trial were specific enough to preserve an issue for appeal. The Court stated that its reasoning was consistent with *Collins v. Wayne Corp.,* 621 F.2d 777 (5th Cir. 1980). See also *United States v. Marshall,* 762 F.2d 419 (5th Cir. 1985) (continuing objection is sufficient to preserve issue for appeal). However, in *Petty v. Ideco,* 761 F.2d 1146 (5th Cir. 1985), the Court refused to permit a party to appeal the use of a videotape when he asked the Trial Judge to entertain objections before the tape was shown and then made no objections after the Judge stated that he would hear specific objections while the tape was shown.

United States v. James T. Barnes & Co., 758 F.2d 146 (6th Cir. 1985): The Court held that an objection to opinion testimony in an employment discrimination action was properly preserved for appeal where the ground of the objection was clear from the context.

United States v. Holland, 880 F.2d 1091 (9th Cir. 1989): In a prosecution arising from a payroll-padding scheme, the Court held that defendant did not preserve an objection to failure to redact a ninety-minute tape recording by making a blanket objection to admission of the tape.

United States v. Dysart, 705 F.2d 1247 (10th Cir.), *cert. denied,* 104 S. Ct. 339 (1983): This case illustrates how a lawyer choosing to use inadmissible evidence in furtherance of trial strategy may lose the chance to complain about its admission on appeal. In a prosecution for threatening the life of the President, the Trial Judge permitted the government's expert to rely on statements made in a pretrial competency examination. Admission of the evidence violated the governing statute and possibly the Fifth Amendment, but defense counsel was aware of the statute and chose to cross-examine extensively on the background material related by the doctor. In light of the defense strategy and the absence of a specific objection, the Court refused to consider on appeal the claim that the expert impermissibly relied on statements made in the competency examination. See also *K-B Trucking Co. v. Riss Int'l Co.,* 763 F.2d 1148 (10th Cir. 1985) (objection to exhibit on grounds of foundation insufficient to preserve a Rule 403 claim, but objection that evidence was cumulative was sufficient).

Wilson v. Attaway, 757 F.2d 1227 (11th Cir. 1985): In a civil rights action in which the plaintiffs claimed that the defendants had unlawfully arrested them, the Court found that Rule 403 cannot be relied upon on appeal if objections under the Rule are not made at trial. Parties failing to object may only rely on the doctrine of plain error, which the Court did not find in the instant case. See also *Collins v. Seaboard Coast Line R.R.*, 675 F.2d 1185 (11th Cir. 1982) (railroad's failure to object to testimony that one of its employees made a racially derogatory remark about the victim and to evidence of accidents occurring after the one giving rise to the instant case preserved no issue for appeal).

Objections — timing

Government of Virgin Islands v. Archibald, 987 F.2d 180 (3d Cir. 1993): Reversing a conviction for aggravated rape of a ten-year-old, the Court held that, when the victim's mother was asked how she happened to know the defendant and answered that the defendant had fathered the child of her fifteen-year-old other daughter, the defendant could not reasonably have been expected to object to the question, and therefore an objection and motion to strike the answer were timely.

Spivey v. United States, 912 F.2d 80 (4th Cir. 1990): In a Federal Tort Claims Act case, the Court held that a proper hearsay objection and motion to strike made nine days after the plaintiff offered a posttrial affidavit were timely.

United States v. Evans, 994 F.2d 317 (7th Cir.), *cert. denied*, 114 S. Ct. 335 (1993): Affirming the defendant's conviction for possession of a firearm by a felon, the Court held that the defendant properly preserved error as to the Trial Judge's prejudicially interrogating the defendant in a skeptical tone by making the objection the next day as the first order of business after completion of the defendant's testimony.

United States v. Potter, 616 F.2d 384 (9th Cir. 1979), *cert. denied*, 449 U.S. 832 (1980): The Court sustained a Rule 403 balancing ruling, which was not accompanied by reasons, in part because the objection to a line of evidence was late. See also *United States v. Lara-Hernandez*, 588 F.2d 272 (9th Cir. 1978) (posttrial evidence claims come too late).

Vallejos v. C.E. Glass Co., 583 F.2d 507 (10th Cir. 1978): The Court held that the proper time to object to evidence such as a stipulation is when it is offered, not in a subsequent motion.

Objections — waiver by offering evidence

Willco Kuwait (Trading) S.A.K. v. deSavary, 843 F.2d 618 (1st Cir. 1988): In a securities and common-law fraud action, the Court held that the Kuwait oil company not only failed to object to redirect testimony by the financier who it had sued, but that it also had waived any objection by eliciting similar testimony on cross-examination.

United States v. Hall, 845 F.2d 1281 (5th Cir.), *cert. denied*, 109 S. Ct. 155 (1988): In a prosecution for forging an endorsement on a stolen treasury check, the Court held that the defendant not only failed to object to the victim's testimony concerning what a "surprise witness" might say, but also opened the door to the victim's testimony when it cross-examined the victim about this witness.

Offers of proof — basic requirement — civil cases

Beech Aircraft Corp. v. Rainey, 109 S. Ct. 439 (1988): Agreeing with the Court of Appeals that the Trial Judge had erred in refusing to permit a plaintiff, who had been called as an adverse witness and asked about a letter he had written to a Navy officer concerning his wife's death, to testify on cross-examination as to other aspects of the letter, the Court held that the plaintiff had preserved for appeal a rule of completeness argument. Justice Brennan reasoned that "the nature of the proposed testimony was abundantly apparent from the very question put by Rainey's counsel," the Trial Court appeared to indicate that it understood counsel to be making a completeness argument, counsel was interrupted by opposing counsel and by the Judge, and "the degree of precision with which counsel is required to argue must be judged, among other things, in accordance with the leeway the court affords him in advancing his arguments."

BWX Electronics, Inc. v. Control Data Corp., 929 F.2d 707 (D.C. Cir. 1991): In a suit alleging breach of contract and fraud after termination of negotiations to purchase a business and a building, the Trial Judge granted the defendant's motion *in limine* excluding evidence allegedly showing improper motive. The Court affirmed judgments for the defendant, holding that the plaintiff's failure to suggest a single piece of tangible evidence supporting its unsubstantiated allegations doomed its challenge to the ruling.

Curreri v. International Bhd. of Teamsters, 722 F.2d 6 (1st Cir. 1983): The Court reversed a judgment against a union in an action for injuries that the plaintiff received when he crossed a picket line, holding it was error to exclude testimony by the union's business agent concerning directions he gave to workers on the first day of the strike, as the instructions were not hearsay but were conduct probative of whether the union instigated violence or attempted to prevent it. Discussing the union's offer of proof, the Court observed that "[m]ere compliance with Rule 103 may, in some situations, be insufficient to preserve for appeal the issue whether evidence was properly excluded." The Court cited pre-Rules cases requiring a party to make clear, after a ruling, that he is still pressing a point so that the Judge might reconsider an exclusionary ruling as the issues in a case become clearer. In *Andrews v. Bechtel Power Corp.,* 780 F.2d 124 (1st Cir. 1985), *cert. denied,* 106 S. Ct. 2896 (1986), an employment discrimination case, the Court refused to excuse a *pro se* litigant from the offer of proof requirement, since there is nothing for an appellate court to review when a litigant fails to indicate the evidence he wishes to offer.

Fischer v. Dallas Fed. Sav. & Loan Assoc., 835 F.2d 567 (5th Cir. 1988): Affirming a judgment for a bank in a class action alleging discriminatory lending practices, the Court held that the plaintiffs failed to make an offer of proof with respect to several documents relating to a federal investigation of the bank. Thus, there was nothing for the Court to review on appeal. See also *James v. Bell Helicopter Co.,* 715 F.2d 166 (5th Cir. 1983) (unsuccessful plaintiff in product liability action could not complain about exclusion of evidence of tests conducted by seller after accident where no offer of proof was made); *Mercado v. Austin Police Dep't,* 754 F.2d 1266 (5th Cir. 1985) (emphasizing importance of offer of proof when Judge excludes the testimony of a witness in whole or in part); *Petty v. Ideco,* 761 F.2d 1146 (5th Cir. 1985) ("[w]here no offer of proof appears of record, there is no way that a party can demonstrate that his substantial rights have been affected''). In *Espino v. City of Kingsville,* 676 F.2d 1075 (5th Cir. 1982), the Court upheld a jury verdict for the City in a civil rights case, noting that because no offer of proof was made with respect to a certain line of questioning, it was impossible for it to determine whether exclusion was error. Decided the same day was *Parliament Ins. Co. v. Hanson,* 676 F.2d 1069 (5th Cir. 1982), where the Court found that a Trial Judge had heard sufficiently from counsel to rule on the admissibility of prior recollection recorded. See also *Gray v. Lucas,* 677 F.2d 1086 (5th Cir. 1982), *cert. denied,* 461 U.S. 910 (1983) (error for Judge to deny opportunity for offer of proof, but substance of claims raised was sufficient for Appellate Court to rule).

Evanston Bank v. Brink's, Inc., 853 F.2d 512 (7th Cir. 1988): Affirming a judgment for a bank that sued an armored car company for breach of contract, the Court declined to consider arguments for admissibility of evidence not raised below, and opined that ''it is incumbent upon the party presenting the evidence to make an appropriate offer of proof describing both the relevance of the evidence and the basis upon which it is being offered in order to properly preserve an issue regarding such evidence for appeal.''

Lee v. Rapid City Area School Dist. No. 51-4, 981 F.2d 316 (8th Cir. 1992) (en banc): In an ADEA action by a teacher whose contract was not renewed, the Trial Court admitted evidence that school administrators had received complaints about the plaintiff from students and parents but refused, on grounds that the evidence was hearsay and the witnesses repeatedly volunteered nonresponsive statements, to allow testimony about the substance of the complaints unless they had been documented. The Court held, *inter alia,* that the defendants had not preserved any error, as their offer of proof referred only generally to the complaints without naming the individuals making them or their specific substance. Four Judges believed the offer of proof was sufficient. In *Fox v. Dannenberg,* 906 F.2d 1253 (8th Cir. 1990), the Court, holding that evidence from the plaintiff's expert engineers had been improperly excluded in a wrongful death case arising out of an automobile accident, noted that the error had been sufficiently preserved by counsel's specific statement describing the witness' anticipated testimony. Putting a proffered witness on the stand is not the only way to make an adequate offer of proof. In *Strong v. Mercantile Trust Co.,* 816 F.2d 429 (8th Cir. 1987), *cert. denied,* 108 S. Ct. 759 (1988), the Court affirmed a judgment for the employer in a suit by an employee who alleged that her discharge was in retaliation for her attendance at an EEOC factfinding conference, concluding that the plaintiff failed to make an adequate offer of proof concerning a statement by one of the defendant's employees. It observed that the Trial Judge had indicated that evidence that had been excluded might be subject to reconsideration upon the presentation of an offer of proof and emphasized ''the importance of expressing precisely the substance of the excluded evidence.'' In *Estes v. Dick Smith Ford, Inc.,* 856 F.2d 1097 (8th Cir. 1988), the Court reversed a judgment in an employment discrimination case and found that prior acts of discrimination against black customers by the service department for which the plaintiff formerly worked should have been admitted. Although the defendant complained that the plaintiff had not established the number of times discrimination occurred or proved that nondiscriminatory reasons might have explained the actions of its employees, the Court concluded that the substance of the evidence was made known and that an offering party did not have to answer all questions that went more to the weight than to the admissibility of evidence.

Price v. Seydel, 961 F.2d 1470 (9th Cir. 1992): In a fraud action by the purchaser of a hotel, the plaintiff attempted to show that the defendant kept two sets of books, one accurate and the other showing greater income in order to induce purchase of the property. The Magistrate Judge excluded evidence of the first set, presuming they were kept for the purpose of defrauding the IRS. The Court noted that exclusion may well have been an abuse of discretion under Rule 404(b), but the plaintiff's attorney never made a clear statement of the theory on which admission was sought. An offer of proof would have avoided the problem.

Polys v. Trans-Colorado Airlines, 941 F.2d 1404 (10th Cir. 1991): The Court held that plaintiffs who brought a personal injury action against an airline had not preserved error for appeal when they made no formal offer of proof following exclusion of their expert's deposition testimony. Elicitation through later testimony of the substance of the previously excluded evidence did not require reconsideration of the ruling without more in the way of explanation or proffer.

Murphy v. City of Flagler Beach, 761 F.2d 622 (11th Cir. 1985): The Court held that a plaintiff in a civil rights case made a proper offer of proof at a conference on evidence questions that was held some time after the plaintiff had been barred from eliciting certain testimony from a witness. Since the plaintiff intended to elicit similar testimony from subsequent witnesses, the Court found that the Trial Judge had a chance to correct the error in his ruling. In *Collins v. Seaboard Coast Line R.R.,* 675 F.2d 1185 (11th Cir. 1982), the Court affirmed a judgment against a railroad in a crossing accident case, approving the Trial Judge's conduct in refusing to rule on the admissibility of a tape recording of a conversation between a railroad claims agent and the accident victim until testimony was offered concerning the mental condition of the victim at the time the tape was made. See also *Perry v. State Farm Fire & Cas. Co.,* 734 F.2d 1441 (11th Cir. 1984), *cert. denied,* 105 S. Ct. 784 (1985) (upholding Trial Judge's refusal to permit an insurance company to ask insured about testimony in a prior divorce proceeding concerning the condition of her house absent an offer of proof that the house was in the same condition at the time of the testimony as at the time of the fire).

Offers of proof — basic requirement — criminal cases

United States v. Wright, 783 F.2d 1091 (D.C. Cir. 1986): The Court held that evidence of a telephone call that one defendant claimed to have received was not hearsay when it was offered in support of a duress defense to prove that the call contained a threat, but found that no offer of proof was made at trial and that the exclusion of the evidence was not plain error. Thus, the Court affirmed a conviction for kidnapping.

United States v. Hudson, 970 F.2d 948 (1st Cir. 1992): After witnesses, including the defendant's brother, testified under a grant of immunity about drug transactions, the defense offered evidence that the witnesses had participated in jailhouse conversations indicating that the defendant was not involved in drugs and that the brother was upset at the defendant for beating him out of gambling money and not taking care of his family. The Court held that the defendants had sufficiently preserved the error in excluding the evidence by asserting that the evidence was admissible as impeachment by inconsistent statement and to show bias, even though much of the colloquy centered on whether the evidence came within a hearsay exception. In *United States v. Smith,* 940 F.2d 710 (1st Cir. 1991), the defendant, charged with being a felon in unlawful possession of firearms, asserted that he had been acting as an undercover agent for the Bureau of Alcohol, Tobacco, and Firearms, but he did not give testimony at a preliminary hearing after it was suggested that by testifying he would waive his self-incrimination privilege. The Court held that, although preliminary hearing testimony might have been used for impeachment at trial, a defendant who testified at such a hearing did not waive the privilege at trial, and that the error in the Trial Judge's ruling excluding the evidence because it was irrelevant was sufficiently preserved by the counsel's representations at the hearing.

United States v. Dennis, 843 F.2d 652 (2d Cir. 1988): The Court held that a defendant in a cocaine conspiracy case could not obtain appellate review with respect to allegedly inconsistent statements by a government witness, since no offer of proof was made as to the substance of the statements. In *United States v. Pugliese,* 712 F.2d 1574 (2d Cir. 1983), the Court affirmed heroin-related convictions, finding that a defendant could not argue that a statement originally offered under the residual exception to the hearsay rule should have been admitted as a declaration against interest. The Court noted that where evidence was improperly admitted under one theory, it might affirm if the evidence should have been admitted anyway under another theory. But it distinguished the instant case, since the defendant never offered the Trial Court a solid ground for admitting the evidence.

United States v. Ballis, 28 F.2d 1399 (5th Cir. 1994): In a prosecution for bank fraud and obstructing investigation of that fraud, there was a dispute as to what the defendant said at two meetings with government agents. The Trial Court sustained a hearsay objection when defense witnesses were called to testify to the defendant's version of the meeting. On appeal, the government argued that the defendant had not sufficiently preserved his objection, because he "proffered" the entire record of the prior motion to dismiss hearing, rather than specifically listing the parts of that testimony that he wished to present. The Court declared, however, that "neither the Rules nor this Circuit require a *formal* offer to preserve error." Rather, all that is required is a sufficient indication that the Trial Court "has been informed as to what counsel intends to show by the evidence and why it should be admitted." In this case, the Trial Judge had chided defense counsel for "spoon feeding" the Court, and expressed an "intimate familiarity" with the challenged statements on the basis of having tried related cases and ruled on the motion to dismiss. The Court of Appeals concluded that even a general proffer of evidence was sufficient to preserve review under these circumstances. In *United States v. Mejia,* 844 F.2d 209 (5th Cir. 1988), the Court declined to consider whether testimony from the defendant's attorney should have been admitted to demonstrate the defendant's innocent state of mind, since no claim was made at trial that the testimony came within a hearsay exception.

United States v. Clark, 918 F.2d 843 (9th Cir. 1990): The Court affirmed convictions of perjury offenses, holding that an offer of proof asserted to have been made off the record did not preserve for appeal a defendant's argument that evidence was erroneously excluded. In *United States v. Cutler,* 676 F.2d 1245 (9th Cir. 1982), a defendant charged with mail fraud and arson tried to show that an employee of his was the guilty party, but the Court upheld a ruling excluding *modus operandi* evidence concerning the employee because the defendant failed to demonstrate by a proper offer of proof that the evidence would amount to a "signature" that could be associated with the employee.

United States v. Willie, 941 F.2d 1384 (10th Cir. 1991), *cert. denied*, 112 S. Ct. 1200 (1992): In a tax protestor's trial for tax evasion, the defendant offered a series of documents, including the Constitution and a Navajo Treaty, to show the basis for his belief that he was not required to file tax returns; all were excluded as irrelevant. Affirming, the Court held that the defendant failed to preserve the issue for appeal because the purpose for which the evidence was offered was not clear, even though the substance of the evidence was presented, and that there was no plain error. A dissenting Judge considered the evidence relevant and its exclusion prejudicial error.

United States v. West, 898 F.2d 1493 (11th Cir. 1990), *cert. denied*, 111 S. Ct. 685 (1991): In a trial for solicitation of murder, the Trial Judge excluded testimony as to unrecorded statements by an informant to the defendant, which the defendant argued on appeal would have shed light on his defense that he lacked criminal intent. The Court said that the defendant was improperly prevented from testifying to the effect of the informant's statements on his state of mind, but as he made no attempt to inform the Judge of the nature of the informant's statements, the Court was unable to determine whether their exclusion substantially prejudiced his rights.

Offers of proof — cross-examination

Wright v. Hartford Acc. & Indem. Co., 580 F.2d 809 (5th Cir. 1978): The defendant cross-examined the plaintiff's expert at a deposition in a worker's compensation case. The plaintiff's motion *in limine* to exclude this cross-examination was granted and the plaintiff objected both times the defendant offered the testimony at trial. The evidence was excluded after the defendant provided no authority supporting its admission in response to the Trial Judge's request. Affirming a judgment for the plaintiff, the Court observed: "The arguments for a more relaxed requirement of an offer of proof on cross-examination ... are inapplicable, when, as in this case, the evidence is deposition testimony, counsel is forewarned of the objection, and the trial judge specifically requests that counsel provide support for admitting the evidence."

Offers of proof — response by objecting party

Gilchrists v. Bolger, 733 F.2d 1551 (11th Cir. 1984): The Court upheld a ruling denying class certification in an employment discrimination action, finding that an offer of proof as to class size failed to demonstrate that the members of the class were so numerous that joinder was impractical. In a footnote, the Court observed that the Trial Judge wisely permitted defense counsel to comment on the offer of proof in an effort to ascertain whether there were matters in the offer that were uncontroverted.

Summary judgment

Movie 1 & 2 v. United Artists Commun., Inc., 909 F.2d 1245 (9th Cir. 1990), *cert. denied*, 111 S. Ct. 2852 (1991), 112 S. Ct. 866 (1992): The Trial Court granted summary judgment for the defendants in an antitrust action involving film distribution rights after excluding from evidence statements by an employee of a defendant. The appellees argued that a plain error standard under Rule 103(d) applied because the appellants did not address appellees' specific objections in their responsive papers or in oral argument on the summary judgment motion. But the Court held Rule 103(d) does not apply where the evidence was made known to the Trial Court, so the *de novo* standard of review was applicable.

Use of incompetent evidence

United States v. Jamerson, 549 F.2d 1263 (9th Cir. 1977): Affirming a conviction for knowing transportation of a stolen vehicle in interstate commerce, the Court, citing Rule 103, held that testimony introduced without objection becomes part of the record and may be considered for its probative value by the trier of fact.

RULE 103(c) — HEARING OF JURY

United States v. Nace, 561 F.2d 763 (9th Cir. 1977): Although it affirmed loansharking convictions, the Court indicated that the government should use Rule 103(c) and should broach highly inflammatory material outside of the jury's presence in order to avoid possible mistrials.

United States v. Wolf, 561 F.2d 1376 (10th Cir. 1977): The Court held it was improper, because of the possible prejudicial effect, for the government to ask an accused who had admitted a prior conviction a general question whether he had been convicted of any other felony, unless it was prepared to prove a crime admissible under Rule 609.

RULE 103(d) — PLAIN ERROR

Examples of plain error

Government of Virgin Islands v. Joseph, 685 F.2d 857 (3d Cir. 1982): The Court found plain error in the submission to a jury of two critical documents not admitted in evidence and reversed the appellant's convictions for assault, robbery, and rape. In *Teen-Ed, Inc. v. Kimball Int'l, Inc.,* 620 F.2d 399 (3d Cir. 1980), the Court vacated a judgment awarding the plaintiff one dollar for breach of contract, even though the evidence point that was determinative on appeal was not raised below. The Court said that the appellant's counsel was not solely to blame, since ''appellee's counsel also failed to assist the court in the proper resolution of a very difficult evidentiary problem'' and went on to find that ''fundamental dictates of fairness and justice'' required a new trial on the issue of damages.

United States v. Osborne, 532 F. Supp. 857 (W.D. Va. 1982): Awarding a new trial to a defendant convicted of conspiracy to violate gun laws, the Trial Judge found that he had committed plain error in failing to give *sua sponte* specific cautionary instructions regarding the limited use of a guilty plea of a coconspirator witness called and impeached by the government.

United States v. Escobar, 674 F.2d 469 (5th Cir. 1982): The Court reversed a conviction for marijuana offenses because, in explaining how his attention focused on the defendant, a police officer related computer information that stated the defendant was a suspected marijuana smuggler. The evidence was hearsay, clearly prejudicial, and was not offered for any proper limited purpose. Even though the defendant raised only a hearsay objection at trial, the Court also found plain error under Rule 404(b).

Williams v. Wal-Mart Stores, Inc., 922 F.2d 1357 (8th Cir. 1990): The Court reversed a judgment for the defendant in a personal injury action brought by a store customer who allegedly suffered back injuries when a shelf display collapsed on him. It was plain error to preclude the plaintiff from asking his medical experts whether he experienced a trauma to his back.

United States v. Baez, 703 F.2d 453 (10th Cir. 1983): In a drug conspiracy case, the Court found plain error in a statement by the Trial Judge to the jury that two codefendants had pleaded guilty.

Relationship to harmless error

United States v. Armijo, 5 F.3d 1229 (9th Cir. 1993): The Court held it was plain error in a drug prosecution to admit a prior inconsistent statement not given under oath without a limiting instruction, but the error did not affect substantial rights, so there was no authority to correct it. In *United States v. Wilson*, 690 F.2d 1267 (9th Cir. 1982), *cert. denied*, 464 U.S. 867 1983), the Court found plain error in the admission of police officers' testimony concerning statements made by a suspect before *Miranda* warnings were given, but it found the error to be harmless beyond a reasonable doubt.

Stipulation

United States v. McGill, 952 F.2d 16 (1st Cir. 1991): The Court held there was no plain error where the jury was permitted to view a three-hour film in its entirety pursuant to a stipulation of the parties. The film depicted an incident allegedly imitated by the defendant guard when he shot an inmate, and the defendant had apparently not wished the jury to see the relevant scene in isolation.

D. LEGISLATIVE HISTORY

Advisory Committee's Note

Subdivision (a) states the law as generally accepted today. Rulings on evidence cannot be assigned as error unless (1) a substantial right is affected, and (2) the nature of the error was called to the attention of the judge, so as to alert him to the proper course of action and enable opposing counsel to take proper corrective measures. The objection and the offer of proof are the techniques for accomplishing these objectives. For similar provisions see Uniform Rules 4 and 5; California Evidence Code §§ 353 and 354; Kansas Code of Civil Procedure §§ 60-404 and 60-405. The rule does not purport to change the law with respect to harmless error. See 28 U.S.C. § 2111, F.R. Civ. P. 61, F.R. Crim. P. 52, and decisions construing them. The status of constitutional error as harmless or not is treated in Chapman v. California, 386 U.S. 18, 87 S. Ct. 824, 17 L. Ed. 2d 705 (1967), *reh. denied, id.* 987, 87 S. Ct. 1283 (1967).

Subdivision (b). The first sentence is the third sentence of Rule 43(c) of the Federal Rules of Civil Procedure virtually verbatim. Its purpose is to reproduce for an appellate court, insofar as possible, a true reflection of what occurred in the trial court. The second sentence is in part derived from the final sentence of Rule 43(c). It is designed to resolve doubts as to what testimony the witness would have in fact given, and, in nonjury cases, to provide the appellate court with material for a possible final disposition of the case in the event of reversal of a ruling which excluded evidence. See 5 Moore's Federal Practice § 43.11 (2d ed. 1968). Application is made discretionary in view of the practical impossibility of formulating a satisfactory rule in mandatory terms.

Subdivision (c). This subdivision proceeds on the supposition that a ruling which excludes evidence in a jury case is likely to be a pointless procedure if the excluded evidence nevertheless comes to the attention of the jury. Bruton v. United States, 389 U.S. 818, 88 S. Ct. 126, 19 L. Ed. 2d 70 (1968). Rule 43(c) of the Federal Rules of Civil Procedure provides: "The court may require the offer to be made out of the hearing of the jury." In re McConnell, 370 U.S. 230, 82 S. Ct. 1288, 8 L. Ed. 2d 434 (1962), left some doubt whether questions on which an offer is based must first be asked in the presence of the jury. The subdivision answers in the negative. The judge can foreclose a particular line of testimony and counsel can protect his record without a series of questions before the jury, designed at best to waste time and at worst "to waft into the jury box" the very matter sought to be excluded.

Subdivision (d). This wording of the plain error principle is from Rule 52(b) of the Federal Rules of Criminal Procedure. While judicial unwillingness to be constricted by mechanical breakdowns of the adversary system has been more pronounced in criminal cases, there is no scarcity of decisions to the same effect in civil cases. In general, see Campbell, Extent to Which Courts of Review Will Consider Questions Not Properly Raised and Preserved, 7 Wis. L. Rev. 91, 160 (1932); Vestal, Sua Sponte Consideration in Appellate Review, 27 Fordham L. Rev. 477 (1958-59); 64 Harv. L. Rev. 652 (1951). In the nature of things the application of the plain error rule will be more likely with respect to the admission of evidence than to exclusion, since failure to comply with normal requirements of offers of proof is likely to produce a record which simply does not disclose the error.

House Subcommittee on Criminal Justice Notes

The Rules submitted by the Court used the terms "judge" and "court" interchangeably. The Subcommittee determined that the term "court" should be preferred unless plainly inappropriate in the context of a rule since "court" has the advantage of including cases tried by multi-judge courts. Amendments of "judge" to "court" with concomitant changes in pronoun references appear throughout the Rules.

Report of the House and Senate Conferences

The House bill contains the word "judge." The Senate amendment substitutes the word "court" in order to conform with usage elsewhere in the House bill.

The Conference adopts the Senate amendment.

RULE 104

A. OFFICIAL TEXT

Rule 104. Preliminary Questions

(a) *Questions of admissibility generally.* — Preliminary questions concerning the qualification of a person to be a witness, the existence of a privilege, or the admissibility of evidence shall be determined by the court, subject to the provisions of subdivision (b). In making its determination it is not bound by the rules of evidence except those with respect to privileges.

(b) *Relevancy conditioned on fact.* — When the relevancy of evidence depends upon the fulfillment of a condition of fact, the court shall admit it upon, or subject to, the introduction of evidence sufficient to support a finding of the fulfillment of the condition.

(c) *Hearing of jury.* — Hearings on the admissibility of confessions shall in all cases be conducted out of the hearing of the jury. Hearings on other preliminary matters shall be so conducted when the interests of justice require, or when an accused is a witness and so requests.

(d) *Testimony by accused.* — The accused does not, by testifying upon a preliminary matter, become subject to cross-examination as to other issues in the case.

(e) *Weight and credibility.* — This rule does not limit the right of a party to introduce before the jury evidence relevant to weight or credibility.

B. EDITORIAL EXPLANATORY COMMENT

Questions of admissibility

Rule 104 allocates responsibility between the Judge and jury for deciding preliminary questions of fact upon which the admissibility of evidence depends. The Rule preserves the force of exclusionary rules of evidence by assuring that inadmissible evidence will generally not be brought before the jury. At the same time, the Rule assures that the jury will be the factfinder as to all substantive issues in the case.

The determination of whether certain evidence should be admitted at trial cannot be made until preliminary questions of fact are resolved. For example, if one party wants to introduce out-of-court statements of a declarant who is dead at the time of trial for their truth, and the other party objects, some exception to the hearsay rule will have to be found. If the offering party claims that the statement is a declaration against interest, the Court will have to determine whether a reasonable person in the declarant's position would have perceived it to be against the requisite interest. Factfinding is necessary.

Another example is an attempt by the prosecution in a criminal case to introduce evidence of a confession by the defendant. If the defendant claims that the confession was coerced, a finding of voluntariness will have to be made before the confession can be introduced. Once again, factfinding is required. Ordinarily, the Trial Judge decides the preliminary questions of fact that condition the admissibility of evidence.

"Competency" versus conditional relevance

Under Rule 104, the Trial Judge decides preliminary questions of fact relating to competency. Competency is a word of art that really stands for all of the technical rules of evidence. Competency is used in contradistinction to relevancy. Suppose, for instance, a defendant is charged with receiving stolen property. The prosecution contends that the defendant was in Philadelphia on a given day. This may only be relevant if the stolen goods were also in Philadelphia on the same day; thus, the relevance of one piece of evidence depends on the existence of another piece. Since it is generally believed that the jury is capable of deciding the truth of both propositions equally well, it is thought that there is no reason to take either of these questions from the jury. The whole idea of a jury system is that the jury will apply logic and experience in reaching its conclusions, and will reject a conclusion unsupported by the evidence. The decision that must be made is one of connection, and the jurors can easily ignore the evidence if no connection is established. The role of the Trial Judge in these circumstances is merely to determine whether there is enough evidence for a jury to find both facts.[1]

This is often referred to as connecting one piece of evidence up with another piece of evidence. If the connection cannot be made, then both pieces of evidence should be rejected, since the relevance of each part of the evidence depends upon the existence of some other part.[2] For example, in a case where notice is an issue, the relevancy of a shouted-out warning is dependent upon whether the shout was heard. Rule 104(b) allocates to the jury the responsibility to determine whether a condition of fact has been met whenever the relevancy of proffered evidence depends on a factual condition.

When a competency issue is raised, the problem is not whether evidence is relevant. A competency objection maintains that evidence, even if relevant, still should be

---

1. See, e.g., United States v. 478.34 Acres of Land, 578 F.2d 156 (6th Cir. 1978) (Trial Judge in condemnation case must determine that there is sufficient factual support for a jury to find that property is adaptable and needed or likely to be needed in the reasonably near future, but must leave the decision whether or not to believe the evidence to the jury).

2. See, e.g., United States v. Snow, 517 F.2d 441 (9th Cir. 1975) (name tape on briefcase admitted over hearsay objection as circumstantial evidence to show defendant's ownership of briefcase and knowing possession of unregistered firearm contained therein, but only after briefcase itself had been admitted upon proper foundation; briefcase and name tape concealed from jury by order of Trial Judge until proper foundation established); United States v. Stearns, 550 F.2d 1167 (9th Cir. 1977) (admissibility of photographs depends upon foundation evidence, photographs may be admitted conditionally, but Trial Judge should ensure that foundation is subsequently laid).

excluded. Competency rules, which include most of the evidence rules that exist, serve as screening devices to protect against certain special problems — such as unreliability, confusion, and governmental error — or as special guarantees of privacy or some other social policy.

Examples of competency rules include: (1) the hearsay rule, and the admissibility requirements of the hearsay exceptions (such as whether the declarant, whose statement is proffered as an excited utterance, was in fact speaking while under the influence of a startling event); (2) the rules on privilege (such as whether a client was seeking legal advice from an attorney for purposes of the attorney-client privilege); (3) rules mandating qualifications for testifying witnesses (such as whether a person is qualified as an expert);[3] and (4) rules mandating exclusion of illegally obtained evidence.[4]

Examples of conditional relevancy include: (1) whether a witness has a basis of personal knowledge from which to testify; and (2) whether a document has been properly authenticated.[5]

While Rule 104 distinguishes "competency" from "relevancy," it would be a mistake to conclude that the Judge has no role in determining questions of relevancy. The question of whether evidence is relevant within the meaning of Rule 401 is one for the Trial Judge. Likewise, it is for the Judge to determine, under Rule 403, whether the probative value of proffered evidence is substantially outweighed by prejudice, confusion, and delay. Even questions of conditional relevancy, specifically allocated to the jury under Rule 104(b), are subject to the Trial Court's determination that a reasonable juror could find the existence of the predicate facts.

---

3. See Kingsley Assoc. v. Del-Met, Inc., 918 F.2d 1277 (6th Cir. 1990) (qualification of witness to testify as expert "unquestionably" raises a preliminary question for the Trial Court under Rule 104).

4. See, e.g., United States v. Lang, 8 F.3d 268 (5th Cir. 1993), in which the defendant moved to suppress evidence as illegally obtained, while the prosecution argued that the evidence was found in plain view; the question of whether the evidence was found in plain view was within the sole province of the Trial Court, and it was reversible error to leave this question to the jury:

> The cocaine's relevancy did not depend upon the fulfillment of a condition of fact, as the cocaine would have been relevant to show Lang's guilt of the charged offense notwithstanding whether officer Young saw the cocaine in plain view. Although relevant, the cocaine would have been excluded for policy reasons underlying the Fourth Amendment.

Compare United States v. Noll, 600 F.2d 1123 (5th Cir. 1979) (no reversible error when Trial Judge submitted Fourth Amendment question to jury, because the Trial Court had already independently decided that the evidence was admissible, and defendant could only benefit by allowing the jury an opportunity to reject the Judge's ruling).

5. See, e.g., United States v. Branch, 970 F.2d 1368 (4th Cir. 1993) (the question of authenticity is really one of conditional relevance; a document or tape is not relevant unless it is what the proponent purports it to be; as a question of conditional relevance, the admissibility question is the same as that provided by Rule 104(b) — the proponent must offer a foundation from which the jury could reasonably find that the evidence is what the proponent says it is; this is a liberal standard favorable to admitting the evidence).

Where the preliminary question mirrors the ultimate question

In some cases, the preliminary question to be decided by the Trial Judge is the same question as that to be ultimately decided by the jury. For example, suppose a plaintiff is injured in a car accident, and sues the employer of the other driver. At the scene, the other driver made a statement admitting fault. This is not admissible against the employer unless the other driver was an agent speaking about a matter within the scope of employment. Yet the questions of agency and scope of employment may be the very questions the jury will have to decide. Another example of a confluence of preliminary questions and ultimate issues occurs in conspiracy cases. A statement is not admissible as coconspirator hearsay unless the declarant and the defendant are coconspirators; the jury may well have to decide the same question.

Where the preliminary question mirrors the ultimate question, the Trial Judge who excludes the evidence for insufficient proof of the preliminary fact will often preempt the jury. But this is not particularly troublesome. The law of evidence is based on the assumption that a litigant will not get to the jury unless she has enough evidence which the Trial Judge finds to be admissible. There is no good reason for the Trial Judge to treat "mirror" admissibility questions differently from any other question of admissibility.

Inapplicability of rules

The Rules of Evidence do not apply to preliminary fact determinations, except that rules of privilege do apply. This is because many of the Rules are justified on the basis of the inability of the jury to handle certain kinds of evidence, something that is not a concern when the Trial Judge alone decides questions. With respect to privileges, however, disclosure at any stage would destroy the purpose of the privilege.

Exclusion of jurors from preliminary determinations

Subdivision (c) of the Rule provides that hearings concerning the admissibility of confessions must be conducted outside the hearing[6] of the jury, and that other hearings shall be so conducted when the interests of justice require it. The mandatory aspect of the Rule tracks constitutional law. In *Jackson v. Denno,* 378 U.S. 368 (1964), the Court held that a Judge must, upon objection, make a determination of the voluntariness of the accused's confession prior to its introduction at trial. A fair reading of *Jackson* is that the hearing must be held outside the hearing of the jury. Also, after *Jackson,* a Trial Judge may not inform the jury that she has found the defendant's confession to be voluntary, even if the Judge instructs the jury that they can reject the finding if they wish. Giving the jury this information tends to subvert the jury's role of weighing the confession.

---

6. The Rule uses the word "hearing" rather than "presence" in order to specify that the jury need not always be physically excused; a brief sidebar conference may suffice to protect the parties.

Courts have held that in search and seizure cases, a suppression hearing should be held outside the hearing of the jury.[7] As a practical matter this will almost always be the case, because Rule 104(c) requires exclusion of the jury if the accused is a witness and so requests; ordinarily, the defendant is a witness at the suppression hearing, and there is no upside to the defendant in having the jury listen to suppression hearing testimony. At any rate, pursuant to Federal Rule of Criminal Procedure 41, suppression hearings are likely to be held long before trial and well before the jury is empanelled.

In contrast, in *Watkins v. Sowders,* 449 U.S. 341 (1981), the Court found no constitutional error when the Trial Court conducted a hearing in the presence of the jury on the admissibility of identification testimony. The *Watkins* Court distinguished *Jackson,* where the admissibility question related to the voluntariness of the defendant's confession. The Court explained that *Jackson* was based on the concern that the jury may give credit to the defendant's confession even if it was found to be involuntary; this was because involuntary confessions could still be probative and reliable. The Court found no such danger with respect to pretrial identification evidence; if the identification was so suggestive as to be unreliable under due process standards, the jury would be unlikely to give it any consideration at trial. The Court did state, however, that a "judicial determination outside the presence of the jury of the admissibility of identification evidence may often be advisable." But it was not constitutionally required.

Sometimes the Trial Judge will find it more efficient to make a determination of admissibility after much of the evidence is already before the jury. For example, in a conspiracy case, the Trial Judge may admit statements by alleged coconspirators on the condition that before resting, the prosecution show by a preponderance of the evidence that there was a conspiracy.[8] Failure to connect up the evidence will result in the Judge either declaring a mistrial, or, at the very least, instructing the jury to disregard all of the statements of the alleged coconspirator with respect to anyone other than the declarant himself.[9] Reviewing courts have sometimes stated a preference for separate hearings as to the admissibility of coconspirator hearsay, but they also recognize that the Trial Judge

---

7. See, e.g., United States v. Bear Killer, 534 F.2d 1253 (8th Cir.), *cert. denied,* 429 U.S. 846 (1976).

8. In these circumstances, some defendants have sought a provisional instruction to the jury to disregard the coconspirator statement "for the time being." Most Courts have found such an instruction to be unwise, because if the Judge ultimately finds that the coconspirator exception applies, the provisional instruction must be undone. This may tend to highlight the coconspirator's statement, and may even signal to the jury that the Trial Judge has found the existence of a conspiracy. See United States v. Drougas, 748 F.2d 8 (1st Cir. 1984) (Trial Judge properly rejected provisional instruction as to coconspirator hearsay: "the retraction of the limiting instruction can appear to be a judicial endorsement of the conspiracy").

9. See United States v. Helmel, 769 F.2d 1306 (8th Cir. 1985) (failure to grant mistrial was error where drug ledger was conditionally admitted as coconspirator hearsay, and the government ultimately failed to connect the defendant to the declarant); United States v. Vinson, 606 F.2d 149 (6th Cir. 1979) (if coconspirator hearsay is conditionally admitted and the government subsequently fails to establish the conspiracy, the Trial Court "should, on defendant's motion, declare a mistrial unless convinced that a cautionary jury instruction would shield the defendant from prejudice").

should have discretion to leave the admissibility question for trial.[10] The predicate question of conspiracy is often the question to be decided on the merits at trial. Thus, an ironclad rule requiring an admissibility hearing for all coconspirator hearsay would result in much duplication of time and effort — a trial before the trial.

In practice, it may be possible for the Trial Judge, at an early stage, to at least rule conditionally on the admissibility of the coconspirator hearsay.[11] Such an early ruling might be possible on the basis of documents marked for trial, suppression hearing testimony, argument of the parties, and perhaps a few witnesses. The early, conditional ruling would have the effect of providing some predictability for the parties.

Of course, if the Trial Judge does find sufficient evidence of conspiracy to admit the hearsay statement, she should not inform the jury about this finding, since this could improperly influence the jury in its ultimate determination of the conspiracy issue.[12]

Excluding the jury in the interests of justice

Rule 104(c) provides for excluding the jury from preliminary determinations if the "interests of justice" so require. This provision is deliberately vague, and much discretion is left to the Trial Judge. Generally speaking, four factors are pertinent to whether discretion should be exercised to exclude the jury:

(1) If disclosure to the jury would result in substantial prejudice, this clearly cuts in favor of a hearing away from the jury.[13] For example, if there is a viable claim of privilege, this should be resolved outside the hearing of the jury; otherwise, the very reason for the privilege is undermined. Likewise, jurors should be excluded from a hearing concerning the admissibility of a statement of a murder victim that implicates the accused. On the other hand, there is often no reason to exclude the jury from the presentation of foundational evidence as to the qualification of an expert witness. If the Trial Judge finds that the expert is unqualified, there is little risk that the jury will be prejudiced against the party.

---

10. See United States v. Radeker, 664 F.2d 242 (10th Cir. 1981) (Trial Judge should ordinarily determine the predicate facts of the coconspirator exception before the hearsay is introduced; but the court notes a "limited exception" for provisionally admitting the hearsay at trial, where it is "not reasonably practical" to establish the existence of a conspiracy first); United States v. Isabel, 945 F.2d 1193 (1st Cir. 1991) (pretrial hearing may be preferable, but Trial Court has discretion to provisionally admit coconspirator hearsay).

11. See United States v. Cox, 923 F.2d 519 (7th Cir. 1991), discussed in the annotations, in which the Trial Court received a limited pretrial proffer and made a conditional ruling.

12. See United States v. Peters, 791 F.2d 1270 (7th Cir. 1986) (error, though harmless, for the Trial Court to give an instruction to the jury explaining its ruling on coconspirator hearsay; such an instruction may alert the jury that the Trial Judge has found a conspiracy and could influence the jury's deliberations; at most, the Trial Court should issue a cautionary instruction that the coconspirator's statement was not subject to cross-examination). See also United States v. Bartley, 855 F.2d 547 (8th Cir. 1988), discussed in the annotations, where the Appellate Court cautioned against an instruction that the Trial Judge had found a party's expert to be qualified.

13. See also Federal Rule 103(c), which provides that proceedings on objections and offers of proof must be conducted, "to the extent practicable, so as to prevent inadmissible evidence from being suggested to the jury by any means."

(2) If the Trial Judge can see that admissibility is doubtful, this cuts in favor of excluding the jury. Conversely, there is little risk in including the jury if admissibility is a foregone conclusion.

(3) If the same evidence is relevant to weight as well as to admissibility, this should cut in favor of allowing the jury to hear the foundation proof.

(4) The Trial Judge must take into account the cumulative effect of juror exclusions. The jury may be understandably disenchanted if it is repeatedly and pointedly excluded from what are obviously important decisions. It may also be that the speculations of an excluded juror would be more prejudicial to one of the parties than the proffered evidence itself.

Conspirator statement

One of the most complex problems associated with Rule 104(a), and to some extent with subdivision (b) of the Rule as well, relates to a preliminary ruling that is mentioned above: What evidence may a Trial Judge consider in ruling on the admissibility of conspirators' statements under Rule 801(d)(2)(E)? We are reserving our lengthy discussion on this question for Rule 801. For now, it is important to note that the preliminary questions as to the admissibility of a coconspirator statement — whether the statement was made during the course and in furtherance of the conspiracy and whether the declarant and defendant were in fact coconspirators — are left to the Trial Judge under Rule 104(a).[14] A contrary rule, leaving the question to the jury as one of conditional relevancy, would undermine the protection otherwise afforded by the hearsay rule, since the jury would be likely to consider the coconspirator's statement for its truth even if the predicate facts are not established.

Testimony by accused

Rule 104(d) allows an accused to testify upon a preliminary matter in a criminal case (such as his standing to contest a search, or the involuntariness of his confession) without the risk of opening himself to cross-examination as to other issues in the case, i.e., issues other than those that relate to the preliminary question. But this does not mean that the accused pays no price for testifying on preliminary issues. The question arises as to whether his statements can be used against him for impeachment purposes. The Supreme Court has left this question open. See *United States v. Salvucci,* 448 U.S. 83 (1980). Most lower courts have held that the testimony of the accused on a preliminary matter *can* be used to impeach the defendant should he testify at trial.[15]

Defense counsel must therefore be aware that when the accused testifies on a preliminary matter, he may have little choice but to exercise his right *not* to testify at trial. For example, if the defendant seeks to establish standing at the suppression hearing

---

14. Bourjaily v. United States, 483 U.S. 171 (1987).

15. See, e.g., United States v. Quesada-Rosadal, 685 F.2d 1281 (11th Cir. 1982) ("prior inconsistent statements given at a suppression hearing can be used to impeach a defendant's trial testimony, whether given during direct or cross-examination").

by testifying that he possessed and controlled the drugs in issue, he would generally be foolhardy to testify at trial that he did not possess the drugs. Conversely, if the defendant wishes to testify at trial, he may well have to forgo a suppression motion. This is ironic because the Supreme Court provided immunity for the defendant's suppression hearing testimony in order to prevent him from being placed in the dilemma of having to sacrifice one constitutional right (the Fourth Amendment) for another (the Fifth Amendment). See *Simmons v. United States,* 390 U.S. 377 (1968). And yet the "impeachment exception" presents this very dilemma.

It is important to note that if the accused testifies on a preliminary matter, he is entitled to testify outside the jury's hearing. The Rule appears to suggest that, confession cases aside, an accused "waives" this right by not specifically requesting it.

Burdens of proof as to preliminary facts

Who bears the burden of proof on preliminary fact questions? And what standard of proof is to be employed? Nothing in the Rule answers either of these questions. But the Supreme Court has, in several cases, established the proposition that the moving party has the burden of proving admissibility requirements pertaining to competency by a preponderance of the evidence. Where the objection goes to conditional relevance, the proponent must show that a reasonable juror could believe the preliminary fact by a preponderance of the evidence.

In *Bourjaily v. United States,* 483 U.S. 171 (1987), the Supreme Court held that the preponderance of the evidence standard governs preliminary factfinding under Rule 801(d)(2)(E). It also held that Rules 104(a) and 1101(d)(1) demonstrate a plain congressional intent to permit courts to consider the contents of challenged conspirator statements in making preliminary factual determinations. It left undecided, however, whether a court may rely solely on conspirator statements to find that Rule 801(d)(2)(E) is satisfied.[16]

Although the Court addressed only conspirator statements in *Bourjaily,* it reasoned that the preponderance standard had been used successfully to determine the admissibility of confessions and evidence seized pursuant to searches conducted under Fourth Amendment standards. Subsequently, in *Huddleston v. United States,* 485 U.S. 681 (1988), the defendant challenged the admissibility of other act evidence that was admitted to prove knowledge that he was dealing with stolen property. Chief Justice Rehnquist wrote for a unanimous Court as it concluded that when other act evidence is offered under Rule 404(b) for a proper purpose, the Trial Court must decide whether it satisfies the conditional relevance standard and need not engage in preliminary factfinding. The Chief Justice described the proper judicial approach to conditional relevance in the following language: "The court simply examines all the evidence in the case and decides whether the jury could reasonably find the conditional fact — here, that the television sets were stolen — by a preponderance of the evidence."

---

16. The use of the coconspirator statement to prove its own admissibility is discussed in more detail in the commentary to Rule 801.

Finally, in the recent case of *Daubert v. Merrell Dow Pharmaceuticals,* 113 S. Ct. 2786 (1993), the Court held that the proponent of scientific expert testimony had the burden of establishing its admissibility by a preponderance of the evidence. The *Daubert* Court relied on Rule 104 and *Bourjaily.* Given this line of cases, it can be fairly stated that the offering party must ordinarily establish competency requirements by a preponderance of the evidence.[17]

One wrinkle on this general principle pertains to privileges. There, it is the party seeking to exclude the evidence who has the burden of establishing, by a preponderance of the evidence, that a privilege exists. Once this burden has been met, the proponent of the evidence has the burden of establishing, by *prima facie* evidence, that an exception to the privilege (such as the crime-fraud exception to the attorney-client privilege) exists. See *United States v. Zolin,* 491 U.S. 554 (1989).

In camera review

In *United States v. Zolin,* 491 U.S. 554 (1989), the Supreme Court unanimously held (Justice Brennan not participating) that Rule 104(a) does not prohibit use of *in camera* review procedures when a District Court rules on privilege claims. The Court set forth the showing required to warrant *in camera* review in the context of a claim that the crime or fraud exception to the attorney-client privilege warrants disclosure. The Court's analysis is discussed in the Editorial Explanatory Comment to Rule 501.[18]

Evidence relating to weight

Rule 104(e) provides that after the Trial Judge makes a determination on a preliminary question of fact, the party opposing the ruling is still entitled to introduce before the jury evidence that relates to the weight or credibility of certain evidence. For instance, even if the Judge determines that a confession was not coerced, the defendant is entitled to introduce evidence of coercion at trial, because this goes to the weight of the evidence.[19] Where the preliminary testimony is from a witness who becomes unavailable for trial, the testimony will probably be admissible under Rule 804(b)(1).

---

17. See, e.g., Miller v. Keating, 754 F.2d 507 (3rd Cir. 1985) (proponent must establish admissibility of an excited utterance by a preponderance of the evidence).

18. See also United States v. Branch, 970 F.2d 1368 (4th Cir. 1993) (because authenticity of a document must be established to the jury, an *in camera* hearing cannot replace the presentation of evidence of authenticity at trial; holding a preliminary hearing, as the Court did in this case, cannot be used to streamline the trial by excusing proof of authenticity; still, an *in camera* hearing is not itself error and indeed may be a good idea; it ensures that the jury will not be tainted by hearing prejudicial evidence where the proponent cannot show in advance that he will be able to provide an adequate foundation for admission).

19. See 18 U.S.C. § 3501(a):

> If the trial judge determines that the confession was voluntarily made it shall be admitted in evidence and the trial judge shall permit the jury to hear relevant evidence on the issue of voluntariness and shall instruct the jury to give such weight to the confession as the jury feels it deserves under all the circumstances.

C. ANNOTATED CASES

RULE 104(a) — QUESTIONS OF ADMISSIBILITY GENERALLY

Informing the jury about preliminary determinations

United States v. Tracy, 12 F.3d 1186 (2d Cir. 1993): In the prosecution of two leaders of a large drug trafficking conspiracy, the Trial Judge told the jury that statements proffered as coconspirator statements were admitted on a conditional basis and later told them that the government had proved the existence of a conspiracy to his satisfaction, so that the statements were admissible against both defendants. The Court held that the Judge's comments were inappropriate because, while it might be proper to alert the jury that there may be a later ruling to disregard conditionally admitted evidence, the jury should not be told what facts the Judge believes have been established when making a determination of admissibility. The error was harmless, however.

Inapplicability of rules

Precision Piping & Instruments, Inc. v. E.I. du Pont de Nemours & Co., 951 F.2d 613 (4th Cir. 1991): The Court affirmed a judgment on a directed verdict for the defendants in an antitrust action, holding there was no error in excluding statements offered under Rule 801(d)(2)(E) because the preliminary showing of a conspiracy was insufficient. In making that determination, the Trial Judge acted properly in weighing the credibility and reliability of evidence, including hearsay statements.

United States v. York, 933 F.2d 1343 (7th Cir.), *cert. denied,* 112 S. Ct. 321 (1991): The Court affirmed convictions for mail fraud and arson, holding there was no error in permitting the government to conduct a *voir dire* in the jury's presence focusing on prior unprofessional conduct by a pathologist called as an expert. The defendant had qualified the witness before the jury, the questions were relevant to the weight to be accorded the expert's testimony, the prosecutor had a good faith basis for the questions, and qualification is a preliminary question to which Rule 608(b) does not apply.

In re Coordinated Pretrial Proceedings, 906 F.2d 432 (9th Cir. 1990), *cert. denied,* 111 S. Ct. 2274 (1991): Reversing a summary judgment granted for defendants in an antitrust conspiracy case, the Court held that a declarant's out-of-court statements could be considered in determining the preliminary question under Rule 801(d)(2)(D) of the scope of his duties.

In limine rulings

United States v. Russell, 919 F.2d 795 (1st Cir. 1990): In a prosecution for illegal possession of firearms, the Trial Judge granted a motion to suppress a gun found in the arresting trooper's car on the ground that there was no evidence connecting it with the defendants. Reversing, the Court noted that as a general rule, when a pretrial motion raises a question of fact — especially one involving credibility — that is intertwined with issues on the merits, resolution of the question of fact thus raised must be deferred until trial.

Procedure

Gentile v. County of Suffolk, 926 F.2d 142 (2d Cir. 1991), *aff'g* 129 F.R.D. 435 (E.D.N.Y. 1990): When the plaintiffs in a civil rights action offered a state investigation commission report as evidence of the defendant County's failure to investigate and discipline cases of employee misconduct, the Trial Judge made a preliminary finding of the report's trustworthiness under Rule 803(8)(C), but deferred a final ruling on admissibility until after a posttrial hearing. The Court affirmed a judgment for the plaintiffs, holding the defendants were not entitled as a matter of law to a trustworthiness hearing and there was no abuse of discretion in following the procedure in this case, where the defendants had pretrial notice that the report would be offered but did not request an evidentiary hearing until the third day of trial and did not controvert the presumption favoring admission of the report. A dissenting Judge argued that the defendants had not been given an adequate opportunity to challenge the trustworthiness of the report.

United States v. Cox, 923 F.2d 519 (7th Cir. 1991): In ruling on the admissibility of a coconspirator's statements, the Trial Court followed the permissible procedure of having a pretrial proffer, making a conditional ruling, and making an ultimate ruling at the end of the government's case, but required as a matter of policy that the preliminary proffer be *ex parte.* The procedure withheld the evidence from the defendant's counsel up through oral argument on appeal. Although it expressed its concern and bewilderment over this policy when there was no reasonable justification for sealing, the Court nevertheless held there was no reversible error.

Resubmission to jury

United States v. Lang, 8 F.3d 268 (5th Cir. 1993): The Court vacated a cocaine possession conviction because the question of whether cocaine seized from the defendant was admissible under the plain view exception to the warrant requirement was submitted to the jury. The dissenting Judge believed that the jury was only given the opportunity to reject the Trial Judge's admissibility decision and argued that while the procedure was improper, it caused no harm to the defendant. In *United States v. Gomez,* 947 F.2d 737 (5th Cir. 1991) (per curiam), *cert. denied,* 112 S. Ct. 1504 (1992), the Court affirmed convictions for drug offenses, holding that the issue of whether a telephone conversation with the defendant had been recorded with the consent required for admissibility is decided only by the Trial Judge and need not be resubmitted to the jury.

Standard of proof

Bourjaily v. United States, 107 S. Ct. 2775 (1987): This case, discussed in the Editorial Explanatory Comment, *supra,* establishes the preponderance of the evidence standard for preliminary factfinding associated with coconspirator statements.

RULE 104(b) — RELEVANCY CONDITIONED ON FACT

Act of remaining silent

United States v. Cummiskey, 728 F.2d 200 (3d Cir. 1984), *cert. denied,* 471 U.S. 1005 (1985): The Court read the Supreme Court's decision in *Doyle v. Ohio,* 426 U.S. 610 (1976), as holding that "when the action of remaining silent occurs after the witness has received *Miranda* warnings, that action is not relevant as a prior inconsistent assertion." Since the relevance of the silence depends on the absence of warnings, the Court held that "when a testifying defendant makes an objection to the prosecutor's cross-examination with respect to postarrest silence, it is the prosecutor's burden, under Rule 104(b), to establish that *Miranda* warnings were not given prior to the silence relied upon for impeachment purposes."

Affidavit of counsel

United States v. Flores Perez, 849 F.2d 1 (1st Cir. 1988): Affirming a firearms conviction, the Court held that it was permissible to consider facts stated in an affidavit of the defendant's lawyer in determining the admissibility of other acts evidence. But it also held that the fact that charges were brought against a defendant was not evidence of other acts and that a jury should not be told about other charges.

Failure to connect up

Tate v. Robbins & Myers, Inc., 790 F.2d 10 (1st Cir. 1986): The Court affirmed a judgment for the defendant in a product liability suit claiming that the manufacturer breached its continuous duty to warn. It found that evidence of a manual published in 1980 was properly excluded, where the plaintiff offered no evidence that the manufacturer knew that the operator possessed a 1943 hoist.

United States v. Cote, 744 F.2d 913 (2d Cir. 1984): In a prosecution for transportation of stolen firearms, the government offered evidence concerning two burglaries and several weapons sales that was never connected to the defendant in any way. The Court reversed the convictions, indicating that it had been offered no explanation for the government's introducing irrelevant evidence that it knew or should have known could not be connected to the defendant. The Court noted that it appreciated "the need for leeway so counsel may select the most persuasive order of proof," but added that "representations, express or implied, that otherwise irrelevant evidence will be tied to a defendant should not be made without a good faith and objectively reasonable belief that the missing links will in fact be supplied."

United States v. Anderson, 933 F.2d 1261 (5th Cir. 1991): A defendant's conviction for arson of a furniture warehouse was reversed because the Trial Judge had not determined that jurors could find by a preponderance that each of four previous fires involving the defendant's furniture factory had involved arson and that the defendant was involved. The evidence had been admitted over objection, and there was no later proof on the issue, so the objection was sufficient to preserve any error and no motion to strike was necessary.

In-court demonstrations

United States v. Hart, 729 F.2d 662 (10th Cir. 1984), *cert. denied,* 105 S. Ct. 914 (1985): The Court affirmed firearms convictions, finding that the Trial Judge properly refused to permit defense counsel to ask a witness, who testified that the defendant opened a gun case with a hairpin, to demonstrate in court with a pin how the defendant bent and used the pin. The defense made no claim or showing that the pin produced in court was similar to the one used by the defendant.

Nature of evidentiary hearing

United States v. Leight, 818 F.2d 1297 (7th Cir.), *cert. denied,* 108 S. Ct. 356 (1987): The Court affirmed a mother's conviction for murdering her infant son. Since there was clear and convincing evidence that the defendant had inflicted injuries upon two of her other children, the Court held that the admission of this evidence was proper at trial. It declined "to hold that every Rule 104 hearing must be a full-blown trial in which both sides may present every available piece of evidence." Instead, the Court concluded that Trial Judges must decide in light of the circumstances of particular cases "what and how much evidence" is necessary to make a finding of clear and convincing evidence.

Personal knowledge

United States v. Owens-El, 699 F. Supp. 815 (C.D. Cal. 1988), *aff'd,* 889 F.2d 913 (9th Cir. 1989): The Trial Judge ruled that when a question is raised as to whether a witness has sufficient personal knowledge to satisfy Rule 602, the testimony will be excluded only when no reasonable jury could conclude that the witness has personal knowledge. In the instant case, the jury could determine that there was evidence — e.g., placement of wounds — to support the conclusion that an assault victim had sufficient personal knowledge to make an out-of-court identification, even though the victim was later unable to testify as to the basis upon which he made his identification.

Punitive damages

Wolf v. Procter & Gamble Co., 555 F. Supp. 613 (D.N.J. 1982): The Court ruled *in limine* in an action against the manufacturer and distributor of a tampon to recover for toxic shock syndrome that punitive damages could be mentioned in the plaintiff's opening statement, but that no evidence of the defendant's financial condition could be offered until plaintiff established a *prima facie* case of entitlement to punitive damages.

Receipts of documents

In re Related Asbestos Cases, 543 F. Supp. 1142 (N.D. Cal. 1982): In an asbestos-related product liability case, the Court ruled that documents of one company could be used against a second company to show notice of a hazard as long as the plaintiffs could show that the second company received the documents when it purchased an asbestos insulation product from the first company. Admission of the documents was dependent on the proof of receipt.

Standard of proof

Huddleston v. United States, 108 S. Ct. 1496 (1988): This case, discussed in the Editorial Explanatory Comment, *supra,* establishes the standard for conditional relevancy: sufficient evidence for a jury to find the fact by a preponderance of the evidence.

MDU Resources Group v. W.R. Grace & Co., 14 F.3d 1274 (8th Cir.), *cert. denied,* 115 S. Ct. __ (1994): Reversing a judgment for the defendant in an action by a building owner for expenses in removing asbestos fireproofing, the Court held it was error to exclude documents offered to show the defendant's awareness of asbestos dangers in 1968 when the building was constructed. The documents came from the defendant's sole custody and control and the defendant did not provide the plaintiff with evidence necessary for it to establish the date they were received, so the jury could have inferred they were received when the plaintiff said. Furthermore, the documents contained other evidence supporting the inference, so there was a sufficient basis to make a preliminary determination that relevancy had been established and to admit the documents, leaving the question of when the defendant received them, and their relevance to the liability issue, to the jury.

RULE 104(c) — HEARING OF JURY

United States v. Odom, 736 F.2d 104 (4th Cir. 1984): In a mail fraud prosecution arising out of a fraudulent absentee voting scheme, the Court rejected an argument that the Trial Judge erred in not holding an *in camera* hearing on the competency of residents of a nursing home to testify. The Court cited Rule 104(c) and noted that it requires an *in camera* hearing in only one instance. It concluded that a Trial Judge has "great latitude in the procedure he may follow in determining the competency of a witness to testify."

United States v. Bartley, 855 F.2d 547 (8th Cir. 1988): The Court upheld a cocaine distribution conviction. It found that an expert was qualified to identify cocaine and that "there is no requirement that the court specifically make that finding in open court upon proffer of the offering party," since "[s]uch an offer and finding by the Court might influence the jury in its evaluation of the expert and the better procedure is to avoid an acknowledgement of the witnesses' expertise by the Court."

RULE 104(d) — TESTIMONY BY ACCUSED

United States v. Smith, 940 F.2d 710 (1st Cir. 1991): The defendant, charged with being a felon in unlawful possession of firearms, asserted that he had been acting as an undercover agent for the Bureau of Alcohol, Tobacco and Firearms, but he did not give testimony at a preliminary hearing after it was suggested that by doing so he would waive his self-incrimination privilege. The Court noted that, although preliminary hearing testimony might have been used for impeachment at trial, the accused would not waive the privilege by testifying at a preliminary hearing.

United States v. Gomez-Diaz, 712 F.2d 949 (5th Cir. 1983), *cert. denied,* 104 S. Ct. 731 (1984): The Court affirmed drug convictions, finding that the defendant consented to X-rays of his body. It rejected his contention that the Magistrate should have permitted him to take the stand during a suppression hearing to answer a single question: whether he verbally agreed to the X-ray. The Court reasoned that if appellant chose to testify, he could have been cross-examined "on any matter that occurred during his detention by customs officials which related to the issue of consent," since this was not examination on a new issue.

United States v. Williams, 754 F.2d 672 (6th Cir. 1985): Affirming a conviction for possessing cocaine, the Court held that the Trial Judge properly compelled the defendant to state during a suppression hearing whether he knew that he was carrying drugs, after he testified that he was not exhibiting signs of nervousness before being stopped by an officer in an airport.

United States v. Roberts, 14 F.3d 502 (10th Cir. 1993): Affirming the defendant's conviction for drug trafficking offenses, the Court held there was no error in permitting him to be asked at a suppression hearing about the indictment itself. Once the defendant took the stand to challenge the voluntariness of his confession on the ground he was substantially under the influence of drugs, it was appropriate to question him about his awareness and mental capacity to run a business at that time.

United States v. Quesada-Rosadal, 685 F.2d 1281 (11th Cir. 1982): The Court held that prior inconsistent statements given at a suppression hearing can be used to impeach a defendant's trial testimony, whether those statements were made during direct or cross-examination.

D. LEGISLATIVE HISTORY

Advisory Committee's Note

Subdivision (a). The applicability of a particular rule of evidence often depends upon the existence of a condition. Is the alleged expert a qualified physician? Is a witness whose former testimony is offered unavailable? Was a stranger present during a conversation between attorney and client? In each instance the admissibility of evidence will turn upon the answer to the question of the existence of the condition. Accepted practice, incorporated in the rule, places on the judge the responsibility for these determinations. McCormick § 53; Morgan, Basic Problems of Evidence 45-50 (1962).

To the extent that these inquiries are factual, the judge acts as a trier of fact. Often, however, rulings on evidence call for an evaluation in terms of a legally set standard. Thus when a hearsay statement is offered as a declaration against interest, a decision must be made whether it possesses the required against-interest characteristics. These decisions, too, are made by the judge.

In view of these considerations, this subdivision refers to preliminary requirements generally by the broad term "questions," without attempt at specification.

This subdivision is of general application. It must, however, be read as subject to the special provisions for "conditional relevancy" in subdivision (b) and those for confessions in subdivision (d).

If the question is factual in nature, the judge will of necessity receive evidence pro and con on the issue. The rule provides that the rules of evidence in general do not apply to this process. McCormick § 53, p. 123, n. 8, points out that the authorities are "scattered and inconclusive," and observes: "Should the exclusionary law of evidence, 'the child of the jury system' in Thayer's phrase, be applied to this hearing before the judge? Sound sense backs the view that it should not, and that the judge should be empowered to hear any relevant evidence, such as affidavits or other reliable hearsay." This view is reinforced by practical necessity in certain situations. An item, offered and objected to, may itself be considered in ruling on admissibility, though not yet admitted in evidence. Thus the content of an asserted declaration against interest must be considered in ruling whether it is against interest. Again, common practice calls for considering the testimony of a witness, particularly a child, in determining competency. Another example is the requirement of Rule 602 dealing with personal knowledge. In the case of hearsay, it is enough, if the declarant "so far as appears [has] had an opportunity to observe the fact declared." McCormick § 10, p. 19.

If concern is felt over the use of affidavits by the judge in preliminary hearings on admissibility, attention is directed to the many important judicial determinations made on the basis of affidavits. Rule 47 of the Federal Rules of Criminal Procedure provides: "An application to the court for an order shall be by motion.... It may be supported by affidavit." The Rules of Civil Procedure are more detailed. Rule 43(e), dealing with motions generally, provides: "When a motion is based on facts not appearing of record the court may hear the matter on affidavits presented by the respective parties, but the court may direct that the matter be heard wholly or partly on oral testimony or depositions." Rule 4(g) provides for proof of service by affidavit. Rule 56 provides in detail for the entry of summary judgment based on affidavits. Affidavits may supply the foundation for temporary restraining orders under Rule 65(b).

The study made for the California Law Revision Commission recommended an amendment to Uniform Rule 2 as follows: "In the determination of the issue aforesaid [preliminary determination], exclusionary rules shall not apply, subject, however, to Rule 45 and any valid claim of privilege." Tentative Recommendation and a Study Relating to the Uniform Rules of Evidence (Article VIII, Hearsay), Cal. Law Revision Comm'n, Rep., Rec. & Studies, 470 (1962). The proposal was not adopted in the California Evidence Code. The Uniform Rules are likewise silent on the subject. However, New Jersey Evidence Rule 8(1), dealing with preliminary inquiry by the judge, provides: "In his determination the rules of evidence shall not apply except for Rule 4 [exclusion on grounds of confusion, etc.] or a valid claim of privilege."

Subdivision (b). In some situations, the relevancy of an item of evidence, in the large sense, depends upon the existence of a particular preliminary fact. Thus when a spoken statement is relied upon to prove notice to X, it is without probative value unless X heard it. Or if a letter purporting to be from Y is relied upon to establish an admission by him, it has no probative value unless Y wrote or authorized it. Relevance in this sense has been labelled "conditional relevancy." Morgan, Basic Problems of Evidence 45-46 (1962). Problems arising in connection with it are to be distinguished from problems of logical relevancy, e.g., evidence in a murder case that accused on the day before purchased a weapon of the kind used in the killing, treated in Rule 401.

If preliminary questions of conditional relevancy were determined solely by the judge, as provided in subdivision (a), the functioning of the jury as a trier of fact would be greatly restricted and in some cases virtually destroyed. These are appropriate questions for juries. Accepted treatment, as provided in the rule, is consistent with that given fact questions generally. The judge makes a preliminary determination whether the foundation evidence is sufficient to support a finding of fulfillment of the condition. If so, the item is admitted. If after all the evidence on the issue is in, pro and con, the jury could reasonably conclude that fulfillment of the condition is not established, the issue is for them. If the evidence is not such as to allow a finding, the judge withdraws the matter from their consideration. Morgan, *supra;* California Evidence Code § 403; New Jersey Rule 8(2). See also Uniform Rules 19 and 67.

The order of proof here, as generally, is subject to the control of the judge.

Subdivision (c). Preliminary hearings on the admissibility of confessions must be conducted outside the hearing of the jury. See Jackson v. Denno, 378 U.S. 368, 84 S. Ct. 1774, 12 L. Ed. 2d 908 (1964). Otherwise, detailed treatment of when preliminary matters should be heard outside the hearing of the jury is not feasible. The procedure is time consuming. Not infrequently the same evidence which is relevant to the issue of establishment of fulfillment of a condition precedent to admissibility is also relevant to weight or credibility, and time is saved by taking foundation proof in the presence of the jury. Much evidence on preliminary questions, though not relevant to jury issues, may be heard by the jury with no adverse effect. A great deal must be left to the discretion of the judge who will act as the interests of justice require.

Subdivision (d). The limitation upon cross-examination is designed to encourage participation by the accused in the determination of preliminary matters. He may testify concerning them without exposing himself to cross-examination generally. The provision is necessary because of the breadth of cross-examination under Rule 611(b).

The rule does not address itself to questions of the subsequent use of testimony given by an accused at a hearing on a preliminary matter. See Walder v. United States, 347 U.S. 62 (1954); Simmons v. United States, 390 U.S. 377 (1968); Harris v. New York, 401 U.S. 222 (1971).

Subdivision (e). For similar provisions see Uniform Rule 8; California Evidence Code § 406; Kansas Code of Civil Procedure § 60-408; New Jersey Evidence Rule 8(1).

[The entire Advisory Committee Note accompanying the gender-neutralizing changes effective October 1, 1987 is as follows: "The amendments are technical. No substantive change is intended."]

House Subcommittee on Criminal Justice Notes

The Subcommittee adopted the March 1971 draft version of subdivision (c). Although recognizing that in some instances duplication of evidence would occur and that the procedure could be subject to abuse, the Subcommittee felt that a proper regard for the right of an accused not to testify generally in the case requires that he be given an option to testify out of the presence of the jury on preliminary matters.

Report of the House Committee on the Judiciary

Rule 104(c) as submitted to the Congress provided that hearings on the admissibility of confessions shall be conducted outside the presence of the jury and hearings on all other preliminary matters should be so conducted when the interests of justice require. The Committee amended the Rule to provide that where an accused is a witness as to a preliminary matter, he has the right, upon his request, to be heard outside the jury's presence. Although recognizing that in some cases duplication of evidence would occur and that the procedure could be subject to abuse, the Committee believed that a proper regard for the right of an accused not to testify generally in the case dictates that he be given an option to testify out of the presence of the jury on preliminary matters.

The Committee construes the second sentence of subdivision (c) as applying to civil actions and proceedings as well as to criminal cases, and on this assumption has left the sentence unamended.

Report of the Senate Committee on the Judiciary

Under Rule 104(c) the hearing on a preliminary matter may at times be conducted in front of the jury. Should an accused testify in such a hearing, waiving his privilege against self-incrimination as to the preliminary issue, Rule 104(d) provides that he will not generally be subject to cross-examination as to any other issue. This rule is not, however, intended to immunize the accused from cross-examination where, in testifying about a preliminary issue, he injects other issues into the hearing. If he could not be cross-examined about any issues gratuitously raised by him beyond the scope of the preliminary matters, injustice might result. Accordingly, in order to prevent any such unjust result, the committee intends the rule to be construed to provide that the accused may subject himself to cross-examination as to issues raised by his own testimony upon a preliminary matter before a jury.

Citations to Hearings and Debates

Letter from Edward W. Cleary to Herbert E. Hoffman, March 22, 1973, in Supp. to Hearings on Proposed Rules of Evidence Before the Subcomm. on Criminal Justice of the House Comm. on the Judiciary, 93rd Cong., 1st Sess., at 3-4 (1973).

RULE 105

A. OFFICIAL TEXT

Rule 105. Limited Admissibility

When evidence which is admissible as to one party or for one purpose but not admissible as to another party or for another purpose is admitted, the court, upon request, shall restrict the evidence to its proper scope and instruct the jury accordingly.

B. EDITORIAL EXPLANATORY COMMENT

Purpose of the Rule

Most of the rules of exclusion found in the Federal Rules are purpose-specific — exclusion depends upon the purpose for which the evidence is offered. For example, the hearsay rule excludes out-of-court statements only if they are offered for the purpose of proving the truth of the statement; and Rule 404(b) excludes prior bad acts but only if they are offered to prove propensity. The corollary to these purpose-specific exclusionary rules is that the same evidence may be admissible if offered for one purpose but inadmissible if offered for another. Rule 105 provides the mechanism with which the Trial Judge must deal with evidence offered for a "good" purpose, where that same evidence could be used by the factfinder for a "bad" purpose. The purpose of the Rule is to allow for admission of the evidence for the limited "good" purpose, but to provide protection by way of limiting instruction to the nonoffering party who will be prejudiced by the "bad" purpose.

Burden on parties to object

When evidence is admitted for a limited purpose, or against only one party, the Judge must instruct the jury as to the proper scope of the evidence if requested to do so. The plain language of the Rule imposes a mandatory duty to instruct "upon request." Rule 105 makes clear that the burden is on the party who wants the instruction to ask for it.[1] Thus, the Trial Judge apparently has no duty to raise the point *sua sponte.*

---

1. See United States v. Capital Sav. Ass'n, 576 F. Supp. 790 (N.D. Ind. 1983), and Gray v. Busch Entertainment Corp., 886 F.2d 14 (2d Cir. 1989), both discussed in the annotations *infra*, where the Courts held that the failure to ask for a limiting instruction meant that the proffered evidence could be used for any purpose.

Sua sponte instructions

There is nothing in the Rule that *prohibits* the Trial Judge from providing a limiting instruction *sua sponte*. Indeed there are some cases where it would be in the interests of justice for the Judge to give an instruction even if no request is made. For example, in *United States v. Copelin,* 996 F.2d 379 (D.C. Cir. 1993), the defendant's credibility was impeached with a prior bad act. The Trial Court failed to give a limiting instruction that the bad act could be used only for impeachment purposes. The Court of Appeals found the absence of an instruction to be plain error. The Court declared that there is a "huge presumption" of plain error when a Trial Judge admits impeachment evidence against a criminal defendant and omits a cautionary instruction; the risk is ordinarily too great that the jury will use the prior bad act for the impermissible inference that the defendant committed the crime charged. The presumption of plain error was not overcome in *Copelin,* since the defendant was impeached with evidence of drug activity, and he was being tried on a drug charge.[2]

On the other hand, there is often good reason for a Trial Court to avoid giving an instruction that is not requested. The party who is otherwise entitled to an instruction may have made a strategic decision that she is better off without one, i.e., that an instruction will only serve to emphasize the evidence that the jury has heard, and may suggest a use to which the evidence could be put that the jury might not even have thought about. A Trial Judge should not lightly override what might be a strategic decision. Thus, the Trial Judge is caught between the risk of reversal for plain error, and the risk of overriding a legitimate strategic decision of counsel.

Whenever it is likely that an Appellate Court would hold the failure to give a limiting instruction to be plain error, a Trial Judge is well advised to rule *sua sponte* that a limiting instruction should be given. However, the best approach for a Trial Judge who is concerned about invading the strategy of counsel is to make a record outside the presence of the jury as to the reasons for counsel's failure to seek a limiting instruction, and to give an instruction unless counsel explicitly waives it as a matter of trial strategy.

Former Chief Justice Burger, as well as several influential Judges of lower Federal Courts, have stated in recent years that the quality of trial advocacy is quite low. They have suggested that many trial lawyers inadequately protect the interests of their clients. We believe that it is consistent with the philosophy of the adversary system and with the impartial posture required of a Trial Judge for the Judge to inquire of counsel whether a limiting instruction has been inadvertently overlooked during the course of the trial. In other words, it should be permissible for a Trial Judge to assure clients that careless

---

2. See also United States v. Garcia, 530 F.2d 650 (5th Cir. 1976) (plain error for failure to give limiting instruction after impeachment with a prior inconsistent statement). Compare Government of the Virgin Islands v. Mujahid, 990 F.2d 111 (3d Cir. 1993) (where a coconspirator's guilty plea is offered for credibility purposes, the Trial Judge must give a limiting instruction that the plea is completely inadmissible in assessing the defendant's guilt; in this case, the Trial Court's instruction warned the jury that it should not give undue weight to an accomplice who has pleaded guilty; this instruction was insufficient, since it made no reference to the fact that the jury could not in any way use the guilty plea as proof of the defendant's guilt; however, the defendant did not object to the instruction at trial, and the error did not rise to the level of plain error).

lawyers will not deny clients the protection afforded by limiting instructions. A Trial Judge who is too quick to give an instruction *sua sponte* runs the risk that a lawyer who appears careless at trial will prevail on appeal by urging that the Trial Judge invaded the province of counsel by denying the opportunity to forgo an instruction. But the Trial Judge who makes a careful record of the reasons why an instruction was (or was not) given is very likely to be sustained on appeal. See generally Saltzburg, *The Unnecessarily Expanding Role of the American Trial Judge,* 64 Va. L. Rev. 1 (1978).

Relationship to Rule 403

Counsel should pay particular attention to the relationship between Rules 105 and 403. The mere fact that evidence is admissible for a limited purpose does not require that the evidence be admitted. Rule 105 does not purport to state that a limiting instruction is a panacea in all situations. If the prejudicial effect of evidence substantially outweighs its probative value, despite a limiting instruction, then the nonoffering party can argue that the evidence should be completely excluded because any limiting instruction would be inadequate.

Rules 403 and 105 are interrelated, because a Judge in determining the prejudice to be suffered from proffered evidence must necessarily take into account whether this prejudice can be sufficiently ameliorated by a limiting instruction.[3] The more effective the instruction in controlling prejudice, the less prejudice is taken into account in the Rule 403 balancing process. This means that the offering party should be prepared to argue that a limiting instruction will cure the negative effect of the evidence, while the nonoffering party must articulate why the instruction will not suffice. It is well recognized that in some cases a limiting instruction will be insufficient, and proffered evidence must be altogether excluded under Rule 403.[4]

Form of requests

The Rule directs the Trial Judge to restrict evidence to its proper scope and to instruct the jury accordingly if a request is made, but it does not articulate the requirements of a proper request. We suggest that an analogy be drawn to Rule 103, sections (a)(1) and (2), which require a specific objection or a reasonably definite offer of proof.[5] Counsel

---

3. See, e.g., Mauldin v. Upjohn Co., 697 F.2d 644 (5th Cir. 1983) (reports concerning adverse reactions to drugs made by defendant were admissible to prove notice; no error under Rule 403 to admit them where the Trial Judge instructed the jury that the reports could be considered solely for notice and not for the truth of their contents).

4. See, e.g., Carter v. District of Columbia, 795 F.2d 116 (D.C. Cir. 1986) (in suit claiming excessive force during an arrest, it was error to admit evidence of complaints filed against members of the police force who were not defendants in the case; although the Trial Court "gave adequate, if not model, instructions as to the limited purpose for which the evidence should be considered," those instructions were insufficient to protect against the danger of unfair prejudice).

5. See, e.g., United States v. Dozier, 672 F.2d 531 (5th Cir. 1982) (in extortion trial, Trial Court instructed the jury to consider a victim's characterization of defendant's conduct as "extortion" only as evidence of the victim's perception and not as a conclusive legal opinion: "If the defense, having lost the

should not be permitted to request that "the Court do whatever is legal and correct." Rather, counsel should seek to illuminate all concerns for the Court and to suggest appropriate actions. But to avoid reversals for plain error, the Court will sometimes have to act on its own.

It is our view that lawyers who want a good limiting instruction will suggest specific language to the Court and not just say, "May I have a limiting instruction?"[6]

Timing and content of instructions

It is ordinarily preferable to give a limiting instruction immediately when the challenged evidence is introduced.[7] Otherwise, the passage of time and accumulation of other evidence may impair the usefulness of the instruction. However, reviewing courts have generally held that the timing of an instruction is a matter of Trial Court discretion. Thus, the Trial Judge may decide to delay a limiting instruction and include it with the general charge to the jury at the end of the case.[8] In some cases, however, an immediate instruction may be required, because a delayed instruction would be tantamount to giving none at all. For example, where the failure to give any instruction would be so serious as to amount to plain error, there is a strong argument that a Trial Court must give it immediately upon the introduction of the evidence.[9]

Usually, the most effective limiting instruction is one that specifies and prohibits the impermissible use of the evidence; indeed, some courts have required a "prohibited use" instruction.[10] Despite these rulings, there is no requirement in the language of Rule 105 that a limiting instruction actually articulate and prohibit the impermissible use of the evidence. Indeed, it may be appropriate in some cases to craft an instruction that specifies only a permissible use, and says nothing about forbidden uses, so as not to give the jury any ideas.[11] Most Courts have held that while a prohibited use instruction is ordinarily

---

argument on general admissibility, desired a more precise limiting instruction on the extent to which the jury should consider such testimony, it could, and should, have requested one. See Fed. R. Evid. 103(a)(1), 105.").

6. See, e.g., United States v. Thirion, 813 F.2d 146 (8th Cir. 1987) (request for limiting instruction properly denied where counsel did not specifically identify the portions of the testimony to be limited).

7. See United States v. Kerr, 981 F.2d 1050 (9th Cir. 1992) (prosecutor impermissibly vouches for credibility of government witness; instructions did not neutralize the harm where "they did not mention the specific statements of the prosecutor and were not given immediately after the damage was done").

8. United States v. Sliker, 751 F.2d 477 (2d Cir. 1984) (no error where Trial Judge "chose to delay the limiting instruction until the final charge"); Lubbock Feed Lots, Inc. v. Iowa Beef Processors, Inc., 630 F.2d 250 (5th Cir. 1980) ("Although generally more effective at the time the evidence is presented, limiting instructions may be requested and given as part of the court's final instructions to the jury.").

9. See, e.g., Jones v. United States, 385 F.2d 296 (D.C. Cir. 1967) (plain error not to give immediate instruction that prior inconsistent statement could only be used for impeachment purposes).

10. See, e.g., Government of the Virgin Islands v. Mujahid, 990 F.2d 111 (3d Cir. 1993) ("The instruction to the jury must deal precisely with the issue of how the ... evidence can and cannot be used").

11. See Federal Judicial Center Pattern Jury Instruction No. 18 (limiting the jury's consideration to one purpose without disclosing impermissible purposes). See also Borunda v. Richmond, 860 F.2d 937 (9th Cir. 1988) (while "forbidden use" instruction may be preferred, it is not required by Rule 105).

preferable, the Trial Judge has discretion in crafting an appropriate limiting instruction.[12]

The Trial Judge is not bound by the exact language of an instruction proffered by counsel, even if it correctly states the law. Rule 105 imposes a mandatory duty to give a limiting instruction upon request, but it does not require the Court to give the exact instruction requested.[13]

Constitutional limitations

The doctrine of limited admissibility rests on the assumption that the jury, when instructed to ignore evidence insofar as it proves a certain, impermissible point, will in fact follow the instruction. This assumption reaches its breaking point where two or more criminal defendants are tried together, and statements are admissible against one defendant but not another. The Supreme Court has held that, in some circumstances, a limiting instruction is constitutionally insufficient to protect the rights of a criminal defendant. The leading case, of course, is *Bruton v. United States,* 389 U.S. 818 (1967),[14] where Bruton's codefendant, Evans, confessed; the confession was admissible against Evans but not against Bruton. The Court held that a limiting instruction — to use the confession only against Evans, and not against Bruton — was insufficient to protect Bruton's right to confrontation, because the hearsay statement was "powerfully incriminating" as to Bruton, and the jury would be very unlikely to follow the instruction. The Court reasoned that the instruction was an especially difficult one for laypersons to follow, because it required the jury to affirmatively use the evidence against Evans, but not at all against Bruton. Such mental gymnastics were considered beyond the power of any juror; the jury was asked to do more than simply ignore evidence which had come before it or to use the evidence for one purpose but not for another. Therefore, Evans' confession could not be admitted, even against Evans, in a joint trial with Bruton, because admission against Evans was tantamount to admission against Bruton.

Bruton was extended to "interlocking" confessions (i.e., where both codefendants confess, but neither defendant's confession is admissible against the other) in *Cruz v. New York,* 481 U.S. 186 (1987). However, in *Richardson v. Marsh,* 481 U.S. 200 (1987), the Court held that the Confrontation Clause is not violated where a codefendant's confession

---

12. See Hale v. Firestone Tire & Rubber Co., 820 F.2d 928 (8th Cir. 1987) (in product liability suit, Trial Judge instructed jury that certain evidence was offered for the purpose of notice of allegations of claims of defect; although it "would have been better had the trial court specifically directed the jury not to consider the evidence as proof of defect," there was no abuse of discretion; Rule 105 "does not require all limiting instructions to contain prohibited use language").

13. See United States v. Dray, 901 F.2d 1132 (1st Cir. 1990) (no error in refusing to instruct the jury that documents proffered by the government had not been mailed, where the Trial Judge had already instructed the jury that the case was not about mail fraud, but rather that it was a conspiracy case, and the Trial Judge had "painstakingly explained the difference").

14. See also Jackson v. Denno, 378 U.S. 368 (1964) (instruction to jury, to consider defendant's confession only if it finds that it was voluntarily made, held constitutionally insufficient to protect the defendant against the use of an involuntary confession). But see Spencer v. Texas, 385 U.S. 554 (1967) (instruction as to appropriate use of prior crimes evidence was constitutionally sufficient).

is redacted to eliminate any reference to the defendant's existence, and proper limiting instructions are provided.[15] Also, it is well-established that there is no *Bruton* problem if the confessing codefendant takes the stand and is available for cross-examination; in that case, the defendant's right to confrontation is assured.[16] Finally, *Bruton* is not applicable where the confessing defendant's statement is admissible against the codefendant under a hearsay exception which satisfies the Confrontation Clause.[17]

C. ANNOTATED CASES

Exhibits

United States v. Capital Savings Ass'n, 576 F. Supp. 790 (N.D. Ind. 1983): The Court entered a judgment for the United States against a bank in an action to recover money withdrawn by a taxpayer that was subject to a levy. It rejected the bank's argument that the government had failed to show that it had satisfied the prerequisites for a valid levy, since a government exhibit indicated that they had been satisfied. Although the bank complained that it had assumed the exhibit was offered for a limited purpose only, the Court said that the bank never requested a limitation on its use and that, absent a request, the exhibit could be used for any valid purpose.

Impeachment evidence

United States v. Copelin, 996 F.2d 379 (D.C. Cir. 1993): The Court reversed a cocaine distribution conviction, holding that although the Trial Judge properly permitted the prosecution to ask the defendant about testing positive on drug tests to impeach his statements that he had only seen drugs advertised on television, the failure to instruct the jury on the permissible use of the defendant's positive tests was plain error. The Court stated that "[w]e do not hold that it is *per se* plain error for a district judge to neglect to offer an immediate limiting instruction whenever evidence is admitted only for purposes of impeachment," but "this Circuit's cases indicate that there is a huge presumption of plain error when a trial judge omits a cautionary instruction when admitting impeachment evidence to which a jury could give substantial effect against a criminal defendant."

Gray v. Busch Entertainment Corp., 886 F.2d 14 (2d Cir. 1989): The Court held that after a witness denied making a statement to a nurse employed by the defendant, it was permissible to offer the defendant's business record which recorded the statement to impeach the witness. Although the record was only admissible for impeachment purposes,

---

15. For more discussion of the *Bruton* problem and the role of limiting instructions, see United States v. Washington, 952 F.2d 1402 (D.C. Cir. 1991) (limiting instructions are sufficient so long as the codefendant's statement does not create an "inevitable association" with the defendant), and the cases cited therein.

16. United States v. Morrow, 923 F.2d 427 (6th Cir. 1991) (no *Bruton* violation "where the codefendant testifies and is subject to cross-examination"); United States v. Zane, 495 F.2d 683 (2d Cir. 1974).

17. See United States v. Vazquez, 857 F.2d 857 (1st Cir. 1988) (codefendant's hearsay statement admissible as an excited utterance; admitting it against defendant did not violate the *Bruton* rule).

the plaintiff failed to request an instruction, and the Court held that the general hearsay objection made by the plaintiff was insufficient to preserve for appeal a complaint that the evidence should have been admitted only for a limited purpose.

United States v. Barnes, 586 F.2d 1052 (5th Cir. 1978): Affirming convictions on drug offenses, the Court held that the Trial Judge did not err in failing to give the jury a limiting instruction on the use of prior inconsistent statements of a codefendant. Except in limited circumstances identified in *United States v. Sisto,* 534 F.2d 616 (5th Cir. 1976), the Court indicated that in most cases a limiting instruction will only be given upon request. Rule 105 requires a request for such an instruction and, unless such a request were made, only plain error would require a reversal. Plain error would seem to require a showing of great prejudice in a context in which the need for a limiting instruction is obvious.

Sherman v. Burke Contracting, Inc., 891 F.2d 1527 (11th Cir.), *cert. denied,* 111 S. Ct. 353 (1990): When a witness denied that the defendant had urged him to fire the plaintiff for making an EEOC complaint against the defendant, the plaintiff introduced a surreptitious tape recording in which the witness had previously recounted the conversation with the defendant. The Court held that although an instruction limiting use of the recording to impeachment purposes would have been correct, the Trial Judge had no duty to give the instruction *sua sponte,* and counsel's failure to request one did not result in a manifest miscarriage of justice.

Motive

Staniewicz v. Beecham, Inc., 687 F.2d 526 (1st Cir. 1982): Affirming a judgment for an employer in an age discrimination suit, the Court found that the results of a telephone audit conducted by the plaintiff's superior were not hearsay, since they were offered only to show why a meeting was called with appellant that ultimately led to his resignation. The Court rejected a complaint that no limiting instruction had been given, as none had been requested.

Other accidents

Hale v. Firestone Tire & Rubber Co., 820 F.2d 928 (8th Cir. 1987): Although the Court affirmed the liability portion of a judgment for a husband and wife who sued following a wheel rim explosion that injured the husband, it indicated that the Trial Judge's limiting instruction — that evidence of other accidents was admitted to prove notice of the alleged defect — would have been better if the Court had included a specific direction that the evidence could not be used to prove a defect.

Other crimes and acts

United States v. Lewis, 693 F.2d 189 (D.C. Cir. 1982): The Court, upholding convictions for transporting forged securities, concluded that the Trial Judge did not err in failing to give a limiting instruction when uncharged acts were admitted to prove a scheme. No instruction was requested and the Court indicated that reversal for failure to give an instruction *sua sponte* occurs only "when evidence that substantially prejudices a defendant is admitted without an immediate cautioning instruction as to its permissible uses."

United States v. Echeverri-Jaramillo, 777 F.2d 933 (4th Cir. 1985), *cert. denied,* 106 S. Ct. 1237 (1986): Although the Court stated that ordinarily a limiting instruction should be given when other crimes evidence is admitted, it found that no request for an instruction was made in this case and affirmed a defendant's drug convictions.

United States v. Liefer, 778 F.2d 1236 (7th Cir. 1985): Affirming convictions for conspiracy to distribute marijuana, the Court held that a Trial Judge's failure to give a limiting instruction concerning prior criminal acts will only be reversible error if it qualifies as plain error.

United States v. Unruh, 855 F.2d 1363 (9th Cir.), *cert. denied,* 109 S. Ct. 513 (1988): In a prosecution for misapplication of bank funds, the Court suggested that defense counsel should have requested a more specific instruction with respect to the use of evidence if they believed that the Trial Judge's proposed instruction was inadequate. In *Borunda v. Richmond,* 885 F.2d 1384 (9th Cir. 1988), the Court held there was no error in admitting evidence of the plaintiffs' prior acquittals in a state criminal proceeding, which was offered as part of proof that they expended funds following the arrest which they claimed was unlawful. The Court observed that the Trial Judge gave a limiting instruction and that the defendants, who did not request a more elaborate instruction, could not complain on appeal that a more precise instruction was required. In *United States v. Potter,* 616 F.2d 384 (9th Cir. 1979), *cert. denied,* 449 U.S. 832 (1980), the Court said that limiting instructions should ordinarily be given when Rule 404(b) evidence is admitted against a criminal defendant, but found no error in the failure of the Trial Judge to instruct *sua sponte.*

United States v. Bridwell, 583 F.2d 1135 (10th Cir. 1978): In this drug case, the Court noted that a jury instruction on the proper use of other crimes evidence generally must be given only upon the request of a defendant, not *sua sponte* by the Trial Judge. But the Court also said that "[d]efendant's counsel is ordinarily under an obligation to request a cautionary instruction."

United States v. Rodriguez, 765 F.2d 1546 (11th Cir. 1985): The Court indicated that it would have been better practice in a drug prosecution to give a limiting instruction when evidence of guns found on the dashboard of a car was admitted, but it held that it was not error to fail to give an instruction when no request for one was made.

Other defendants' convictions

United States v. Ramirez, 973 F.2d 102 (2d Cir. 1992): The Court reversed the defendant's conviction for narcotics and firearms offenses, holding it was error to refuse to instruct the jury that they should not consider a testifying codefendant's guilty plea as evidence of the defendant's guilt.

United States v. Werme, 939 F.2d 108 (3d Cir. 1991), *cert. denied,* 112 S. Ct. 1165 (1992): Affirming a conviction for conspiracy to violate the Travel Act, the Court noted that evidence of another party's guilty plea is not admissible to prove the defendant's guilt but may be admitted to show the witness' bias. The Court held it was error, but harmless, to fail to give a requested limiting instruction when a coconspirator's guilty plea was introduced. See also *Government of Virgin Islands v. Mujahid,* 990 F.2d 111 (3d Cir. 1993) (error, but harmless, merely to instruct jury to be cautious in evaluating cooperating witness without telling them witness' guilty plea could not be considered evidence of defendant's guilt).

United States v. Christian, 786 F.2d 203 (6th Cir. 1986): The Court affirmed drug convictions, holding there was no plain error in the failure to give a limiting instruction *sua sponte* concerning a codefendant's guilty plea.

United States v. Lawrence, 934 F.2d 868 (7th Cir.), *cert. denied,* 112 S. Ct. 372 (1991): Affirming tax evasion convictions arising out of a "skimming" scheme, the Court held there was no abuse of discretion in giving, at the government's instance, an instruction to carefully consider testimony from a prosecution witness who had been given immunity. Although the instruction is ordinarily given on behalf of the defense, the witness was basically a hostile witness, and Rule 607 permits any party to attack a witness' credibility.

United States v. Roth, 736 F.2d 1222 (8th Cir.), *cert. denied,* 469 U.S. 1058 (1984): The Court affirmed loansharking convictions, observing that admission of "evidence that a codefendant has pled guilty to the same offense is not error unless elicited as substantive proof of the defendant's guilt. Such evidence is clearly admissible to show the witness' acknowledgement of participation in the offense, or to reflect on his credibility." An instruction to the jury on the proper use of the conviction should be given when it is requested.

United States v. Harris, 738 F.2d 1068 (9th Cir. 1984): The Court said that it was unfortunate that the jury was instructed not to speculate on the reasons why two coconspirators pleaded guilty and testified for the government. The defendants attempted to use the pleas to prove that the coconspirators had a motive to testify as the government wanted, and the instruction tended to undercut the attempt at impeachment. However, the Court found that another instruction fairly informed the jury that it should carefully examine the testimony of confessing codefendants.

United States v. Austin, 786 F.2d 986 (10th Cir. 1986): The Court reversed two defendants' marijuana convictions because the government informed the jury that ten coconspirators had been previously tried and convicted for their parts in the alleged conspiracy. It concluded that the government engaged in "blatantly impermissible use of these convictions" and that it was plain error for the Trial Judge to have admitted evidence that two of the conspirators who testified had been convicted without giving the jury a limiting instruction.

Right to an instruction

United States v. Washington, 592 F.2d 680 (2d Cir. 1979): The Court held that it was error in a case charging assault on a federal officer for the Trial Judge to refuse to instruct the jury that the fact that the defendant was previously convicted of a felony, the nature of which was not disclosed, could be considered only for a limited purpose.

United States v. Werme, 939 F.2d 108 (3d Cir. 1991), *cert. denied,* 112 S. Ct. 1165 (1992): Affirming a conviction for conspiracy to violate the Travel Act, the Court noted that evidence of another party's guilty plea is not admissible to prove the defendant's guilt but may be admitted to show the witness' bias. The Court held it was error (but harmless) to fail to give a requested limiting instruction when a coconspirator's guilty plea was introduced.

Hale v. Firestone Tire & Rubber Co., 756 F.2d 1322 (8th Cir. 1985): In a product liability action brought against manufacturers of a tire rim which separated and struck one of the plaintiffs as he attempted to inflate a truck tire, the Court found that the Trial Judge erred in refusing to give a limiting instruction when evidence was admissible for a limited purpose with respect to only one of the defendants. Subsequently, in *Sprynczynatyk v. General Motors Corp.,* 771 F.2d 1112 (8th Cir. 1985), *cert. denied,* 475 U.S. 1046 (1986), the Court reversed a judgment for a plaintiff who brought an action alleging product liability and negligence in the design of automobile brakes, because the Trial Judge erred in admitting videotapes of a hypnotic session and in rejecting the defendant's request for a limiting instruction explaining that the videotapes were admitted only to evaluate the opinions of an expert witness. Since the tapes were important evidence and the jury was permitted to consider the truth of the contents, the Court held that the error was prejudicial to the defendant.

Settlements

Borcklesby v. United States, 767 F.2d 1288 (9th Cir. 1985), *cert. denied,* 474 U.S. 1101 (1986): The Court affirmed a judgment against the manufacturer of an approach chart in a case arising out of an airline crash. It held that the Trial Judge properly admitted evidence of a compromise settlement between the manufacturer and the United States to attack the credibility of witnesses for the manufacturer and the government, and that the Trial Judge was not obliged to give a limiting instruction concerning the proper use of the evidence where no request for such an instruction was made.

State of mind

United States v. Dozier, 672 F.2d 531 (5th Cir.), *cert. denied,* 459 U.S. 943 (1982): In the course of affirming Hobbs Act and RICO convictions, the Court stated that if the defendant wanted a more particularized limiting instruction regarding testimony by government witnesses as to why they gave money to him, he "could, and should, have requested one."

Tactical choice

United States v. Brandon, 17 F.3d 409 (1st Cir.), *cert. denied,* 115 S. Ct. __ (1994): After a witness in a bank fraud prosecution mentioned that two of the defendants were Jewish, defense counsel moved to dismiss and for a mistrial on the grounds that the testimony invited an impermissible inference that members of the same religion would be more likely to join a conspiracy and may have provoked anti-Semitic feelings. When the Trial Judge offered to try to ferret out any anti-Semitism on the jury, the counsel requested only dismissal, not further questioning of the jury, and expressed displeasure with the possibility of providing curative instructions that "would only magnify the problem." Affirming, despite the possible inappropriateness of the testimony, the Court found that the level of prejudice, if any, was not sufficiently significant to overturn the decision to accept "the defendants' tactical choice to forgo more appropriate methods of addressing the potential prejudice in favor of the unrealistic and unnecessary solution of a dismissal or a new trial."

Timing of instruction

United States v. Garcia, 848 F.2d 1324 (2d Cir. 1988), *rev'd on other grounds,* 490 U.S. 858 (1989): Affirming narcotics-related convictions, the Court held that it was not an abuse of discretion to decline to give a limiting instruction at the time physical evidence was admitted against some, but not all defendants, where the Judge instead instructed the jury on the admissibility of evidence in the general charge at the close of trial. In our judgment, the better practice is to give an instruction at the time evidence is offered, provided that a specific request is made for an instruction. In the instant case, the jury might well have assumed that all physical evidence was admissible against all defendants, especially in view of the fact that when conspirator statements were not admissible against all the Judge had so indicated. A timely limiting instruction works to guarantee that a jury does not incorrectly assume for much of a trial that evidence is admissible against all defendants and that it is not necessary for the jury to disabuse itself of the assumption at the last moment.

D. LEGISLATIVE HISTORY

Advisory Committee's Note

A close relationship exists between this rule and Rule 403 which requires exclusion when "probative value is substantially outweighed by the danger of unfair prejudice, confusion of the issues, or misleading the jury." The present rule recognizes the practice of admitting evidence for a limited purpose and instructing the jury accordingly. The availability and effectiveness of this practice must be taken into consideration in reaching a decision whether to exclude for unfair prejudice under Rule 403. In Bruton v. United States, 389 U.S. 818, 88 S. Ct. 126, 19 L. Ed. 2d 70 (1968), the Court ruled that a limiting instruction did not effectively protect the accused against the prejudicial effect of admitting in evidence the confession of a co-defendant which implicated him. The decision does not, however, bar the use of limited admissibility with an instruction where the risk of prejudice is less serious.

Similar provisions are found in Uniform Rule 6; California Evidence Code § 355; Kansas Code of Civil Procedure § 60-406; New Jersey Evidence Rule 6. The wording of the present rule differs, however, in repelling any implication that limiting or curative instructions are sufficient in all situations.

Report of the House Committee on the Judiciary

Rule 106 as submitted by the Supreme Court (now Rule 105 in the bill) dealt with the subject of evidence which is admissible as to one party or for one purpose but is not admissible against another party or for another purpose. The Committee adopted this Rule without change on the understanding that it does not affect the authority of a court to order a severance in a multi-defendant case.

RULE 106

A. OFFICIAL TEXT

Rule 106. Remainder of or Related Writings or Recorded Statements

When a writing or recorded statement or part thereof is introduced by a party, an adverse party may require the introduction at that time of any other part or any other writing or recorded statement which ought in fairness to be considered contemporaneously with it.

B. EDITORIAL EXPLANATORY COMMENT

Purpose

Rule 106 codifies the standard common-law rule that when a writing or recorded statement or a part thereof is introduced by any party, an adverse party can obtain admission of the entire statement or any other writing or recording so closely related that in fairness it too should be admitted.[1] Where the Trial Court finds that fairness requires the admission of additional evidence, the proponent must decide whether all of the evidence should be omitted, or whether to forgo the use of the originally proffered portions.[2]

The Rule by its terms applies to separate writings and recordings as well as to excised portions of a single writing or recording. Thus, if the offering party proffers a reply letter, a Court might find it necessary to place the letter in context by admitting the letter to which reply was made.[3]

The only change from the common law in Rule 106 is that the party who wants to complete the record is entitled to compel the offer of the additional information at the time the proponent offers the partial evidence, rather than waiting until a later stage of the trial. Thus, Rule 106 is a procedural device governing the timing of completion

---

1. The Court decides what is closely related. See Government of the Virgin Islands v. Archibald, 987 F.2d 180 (3d Cir. 1993) (doctrine of completeness is based on the need to elaborate upon subject matter that was incompletely set forth by the adversary; subject matter of witness' cross-examination was whether she ever overheard her daughters talking about the defendant; the response on redirect was beyond the subject matter because she testified to *what her daughter told her* about the defendant; the principle of completeness does not apply to "separate utterances or occurrences pertaining to a different subject.").

2. See American Bald Eagle v. Bhatti, 9 F.3d 163 (1st Cir. 1993) (where portions of document were taken out of context, the Trial Court did not err in allowing the proponent of the portions to "choose whether the entire documents or no portion thereof would be admitted").

3. Whether a separate document must be admitted will, of course, depend on the facts. See United States v. Boyland, 898 F.2d 230 (1st Cir. 1990) (where certain personnel orders taken from a file were admitted, there was no need to admit other items from the file because the personnel orders were "complete in and of themselves").

evidence. It means that the adverse party need not wait until cross-examination or rebuttal. As such, the Rule reduces the risk that a writing or recording will be taken out of context and that an initial misleading impression will take hold in the mind of the jury.[4]

The Rule does not mean that an entire writing or recording is automatically admissible whenever part of it is introduced. As one Court put it, the remainder of a writing or recording is only admissible when necessary "to (1) explain the admitted portion, (2) place the admitted portion in context, (3) avoid misleading the trier of fact, or (4) insure a fair and impartial understanding."[5] As another Court stated, "the trial judge need only admit the remaining portions of the statement which are needed to clarify or explain the portion already received."[6]

While Rule 106 by its terms applies only to writings and recordings, the principle of completeness embodied in the Rule has been applied to the introduction of oral out-of-court statements as well. Whether this is mandated by Rule 106 or by Rule 611 is unimportant. The important point is that a party cannot introduce a portion of an oral statement where that portion would be misleading; the adversary is entitled to have the entire statement introduced at one time, insofar as that is necessary to correct any misimpression that the initially proffered portion would create.[7]

As simple as Rule 106 is on its face, it was not without opposition. The Department of Justice contended that the Rule could disrupt an orderly presentation, particularly in complicated fraud and antitrust cases.[8] The Department favored limiting the Rule to the same document. As the Rule indicates, the Department failed to achieve a change in the wording. Alternatively, the Department asked that the Rule be clarified so that only evidence otherwise admissible could be introduced into evidence under this provision. Although no change in wording was forthcoming, none was needed since Rule 106

---

4. See Beech Aircraft Corp. v. Rainey, 488 U.S. 153 (1988) (the rule of completeness protects against the "danger that an out-of-context statement may create such prejudice that it is impossible to repair by a subsequent presentation of additional material"); United States v. Haddad, 10 F.3d 1252 (7th Cir. 1993) ("The whole statement should be admitted in the interest of completeness and context, to avoid misleading inferences, and to help insure a fair and impartial understanding of the evidence.").

5. United States v. Soures, 736 F.2d 87, 91 (3d Cir. 1984) (second day of grand jury testimony not admissible under Rule 106 merely because first day of grand jury testimony was admitted). See also United States v. Lewis, 954 F.2d 1386 (7th Cir. 1992) (Trial Court admitted a statement by the defendant: "If I did it, I wouldn't tell you"; Rule 106 did not require introduction of the remainder of the statement, "I would consult with an attorney first"; the admitted portion was not misleading in light of the omitted portion); United States v. LeFevour, 798 F.2d 977 (7th Cir. 1986) (where portion of tape is introduced, Rule 106 does not require the introduction of an entirely separate conversation, on a different subject matter, that also happened to be on the tape). See also United States v. Pendas-Martinez, 845 F.2d 938 (11th Cir. 1988) (where prosecution witness was cross-examined about a report, it was error to allow the prosecution to admit the entire report; defense counsel had not offered any specific portion of the report "for which the remainder was relevant and necessary to harmonize the introduced portions").

6. United States v. Haddad, 10 F.3d 1252, 1259 (7th Cir. 1993).

7. Id. (while Rule 106 applies by its terms to written or recorded statements, "Rule 611(a) gives the district courts the same authority with respect to oral statements and testimonial proof"); United States v. Lewis, 954 F.2d 1386 (7th Cir. 1992) (applying Rule 106 analysis to oral statements and testimonial proof). See also the discussion of prior consistent statements, infra.

8. The Department's position is asserted in the Rakestraw letter cited in Section D, infra.

instructs the Judge to determine whether evidence "ought in fairness to be considered with" other evidence. Such a determination obviously requires the Judge to know what the offered evidence purports to be and that it is relevant. Although the Rule is less clear regarding admissibility of hearsay and other objectionable evidence, nothing in it purports specifically to override other rules of exclusion.[9]

On the other hand, evidence that might be inadmissible initially can become admissible as fair response to evidence introduced by an adversary.[10] Rule 106 is consistent with the "open door" principle.[11] So, for example, a statement in a writing or recording that might otherwise be inadmissible hearsay can become admissible if relevant for "background"; and "background" is another way of saying "context"; and placing a portion of a writing or recording in "context" is what Rule 106 is all about.[12]

Of course, if evidence is otherwise inadmissible on grounds such as hearsay, and it becomes admissible only by way of Rule 106, then the original proponent of the writing or recording is entitled to a limiting instruction under Rule 105.

Timing

This is one of the rare examples of an evidence rule that permits one party to require another party to introduce more evidence than the latter desires to offer, or at least to have the latter party's case-in-chief interrupted while additional evidence is offered. Contrast Rule 106 with the typical approach to oral trial testimony. Questions asked on direct examination may produce a story that is shaded to the advantage of the party calling the witness. Yet, clarification does not occur until cross-examination. Thus, the Rule provides protection against initial offers of incomplete writings and recordings that is not provided against initial offers of incomplete testimony. The reason for limiting the

---

9. See USFL v. NFL, 842 F.2d 1335 (2d Cir. 1988) (Rule 106 "does not compel admission of otherwise inadmissible hearsay evidence"). Also, introduction of one person's out of court statements does not mean that other people's statements also must be admitted. See, e.g., United States v. Jamar, 561 F.2d 1103 (4th Cir. 1977) (Rule held inapplicable as to preliminary hearing testimony of nonparty which might have corroborated defense to perjury charge based on appellant's preliminary hearing testimony).

10. Cf. Rule 404(a), which provides that the prosecution cannot introduce character evidence except in response to character evidence proffered by the defendant. United States v. Beverly, 5 F.3d 633 (2d Cir. 1993) (impeachment with prior bad acts permissible even though it would have been error to introduce this evidence had defendant not testified: "Once a defendant has put certain activity in issue by offering innocent explanations for or denying wrongdoing, the government is entitled to rebut by showing that the defendant has lied.").

11. See United States v. Sutton, 801 F.2d 1346 (D.C. Cir. 1986) ("Rule 106 can adequately fulfill its function only by permitting the admission of some otherwise inadmissible evidence when the court finds in fairness that that proffered evidence should be considered contemporaneously."); United States v. LeFevour, 798 F.2d 977 (7th Cir. 1986) (otherwise inadmissible evidence is admissible under Rule 106 where it is "necessary to correct a misleading impression").

12. United States v. Haddad, 10 F.3d 1252, 1258 (7th Cir. 1993) (defendant's statement that he knew that marijuana was under the bed, but that he did not know that a gun was under the bed, was improperly redacted to exclude the statement about the gun: "Ordinarily, a defendant's self-serving, exculpatory, out-of-court statements would not be admissible. But here the exculpatory remarks were part and parcel of the very statement a portion of which the Government was properly bringing before the jury, i.e., the defendant's admission about the marijuana.").

Rule to writings and recordings, at least as to timing, was that a process of immediate interruption was thought to be unwieldy for witness testimony.

Under Rule 106, a Trial Judge applying concepts of "fairness" must take into account the possible disruption of a party's order of proof, and balance that against the risk to the adversary that a misimpression could not be undone at a later point.

Rule 106 authorizes the introduction of completeness evidence during the initial presentation of the writing or recording, but it does not *require* the adversary to introduce the material at that point. The adversary may in some cases find it more effective to present the completion evidence on cross-examination or rebuttal.[13]

Relationship to best evidence rule

Rule 106 serves as a reminder that it may be very important to determine whether a writing or oral testimony is offered as evidence. If a writing is offered, special rules may govern its introduction. Rule 106 is one of the best examples. See also Rules 803(5) and 803(18). One theme concerning writings seems to run through the Rules: writings, it is feared, may have undue impact on a trier of fact, especially a jury. Thus, special controls have been developed to govern the admissibility of writings.

One of these controls is the Best Evidence Rule, found in Article X (Rules 1001-1008). There is a relationship between the Best Evidence Rule and Rule 106, and it has not received much attention. If a witness is permitted to testify about the contents of a missing writing — when a writing has been lost, for example — what impact should Rule 106 have? Plainly, the Rule should be read to permit the questioning of the witness on cross-examination about related writings or parts of the missing writing that are necessary for a full understanding of the meaning of the terms of the writing already in evidence. But when the production of a writing is excused and oral testimony is accepted, the writing itself is not present and there is no danger that it will have an undue impact on the jury. Thus, there is not an immediate need to interrupt direct examination with questions by an opposing party. That is, the timing provisions of Rule 106 should not be applicable in these circumstances. However, the spirit of both this Rule[14] and Rule 611 suggests that a broad view of the "scope of direct examination" should be taken to

---

13. See Advisory Committee Comment to Rule 106 ("The rule does not in any way circumscribe the right of the adversary to develop the matter on cross-examination or as part of his own case.").

14. The spirit of this Rule has resulted in the admission of documents to which one party has made reference at trial in order to clarify for the trier of fact the contents of the documents. See, e.g., United States v. Baron, 602 F.2d 1248 (9th Cir.), *cert. denied,* 444 U.S. 967 (1979), a case in which defense counsel attempted to impeach the key government witness in a bribery case by referring to the witness' prior memoranda in order to suggest that they really were consistent with trial testimony. See also United States v. Rubin, 609 F.2d 51 (2d Cir. 1979), *aff'd,* 449 U.S. 424 (1981) (holding that government could introduce memos not even written by a witness but used to refresh recollection when defense counsel asked questions about the memos); United States v. Juarez, 549 F.2d 1113 (7th Cir. 1977) (reports of government agent used by defense counsel in cross-examination properly admitted under Rules 106 and 801(d)(1)(B) even though neither Rule "literally applicable" since witness' testimony not as good as reports in determining whether reports constituted accurate summaries).

assure that full and fair cross-examination occurs and that testimony about documents is placed in proper context.[15]

Use by proponent

A proponent may not invoke Rule 106 as a means of admitting otherwise inadmissible portions of a writing or recording. Rule 106 is designed to benefit the adversary by providing a complete rendering of a writing or recording; if the adversary does not wish to invoke the Rule, the proponent cannot do so in the guise of completeness. On the other hand, the adversary may not use "completeness" as an excuse to admit otherwise inadmissible portions of a writing or recording, where such portions do not in fact provide meaningful context for the material already admitted.[16]

Tape recordings

How does the rule of completeness apply to tape recordings where part of the recording is inaudible? The question is whether the inaudible portions would provide important context, or would alleviate misimpressions. If so, Rule 106 could be invoked to either require the audible portions to be summarized or recharacterized,[17] or to require exclusion of the entire recording. But of course the Trial Court must engage in some supposition in determining whether the inaudible portions are necessary to give a complete account.[18] The admissibility of portions of a tape where other portions are

---

15. See, e.g., United States v. Alvarado, 882 F.2d 645 (2d Cir. 1989) (Rule 611(a) basically applies Rule 106 to oral statements); United States v. Castro, 813 F.2d 571 (2d Cir. 1987) (while Rule 106 concerns only written or recorded statements, Rule 611 permits a Court to require a party to provide a fair context for an oral statement).

16. See, e.g., United States v. Wright, 826 F.2d 938 (10th Cir. 1987) (Rule 106 does not require that "portions of a writing which are neither explanatory of the previously introduced portions nor relevant to the introduced portions be admitted"; the Rule does not mean that if any part of a statement is to be admitted, then the entire statement is to be admitted).

17. See United States v. Phelps, 733 F.2d 1464 (11th Cir. 1984) (Trial Judge read a summary of a tape to a jury, because he was concerned about inaudible portions; no abuse of discretion).

18. Sometimes the problem with a tape recording is not whether inaudible portions render it incomplete, but rather whether the tape "says" what the proponent says it does. The adversary may dispute the proponent's interpretation of what the declarants stated on the tape. This dispute is a question of authentication: is the document or recording what the proponent says it is? See, e.g., United States v. West, 948 F.2d 1042 (6th Cir. 1991) (defendant argued that transcripts of taped conversations should not have been admitted because they were inaccurate; the Court noted that the preferred practice for determining the accuracy of transcriptions is to have both parties stipulate to accuracy; if no stipulation is made, the transcriber should attest to the accuracy of the transcripts and the Court should make an independent determination of accuracy by listening to the tapes outside the jury's presence; the least preferred method is to allow each party to prepare a transcript for the jury; in this case, the Court of Appeals found that the Trial Court had properly made an independent determination of accuracy, and that the transcriber had testified to the accuracy of the transcription). For a further discussion of the question of accuracy of a tape recording, see the commentary and annotations to Rule 901.

inaudible is necessarily committed to the discretion of the Trial Court.[19] Generally speaking, the chance of exclusion should increase with the percentage of inaudible material on the tape.[20] However, the presumption should be that the audible portions are admissible if relevant, and that the risk presented by inaudible portions can be rectified by an appropriate limiting instruction.[21]

Prior consistent statements

Rule 106 has sometimes been invoked to allow the admission of a prior consistent statement of a testifying witness. This can occur when the witness is impeached with a prior *inconsistent* statement, and counsel argues that another statement consistent with the in-court testimony will serve to explain away the alleged inconsistency. Thus, the argument is that an inconsistent statement was taken out of context, and that a consistent statement must be introduced in order to alleviate the misimpression.

Where both statements — consistent and inconsistent — are contained in a recording or writing, then Rule 106 applies by its terms. For example, in *United States v. Pierre,* 781 F.2d 329 (2d Cir. 1986), a DEA agent testified to an inculpatory statement made by Pierre in an interview. On cross-examination, he was confronted with the handwritten notes he took during the interview. These notes contained a series of "fragmentary phrases," and did not mention Pierre's inculpatory statement. On redirect, the Trial Court permitted the witness to testify that he had prepared typewritten notes three days after the interview, and he was allowed to read these notes. The typewritten notes included Pierre's inculpatory statement. The Court of Appeals relied on Rule 106 and held that admission of a prior consistent statement is warranted "when the consistent statement will amplify or clarify the allegedly inconsistent statement." In *Pierre,* the consistent statement could explain the alleged inconsistency as follows: the inculpatory statement was not included in the original notes because the officer was just jotting down certain phrases in the heat of the moment; after the interview, and while preparing the formal report, the witness had the opportunity to write down the inculpatory statement for the first time. He did not need to write the statement down initially, since it was something that he was unlikely to forget.

While Rule 106 does not explicitly apply if either the prior inconsistent statement or the consistent statement are oral rather than written, it is clear that the reasoning of the

---

19. United States v. Devous, 764 F.2d 1349 (10th Cir. 1985) ("admissibility of tape recordings that are partially inaudible lies within the sound discretion of the trial court"); United States v. Enright, 579 F.2d 980 (6th Cir. 1978) (no abuse of discretion where Trial Court carefully considered, and rejected, defense argument that audible portions of a tape could be taken out of context due to the fact that much of the tape, alleged to be clarification, was inaudible).

20. See United States v. Brinklow, 560 F.2d 1008 (10th Cir. 1977) (tape recording is admissible unless the inaudible portions are so substantial as to render the tape untrustworthy; this question is left to the sound discretion of the Trial Judge).

21. See United States v. Arango-Correa, 851 F.2d 54 (2d Cir. 1988) (there is a "clear preference for the admission of recordings notwithstanding some ambiguity or inaudibility, as long as the recordings are probative").

Rule should still apply.[22] As the Court in *Pierre* put it: "It matters not whether such use is deemed a permissible type of rehabilitation or only an invocation of the principle of completeness, though not a precise use of Rule 106."

Note that where the prior consistent statement will explain an alleged inconsistency, it is admissible under the principle of completeness even if it is not admissible under the terms of Rule 801(d)(1)(B).[23] For example, in *Pierre,* there was no charge that the witness had recently fabricated his testimony, or that he had an improper motive. These are conditions for admissibility under Rule 801(d)(1)(B); but that Rule deals with the substantive use of prior consistent statements.[24] Where a consistent statement is admissible to explain an inconsistency, and yet is not admissible as substantive evidence under Rule 801(d)(1)(B), the adversary is entitled to a limiting instruction as to the appropriate use of the evidence.

For more treatment of these issues, see the annotated cases under the heading "Relationship to consistent statements."

C. ANNOTATED CASES

Books relied upon

United States v. Latham, 754 F.2d 747 (7th Cir. 1985): The Court found that the Trial Judge properly excluded books that the defendant claimed to have relied on in deciding not to file tax returns and admitted only portions that the defendant quoted during his testimony. The books contained only general criticism of the Tax Code and did not relate to the charges made against the defendant.

Burden of invoking the rule

United States v. Sweiss, 814 F.2d 1208 (7th Cir.), *aff'd,* 812 F.2d 1023 (1987): In an arson prosecution, the Court held that Rule 106 gave a defendant a right to offer a tape recording of a conversation between himself and the main prosecution witness if the recording were relevant to explain later recorded statements that were admitted. In this case, however, the defendant failed to specify the portions of the recording that would qualify or explain the other recordings, so it was no abuse of discretion to refuse to admit the tape recording.

United States v. Larranaga, 787 F.2d 489 (10th Cir. 1986): The Court affirmed a perjury conviction, finding no error in the exclusion of the defendant's entire grand jury testimony after the government introduced portions relevant to the perjury charge. The

---

22. See United States v. Tarantino, 846 F.2d 1384 (D.C. Cir.) ("The opposing party may not pick and choose among prior statements to create an appearance of confict and then object when this appearance is rebutted by means of a fuller version of the same prior statements."), *cert. denied,* 488 U.S. 840, 867 (1988).

23. See United States v. Brennan, 798 F.2d 581 (2d Cir. 1986) ("prior consistent statements may be admissible for rehabilitation even if not admissible under Rule 801(d)(1)(B)").

24. See United States v. Pierre, *supra* (rules on substantive admissibility do not control use of evidence for rehabilitation).

Court found that the defendant had not invoked Rule 106 and had failed to claim that other portions should have been admitted "in fairness."

Experts' reports

Engebretsen v. Fairchild Aircraft Corp., 21 F.3d 721 (6th Cir. 1994): Affirming a defendant's judgment in a product liability case, the Court held that reports containing opinions of defense expert witnesses as well as prejudicial hearsay should not have been admitted under Rules 702 and 703 simply because the experts testified. Rule 702 permits admission of expert opinion *testimony,* and Rule 703 permits an expert to base an opinion on inadmissible evidence but not to introduce that evidence for its truth. However, where the plaintiff extensively cross-examined the witnesses regarding the reports, the door was opened to their admission under the rule of completeness.

Films, movies, etc.

Brewer v. Jeep Corp., 724 F.2d 653 (8th Cir. 1983): A judgment for the defendant in an action by an injured driver was upheld on appeal, as the Court ruled that the Trial Judge properly refused to admit into evidence a film commissioned by the company, which dealt with Jeep rollovers, unless a companion report written by the film-makers was also admitted.

Hearsay in documents

Engebretsen v. Fairchild Aircraft Corp., 21 F.3d 721 (6th Cir. 1994): See annotation under "Experts' reports," *supra.*

Haygood v. Auto-Owners Ins. Co., 995 F.2d 1512 (11th Cir. 1993): As evidence that the plaintiff had made material misstatements in a claim for fire damage to his house, the defendant insurer offered part of his statement under oath indicating he was current on all of his obligations at the time, which was inconsistent with other evidence indicating that he was delinquent. The Court held it was error (but harmless) to admit under Rule 106 another part of his statement showing he had a "1A" credit rating, as that hearsay within hearsay was not needed to qualify or place in context the statement about being current on all obligations.

Impeachment versus substantive evidence

United States v. Pierre, 781 F.2d 329 (2d Cir. 1986): After the defense in a heroin prosecution elicited testimony from an agent that his notes of his interview with the defendant contained no reference to the defendant's refusal to make a controlled delivery, the Trial Judge admitted evidence that the agent's formal report mentioned the refusal. Holding that the evidence was properly admitted, the Court observed in a footnote that Rule 106 is silent as to the permissible uses of a document offered for completeness. It reasoned that "[w]here the first document is introduced not as substantive evidence but only to impeach credibility, the document offered for completeness would seem to be appropriately introduced also not as substantive evidence but only to rehabilitate credibility.''

United States v. Myers, 972 F.2d 1566 (11th Cir. 1992), *cert. denied,* 113 S. Ct. 1813 (1993): In a civil rights prosecution of an officer for using a stun gun on arrestees, the Court held there was no abuse of discretion in limiting admission of a statement made by the defendant during an internal affairs investigation to the parts concerning the number of times he had used the stun gun, as the prosecutor had introduced the statement only to impeach the defendant on that issue. The parts consistent with the defendant's trial testimony were admitted for rehabilitation, but the parts of the statement dealing with the circumstances and the defendant's motivation were not admissible under the Rule.

Opinion in document

Polk v. Yellow Freight Sys., 876 F.2d 527 (6th Cir. 1989): The Court held in a wrongful discharge case that the defendant's attempt to rebut a witness' testimony by quoting from an investigator's report was properly conditioned on also admitting the investigator's conclusion in the report about the incident because the conclusion was relevant to whether the defendant's action was pretextual.

Oral statements

United States v. Tarantino, 846 F.2d 1384 (D.C. Cir.), *cert. denied,* 109 S. Ct. 108, 174 (1988): Affirming drug conspiracy convictions, the Court held that prior statements by a government witness were properly offered on redirect examination, since the defense had used portions of the statements on cross-examination and the government merely wished to rebut the use of the statements by showing the portions in context.

United States v. Maccini, 721 F.2d 840 (1st Cir. 1983): Affirming convictions for conspiracy and submitting a false statement, the Court cited Rule 106 as support for upholding a ruling that permitted the prosecutor, during defense cross-examination of a government witness, to have portions of the witness' grand jury testimony read to the jury in addition to those that defense counsel read. While technically Rule 106 does not seem to cover oral statements, we believe that the philosophy of the Rule properly extends to this situation and that the Trial Judge has authority under Rule 611(a), as well as Rule 106, to control the scope and order of proof so that a jury is not confused or misled.

United States v. Castro, 813 F.2d 571 (2d Cir.), *cert. denied,* 108 S. Ct. 137 (1987): In a cocaine prosecution, the government offered evidence of a statement made by one nontestifying defendant that implicated another. The Trial Judge ruled that no part of the statement relating to the other defendant could be adduced. Rejecting the defendant's argument that the ruling violated Rule 106, the Court noted that Rule 106 governs only writings, but observed that even the substance of oral statements must be presented fairly and that the Trial Judge can utilize Rule 611(a) to ensure fairness. It found in this case that the essential point the defendant who made the statement wanted to convey — i.e., he had denied ownership of the cocaine — was conveyed to the jury. Thus, the Trial Judge reasonably balanced interests of judicial economy in trying defendants jointly against the unfairness of using a redacted statement, and any error was harmless. In *United States v. Terry,* 702 F.2d 299 (2d Cir.), *cert. denied,* 103 S. Ct. 2095 (1983), a narcotics case, the Court held it was error (but harmless) to admit testimony that defendants refused to supply palm prints pursuant to court order while excluding statements made by the defendants that they wanted their lawyers present when the prints were taken. Although the statements were not required to be admitted under Rule 106 since they were oral statements, not writings, they qualified for admission under Rule 803(3).

Government of Virgin Islands v. Archibald, 987 F.2d 180 (3d Cir. 1993): The mother of a ten-year-old victim of aggravated rape was asked on cross-examination whether she had ever heard the victim discussing the defendant with her fifteen-year-old sister, who was the defendant's girlfriend. Reversing the conviction, the Court held that the question did not open the door to redirect examination of the mother as to whether the fifteen-year-old might have told the mother she observed the defendant and the victim together. The Court stated that "[t]he principle of completeness does not apply ... to separate utterances or occurrences pertaining to a different subject."

United States v. Smith, 792 F.2d 441 (4th Cir. 1986), *cert. denied,* 107 S. Ct. 892 (1987): Upholding a defendant's convictions for his involvement in burning a barn, the Court held there was no error in rejecting the defendant's request that a codefendant's prior testimony at his own trial in which he recanted a confession be admitted during the government's case at the same time when the codefendant's confession was admitted as evidence.

United States v. Haddad, 10 F.3d 1252 (7th Cir. 1993): In a prosecution for possession of a firearm by a felon, an officer testified that the defendant admitted when arrested knowing marijuana was under his bed, but the defense was not permitted to elicit from the officer that the defendant had denied knowledge of a gun found under the bed at the same time. The Court held it was error (but harmless) to preclude the testimony, which was part and parcel of the inculpatory statement. In *United States v. Bigelow,* 914 F.2d 966 (7th Cir. 1990), *cert. denied,* 111 S. Ct. 1077 (1991), the Court affirmed loansharking convictions, holding that testimony regarding one defendant's oral admission was properly admitted without part of the statement inculpating another defendant. The Rule applies only to written or recorded statements; in any event, it would not be possible to redact the excluded portion in such a way as to protect the codefendant's *Bruton* rights. See also *United States v. Harvey,* 959 F.2d 1371 (7th Cir. 1992) (exculpatory statements were not admissible, as they were oral rather than written and they were not relevant). In *United States v. Draiman,* 784 F.2d 248 (7th Cir. 1986), the Court affirmed a defendant's mail fraud conviction arising from his filing fraudulent insurance claims following a burglary. After the defendant elicited on cross-examination of a detective a statement by one of the burglars tending to show that the burglars were capable of hauling away a lot of material, the government was properly permitted to elicit on redirect the burglar's statement that $25,000 of merchandise had been taken. The Court stated that the defendant "could not open it [the statement] up to seek only as much as would leave a favorable, but erroneous, impression with the jury."

United States v. Woolbright, 831 F.2d 1390 (8th Cir. 1987): In a drug prosecution, the defendant successfully offered a statement by a female companion that a suitcase containing the drugs belonged to her. The government responded by offering her statement that she and the defendant were on a "honeymoon trip." Although the defendant and the woman were not married, the statement was offered to establish that the pair had more than a casual relationship. The Court held that the statement was not admissible under Rule 106, since the Rule is limited to writings, and neither it nor Rule 611 empowers a court to admit unrelated hearsay even in a writing. The statement was held properly admitted under a residual hearsay exception, however.

Oral testimony about writings

Beech Aircraft Corp. v. Rainey, 488 U.S. 153 (1988): The Supreme Court agreed with the Court of Appeals, 784 F.2d 1523 (1986), *reinstated,* 827 F.2d 1498 (11th Cir. 1987) (en banc), that a Trial Judge had erred in refusing to permit a plaintiff, who had been called as an adverse witness and asked about a letter he had written to a Navy officer concerning his wife's death, to testify on cross-examination as to other aspects of the letter. The Court reasoned that, whether or not Rule 106 actually applied to the facts, "[c]learly the concerns underlying Rule 106 are relevant here, but, as the general rules of relevancy permit a ready resolution to this case, we need go no further in exploring the scope and meaning of Rule 106." The Court held that "when one party has made use of a portion of a document, such that misunderstanding or distortion can be averted only through presentation of another portion, the material required for completeness is *ipso facto* relevant and therefore admissible under Rules 401 and 402."

Otherwise inadmissible evidence offered to complete

United States v. Sutton, 801 F.2d 1346 (D.C. Cir. 1986): In a prosecution arising out of a conspiracy to bribe federal officials, the Court reasoned that "Rule 106 can adequately fulfill its function only by permitting the admission of some otherwise inadmissible evidence when the court finds in fairness that the proffered evidence should be considered contemporaneously." It added, however, that "the provision of Rule 106 grounding admission on 'fairness' reasonably should be interpreted to incorporate the common-law requirements that the evidence be relevant, and be necessary to qualify or explain the already introduced evidence allegedly taken out of context" and that "[i]n almost all cases we think Rule 106 will be invoked rarely and for a limited purpose." The Court found error in the exclusion of portions of recorded conversations that the defense offered after the government introduced portions of the recordings, but it found the error to be harmless. Our view is that the opinion may address a nonproblem. When portions of a conversation are relevant to explain or to place in context other portions of a conversation that have been admitted, they almost never fall within the proscription of other rules of evidence, because they are not offered for their truth or to establish an independent proposition; they are offered to provide the context in which other evidence must be viewed. Of course, in some situations, evidence qualifying for admission under Rule 106 would be excluded under Rule 403, since the probative value of the context evidence might pale before the probability that a jury would use the evidence for a prohibited purpose.

97

United States v. Nixon, 779 F.2d 126 (2d Cir. 1985): Although the error was harmless, the Court found in a narcotics case that the government erred in introducing a telex containing a witness' description of a defendant. Since the agent who sent the telex never testified, the telex was hearsay and could not be admitted under any exception. Although the government sought to rely upon Rule 106, the Court concluded that the Rule could not be used where the evidence was not admissible under the hearsay rule. In *United States Football League v. National Football League,* 842 F.2d 1335 (2d Cir. 1988), the Court affirmed a judgment awarding the plaintiff $1 on antitrust claims and held that the Trial Judge ruled properly in excluding a letter, even though a reply letter was admitted. It said that "[t]he doctrine of completeness, Fed. R. Evid. 106, does not compel admission of otherwise inadmissible hearsay evidence."

United States v. Costner, 684 F.2d 370 (6th Cir. 1982): The Court reversed a conviction for making a false statement to a bank in order to obtain a loan, because the Trial Judge improperly admitted portions of a document that were hearsay and were not related to a portion that appellant had previously offered. The Court observed that "Rule 106 is intended to eliminate the misleading impression created by taking a statement out of context. The rule covers an offer of proof problem; it is not designed to make something admissible that should be excluded."

United States v. Pendas-Martinez, 845 F.2d 938 (11th Cir. 1988): The Court reversed a conviction for marijuana offenses, holding that a Coast Guard officer's handwritten report of events on the night of a chase of a small boat from which marijuana was thrown was improperly admitted. Without deciding whether Rule 106 permitted the admission of otherwise inadmissible evidence, the Court concluded that the concept of completeness embodied in the Rule did not require admission of the entire report where nothing was read out of context during cross-examination that required admission of the whole to correct a misleading impression.

Prejudicial material in documents

United States v. Brown, 720 F.2d 1059 (9th Cir. 1983): The Court reversed convictions of numerous defendants convicted of a conspiracy to distribute heroin. It found that the government had sufficient evidence of conspiracy and the defendants' connection therewith, but it held that the prosecutor acted improperly in bringing to the jury's attention the fact that as part of plea bargain agreements several government witnesses agreed to submit to polygraph tests. The Court recognized that the government is entitled to bring out the fact that it has made a bargain with a witness, but it refused to permit the government to elicit every fact that might be mentioned in the agreement. And it rejected the government's argument that since the defense insinuated that the witnesses had been made promises not revealed in their written agreements with the government, the polygraph was properly mentioned. The Court found that the defense never implied that the polygraph provision was not in the writing, so there was no reason to offer it as evidence except for the improper purpose of rehabilitating witnesses through reliance on the polygraph.

Prior testimony

United States v. Soures, 736 F.2d 87 (3d Cir. 1984), *cert. denied,* 105 S. Ct. 914 (1985): Affirming a defendant's conviction for receiving kickbacks, the Court found that the Trial Judge properly admitted some portions of the defendant's grand jury testimony and excluded others. The Court cited Rule 106 and commented that "[t]he Rule does not require introduction of portions of a statement that are neither explanatory of nor relevant to the passages that have been admitted."

United States v. Walker, 652 F.2d 708 (7th Cir. 1981): A conviction for extortion was reversed because the Trial Judge admitted selected portions of the appellant's testimony in a first trial that ended in a mistrial but excluded other relevant portions that explained the excerpts that were admitted.

Redacted statements

United States v. Marin, 669 F.2d 73 (2d Cir. 1982): The Court approved a ruling in a drug case that admitted one defendant's statement without the part attributing possession and control of narcotics to a codefendant. The Court said that "[t]he completeness doctrine does not require introduction of portions of a statement that are neither explanatory of nor relevant to the admitted passages" and found that the deleted portion was inadmissible, self-serving hearsay.

Frymire-Brinati v. KPMG Peat Marwick, 2 F.3d 183 (7th Cir. 1993): The Court reversed a judgment for investors who sued an accounting firm, holding, *inter alia,* that the Trial Judge erred in permitting the plaintiffs to compress the defendant's discovery responses into a three-page narrative and in denying the defendant's request to have its statements restored to their original context. The Court stated that "[a]n admission depicts the party in its own words; Peat Marwick was entitled to have the jury see those words rather than a precis that the adverse party thought would depict the speaker in the worst light." In *United States v. Velasco,* 953 F.2d 1467 (7th Cir. 1992), a cocaine conspiracy prosecution, the government introduced a portion of one defendant's postarrest statement to prove his knowledge, but the defendant was not permitted to introduce the remainder. The Court held there was no abuse of discretion, as the rest of the statement referred only to a nontestifying codefendant (and therefore would be inadmissible under *Bruton*) and others whose activities were irrelevant in the case.

United States v. Dorrell, 758 F.2d 427 (9th Cir. 1985): In a prosecution for injuring government property and illegally entering a military reservation, the Court held that the Trial Judge properly redacted a defendant's statement to eliminate references to political and religious motivations that were not relevant.

United States v. Lopez, 898 F.2d 1505 (11th Cir. 1990): One defendant argued that introduction of his redacted postarrest statement at his trial with another for drug offenses violated the rule of completeness. The Court affirmed the convictions, holding there was no error in admitting the statement, when the redaction was made to protect the *Bruton* rights of a codefendant and it did not distort the meaning of the statement or exclude information substantially exculpatory of the nontestifying defendant.

Relationship to consistent statements

United States v. Harris, 761 F.2d 394 (7th Cir. 1985): Affirming convictions for forging papers and illegally receiving government funds pursuant to a job training statute, the Court held that the general rule governing prior consistent statements — i.e., "the motive to fabricate must not have existed at the time the statements were made or they are inadmissible" — "need not be met to admit into evidence prior consistent statements which are offered solely to rehabilitate a witness rather than as evidence of the matters asserted in those statements." The Court added:

> This use of prior consistent statements for rehabilitation is particularly appropriate where, as here, those statements are part of a report or interview containing inconsistent statements which have been used to impeach the credibility of the witness. Prior consistent statements which are used in this matter are relevant to whether the impeaching statements really were inconsistent within the context of the interview, and if so, to what extent.... This rehabilitative use of prior consistent statements is also in accord with the principle of completeness promoted by Rule 106.

United States v. Blankinship, 784 F.2d 317 (8th Cir. 1986): The Court affirmed the admission of an entire extrajudicial written statement of a postal employee who the defendant was charged with assaulting. Since the defendant's counsel used portions of the statement to suggest recent fabrication, the Court reasoned that it was important for the factfinder to see the entire statement in order to assess the seriousness of any inconsistencies. In *United States v. Andrade,* 788 F.2d 521 (8th Cir.), *cert. denied,* 107 S. Ct. 462 (1986), the Court affirmed convictions arising out of a scheme to use fraudulent credit cards to buy and later cash-in airline tickets. There was no error in admitting evidence of one agent's notes concerning an interview with a defendant, where the defense had questioned two other witnesses concerning the notes and left impressions that there might have been inaccuracies in the notes and collaboration between government witnesses. The Court held that the rehabilitation was proper and it fell within Rule 106.

United States v. Myers, 972 F.2d 1566 (11th Cir. 1992), *cert. denied,* 113 S. Ct. 1813 (1993): In a civil rights prosecution of an officer for using a stun gun on arrestees, the Court held there was no abuse of discretion in limiting admission of a statement made by the defendant during an internal affairs investigation to the parts concerning the number of times he had used the stun gun, as the prosecutor had introduced the statement only to impeach the defendant on that issue. The parts consistent with the defendant's trial testimony were admitted for rehabilitation, but the parts of the statement dealing with the circumstances and the defendant's motivation were not admissible under the Rule.

Relevance requirement

United States v. Crosby, 713 F.2d 1066 (5th Cir.), *cert. denied,* 104 S. Ct. 506 (1983): The Court affirmed convictions for kidnapping offenses, rejecting the defendant's argument that he should have been permitted to play for the jury portions of a tape recording of the negotiations between himself and the police while he was holding a hostage. The Court interpreted the Trial Judge's ruling to require that the defense show that the portion of the tape it wished to play was relevant, and it observed that promises of immunity in a hostage situation are irrelevant to guilt or innocence.

United States v. Harvey, 959 F.2d 1371 (7th Cir. 1992): The Court affirmed mail fraud convictions, holding there was no abuse of discretion in precluding cross-examination of a postal inspector about statements from the defendant that his funding sources were "hustlers," as the statements were made when he had time to reflect and perhaps misrepresent his thoughts and were, in any event, not probative of whether he had an intent to defraud. Moreover, there was no showing the statements qualified or explained the witness' direct testimony. In *United States v. Lewis,* 954 F.2d 1386 (7th Cir. 1992), the defendant, when questioned about a postarrest statement, was asked whether he had told agents that he had not obtained any drugs from an accomplice but that if he had he would not tell the FBI; on redirect, he was not permitted to add that he had said he would not tell the FBI without talking to an attorney first. Affirming the defendant's conviction for a cocaine conspiracy, the Court said it might have admitted the completing statement but held there was no abuse of discretion, as the statement had only minimal significance. In *United States v. Velasco,* 953 F.2d 1467 (7th Cir. 1992), a cocaine conspiracy prosecution, the government introduced a portion of one defendant's postarrest statement to prove his knowledge, but the defendant was not permitted to introduce the remainder. The Court held there was no abuse of discretion, as the rest of the statement referred only to a nontestifying codefendant (and therefore would be inadmissible under *Bruton*) and others whose activities were irrelevant in the case.

United States v. Wright, 826 F.2d 938 (10th Cir. 1987): Affirming fraud convictions, the Court held that portions of a diary were properly excluded while others were admitted. The portions excluded were not relevant to trial issues nor were they explanatory of other portions that were admitted.

Scientific articles

Marsee v. United States Tobacco Co., 866 F.2d 319 (10th Cir. 1989): Affirming a judgment against a plaintiff who claimed that her son developed oral cancer from using snuff, the Court held that the defendant was properly permitted to introduce scientific articles in addition to those introduced by the plaintiff in order to rebut a claim that the then-existing scientific and medical evidence "as a whole" tended to show that the product was dangerous.

Tape recordings

In re Air Crash Disaster, 635 F.2d 67 (2d Cir. 1980): The Court affirmed the Trial Judge's decision refusing to allow the playing of one channel of the cockpit recorder by itself and requiring the entire tape to be played with volume adjustments to make the tape clearer.

United States v. Garrett, 716 F.2d 257 (5th Cir. 1983), *cert. denied,* 104 S. Ct. 1910 (1984): The Court affirmed Travel Act convictions, finding no error in the admission of part of a tape recording for the government and rejection of another part offered by a defendant. The Court said that Rule 106's completeness doctrine "does not require introduction of portions of a statement that are neither relevant to nor explanatory of the admitted passages." In *United States v. Crosby,* 713 F.2d 1066 (5th Cir.), *cert. denied,* 104 S. Ct. 506 (1983), the Court affirmed convictions for kidnapping offenses, rejecting the defendant's argument that he should have been permitted to play for the jury portions of a tape recording of the negotiations between himself and the police while he was holding a hostage. The Court interpreted the Trial Judge's ruling to require that the defense show that the portion of the tape it wished to play was relevant, and it observed that promises of immunity in a hostage situation are irrelevant to guilt or innocence.

United States v. LeFevour, 798 F.2d 977 (7th Cir. 1986): Affirming the convictions of a former state court judge, the Court found no error in the admission of part of a tape recording and the exclusion of a part offered by the defendant. It found that no misleading impression was created by the playing of only part of the tape, and the part that the defendant desired to play was irrelevant.

Timing

United States v. Southland Corp., 760 F.2d 1366 (2d Cir.), *cert. denied,* 474 U.S. 825 (1985): The Court affirmed convictions of a corporation and a lawyer for conspiring to defraud the United States, although it found that the lawyer should have been permitted to introduce certain portions of grand jury testimony immediately after the prosecutor introduced an excerpt from the testimony. The Court cited Rule 106 and referred to it as "a principle of simple fairness, long antedating the Federal Rules of Evidence."

D. LEGISLATIVE HISTORY

Advisory Committee's Note

The rule is an expression of the rule of completeness. McCormick § 56. It is manifested as to depositions in Rule 32 (a)(4) of the Federal Rules of Civil Procedure, of which the proposed rule is substantially a restatement.

The rule is based on two considerations. The first is the misleading impression created by taking matters out of context. The second is the inadequacy of repair work when delayed to a point later in the trial. See McCormick § 56; California Evidence Code § 356. The rule does not in any way circumscribe the right of the adversary to develop the matter on cross-examination or as part of his own case.

For practical reasons, the rule is limited to writings and recorded statements and does not apply to conversations.

[The entire Advisory Committee Note accompanying the gender-neutralizing changes effective October 1, 1987 is as follows: "The amendments are technical. No substantive change is intended."]

Citations to Hearings and Debates

Letter from Edward W. Cleary to Herbert E. Hoffman, March 28, 1973, in Supp. to Hearings on Proposed Rules of Evidence Before the Subcomm. on Criminal Justice of the House of Comm. on the Judiciary, 93rd Cong., 1st Sess., at 4-5 (1973).

Letter from W. Vincent Rakestraw to Hon. James O. Eastland, June 14, 1974, in Hearings on H.R. 5463 (Federal Rules of Evidence) Before the Senate Comm. on the Judiciary, 93rd Cong., 2d Sess., at 121-22, 126 (1974).

ARTICLE II. JUDICIAL NOTICE

RULE 201

A. OFFICIAL TEXT

Rule 201. Judicial Notice of Adjudicative Facts

(a) *Scope of rule.* — This rule governs only judicial notice of adjudicative facts.

(b) *Kinds of facts.* — A judicially noticed fact must be one not subject to reasonable dispute in that it is either (1) generally known within the territorial jurisdiction of the trial court or (2) capable of accurate and ready determination by resort to sources whose accuracy cannot reasonably be questioned.

(c) *When discretionary.* — A court may take judicial notice, whether requested or not.

(d) *When mandatory.* — A court shall take judicial notice if requested by a party and supplied with the necessary information.

(e) *Opportunity to be heard.* — A party is entitled upon timely request to an opportunity to be heard as to the propriety of taking judicial notice and the tenor of the matter noticed. In the absence of prior notification, the request may be made after judicial notice has been taken.

(f) *Time of taking notice.* — Judicial notice may be taken at any stage of the proceeding.

(g) *Instructing jury.* — In a civil action or proceeding, the court shall instruct the jury to accept as conclusive any fact judicially noticed. In a criminal case, the court shall instruct the jury that it may, but is not required to, accept as conclusive any fact judicially noticed.

B. EDITORIAL EXPLANATORY COMMENT

Kinds of facts

Both at common law and under the Federal Rules, most proof is presented by means of testimonial evidence or by the offering of real evidence. But there is an exception to the requirement that a party who relies on a certain proposition must prove it; the exception is judicial notice. Professor Kenneth Culp Davis has suggested a distinction between two kinds of judicial notice: (1) judicial notice of legislative facts, and (2) judicial notice of adjudicative facts. As Professor Davis noted in a letter to the House Subcommittee [cited in Section D, *infra*]:

> A rule on judicial notice cannot lump together the facts about the parties and the facts that are used for lawmaking. The two kinds of facts are quite different. *Judicial practices about the two kinds of facts are and always have been quite different.* Facts pertaining to the parties should not be judicially noticed but should be developed through the evidence unless the facts are unlikely to be questioned. But facts that help a judge determine what the law ought to be often cannot be proved with evidence; they are a part of a judge's thinking and they often have to be the subject of judicial notice. (Emphasis in original).

This is the only Rule dealing with judicial notice. It covers only what Davis refers to as adjudicative facts — facts which concern the "who, what, when, where, and why" of the case before the Court. Judicial notice of legislative facts — facts and policy assumptions used by the Court in the process of construing a statute or developing the law — is intentionally left unrestricted. A Court can rely on legislative facts and assumptions even if they are subject to dispute and are not verifiable.[1]

To be judicially noticed a fact must be either one generally known within the territorial jurisdiction of the Trial Court or one that is capable of accurate and ready determination by resort to sources whose accuracy cannot reasonably be questioned. Thus, there are two different types of indisputable adjudicative facts subject to judicial notice under Rule 201. The first is a fact so well known that it would be a waste of judicial resources to require proof; reasonably well-informed people simply could not differ as to the fact.[2] This indisputability requirement is not satisfied merely because the

---

1. See, e.g., Brown v. Board of Educ., 347 U.S. 483 (1954), where the Court cited a number of authorities for the proposition that segregated schools have a detrimental effect on African-American children. One commentator has stated that the authorities relied on in *Brown* were not so indisputable as to "allow the Court to find as a fact, irrefutable in all future cases," that segregation was harmful. Kaplan, *Segregation Litigation and the Schools,* 58 NW. U. L. REV. 157 (1963). However, indisputability is not required where a legislative fact is used. The finding in *Brown* was a legislative fact because it was used to support a policy decision and to develop the law.

2. See Wooden v. Missouri Pac. R.R., 862 F.2d 560 (5th Cir. 1989) ("judicial notice applies to self-evident truths that no reasonable person could question, truisms that approach platitudes or banalities"; Court could not take judicial notice of the fact that working in a cloud of silicon dust without respiratory gear could cause severe lung disease). See also King v. New Hampshire Dep't of Resources & Econ. Dev., 420 F. Supp.

Trial Judge learns of a fact through personal experience. The matter must be generally known by reasonably well-informed people.[3] However, it is not required that the fact be *universally* known. The Rule requires general knowledge "within the territorial jurisdiction" of the Trial Court. Thus, it may not be universally known that Nebraska has a unicameral legislature; but that fact is generally known in Nebraska.[4]

The second type of adjudicative fact which can be judicially noticed under the Rule is one which is capable of ready verification through sources whose reliability cannot reasonably be questioned. This prong of adjudicative fact is the one more often relied upon, because a fair argument can be made that most facts are not generally known, but yet that many of these facts can be reliably verified. For example, there may be some argument as to whether the names of the current Justices of the United States Supreme Court are "generally known" even to reasonably well-informed people. Yet it is clear that these names can be readily verified through an unimpeachable source.[5]

It should be noted that the categories of indisputable adjudicative facts are limited and intentionally so. The point of going to trial is to give both parties a chance to examine each other's evidence and to present all sides to the trier-of-fact. Our system disfavors short-cutting the trial process. So for example, a Trial Judge who resorts to outside sources to determine an adjudicative fact should resist the temptation to decide the entire case on the basis of his or her own independent research. Counsel should be permitted to examine the sources relied upon, to suggest other sources, and to present argument about the meaning of the sources upon which the Trial Judge might be prepared to rule.[6]

As we state in the next paragraph, there is no reason to quarrel with the basic distinction between adjudicative and legislative facts. But the labels may be difficult to apply in many cases. One of the authors of this Manual was the Reporter for the Supreme Court of Alaska when it drafted its evidence code. The following quotation is drawn from the Reporter's Comment that accompanied Alaska Rule 201. Although the Alaska Rule

---

1317 (D.N.H. 1976), *aff'd,* 562 F.2d 80 (1st Cir. 1977) (judicial notice taken of the fact that the position for which the plaintiff applied, as a meter patrol officer, was "not particularly different from the job performed by the myriad of meter maids who can be seen performing their jobs daily" and "that no special education or skill is needed to perform the job ...").

3. See United States v. Sorrells, 714 F.2d 1522 (11th Cir. 1983) (Trial Court cannot take judicial notice of informant's reliability based on the Court's personal experience with the informant); United States v. Lewis, 833 F.2d 1380 (9th Cir. 1987) (Trial Judge erred in taking judicial notice of effects of surgery on the defendant, where the Judge relied solely on his own personal experience).

4. See, e.g., United States v. Evans, 994 F.2d 317 (7th Cir. 1993) (no error in taking judicial notice that a certain area was a high crime area); Norman v. Housing Auth. of Montgomery, 836 F.2d 1292 (11th Cir. 1988) (Trial Court properly took judicial notice of the prevailing hourly rate for bookkeepers in the Montgomery area).

5. See Terrebonne v. Blackburn, 646 F.2d 997 (5th Cir. 1981) (proper to take judicial notice of pardons and commutations recommended by Board of Pardons, by reference to information compiled in Department of Corrections Statistical Report).

6. See Oneida Indian Nation v. New York, 691 F.2d 1070 (2d Cir. 1982) (in an action by Indian tribes to invalidate land purchases executed prior to adoption of the Constitution, the Trial Judge should not have dismissed the claim on the basis of his own interpretation of the Articles of Confederation, their legislative history, and contemporary accounts; the Trial Court erred in failing to allow the parties to argue the meaning of the sources and to suggest other sources).

does not use the terms adjudicative and legislative fact, it covers approximately the same ground as the Federal Rule, and the Comment may help Judges and lawyers understand when formal procedures are to be employed in taking judicial notice.

One aspect not covered by Rule 201 involves assumptions made by the court in its determination of policy; e.g., that a particular change in the law would probably do more harm than good. This is not the sort of fact question that, in a jury trial, would normally be put to the jury, and so is not subsumed by Rule 201's definition of "judicial notice of fact." Rather than findings of fact, these are policy determinations made by the court acting in its lawmaking capacity. The court as lawmaker is held to the same standard as the legislature is for the veracity of its inferences: it must be rational. The court taking judicial notice of a fact as that term is used in Rule 201 is held to a different and more demanding standard — the same standard required for it to direct a verdict; it must be right, meaning that rational minds would not dispute the fact that the court notices.

Stated more specifically, Rule 201 does not bar:

(1) Common law rule-making on the basis of factual assumptions based on the court's familiarity with non-evidence sources. See, e.g., Kaatz v. State, 540 P.2d 1037 (Alaska 1975).

(2) Rule-making pursuant to a constitutional grant of authority on the basis of disputable factual assumptions.

(3) Constitutional interpretation based upon disputable factual assumptions — for example the balancing of interests in the vague area of due process.

(4) Judicial creation of remedies assumed to be necessary to carry out the legislative intent of a statute.

. . . .

Alaska Rule 201 requires a determination of whether a question is one normally decided by the trier of fact or is the sort properly left to the maker of law. While this determination is not always easy to make, it is one that courts have coped with for many years. Simply stated, the guiding principle should be: if the fact involved tends to show that general conduct X is or is not, or should or should not, be against the law (or unconstitutional), it is for the court to consider freely; if the fact involved tends to prove an instance of X, it is a question for the trier of fact and covered by Rule 201.

"Legislative" facts

The most serious problem with Rule 201 may be its total failure to address legislative facts. Thus, if something is a "legislative" fact, it may be judicially noticed even though none of the requirements of Rule 201 — most importantly, indisputability and notice — are met. For example, a Court may decide to extend strict liability in tort on the assumption that defendants and their insurers can spread the cost. Or it may decide to expand the attorney-client privilege to protect the communications between low-level corporate agents and corporate counsel, on the assumption that a less generous privilege would deter the free flow of communication necessary to guarantee the attorney's effectiveness. These are factual assumptions that are disputable, yet they are legislative facts and the Court is not bound, when making policy choices, to adhere to Rule 201. If the law is to develop, then Courts must respond to changed conditions and new ideas, before the conditions and ideas become indisputable.

Although we do not challenge either the basic distinction between adjudicative and legislative facts or the need to treat them differently for purposes of judicial notice, we are greatly troubled by the implications of the Advisory Committee's Note that it is acceptable for Courts to take judicial notice of important legislative facts without affording the parties an opportunity to be heard. The Note indicates that evidence of legislative facts should be taken in appropriate situations, but implies that such situations will be rare. Certainly no one would seriously contend that evidence should be taken or argument heard on all the thousands of nonevidence facts discussed by Professor Davis in *A System of Judicial Notice Based on Fairness and Convenience,* PERSP. OF L. 69, 73 (1974). But when a Judge departs from the theories, evidence, and arguments of the parties to embrace a new approach, we favor participation by the parties.[7] The line between consulting and relying upon material facts not addressed by the parties and general background reading may be a fine one. Yet if one has to choose between too much or too little participation by the parties, we would favor the former. We do not claim Judges cannot rely on a broad range of facts to force the law forward. We suggest only that the parties should be permitted to participate in the march. In fact, it may be necessary to remind Trial Judges that Davis' dichotomy may be a useful tool, but that it is dangerous to attempt to use the tool as if it were a sharply honed device designed to split hairs.[8] If a fact or set of facts is likely to be critical to a decision on the law to be applied to parties, there is every reason to want the parties to be heard on the factual question. Evidence need not always be taken. Briefs may work better in many situations. But some chance for the parties to be heard on decisive legislative facts is desirable.[9]

Procedure

According to the Rule, which is consistent with most common-law authority, a Court may take judicial notice upon its own motion. The reason for this is that if judicial notice is truly a means of conserving scarce judicial resources, the parties should not be totally free to impose unnecessary burdens on the Court. Thus, even without a motion by a party, a Court has the discretion to take judicial notice in appropriate circumstances. In

---

7. Cf. 5 U.S.C. § 556(e) (hearing upon timely request under Administrative Procedure Act).

8. See DAVIS, JUDICIAL NOTICE, 1969 LAW AND THE SOCIAL ORDER, 513, 515:

> The ultimate principle is that extra-record facts should be assumed whenever it is convenient to assume them, except that convenience should always yield to the requirement of procedural fairness that parties should have an opportunity to meet in the appropriate fashion all facts that influence the disposition of the case.

9. See, e.g., Bulova Watch Co. v. K. Hattori & Co., 508 F. Supp. 1322 (E.D.N.Y. 1981) (in ruling on a motion to dismiss for lack of jurisdiction, Trial Court took judicial notice of materials concerning the history and development of multinational corporations like the defendant; the Court issued a provisional ruling and invited the parties "to be heard on the propriety of taking judicial notice and the tenor of the matter noticed").

contrast to this discretionary power, a Judge must take judicial notice when requested to do so by a party who supplies the necessary information. In order to be fair to both parties, the party opposing the taking of judicial notice is entitled to be heard. An opposing party who has notice prior to a Court ruling may make a presentation. If prior notification is not given, a request for the abandonment of judicial notice may be made after the Trial Court's ruling. In jury trials, it is clearly preferable for the parties to receive an opportunity to be heard before the judicially noticed matter is introduced.

Effect of judicial notice

There has been a great division of authority as to whether once judicial notice is taken the opposing party should have a chance to introduce facts that rebut the facts judicially noticed. According to the Rule, in civil cases the Court shall instruct the jury to accept as conclusive any fact judicially noticed. This means that the opposing party cannot present contradictory evidence on the fact once it has been judicially noticed; the time for presenting such evidence is when the matter is heard by the Trial Judge under Rule 201(e).

In a criminal case, the Court can only instruct the jury that it may, but is not required to, accept as conclusive the facts judicially noticed. The reason that judicially noticed facts are not binding on the jury in criminal cases is because of a concern for the defendant's Sixth Amendment right to jury trial. Since the Trial Judge cannot direct a verdict for the prosecution,[10] neither can the Judge grant a "partial" directed verdict by way of judicial notice. In effect, Rule 201 treats judicial notice in criminal cases on a par with a permissible inference.[11] This would seem to permit the party, usually the defendant, against whom notice is taken, to offer evidence to rebut the noticed fact (although relevant evidence of a fact not reasonably disputed should be hard to find). The real advantage of judicial notice in a criminal case is to excuse the prosecution (or the defendant in the rare case in which the defense takes advantage of judicial notice) from having to make a formal presentation of evidence to establish a point. Judicial notice spares the expense of proof.

The Rule requires the Trial Judge to send all disputed fact questions to the jury. If an issue is disputed, the jury is permitted to reject facts even if the Trial Judge regards this as unreasonable.

The Federal Judicial Center has proposed the following jury instruction with respect to judicially noticed facts in criminal cases:

> Even though no evidence has been introduced about it, I have decided to accept as proved the fact that [e.g., the city of San Francisco is north of the city of Los Angeles]. I believe that this fact is of such common knowledge [or alternative justification per rule 201(b)(2) of the Federal Rules of Evidence] that

---

10. See Sullivan v. Louisiana, 113 S. Ct. 2078 (1993) (Sixth Amendment prohibits directed verdict for prosecution).

11. For a further discussion of permissible inferences in criminal cases, see S. SALTZBURG & D. CAPRA, AMERICAN CRIMINAL PROCEDURE 876-885 (4th ed. West 1992).

it would be a waste of our time to hear evidence about it. Thus, you may treat it as proved, even though no evidence was brought out on the point. Of course, with this fact, as with any fact, you will have to make the final decision and you are not required to agree with me.[12]

Jury instructions

If the Judge in a criminal case takes judicial notice of facts and instructs the jury that they may find the facts as noticed, what additional instructions may be needed?

It may well be necessary for the Judge to assure the jury that factfinding is its function. Normally the Judge will tell the jury that it is the sole judge of the credibility of the witnesses and that the existence or nonexistence of particular facts is a matter for the jury to decide. If this is the only instruction given, however, and if the Judge attempts to take judicial notice of facts, there is the possibility that an Appellate Court would reverse on the ground that the jury was misled as to precisely what the effect of judicial notice was. Since the Rule clearly permits the jury to reject the Judge's notice in a criminal case, there seems to be no reason for the Judge to be anything but explicit on this point.[13]

Judicial notice on appeal

Because of the special recognition in the Rule of the jury's role, an Appellate Court must be careful not to judicially notice facts in a way that would deprive a litigant of jury consideration of those facts. For example, in reviewing a criminal case tried to a jury, an Appellate Court should not take judicial notice of an adjudicative fact in order to find that the evidence was sufficient for a conviction. To do so would be tantamount to the use of a binding instruction concerning a judicially noticed fact at trial, which is prohibited under Rule 201(g); it would be the same as directing the jury to find a fact upon which no evidence was introduced.[14] The same concerns would not apply to

---

12. Federal Judicial Center Pattern Criminal Jury Instructions, No. 7. The Commentary to the Instruction states: "The Committee recommends that the instruction regarding judicial notice be given at the time notice is taken."

13. See United States v. Anderson, 528 F.2d 590 (5th Cir.), *cert. denied,* 429 U.S. 837 (1976) (Trial Judge instructed the jury after taking judicial notice, "you are allowed to accept that as a fact proven before you just as though there had been evidence to that effect before you''; Appellate Court noted that Trial Judge failed to instruct the jury in the words of subsection (g) that the jury "may, but is not required to, accept as conclusive any fact judicially noticed," but held that the variance in the rule did not amount to reversible error).

14. See e.g., United States v. Bliss, 642 F.2d 390 (10th Cir. 1981) (Appellate Court declines to take judicial notice that bank was member of Federal Reserve System; in absence of proof below, the taking of judicial notice would be tantamount to a partial directed verdict); United States v. Thomas, 610 F.2d 1166 (3d Cir. 1979) (provision for judicial notice on appeal "is modified by subsection (g)''; Appellate Court is not permitted to undermine the jury's right to ignore a court's factual conclusion); United States v. Hones, 580 F.2d 219 (6th Cir. 1978):

Rule 201(g) plainly contemplates that the jury in a criminal case shall pass upon facts which are judicially noticed. This it could not do if this notice were taken for the first time after it had been

appellate judicial notice in the context of review of civil trials or criminal nonjury trials.[15]

The provision for mandatory judicial notice in Rule 201(d) should not be automatically applied on appeal, if the party could have and yet failed to raise the issue at trial. A requirement of mandatory judicial notice on appeal would, in these circumstances, conflict with the provisions of Rule 103, which require timely objection and an offer of proof. Consequently, if the party missed an opportunity to raise the issue at trial, an Appellate Court should judicially notice a fact in the party's favor only if the Trial Court's failure to do so was plain error. This is particularly true where the asserted ground of indisputability is that the fact could have been readily verified by accurate sources. The party's failure to raise the issue at trial means that the Trial Judge was never directed to any sources.

Judicial notice of law

There is no provision in the Rule with respect to so-called judicial notice of law.[16] Rule 44.1 of the Federal Rules of Civil Procedure and Rule 26.1 of the Federal Rules of Criminal Procedure provide a method for invoking the law of a foreign country. These rules received praise from the Advisory Committee, which concluded that questions involving determination of law are better left for the procedural rules. At common law, it was likely that a Court would take judicial notice of domestic law, i.e., the law of the jurisdiction in which the Court sat. As for the law of sister states (usually noticed by Federal Courts, but not by State Courts) and the law of foreign countries, these were often matters to be pleaded and proved, although various presumptions might be invoked to make proof easier. There seems to be a movement to permit the Judge to decide what the law is in any jurisdiction when it is necessary to determine such law to decide a case.[17]

Given the federal procedural rules already enacted and the favorable commentary contained in the Advisory Committee Note, in most cases Federal Judges will utilize a procedure that permits the Judge to determine all questions of law. It does not seem unwise, however, to require a party who asks the Court to take judicial notice of law to do some of the digging that is necessary to discover the law. All that the procedural rules and the current trend provide is that the Court itself is free to consult its own sources and

---

discharged and the case was on appeal. We, therefore, hold that Rule 201(f), authorizing judicial notice at the appellate level, must yield in the face of the express congressional intent manifested in 201(g) for criminal jury trials.

15. See Government of Canal Zone v. Burjan, 596 F.2d 690 (5th Cir. 1979) (Court of Appeals can take judicial notice of a fact in reviewing criminal nonjury trial, because concerns of Rule 201(g) are not at stake).

16. But courts occasionally cite Rule 201 as authority for judicial notice of law. See United States v. Holmes, 414 F. Supp. 831 (D. Md. 1976) (army regulation judicially noticed under Rule 201(b)(2)). On the subject of proof of international and foreign law, see Symposium, 18 VA. J. INT'L 689 (1978).

17. See Toney v. Burris, 829 F.2d 622, 626 (7th Cir. 1987) ("Federal courts must take judicial notice of the statutory and common law of any state of the union without pleading or proof."); United States v. Atwell, 71 F.R.D. 357 (D. Del. 1976), aff'd, 559 F.2d 1209 (3d Cir. 1977) (law of sister state judicially noticed).

to attempt to determine the appropriate law on the basis of all available statutes, decisions and other sources.

Application to facts of case

In most cases, there are some underlying facts which are so obvious as to be subject to judicial notice. But this is often of little importance, because in most cases there is significant dispute between the parties as to whether and how a particular judicially noticed fact would be applicable to the facts of the case. For example, in *Wooden v. Missouri Pacific R.R.,* 862 F.2d 560 (5th Cir. 1989), plaintiff was exposed to silicon dust while he worked for a Railroad. He contracted silicosis, and sued the Railroad for failing to provide him with a respiratory mask. Plaintiff sought judicial notice of the fact that "it was common knowledge in the late 1950's that working in a cloud of silicon dust without respiratory gear could cause severe lung diseases." The Court held that judicial notice was not required, because the application of the "indisputable" fact was in dispute:

> The essential defect in Wooden's argument is that the fact he asks be noticed is closely joined to an obviously, and legitimately, controverted issue: even if it was common knowledge in 1955 that inhaling silica dust could lead to lung disease, that does not resolve the crucial question of whether the Railroad should have known that the *particular* concentration of dust to which Wooden was exposed entailed a significant risk of silicosis. To notice the fact that some concentrations of silica dusts were known to be harmful would only confuse the jury's consideration of whether the Railroad did know, or should have known, a particular substance to be harmful.[18]

The result in *Wooden* is consistent with Rule 403. Essentially, the Court held that the application of judicial notice would only be marginally probative, because it would not factor in the degree of exposure. For that very reason, the judicially noticed fact might confuse the jury into thinking that the Railroad should have known that any exposure could be harmful.[19]

In other circumstances, a judicially noticed fact may be only conditionally relevant; satisfying Rule 201 is obviously insufficient in these circumstances. The requirements of Rule 104(b) must also be met. For example, in *United States v. Southard,* 700 F.2d 1 (1st Cir. 1983), the prosecution sought to establish that the defendant knew that a telephone call was made to him from out-of-state. The defendant knew the caller had made a call from the New Haven area, and then, fifteen minutes later, placed a call to the defendant in Rhode Island. The Trial Court took judicial notice that "no one could

---

18. See also United States v. Judge, 846 F.2d 274 (5th Cir. 1988) (judicial notice of DEA inventory regulations would not be helpful because the application of the regulations "to the facts presented here is subject to reasonable dispute").

19. See also Laster v. Celotex Corp., 587 F. Supp. 542 (S.D. Ohio 1984) (taking "judicial notice that the inhalation of asbestos *may* cause asbestosis under certain conditions would have no appreciable impact on the length of expert testimony").

have driven from New Haven, Connecticut to the Rhode Island line in 15 minutes.'' But the Court of Appeals reversed, on the ground that the prosecution presented no evidence from which it could be found that the defendant "knew or should have known the driving time between New Haven, Connecticut and the Rhode Island line." Thus, the prosecution failed to ask "the questions necessary for the judicially-noticed fact to become operative," such as whether the defendant had a car, whether he had ever driven to New Haven, whether he had ever studied geography, etc.

Relationship to discovery rules

Counsel in civil cases should be aware of Rule 36 of the Federal Rules of Civil Procedure, which permits one party to ask the other to admit certain facts. More can be accomplished by way of admissions than by way of judicial notice. Failure of the party upon whom a request for admissions is made to admit may result in sanctions under Rule 37 of the procedural rules. Sanctions may not be effective, however, if the party refusing to admit is judgment-proof. More importantly, it may be that a party who seeks the admission cannot afford to prove the facts unless judicial notice is taken. Summary judgment is another possible alternative. Also, a pretrial conference may produce agreement on many issues, thus avoiding unnecessary trial issues.

It has been held that the requirements of Rule 201 are not specifically applicable when a Court is asked to rule on a discovery matter, such as a motion to compel or for a protective order.[20] This does not mean that a Court's use of judicial notice in passing on a discovery motion is unreviewable, however. As one Court put it: "Discovery is not made subject to the same evidence rules that would apply at trial, but Rule 201 does supply a well-accepted standard for judicial notice, and radical departure from this standard could amount to an abuse of the trial court's discretion in overseeing the discovery process."[21]

Relationship to other doctrines

From the cases decided thus far under Rule 201, it is apparent that too often the term judicial notice is used to describe an action of a Trial Judge or an Appellate Court which is better characterized in another way. For example, judicial factfinding may sometimes be confused with the concept of taking judicial notice. When a Trial Judge draws inferences from a writing, the Judge is not taking judicial notice; she is engaging in factfinding and Rule 201 does not apply. Another example of confusion among concepts is the use of Rule 201 where another Rule would be more appropriate — for example,

---

20. See Marshall v. Bramer, 828 F.2d 355 (6th Cir. 1987) (in taking judicial notice of a fact pertinent to plaintiff's discovery demand, "the judge here was not finding the adjudicative facts of the case"; he simply determined, on the basis of the noticed fact, that the defendant probably had custody of certain discoverable information).

21. Marshall v. Bramer, 828 F.2d 355, 358 (6th Cir. 1987) (no abuse of discretion where Trial Court took judicial notice of the fact that the Ku Klux Klan is a violent, racist organization).

the hearsay rule.[22] A document that qualifies for admission into evidence under the hearsay rule becomes evidence in the case; it can be used without the necessity of taking judicial notice under Rule 201.

Relationship to plain error

One of the most difficult distinctions to make is the distinction between a ruling on a claim of plain error under Rule 103(d) and the taking of judicial notice. By definition, plain error signifies that a point was not properly raised in the Lower Court. Because evidence on the point is not in the record, in deciding whether a miscarriage of justice occurred, a reviewing Court often will go outside the record to evaluate the importance of the error. Although the actions of the reviewing Court look very much like the taking of judicial notice, the Court actually is doing something slightly different from taking notice. The Court is not conclusively finding any facts; it is making an educated guess as to the significance of an error. Often the reviewing Court will be willing to concede that the question of whether or not the error was harmful is fairly debatable. But having conceded this, the Court may find no plain error, not because it conclusively determines that a fact is true or false, but because it determines that the party who failed to properly preserve the point for appeal has not been damaged enough to warrant a reversal. Actually, the reviewing Court is not engaged in the kind of factfinding associated with judicial notice of adjudicative facts; it is making a judgment about the requirements of fair procedure based upon an educated guess in an area of uncertainty.

C. ANNOTATED CASES

RULE 201(a) — SCOPE OF RULE

Administrative notice

Llana-Castellon v. INS, 16 F.3d 1093 (10th Cir. 1994): Although the Court noted that the scope of administrative notice may be somewhat broader than judicial notice because of an agency's specialized expertise, it held that the Board of Immigration Appeals denied aliens due process by overturning an Immigration Judge's finding that the aliens had a well-founded fear of prosecution on the basis of administrative notice that control of the government in Nicaragua had changed and by denying the aliens an opportunity to be heard on the issue.

Notice of law

Siderius, Inc. v. M.V. "Amilla," 880 F.2d 662 (2d Cir. 1989): In an action by a manufacturer against a shipowner and ship charterer for cargo damage, the Trial Court

---

22. See, e.g., United States v. Posner, 405 F. Supp. 934 (D. Md. 1975) (judicial notice taken of an affidavit that might have qualified under Rule 803(8)).

looked to the New York Produce Exchange Interclub Agreement in apportioning damages between the defendants. The Court held that the charterer was not entitled to notice before the Judge referred to the Agreement because it was more like law, to which Rule 201 has no application, than an adjudicative fact. Even if the Agreement were considered an adjudicative fact, adequate notice was given by its incorporation by reference in one of the parties' key joint exhibits, the charter party between them.

RULE 201(b) — KINDS OF FACTS

Business or government custom

Eagle-Picher Indus. v. Liberty Mut. Ins. Co., 682 F.2d 12 (1st Cir. 1982), *cert. denied,* 460 U.S. 1028 (1983): In a suit by a manufacturer of asbestos products for a declaratory judgment as to rights and liabilities of various insurers, the Court declined to take judicial notice of the drafting history of standardized insurance policies that were at issue.

Pina v. Henderson, 752 F.2d 47 (2d Cir. 1985), *rev'g* 586 F. Supp. 1452 (E.D.N.Y. 1984): The District Court granted habeas corpus relief to a state prisoner, finding that the prosecution failed to reveal in a timely fashion to the petitioner that a codefendant had admitted sole responsibility for the crime charged. The Court took judicial notice of the fact that it was common practice for the police to make a record of statements made by suspects and that the record would have been similar to the one found in the petitioner's probation report. The Court of Appeals reversed, holding that judicial notice was inappropriate when the fact noticed was an essential part of the party's case and was not clearly beyond dispute. In *Sinatra v. Heckler,* 566 F. Supp. 1354 (E.D.N.Y. 1983), the Court, remanding a case to the Social Security Administration for consideration of whether the plaintiff's request for a hearing was untimely, took judicial notice that in the year-end holiday season a number of federal employees take vacations and that the mails are heavily burdened and sometimes slowed by the increase in mailings. See also *Antco Shipping Co. v. Sidermar S.P.A.,* 417 F. Supp. 207 (S.D.N.Y. 1976) (judicial notice as to purpose of phrase in contract could not be taken where alternative theories were plausible, so that there was a reasonable dispute), *aff'd,* 553 F.2d 93 (2d Cir. 1977).

United States v. George, 971 F.2d 1113 (4th Cir. 1992): Remanding a suppression order in a racketeering case for a determination of whether hacksaw blades seized from the defendant's truck would have been an inevitable discovery in a lawful inventory search, the Court said that judicial notice should be taken of the county police's published policies and procedures for inventory searches. See also *Raleigh-Durham Airport Auth. v. Delta Air Lines,* 429 F. Supp. 1069 (D.N.C. 1976) (judicial notice taken of interdependence of parties in suit for airport landing fees, as well as of nationwide practice of establishing, by process of negotiation, rates to be charged for airport landing fees and space rental).

Harcon Barge Co. v. D & G Boat Rentals, Inc., 746 F.2d 278 (1984), *aff'd en banc,* 784 F.2d 665 (5th Cir.), *cert. denied,* 479 U.S. 930 (1986): The Court took judicial notice as to the uniform practice of the clerks of District Courts within the Circuit with respect to signifying the date of entry of an order or a judgment. See also *Lawrence v.*

Commodity Futures Trading Comm'n, 759 F.2d 767 (9th Cir. 1985) (claim of associated person of commodity broker that suspension would cause broker to lose customers and income was not proper subject of judicial notice).

Calendar and time

Lloyd v. Cessna Aircraft Co., 430 F. Supp. 25 (E.D. Tenn. 1976): When one party to this litigation served notice on opposing parties of an intention to take a deposition, the District Court quashed the notice on the ground that it gave opposing counsel insufficient time to get ready for the depositions. The Court took judicial notice of the fact that one of the days between the time of notice and the scheduled deposition was a national holiday.

Copyrights, patents, trademarks

Eden Toys, Inc. v. Marshall Field & Co., 675 F.2d 498 (2d Cir. 1982): Affirming summary judgment for the defendant in a copyright infringement action, the Court said that the traditional features of a "snowman" are generally enough known to be judicially noticed. See also *Nestle Co. v. Chester's Mkt., Inc.,* 571 F. Supp. 763 (1983) (taking judicial notice of dictionary and cookbook excerpts, Court concluded "Toll House" was a generic term that could not be claimed by Nestle as its trademark), *vacated on settlement,* 609 F. Supp. 588 (D. Conn. 1985).

Marcyan v. Nissen Corp., 578 F. Supp. 485 (N.D. Ind. 1982), *aff'd,* 725 F.2d 687 (1983): In the course of finding for the defendants in a patent infringement case involving an exercise device with an invertible handlebar, the Court took judicial notice of the fact that handlebars of bicycles are routinely inverted and have been for some time.

Metro Publishing, Ltd. v. San Jose Mercury News, 987 F.2d 637 (9th Cir. 1993): In the course of reversing the denial of a motion for a preliminary injunction in a trademark infringement action, the Court held that the fact that titles of newspapers and magazine columns have been registered as trademarks by the U.S. Patent and Trademark Office could be the subject of judicial notice once certified copies of registrations taken from the Principal Register were presented to the Court.

B.V.D. Licensing Corp. v. Body Action Design, Inc., 846 F.2d 727 (Fed. Cir. 1988): In a trademark infringement case, the Court held that dictionaries and encyclopedias may be consulted and judicial notice of their contents taken when a Court determines the familiarity of a word or a mark. A concurring opinion suggested that judicial notice "is not acknowledged as often as it should be" and that "[i]t is available at the appellate level, even if not used by the trial tribunal, and may support or undermine that tribunal's conclusions."

Current events

Washington Post v. Robinson, 935 F.2d 282 (D.C. Cir. 1991): The government had argued that sealing a plea agreement was justified by the danger of compromising an ongoing criminal investigation or embarrassing innocent parties, but the Court vacated the sealing order, taking judicial notice of the current newspaper publicity surrounding the investigation and the defendant's involvement and cooperation in that investigation.

Barnes v. Bosley, 568 F. Supp. 1406 (E.D. Mo. 1983), *modified,* 745 F.2d 501 (8th Cir. 1984), *cert. denied,* 105 S. Ct. 2022 (1985): In an action by discharged public employees claiming that they were victims of politically motivated action, the Court took judicial notice that the Democratic Party was currently in firm control of political offices within the City of St. Louis.

Orantes-Hernandez v. Smith, 541 F. Supp. 351 (C.D. Cal. 1982): In the course of granting injunctive relief against the Immigration and Naturalization Service's treatment of Salvadoran aliens, the Court took judicial notice that El Salvador was in the midst of a civil war that created a substantial danger of violence to civilians residing there and that both government forces and guerrillas had been responsible for human rights violations and political persecution.

Economic information

Cardio-Medical Assocs. v. Crozer-Chester Med. Center, 721 F.2d 68 (3d Cir. 1983): Holding that an antitrust plaintiff's allegations were sufficient to state a claim, the Court found that the District Judge erred in taking judicial notice of the proposition that it was "logically inconceivable" that the defendants' conduct affected the interstate movement of patients seeking cardiological therapy. This, said the Court of Appeals, "[c]learly ... is reasonably disputable." In *Varlack v. SWC Caribbean, Inc.,* 550 F.2d 171 (3d Cir. 1977), a personal injury action, the Court noted that a Trial Judge is empowered to take judicial notice of the appropriate discount rate to be applied to a lump sum payment in a tort action. See also *Fox v. Kane-Miller Corp.,* 398 F. Supp. 609 (D. Md. 1975) (judicial notice of the rate of inflation), *aff'd,* 542 F.2d 915 (4th Cir. 1976).

Transorient Navigators Co., S.A. v. M/S Southwind, 788 F.2d 288 (5th Cir. 1986): The Court held in an admiralty case that a Trial Judge may take judicial notice of prevailing interest rates. See also *Mainline Inv. Corp. v. Gaines,* 407 F. Supp. 423 (N.D. Tex. 1976) (taking judicial notice of economic events in the oil industry, in determining whether breach of contract was excused by "act of God or other extraordinary cause" over which party had no control).

Ohio River Co. v. Peavey Co., 731 F.2d 547 (8th Cir. 1984): In an admiralty case, the Court held that the Trial Judge could not take judicial notice that a 10 percent rate was appropriate for prejudgment interest, where evidence was offered to the contrary.

Grason Elec. Co. v. Sacramento Mun. Util. Co., 571 F. Supp. 1504 (E.D. Cal. 1983): In the course of denying summary judgment for the plaintiff in an antitrust case using a "monopoly leveraging" theory, the Court took judicial notice that "there is no alternative to which consumers could readily turn should they desire to live their lives as they presently do, but without electricity." This notice led the Court to conclude that the relevant product market was electrical energy and that the relevant geographic market was the area in which the defendant utility operated, since it had no competitors.

Facts about litigants

Peters v. Delaware R. Port Auth., 16 F.3d 1346 (3d Cir.), *cert. denied,* 115 S. Ct. __ (1994): Determining in a civil rights action by the Secretary of the Port Authority, who had been discharged because he was Republican, that party affiliation is an appropriate requirement for effective performance in the position, the Court took judicial notice from newspaper accounts of the part played by political considerations in the Authority's operations. In *Hinton v. Department of Justice,* 844 F.2d 126 (3d Cir. 1988), the Court declined to take judicial notice of FBI affidavits predicting the time and cost of preparing an index to documents in response to a Freedom of Information Act request. In *City of New Brunswick v. Borough of Milltown,* 686 F.2d 120 (3d Cir. 1982), *cert. denied,* 459 U.S. 1201 (1983), a suit by a city against a borough and a county utilities authority to void a contract concerning sewage disposal, the Court refused to take judicial notice of the amount of sewage flowing from the borough into a plant. It observed that "[t]he doctrines of 'legislative facts' and 'judicial notice' are not talismans by which gaps in a litigant's evidentiary presentation before the district court may be repaired on appeal."

Haavistola v. Community Fire Co., 6 F.3d 211 (4th Cir. 1993): In reversing summary judgment granted a volunteer fire company in a Title VII and § 1983 sex discrimination action, the Court held it was an abuse of discretion to take judicial notice of the defendant's status as a State actor. In *Washington Metro. Area Transit Auth. v. One Parcel of Land,* 706 F.2d 1312 (4th Cir.), *cert. denied,* 104 S. Ct. 238 (1983), an eminent domain case, the Court took judicial notice of the fact that a mass transit system consisted of very substantial personal and real property.

Wooden v. Missouri Pac. R.R., 862 F.2d 560 (5th Cir. 1989): In a suit by a railroad employee alleging that he contracted silicosis from tamping gravel, the Court held that judicial notice could not be taken of the fact that it was common knowledge in the 1950s that working in a cloud of silicon dust without respiratory gear could cause severe lung disease.

Brown & Williamson Tobacco Corp. v. Jacobson, 827 F.2d 1119 (7th Cir. 1987), *cert. denied,* 108 S. Ct. 1302 (1988): The Court held that a Trial Judge could not take judicial notice that media coverage of a verdict in favor of a cigarette manufacturer who successfully proved actual malice in a television broadcast was "fair." The Court found error in the Judge's reliance on the noticed fact as justification for reducing a compensatory damage award.

Bethel Conservative Mennonite Church v. Commissioner, 746 F.2d 388 (7th Cir. 1984), the Court reversed the Commissioner's determination that the Church was not qualified for exemption from federal income tax. Taking judicial notice of church documents that detailed the history of "mutual aid practices," the Court found that a medical aid plan was similar to the other mutual aid plans that the group used to further a strongly-held religious belief that its members must "bear one another's burdens."

Holloway v. Lockhart, 813 F.2d 874 (8th Cir. 1987): The Court reversed summary judgments for prison guards and officials in a suit by an inmate who alleged that the defendants used or approved the use of tear-gas that caused him an unconstitutional injury. The Court found that the Trial Judge erred in adopting findings of fact concerning the reasonableness of the defendants' actions that were made in another lawsuit arising out of the same tear-gas incident, since the plaintiff could not be estopped by the findings and they were not the kind of findings as to which judicial notice could be taken.

Storm Plastics, Inc. v. United States, 770 F.2d 148 (10th Cir. 1985): Reversing a judgment for the government in a suit involving excise taxes on fishing lures, the Court held that the Trial Judge improperly took judicial notice of the quality of the plaintiff's fishing lures. This was neither a subject generally known in the community nor one capable of accurate and ready determination by plainly accurate sources.

Cofield v. Alabama Pub. Serv. Comm'n, 936 F.2d 512 (11th Cir. 1991): Affirming in part an order requiring an inmate to seek prefiling approval of any complaints or papers he filed in the future, the Court held that judicial notice should not have been taken of a newspaper article as proof that the inmate had access to thousands of dollars hidden somewhere. Just because a statement appears in a newspaper does not establish that the fact is capable of accurate and ready determination by resort to sources whose accuracy cannot reasonably be questioned. In *Nationalist Movement v. City of Cumming,* 913 F.2d 885, *vacated & reh'g en banc granted,* 921 F.2d 1125 (1990), *panel opinion reinstated,* 934 F.2d 1482 (11th Cir. 1991), *aff'd,* 112 S. Ct. 2395 (1992), the Court held there had been no error in taking judicial notice that the plaintiff organization's rallies were often loud and attracted boisterous and sometimes violent counter-demonstrators. The Trial Judge's observations were apparently based on local and national media accounts, as well as on public records, of the organization's marches and counter-marches in the county. In any event, because the plaintiffs had not requested a hearing under Rule 201(e), the judicial notice issue was nonappealable.

Fees, salaries, etc.

In re Olson, 884 F.2d 1415 (D.C. Cir. 1989): In ruling on an attorney's fee application, the Court said that it would take judicial notice that an attorney's billing rate of $260 per hour was reasonable, as his legal abilities were generally well known within the Circuit.

Ursic v. Bethlehem Mines, 719 F.2d 670 (3d Cir. 1983): The Court found that an attorney for a successful plaintiff in an action claiming wrongful discharge in violation of the federal retirement security statute was not entitled to a bonus established by the District Court. The Court took judicial notice of the attorney's fees charged by able counsel in the Western District of Pennsylvania. See also *Whitman v. Fuqua,* 561 F. Supp. 175 (W.D. Pa. 1983) (in considering joint motion for approval of attorneys' fees in bitter corporate control contest, Court was entitled to "take notice of the customary rates in the community for attorneys of comparable standing, skill and experience").

Rutherford v. Sea-Land Serv., 575 F. Supp. 1365 (N.D. Cal. 1983): The Court took judicial notice that the eight dollars per day provided for in a collective bargaining agreement was an unreasonably low sum for obtaining a room and three meals in the San Francisco Bay area.

General information

United States v. Simon, 842 F.2d 552 (1st Cir. 1988): Affirming a defendant's drug-related convictions, the Court held that the Trial Judge was not required to take judicial notice of the facts that there is a University of the West Indies in Jamaica and that Rastafarians use marijuana as part of their religion. It concluded that no showing was made that these facts were either generally known or capable of accurate and ready determination by sources that could not reasonably be questioned. See also *United States v. Bourque,* 541 F.2d 290 (1st Cir. 1976) (not proper for District Court to take judicial notice of whether the Internal Revenue Service ever loses tax returns).

Caulfield v. Board of Educ., 486 F. Supp. 862 (E.D.N.Y. 1979), *aff'd,* 632 F.2d 999 (2d Cir. 1980), *cert. denied,* 450 U.S. 1030 (1981): In a civil rights action challenging an agreement between local and federal education officials designed to remedy statutory violations, the Court took judicial notice of the fact that historically in New York City women comprised a large percentage of the teaching force, particularly at lower school levels.

Record Museum v. Lawrence Township, 481 F. Supp. 768 (D.N.J. 1979): The Court took judicial notice of "the phenomenon known as the counterculture of the seventies." See also *Newark Morning Ledger Co. v. United States,* 416 F. Supp. 689 (D.N.J. 1975) (taking judicial notice in income tax case that plaintiff was New Jersey's largest and only statewide newspaper, both on weekdays and on Sunday), *aff'd,* 539 F.2d 929 (3d Cir. 1976).

Conway v. Chemical Leaman Tank Lines, Inc., 610 F.2d 360 (5th Cir. 1980): The Court of Appeals refused to take judicial notice of the reaction times of truck drivers, since the cited treatise referred only to "normal" reaction times and no request had been made for judicial notice until the appeal following a third trial. In *Blacks United for Lasting Leadership, Inc. v. City of Shreveport,* 71 F.R.D. 623 (W.D. La. 1976), *remanded on other grounds,* 571 F.2d 248 (5th Cir. 1978), the District Judge, holding that at-large elections for the mayor and city commissioners unconstitutionally diluted black voting strength, took judicial notice that until recently *de jure* segregation under both a state statute and a local ordinance affected the lives of all black persons in ways described by the Court. The Court also took judicial notice of a 1974 city-wide census in order to supplement evidence introduced at trial based on the 1970 Census. Finally, the Court judicially noticed that, in contrast to the government's concern for the condition of streets in black neighborhoods, similar streets located in more affluent neighborhoods were not permitted to lapse into such disrepair. See also *Clark v. South Cent. Bell Tel. Co.,* 419 F. Supp. 697 (W.D. La. 1976) (Court refused to take judicial notice of black population of particular parish in employment discrimination suit, where source of information not placed before Court).

United States v. Deckard, 816 F.2d 426 (8th Cir. 1987): The Court affirmed a defendant's conviction for an illegal wiretap, holding there was no error in taking judicial notice that interstate communications were carried over the telephone company's lines. The Trial Judge had properly instructed the jury that it could, but was not required to, accept as conclusive a fact that was judicially noticed.

United States v. Baker, 641 F.2d 1311 (9th Cir. 1981): The Court said that nonparties to an injunction must have actual notice of it before they can be held in criminal contempt for violating it and that judicial notice of "actual notice" could not be taken on the basis of "unproved, widespread publicity." In *Neeld v. National Hockey League,* 594 F.2d 1297 (9th Cir. 1979), the Court took judicial notice that ice hockey is a rough, physical contact sport that must be dangerous for a player who has only one eye and cannot see other players on his blind side.

United Klans of Am. v. McGovern, 453 F. Supp. 836 (N.D. Ala. 1978), *aff'd,* 621 F.2d 152 (5th Cir. 1980): The District Court took judical notice that the plaintiff organization was a "white hate" organization.

Geography

United States v. Southard, 700 F.2d 1 (1st Cir.), *cert. denied,* 104 S. Ct. 89 (1983): The Court reversed a gambling conviction in a bench trial because the District Judge took judicial notice in a bench trial that "no one could have driven from New Haven, Connecticut to the Rhode Island line in 15 minutes," and used this as the basis for concluding that the defendant knew that a key telephone call had been made from out of state. The Court said that notice of the facts might have been proper, but that such notice could not support a finding that the defendant actually knew the facts, since there was no evidence that the defendant knew the distances that were judicially noticed.

United States v. Ramirez, 910 F.2d 1069 (2d Cir.), *cert. denied,* 111 S. Ct. 531 (1990): Affirming the defendant's sentence for a drug offense, the Court held that the sentencing Court could take judicial notice that New York had no firearms manufacturers and conclude that a handgun illegally in the defendant's possession came from interstate commerce.

Berkshire Fashions, Inc. v. M.V. Hakusan II, 954 F.2d 874 (3d Cir. 1992): An admiralty action seeking to recover for loss of umbrellas to be shipped from Taiwan to New Jersey was dismissed for lack of subject matter jurisdiction on the ground that the bill of lading did not contemplate carriage by sea alone. In reversing for further factfinding, the Court held that while it would be proper to notice judicially that a purely maritime route was elongated, it would be inappropriate to take judicial notice that parties would never contract for shipment over that geographical distance. See also *Deary v. Evans,* 570 F. Supp. 189 (D.V.I. 1983) (taking judicial notice, in action for a false arrest arising out of a bank robbery investigation, that a downtown business area was small and that two buildings were within several blocks of one another), *aff'd in part & rev'd in part,* 746 F.2d 185 (3d Cir. 1984).

United States v. Lossiah, 537 F.2d 1250 (4th Cir. 1976): The Court of Appeals approved the District Court's judicial notice that a certain town was within the Cherokee Indian Reservation, but reversed on another ground. See also *Otto v. Alper,* 489 F. Supp. 953 (D. Del. 1980) (judicial notice that Rehoboth Bay in Delaware is navigable waterway for purposes of admiralty jurisdiction).

United States v. Anderson, 528 F.2d 590 (5th Cir.), *cert. denied,* 429 U.S. 837 (1976): Affirming a conviction for assault with intent to do bodily harm, the Court approved taking judicial notice that the Federal Correctional Institution in Tallahassee,

Fla., where the assault was proved to have taken place, was "within the special maritime and territorial jurisdiction of the United States." See also *Smith v. Hustler, Inc.,* 514 F. Supp. 1265 (W.D. La. 1981) (taking judicial notice in admiralty case that lake on which accident occurred was not "navigable," a fact generally known in the community).

Northwest Airlines v. County of Kent, Mich., 955 F.2d 1054 (6th Cir. 1992), *aff'd on other grounds,* 114 S. Ct. 855 (1994): In an action by airlines over the reasonableness of rates charged by an airport, judicial notice was taken that the airport was located less than an hour and a half from two airports serviced by major airlines. In *United States v. Blunt,* 558 F.2d 1245 (6th Cir. 1977), the Court affirmed a conviction for assault with a deadly weapon, noting that the Trial Judge would have been correct in taking judicial notice under Rule 201 of the fact that the federal prison in which the assault giving rise to the instant prosecution took place was within the special territorial jurisdiction of the United States.

Lowrance v. Pflueger, 878 F.2d 1014 (7th Cir. 1989): The plaintiff in this § 1983 action had been arrested in Kenosha, Wis., for kidnapping his daughter from her mother's custody in Tennessee. In holding that the defendant sheriff in Tennessee had reasonable cause when alleging in an affidavit supporting an arrest warrant that the defendant was in Kenosha and might take the girl to Canada, the Court took judicial notice that Kenosha was several hundred miles north of Tennessee, in the general direction of Canada, and less than 300 miles from a Canadian port of entry.

Horton v. Taylor, 585 F. Supp. 224 (W.D. Ark. 1984), *rev'd on other grounds,* 767 F.2d 471 (8th Cir. 1985): The Court took judicial notice that a county was predominantly rural and was located in mountainous regions.

United States v. Perez, 776 F.2d 797 (9th Cir. 1985): The Court, sustaining a conviction for drug importation, took judicial notice of the fact that a trip between Guam and an Island in the Trust Territory of the Pacific Islands must have involved travel through international waters.

United States v. Garcia, 672 F.2d 1349 (11th Cir. 1982): The Court found that a Trial Judge was entitled to take judicial notice that a location was well beyond the three mile territorial limit of the United States. It also reminded Trial Judges that where they are taking notice they should notify the parties and give them a chance to be heard.

Historical information

Oneida Indian Nation v. New York, 691 F.2d 1070 (2d Cir. 1982): In an action by the Nation to invalidate land purchases by New York from Indian tribes prior to the adoption of the Constitution, the Court said that the District Judge should not have taken judicial notice of various historical materials in order to interpret the Articles of Confederation. The historical material had not been subject to cross-examination, and the Court of Appeals remanded for an evidentiary hearing.

Korematsu v. United States, 584 F. Supp. 1406 (N.D. Cal. 1984): In a landmark case, the Court utilized the writ of *coram nobis* to vacate the conviction (which had been affirmed by the Supreme Court in 1944, 323 U.S. 214) of an American citizen of Japanese ancestry who had violated an order excluding persons of such ancestry from various places after the United States declared war on Japan in 1941. In making its ruling, the Court declined to take judicial notice of certain adjudicative facts — i.e., that there was no military necessity for relocation and detention of ethnic Japanese and that the government had failed to disclose crucial information to courts considering the military necessity question. Even though the government did not oppose judicial notice, the Court expressed its view that notice of the ultimate facts in a case was inappropriate. Instead, the Court suggested that a report of a Congressional Commission on Wartime Relocation could be considered under Rule 803(8) and that certain internal government documents either were not hearsay and admissible to show notice to the government or they satisfied one or more hearsay exceptions.

Judicial records and proceedings

Reiner v. Washington Plate Glass Co., 711 F.2d 414 (D.C. Cir. 1983): In a bankruptcy proceeding the Court took judicial notice on appeal of the records of the District of Columbia Recorder of Deeds and the dates a corporation surrendered its charter and was reincorporated. In *United States v. Haldeman,* 559 F.2d 31 (D.C. Cir. 1976), *cert. denied,* 431 U.S. 933 (1977), the Court said: "The District Judge could surely take judicial notice, in a preliminary hearing merely on the admissibility of certain evidence, that ... testimony [read into the record by the government] was in fact presented in a hearing at which he presided on a not unrelated matter." In *Washington Mobilization Comm. v. Cullinane,* 566 F.2d 107 (D.C. Cir. 1977), the Court took judicial notice of an exhibit filed in another case pending before it.

Kowalski v. Gagne, 914 F.2d 299 (1st Cir. 1990): The Court affirmed a judgment for the plaintiff in a wrongful death action brought by the widow against the man convicted of murdering her husband, holding that the conviction was properly established by judicial notice rather than a certified copy.

Liberty Mut. Ins. Co. v. Rotches Pork Packers, Inc., 969 F.2d 1384 (2d Cir. 1992): Reversing a judgment for the subrogee of a bankrupt meat packer, the Court held it was error to take judicial notice of a Bankruptcy Court's orders in order to prove that a statutory trust had been created, as judicial notice of documents filed in another court may be used only to establish the fact of the other litigation and related filings, not the truth of matters asserted in the filings. In *West v. Village of Morrisville,* 728 F.2d 130 (2d Cir. 1984), the Court, in directing a District Court to abstain pending a state court determination on disputed questions of state law, took judicial notice that prompt resolution of a claim is possible in Vermont courts.

O'Neill v. Heckler, 579 F. Supp. 979 (E.D. Pa. 1984): Although the Court dismissed a complaint seeking review of the denial of disability benefits on the ground that the complaint was not filed in a timely manner, it took judicial notice that the complaint was actually filed, along with a motion to proceed *in forma pauperis,* before the Court clerk stamped "filed" on it.

Colonial Penn Ins. Co. v. Coil, 887 F.2d 1236 (4th Cir. 1989): The Court took judicial notice of plaintiffs' postsettlement guilty pleas to arson accessory charges in setting aside a settlement of a suit under a fire policy.

United States v. Pierre, 932 F.2d 377 (1991), *on reh'g en banc,* 958 F.2d 1304 (5th Cir.), *cert. denied,* 113 S. Ct. 280 (1992): Reviewing convictions for cocaine possession with intent to distribute because of an allegedly illegal border search, the Court took judicial notice of testimony given by the officer in a previous case concerning his practice of, and purposes in, putting his head through the open window of vehicles stopped at the border. In *In re Missionary Baptist Found. of Am., Inc.,* 712 F.2d 206 (5th Cir. 1983), the Court found no error in a Bankruptcy Judge's taking judicial notice of a record developed in the same bankruptcy case, but in a different proceeding. See also *MacMillan Bloedel Ltd. v. Flintkote Co.,* 760 F.2d 580 (5th Cir. 1985) (upholding summary judgment for a seller in a suit by the buyer of corporate assets and observing that "[a] court may take judicial notice of related proceedings and records in cases before the same court"); *Kinnett Dairies, Inc. v. Farrow,* 580 F.2d 1260 (5th Cir. 1978) (in absence of any complaint or claim by party that procedure violated due process, no error in Trial Court's taking judicial notice of materials in its files from prior proceedings even though one of the parties in the instant case had not been a party in the prior proceedings). In *United States v. Hawkins,* 566 F.2d 1006 (5th Cir.), *cert. denied,* 439 U.S. 848 (1978), the Court took judicial notice of a jury selection plan for one Federal District that was on file with the Court.

United States v. Garland, 991 F.2d 328 (6th Cir. 1993): The Court vacated a defendant's conviction for fraud arising out of what he claimed was a failed attempt to buy cocoa beans from Ghana. While his appeal was pending, a court in Ghana convicted two Ghanians of defrauding Garland in connection with the cocoa bean transaction. The Court determined that judicial notice should be taken of the Ghanian judgment and findings and that the evidence was sufficient newly discovered evidence to warrant a new trial.

Green v. Warden, 699 F.2d 364 (7th Cir.), *cert. denied,* 461 U.S. 960 (1983): The Court took judicial notice of a prisoner's extensive record of litigation and of the subject matter of his lawsuits and entered an injunction barring future actions in the District Courts and the Court of Appeals for the Seventh Circuit without first obtaining leave of court. In *Zell v. Jacoby-Bender, Inc.,* 542 F.2d 34 (7th Cir. 1976), the Court of Appeals refused to take judicial notice of documents filed by the same plaintiff in a companion case involving the same parties that was pending before the same District Court.

United States v. Wilson, 631 F.2d 118 (9th Cir. 1980): The Court reversed a bail-jumping conviction, holding it was error to take judicial notice of the fact that the defendant was absent from the jurisdiction of the court for approximately seven months, where the warrant for arrest showed only the date of arrest and not the date on which the defendant was taken into state custody. See also *Wyle v. Bank Melli,* 577 F. Supp. 1148 (N.D. Cal. 1983) (declining judicial notice of the large number of legal proceedings around the country involving the Bank Melli and the nation of Iran, but finding "fraud in the transaction" on the part of the Bank Melli in its effort to force payment pursuant to a letter of credit).

Meredith v. Beech Aircraft Corp., 18 F.3d 890 (10th Cir. 1994): The plaintiff claimed that the defendant discriminated against her on the basis of her sex in connection with a promotion, and the Trial Court granted summary judgment, taking into consideration another case in which a District Judge had decided that the defendant had discriminated on grounds of sex in connection with the very same promotion. The Court held it was error to take judicial notice of the determination in the other action, because the fact that the plaintiff in the other action was the most qualified for the position was not a "kind of universal truth." Moreover, the plaintiff could not be collaterally estopped because she was not a party in the earlier case. In *St. Louis Baptist Temple, Inc. v. FDIC,* 605 F.2d 1169 (10th Cir. 1979), the Court said that judicial notice "of proceedings in other courts, both within and without the federal judicial system," may be taken "if those proceedings have a direct relation to matters at issue." In *Rogers v. United States,* 575 F. Supp. 4 (D. Mont. 1983), an action by the holder of unpatented mining claims against the Bureau of Land Management challenging the Bureau's determination that the holder's claims were invalid, the Court took judicial notice of certain state court records that were not before the agency when it made its determination. The holder was challenging the constitutionality of an irrebuttable presumption, and the first opportunity to rely on the records arose in the District Court.

Coney v. Smith, 738 F.2d 1199 (11th Cir. 1984): The Court took judicial notice of state court proceedings to decide whether a search and seizure claim had been decided.

Schapansky v. Department of Transp., 735 F.2d 477 (Fed. Cir.), *cert. denied,* 469 U.S. 1018 (1984): In the course of affirming a Merit Systems Protection Board's permanent removal of an air traffic controller, the Court took judicial notice, at the former controller's request, of materials in his "Supplemental Appendix" that had been used in a case argued together with his and several others' before the Board.

Medical information

Hardy v. Johns-Manville Sales Corp., 681 F.2d 334 (5th Cir. 1982): In an asbestos-related product liability action, the Court refused to take judicial notice that asbestos causes cancer, as that proposition was inextricably linked to a host of disputed issues.

United States v. Johnson, 979 F.2d 396 (6th Cir. 1992): The defendant, who pleaded guilty to bank fraud, claimed a downward departure in sentencing because of a Severe Adjustment Disorder. Taking judicial notice of the definition of the disorder in the American Psychiatric Association's diagnostic manual, the Court held that the defendant failed to establish the existence of such a condition.

Hines v. Secretary of Health & Human Servs., 940 F.2d 1518 (Fed. Cir. 1991): Reviewing a Vaccine Act proceeding, the Court noted that the incubation period of measles is the sort of well-known medical fact of which judicial notice may be taken.

Official records

Massachusetts v. Westcott, 431 U.S. 322 (1977): Westcott was convicted of illegally fishing in Massachusetts waters under a statute directed at nonresidents. The Massachusetts Supreme Judicial Court ordered the complaint against him dismissed on the ground that the statute violated the privileges and immunities clause of Art. IV, § 3, cl. 2 of the United States Constitution. Citing Rule 201(b), the Supreme Court took judicial notice of the fact that Westcott was "federally enrolled and licensed" to fish, and vacated and remanded for consideration of whether federal preemption, rather than a constitutional argument, should govern the case.

Joseph v. United States Civil Serv. Comm'n, 554 F.2d 1140 (D.C. Cir. 1977): In an action by District of Columbia residents challenging a Hatch Act exemption by the Civil Service Commission, the Court took "judicial notice of certain facts with respect to the candidates for seats on the District of Columbia City Council which to some extent fill in the generalized allegations of appellants' affidavits." The Court said it was noting "matters of public record which could be unquestionably demonstrated from easily accessible sources of indisputable accuracy." Compare *Melong v. Micronesian Claims Comm'n,* 643 F.2d 10 (D.C. Cir. 1980) (refusing to notice 172 pages of unauthenticated documents involving Claims Commission).

Kramer v. Time Warner, Inc., 937 F.2d 767 (2d Cir. 1991): Affirming dismissal of a securities action, the Court held that a District Court may consider relevant documents filed with the SEC in determining a motion to dismiss, even though those documents were not part of the complaint. In *Wiscope v. Commodity Futures Trading Comm'n,* 604 F.2d 764 (2d Cir. 1979), the Court held that in proceedings before the Commodity Futures Trading Commission official notice should not have been taken of an edited transcript of a Commission meeting with its staff, since the transcript was not usually kept as a public record. In fact, it was created for the purpose of this proceeding.

United States v. 97.19 Acres, 511 F. Supp. 565 (D. Md. 1981): In a condemnation case, the Court approved the judicial notice by the Magistrate of the final rate of interest on corporate debt obligations as set forth in the Federal Reserve Bulletin for 1980.

United States v. Judge, 846 F.2d 274 (5th Cir. 1988): In a cocaine prosecution, the Court remanded for a determination of whether an inventory was conducted pursuant to standard procedure. It declined to take notice of certain regulations that the government submitted from the DEA's manual for two reasons: (1) the regulations were not part of the record below; (2) only selected portions of the manual were submitted, so the Court could not be sure that additional portions were necessarily irrelevant.

Robbins v. B & B Lines, Inc., 830 F.2d 648 (7th Cir. 1987): The Court took judicial notice of arbitration association rules that were incorporated by reference in pension fund rules that governed an arbitration and were referred to by both parties in their briefs. See also *Orlando v. Wizel,* 443 F. Supp. 744 (W.D. Ark. 1978) (judicial notice taken of the official capacity of a Judge).

Nugget Hydroelectric, L.P. v. Pacific Gas & Elec. Co., 981 F.2d 429 (9th Cir. 1992), *cert. denied,* 113 S. Ct. 2326 (1993): The Court held, in an antitrust case in which a defendant claimed immunity under the state action doctrine, that the Trial Judge could take judicial notice of published decisions of the California Public Power Commission. In *Mack v. South Bay Beer Distribs., Inc.,* 798 F.2d 1279 (9th Cir. 1986), the Court reversed a judgment based on collateral estoppel principles in an age discrimination action, but it stated that a court may take judicial notice of the records and reports of administrative bodies. See also *Haye v. United States,* 461 F. Supp. 1168 (C.D. Cal. 1978) (in action to quiet title and enjoin enforcement of federal tax lien, Court took notice of recorded deeds, recorded notice of a lien, and county general index).

Melton v. City of Oklahoma City, 879 F.2d 706 (1989), *modified on other grounds en banc,* 928 F.2d 920 (10th Cir.), *cert. denied,* 112 S. Ct. 296 (1991): In this civil rights action by a discharged police officer against the city and police officials, the Court took judicial notice of state laws and local ordinances in determining, on the issue of the municipality's liability, whether the unconstitutional action had been taken by a "final policymaker" identified by statute.

Powers v. United States, 996 F.2d 1121 (11th Cir. 1993): In a Federal Tort Claims Act action in which the plaintiff alleged that the availability of federally subsidized flood insurance had not been sufficiently publicized, the Court took judicial notice of the *Code of Federal Regulations* and other government publications publicizing the insurance.

Performance of equipment

Granholm v. TFL Express, 576 F. Supp. 435 (S.D.N.Y. 1983, and 1984): In an admiralty action, the Court took judicial notice that service lives of radar sets are finite and that indiscriminate use could cause radar to fail when it was most needed.

Personal knowledge of court

Fultz v. Rose, 833 F.2d 1380 (9th Cir. 1987), *cert. denied,* 108 S. Ct. 2824 (1988): Reversing an order suppressing a confession, the Court held that the Judge had erred in relying upon his personal experience concerning the effects of a general anesthetic following an operation. The Court observed that the record was silent as to the Judge's surgical procedure and the type of anesthetic with which he had experience, and concluded that the parties had no fair opportunity to respond to the facts that the Judge was noticing.

In re National Airlines, Inc., 434 F. Supp. 269 (S.D. Fla. 1977): The District Court entered a judgment for the defendants, rejecting a claim that the airline's flight attendant weight program discriminated against women. The Court concluded that absent discrimination, the airline could choose "to have a lean lithe corps," or "stocky, robust flight attendants," and noted:

> To the extent permitted by Federal Evidence Rule 201 the court can take judicial notice that in southern Florida, National's flight attendants enjoy a reputation for competence as well as good looks. The court's judicial notice is supplemented by personal experience gained from more than 100 flights aboard National Airlines and a total of more than 500 flights aboard 24 United States commercial air carriers.

We respectfully observe that such personal, rather than general, knowledge is not a permissible basis for judicial notice under the Rule.

Scientific facts

United States v. Jakobetz, 955 F.2d 786 (2d Cir.), *cert. denied,* 113 S. Ct. 104 (1992): Affirming the defendant's conviction for kidnapping, the Court held that, given the findings made by the District Court and after careful consideration and review on appeal, in future cases, judicial notice could properly be taken of the general acceptability of the general theory and the use of the specific techniques of DNA profiling.

United States v. Bonds, 12 F.3d 540 (6th Cir. 1993): The Court held, in a conspiracy and firearms prosecution, that it would not take judicial notice of a National Academy of Sciences report on DNA testing. The report was published more than a year after the defendants' convictions and so was not available at the admissibility hearing or the suppression hearings; moreover, there was considerable dispute over the significance of its contents, so it was not an appropriate subject of judicial notice.

Technological facts

Carley v. Wheeled Coach, 991 F.2d 1117 (3d Cir.) *cert. denied,* 114 S. Ct. 191 (1993): The defendant manufacturer of a government ambulance involved in a roll-over accident asserted a government contractor defense, which required that it warn the government of dangers in the use of its product known to it but not the government. Reversing summary judgment for the defendant, the Court held it was error to find the government's equal knowledge by taking judicial notice that vehicles with a high center of gravity have rollover problems. Most people probably know little, if anything, about how high centers of gravity cause vehicular accidents.

Weather

Newman v. Village of Hinsdale, 592 F. Supp. 1307 (N.D. Ill. 1984), *aff'd,* 767 F.2d 925 (7th Cir. 1985): To determine the amount of snowfall on a given day, the Court indicated that it would take judicial notice of the records of the National Oceanic and Atmospheric Administration.

RULE 201(e) — OPPORTUNITY TO BE HEARD

Cooperativa de Ahorro y Credito Aguada v. Kidder, Peabody & Co., 993 F.2d 269 (1st Cir. 1993): The Court held that the Trial Judge improperly dismissed a securities action as time barred on the basis of judicial notice of articles in the national press that had not been submitted by either party, where the parties had not been given an opportunity to be heard with respect to the material noticed.

Chen v. Metropolitan Ins. & Annuity Co., 907 F.2d 566 (5th Cir. 1990): In an action on a double indemnity provision in a life insurance policy where the insurer defended on the ground that the insured's death by drinking too much brandy was not an "accident" and was caused by a "drug" within the meaning of the policy, the Court reversed a summary judgment for the defendant, noting that although it is usually the party's burden to request a hearing to challenge the taking of judicial notice, here the judicial notice taken that alcohol is a drug involved a matter of contractual interpretation reviewable as a matter of law.

Castillo-Villagra v. INS, 972 F.2d 1017 (9th Cir. 1992): The Court reversed an order of the Board of Immigration Appeals which denied Nicaraguans political asylum on the ground that removal of the Sandinista government had removed the threat to the petitioners. The Court held it was error to take administrative notice of the election and its effects subsequent to the filing of briefs with the BIA and without any opportunity for the petitioners to be heard on the effects of Sandinistas retaining power over the police and the military.

In re Calder, 907 F.2d 953 (10th Cir. 1990): The Court affirmed denial of discharge in bankruptcy, holding that the Bankruptcy Court was not required to give the debtor prior notice before taking judicial notice of the contents of his petition in deciding whether to deny discharge for material false statements. The burden rested with the debtor to request a hearing to challenge the propriety of taking judicial notice even after notice had been taken.

RULE 201(f) — TIME OF TAKING NOTICE

Bulova Watch Co. v. K. Hattori & Co., 508 F. Supp. 1322 (E.D.N.Y. 1981): Ruling on a motion to dismiss for lack of personal jurisdiction, the District Court said that not only could judicial notice be employed at this stage of the proceeding, but also that the judgment to be made was a mixed question of fact and law which permitted broader, more flexible judicial notice than is typically allowed in connection with standard adjudicative facts.

Colonial Leasing Co. v. Logistics Control Group Int'l, 762 F.2d 454, *reh'g granted in part on other grounds,* 770 F.2d 479 (5th Cir. 1985): The Court reversed a judgment for a purported creditor who sued a purported debtor and a third party alleging a fraudulent transfer of assets. It found that the Trial Judge erred in taking judicial notice of an Oregon state court judgment after a trial in which the Judge had excluded such evidence. Although the judgment was admissible and its existence was the proper subject of judicial notice, the Court of Appeals reasoned that since the transferee declined to produce evidence at trial when the plaintiff failed to establish a *prima facie* case and since the judicial notice that established the *prima facie* case took place after trial, the transferee was deprived of an opportunity to adduce evidence on a critical fact. The case serves as a reminder that in a jury trial, judicial notice ordinarily will be required before the jury returns its verdict if it is to have any effect. In *Government of Canal Zone v. Burjan,* 596 F.2d 690 (5th Cir. 1979), the Court held that judicial notice may be taken under Rule 201 of governmental boundaries. Since this case was a bench trial, the Court found no problem with subdivision (g), even though no request for judicial notice was made in the Trial Court.

United States v. Bonds, 12 F.3d 540 (6th Cir. 1993): The Court held, in a conspiracy and firearms prosecution, that it would not take judicial notice of a National Academy of Sciences report on DNA testing. The report was published more than a year after the defendants' convictions and so was not available at the *Frye* hearing or the suppression hearings; moreover, there was considerable dispute over the significance of its contents, so it was not an appropriate subject of judicial notice.

United States v. Wessels, 12 F.3d 746 (8th Cir. 1993), *cert. denied,* 115 S. Ct. __ (1994): During the defendant's sentencing for drug offenses, the Judge took judicial notice that a particular type of methamphetamine had been involved, on the ground that none of the 50-some cases in the state with which the Judge was familiar involved the alternative type. The Court remanded, holding that the particular type was essential to the calculation of the proper sentence and the government rather than the defendant bore the burden of producing evidence on the issue.

RULE 201(g) — INSTRUCTING JURY

United States v. Mentz, 840 F.2d 315 (6th Cir. 1988): The Court reversed a conviction for bank robbery, finding that the Trial Judge invaded the province of the jury and violated the Sixth Amendment by instructing the jury that banks were insured by the Federal Deposit Insurance Corporation. One Judge would have found the erroneous instruction to have been harmless error.

United States v. Jones, 580 F.2d 219 (6th Cir. 1978): In the defendant's trial for illegally intercepting telephone conversations of his estranged wife, the government introduced evidence that appellant had tapped a telephone furnished by South Central Bell Telephone Company, but offered no evidence to show that the company was at the time a "person engaged as a common carrier in providing or operating ... facilities for the transmission of interstate or foreign communications." After the jury convicted on three of five counts, the District Judge granted the defendant's motion for a judgment of acquittal on the ground that the government failed to prove that the tapped conversation was a wire communication covered by the statute. The Court examined the legislative history of Rule 201(g) and concluded that it could not take judicial notice of the common carrier status of the telephone company involved in the case, because "[a]s enacted by Congress, Rule 201(g) plainly contemplates that the jury in a criminal case shall pass upon facts which are judicially noticed. This it could not do if this notice were taken for the first time after it had been discharged and the case was on appeal." To the extent that subdivision (f) authorizes judicial notice at the appellate level, that subdivision, said the Court, "must yield in the face of the express congressional intent manifested in 201(g) for criminal jury trials."

United States v. Gould, 536 F.2d 216 (8th Cir. 1976): At the trial of a cocaine importation conspiracy, two expert witnesses for the government testified that a powdered substance seized from someone working with the defendants was cocaine hydrochloride. The statute penalized conduct relating to controlled substances and defined a controlled substance as being, *inter alia,* any "derivative ... of coca leaves." Although there was no direct evidence to indicate that cocaine hydrochloride is a derivative of coca leaves, the District Court instructed the jury: "If you find the substance was cocaine hydrochloride, you are instructed that cocaine hydrochloride is a Schedule II controlled substance under the laws of the United States." The Court of Appeals had no difficulty concluding that the fact that cocaine hydrochloride is derived from coca leaves is, if not common knowledge, at least a matter which is capable of certain, easily accessible and indisputably accurate verification. It then characterized the judicial notice as notice of a legislative fact, rather than an adjudicative fact, and approved the binding instruction given by the District Judge to the jury. The Court stated that "[l]egislative facts are established truths, facts or pronouncements that do not change from case to case but apply universally, while adjudicative facts are those developed in a particular case." The Court stated that this is not a fact that would traditionally go to the jury. To rule otherwise, in the view of the Court of Appeals, "would be preposterous, ... permitting juries to make conflicting findings on what constitutes controlled substances under federal law.'' See also *United States v. Berrojo,* 628 F.2d 368 (5th Cir. 1980) (failure to instruct the jury that it was not required to accept that cocaine hydrochloride was a controlled substance was not plain error).

United States v. Bliss, 642 F.2d 390 (10th Cir. 1981): In affirming postverdict judgments of acquittal in a case charging falsification of bank records, the Court cited *United States v. Jones, supra,* and concluded that acquittal was proper because the government had offered no evidence that the bank was a member of the Federal Reserve System and had not requested that judicial notice be taken of the fact. In *United States v. Piggie,* 622 F.2d 486 (10th Cir.), *cert. denied,* 449 U.S. 863 (1980), the Court found no error in taking judicial notice that Leavenworth Penitentiary is United States territory. Although the Trial Judge did not instruct in the language of subdivision (g), no request for any instruction was made, and there really was no dispute about the fact.

D. LEGISLATIVE HISTORY

Advisory Committee's Note

Subdivision (a). This is the only evidence rule on the subject of judicial notice. It deals only with judicial notice of ''adjudicative'' facts. No rule deals with judicial notice of ''legislative'' facts. Judicial notice of matters of foreign law is treated in Rule 44.1 of the Federal Rules of Civil Procedure and Rule 26.1 of the Federal Rules of Criminal Procedure.

The omission of any treatment of legislative facts results from fundamental differences between adjudicative facts and legislative facts. Adjudicative facts are simply the facts of the particular case. Legislative facts, on the other hand, are those which have relevance to legal reasoning and the lawmaking process, whether in the formulation of a legal principle or ruling by a judge or court or in the enactment of a legislative body. The terminology was coined by Professor Kenneth Davis in his article An Approach to Problems of Evidence in the Administrative Process, 55 Harv. L. Rev. 364, 404-07 (1942). The following discussion draws extensively upon his writings. In addition, see the same author's Judicial Notice, 55 Colum. L. Rev. 945 (1955); Administrative Law Treatise, ch. 15 (1958); A System of Judicial Notice Based on Fairness and Convenience, in Perspectives of Law 69 (1964).

The usual method of establishing adjudicative facts is through the introduction of evidence, ordinarily consisting of the testimony of witnesses. If particular facts are outside the area of reasonable controversy, this process is dispensed with as unnecessary. A high degree of indisputability is the essential prerequisite.

Legislative facts are quite different. As Professor Davis says:

> My opinion is that judge-made law would stop growing if judges, in thinking about questions of law and policy, were forbidden to take into account the facts they believe, as distinguished from facts which are ''clearly ... within the domain of the indisputable.'' Facts most needed in thinking about difficult problems of law and policy have a way of being outside the domain of the clearly indisputable.

A System of Judicial Notice Based on Fairness and Convenience, *supra,* at 82.

An illustration is Hawkins v. United States, 358 U.S. 74, 79 S. Ct. 136, 3 L. Ed. 2d 125 (1958), in which the Court refused to discard the common law rule that one spouse could not testify against the other, saying, ''Adverse testimony given in criminal proceedings would, we think, be likely to destroy almost any marriage." This conclusion has a large intermixture of fact, but the factual aspect is scarcely "indisputable." See Hutchins and Slesinger, Some Observations on the Law of Evidence — Family Relations, 13 Minn. L. Rev. 675 (1929). If the destructive effect of the giving of adverse testimony by a spouse is not indisputable, should the Court have refrained from considering it in the absence of supporting evidence?

> If the Model Code or the Uniform Rules had been applicable, the Court would have been barred from thinking about the essential factual ingredient of the problems before it, and such a result would be obviously intolerable. What the law needs at its growing points is more, not less, judicial thinking about the factual ingredients of problems of what the law ought to be, and the needed facts are seldom "clearly" indisputable.

Davis, *supra,* at 83.

Professor Morgan gave the following description of the methodology of determining domestic law:

> In determining the content or applicability of a rule of domestic law, the judge is unrestricted in his investigation and conclusion. He may reject the propositions of either party or of both parties. He may consult the sources of pertinent data to which they refer, or he may refuse to do so. He may make an independent search for persuasive data or rest content with what he has or what the parties present.... [T]he parties do no more than to assist; they control no part of the process.

Morgan, Judicial Notice, 57 Harv. L. Rev. 269, 270-71 (1944).

This is the view which should govern judicial access to legislative facts. It renders inappropriate any limitation in the form of indisputability, any formal requirements of notice other than those already inherent in affording opportunity to hear and be heard and exchanging briefs, and any requirement of formal findings at any level. It should, however, leave open the possibility of introducing evidence through regular channels in appropriate situations. See Borden's Farm Products Co. v. Baldwin, 293 U.S. 194, 55 S. Ct. 187, 79 L. Ed. 281 (1934), where the cause was remanded for the taking of evidence as to the economic conditions and trade practices underlying the New York Milk Control Law.

Similar considerations govern the judicial use of non-adjudicative facts in ways other than formulating laws and rules. Thayer described them as a part of the judicial reasoning process.

> In conducting a process of judicial reasoning, as of other reasoning, not a step can be taken without assuming something which has not been proved; and the capacity to do this with competent judgment and efficiency, is imputed to judges and juries as part of their necessary mental outfit.

Thayer, Preliminary Treatise on Evidence 279-80 (1898).

As Professor Davis points out, A System of Judicial Notice Based on Fairness and Convenience, in Perspectives of Law 69, 73 (1964), every case involves the use of hundreds or thousands of non-evidence facts. When a witness in an automobile accident case says "car," everyone, judge and jury included, furnishes, from non-evidence sources within himself, the supplementing information that the "car" is an automobile, not a railroad car, that it is self-propelled, probably by an internal combustion engine, that it may be assumed to have four wheels with pneumatic rubber tires, and so on. The judicial process cannot construct every case from scratch, like Descartes creating a world based on the postulate *Cogito, ergo sum.* These items could not possibly be introduced into evidence, and no one suggests that they be. Nor are they appropriate subjects for any formalized treatment of judicial notice of facts. See Levin and Levy, Persuading the Jury with Facts Not in Evidence: The Fiction-Science Spectrum, 105 U. Pa. L. Rev. 139 (1956).

Another aspect of what Thayer had in mind is the use of non-evidence facts to appraise or assess the adjudicative facts of the case. Pairs of cases from two jurisdictions illustrate this use and also the difference between non-evidence facts thus used and adjudicative facts. In People v. Strook, 347 Ill. 460, 179 N.E. 821 (1932), venue in Cook County had been held not established by testimony that the crime was committed at 7956 South Chicago Avenue, since judicial notice would not be taken that the address was in Chicago. However, the same court subsequently ruled that venue in Cook County was established by testimony that a crime occurred at 8900 South Anthony Avenue, since notice would be taken of the common practice of omitting the name of the city when speaking of local addresses, and the witness was testifying in Chicago. People v. Pride, 16 Ill. 2d 82, 156 N.E.2d 551 (1951). And in Hughes v. Vestal, 264 N.C. 500, 142 S.E.2d 361 (1965), the Supreme Court of North Carolina disapproved the trial judge's admission in evidence of a state-published table of automobile stopping distances on the basis of judicial notice, though the court itself had referred to the same table in an earlier case in a "rhetorical and illustrative" way in determining that the defendant could not have stopped her car in time to avoid striking a child who suddenly appeared in the highway and that nonsuit was properly granted. Ennis v. Dupree, 262 N.C. 224, 136 S.E.2d 702 (1964). See also Brown v. Hale, 263 N.C. 176, 139 S.E.2d 210 (1964); Clayton v. Rimmer, 262 N.C. 302, 136 S.E.2d 562 (1964). It is apparent that this use of non-evidence facts in evaluating the adjudicative facts of the case is not an appropriate subject for a formalized judicial notice treatment.

In view of these considerations, the regulation of judicial notice of facts by the present rule extends only to adjudicative facts.

What, then, are "adjudicative" facts? Davis refers to them as those "which relate to the parties," or more fully:

> When a court or an agency finds facts concerning the immediate parties — who did what, where, when, how, and with what motive or intent — the court or agency is performing an adjudicative function, and the facts are conveniently called adjudicative facts....
>
> Stated in other terms, the adjudicative facts are those to which the law is applied in the process of adjudication. They are the facts that normally go to the jury in a jury case. They relate to the parties, their activities, their properties, their businesses.

2 Administrative Law Treatise 353.

Subdivision (b). With respect to judicial notice of adjudicative facts, the tradition has been one of caution in requiring that the matter be beyond reasonable controversy. This tradition of circumspection appears to be soundly based, and no reason to depart from it is apparent. As Professor Davis says:

> The reason we use trial-type procedure, I think, is that we make the practical judgment, on the basis of experience, that taking evidence, subject to cross-examination and rebuttal, is the best way to resolve controversies involving disputes of adjudicative facts, that is, facts pertaining to the parties. The reason we require a determination on the record is that we think fair procedure in resolving disputes of adjudicative facts calls for giving each party a chance to meet in the appropriate fashion the facts that come to the tribunal's attention, and the appropriate fashion for meeting disputed adjudicative facts includes rebuttal evidence, cross-examination, usually confrontation, and argument (either written or oral or both). The key to a fair trial is opportunity to use the appropriate weapons

(rebuttal evidence, cross-examination, and argument) to meet adverse materials that come to the tribunal's attention.

A System of Judicial Notice Based on Fairness and Convenience, in Perspectives of Law 69, 93 (1964).

The rule proceeds upon the theory that these considerations call for dispensing with traditional methods of proof only in clear cases. Compare Professor Davis' conclusion that judicial notice should be a matter of convenience, subject to requirements of procedural fairness. *Id.*, 94.

This rule is consistent with Uniform Rule 9(1) and (2) which limit judicial notice of facts to those "so universally known that they cannot reasonably be the subject of dispute," those "so generally known or of such common notoriety within the territorial jurisdiction of the court that they cannot reasonably be the subject of dispute," and those "capable of immediate and accurate determination by resort to easily accessible sources of indisputable accuracy." The traditional textbook treatment has included these general categories (matters of common knowledge, facts capable of verification), McCormick §§ 324, 325, and then has passed on into detailed treatment of such specific topics as facts relating to the personnel and records of the court, *id.* § 327, and other governmental facts, *id.* § 328. The California draftsmen, with a background of detailed statutory regulation of judicial notice, followed a somewhat similar pattern. California Evidence Code §§ 451, 452. The Uniform Rules, however, were drafted on the theory that these particular matters are included within the general categories and need no specific mention. This approach is followed in the present rule.

The phrase "propositions of generalized knowledge," found in Uniform Rule 9(1) and (2) is not included in the present rule. It was, it is believed, originally included in Model Code Rules 801 and 802 primarily in order to afford some minimum recognition to the right of the judge in his "legislative" capacity (not acting as the trier of fact) to take judicial notice of very limited categories of generalized knowledge. The limitations thus imposed have been discarded herein as undesirable, unworkable, and contrary to existing practice. What is left, then, to be considered, is the status of a "proposition of generalized knowledge" as an "adjudicative" fact to be noticed judicially and communicated by the judge to the jury. Thus viewed, it is considered to be lacking practical significance. While judges use judicial notice of "propositions of generalized knowledge" in a variety of situations: determining the validity and meaning of statutes, formulating common law rules, deciding whether evidence should be admitted, assessing the sufficiency and effect of evidence, all are essentially nonadjudicative in nature. When judicial notice is seen as a significant vehicle for progress in the law, these are the areas involved, particularly in developing fields of scientific knowledge. See McCormick 712. It is not believed that judges now instruct juries as to "propositions of generalized knowledge" derived from encyclopedias or other sources, or that they are likely to do so, or, indeed, that it is desirable that they do so. There is a vast difference between ruling on the basis of judicial notice that radar evidence of speed is admissible and explaining to the jury its principles and degree of accuracy, or between using a table of stopping distances of automobiles at various speeds in a judicial evaluation of testimony and telling the jury its precise application in the case. For cases raising doubt as to the propriety of the use of medical texts by lay triers of fact in passing on disability claims in administrative proceedings, see Sayers v. Gardner, 380 F.2d 940 (6th Cir. 1967); Ross v. Gardner, 365 F.2d 554 (6th Cir. 1966); Sosna v. Celebrezze, 234 F. Supp. 289 (E.D. Pa. 1964); Glendenning v. Ribicoff, 213 F. Supp. 301 (W.D. Mo. 1962).

Subdivisions (c) and (d). Under subdivision (c) the judge has a discretionary authority to take judicial notice, regardless of whether he is so requested by a party. The taking of judicial notice is mandatory, under subdivision (d), only when a party requests it and the necessary information is supplied. This scheme is believed to reflect existing practice. It is simple and workable. It avoids troublesome distinctions in the many situations in which the process of taking judicial notice is not recognized as such.

Compare Uniform Rule 9 making judicial notice of facts universally known mandatory without request, and making judicial notice of facts generally known in the jurisdiction or capable of determination by resort to accurate sources discretionary in the absence of request but mandatory if request is made and the information furnished. But see Uniform Rule 10(3), which directs the judge to decline to take judicial notice if available information fails to convince him that the matter falls clearly within Uniform Rule 9 or is insufficient to enable him to notice it judicially. Substantially the same approach is found in California Evidence Code §§ 451-453 and in New Jersey Evidence Rule 9. In contrast, the present rule treats alike all adjudicative facts which are subject to judicial notice.

Subdivision (e). Basic considerations of procedural fairness demand an opportunity to be heard on the propriety of taking judicial notice and the tenor of the matter noticed. The rule requires the granting of that opportunity upon request. No formal scheme of giving notice is provided. An adversely affected party may learn in advance that judicial notice is in contemplation, either by virtue of being served with a copy of a request by another party under subdivision (d) that judicial notice be taken, or through an advance indication by the judge. Or he may have no advance notice at all. The likelihood of the latter is enhanced by the frequent failure to recognize judicial notice as such. And in the absence of advance notice, a request made after the fact could not in fairness be considered untimely. See the provision for hearing on timely request in the Administrative Procedure Act, 5 U.S.C. § 556(e). See also Revised Model State Administrative Procedure Act (1961), 9C U.L.A. § 10(4) (Supp. 1967).

Subdivision (f). In accord with the usual view, judicial notice may be taken at any stage of the proceedings, whether in the trial court or on appeal. Uniform Rule 12; California Evidence Code § 459; Kansas Rules of Evidence § 60-412; New Jersey Evidence Rule 12; McCormick § 330 p. 712.

Subdivision (g). Much of the controversy about judicial notice has centered upon the question whether evidence should be admitted in disproof of facts of which judicial notice is taken.

The writers have been divided. Favoring admissibility are Thayer, Preliminary Treatise on Evidence 308 (1898); 9 Wigmore § 2567; Davis, A System of Judicial Notice Based on Fairness and Convenience, in Perspectives of Law, 69, 76-77 (1964). Opposing admissibility are Keeffe, Landis and Shaad, Sense and Nonsense about Judicial Notice, 2 Stan. L. Rev. 664, 668 (1950); McNaughton, Judicial Notice — Excerpts Relating to the Morgan-Wigmore Controversy, 14 Vand. L. Rev. 779 (1961); Morgan, Judicial Notice, 57 Harv. L. Rev. 269, 279 (1944); McCormick 710-11. The Model Code and the Uniform Rules are predicated upon indisputability of judicially noticed facts.

The proponents of admitting evidence in disproof have concentrated largely upon legislative facts. Since the present rule deals only with judicial notice of adjudicative facts, arguments directed to legislative facts lose their relevancy.

Within its relatively narrow area of adjudicative facts, the rule contemplates there is to be no evidence before the jury in disproof. The judge instructs the jury to take judicially noticed facts as established. This position is justified by the undesirable effects of the opposite rule in limiting the rebutting party, though not his opponent, to admissible evidence, in defeating the reasons for judicial notice, and in affecting the substantive law to an extent and in ways largely unforeseeable. Ample protection and flexibility are afforded by the broad provision for opportunity to be heard on request, set forth in subdivision (e).

Authority upon the propriety of taking judicial notice against an accused in a criminal case with respect to matters other than venue is relatively meager. Proceeding upon the theory that the right of jury trial does not extend to matters which are beyond reasonable dispute, the rule does not distinguish between criminal and civil cases. People v. Mayes, 113 Cal. 618, 45 P. 860 (1896);

Ross v. United States, 374 F.2d 97 (8th Cir. 1967). Cf. State v. Main, 94 R.I. 338, 180 A.2d 814 (1962); State v. Lawrence, 120 Utah 323, 234 P.2d 600 (1951). [This treatment was rejected by the Congress, which provided that notice is not conclusive in criminal cases. Ed.]

Note on Judicial Notice of Law

By rules effective July 1, 1966, the method of invoking the law of a foreign country is covered elsewhere. Rule 44.1 of the Federal Rules of Civil Procedure; Rule 26.1 of the Federal Rules of Criminal Procedure. These two new admirably designed rules are founded upon the assumption that the manner in which law is fed into the judicial process is never a proper concern of the rules of evidence but rather of the rules of procedure. The Advisory Committee on Evidence, believing that this assumption is entirely correct, proposes no evidence rule with respect to judicial notice of law, and suggests that those matters of law which, in addition to foreign-country law, have traditionally been treated as requiring pleading and proof and more recently as the subject of judicial notice be left to the Rules of Civil and Criminal Procedure.

House Subcommittee on Criminal Justice Notes

June 28, 1973

As proposed, Article II was restricted by subdivision (a) to "adjudicative" facts, as contrasted with "legislative" facts. The import of both terms was discussed in the Advisory Committee's note, but the Subcommittee nonetheless felt that the distinction was not clear and would breed litigation. The Subcommittee also felt that differing treatment for the two types of facts was unjustified. Accordingly, subdivision (a) was deleted.

As proposed, subdivision (g) would have precluded a judge from admitting evidence in disproof of facts of which judicial notice had been taken. Believing that judicial notice should be treated on the same basis as any other evidence which is admitted — subject to refutation — the Subcommittee deleted this subdivision.

October 10, 1973

Being of the view that a mandatory instruction to a jury in a criminal case to accept as established any fact judicially noticed was inappropriate because contrary to the spirit of the Sixth Amendment right to a jury trial, the Subcommittee adopted the 1969 Advisory Committee draft of subsection (g) allowing a mandatory instruction in civil actions and proceedings, but not in criminal cases. [The Reader will note that the June 28 change relating to section (a) was abandoned, and the change relating to section (g) was modified.]

Report of the House Committee on the Judiciary

Rule 201(g) as received from the Supreme Court provided that when judicial notice of a fact is taken, the court shall instruct the jury to accept that fact as established. Being of the view that mandatory instruction to a jury in a criminal case to accept as conclusive any fact judicially noticed is inappropriate because contrary to the spirit of the Sixth Amendment right to a jury trial, the Committee adopted the 1969 Advisory Committee draft of this subsection, allowing a mandatory instruction in civil actions and proceedings and a discretionary instruction in criminal cases.

Citations to Hearings and Debates

Letter from Kenneth Culp Davis to Hon. William L. Hungate, August 7, 1973, in Supp. to Hearings on Proposed Rules of Evidence Before the Subcomm. on Criminal Justice of the House Comm. on the Judiciary, 93rd Cong., 1st Sess., at 312-17 (1973).

Letter from Hon. Roszel C. Thomsen to Hon. James O. Eastland, May 22, 1974, and accompanying material, Hearings on H.R. 5463 (Federal Rules of Evidence) Before the Senate Comm. on the Judiciary, 93rd Cong., 2d Sess., at 53-54, 55-56 (1974).

Testimony of Hon. Charles W. Joiner, June 4, 1974, Hearings on H.R. 5463 (Federal Rules of Evidence) Before the Senate Comm. on the Judiciary, 93rd Cong., 2d Sess., at 35 (1974).

Testimony and Prepared Statement of Richard H. Keating, June 5, 1974, Hearings on H.R. 5463 (Federal Rules of Evidence) Before the Senate Comm. on the Judiciary, 93rd Cong., 2d Sess., at 127, 133-37 (1974).

Letter from W. Vincent Rakestraw to Hon. James O. Eastland, June 14, 1974, in Hearings on H.R. 5463 (Federal Rules of Evidence) Before the Senate Comm. on the Judiciary, 93rd Cong., 2d Sess., at 121-23, 126 (1974).

RULE 301

A. OFFICIAL TEXT

Rule 301. Presumptions in General in Civil Actions and Proceedings

In all civil actions and proceedings not otherwise provided for by Act of Congress or by these rules, a presumption imposes on the party against whom it is directed the burden of going forward with evidence to rebut or meet the presumption, but does not shift to such party the burden of proof in the sense of the risk of nonpersuasion, which remains throughout the trial upon the party on whom it was originally cast.

B. EDITORIAL EXPLANATORY COMMENT

Effect of a presumption

There has been substantial disagreement among common law Courts regarding the proper weight to be given a presumption. In some Courts, a presumption would place the burden of persuasion on the party opposing the fact presumed to establish its nonexistence, once the party invoking the presumption establishes the basic fact giving rise to it. In other Courts, the presumption vanishes upon the introduction of evidence that would support a finding of the nonexistence of the presumed fact. The practical difference between these views — known respectively as the Morgan and Thayer views[1] — is in the quantity and quality of evidence required to overcome the presumption. Under the Morgan view, the opponent of the presumption must establish, by a preponderance of the evidence in a civil case, the nonexistence of the presumed fact. Under the Thayer view, the opponent must merely offer credible evidence sufficient to support a finding contrary to the presumed fact in order to take the presumption out of the case.[2]

The Federal Rule provides that a presumption imposes on the party against whom it is directed the burden of going forward with evidence to rebut the presumption. But the

---

[1]. The Thayer view, which is the view adopted in Rule 301, has also been described as the "bursting bubble" theory. The theory is that the presumption ceases to exist when contrary evidence as to the presumed fact is introduced.

[2]. For general discussions of presumptions, see BASIC PROBLEMS OF EVIDENCE, ch. 3 (M. Martin 6th ed. 1988); Ladd, *Presumptions in Civil Actions*, 1977 ARIZ. ST. L.J. 275.

burden of persuasion remains with the party on whom it was originally cast, despite an Advisory Committee preference for shifting the burden. The Advisory Committee was of the view that a presumption would have too slight an effect if it merely served to shift the burden of going forward.[3] But Congress rejected this concern. As adopted, Rule 301 operates merely as a procedural device to shift the burden of producing evidence, exposing the opponent of the presumption to the risk of an adverse result on a directed verdict if he fails to present enough evidence to support a finding of the nonexistence of the presumed fact.

The Rule does not itself determine whether a particular presumption applies; that is left to substantive law.[4] Generally speaking, presumptions are based on one or more of the following rationales: (1) one party has superior access to proof; (2) social or economic policies warrant a presumption; (3) experience indicates the high probability of a given conclusion from a given set of facts; (4) a presumption will promote efficiency and convenience. The annotated cases under this Rule contain many examples of substantive law presumptions.

The Rule does not say anything about the original placement of the burden of proof, the degree of proof required to meet that burden, or the burden of production. Again, these questions are governed by substantive law.[5] Even the procedural effect of a presumption may be governed by other law, rendering Rule 301 by its terms inoperative.[6]

---

3. The Advisory Committee was persuaded by Morgan's critique of the Thayer view on presumptions. Morgan's critique is well-stated in the following passage:

> If a policy is strong enough to call a presumption into existence, it is hard to imagine it so weak as to be satisfied by the bare recital of words on the witness stand or the reception in evidence of a writing. And if the judicial desire for the result expressed in a presumption is buttressed by either the demands of procedural convenience or is in accord with the usual balance of probability, it is little short of ridiculous to allow so valuable a presumption to be destroyed by the introduction of evidence without actual persuasive effect.

Morgan, *Instructing the Jury upon Presumptions and Burden of Proof,* 47 HARV. L. REV. 59, 82 (1933).

4. See, e.g., Clay v. Traders Bank of Kansas City, 708 F.2d 1347 (8th Cir. 1983) (applying presumption in 28 U.S.C. § 547(f), that an entity is insolvent for the ninety-day period preceding the filing of a bankruptcy petition; Court notes that Rule 301 controls the effect of this presumption, and therefore the burden of persuasion "remains on the party in favor of whom the presumption applies"). See also 28 U.S.C. § 2254(d) (habeas actions; presumption of correctness of state court factual findings); Sumner v. Mata, 449 U.S. 539 (1981) (applying § 2254(d)).

5. See, e.g., Santosky v. Kramer, 455 U.S. 745 (1982) (Due Process Clause requires that before a state may terminate parental rights of a natural parent, it must establish cause by a standard of clear and convincing evidence).

6. See Alabama By-Products v. Killingsworth, 733 F.2d 1511 (11th Cir. 1984) (Rule 301 does not apply to the presumption that a coal miner, employed for ten years and suffering from pneumoconiosis, is totally disabled; under the plain terms of the statute and regulation at issue, "the burden of persuasion or proof shifts to the operator on rebuttal"); Tenneco Chems., Inc., v. William T. Burnett & Co., 691 F.2d 658 (4th Cir. 1982) (construing 35 U.S.C. § 282, the Court concludes that the statutory presumption of patent validity "does not merely shift the burden of coming forward with evidence of invalidity to the party contesting the patent but shifts the ultimate burden of establishing invalidity by clear and convincing evidence"); Plough, Inc. v. Mason & Dixon Lines, 630 F.2d 468 (6th Cir. 1980):

The legislative history is rather clear that the Congress intended the words "civil actions and proceedings" to cover all proceedings that are reached by the Federal Rules of Evidence under Rule 1101. The major exception, explicit in the Rule, is criminal cases. The Advisory Committee proposed a Rule 303 to govern presumptions in criminal cases, but this proposal was rejected by Congress. In criminal cases, the use of presumptions presents a sensitive constitutional inquiry, because of the beyond the reasonable doubt standard of proof.[7]

Jury instructions and permissible inferences

An example may help to illustrate how the Rule works in practice. If there is a presumption that a letter once mailed is received, and one party to litigation introduces evidence of mailing, an opposing party must produce evidence of nonreceipt to rebut the presumption or the Judge will find that receipt is established on the basis of the evidence of mailing together with the presumption; if there is no rebuttal evidence, the jury is instructed that it *must* find the presumed fact.[8] If evidence sufficient to support a finding of nonreceipt is offered, the presumption disappears. This is true regardless of the strength of the evidence on mailing, and regardless of whether the Judge actually believes the evidence of nonreceipt.

Even though a presumption disappears when sufficient contrary evidence is offered, there is nothing in the plain meaning of the Rule that prevents the Judge from instructing the jury that it *may* infer one fact from another — in the above example, that receipt may be inferred from mailing, despite some evidence of nonreceipt. In short, the Judge may relay to the jury information about a permissible inference.[9]

It is arguable that Congress intended to codify the "bursting bubble" theory of presumptions and that giving *any* effect to a presumption once it is rebutted is improper. We find support for our approach, however, in the last paragraphs of the Senate Report and the Conferees' Report.[10] It is important to note that nothing in the Rule requires the

---

It is immediately apparent that Rule 301 does not affect the burden of proof in Carmack Amendment cases. For well articulated reasons Congress chose to place the burden of proof on a carrier in whose hands goods are damaged rather than on the shipper. This is more than a burden of going forward with the evidence. It is a true burden of proof in the sense of the risk of nonpersuasion and it remains on the carrier once the prima facie showing has been made.

7. For a further discussion of presumptions and burden-shifting in criminal cases, see S. SALTZBURG & D. CAPRA, AMERICAN CRIMINAL PROCEDURE 855-85 (West 4th ed. 1992).

8. See the discussion below as to the mandatory nature of an unrebutted presumption.

9. See Howing Co. v. Nationwide Corp., 927 F.2d 262 (6th Cir. 1991) (failure to state information in a proxy statement triggers a presumption that the information was significant to investors; if the defendant offers evidence that the information was insignificant, the presumption drops from the case, but the jury may still "infer that the information would be significant" unless the defendant offers contrary proof so compelling as to require a finding in its favor).

10. See H.R. Conf. Rep. No. 93-1597, 93d Cong., 2d Sess. 5-6 (1974):

If the adverse party does offer evidence contradicting the presumed fact, the court cannot instruct the jury that it may *presume* the existence of the presumed fact from proof of the basic facts. The court

Judge to single out an inference that derives from a presumption and instruct the jury concerning it; however, the Judge has discretion to do so, at least where the evidence of nonexistence of the presumed fact is not so compelling as to *require* the jury to find its nonexistence.

In his article, *Construing Rule 301: Instructing the Jury on Presumptions in Civil Actions and Proceedings,* 63 VA. L. REV. 281 (1977), the late Professor Louisell discussed the various approaches to presumptions and articulated the approach chosen by Congress in Rule 301. A major contribution of the article is its discussion of the various kinds of instructions that a judge should give a jury depending on whether a presumption is unrebutted or whether a presumption is matched by rebuttal evidence. Professor Louisell agreed with us that an inference instruction — i.e., that the proved fact giving rise to a presumed fact that is rebutted can be used as an inference of the proved fact even after the rebuttal evidence is offered — is permissible if two conditions are met:

> First, the facts established by the evidence or supported by sufficient evidence to enable the jury to find their existence ... must themselves be a sufficient basis in logic and reason to support a finding of the presumed fact. Second, the adversary's proof of the nonexistence of the presumed fact must not be so strong as to require a finding of its nonexistence as a matter of law (footnote omitted).

Professor Louisell also made the following suggestion concerning instructions that should be given to the jury:

> Where the presumption in question rests mostly or entirely upon policy grounds, the jury should be told that upon finding the basic facts it should also find the presumed fact unless upon all the evidence in the case it finds that the nonexistence of the presumed fact is at least as probable as its existence. Where the presumption in question rests mostly or entirely upon inherent logic or probability, the jury should be told that the basic facts are strong evidence of the presumed fact. The instruction should further inform the jury that upon finding the basic facts it should therefore find the presumed fact to exist unless upon all the evidence it believes that the nonexistence of the presumed fact is at least as probable as its existence (footnotes omitted).

Professor Louisell argued that his proposed instructions are consistent with the intent of Congress and do not give too much weight to presumptions. We find ourselves in disagreement. First, we believe that the instructions are too complicated and will confuse the jury. The proposed instruction for presumptions resting on policy grounds does nothing more than restate the ordinary burden of persuasion, but it does so in a way that must confuse the jury as to the meaning of the instruction. As for the instruction concerning logic and probability, except for the last sentence which is as problematic as the instruction concerning presumptions resting on policy grounds, it is understandable

---

may, however, instruct the jury that it may infer the existence of the presumed fact from proof of the basic facts.

and is probably consistent with the traditional power of federal judges to comment on the weight of evidence. The problem with it is that the proved facts giving rise to presumptions are not always strong evidence of the presumed fact; the fact that there is a logical connection does not mean that it is strong. Moreover, Congress was aware of the possibility of providing for such an instruction since it debated whether to incorporate such language in the proposed, but rejected, Rule 303, which was to deal with criminal cases. Finally, Professor Louisell's dichotomy between presumptions resting on policy grounds and presumptions resting on probability is a problematic one. Many presumptions are based on both policy and probability — such as the presumption that a bailee is responsible for damaged goods that were originally received in good order.

We believe that Congress intended that presumptions would be treated uniformly under Rule 301 and that the uniform treatment would be the "bursting bubble" approach in which a rebutted presumption disappears, leaving the Trial Judge free to give an inference instruction. If a Judge wishes to use the power to comment in addition to the inference instruction, this is not a violation of the spirit of Rule 301, but it should be done on a case-by-case basis, not in every case that falls within the Rule.

Dispute as to facts underlying the presumption

A presumption is established by proof of certain underlying facts. For example, the presumption that a letter once mailed is received comes into play only after proof that the letter was mailed. But what happens if the underlying facts are themselves in dispute? What if the plaintiff testifies that he mailed a letter, but the defendant calls a witness who testifies that he saw the plaintiff throw the letter in the trash? If jurors could decide either way as to the underlying facts, then they must be allowed to do so. It would be proper to instruct on the presumption, assuming no contrary evidence is presented as to the presumed fact — e.g., no evidence of nonreceipt. But the instruction must be conditional; it must emphasize that the presumption comes into play only if the jury is satisfied that the underlying fact has been proven.

It may also be appropriate in some cases to instruct the jury that if the underlying fact is not found, then the presumed fact *cannot* be found. This will occur where the presumed fact cannot exist without the basic underlying fact, or where there is no other evidence that supports the existence of the presumed fact. Thus, if the jury could not find that a letter was mailed, and there is no other evidence that the letter was delivered by other means, then it cannot find that the letter was received.

"Presumptions" are not evidence

While the Senate Report and the Conferees' Report do not explicitly state that the word "presumption" shall not be used before the jury, this seems to be the intent in view of the comments that a presumption is not evidence.[11]

---

11. See Panduit Corp. v. All States Plastic Mfg. Co., 744 F.2d 1564 (Fed. Cir. 1984) (a presumption "does not enjoy the status of evidence"; therefore if the presumed fact has been rebutted, the presumption "does not linger to be weighed against the evidence").

Rebuttal evidence

The Rule does not explicitly state how much opposing evidence is needed to turn a presumption into a permissible inference. However, the only logical conclusion is that the opponent must produce the same amount of evidence necessary to avoid a directed verdict or peremptory instruction in the usual context of a civil case. Given the language of the Rule — requiring as it does that a party opposing a presumption come forward with evidence to rebut it, but not necessarily with sufficient evidence to carry a burden of persuasion — and given that the Congress was trying to give some weight to presumptions but not too much weight — the requirement of enough evidence for a reasonable person to find the fact is all that is intended.[12] If less proof were satisfactory, the presumption would be worth little because it would be almost automatically rebuttable; and one of the purposes of the Rule as drafted is to give the presumption sufficient, but not overwhelming, weight.

Peremptory instructions

Neither the Rule itself nor its legislative history clearly indicates whether a party favored by a presumption is entitled to a peremptory instruction or a partial directed verdict if the party against whom the presumption operates fails to offer any rebuttal evidence. Under the Thayer view of presumptions, where there is no rebuttal evidence the instruction to the jury would be a binding instruction. But the Conferees' Report contains a sentence that states that "the court will instruct the jury that if it finds the basic facts, it *may* presume the existence of the presumed fact" (emphasis added) when "the adverse party offers no evidence contradicting the presumed fact." Despite the language of the Conferees' Report, we believe that the best reading of Rule 301 is that a peremptory instruction is mandated upon request, when the party against whom a presumption operates offers no proof to rebut the presumption.[13] It appears that the Conferees confused a presumption with a permissible inference; but that should have no bearing on how the Rule is applied.

Our reasoning is as follows: The Advisory Committee believed that the choice was between the Thayer approach and the Morgan approach. It spoke of no middle ground. When the Subcommittee on Criminal Justice received the Rule from the Supreme Court, it refused to go along with the Morgan approach of shifting the ultimate burden of persuasion. But it said that it thought that the "bursting bubble" or Thayer approach to presumptions gave presumptions too slight an effect. It made clear its intent to opt for

---

12. See, e.g., Sinatra v. Heckler, 566 F. Supp. 1354 (E.D.N.Y. 1983) ("In order to rebut the presumption that a notice of reconsideration is received five days after it is dated, the claimant must adduce evidence that would be sufficient to overcome a directed verdict."); In re Dodd, 82 B.R. 924 (Bankr. N.D. Ill. 1987) (under Rule 301, "a party may rebut a presumption by introducing evidence which would support a finding of the nonexistence of the presumed fact").

13. See A.C. Aukerman Co. v. R.L. Chaides Constr. Co., 960 F.2d 1020 (Fed. Cir. 1992) (where presumption applies, the presumed fact "*must* be inferred, absence rebuttal evidence").

a provision that gave presumptions more force than they would have under the Thayer view. This was the approach taken by the House Judiciary Committee.[14]

The Senate Judiciary Committee wisely rejected the confusing language chosen by the House. But the Senate Judiciary Committee was so concerned with demonstrating that a treatment of presumptions as evidence was improper that it failed to explain whether it really meant to say that the traditional Thayer approach, which did not treat presumptions as evidence, was not to be followed. The confusion engendered by the Senate Judiciary Committee Report continued in the Conferees' Report. The only change that the Senate Committee stated that it wanted to make was deletion of the provision in the House draft that would have treated presumptions as evidence. The Senate Committee did not indicate that it wanted to weaken the traditional force of presumptions. Certainly, it is doubtful that the House would have joined in the adoption of an approach to presumptions that gives them less force than the Thayer approach did.

Thus, we conclude that the Senate Committee, and ultimately the Conferees, were confused as to the traditional Thayer approach to presumptions and that there is no demonstrable intention on the part of the Congress to depart from the traditional approach. We recognize that the language of both the Senate Committee Report and the Conferees' Report can be read otherwise, but we do not believe that the cryptic wording concerning a permissive instruction to be given a jury represents the view of the House Committee, which wanted to strengthen the force of presumptions, or the Senate Committee, which only wanted to assure that presumptions were not treated as evidence. We believe that both Houses of Congress thought they were adopting the Thayer approach and that the Rule should be read as if they did.

Conflicting presumptions

The familiar problem of conflicting presumptions is no longer a great problem in cases where both presumptions are rebutted, since both presumptions become, at most, inferences. Even in these cases, however, it may be difficult to draft a satisfactory jury instruction to cover conflicting permissible inferences. When no rebuttal evidence is offered, the stronger presumption should predominate. The Court must determine which is the stronger presumption based on policy and probability.[15] In the unlikely situation that the presumptions are in equipoise in terms of social policy and probability, they should both be discarded.

---

14. The House Rule provided that in civil cases, a presumption imposed on the party against whom it was directed the burden of going forward with the evidence. Moreover, even if the party produced evidence, a presumption was sufficient evidence of the fact presumed to be considered by the trier-of-fact. One confusing thing about the House Rule was that it did not indicate whether the Judge was supposed to tell the jury that there was such a thing as a presumption operating in the case. And, if the jury was to be told of the presumption, deciding what it should be told would not have been easy.

15. But see Legille v. Dann, 544 F.2d 1 (D.C. Cir. 1976) (where two presumptions conflict, the dispute should go to trial and there is no reason to prefer one over the other unless one has a particularly firm grounding in social policy). This case is discussed in the Annotations to this Rule.

Judicially-created presumptions

No mention is made in the Rule of judicial power to create presumptions. But the Courts can and have created and applied presumptions as a matter of Federal common law when necessary to further congressional policy (i.e., when Congress would have wanted a presumption created).[16] In admiralty cases, where Federal Courts exercise common-law power, judicially created presumptions have been found to be outside the scope of Rule 301, as the cases annotated *infra* indicate.[17]

Rule 301 does not bar the creation of different kinds of presumptions in special rules adopted by the Supreme Court. See, e.g., Rule 9(a) of the Rules Governing Section 2254 Cases in the United States District Courts and the parallel Rule 9(a) of the Rules Governing Section 2255 Proceedings for the United States District Courts.

Congressional intent in enacting statutes

Quite surprisingly, some commentators appear to assume that Rule 301 requires the plaintiff to bear the burden of proof in civil cases on all issues unless Congress explicitly requires otherwise.[18]

We believe that Rule 301 need not stand in the way of judicial interpretation of legislation so that it places the burden of proof on defendants on certain issues; as stated previously, Rule 301 is simply a procedural device that does not allocate the burden of proof. While the line separating presumptions that shift burdens of persuasion from rulings placing burdens of persuasion in the first instance is not clear, we hold the view that a judicial decision that requires a civil defendant to bear the burden of proving issue *D* after plaintiff proves issues *A, B,* and *C* is generally not a decision about presumptions within the meaning of Rule 301. In such a case all four issues are material to the outcome. Rule 301 will usually apply when one fact is used as a bridge to another, and only by travelling the bridge is a material issue reached. For example, under a statute like 42 U.S.C. § 1982, plaintiffs might have the burden of proving that (1) African-Americans were treated more poorly than whites under similar circumstances, and (2) that defendants knew or had reason to know of the disparity; and defendants might have the burden of showing a nonracial reason for any disparity in the particular case. One could employ presumptions, but one need not.[19]

---

16. See, e.g., A.C. Aukerman Co. v. R.L. Chaides Constr. Co., 960 F.2d 1020 (Fed. Cir. 1992) (presumption of laches upon proof that six years elapsed between infringement and patentee's knowledge); Neal v. Secretary of Navy, 639 F.2d 1029 (3d Cir. 1981) (applying presumption that personnel involved in official decisionmaking will faithfully discharge their duties).

17. See, e.g., James River Parishes Co., 686 F.2d 1129 (5th Cir. 1982) (in an admiralty case, the court employs the presumption that when a drifting vessel causes damage, the vessel was adrift through negligence).

18. See, e.g., Brown, Giveller, & Lubin, *Treating Blacks As If They Were White: Problems of Definition and Proof in Section 1982 Cases,* U. PA. L. REV. 1, 35-42 (1975).

19. For an example of how important it is for the Courts to ascertain the intent of Congress and to allocate burdens of production and persuasion in accordance with congressional intent, see Nashville Gas Co. v. Satty, 434 U.S. 136 (1977). See also Ansel v. Weinberger, 529 F.2d 304 (6th Cir. 1976); Mendez, *Presumptions of Discriminatory Motive in Title VII Disparate Treatment Cases,* 32 STAN. L. REV. 1129 (1980).

Conclusive presumptions

Ordinarily, a "conclusive" presumption is essentially a rule of law, rather than a presumption as that term is used in Rule 301. Thus, a conclusive presumption that a child under the age of seven is incapable of forming a criminal intent is really a legal rule that children under seven are not criminally responsible.

C. ANNOTATED CASES

Admiralty cases

City of Boston v. S.S. Texaco Texas, 773 F.2d 1396 (1st Cir. 1985): The Court followed the holding in *James v. River Parishes Co., infra,* and held that Rule 301 does not disturb the well-settled rule that "when a vessel under its own power collides with an anchored vessel or a navigational structure, the burden of proving absence of fault or *vis major* rests on the pilot vessel."

Brunet v. United Gas Pipeline Co., 15 F.3d 500 (5th Cir. 1994): In an admiralty limitation action brought by owners of a pushboat that came into contact with a gas pipeline, the Court held that a moving vessel colliding with a stationary object, including an obstruction to navigation known to the mariner, is presumed to be at fault and the presumption shifts the burdens of producing evidence and of persuasion onto the moving vessel. In an action by a deckhand on a moored vessel who was injured when it was struck by a drifting barge, *James v. River Parishes Co.,* 686 F.2d 1129 (5th Cir. 1982), the plaintiff offered no proof of negligence and instead relied on a presumption of negligence. A majority of the Court held that the law imposed the burden of persuasion on the negligence question on the party whose vessel was adrift. One dissenter argued that Rule 301 was applicable and that the plaintiff should have borne the burden of persuasion. In our view the majority was correct. Although Congress' decisions concerning burdens of persuasion would provide exceptions to Rule 301 in other areas, judicial rulings in admiralty cases make up the bulk of admiralty law, and longstanding precedents should not be disturbed absent some indication that in drafting Rule 301 Congress intended to change prior holdings.

Hood v. Knappton Corp., 986 F.2d 329 (9th Cir. 1993): In a negligence action by boaters against the owner of a log raft that had drifted into collision with their boats, the Court held that the rule in *The Louisiana,* 70 U.S. (3 Wall.) 164 (1866), that the owner of a drifting vessel bears the burden of persuasion on the fault issue, remains the law of the Circuit, notwithstanding Rule 301.

Attorney disqualification

Panduit Corp. v. All States Plastic Mfg. Co., 744 F.2d 1564 (Fed. Cir. 1984): In a patent infringement suit, the Court reversed an order that had disqualified a law firm because one of its attorneys had previously worked on related matters for another firm that had represented an opposing party. The District Court had relied upon the presumptions that a party who performed legal services for a client received confidential information and that attorneys within a firm share each other's confidential information, but the Court of Appeals found that the presumptions had been rebutted and that under Rule 301 the burden remained on the party seeking disqualification to demonstrate that it was necessary.

Bail Reform Act of 1984

United States v. Jessup, 757 F.2d 378 (1st Cir. 1985): In an opinion sustaining the presumption in the Bail Reform Act of 1984 that a defendant charged with a serious drug offense poses a serious risk of flight, the Court concluded that Congress shifted only the burden of production on the flight issue to the defendant, and that the government continued to bear the burden of persuasion with respect to likelihood of flight. The Court also concluded, however, that the presumption did not disappear when the defendant offered rebuttal evidence. Instead, it adopted a "middle ground" that requires Judges and Magistrates to consider Congress' finding that suspects charged with serious drug offenses pose special risks of flight and to weigh that finding when deciding whether the government has satisfied its persuasion burden. Thus, Rule 301 was inapplicable because the statutory presumption was controlled by other law.

United States v. Freitas, 602 F. Supp. 1283 (N.D. Cal. 1985): The Court held that the rebuttable presumption against pretrial release under some circumstances created by the Bail Reform Act of 1984 did not shift the burden of proof to the defendant. The statute shifts only the burden of production and requires the government to prove dangerousness by clear and convincing evidence.

Bankruptcy cases

In re Yoder Co., 758 F.2d 1114 (6th Cir. 1985): The Court reversed a judgment that a product liability claim was barred for failure to file a timely proof of claim. The Bankruptcy Court had relied mainly on a presumption of receipt arising from evidence that notice of the "bar date" was sent to the claimant, but the Court of Appeals held that "a presumption has no probative effect once rebutted." There was no evidence that the claimant had received notice, and the only alleged mailing had been to his lawyer, who testified that he received no mailing. Because there was no evidence of notice, the Court concluded that the proof of claim should have been filed.

Clay v. Traders Bank, 708 F.2d 1347 (8th Cir. 1983): In a bankruptcy appeal, the Court interpreted 11 U.S.C. § 547(f), which creates a presumption that a debtor was insolvent ninety days before filing a petition, as imposing a burden on a party claiming that the debtor was solvent during the ninety-day period to offer evidence rebutting the presumption. The burden of persuasion did not shift as a result of the presumption.

In re East Coast Brokers & Packers, Inc., 961 F.2d 1543 (11th Cir. 1992): The Court reversed an order denying relief from the automatic stay and turnover of property in a bankruptcy proceeding, holding that the evidence presented was sufficient to raise the presumption of mailing to establish receipt by the debtor of notices of intent to preserve trust benefits under the Perishable Agricultural Commodities Act.

Civil rights cases

Patterson v. McLean Credit Union, 109 S. Ct. 2363 (1989): In this racial harassment and promotion-discrimination case brought under 42 U.S.C. § 1981, the Supreme Court held that on the promotion claim the plaintiff had an initial burden of proving, by a preponderance of the evidence, a *prima facie* case of discrimination; that when she did so, by showing she was qualified but defendant filled the position with a white person after rejecting her, an inference of discrimination arose, which imposed a burden on defendant to present evidence of a legitimate nondiscriminatory reason for the action; and that when defendant presented evidence the white applicant was better qualified, the presumption of discrimination was rebutted and plaintiff retained the final burden of persuading the jury of intentional discrimination. The District Court had erred by instructing the jury that plaintiff was required to show she was better qualified than the person chosen in order to show defendant's stated reasons were pretextual and satisfy her burden of proof; the Supreme Court held that showing she was better qualified was only one of the ways plaintiff might prove intentional discrimination.

Jund v. Town of Hempstead, 941 F.2d 1271 (2d Cir. 1991): In a RICO and civil rights action arising out of a coercive political contributions scheme, the Trial Judge instructed the jury that they could infer, because there was a coercive policy in 1973-76, that there was such a policy in 1978. Reinstating a verdict for the plaintiff, the Court held that it would have been proper to instruct the jury on the general presumption of the continuance of a status or condition once proved to exist, so it was not improper to shift the burden to the defendants to prove that the coercive practice did not continue in 1978.

United States v. City of Chicago, 411 F. Supp. 218 (N.D. Ill. 1976), *modified,* 549 F.2d 415 (7th Cir.), *cert. denied,* 434 U.S. 875 (1977): The District Court held that the City defendants failed to establish the validity of certain promotion examinations that had a disproportionate impact upon Black and Hispanic candidates for patrolman and sergeant positions. The Court noted that Rule 301, which provides that a presumption does not shift the burden of proof (in the sense of the risk of nonpersuasion), has no application in suits under the Civil Rights Act of 1964 because such suits are cases in which an Act of Congress allocates the burden of proof. In the course of its opinion, the Court indicated that it regretted using the word presumption at all in an earlier opinion.

Smiddy v. Varney, 665 F.2d 261 (9th Cir. 1981), *cert. denied,* 459 U.S. 829 (1982): In a civil rights suit alleging false arrest by police officers, the Court held that there is a presumption that a district attorney files complaints on the basis of an independent judgment and, unless rebutted, that presumption immunizes officers from liability for any time period after the complaint is filed. The Court added: "Where the plaintiff has introduced evidence to rebut the presumption, the burden remains on the defendant to prove that an independent intervening cause cuts off his tort liability. Fed. R. Evid. 301. If for reasons of privilege or otherwise the relevant evidence is not available, no presumption will arise."

Conflicting presumptions

Legille v. Dann, 544 F.2d 1 (D.C. Cir. 1976): In this patent case the applicant relied on the presumption of regularity of the mails and the Commissioner of Patents relied upon a presumption of regularity in its office. The Trial Judge granted summary judgment on the basis of the first presumption, but a divided Court of Appeals reversed. The majority said that ''we perceive no legal or practical justification for preferring either of the two involved presumptions over the other.'' The Court seemed to recognize that a presumption might survive a battle of presumptions if its grounding in policy were firm enough, but held that when two presumptions were based on probabilities, proof of the basic facts as to both resulted in their disappearance, leaving only any inferences from the evidence of the basic facts that the trier might wish to draw. Although there is support in the literature for the Court's approach, in a case like this there is no evidence concerning the specific documents in issue and their handling by the Patent Office, so even at trial the two presumptions (having become permissible inferences) will be all that the trier of fact has to work with. Thus, it might make better sense to decide as a matter of law which presumption should prevail; there is little reason to allow different triers of fact to come to different conclusions about the reliability of Patent Office procedures.

Employment discrimination cases

St. Mary's Honor Center v. Hicks, 113 S. Ct. 2742 (1993): The Supreme Court noted that the *McDonnell Douglas* presumption in employment discrimination cases operates like all presumptions under the Rule in that it imposes a burden on the defendant to produce admissible evidence to rebut the *prima facie* case, but it does not shift the plaintiff's ultimate burden of proving that the defendant intentionally discriminated. In *Price Waterhouse v. Hopkins,* 109 S. Ct. 1775 (1989), the Court held that once a plaintiff in a mixed-motive, disparate-treatment Title VII case shows that gender played a motivating part in an employment decision, the defendant may avoid a finding of liability only by proving by a preponderance of the evidence that it would have made the same decision even if it had not allowed gender to play such a role. See also *Patterson v. McLean Credit Union,* discussed *supra* under ''Civil rights cases.'' In *Texas Dep't of Community Affairs v. Burdine,* 450 U.S. 248 (1981), the Court held that once the plaintiff in a Title VII case makes a showing that she applied for an available position for which she was qualified but was rejected under circumstances that give rise to an inference of unlawful discrimination, there is a presumption of discrimination that imposes upon a defendant the burden of producing evidence that the employment decision was made for a legitimate, nondiscriminatory reason. ''It is sufficient if the defendant's evidence raises a genuine issue of fact....'' The plaintiff retains the burden of persuasion *if* the presumption is rebutted.

Reeves v. General Foods Corp., 682 F.2d 515 (5th Cir. 1982): In an age discrimination suit, the Court affirmed a judgment for the plaintiff. The Court reasoned that although a plaintiff's proof that established a *prima facie* case of discrimination might not be sufficient to warrant sending a case to the jury after an employer submitted evidence of nondiscriminatory reasons for a discharge, in this case the plaintiff offered sufficient evidence to support the jury verdict.

Labor cases

NLRB v. Tahoe Nugget, Inc., 584 F.2d 293 (9th Cir. 1978), *cert. denied,* 442 U.S. 921 (1979): A burden of persuasion placed on an employer as a result of a presumption was held to govern, notwithstanding Rule 301.

American Coal Co. v. Benefits Review Bd., 738 F.2d 387 (10th Cir. 1984): The Court affirmed an award of benefits to an employee claiming a black lung illness. It rejected the employer's argument that Rule 301 governed administrative proceedings and found that Congress delegated to the Secretary of Labor authority to designate how the presumptions set forth in the statute could be rebutted. In *Presbyterian/St. Luke's Med. Center v. NLRB*, 653 F.2d 450 (10th Cir. 1981), the Court found that under Rule 301 the General Counsel must prove that an unfair labor practice occurred and that the burden of persuasion as to the appropriateness of a bargaining unit had been improperly shifted to the employer.

Miscellaneous cases

Beck v. Somerset Technologies, Inc., 882 F.2d 993 (5th Cir. 1989): The Court affirmed the grant of summary judgment to the defendant corporate successors to the manufacturer of machinery in which plaintiff was injured on the ground that the plaintiff's employer had been given notice of the defects before the injury. The defendant's summary judgment record included a copy of a properly addressed letter to the employer and signed return postcards, and the resulting presumption of receipt was not met by an affidavit from one of the employer's employees that he did not remember receiving the warning letter or the person who signed the return receipt. In *Pennzoil Co. v. Federal Energy Regulatory Comm'n*, 789 F.2d 1128 (5th Cir. 1986), the Court found that the FERC misconstrued a previous decision, and vacated and remanded proceedings involving rates charged by natural gas producers. The earlier decision affirmed procedures that created a rebuttable presumption that an assertion by a producer and a purchaser that they intended in their contract to permit certain rates to be charged was accurate and not unreasonable. A party protesting the rates must bear the "burden of coming forward with substantial evidence of the lack of contractual authority to overcome the presumption." Once the burden is borne, the presumption disappears, which the Court observed is also true under Rule 301.

Howing Co. v. Nationwide Corp., 927 F.2d 263 (6th Cir.), *vacated,* 112 S. Ct. 39 (1991): Reversing a summary judgment for the defendant in a securities action by minority public shareholders arising from a freeze-out merger, the Court held that the specific language of the instructions to SEC proxy rules creates a presumption that a discussion of book, going concern, and liquidation value in the proxy statement would be material to a reasonable investor. In this case, the defendants did not rebut the presumption so as to avoid trial because they did not establish the lack of significance of the omitted information with sufficient clarity. In *Plough, Inc. v. Mason & Dixon Lines*, 630 F.2d 468 (6th Cir. 1980), the Court vacated a judgment for a motor carrier charged with injury to shipped goods, finding that the District Court misallocated the burden of persuasion. Noting that the Supreme Court has interpreted Congress' intent in the 1906 Carmack Amendment to the Interstate Commerce Act as codifying the common-law rule that a carrier is liable for damage to goods except when it can make certain special showings that it was not responsible for the damage, the Court said that Rule 301 did not bar placement of the burden of persuasion on the carrier, since Congress had placed it there.

Godfrey v. United States, 997 F.2d 335 (7th Cir. 1993): The Court reversed denial of a taxpayer's claim for interest on a delayed refund check, holding that a computer transcript indicating that refund of an overpayment had been authorized was insufficient to create a presumption of delivery, absent any evidence indicating regular procedures for mailing refund checks after authorization of refunds.

United States v. Redondo-Lemos, 27 F.3d 439 (9th Cir. 1994): The Court reversed a determination that the U.S. Attorney's office had discriminated on the basis of gender while plea bargaining, holding that, even if the District Court did not believe them, the government's gender-neutral explanations for its plea bargaining decisions rebutted the presumption of discrimination raised by the defendant's prima facie case, so the presumption simply dropped out of the picture. In *Anderson v. United States,* 966 F.2d 487 (9th Cir. 1992), a taxpayer's suit for a refund, the Court held that the government had not rebutted the common-law presumption of receipt that arose on the taxpayer's proof of mailing her return.

Pennsylvania v. United States, 643 F.2d 758 (Ct. Cl.), *cert. denied,* 454 U.S. 826 (1981): The Court found that since Congress did not provide otherwise, a presumption for reimbursement of a State under the Federal-Aid Highways Act related only to the burden of production of evidence, not to the ultimate burden of persuasion.

Patent and copyright cases

Legille v. Dann, 544 F.2d 1 (D.C. Cir. 1976): In this patent case the applicant relied on the presumption of regularity of the mails and the Commissioner of Patents relied upon a presumption of regularity in its office. The Trial Judge granted summary judgment on the basis of the first presumption, but a divided Court of Appeals reversed. The majority said that "we perceive no legal or practical justification for preferring either of the two involved presumptions over the other." The Court seemed to recognize that a presumption might survive a battle of presumptions if its grounding in policy were firm enough, but held that when two presumptions were based on probabilities, proof of the basic facts as to both resulted in their disappearance, leaving only any inferences from the evidence of the basic facts that the trier might wish to draw. Although there is support in the literature for the Court's approach, in a case like this there is no evidence concerning the specific documents in issue and their handling by the Patent Office, so even at trial the two presumptions (having become permissible inferences) will be all that the trier of fact has to work with. Thus, it might make better sense to decide as a matter of law which presumption should prevail; there is little reason to allow different triers of fact to come to different conclusions about the reliability of Patent Office procedures.

Keeler Brass Co. v. Continental Brass Co., 862 F.2d 1063 (4th Cir. 1988): Affirming a judgment for defendants in a copyright infringement case, the Court analogized to Rule 301 in holding that the establishment of a *prima facie* case creates a presumption of copying that can be rebutted with evidence of independent creation. It concluded that if the presumption is rebutted, the plaintiff has the ultimate burden of persuading the trier of fact that there was copying. In *Tenneco Chems., Inc. v. William T. Burnett & Co.,* 691 F.2d 658 (4th Cir. 1982), the Court, reviewing challenges to two patents, observed that the statutory presumption of patent validity requires a party challenging a patent not only to produce evidence of invalidity, but also to prove invalidity by clear and convincing evidence.

Selle v. Gibb, 567 F. Supp. 1173 (N.D. Ill. 1983), *aff'd,* 741 F.2d 896 (7th Cir. 1984): In a suit alleging the infringement of a copyright on a song, the Court entered a judgment n.o.v. for the defendants. It reasoned that the plaintiff's evidence that his song was similar to one put out by the defendants supported an inference that the defendants might have had access to the plaintiff's song, but that the undisputed testimony demonstrated that the defendants had never heard of the plaintiff or his music. The Court relied on the traditional analysis of presumptions in concluding that "[w]here the case of a plaintiff is based on an inference or inferences, it must fail upon proof of undisputed facts inconsistent with such inference or inferences."

A.C. Aukerman Co. v. R.L. Chaides Constr. Co., 960 F.2d 1020 (Fed. Cir. 1992) (en banc): The Court reversed summary judgment for the defendant in a patent infringement case, holding that the presumption of laches arising from a six-year delay in bringing suit may be eliminated by offering evidence to show an excuse for the delay or that the delay was reasonable, and that (contrary to the decision below and suggestions in recent patent cases) at all times the defendant bears the ultimate burden of persuasion on the affirmative defense of laches. In *Solder Removal Co. v. United States Int'l Trade Comm'n,* 582 F.2d 628 (C.C.P.A. 1978), the Court noted that the statutory presumption of patent validity under 35 U.S.C. § 282 must be given precedence over Rule 301. Because a specific statute governs the matter, "a party asserting invalidity [must] bear not only the presumption-generated burden of going forward with proof but also the burden of persuasion on that issue."

Social security cases

Chavis v. Heckler, 577 F. Supp. 201 (D.D.C. 1983): The Court granted the plaintiff's motion for summary judgment in an action seeking supplementary security income, on the ground that the agency had not given notice reasonably calculated to reach the plaintiff. The plaintiff had notified the agency to send correspondence to his post office box, not his home, because of chronic problems with the handling of mail; but the agency made a clerical mistake and sent a notice of termination to the home. The Court noted that the statutory presumption that a mailed letter is received is rebuttable and disappeared in this case when the plaintiff testified before an Administrative Law Judge that he never received the notice.

Sinatra v. Heckler, 566 F. Supp. 1354 (E.D.N.Y. 1983): The Court remanded a case to the Social Security Administration for consideration of whether the plaintiff's request for a hearing was untimely. Reasoning that Rule 301 was persuasive authority even for agency presumptions, the Court ruled that the presumption under SSA regulations that a letter is received five days after its date is rebuttable. It declined to decide whether a bare affidavit by a claimant denying receipt of a letter would be sufficient rebuttal evidence to thwart the presumption, because judicial notice of the usual delay in mail delivery associated with the year-end holiday season supported the claimant.

Patti v. Schweiker, 669 F.2d 582 (9th Cir. 1982): The Court reversed a District Court that had upheld the termination of social security benefits. It recognized that "when a claimant is entitled to the benefit of a presumption that her disability still exists, the burden is still on her to prove her case,'' but the Court found that there was insufficient rebuttal evidence to warrant disregard of the presumption in this case.

D. LEGISLATIVE HISTORY

Advisory Committee's Note

This rule governs presumptions generally. See Rule 302 for presumptions controlled by state law and Rule 303 for those against an accused in a criminal case. [The latter rule was deleted by Congress. Ed.]

Presumptions governed by this rule are given the effect of placing upon the opposing party the burden of establishing the nonexistence of the presumed fact, once the party invoking the presumption establishes the basic facts giving rise to it. The same considerations of fairness, policy, and probability which dictate the allocation of the burden of the various elements of a case as between the prima facie case of a plaintiff and affirmative defenses also underlie the creation of presumptions. These considerations are not satisfied by giving a lesser effect to presumptions. Morgan and Maguire, Looking Backward and Forward at Evidence, 50 Harv. L. Rev. 909, 913 (1937); Morgan, Instructing the Jury upon Presumptions and Burden of Proof, 47 Harv. L. Rev. 59, 82 (1933); Cleary, Presuming and Pleading: An Essay on Juristic Immaturity, 12 Stan. L. Rev. 5 (1959). [This approach was rejected by the Congress. Ed.]

The so-called "bursting bubble" theory, under which a presumption vanishes upon the introduction of evidence which would support a finding of the nonexistence of the presumed fact, even though not believed, is rejected as according presumptions too "slight and evanescent" an effect. Morgan and Maguire, *supra,* at p. 913. [This approach was adopted by the Congress. Ed.]

In the opinion of the Advisory Committee, no constitutional infirmity attends this view of presumptions. In Mobile, J. & K. C. R. Co. v. Turnipseed, 219 U.S. 35, 31 S. Ct. 136, 55 L. Ed. 78 (1910), the Court upheld a Mississippi statute which provided that in actions against railroads proof of injury inflicted by the running of trains should be prima facie evidence of negligence by the railroad. The injury in the case had resulted from a derailment. The opinion made the points (1) that the only effect of the statute was to impose on the railroad the duty of producing some evidence to the contrary, (2) that an inference may be supplied by law if there is a rational connection between the fact proved and the fact presumed, as long as the opposite party is not precluded from presenting his evidence to the contrary, and (3) that considerations of public policy arising from the character of the business justified the application in question. Nineteen years later, in Western & Atlantic R. Co. v. Henderson, 279 U.S. 639, 49 S. Ct. 445, 73 L. Ed. 884 (1929), the Court overturned a Georgia statute making railroads liable for damages done by trains, unless the railroad made it appear that reasonable care had been used, the presumption being against the railroad. The declaration alleged the death of plaintiff's husband from a grade crossing collision, due to specific acts of negligence by defendant. The jury were instructed that proof of the injury raised a presumption of negligence; the burden shifted to the railroad to prove ordinary care; and unless it did so, they should find for the plaintiff. The instruction was held erroneous in an opinion stating (1) that there was no rational connection between the mere fact of collision and negligence on the part of anyone, and (2) that the statute was different from that in *Turnipseed* in imposing a burden upon the railroad. The reader is left in a state of some confusion. Is the difference between a derailment and a grade crossing collision of no significance? Would the *Turnipseed* presumption have been bad if it had imposed a burden of persuasion on defendant, although that would in nowise have impaired its "rational connection"? If *Henderson* forbids imposing a burden of persuasion on defendants, what happens to affirmative defenses?

Two factors serve to explain *Henderson*. The first was that it was common ground that negligence was indispensable to liability. Plaintiff thought so, drafted her complaint accordingly, and relied upon the presumption. But how in logic could the same presumption establish her alternative grounds of negligence that the engineer was so blind he could not see decedent's truck and that he failed to stop after he saw it? Second, take away the basic assumption of no liability without fault, as *Turnipseed* intimated might be done ("considerations of public policy arising out of the character of the business"), and the structure of the decision in *Henderson* fails. No question of logic would have arisen if the statute had simply said: a prima facie case of liability is made by proof of injury by a train; lack of negligence is an affirmative defense, to be pleaded and proved as other affirmative defenses. The problem would be one of economic due process only. While it seems likely that the Supreme Court of 1920 would have voted that due process was denied, that result today would be unlikely. See, for example, the shift in the direction of absolute liability in the consumer cases. Prosser, The Assault upon the Citadel (Strict Liability to the Consumer), 69 Yale L.J. 1099 (1960).

Any doubt as to the constitutional permissibility of a presumption imposing a burden of persuasion of the nonexistence of the presumed fact in civil cases is laid at rest by Dick v. New York Life Ins. Co., 359 U.S. 437, 79 S. Ct. 921, 3 L. Ed. 2d 935 (1959). The Court unhesitatingly applied the North Dakota rule that the presumption against suicide imposed on defendant the burden of proving that the death of insured, under an accidental death clause, was due to suicide.

"Proof of coverage and of death by gunshot wound shifts the burden to the insurer to establish that the death of the insured was due to his suicide." 359 U.S. at 443, 79 S. Ct. at 925.

"In a case like this one, North Dakota presumes that death was accidental and places on the insurer the burden of proving that death resulted from suicide." *Id.* at 446, 79 S. Ct. at 927. [See also the *Usery* case, discussed in Section B, *supra*. Ed.]

The rational connection requirement survives in criminal cases, Tot v. United States, 319 U.S. 463, 63 S. Ct. 1241, 87 L. Ed. 1519 (1943), because the Court has been unwilling to extend into that area the greater-includes-the-lesser theory of Ferry v. Ramsey, 277 U.S. 88, 48 S. Ct. 443, 72 L. Ed. 796 (1928). In that case the Court sustained a Kansas statute under which bank directors were personally liable for deposits made with their assent and with knowledge of insolvency, and the fact of insolvency was *prima facie* evidence of assent and knowledge of insolvency. Mr. Justice Holmes pointed out that the state legislature could have made the directors personally liable to depositors in every case. Since the statute imposed a less stringent liability, "the thing to be considered is the result reached, not the possibly inartificial or clumsy way of reaching it." *Id.* at 94, 48 S. Ct. at 444. Mr. Justice Sutherland dissented: though the state could have created an absolute liability, it did not purport to do so; a rational connection was necessary, but lacking, between the liability created and the prima facie evidence of it; the result might be different if the basis of the presumption were being open for business.

The Sutherland view has prevailed in criminal cases by virtue of the higher standard of notice there required. The fiction that everyone is presumed to know the law is applied to the substantive law of crimes as an alternative to complete unenforceability. But the need does not extend to criminal evidence and procedure, and the fiction does not encompass them. "Rational connection" is not fictional or artificial, and so it is reasonable to suppose that Gainey should have known that his presence at the site of an illicit still could convict him of being connected with (carrying on) the business, United States v. Gainey, 380 U.S. 63, 85 S. Ct. 754, 13 L. Ed. 2d 658 (1965), but not that Romano should have known that his presence at a still could convict him of possessing it, United States v. Romano, 382 U.S. 136, 86 S. Ct. 279, 15 L. Ed. 2d 210 (1965).

In his dissent in Gainey, Mr. Justice Black put it more artistically:

> It might be argued, although the Court does not so argue or hold, that Congress if it wished could make presence at a still a crime in itself, and so Congress should be free to create crimes which are called "possession" and "carrying on an illegal distillery business" but which are defined in such a way that unexplained presence is sufficient and indisputable evidence in all cases to support conviction for those offenses. See Ferry v. Ramsey, 277 U.S. 88, 48 S. Ct. 443, 72 L. Ed. 796. Assuming for the sake of argument that Congress could make unexplained presence a criminal act, and ignoring also the refusal of this Court in other cases to uphold a statutory presumption on such a theory, see Heiner v. Donnan, 285 U.S. 312, 52 S. Ct. 358, 76 L. Ed. 772, there is no indication here that Congress intended to adopt such a misleading method of draftsmanship, nor in my judgment could the statutory provisions if so construed escape condemnation for vagueness, under the principles applied in Lanzetta v. New Jersey, 306 U.S. 451, 59 S. Ct. 618, 83 L. Ed. 888, and many other cases.

380 U.S. at 84, n. 12, 85 S. Ct. at 766.

And the majority opinion in *Romano* agreed with him:

> It may be, of course, that Congress has the power to make presence at an illegal still a punishable crime, but we find no clear indication that it intended to so exercise this power. The crime remains possession, not presence, and with all due deference to the judgment of Congress, the former may not constitutionally be inferred from the latter.

382 U.S. at 144, 86 S. Ct. at 284.

The rule does not spell out the procedural aspects of its application. Questions as to when the evidence warrants submission of a presumption and what instructions are proper under varying states of fact are believed to present no particular difficulties.

House Subcommittee on Criminal Justice Notes

Being persuaded that the term "cases" might be construed to exclude certain bankruptcy and other civil proceedings, the Subcommittee determined to use the phrase "actions and proceedings" to include all types of civil litigation, and to use the term "cases" to include all criminal litigation. Such changes in terminology appear consistently throughout the Rules.

The word "civil" was added to effectuate the Subcommittee's decision not to deal with the question of presumptions in criminal cases. See Rule 303.

With respect to the weight to be given a presumption in a civil case, the Subcommittee agreed with the conclusion reflected in the Court's version that the so-called "bursting bubble" theory of presumptions, whereby a presumption vanishes upon the appearance of any contradicting evidence by the other party, gives to presumptions too slight an effect. On the other hand, the Subcommittee believed that the rule proposed by the Court, whereby a presumption permanently alters the burden of persuasion, no matter how much contradicting evidence is introduced — a view adopted by only a few courts — lent too great a force to presumptions. The Subcommittee accordingly adopted an intermediate position under which a presumption does not vanish upon the introduction of contradicting evidence, and does not change the burden of persuasion; instead it is merely deemed sufficient evidence of the fact presumed to be considered by the jury or other finder of fact.

Report of the House Committee on the Judiciary

Rule 301 as submitted by the Supreme Court provided that in all cases a presumption imposes on the party against whom it is directed the burden of proving that the nonexistence of the presumed fact is more probable than its existence. The Committee limited the scope of Rule 301 to "civil actions and proceedings" to effectuate its decision not to deal with the question of presumptions in criminal cases. [Rejected Rule 303 is set forth in Part Three of this Manual. Ed.] With respect to the weight to be given a presumption in a civil case, the Committee agreed with the judgment implicit in the Court's version that the so-called "bursting bubble" theory of presumptions, whereby a presumption vanishes upon the appearance of any contradicting evidence by the other party, gives to presumptions too slight an effect. On the other hand, the Committee believed that the Rule proposed by the Court, whereby a presumption permanently alters the burden of persuasion, no matter how much contradicting evidence is introduced — a view shared by only a few courts — lends too great a force to presumptions. Accordingly, the Committee amended the Rule to adopt an intermediate position under which a presumption does not vanish upon the introduction of contradicting evidence, and does not change the burden of persuasion; instead it is merely deemed sufficient evidence of the fact presumed to be considered by the jury or other finder of fact.

Report of the Senate Committee on the Judiciary

This rule governs presumptions in civil cases generally. Rule 302 provides for presumptions in cases controlled by State law.

As submitted by the Supreme Court, presumptions governed by this rule were given the effect of placing upon the opposing party the burden of establishing the nonexistence of the presumed fact, once the party invoking the presumption established the basic facts giving rise to it.

Instead of imposing a burden of persuasion on the party against whom the presumption is directed, the House adopted a provision which shifted the burden of going forward with the evidence. They further provided that "even though met with contradicting evidence, a presumption is sufficient evidence of the fact presumed, to be considered by the trier of fact." The effect of the amendment is that presumptions are to be treated as evidence.

The committee feels the House amendment is ill-advised. As the joint committees (the Standing Committee on Practice and Procedure of the Judicial Conference and the Advisory Committee on the Rules of Evidence) stated: "Presumptions are not evidence, but ways of dealing with evidence." This treatment requires juries to perform the task of considering "as evidence" facts upon which they have no direct evidence and which may confuse them in performance of their duties. California had a rule much like that contained in the House amendment. It was sharply criticized by Justice Traynor in *Speck v. Sarver* and was repealed after 93 troublesome years.

Professor McCormick gives a concise and compelling critique of the presumption as evidence rule:

> Another solution, formerly more popular than now, is to instruct the jury that the presumption is "evidence," to be weighed and considered with the testimony in the case. This avoids the danger that the jury may infer that the presumption is conclusive, but it probably means little to the jury, and certainly runs counter to accepted theories of the nature of evidence.

For these reasons the committee has deleted that provision of the House-passed rule that treats presumptions as evidence. The effect of the rule as adopted by the committee is to make clear that while evidence of facts giving rise to a presumption shifts the burden of coming forward with evidence to rebut or meet the presumption, it does not shift the burden of persuasion on the existence of the presumed facts. The burden of persuasion remains on the party to whom it is allocated under the rules governing the allocation in the first instance.

The court may instruct the jury that they may infer the existence of the presumed fact from proof of the basic facts giving rise to the presumption. However, it would be inappropriate under this rule to instruct the jury that the inference they are to draw is conclusive. [Footnotes deleted.]

Report of the House and Senate Conferees

The House bill provides that a presumption in civil actions and proceedings shifts to the party against whom it is directed the burden of going forward with evidence to meet or rebut it. Even though evidence contradicting the presumption is offered, a presumption is considered sufficient evidence of the presumed fact to be considered by the jury. The Senate amendment provides that a presumption shifts to the party against whom it is directed the burden of going forward with evidence to meet or rebut the presumption but it does not shift to that party the burden of persuasion on the existence of the presumed fact.

Under the Senate amendment, a presumption is sufficient to get a party past an adverse party's motion to dismiss made at the end of his case-in-chief. If the adverse party offers no evidence contradicting the presumed fact, the court will instruct the jury that if it finds the basic facts, it may presume the existence of the presumed fact. If the adverse party does offer evidence contradicting the presumed fact, the court cannot instruct the jury that it may *presume* the existence of the presumed fact from proof of the basic facts. The court may, however, instruct the jury that it may infer the existence of the presumed fact from proof of the basic facts.

The Conference adopts the Senate amendment.

Citations to Hearing and Debates

Letter from James F. Schaeffer to Hon. William L. Hungate, June 25, 1973, and accompanying material, in Supp. to Hearings on Proposed Rules of Evidence Before the Subcomm. on Criminal Justice of the House Comm. on the Judiciary, 93rd Cong., 1st Sess., at 130-34 (1973).

Letter from Hon. Roszel C. Thomsen to Hon. James O. Eastland, May 22, 1974, and accompanying material, in Hearings on H.R. 5463 (Federal Rules of Evidence) Before the Senate Comm. on the Judiciary, 93rd Cong., 2d Sess., at 53-54, 56-58 (1974).

Testimony of Edward W. Cleary, June 4, 1975, Hearings on H.R. 5463 (Federal Rules of Evidence) Before the Senate Comm. on the Judiciary, 93rd Cong., 2d Sess., at 47-48 (1974).

Testimony and Prepared Statement of Paul F. Rothstein, June 5, 1974, Hearings on H.R. 5463 (Federal Rules of Evidence) Before the Senate Comm. on the Judiciary, 93rd Cong., 2d Sess., at 267-69 (1974).

RULE 302

A. OFFICIAL TEXT

Rule 302. Applicability of State Law in Civil Actions and Proceedings

In civil actions and proceedings, the effect of a presumption respecting a fact which is an element of a claim or defense as to which State law supplies the rule of decision is determined in accordance with State law.

B. EDITORIAL EXPLANATORY COMMENT

Deference to state law

Rule 302 provides that whenever a Federal Court in a civil case looks to state law to find the rule of decision with respect to a claim or a defense, state law will also govern with respect to the effect of a presumption. In other words, just as Federal Courts normally follow state rules regarding burdens of proof and standards of proof, they will also borrow state law regarding the treatment of a presumption.[1] This is neither surprising nor unusual, given that a presumption serves an important function in allocating responsibility between parties to bring forth evidence. Moreover, to the extent that a presumption places the burden of persuasion on the party against whom the presumption operates, it seems that it is part and parcel of the state substantive law, proper deference to which requires the Federal Court to follow the state law. *Erie R.R. v. Tompkins,* 304 U.S. 64 (1938) is, of course, the most relevant case. Although *Erie* involved on its facts only the diversity jurisdiction of the Federal Courts, its general thesis concerning the manner in which Federal Courts must observe state substantive law is clearly important in explaining why Federal Courts follow state law regarding presumptions.

State law may provide the rule of decision even in a nondiversity case, and where that is so, Rule 302 provides that state law controls the effect of a presumption concerning a fact that is an element of the claim or defense.[2]

Nothing in this Comment or elsewhere in this Manual is intended to suggest that Congress is without constitutional power to abolish Rule 302 and to bring all presumptions under the umbrella of Rule 301. Congress (not the Supreme Court) may possess such power. See Ely, *The Irrepressible Myth of Erie,* 87 HARV. L. REV. 693 (1974);

---

1. See, e.g., Monger v. Cessna Aircraft Co., 812 F.2d 402 (8th Cir. 1987) (in diversity action for negligence, court applied state law presumption that a pilot acted with due care, and also held that the evidence presented by the plaintiff was sufficient, under state law, to overcome the presumption).

2. See Maternally Yours, Inc. v. Your Maternity Shop, Inc., 234 F.2d 538 (2d Cir. 1956) ("the *Erie* doctrine applies, whatever the ground for federal jurisdiction to any issue or claim which has its source in state law").

Hanna v. Plumer, 380 U.S. 460 (1965). In fact, our proposed treatment of federal-state conflict when federal and state presumptions arise in a single case, which we offer below, suggests some such power and also suggests that Rule 301 should be interpreted in some cases as an exercise of the power. Putting the question of power aside, Rule 302 can be understood as an expression of Congress' concern about comity and respect for state law — much like Rules 501 and 601 in that regard. See Mishkin, *Some Further Last Words on Erie — The Thread,* 87 Harv. L. Rev. 1682 (1974).

Element of a claim or defense

Because Rule 302 has not been subjected to much judicial analysis, it remains difficult to determine when "a fact ... is an element of a claim or defense ... to which state law supplies the rule of decision."

Apparently, Congress was of the view that where Federal Courts traditionally deferred to state presumptions, Rule 302 would require continued deference.

Some commentators have suggested that Rule 302 should be read restrictively. Judge Weinstein and Professor Berger suggest that "[i]n cases of doubt, the policy embodied in Rule 302 suggests the application of federal rather than state law, since the draftsmen of the Rule deliberately chose to interpret *Erie* as narrowly as possible." 1 Weinstein's Evidence ¶ 302[01]. With this we respectfully disagree. It is apparent that the Congress intended to defer to state law whenever state law provides the rule of decision and a particular presumption is important to furthering state policies.

Our suggestion is that Federal Judges should defer to state rules on presumptions whenever they are in doubt in a case otherwise governed by state law.[3] Federal Courts should not jump to premature conclusions that presumptions are not expressions of a state's policy toward its litigants. While a certain presumption may appear to be based only on logic and experience, the fact is that most presumptions are based on a combination of logic, probability, policy, and a consideration of access to proof. At least some, and probably most of these considerations can be considered substantive.[4] For example, the presumption that a death was the result of accident rather than suicide may be based somewhat on probability; but it also reflects the state's substantive concern that where access to proof is difficult, the burden should be placed on the insurer.

Whenever a Federal Judge is compelled to follow state law generally, it makes good sense for the Judge to use state law on presumptions as well. It is difficult to see a substantial federal interest in applying federal law in those circumstances. Perhaps the most that can be said is that if the presumption is clearly designed only to operate for purposes of judicial convenience, the presumption is purely procedural, and the Court may apply the federal law if there is a conflict.

---

3. See, e.g., In re Jackson, 28 B.R. 559 (Bankr. D. Pa. 1983) (Court applied Pennsylvania law to determine that the burden of proof of establishing the existence of a partnership is placed on the party who seeks to prove its existence).

4. See, e.g., In re Bahre, 23 B.R. 460 (Bankr. D. Conn. 1982) (where Court applied the state bankruptcy statute, the effect of the state presumption that an intrafamily conveyance was made without consideration was held a matter of state law).

The distinction proposed by the Advisory Committee — between "tactical" presumptions to be governed by federal law and presumptions as to an element of a claim or defense to be governed by state law — is problematic because it is so vague. The distinction also ignores the fact that certain presumptions may embody substantive state policy even if they are "tactical." The distinction proposed by the Advisory Committee is certainly not mandated by the words of the Rule itself. So again, we conclude that state law presumptions are "presumptively" applicable wherever state law provides the rule of decision.

Federal and state claims joined

Where state and federal claims are joined together in a given case, and where the federal law, statutory or otherwise, would treat a presumption one way, while state law would treat it differently, the determination of governing law may be difficult. Although the Federal Rule does not address this problem, there are three possible solutions. First, a Court could read Rule 302 as applying only in cases in which the presumption that relates to a fact that is an element of a claim or defense governed by state law has no bearing on any federal question involved in the case. Such a reading would mean that federal law would predominate whenever there are conflicting presumptions. Or, this Rule could be read literally, in which case the rule of decision would be determined in accordance with state law, meaning that state law would predominate whenever there are conflicting presumptions. There is also a third possibility, which is to treat the presumption differently in dealing with the federal and state claims.

The third view is probably the correct view with respect to a presumption that is not met by conflicting evidence. In other words, if the sole issue is whether a presumption standing alone is sufficient for the party utilizing it to take his case to the jury, or perhaps to prevent the other party's case from going to the jury, there is no reason why the presumption cannot be treated differently when it is applied to the federal and to the state claims. The Trial Judge should have little difficulty applying the presumption rules in making the respective peremptory rulings.

Once conflicting evidence is introduced, however, the situation is complicated. Of course, so long as the federal and state rules are identical, there is no problem. But when they are divergent, there is the danger of confusion in instructing the jury. If the state law places the burden of proof on the party against whom a presumption operates, it may appear that the Judge can give a simple instruction to the jury with respect to burden of proof on the state claim and then proceed to follow Rule 301 with respect to the federal claim and tell the jury about the permissible inference it is entitled to draw. But once the jury is told about both the burden of proof and the permissible inference, it is possible that there may be a double burden on the party against whom the presumption operates.

An appropriate solution would be to follow the Federal Rule and to apply it to both claims in some but not all cases. Since Rule 302 apparently reflects notions of comity and the proper relationship of federal and state courts in a federal system, there is no reason to give it a wooden and inflexible reading. Comity works both ways, and one jurisdiction's interests may have to accommodate the other's at times. Given that Congress has firmly expressed its view as to the proper treatment of presumptions in Rule 301, given that Congress knew that a choice might have to be made when federal and state claims are brought together, and given the Supremacy Clause, it would seem that state law should give way to federal law when there is a federal cause of action in the case and when the use of conflicting presumptions would be confusing to the jury or unfair to a litigant.

But this assumption need not necessarily be unyielding. It might give way to state interests in cases in which it is apparent that the state presumption is critical to proper application of state law, whereas the federal presumption upon close scrutiny seems relatively unimportant in the federal scheme. In such cases, the state law could govern both claims. Where a presumption expresses both strong state and federal policies, a severance might well be the appropriate course.

For example, suppose both federal and state courts have a presumption that a state of affairs, once proved to exist, continues as long as is usual with things of that nature. Assume that a plaintiff sues to recover damages for various violations of federal securities laws from directors and officers of a corporation and that state common-law claims are joined by pendent jurisdiction to the federal claims. Once an illegality is demonstrated to have occurred at one point in time, an issue may arise as to whether it continued for some period. The presumption may be useful to assist a plaintiff in proving a continuing state of affairs. If federal and state law differ as to the effect of the presumption, which governs? Our suggestion is that ordinarily the Federal Rule would govern both claims. This is somewhat analogous to the theory in common-law jurisdictions that when conflicting presumptions appear, often one must predominate.[5] This is also similar to the result adopted by the Courts under Rule 501, in pendent jurisdiction cases where the state and federal rules on privilege are in conflict. Courts have held that the federal law of privilege applies to both the federal and to the pendent state claims.[6] This is justified in the interest of consistency, and in recognition of the importance of the federal cause of action.

The states that have followed the federal lead and adopted codes of evidence have not been quick to adopt identical versions of Rule 301.[7] This would seem to suggest that over time the possibility that federal presumption rules will differ from state presumption rules is a real one. It is encouraging, however, to note that to date there are almost no reported cases in which the conflict between federal and state rules appears to have presented a problem for Federal Judges.

C. ANNOTATED CASES

Conflicting state presumptions

Melville v. American Home Assur. Co., 443 F. Supp. 1064 (E.D. Pa. 1977), *rev'd on other grounds*, 584 F.2d 1306 (3d Cir. 1978): In a diversity action to recover the

---

5. See the discussion of conflicting presumptions in the Editorial Explanatory Comment to Rule 301.

6. See, e.g., Hancock v. Hobbs, 967 F.2d 462 (11th Cir. 1992) (federal law of privilege provides the rule of decision where the Court's jurisdiction is predicated upon a federal question, even if the witness-testimony is relevant to a pendent state law count that is controlled by a contrary state law of privilege: "It would be impractical to apply two different rules of privilege to the same evidence before a single jury.").

7. See G. JOSEPH & S. SALTZBURG, EVIDENCE IN AMERICA § 8.2 (Michie 1989) (only about half of the states with federal-based codes of evidence follow the "bursting bubble" presumption of Federal Rule 301).

proceeds of an insurance policy, the District Court cited Rule 302 as persuasive authority for its conclusion that presumptions often are more "substantive" than "procedural." The Court carefully observed that although Rule 302 directs the application of state law, it does not set forth a formula for deciding which state's law should apply in a case when several states' laws arguably govern.

Inference

Herbert v. Wal-Mart Stores, Inc., 911 F.2d 1044 (5th Cir. 1990): Appealing a diversity slip-and-fall case for allegedly inadequate damages, the plaintiff argued that the District Court erred in refusing to draw an adverse inference from the defendant's failure to call a witness purportedly under its control. In the course of affirming, the Court noted that the Rule did not apply to the state uncalled-witness rule, because it merely permits an inference and does not create a true presumption.

Presumptive authenticity

In re Bobby Boggs, Inc., 819 F.2d 574 (5th Cir. 1987): In a bankruptcy dispute over entitlement to a subcontractor's funds, the Court held that there was ample evidence to authenticate certain bonds issued by a surety that was defunct at the time of trial. It observed in a footnote that state law made the presence of the bonds in a defunct insurer's files presumptively authentic. Without deciding whether the state presumption would, standing alone, have been sufficient to satisfy Rule 901, the Court reasoned that the failure of the opposing party to offer any evidence to suggest that the bonds were not authentic supported their admissibility.

Use of state presumption

Bernier v. Board of County Rd. Comm'rs, 581 F. Supp. 71 (W.D. Mich. 1983): Ruling *in limine* in a wrongful death action involving a claim that the deceased was killed because the county failed to properly mark an intersection, the Court interpreted a state statute creating a presumption that a person with less than 0.07 percent alcohol in his blood was not under the influence of intoxicating liquor. It found that the presumption did not entitle the plaintiff to judgment as a matter of law on the defendant's affirmative defense of intoxication, but indicated that the language of the state statute that created the presumption might be introduced to the jury if relevant at the time it was offered. The Court expressed some doubts as to whether the presumption would be relevant if the defendant's evidence showed that the deceased's consumption of alcohol affected his ability to control his vehicle.

D. LEGISLATIVE HISTORY

Advisory Committee's Note

A series of Supreme Court decisions in diversity cases leaves no doubt of the relevance of Erie Railroad Co. v. Tompkins, 304 U.S. 64, 58 S. Ct. 817, 82 L. Ed. 1188 (1938), to questions of burden of proof. These decisions are Cities Service Oil Co. v. Dunlap, 308 U.S. 208, 60 S. Ct. 201, 84 L. Ed. 196 (1939), Palmer v. Hoffman, 318 U.S. 109, 63 S. Ct. 477, 87 L. Ed. 645 (1943), and Dick v. New York Life Ins. Co., 359 U.S. 437, 79 S. Ct. 921, 3 L. Ed. 2d 935 (1959). They involved burden of proof, respectively, as to status as bona fide purchaser, contributory negligence, and nonaccidental death (suicide) of an insured. In each instance the state rule was held to be applicable. It does not follow, however, that all presumptions in diversity cases are governed by state law. In each case cited, the burden of proof question had to do with a substantive element of the claim or defense. Application of the state law is called for only when the presumption operates upon such an element. Accordingly the rule does not apply state law when the presumption operates upon a lesser aspect of the case, i.e., "tactical" presumptions.

The situations in which the state law is applied have been tagged for convenience in the preceding discussion as "diversity cases." The designation is not a completely accurate one since *Erie* applies to any claim or issue having its source in state law, regardless of the basis of federal jurisdiction, and does not apply to a federal claim or issue, even though jurisdiction is based on diversity. Vestal, Erie R.R. v. Tompkins: A Projection, 48 Iowa L. Rev. 248, 257 (1963); Hart and Wechsler, The Federal Courts and the Federal System, 697 (1953); 1A Moore, Federal Practice § 0.305[3] (2d ed. 1965); Wright, Federal Courts, 217-18 (1963). Hence the rule employs, as appropriately descriptive, the phrase "as to which state law supplies the rule of decision." See A.L.I. Study of the Division of Jurisdiction Between State and Federal Courts, § 2344(c), p. 40, P.F.D. No. 1 (1965).

ARTICLE IV. RELEVANCY AND ITS LIMITS

RULE 401

A. OFFICIAL TEXT

Rule 401. Definition of "Relevant Evidence"

"Relevant evidence" means evidence having any tendency to make the existence of any fact that is of consequence to the determination of the action more probable or less probable than it would be without the evidence.

B. EDITORIAL EXPLANATORY COMMENT

Basic definition

This Rule defines the term "relevant evidence." The definition provides that evidence is relevant if it has *any* tendency to make the existence of a material fact more probable or less probable than it would be without the evidence. The question for the Trial Judge is whether a reasonable person would find the probability of a consequential fact to be altered, one way or the other, by the proffered evidence.

Rule 401 is purely definitional, and has no operational effect on its own. Therefore, Rule 401 is usually cited together with Rule 402 (providing that relevant evidence is generally admissible) or, more frequently, with Rule 403 (providing that evidence even though relevant may be excluded on grounds of prejudice, confusion or delay).

The important thing for the Judge and for counsel to remember is that the evidence does not by itself have to prove the ultimate proposition for which it is offered; nor does it have to make that ultimate proposition more probable than not. To be relevant it is enough that the evidence has a *tendency* to make a consequential fact even the least bit more probable or less probable than it would be without the evidence. The question of relevance is thus different from whether a mass of evidence is *sufficient* to prove a point.[1]

An example may help to clarify the difference between relevance, preponderance, and sufficiency. Assume that a defendant is charged with an armed robbery committed by someone carrying a handgun. The prosecution wants to offer into evidence testimony that the defendant owned a hand gun prior to the time the robbery was committed. Defendant claims the evidence is irrelevant. Certainly this evidence, standing alone, does not make it more probable than not that the defendant committed the crime. Furthermore, it is *a fortiori* not sufficient to prove beyond a reasonable doubt that the defendant committed the crime. But it is a piece of evidence, the existence of which makes it somewhat more likely that the defendant committed the crime than if there were no such evidence. This evidence, in other words, has some tendency to make it more likely that the defendant is guilty than if no such evidence existed. Thus, relevancy is a threshold admissibility standard to be applied by the Trial Judge. It is up to the trier of fact to weigh the evidence and to determine whether the entirety of the evidence is sufficient to prove a point.

It should be emphasized that "any tendency" is enough. The fact that the evidence is of weak probative value does not make it irrelevant. However, when the Judge strikes a balance between the negative and positive features of evidence, as often must be done under Rule 403, the minimal value of the evidence may become important. But the fact remains that evidence may be relevant even though it is weak.[2]

Notice that the Rule does not explicitly treat "materiality" as a separate concept. Both traditional requirements of relevance analysis — that evidence must relate to issues that are properly in dispute and that it must shed some light on those issues — are combined

---

1. See, e.g., Douglass v. Eaton Corp., 956 F.2d 1339 (6th Cir. 1992) (Trial Court ruling on whether evidence is relevant may not consider the sufficiency or weight of the evidence; even if the evidence is insufficient to prove the point for which it is offered, the Trial Court "may not exclude the evidence if it has even the slightest probative worth," unless some other Rule such as 403 warrants exclusion); Smith v. Georgia, 684 F.2d 729 (11th Cir. 1982) ("Of course, evidence need not prove the proposition for which it is offered to be probative. Rule 401 states that evidence is relevant if it makes the existence of any fact more probable or less probable than it would be without the evidence.").

2. See United States v. Curtis, 568 F.2d 643 (9th Cir. 1978). In the course of affirming a conviction for murder, the Court of Appeals observed that "Rule 401 ... contains a very expansive definition of relevant evidence," and approved the introduction of evidence suggesting that appellant committed rape or attempted rape.

into one rule. Whether an issue is properly in dispute is, of course, determined by the substantive law.[3]

Direct and circumstantial evidence

The difficult relevance issues involve circumstantial, as opposed to direct, evidence. The only question to be asked in regard to direct evidence is whether it relates to an issue that is properly in dispute — i.e., one that is of consequence to the action under Rule 401 (what was called a material issue at common law). If direct eyewitness testimony, for instance, is offered that the defendant in our previous robbery example was the robber, the evidence is clearly relevant, since it relates to a proposition provable in the case. No inferences are required between the proof itself and the ultimate fact to be established. If, however, the testimony proves the robber wore a blue coat and the defendant owns a blue coat, this is circumstantial evidence and the Judge must decide whether, if believed, it makes a disputed fact more or less probable. It is here that hard questions arise.

There is no litmus test or simple formula for applying the general definition. Logic and experience together must supply the Judge with skills in determining whether a given piece of evidence tends to prove a disputed proposition.[4] Sometimes expert witnesses may be necessary to assist the Court in making a relevance determination. And the Trial Judge should consider not only whether the admission of evidence is likely to advance the cause, but also whether its absence might produce negative inferences that would unfairly hurt a party — i.e., the absence of evidence might be probative to a jury.[5]

All this is not to say that circumstantial evidence is less important or less significant than direct evidence. To the contrary, in some cases, circumstantial evidence (e.g., a large amount of trace money from a bank robbery) may indeed have more weight than direct evidence (e.g., dubious or fleeting eyewitness testimony).[6]

---

3. See, e.g., Phillips v. Western Co. of N. Am., 953 F.2d 923 (5th Cir. 1992) (where substantive law prohibits a setoff for collateral benefits already received by an injury victim, evidence of such benefits has no relevance to the case and is inadmissible).

4. See, e.g., United States v. Grier, 866 F.2d 908 (7th Cir. 1989) (in a drug conspiracy case, evidence was presented of a note found in the apartment of Harper's codefendant; the note contained Harper's name and telephone number; this was probative of conspiracy between the codefendant and Harper, and admissible under Rules 401 and 402, because it tended "to make Harper's involvement in the conspiracy more probable than it would be without the evidence" even though the note would not be sufficient to convict; the note was circumstantial evidence that "Harper was participating in the conspiracy and aware of its magnitude"); United States v. Contenti, 735 F.2d 628 (1st Cir. 1984) (in a mail fraud case alleging that defendant burned down a building he owned in order to collect insurance proceeds, evidence that the defendant took out loans from loansharks shortly before and after the fire was relevant and admissible; it tended to prove the defendant's poor financial condition, thus providing motivation to burn down the building to obtain insurance proceeds; question of "weight and value" of such evidence was for the jury).

5. See generally Saltzburg, *A Special Aspect of Relevance: Countering Negative Inferences Associated with the Absence of Evidence*, 66 CAL. L. REV. 1011 (1978).

6. See, e.g., United States v. Russell, 919 F.2d 795 (1st Cir. 1990) (circumstantial evidence is not some form of second-rate evidence, and in appropriate cases it may be given as much or more weight than direct evidence); Madison v. Deseret Livestock Co., 574 F.2d 1027, 1036 (10th Cir. 1978) ("inferences from

Standard of review

There is a good argument that the standard of review for pure relevance determinations should be *de novo*.[7] Unlike Rule 403, which requires a balancing process that is trial-sensitive, and which thus warrants a deferential standard of review, the question of whether evidence is relevant is one based in experience and logic. For example, the Appellate Court need not be constrained by a ''cold record'' in deciding whether a defendant's poor financial condition is probative of a motive to commit a crime. The Appellate Court and the Trial Court are ordinarily in equally good positions to determine whether such an inference can be drawn in logic and experience; trial context is not important. Many Appellate Courts do not see it that way, however. There are a number of cases stating broadly that the Trial Court ''possesses broad discretion in determining the relevance of proffered evidence.''[8]

Of course, it must be remembered that very few rulings are ''pure'' relevance rulings. Ordinarily, the objection to proffered evidence is not that it is totally irrelevant, but rather that the probative value of the evidence is so minimal that it is substantially outweighed by the negative factors of prejudice, confusion and delay. This is a Rule 403 question, which for good reason is governed by a deferential, abuse-of-discretion standard of review.[9]

Disputed issues

The first sentence of the final paragraph of the Advisory Committee's Note, *infra,* states that ''[t]he fact to which the evidence is directed need not be in dispute'' and cites the California Evidence Code in a rather cryptic attempt to support its view. In our view, the wording ''fact that is of consequence to the determination of the action'' requires that all proof be directed to the issues in dispute. Contrary to the suggestion of the Committee, illustrative evidence — such as evidence provided for background or context — would not be barred under such a reading, as long as the illustrative evidence was

---

circumstantial facts may frequently amount to full proof of a given theory, and may on occasion even be strong enough to overcome the effect of direct testimony to the contrary'').

7. See United States v. Donley, 878 F.2d 735 (3d Cir. 1989) (''our standard of review for relevancy rulings is plenary''); United States v. Torniero, 735 F.2d 725 (2d Cir. 1984) (pure relevance question is a ''question of law'').

8. United States v. Laughlin, 772 F.2d 1382, 1392 (7th Cir. 1985). See also Beacham v. Lee-Norse, 714 F.2d 1010 (10th Cir. 1983) (question of relevancy is ''committed to the discretion of the trial court''); United States v. Dunn, 805 F.2d 1275, 1281 (6th Cir. 1986) (''the trial court has broad discretion in determining the relevancy of evidence and in passing on its admissibility under Rule 401'').

9. See United States v. Beasley, 809 F.2d 1273 (7th Cir. 1987):

> When the same evidence has legitimate and forbidden uses, when the introduction is valuable yet dangerous, the district judge has great discretion.... Trial judges have a comparative advantage because they alone see all the evidence in context, and the judicial system as a whole takes advantage of the division of labor.

reasonably related to a disputed issue.[10] We believe the Advisory Committee's Note places undue reliance on Rule 403. Although we would probably reach the same result as the Committee in most cases, we think that it is important to emphasize that the first step in a relevance analysis is to decide whether the trier of fact conceivably could be helped by evidence. If the answer is "no," the evidence should be excluded without reference to a balancing test that requires a specific demonstration of an extant evil before evidence is excluded.[11]

State law

In many instances in which state law provides the rule of decision, it may make sense to consider not only the issues that state courts look to in deciding similar cases, but also the kinds of proof that state courts deem appropriate on certain issues. Even though the Federal Rules apply in all cases unless some specific rule provides otherwise (see, e.g., Rules 302, 501 and 601), it seems appropriate to look to state approaches to legal questions that might be answered in very different ways depending on the types of issues and proof considered.[12] See the cases discussed in the Annotations under the heading "Reference to state law."

At any rate, it is clear that state law in diversity cases determines the issues that are in dispute, and it that way controls whether proffered evidence is relevant. For example, assume that the plaintiff is a mother whose child was run down and killed by a car. Assume further that the plaintiff proffers compelling evidence of emotional distress that she suffered as a result of losing her child. In many states, this evidence is not relevant unless the mother could prove that she was in the "zone of danger" at the time that her child was killed. Where such a state law provides the rule of decision in Federal Court, the evidence is irrelevant under Rule 401. This is because the mother's emotional distress

---

10. See, e.g., United States v. Daly, 842 F.2d 1380, 1388 (2d Cir. 1988). In a racketeering trial against members of an organized crime family, the Trial Court allowed an FBI expert to testify to the nature and structure of the five New York crime families, including membership requirements, rules of conduct, and code of silence; this testimony was relevant background evidence to ultimate issues that were in dispute:

> [T]he trial court may admit evidence that does not directly establish an element of the offense charged, in order to provide background for the events alleged in the indictment. Background evidence may be admitted to show, for example, the circumstances surrounding the events or to furnish an explanation of the understanding or intent with which certain acts were performed.

11. See, e.g., United States v. Hall, 653 F.2d 1002 (5th Cir. 1981) (in a narcotics case, the government relied on testimony of the defendant's coconspirators and had no "controlled buy" or other physical evidence with which to make its case; defendant argued that the coconspirators' uncorroborated testimony was an attempt to "frame" the defendant in order to protect their real source of drug supply; the government called a DEA agent to provide expert testimony to explain that a "controlled buy" was not always possible, especially where the conspiracy has been terminated or where the subject of the investigation is in a managerial position; the Court of Appeals found this testimony irrelevant and reversible error, because the expert "testified to no facts bearing in any manner on the prosecution of [the defendant] or on the investigation leading to that prosecution"; none of the facts to which the DEA agent testified were in dispute, so the "opinion testimony lacked substantial relevance to any matter in issue, and was therefore not admissible").

12. See generally Wellborn, *The Federal Rules of Evidence and the Application of State Law in the Federal Courts,* 55 TEX. L. REV. 371 (1977).

is not "in dispute" under the state's substantive law unless she was in the zone of danger, and it is the state substantive law that determines the issues in dispute in such cases.[13]

Offers of proof

During the course of a trial, it is often unnecessary to require parties to explain how offered evidence relates to the issues in dispute, because the relationship is obvious. There are times, however, when the Trial Judge may be unclear as to the relationship of the evidence to the issues and may require counsel to explain the purpose of an offer. In order for the Trial Judge to give proper limiting instructions under Rule 105 and to strike a proper balance between probative value and prejudicial effect under Rule 403, the Judge must be sure that there is no doubt as to why evidence is being offered. When a doubt arises, the party offering the evidence should be asked to explain.[14]

Relevance and credibility

In determining whether evidence is relevant, the Trial Judge must keep in mind that the credibility of the evidence is a separate issue. For example in *Ballou v. Henri Studios, Inc.*, 656 F.2d 1147 (5th Cir. 1981), a wrongful death action arising from a two-car accident, plaintiffs filed a motion *in limine* to exclude any evidence that the decedent was intoxicated while driving at the time of the accident. At the hearing, defendants proffered a blood test indicating that the decedent had a blood alcohol content of 0.24 percent at the time of his death. Plaintiffs sought to refute the test evidence at the hearing by calling a Mrs. Eisenhower, who saw the decedent just before the accident. Mrs. Eisenhower stated that she had been right next to the decedent, and that he had no alcohol on his breath. The Trial Judge excluded the blood tests "because of the lack of credibility of the tests of alcoholism at the time of the wreck, especially in view of the testimony of Mrs. Eisenhower." The Court of Appeals held that the Trial Court had abused its discretion in excluding the blood tests. The Court concluded that exclusion of evidence on relevance grounds is not permitted merely because "the judge does not find it credible." It reasoned as follows:

> Although we find the court's skepticism about the test results understandable in light of Mrs. Eisenhower's testimony, we cannot sanction the type of credibility choice made by the district court here.... Rather than discounting the probative value of the test results on the basis of its perception of the degree to which the

---

13. See, e.g., Garland v. Herrin, 724 F.2d 16 (2d Cir. 1983) (evidence of parents' emotional distress over the murder of their daughter held irrelevant because "New York law does not permit a bystander to recover for psychic injury for harm inflicted on another").

14. An example is Daskarolis v. Firestone Tire & Rubber Co., 651 F.2d 937 (4th Cir. 1981). In this diversity product liability case, the Court declined to consider whether the Trial Judge erred in excluding a tire offered as demonstrative evidence on the ground that it was not necessary, when defense counsel did nothing to explain its importance.

evidence was worthy of belief, the district court should have determined the probative value of the test results *if true* ... leaving to the jury the difficult choice of whether to credit the evidence (emphasis in original).[15]

It should be noted, however, that the Trial Judge in *Ballou* might have properly excluded the blood tests on other grounds. It is true that the Trial Judge was in error by confusing relevance with credibility. However, evidence is not always admissible merely because it is relevant if believed by the jury. Other rules of evidence may operate to exclude otherwise probative evidence on the grounds that it is *unreliable*. Thus, scientific evidence, such as a blood test, can be excluded under Rule 702 or Rule 403 if the Trial Judge has legitimate and substantial doubts as to its reliability.[16]

Conditional relevancy

By its terms, Rule 401 does not cover the concept of "conditional" relevancy. Evidence is conditionally relevant when its probative value depends upon the existence of another fact. For example, a statement may be probative that a party was aware of a dangerous condition — but only if the party heard the statement. Under Rule 104(b), the proponent of evidence that is conditionally relevant must provide enough evidence to support a finding of the conditional fact. Then the relevance of the evidence is considered under Rules 401-403.

Remoteness

Occasionally, a Trial Judge will exclude evidence on the basis of remoteness, which is to say that the evidence is too far removed in space or time from the proposition that it is offered to prove. For example, assume a two-car accident where the defendant is trying to prove that the plaintiff was not wearing a seatbelt. If the defendant calls a witness who testifies that he saw the plaintiff driving without a seatbelt an hour before the accident, this testimony is undoubtedly relevant; it tends to prove that the plaintiff was not wearing a seatbelt an hour later.[17] On the other hand, if the witness testifies that he saw the plaintiff driving without a seatbelt two years before the accident, the Trial Court is likely to exclude the testimony as too remote (and possibly as character evidence under Rules 404 and 405).

When evidence is excluded as too remote, it is not that it fails to fit the definition of relevant evidence. The definition of relevance in Rule 401 is permissive, to say the least,

---

15. See also United States v. Welsh, 774 F.2d 670, 672 (4th Cir. 1985) ("The credibility of a witness has nothing to do with whether or not his testimony is probative with respect to the fact it seeks to prove.... [T]he law does not consider credibility as a component to relevance.").

16. See the Editorial Explanatory Comment to Rule 702, and Daubert v. Merrell Dow Pharmaceuticals, 113 S. Ct. 2786 (1993), discussed therein.

17. See Hill v. Rolleri, 615 F.2d 886 (9th Cir. 1980) (testimony concerning driver's reckless driving ten minutes before an accident was probative of whether he was engaged in reckless driving at the time of the accident).

and the fact that the plaintiff was not wearing a seatbelt two years earlier has at least *some* tendency to prove that he was not wearing one at the time of the accident. Exclusion on grounds of remoteness is better understood as an exercise of the Trial Court's discretion under Rule 403. That is, the probative value of the evidence is, while not nonexistent, at least minimal due to the gap in time between the fact proffered and the event to be proved. Exclusion results where the minimal probative value is substantially outweighed by the confusion and delay that would result from introducing the evidence.[18]

Illustrations of relevant evidence

No piece of evidence is relevant in itself. It must be evaluated in the light of the facts that are consequential to the action and in the light of logic and experience. So it is not surprising that most rulings on relevance are case-specific. However, over time, certain fact situations have recurred, and some generalizations are possible. Of course, even if a certain class of evidence is relevant in a certain type of case, the evidence in any particular case may be so prejudicial as to warrant exclusion under Rule 403. Also, counsel must remember Rules 404-412, under which classes of undeniably relevant evidence may be excluded because of policy considerations and other concerns. All that said, and with no intent to be exclusive, the following generalizations on relevance can be made:

1. *Similar occurrences.* Evidence of similar incidents or accidents is often offered by plaintiffs, usually in personal injury actions, as relevant on a number of issues, such as to show notice, causation, and/or defect. These occurrences can be found relevant, depending on the degree of similarity and the purpose for which the evidence is offered. If causation or defect is at issue, the occurrence must share "substantial" similarity with the event at issue in the case. In contrast, if the occurrence is offered to prove notice, substantial similarity is not required; the occurrence need only have been of a type that would give notice to a reasonable person as to the condition in issue.[19] Obviously, even

---

18. See, e.g., United States v. Ellzey, 936 F.2d 492 (10th Cir. 1991) (evidence properly excluded under Rule 403 due to the "remote and tenuous link" between the evidence and the charged crime).

19. See, e.g., Four Corners Helicopters, Inc. v. Turbomeca, S.A., 979 F.2d 1434 (10th Cir. 1992):

> Evidence proffered to illustrate the existence of a dangerous condition necessitates a high degree of similarity because it weighs directly on the ultimate issue to be decided by the jury. The requirement of substantial similarity is relaxed, however, when the evidence of other incidents is used to demonstrate notice or awareness of a potential defect....

In this case, plaintiffs offered evidence to prove a design defect and notice thereof and to refute the defendant's assertion that there was no mechanical failure; the Court found that the incidents, though not identical, were substantially similar and were admissible to indicate the existence of a defect; the incidents also met the relaxed requirement of similarity to prove notice, and therefore the Court found they were admissible for all purposes offered by the plaintiffs. See also Johnson v. Ford Motor Co, 988 F.2d 573 (5th Cir. 1993) (evidence of other accidents held inadmissible even for notice since there was no reasonable similarity to the facts at issue; the accidents involved different vehicle models or different years, and none involved the precise mechanical defect at issue in the litigation).

an identical occurrence is not relevant to prove notice if it occurs subsequent to the event in issue.

2. *Consciousness of guilt.* Where a criminal defendant flees prosecution, or bribes a juror, or threatens a witness, or gives a false exculpatory story, this evidence is ordinarily held relevant to the defendant's consciousness of guilt. The inferences work as follows: A person who flees, changes his story, etc., is more likely to believe that he is guilty than a person who has not done any of these things; a person who believes he is guilty is more likely to be guilty than a person who does not; and a person who is guilty is more likely to be guilty of the crime charged than one who is not.[20] Of course, evidence of consciousness of guilt is prejudicial to the defendant, and as such is subject to exclusion if the probative value of the evidence is diminished by a plausible alternative explanation for the defendant's conduct.[21]

3. *Evidence of financial condition.* In criminal cases, evidence of a defendant's poor financial condition before the crime has often been found relevant where the crime charged involved possible financial gain.[22] Conversely, evidence of a sudden aquisition of wealth after the crime charged has been found relevant to prove that the defendant committed the crime.[23]

4. *Government, professional, and industry standards.* Government, professional, and industry standards and regulations are usually held relevant to prove customary practice

---

20. See, e.g., United States v. Tracy, 989 F.2d 1279 (1st Cir. 1993) (evidence of flight by a defendant is admissible as probative of a "guilty mind" if "there is an adequate factual predicate creating an inference of guilt of the crime charged"; a sufficient factual predicate was established in this case; the defendant was scheduled for trial but left the state and did not appear; independent evidence established his drug dealings); United States v. Horton, 873 F.2d 180, 181 (8th Cir. 1989) (no error in admitting the fact that the defendant gave a false name during his pretrial booking interview; "false identification is relevant and admissible to show consciousness of guilt").

21. The Federal Judicial Center suggests the following instruction to be given when evidence of consciousness of guilt is admitted:

_____ testified that, after the crime was supposed to have been committed, the defendant [brief description of behavior, such as flight]. If you believe that the defendant [same brief description], you should keep that in mind when deciding whether the government has proved beyond a reasonable doubt that he committed the crime. On the one hand, you may think that what he did at that time indicated that he knew he was guilty and was attempting to avoid punishment. On the other hand, it is sometimes true that an innocent person will [same brief description] in order to avoid being arrested and charged with a crime.

Federal Judicial Center Pattern Instruction 43 (1982).

22. See, e.g., United States v. Contenti, 735 F.2d 628 (1st Cir. 1984) (evidence of financial distress was relevant to provide motive for burning down a building to collect insurance proceeds).

23. See, e.g., United States v. Chagra, 669 F.2d 241 (5th Cir. 1982) (in narcotics prosecution, evidence that the defendant bought two expensive homes was relevant proof of guilt).

or a standard of care.[24] They have also been found relevant to establish the defendant's knowledge or intent in a criminal case.[25]

5. *Comparable sales to show the value of real property.* Where the fact of consequence is the value of property, evidence of recent sales of similarly situated property has been found relevant.[26] Of course, the greater the time differential, the less probative the sale is as to the current value of the subject property, and the more likely the sale will be excluded under Rule 403.[27]

C. ANNOTATED CASES

Causation and damages

Sir Speedy, Inc. v. L & P Graphics, Inc., 957 F.2d 1033 (2d Cir. 1992): After a jury verdict in an action over breach of a franchise agreement, the Trial Judge ruled that income projections made by the franchisor should not have been admitted in proof of the franchisee's damages because they predated the applicable limitations period. The Court reversed the judgment n.o.v., holding it was error to exclude the documents, as the statute of limitations only bars stale claims and is not a rule of evidence. A suggestion that evidence is too old goes to its relevance and to its weight, which is a matter for the jury.

Blancha v. Raymark Indus., 972 F.2d 507 (3d Cir. 1992): The plaintiffs' theory in an asbestos case was that all asbestos could cause the decedent's mesothelioma; the defendant's expert indicated that asbestos products containing chrysotile did not cause mesothelioma. After a verdict for the defendant, a new trial was granted, first on the ground that the expert's testimony was irrelevant without evidence that the defendant's product contained chrysotile, and later (on reconsideration) on the ground that the jury might have been confused by the expert testimony in the absence of evidence about the defendant's product. Reversing a judgment for the plaintiff on the new trial, the Court held that the expert's testimony was relevant, given the theory advanced and the plaintiffs' burden of proof on proximate causation, and that the danger of confusion did

---

24. See, e.g., Horne v. Owens-Corning Fiberglass Corp., 4 F.3d 276 (4th Cir. 1993) (in a product liability case, OSHA regulations requiring warnings to be placed on asbestos were admissible to show state-of-the-art in the industry); Brown v. Cedar Rapids Iowa City Ry., 650 F.2d 159, 163 (8th Cir. 1981) (allowing admission of "advisory safety codes promulgated by governmental authority as showing an acceptable standard of care").

25. See, e.g., United States v. Head, 641 F.2d 174 (4th Cir. 1981) (IRS manual on employee conduct was relevant to show that the type of conduct the defendant sought to influence was prohibited); United States v. Klauber, 611 F.2d 512 (4th Cir. 1979) (in conviction of lawyer for mail fraud and racketeering, the state Code of Professional Responsibility was relevant to the attitude that the defendant "as a member of the Bar, should have maintained toward practices that were proven").

26. See, e.g., United States v. 179.26 Acres, 644 F.2d 367, 371 (10th Cir. 1981) ("The best evidence of market value of real property in condemnation is, of course, found in sales of comparable land within a reasonable time before the taking.").

27. See, e.g., United States v. 33.90 Acres of Land, 709 F.2d 1012 (5th Cir. 1983) (where there was a time differential of seven or eight years between the proffered sales and the taking, the Trial Court did not err in excluding evidence of the sales).

not so clearly outweigh the probative value of the expert's testimony as to justify exclusion.

Carroll v. Morgan, 17 F.3d 787 (5th Cir. 1994): The Court held in a medical malpractice wrongful death action that evidence showing the decedent's ill health and intemperate lifestyle was relevant to the possible causes of his death and to the issue of damages. His intemperance might have resulted in a reduced life expectancy and, to the extent it included lustful sexual behavior and marital infidelity, was probative of the extent of the survivor's noneconomic loss.

United States v. Morris, 957 F.2d 1391 (7th Cir.), *cert. denied,* 113 S. Ct. 380 (1992): The Court held, in a prosecution for conspiring to defraud the United States arising out of the purchase of a nursing home at an inflated price, that evidence of a 1980 partnership buyback valuation was relevant to the 1984 value of the nursing home partnership.

O'Dell v. Hercules, Inc., 904 F.2d 1194 (8th Cir. 1990): The Court held that the Trial Judge properly excluded evidence of objective symptoms of injury, property marketability, and the plaintiffs' subjective fear resulting from the exposure.

Haney v. Mizell Mem. Hosp., 744 F.2d 1467 (11th Cir. 1984): Affirming a judgment for the defendants in a diversity medical malpractice case, the Court upheld the admission of evidence concerning the plaintiff's use of alcohol and drugs. The evidence was relevant to his ability to communicate with medical personnel following an accident and to his claim for damages.

Civil rights and employment discrimination cases

Taylor v. Western & S. Life Ins. Co., 966 F.2d 1188 (7th Cir. 1992): Affirming in part a judgment for the plaintiffs in a Title VII action, the Court held that prior acts of racial discrimination not included in the EEOC charge were nevertheless relevant to show the plaintiff's reasonableness in believing he had been compelled to resign.

Lee v. Rapid City Area School Dist. No. 51-4, 981 F.2d 316 (8th Cir. 1992) (en banc): In an ADEA action by a teacher whose contract was not renewed, evidence that school administrators had received complaints about the plaintiff from students and parents was admitted but the Trial Judge refused, on grounds that the evidence was hearsay and the witnesses repeatedly volunteered nonresponsive statements, to allow testimony about the substance of the complaints unless they had been documented. The Court held, *inter alia,* that oral complaints were irrelevant because the defendant's agreement with its teachers limited what administrators were permitted to consider in evaluating teachers. Three Judges dissented from this point, on the ground that the ADEA is concerned with whether the defendant's decision was *in fact* based on oral complaints, not with whether such action might have violated the agreement; noncompliance with the agreement might have weakened the administrators' credibility as to their motivation, but it did not render that motive evidence irrelevant.

Consciousness of a weak case — civil cases

McQueeney v. Wilmington Trust Co., 779 F.2d 916 (3d Cir. 1985): The Court reversed a judgment for a seaman in a Jones Act case, holding it was error to exclude evidence suggesting that the seaman had suborned perjury of a proffered witness. The Court found that "subornation of perjury by a party is strong evidence that the party's case is weak" and that there was little chance of "unfair prejudice" in the use of the evidence.

Albrecht v. Baltimore & Ohio R.R., 808 F.2d 329 (4th Cir. 1987): Although the Court reversed a judgment for an employee in an FELA case because of the erroneous admission of subsequent repair evidence, it upheld admission of evidence that the railroad destroyed the ladder on which the plaintiff was standing at the time of the accident. The Court stated that "[w]e should not ... sanction the deliberate destruction of highly relevant evidence."

Dykes v. Raymark Indus., 801 F.2d 810 (6th Cir. 1986), *cert. denied*, 107 S. Ct. 1975 (1987): In an asbestosis action, the Court held there was no error in admitting documents created by a defendant after the last possible date on which the plaintiff's deceased was exposed to asbestos. The documents were consistent with an attitude that the plaintiff claimed existed prior to the deceased's injury and supported a punitive damage award.

S.C. Johnson & Son v. Louisville & N.R.R., 695 F.2d 253 (7th Cir. 1982): Affirming a judgment for a rail carrier in an action by a manufacturer for damages to freight, the Court noted that it is not proper to infer that the contents of evidence that a party has destroyed would have been unfavorable to that party unless the destruction was done in bad faith. In *Coates v. Johnson & Johnson*, 756 F.2d 524 (7th Cir. 1985), the Court affirmed a judgment for an employer in an employment discrimination action. It found that no presumption arose that files destroyed by a plant manager would have been unfavorable to the employer where the files were destroyed only after the manager consulted with the EEOC concerning files that must be maintained and the files were destroyed before litigation was foreseen.

Cerro Gordo Charity v. Fireman's Fund Am. Life Ins. Co., 819 F.2d 1471 (8th Cir. 1987): The Court held that evidence a witness had been threatened in a phone call was admissible, where only one party had a motive to frighten the witness.

Consciousness of guilt — criminal cases

United States v. Perholtz, 842 F.2d 343 (D.C. Cir.), *cert. denied*, 109 S. Ct. 65 (1988): In a racketeering case involving procurement of Postal Service contracts, the Court held that a "script" prepared by one defendant for another person, in an effort to influence what he would say about the scheme, was evidence of consciousness of the defendants' role in the criminal scheme.

United States v. Tracy, 989 F.2d 1279 (1st Cir. 1993): The Court held that evidence of flight by a defendant is admissible as probative of a "guilty mind" if "there is an adequate factual predicate creating an inference of guilt of the crime charged." A sufficient factual predicate was established in this case: the defendant was scheduled for trial but left the state and did not appear, and independent evidence established his drug dealings. In *United States v. Kaplan*, 832 F.2d 676 (1st Cir. 1987), *cert. denied*, 108 S. Ct. 1080 (1988), the Court held that evidence that a lawyer-defendant removed files prior to a government search and that the government could not find them was properly admitted, since a jury could infer that the motive for such action by the defendant was something other than to protect client confidences. In *United States v. Pina,* 844 F.2d 1 (1st Cir. 1988), the Court noted that evidence the defendant allegedly threatened a witness had no probative value, since the witness had completed giving testimony and could not be influenced by the threat. Although the evidence was inflammatory, the Court held that its admission was harmless error.

United States v. Guerrero, 803 F.2d 783 (3d Cir. 1986): The Court affirmed drug convictions, holding that evidence that a defendant threatened an alleged coconspirator to discourage him from testifying was properly admitted with an immediate and appropriate limiting instruction. Although threat evidence may be admitted to prove consciousness of guilt, it can be extremely prejudicial, so the Judge should consider before admitting it "the importance and centrality to the ultimate issue in the case of the fact sought to be proved by the threat evidence, and the availability of other evidence to establish the fact sought to be proven by use of the threat evidence."

United States v. Cook, 580 F. Supp. 948 (N.D. W. Va. 1983), *aff'd,* 782 F.2d 1037 (4th Cir. 1986): Rejecting a new trial motion, the Court held that a jury could consider a defendant's flight as evidence, where he knew he was a suspect in a bombing investigation and he fled in response to an officer's approach only three days after being questioned about involvement in the bombing.

United States v. Myers, 550 F.2d 1036 (5th Cir. 1977), *cert. denied,* 439 U.S. 847 (1978): One ground for reversing the defendant's conviction for bank robbery was an erroneous instruction concerning flight. The Court said that the probative value of flight evidence depends upon the degree of confidence with which four inferences can be drawn: "(1) from the defendant's behavior to flight; (2) from flight to consciousness of guilt; (3) from consciousness of guilt to consciousness of guilt concerning the crime charged; and (4) from consciousness of guilt concerning the crime charged to actual guilt of the crime charged." Because flight evidence is inherently unreliable and dangerous, an instruction regarding the inference to be drawn from flight "is improper unless the evidence is sufficient to furnish reasonable support for all four of the necessary inferences." There must be actual evidence of flight, and the government must be able to show that the flight relates to the crime charged. "The more remote in time the alleged flight is from the commission or accusation of an offense, the greater the likelihood that it resulted from something other than feelings of guilt concerning that offense."

United States v. Touchstone, 726 F.2d 1116 (6th Cir. 1984): Affirming drug convictions, the Court held that the government was properly permitted to present evidence that the defendants fled after the trial commenced. The Court rejected the argument that flight almost three years after the crime charged was of very low probative value and stated that flight evidence "is generally admissible as evidence of guilt and that juries are given the power to determine 'how much weight should be given to such evidence.'"

United States v. Lewis, 797 F.2d 358 (7th Cir. 1986), *cert. denied,* 107 S. Ct. 1308 (1987): The Court affirmed a conviction for attempted extortion, holding that evidence that the defendant moved to a different hotel in New York City and assumed another alias after a warrant was issued for his arrest was properly admitted to show consciousness of guilt. In *United States v. Marks,* 816 F.2d 1207 (7th Cir. 1987), the Court affirmed convictions for conspiring to distribute marijuana, holding that evidence that a defendant threatened a government witness during trial was admissible to prove consciousness of a weak case, notwithstanding the assertion that the threat might have represented righteous indignation against a perjurer.

United States v. Eggleton, 799 F.2d 378 (8th Cir. 1986): Affirming a bank robbery conviction, the Court found that evidence that the defendant used false names and identification and fled after he learned that he was being sought in connection with the robbery was admissible to prove consciousness of guilt. In *United States v. Schepp,* 746 F.2d 406 (8th Cir. 1984), *cert. denied,* 469 U.S. 1215 (1985), the Court affirmed convictions arising out of a car bombing, holding that evidence of the defendant's flight from the city after learning that the FBI had made inquiries about him was properly admitted. See also *United States v. Hall,* 565 F.2d 1052 (8th Cir. 1977) (distortion of handwriting exemplars admissible).

Territory of Guam v. Ojeda, 758 F.2d 403 (9th Cir. 1985): The Court held that a burglary defendant's offer to pay damages to the victim if charges were dropped was admissible, since "statements need not be incriminating to be admissions." It found the offer to be relevant to show consciousness of guilt. In *United States v. Tille,* 729 F.2d 615 (9th Cir.), *cert. denied,* 105 S. Ct. 156, 164 (1984), the Court affirmed RICO convictions, upholding the admission of evidence that the defendant attempted to flee at the time of his arrest. Rejecting an argument that the evidence was not probative absent other evidence that the defendant was aware of the crime for which he was sought, the Court stated that "[t]he probative value of flight evidence depends on all of the circumstances and is a jury question" where "[t]he evidence was sufficient to permit an inference of knowledge of the crime at issue." In *United States v. Guerrero,* 756 F.2d 1342 (9th Cir.), *cert. denied,* 469 U.S. 934 (1984), the Court affirmed convictions for bank robbery and drug offenses, finding that evidence of an escape one day before the defendants were to be arraigned could be used to support an inference of consciousness of guilt. In *United States v. Miller,* 688 F.2d 652 (9th Cir. 1982), a prosecution for receipt of stolen goods, the Court upheld the introduction of photographs of a stolen trailer that showed alterations made after the theft. The photos supported an inference of knowledge that the property was stolen.

United States v. Hammond, 781 F.2d 1536 (11th Cir. 1986): In a prosecution of a pharmacist for illegally distributing controlled substances, the Court upheld the government's questioning of the defendant concerning various means, including offers of money, that he used to attempt to dissuade a witness from testifying. In *United States v. Griffin,* 778 F.2d 707 (11th Cir. 1985), the Court found reversible error in the admission of an agent's testimony that a conspirator had been served with a subpoena before he subsequently disappeared, when there was no charge that the defendant was responsible for the disappearance. In *United States v. De Parias,* 805 F.2d 1447 (11th Cir. 1986), *cert. denied,* 107 S. Ct. 3189 (1987), the Court affirmed extortion convictions, holding that evidence of a defendant's resisting arrest was admissible to demonstrate consciousness of guilt, even though the defendant was suspected of other crimes besides the one charged. Such evidence would be insufficient to prove guilt, however. In *United States v. Nabors,* 707 F.2d 1294 (11th Cir. 1983), *cert. denied,* 104

S. Ct. 1271 (1984), the Court found that evidence that a defendant, the named insured of an airplane, did not make a claim concerning the plane after it burned was admissible to show his involvement in a drug scheme in which the plane was used. The Court found no Fifth Amendment violation in using a failure to make a claim as evidence. See also *United States v. Beard,* 775 F.2d 1577 (11th Cir. 1985), *cert. denied,* 475 U.S. 1030 (1986) (permissible for marshal to testify that defendants switched shirts during trial break).

Consciousness of innocence

United States v. Biaggi, 909 F.2d 662 (2d Cir.), *cert. denied,* 110 S. Ct. 2018 (1990), 111 S. Ct. 1102 (1991): The Court reversed a defendant's convictions in a political corruption case because evidence that he had denied knowledge of others' wrongdoing, at a time when admitting such knowledge would have secured him immunity, was erroneously excluded. This evidence of "consciousness of innocence" tended to preclude a finding that he had knowledge of the wrongdoing.

Criminal cases — defense evidence

United States v. Carriger, 592 F.2d 312 (6th Cir. 1979): Reversing a conviction for income tax evasion, the Court held that certain promissory notes offered by the defendant to show his net worth were relevant and should have been admissible, even though no proof was offered of the underlying transactions.

United States v. Swink, 21 F.3d 852 (8th Cir. 1994): The Court reversed perjury convictions for, *inter alia,* excluding the testimony of the defendant's father. The father was a participant in the events and would have testified that the defendant did not fully understand the bond transactions he had entered into. The Trial Judge erred in concluding that the defendant knew his conduct was illegal, since that was a jury question and the father's testimony might have persuaded the jury that the defendant lacked criminal intent.

United States v. Thompson, 25 F.3d 1558 (11th Cir. 1994): A defendant charged with firearms offenses presented a defense of entrapment by estoppel, alleging that he had been given an oral grant of immunity in exchange for testimony in other cases. The Court held it was error to grant the government's motion *in limine* to exclude the evidence, even if the testimony regarding the alleged immunity agreement was not credible; if there were any basis to support the defendant's contention he had been told he could possess a firearm, the jury should have been permitted to hear the testimony and weigh it.

Economic testimony

Kearns v. Ford Motor Co., 726 F. Supp. 159 (E.D. Mich. 1989): In an action for patent infringement, the Court ruled on a motion *in limine* that evidence of the manufacturer's markup over manufacturing costs was irrelevant in calculating the reasonable royalty that would be negotiated by willing parties in an arm's-length transaction, but that the manufacturer's manufacturing costs would be relevant to that damages computation.

Pierce Packing Co. v. John Morrell & Co., 633 F.2d 1362 (9th Cir. 1980): In a suit for violating federal antitrust and state fair competition laws, the Court held that even though the relevant product market was "pork and pork products," evidence of sales ofunrelated products was admissible to show that the defendant's total sales were profitable and that pork sales were generally more profitable than other sales. The evidence undercut the claim that pork products were sold below marginal cost.

Examples of relevant circumstantial evidence — civil cases

Hobson v. Wilson, 556 F. Supp. 1157 (D.D.C. 1982), *modified,* 737 F.2d 1 (D.C. Cir. 1984), *cert. denied,* 105 S. Ct. 1843 (1985): In an action awarding damages for deprivation of First Amendment rights by police and FBI defendants, the Court concluded that the plaintiffs' FBI files were properly admitted as evidence so that the jury could fully understand the extent of the defendants' efforts to interfere with protected activities. The Court instructed the jury that the individual defendants were responsible only for their own actions. The Court also concluded that a leaflet, anonymously authored by an FBI agent who was not a defendant, that purported to come from an antiwar protestor was properly admitted, since there was credible evidence that such a document would not have been prepared without some review by various defendants.

DCPB, Inc. v. City of Lebanon, 957 F.2d 913 (1st Cir. 1992): The City defended a breach of contract action on the ground that the plaintiff consultant's charges were exorbitant. The Court held that evidence tending to show that the City withheld payment not because of overcharging but for purposes unrelated to the reasonableness of the invoices was probative of the City's real motives and thus relevant.

Schiavone Constr. Co. v. County of Nassau, 717 F.2d 747 (2d Cir. 1983): In an action by a construction company to recover the cost of repair work on a sewage pipeline, the Court held it was proper to admit specifications for backfill material that had been revised when the county attempted to lower the cost of the project. The Court found that the superseded specifications were relevant to the contractor's claim that the materials the county decided to use in later specifications were not suitable.

Cook v. Hoppin, 783 F.2d 684 (7th Cir. 1986): Although the Court reversed a judgment for a landlord in a suit by a tenant's visitor who sustained injuries in a fall from an exterior stairway, it found that a witness was properly permitted to testify that during one evening in the winter of 1979 she had heard two men arguing and had later seen one man lying on the ground near the spot where the plaintiff had fallen. Although she could not place the incident within a strict time frame or identify the fallen man, the Court concluded that the likelihood of two such occurrences happening in one winter was small enough that the evidence was relevant. In *Thronson v. Meisels,* 800 F.2d 136 (7th Cir. 1986), the Court affirmed a judgment for the plaintiffs in a housing discrimination case, holding that evidence of the plaintiffs' financial status was properly admitted to rebut the defendants' explanation that plaintiffs were rejected for housing because they lacked the financial resources to meet rental obligations. The Court also upheld admission of one defendant's statement that rental was denied because the plaintiffs were a "mixed couple," which statement had been admitted solely on the issue of damages.

MDU Resources Group v. W.R. Grace & Co., 14 F.3d 1274 (8th Cir.), *cert. denied,* 115 S. Ct. __ (1994): In an action by a building owner for expenses in removing asbestos fireproofing, the defendant contended that there was no nonasbestos substitute available when the building was constructed in 1968. The plaintiff presented evidence that replacement with a particular substitute was technologically feasible in the early 1970s, but was not permitted to introduce the product's 1943 trademark because the trademark did not by itself show that the product would be an adequate substitute. The Court held that exclusion was an abuse of discretion, since the defendant was denying that a substitute even existed in 1968, not just that it was not feasible then.

Examples of relevant circumstantial evidence — criminal cases

United States v. Fahey, 769 F.2d 829 (1st Cir. 1985): The Court sustained mail and wire fraud convictions, finding that evidence of a television news show's report on the practices of a gold investment company was properly admitted. The company made changes in its sales presentations in response to the broadcast but failed to change the operation of the company. In *United States v. Contenti,* 735 F.2d 628 (1st Cir. 1984), the Court found that the loans made to a defendant before and after a fire were relevant to show his financial position and a motive to burn down his business in order to seek insurance proceeds.

United States v. Amuso, 21 F.3d 1251 (2d Cir.), *cert. denied,* 115 S. Ct. __ (1994): In the prosecution of a mob boss for RICO and other offenses, the Court held there was no abuse of discretion in admitting evidence that a close associate's safe deposit box contained $200,000 in cash in a dog biscuit box. Together with testimony about the way the crime family's business was conducted and the modest incomes reported on the defendant's and his associate's tax returns, the evidence tended to make it more probable he was involved in illegal racketeering activities. In *United States v. Simmons,* 923 F.2d 934 (2d Cir.), *cert. denied,* 111 S. Ct. 2018, 112 S. Ct. 383 (1991), the Court affirmed RICO convictions arising out of a massive heroin distribution conspiracy, holding that evidence that the ringleader referred his attorney to other defendants and made benefactor payments to the attorney on their behalf was probative of a link among them. In *United States v. Diaz,* 878 F.2d 608 (2d Cir.), *cert. denied,* 110 S. Ct. 543 (1989), the Court held that evidence of apparent cocaine-related events near a house on February 20 were relevant in a conspiracy prosecution charging cocaine transactions at that house on May 7 because, together with evidence of other events connecting the house and a nearby public telephone to a conspiracy utilizing the house and the phone in its operations, it had a tendency to make more probable that the house was used on the latter date as a money "stash pad" for the charged cocaine operation. Furthermore, a Customs receipt evidencing the recent seizure of a truck and $999,960 in cash, found in the glove compartment of a vehicle in which all the defendants drove to the house on May 7 and in which two of them departed that day with $1,000,000 in cash, was relevant to the charge that the defendants possessed and concealed the cash proceeds of the conspiracy. In *United States v. Cruz,* 797 F.2d 90 (2d Cir. 1986), *cert. denied,* 107 S. Ct. 1631 (1987), the Court affirmed cocaine convictions, finding no error in the admission of evidence that a defendant had cash and food stamps in his possession when he left a surveillance area of a suspected narcotics exchange. Even though it was not very probative, the evidence was relevant to whether the defendant was the leader of the operation.

United States v. Russell, 971 F.2d 1098 (4th Cir.), *cert. denied,* 113 S. Ct. 1013 (1993): Affirming a murder conviction in a case in which no body or murder weapon was ever found, the Court held the following evidence relevant to the government's theory that the murder had been committed in a storage shed and the body transported to Pennsylvania and disposed of in a mine shaft: testimony that the defendant had purchased a gun; a tape recording of test firings conducted at the shed; testimony that the defendant had discussed the best means for committing suicide; expert testimony about blood splatter from a point-blank shot behind the ear; and testimony about the defendant's familiarity with Pennsylvania mining regions.

United States v. Dursaneau, 19 F.3d 1117 (6th Cir. 1994): In a prosecution for making false statements in a financial affidavit supporting a request for court-appointed counsel, the government sought to prove that the defendant used false names in order to conceal income and real estate. The Court held that evidence found in the defendant's home, including the title of a book about getting new ID and disappearing, a note containing references to deceased parties, and a death certificate and automobile license documents containing names the defendant allegedly used was relevant to prove the defendant was using aliases.

United States v. Sweeney, 688 F.2d 1131 (7th Cir. 1982): In a drug conspiracy case, the Court found that evidence of glassware apparently being used for innocent purposes was properly admitted because it could readily have been assembled into an apparatus for making drugs.

United States v. Westbrook, 896 F.2d 330 (8th Cir. 1990): The Court held in a prosecution for offenses involving amphetamine that the identity of the substance sold or manufactured could be proven by circumstantial evidence, including the name by which members of the conspiracy referred to the substance.

United States v. Blaylock, 20 F.3d 1458 (9th Cir. 1994): The Court reversed a firearm conviction, holding it was error to exclude medical records of the defendant offered to show that he was receiving medical treatment for a bad back at the time of his arrest. These records might have cast doubt on police officers' testimony that they saw the defendant running with a gun in his hand. Further, there was no risk justifying exclusion under Rule 403 that a reasonable jury would be misled by the contents, even without expert interpretation, as the records were written in plain language.

Experts

United States v. Carter, 522 F.2d 666 (D.C. Cir. 1975): The defendant's conviction for offenses related to a burglary was reversed because "doodles" that he made during the trial were admitted into evidence for comparison with a photo of a "doodle" found at the scene of the crime. An FBI agent testified that there was insufficient time to make a comparison of the handwriting and that more experienced agents concluded that there were insufficient points of comparison to warrant a conclusion as to whether the same "doodler" did all of the drawings. The Court concluded (2-1) that without expert evidence to support the comparison, "the exhibits, as offered, were not possessed of probative value."

United States v. Onumonu, 967 F.2d 782 (2d Cir. 1992): The defendant, charged with knowingly smuggling heroin from Nigeria in his alimentary canal, asserted he thought he was smuggling diamonds and offered an expert to testify to the feasibility and prevalence of smuggling diamonds in the same manner from Nigeria. The Court held it was error to exclude the testimony, as it was relevant to the defendant's subjective belief, did not fall under any of the Rule 403 exceptions to admissibility, and would have been helpful to a New York jury unlikely to be familiar with diamond smuggling out of Nigeria and even less so about the feasibility of smuggling diamonds by swallowing condoms. In *United States v. Torniero,* 735 F.2d 725 (2d Cir. 1984), *cert. denied,* 105 S. Ct. 788 (1985), a prosecution for transportation of stolen goods, the government's motion to exclude expert testimony on compulsive gambling was granted. Affirming, the Court stated that "we do not believe that an hypothesis subscribed to by only a small number of professionals establishes that a proposed defense can carry the day on relevance." Assuming arguendo that compulsive gambling could be a mental disease or defect, the Court agreed that there was no demonstrable connection with this mental disease or defect and the offense charged in this case, so the proffered evidence was irrelevant. This result anticipated the Supreme Court's holding in *Daubert v. Merrell Dow Pharmaceuticals, Inc.,* that expert testimony could be excluded on relevance grounds if it did not connect with or "fit" the facts (see Editorial Explanatory Comment to Rule 702).

Blancha v. Raymark Indus., 972 F.2d 507 (3d Cir. 1992): In an asbestos case, the plaintiffs' theory was that all asbestos could cause the decedent's mesothelioma; the defendant's expert indicated that asbestos products containing chrysotile did not cause mesothelioma. After a verdict for the defendant, a new trial was granted, first on the ground that the expert's testimony was irrelevant without evidence that the defendant's product contained chrysotile, and later (on reconsideration) on the ground that the jury might have been confused by the expert testimony in the absence of evidence about the defendant's product. Reversing a judgment for the plaintiff on the new trial, the Court held that the expert's testimony was relevant, given the theory advanced and the plaintiffs' burden of proof on proximate causation, and that the danger of confusion did not so clearly outweigh the probative value of the expert's testimony as to justify exclusion.

United States v. Gillis, 773 F.2d 549 (4th Cir. 1985): The Court affirmed a defendant's convictions for involvement with stolen property and held that expert testimony concerning pathological gambling was properly excluded where there was no causal connection between the condition and the offenses charged.

United States v. Hartmann, 958 F.2d 774 (7th Cir. 1992): A man was murdered as part of a scheme by his wife and others to defraud life insurance companies. The Court held that even though only fraud was charged, it was not an abuse of discretion to admit expert testimony regarding the brutal manner in which the victim was slain, since the evidence provided corroboration and enhanced the credibility of conspirators' out-of-court admissions. In *United States v. Davis,* 772 F.2d 1339 (7th Cir.), *cert. denied,* 474 U.S. 1036 (1985), the Court upheld convictions for defrauding the government, finding no error in exclusion of expert testimony concerning the defendant's compulsive gambling that was offered to support an insanity defense. The Court noted that the witness had not shown that she was qualified to testify on the disputed issues, and that there was no nexus shown between the gambling and the failure to refrain from stealing money.

United States v. Hernando Ospina, 798 F.2d 1570 (11th Cir. 1986): Affirming convictions for various financial reporting requirement offenses growing out of a scheme to launder drug proceeds, the Court found that testimony by dog handlers that narcotic detector dogs reacted positively to the presence of narcotic residue on currency was relevant.

Failure to produce evidence

Simon v. Commissioner, 830 F.2d 499 (3d Cir. 1987): Affirming a Tax Court determination of deficiencies, the Court reasoned that it was permissible to infer from the failure of the taxpayers to adduce testimony from persons who were substantially involved in structuring financial transactions that their testimony would not have supported the taxpayer's claim that the transactions were engaged in to make a profit. In *Gumbs v. International Harvester, Inc.,* 718 F.2d 88 (3d Cir. 1983), the Court vacated a judgment for the plaintiff in a product liability action, noting that it would be improper to instruct the jury that it could draw an adverse inference from the defendant's failure to produce certain evidence. The Court recognized that "[t]he unexplained failure or refusal of a party ... to produce evidence that would tend to throw light on the issues authorizes, under certain circumstances, an inference or a presumption unfavorable to such party," but it found that there was no indication on the facts that the defendant either had the missing evidence or had willfully destroyed it.

Tyler v. White, 811 F.2d 1204 (8th Cir. 1987): Affirming a judgment for prison officers sued by inmates, the Court found it was error (but harmless) to rule that counsel for some defendants could ask the jury to infer from the plaintiffs' failure to call other defendants as witnesses that their testimony would have been unfavorable to the plaintiffs. Where, as in this case, a witness would likely be prejudiced against a party, no such inference is proper.

Identity

United States v. Foster, 986 F.2d 541 (D.C. Cir. 1993): The Court reversed a conviction for distributing crack cocaine because the defense had not been permitted to cross-examine officers about their ability to identify other persons they mentioned in connection with the transaction. The answers to the questions would have made it more or less probable that the officers had correctly identified the defendant, so relevancy objections should have been overruled. Under the Rules, evidence is either relevant or it is not; there is no such thing as "marginally relevant" evidence.

United States v. Ewings, 936 F.2d 903 (7th Cir. 1991): Affirming the defendant's conviction for fraudulently procuring insurance policies on his niece's life, the Court held that evidence he engaged in a colorful spending spree with the insurance proceeds should not have been admitted on the issue of his intent or motive, but it was relevant to rebut his argument that insurance agents who took the applications had committed the fraud.

Illustrative evidence

Wetherill v. University of Chicago, 565 F. Supp. 1553 (N.D. Ill. 1983): The Court ruled *in limine* in a suit against the University and a drug manufacturer that a colposcopic photograph (of the cervix and vagina) taken from a textbook could be used for illustrative purposes.

Impeachment

United States v. Brown, 938 F.2d 1482 (1st Cir.), *cert. denied,* 112 S. Ct. 611 (1991): Affirming convictions for passing counterfeit notes, the Court held it was error, but harmless, to exclude evidence that State court proceedings against a prosecution witness had been dropped the day after he testified, as the evidence clearly went to the issue of bias. In *United States v. Goguen,* 723 F.2d 1012 (1st Cir. 1983), the Court held that evidence about the size of a fire was properly admitted in a prosecution for making a false statement to show that the defendant would have remembered whether he was in the vicinity of the fire.

Schiavone Constr. Co. v. County of Nassau, 717 F.2d 747 (2d Cir. 1983): In an action by a construction company to recover the cost of repair work on a sewage pipeline, the Court held it was proper to admit specifications for backfill material that had been revised when the county attempted to lower the cost of the project. The Court found that the superseded specifications were relevant to the contractor's claim that the materials the county decided to use in later specifications were not suitable.

United States v. Benson, 941 F.2d 598 (1991), *amended,* 957 F.2d 301 (7th Cir. 1992): Reviewing a tax evasion conviction, the Court noted that a witness' statement advising jurors in criminal tax cases to vote not guilty regardless of the law was probative on whether the witness might not regard an oath as binding.

United States v. Spethz, 721 F.2d 1457 (9th Cir. 1983): Affirming convictions on drug charges, the Court found that a book concerning drugs was properly admitted to impeach a father's claim on direct examination that he had no inkling that his son (a defendant) knew about drug dealing, since the father had admitted reading or looking through the book and talking about it with his son.

Whiteley v. OKC Corp., 719 F.2d 1051 (10th Cir. 1983): The Court affirmed a judgment for the plaintiff in a breach of warranty action for personal injuries from defective propane. The Court noted that as a general rule it is impermissible to admit evidence of a party's financial condition "unless necessary to determine the damages sustained," but it found that the defendant opened the door to testimony about its financial condition by eliciting testimony that was intended to show its impecunious condition.

Inconsistent witnesses

United States v. Roman, 728 F.2d 846 (7th Cir.), *cert. denied,* 104 S. Ct. 2360 (1984): The Court affirmed a conviction for conspiring to distribute LSD, rejecting an argument that it was error not to strike the testimony of two witnesses as being too inconsistent and confusing. The credibility of the witnesses was a question for the jury.

Innocent explanations

United States v. Martel, 792 F.2d 630 (7th Cir. 1986): Affirming convictions of a defense contractor and two principal officers for conspiring to make false statements to the United States, the Court held that a letter from an employee of the contractor to one of the individual defendants was properly admitted even though its author testified and offered an innocent explanation for it. The Court observed that "a rule requiring a trial judge to accept as true a witness' testimony would eviscerate the jury's historic function of assessing the credibility of witnesses."

Intent, knowledge, motive, plan

United States v. St. Michael's Credit Union, 880 F.2d 579 (1st Cir. 1989): In a prosecution of a credit union and its bookkeeper for failing to file currency transaction reports, the government offered evidence that the bookkeeper's father was involved in a gambling operation as probative of her motive and intent in failing to file the reports. The Court held that the evidence was irrelevant because there was no evidence the bookkeeper knew of her father's gambling activities, and its admission was prejudicial error because she might have been convicted on guilt by association. In *United States v. Nichols,* 820 F.2d 508 (1st Cir. 1987), the Court affirmed convictions for conspiracy and theft of government property, holding that evidence offered by a defendant who was employed as a Customs officer that Customs may have "set him up" in retaliation for an investigation he had made was irrelevant. It observed that no entrapment defense was raised and no motion was made to dismiss the indictment on vindictive prosecution grounds. In *United States v. Goguen,* 723 F.2d 1012 (1st Cir. 1983), a prosecution for knowingly making a false statement to a grand jury, the Court upheld the exclusion of recantation evidence. It found that a false statement prosecution, unlike a perjury prosecution, which requires proof of an intent to deceive, requires the government to prove only that the defendant knew he was making false statements. The Court reasoned that a later retraction may be excluded as tangential when the only question is knowledge at the time of the testimony.

United States v. Harwood, 998 F.2d 91 (2d Cir.), *cert. denied,* 114 S. Ct. 456 (1993), 893 (1994): The Court held it was error to permit DEA agents to testify that they learned from intelligence sources that the defendant had a large supply of LSD. This was inadmissible hearsay and it could not be offered as "background" to explain why the officers approached the defendant for an undercover buy, because the officers' motive in approaching the defendant were irrelevant to the case. In *United States v. Biaggi,* 909 F.2d 662 (2d Cir.), *cert. denied,* 110 S. Ct. 2018 (1990), 111 S. Ct. 1102 (1991), the Court reversed a defendant's convictions in a political corruption case because evidence that he had denied knowledge of others' wrongdoing, at a time when admitting such knowledge would have secured him immunity, was erroneously excluded. This evidence of "consciousness of innocence" tended to preclude a finding that he had knowledge of the wrongdoing.

United States v. Copple, 24 F.3d 434 (3d Cir. 1994): In a mail fraud prosecution arising from a scheme to invest "pre-need" funds of funeral directors, the Court held that evidence of the extent of the victims' losses could be probative of the defendant's intent to convert the funds to his personal use. However, the victims' testimony about the personal tragedies they suffered was unfairly prejudicial; but the error in admitting that evidence was harmless. In *Williams v. Borough of West Chester, Pa.,* 891 F.2d 458 (3d Cir. 1989), the Court affirmed a summary judgment for the defendants in a civil rights action brought on behalf of an arrestee who hanged himself in his cell, holding that an affidavit stating that the arrestee's suicidal tendencies were widely known in the police department would be admissible to contradict the defendant officers' denial of such knowledge, but it was insufficient to create a genuine issue of material fact.

Aetna Cas. & Sur. Co. v. Guynes, 713 F.2d 1187 (5th Cir. 1983): An insurance company claimed arson by the insureds under a home fire insurance policy, and also that the insureds had misrepresented facts in seeking to recover on the policy. Affirming a judgment for the insureds, the Court held it was proper to exclude evidence that one of the insureds was allegedly involved in a conspiracy with a close relative to commit insurance fraud, since there was no evidence tying that fraud to an intent to commit arson.

United States v. Ewings, 936 F.2d 903 (7th Cir. 1991): Affirming the defendant's conviction for fraudulently procuring insurance policies on his niece's life, the Court held that evidence he engaged in a colorful spending spree with the insurance proceeds should not have been admitted on the issue of his intent or motive, but it was relevant to rebut the defendant's argument that insurance agents who took the applications had committed the fraud. In *United States v. Touloumis,* 771 F.2d 235 (7th Cir. 1985), the Court upheld the admission in an extortionate credit prosecution of a gun found on a person other than the defendant. One means of the defendant's collecting a debt was the threat of violence from this other person.

United States v. Swink, 21 F.3d 852 (8th Cir. 1994): The Court reversed perjury convictions for, *inter alia,* excluding the testimony of the defendant's father. The father was a participant in the events and would have testified that the defendant did not fully understand the bond transactions he had entered into. The Trial Judge erred in concluding that the defendant knew his conduct was illegal, since that was a jury question and the father's testimony might have persuaded the jury that the defendant lacked criminal intent. In *United States v. Eckmann,* 656 F.2d 308 (8th Cir. 1981), the Court reversed a conviction for receiving stolen merchandise, finding it was error to admit evidence showing that other prospective purchasers of the merchandise decided not to buy. This evidence was irrelevant to the appellant's intent and may have suggested to the jury that somehow he should be held to a standard of what others did rather than to a knowledge standard.

United States v. Hernandez-Miranda, 601 F.2d 1104 (9th Cir. 1979): The Court held it was error (but harmless) to admit evidence that a defendant charged with smuggling heroin in an auto had previously carried marijuana across the border in a backpack, since there was no logical basis to connect the two events. Unfortunately, the definition of relevance used by the Court was that it must be "more probable than not" that a person who has knowingly smuggled marijuana on his person will know of the presence of contraband concealed in a vehicle. This is the wrong test of relevance. The evidence would have been relevant if it had "any tendency" to make intent seem more likely than if there were no such evidence. Of course, a Rule 403 balancing analysis still might have warranted exclusion, but the Court never reached the stage of balancing in this case.

United States v. Kelly, 888 F.2d 732 (11th Cir. 1989): The Court reversed a criminal defense attorney's conviction for conspiring with clients to distribute cocaine on the ground, *inter alia,* that he should have been permitted to testify regarding his understanding of his professional obligations as an attorney, as that would have been relevant to the crucial issue of his state of mind regarding his dealings with his clients.

Invocation of privilege

Brink's, Inc. v. City of New York, 539 F. Supp. 1139 (S.D.N.Y. 1982), *aff'd,* 717 F.2d 700 (2d Cir. 1983): The City brought an action against Brink's claiming that the company's employees stole parking meter revenues. Brink's filed a third-party claim for indemnification against 16 employees. In pretrial depositions the suspected employees invoked the privilege against self-incrimination in response to questions about whether they ever stole money or knew of employees who did. The Trial Judge held that the employees could be called to testify against Brink's at trial even though they might well invoke the privilege again, saying that invocation of the privilege was relevant both in the City's action against Brink's and in the company's action for indemnification. After finding that there is no constitutional bar against drawing adverse inferences in a civil case from a witness' invocation of the self-incrimination privilege, the majority in the Court of Appeals agreed that the probative value of the adverse inference was not outweighed by the prejudicial effect of the evidence. One Judge dissented, arguing that "permitting the systematic interrogation of witnesses on direct examination by counsel who knows they will assert the privilege against self-incrimination ... allows juries to draw prejudicial inferences from leading questions put to witnesses, denies parties the right to cross-examine, and is an invitation to sharp practices." See also *Penfield v. Venuti,* 589 F. Supp. 250 (D. Conn. 1984) (defendant's assertion of self-incrimination privilege in response to deposition question concerning his whereabouts at time of car-motorcycle accident could be used as evidence against him at trial, even though he offered to answer the question at a second deposition); *SEC v. Netelkos,* 592 F. Supp. 906 (S.D.N.Y. 1984) (granting SEC injunction against securities laws violations, Court draws adverse inference from defendants' invocation of self-incrimination privilege); *RSO Records, Inc. v. Peri,* 596 F. Supp. 849 (S.D.N.Y. 1984) (adverse inference drawn from defendant's self-incrimination privilege claim in copyright infringement case).

RAD Servs. v. Aetna Cas. & Sur. Co., 808 F.2d 271 (3d Cir. 1987): Affirming a judgment for an insurer in an action by a company to recover costs incurred in disposing of hazardous waste, the Court held that a jury was properly permitted to infer from company agents' invocation during depositions of the self-incrimination privilege with respect to critical facts that their answers would have been adverse to the company. It reasoned that "[a]n employee's self-interest would counsel him to exculpate his employer, if possible.'' Although that was not equally true for past employees, the Court declined to hold invocations of the privilege to be per se inadmissible, since a witness bent on incriminating a former employer would likely offer damaging testimony rather than hope for an adverse inference, and an employer could stymie the discovery process by discharging employees potentially responsible for wrongdoing. In *Lionti v. Lloyd's Ins. Co.,* 709 F.2d 237 (3d Cir.), *cert. denied,* 104 S. Ct. 490 (1983), the insurer alleged in an action on a fire insurance policy that the insured burned down the building. A former employee called by the insurer to rebut a suggestion that this employee actually might have been responsible for the burning invoked the Fifth Amendment when asked whether he was involved in the fire. The insurer subsequently produced an investigator to testify that an hour before testifying, the witness had said that he had nothing to do with the fire. Because the Trial Judge told the jury that the witness' invocation of the privilege had no evidentiary value, the Court concluded that the investigator's testimony could not properly have been used to impeach the witness. Thus, it was hearsay and should not have been admitted, although the error was harmless. The dissenting Judge disagreed with the majority's implicit holding that a nonparty witness' invocation of the privilege could have evidentiary value.

In re Tudor Assoc., Ltd., II, 20 F.3d 115 (4th Cir. 1994): The Court held, in a bankruptcy proceeding to set aside a transfer of the debtor's property on grounds of fraud, that no inference could be drawn from the transferees' proper invocation of the attorney-client privilege to disqualify them as good faith purchasers for value. In *Morley v. Cohen,* 888 F.2d 1006 (4th Cir. 1989), a civil RICO action arising out of an allegedly fraudulent tax shelter, the Court held there had been no abuse of discretion in denying the defendant's motion *in limine* to restrict the scope of cross-examination if he should testify so that he would not have to assert his self-incrimination privilege before the jury regarding a pending criminal investigation of another fraudulent scheme. Drawing an adverse inference from a claim of the privilege is permissible in a civil action.

Farace v. Independent Fire Ins. Co., 699 F.2d 204 (5th Cir. 1983): Judgments for a husband and wife in their suit to recover fire insurance proceeds were affirmed. The Court held there was no error in excluding evidence, offered to impeach the husband, that he had asserted his privilege against self-incrimination in a fire marshal's investigation. The evidence had little probative value, especially since the defendant conceded that the husband cooperated fully in its investigation, and a jury might attach undue weight to the claim of the privilege.

Mayer v. Angelica, 790 F.2d 1315 (7th Cir.), *cert. denied,* 107 S. Ct. 891 (1986): The Court reversed a judgment for the plaintiff in an action alleging racketeering and fraud in the sale of gemstones, holding that the assertion of the privilege at a deposition by a nonparty witness, a codefendant who had settled, could not be used to authenticate letters written by the codefendant. In *Lenard v. Argento,* 699 F.2d 874 (7th Cir.), *cert. denied,* 104 S. Ct. 69 (1983), a civil rights action arising from the plaintiff's arrest at the scene of an auto accident, the Court upheld a ruling barring any inquiry into whether the defendant police officers invoked their self-incrimination privilege during internal police and grand jury investigations. In *Old Security Life Ins. Co. v. Continental Ill. Nat'l Bank & Trust Co.,* 740 F.2d 1384 (7th Cir. 1984), the Court affirmed a judgment for a group insurance fund that had intervened in an action by an insurance company against a bank.

The fund claimed a superior right to any recovery that the insurance company obtained. Since the insurance company failed to prove any malfeasance by the fund's trustees, it was unnecessary to draw an adverse inference against the fund from the fact that three trustees exercised their privilege against self-incrimination.

Cerro Gordo Charity v. Fireman's Fund Am. Life Ins. Co., 819 F.2d 1471 (8th Cir. 1987): A charitable trust created by an insured's brother sued to recover the proceeds of life insurance policies after the insured was murdered; the defense was that the policies were obtained as part of a scheme to defraud the insurer. Affirming a judgment for the defendant, the Court held that the company was properly permitted to call the insured's brother to the stand and to question him, despite knowledge that he would invoke his privilege against self-incrimination. Since the brother had been a member of the charitable entity, there was some reason to believe that he retained loyalty to the entity at the time of trial, and there was some evidence that he might have resigned from the entity as a matter of litigation strategy, so the Court held that it was proper to call the brother and permit the jury to infer from his unwillingness to testify that he probably did the acts alleged against him. However, in *United States v. Doddington,* 822 F.2d 818 (8th Cir. 1987), the Court said that "a defendant does not have the right to call a witness to the stand simply to force invocation of the right against self-incrimination in the presence of a jury," since neither side may benefit from inferences drawn from assertion of the privilege. The entire testimony of a defense witness who refused to answer questions on cross-examination was held properly stricken. In *Rosebud Sioux Tribe v. A & P Steel, Inc.,* 733 F.2d 509 (8th Cir.), *cert. denied,* 105 S. Ct. 565 (1984), a suit arising out of a contract to develop an irrigation system on the Tribe's land, the chairperson of a tribal subsidiary responsible for all land owned by the Tribe gave deposition testimony flatly contradicting the Tribe's complaint. The Tribe unsuccessfully objected to admission of the deposition, while the defendant successfully objected to the Tribe's calling the witness to the stand, since it was clear he would invoke his self-incrimination privilege. After entry of judgment for the defendant, the witness admitted before a federal grand jury that he had perjured himself during the deposition. This was enough, the Court found, to warrant a new trial. The Court went on to say that the Tribe should have been allowed to call the witness to the stand despite his intention to invoke the privilege, reasoning that the Tribe could not cross-examine the witness and "[o]nce the deposition was allowed into evidence, it was necessary to allow the Tribe to call [the] witness in order to offset the unfair advantage A & P gained by being allowed to use the deposition." It cited Rules 501 and 102 in support of its reasoning and commented that permitting the use of the deposition with the witness rendered unavailable amounted to "an unfair manipulation of the rules of evidence and procedure, which succeeded in obscuring the truth."

United States v. Larranaga, 787 F.2d 489 (10th Cir. 1986): The Court affirmed a perjury conviction, finding no error in the exclusion of evidence that a government witness previously refused to testify before a grand jury on self-incrimination grounds, as the evidence lacked probative value. In *United States v. Hart,* 729 F.2d 662 (10th Cir. 1984), *cert. denied,* 105 S. Ct. 914 (1985), the Court affirmed firearms convictions, finding that the Trial Judge properly refused to permit the defendant to force a witness to assert his privilege against self-incrimination before the jury. Since the jury could draw no inference from the privilege claim, the Court found that the defendant had no right to have the jury hear the witness claim his privilege.

Allstate Ins. Co. v. James, 845 F.2d 315 (11th Cir. 1988): The Court reversed a judgment voiding a home insurance policy, concluding that evidence that the homeowners refused to answer questions during a criminal investigation of a fire should have been excluded. The homeowners had cooperated on two occasions and could have inferred that they were the subject of an investigation, so ''[t]he fact that they chose to exercise their Constitutional rights as explained to them upon the advice of their attorney provides little probative evidence of their involvement'' and was prejudicial, particularly because the fire marshal testified concerning the refusal to answer questions and the jury was unaware that the homeowners were exercising their constitutional rights upon advice of counsel.

Irrelevant evidence — civil cases

McDonald v. Piedmont Aviation, Inc., 930 F.2d 220 (2d Cir.), *cert. denied,* 112 S. Ct. 441 (1991): The Court held there was no error in excluding the defendant airline's evidence of a pilot's qualifications in his suit for violation of preferential hiring requirements. Because the airline did not have any of the information at the time it refused to hire the plaintiff, the evidence was irrelevant. In *Schneider v. Revici,* 817 F.2d 987 (2d Cir. 1987), the Court remanded a medical malpractice action for a trial on an assumption of risk defense. The Court identified several items of evidence introduced by the plaintiff that were of doubtful relevance, including a suspension of the defendant's license and a suspension of Medicaid payments to a drug treatment program he administered some twenty years earlier, but declined to disturb the jury's finding of malpractice. Admission of the evidence was harmless, since the jury was told that the license and the payments were reinstated. In *Shatkin v. McDonnell Douglas Corp.,* 727 F.2d 202 (2d Cir. 1984), a suit by the mother of an airline passenger killed in a crash, the Court held there was no error in excluding evidence of her financial needs and of the deceased's probable future income. The mother had offered virtually no evidence that the deceased would support her or of the amount of any support he would offer, and because she was only a secondary beneficiary under the deceased's will, she would have received nothing had his wife lived.

American Home Assur. Co. v. Sunshine Supermarket, 753 F.2d 321 (3d Cir. 1985): In an action on a fire insurance policy, the Trial Judge ruled *in limine* that evidence that the insured was not prosecuted for arson could be admitted if the company relied on opinions by local fire officials that the insured was responsible for the fire. Holding the ruling erroneous, the Court said that evidence of nonprosecution is not very probative, given the different standard of proof in civil and criminal cases and the discretion of a prosecutor not to bring charges. The nonprosecution evidence did not rebut the opinion testimony of fire officials and therefore should have been excluded. In *Leeds v. Cincinnati, Inc.,* 732 F.2d 1194 (3d Cir. 1984), a product liability action, the Court found that a patent document offered by the plaintiff to prove that the defendant had notice of a problem with a machine was properly excluded. New Jersey irrebuttably presumes that a manufacturer has knowledge of the dangerous propensities of its products, so the proffered evidence "was at worst irrelevant and at most cumulative in that it wasted time."

Phillips v. Western Co. of N. Am., 953 F.2d 923 (5th Cir. 1992): In an oil rig worker's Jones Act case, the Court granted a new trial to determine whether disability and other payments he received following the accident were collateral benefits. Given the substantive rule under the Act denying a tortfeasor any reduction of its liability for payments from collateral sources, collateral benefits evidence would be irrelevant and should not be admitted. In *Pregeant v. Pan Am. World Airways,* 762 F.2d 1245 (5th Cir. 1985), the Court held it was error (but harmless) to admit evidence of cockpit conversations that the passengers could not hear in an action seeking damages for preimpact fear on the part of passengers killed in a plane crash. In *Aetna Cas. & Sur. Co. v. Guynes,* 713 F.2d 1187 (5th Cir. 1983), the company claimed arson by the insureds under a home fire insurance policy, and also that the insureds had misrepresented facts in seeking to recover on the policy. Affirming a judgment for the insureds, the Court held it was proper to exclude evidence that one of the insureds was allegedly involved in a conspiracy with a close relative to commit insurance fraud, since there was no evidence tying that fraud to an intent to commit arson. In *Goff v. Continental Oil Co.,* 678 F.2d 593 (5th Cir. 1982), an employment discrimination action, the Court upheld a ruling excluding evidence that the defendant had also discriminated against three other former employees. Since plaintiff alleged individual discrimination, the other acts were irrelevant. Without deciding whether a pattern or practice of discrimination could be proved to support a claim of individualized discrimination, the Court found that the three other claims of discrimination were too sporadic and isolated to establish any pattern or practice.

Turner v. Allstate Ins. Co., 902 F.2d 1208 (6th Cir. 1990): In a former agent's actfon for wrongful discharge, the Court held that statistical evidence offered by the defendant insurance company as tending to prove its good faith or reasonableness was properly excluded when the plaintiff conceded good faith and disputed only that he had falsified documents. A dissenting Judge thought the statistical evidence that a particular discount was given the plaintiff's clients at a rate four times the statewide average was probative on whether he was shorting or defrauding his employer. In *Kelly's Auto Parts, No. 1, Inc. v. Boughton,* 809 F.2d 1247 (6th Cir. 1987), an action by insureds to recover on a fire insurance policy, the Court held that evidence that the insured's sole shareholder was not prosecuted for arson was properly excluded. The Court relied on cases that had reasoned as follows: a criminal prosecution may not be brought as a result of the exercise of prosecutorial discretion based upon factors not relevant to a civil suit, the decision not to prosecute was a type of opinion evidence that was not very helpful, and the burden of persuasion in a criminal prosecution is different from a civil suit. See also *Salamey v. Aetna Cas. & Sur. Co.,* 741 F.2d 874 (6th Cir. 1984) (evidence that an insured's father changed ownership of his store a year after the insured's store burned down was irrelevant in a suit by the insured to recover on a fire insurance policy).

Fortino v. Quasar Co., 950 F.2d 389 (7th Cir. 1991): Reversing judgments for plaintiffs allegedly discharged because of national origin and age discrimination, the Court held that it was error to admit a videotaped speech by one of the defendant's executives that indicated age discrimination, as none of the plaintiffs was in the executive's group and he had no role in their discharge or in that of any other employee. In those circumstances, his comments had no probative value and, being prejudicial, were inadmissible. In *Sherrod v. Berry,* 856 F.2d 802 (7th Cir. 1988) (en banc), the Court reversed a panel opinion and held it was error to admit evidence that the plaintiff was unarmed in a § 1983 action brought against police officers for use of excessive force. The Court said that the evidence was irrelevant to deciding whether the officer acted reasonably, which under the applicable law depended on the circumstances known to him at the time. The evidence was also irrelevant for impeachment and it tended to lead the jury to make its decision on an improper basis. Two Judges dissented on the ground that the evidence was relevant to how the decedent moved before he was attacked by the police officers. In *Lenard v. Argento,* 699 F.2d 874 (7th Cir.), *cert. denied,* 104 S. Ct. 69 (1983), a civil rights action arising from the plaintiff's arrest at the scene of an auto accident, the Court held it was not error to exclude evidence that defendant police officers had been suspended thirty days following their guilty pleas to bribery charges, as the evidence was not probative of the defendant village's intent to condone misconduct.

Campbell v. Vinjamuri, 19 F.3d 1274 (8th Cir. 1994): Affirming a judgment against the plaintiff in a medical malpractice action, the Court held there was no abuse of discretion in excluding evidence that a defendant had failed the board-certifying examination in anesthesiology on several occasions, as his performance on a written or oral examination was not probative of his ability to meet the standard of care of properly positioning the plaintiff's head on the specific occasion.

Irrelevant evidence — criminal cases

United States v. Doe, 903 F.2d 16 (D.C. Cir. 1990): A black American and two Jamaicans were jointly charged with drug offenses. The Court reversed their convictions, in part because a detective was permitted to testify to the *modus operandi* of Jamaican drug dealers and how the market "has been taken over basically by Jamaicans"; comments of the latter sort had no bearing on any issue in the trial and were openly allusive in linking the charges to the defendants solely on the basis of the ancestry of two of them. In *United States v. Carter,* 522 F.2d 666 (D.C. Cir. 1975), the defendant's conviction for offenses related to a burglary was reversed because "doodles" that he made during the trial were admitted into evidence for comparison with a photo of a "doodle" found at the scene of the crime. An FBI agent testified that there was insufficient time to make a comparison of the handwriting and that more experienced agents concluded that there were insufficient points of comparison to warrant a conclusion as to whether the same "doodler" did all of the drawings. The Court concluded (2-1) that without expert evidence to support the comparison, "the exhibits, as offered, were not possessed of probative value."

United States v. Brandon, 17 F.3d 409 (1st Cir.), *cert. denied,* 115 S. Ct. __ (1994): Affirming convictions for bank fraud arising out of a scheme to falsify down payments, the Court held there was no abuse of discretion in excluding defense evidence that 100% financing was common at the time, as a no-down-payment custom does not establish a fake down payment custom and it would have no relevance to whether the defendants knew of, or intended to violate, the bank's down payment requirement. In *United States v. Spinosa,* 982 F.2d 620 (1st Cir. 1992), a prosecution for cocaine distribution, the

Irrelevant evidence — criminal cases (cont'd)

Court held it was an error (but harmless) to admit testimony by a detective that when he called three New York numbers on the defendant's telephone records, two connected to beepers and the third was disconnected. The calls were made six months after the transactions at issue and the detective had no information about who subscribed to the numbers at the earlier time when they were called from the defendant's phone; neither was there any evidence explaining the relevance to drug dealing that two of the numbers connected to beepers rather than to standard telephones. In *United States v. St. Michael's Credit Union,* 880 F.2d 579 (1st Cir. 1989), a prosecution of a credit union and its bookkeeper for failing to file currency transaction reports, the government offered evidence that the bookkeeper's father was involved in a gambling operation as probative of her motive and intent in failing to file the reports. The Court held that the evidence was irrelevant because there was no evidence the bookkeeper knew of her father's gambling activities, and its admission was prejudicial error because she might have been convicted on guilt by association. In *United States v. Nichols,* 820 F.2d 508 (1st Cir. 1987), the Court affirmed convictions for conspiracy and theft of government property, holding that evidence offered by a defendant who was employed as a Customs officer that Customs may have "set him up" in retaliation for an investigation he had made was irrelevant. It observed that no entrapment defense was raised and no motion was made to dismiss the indictment on vindictive prosecution grounds. In *United States v. Goguen,* 723 F.2d 1012 (1st Cir. 1983), a prosecution for knowingly making a false statement to a grand jury, the Court upheld the exclusion of recantation evidence. It found that a false statement prosecution, unlike a perjury prosecution, which requires proof of an intent to deceive, requires the government to prove only that the defendant knew he was making false statements. The Court reasoned that a later retraction may be excluded as tangential when the only question is knowledge at the time of the testimony.

United States v. Harwood, 998 F.2d 91 (2d Cir.), *cert. denied,* 114 S. Ct. 456 (1993), 893 (1994): The Court held it was error to permit DEA agents to testify that they learned from intelligence sources that the defendant had a large supply of LSD. This was inadmissible hearsay and it could not be offered as "background" to explain why the officers approached the defendant for an undercover buy, because the officers' motive in approaching the defendant was irrelevant to the case. In *United States v. Bifield,* 702 F.2d 342 (2d Cir.), *cert. denied,* 461 U.S. 931 (1983), the Court held that a defendant charged with escape could not claim the benefit of a duress defense, and upheld a ruling excluding testimony concerning duress. It rejected the defendant's constitutional claim that the exclusion of the evidence denied him the right to testify in his own behalf.

United States v. Kang, 934 F.2d 621 (5th Cir. 1991): In a prosecution for bribing an IRS agent, the defendant had stipulated to willful commission of the offense and asserted only an entrapment defense. The Court reversed his conviction, finding an abuse of discretion in admitting evidence of the defendant's flight. It was not relevant to show his predisposition or the manner of the government's investigation; thus, it was not only arguably inadmissible under Rule 403 balancing because of the risk of prejudice, but it was also inadmissible under Rule 401 on relevancy grounds. In *United States v. Reeves,* 892 F.2d 1223 (5th Cir. 1990), the Court affirmed convictions for extortion, holding there was no abuse of discretion in excluding evidence, offered on an entrapment defense, of a government witness' remote and unrelated contact with State officials, as it was not pertinent to the defendants' predisposition to commit the crimes charged. In *United States v. Hernandez,* 750 F.2d 1256 (5th Cir. 1985), the Court reversed cocaine convictions because a government witness was permitted to testify that U.S. Customs had identified the defendant as a drug smuggler. The testimony was hearsay and could not be used to prove the state of mind of the witness, a DEA agent, since his state of mind was irrelevant. See also *United States v. Hall,* 653 F.2d 1002 (5th Cir. 1981) (drug convictions reversed because testimony of a drug agent, offered to explain the absence of physical evidence, that it is not always possible to make a "controlled buy" in drug investigations added nothing to the government's case against the defendant).

United States v. Carter, 969 F.2d 197 (6th Cir. 1992): The Court reversed a conviction for selling cocaine to FBI agents, holding it was error to admit evidence of the defendant's purchase of household items, his two bank loan applications, and his failure to file tax returns. As this prosecution did not involve either a continuing criminal enterprise or an allegation that the defendant lacked a legitimate source of income to support an affluent lifestyle, the evidence was irrelevant and extremely prejudicial. In *United States v. Fountain,* 2 F.3d 656 (6th Cir. 1993), the Court held that information regarding the defendant's criminal activity, offered not for its truth but rather to explain why the agents searched where they did, was improperly admitted because the "reason Agent Primak searched the back bedroom simply was not a matter of dispute and was not in issue in this case."

United States v. Young, 20 F.3d 758 (7th Cir. 1994): The Court affirmed a conviction for attempted possession of cocaine with intent to distribute, holding there was no error in an *in limine* ruling that precluded the defendant from introducing evidence that one of the people arrested along with him had been released and not criminally charged. Whether or not the other was charged would not make the facts relating to the defendant's knowledge and participation in the attempted purchase more or less probable. In *United States v. Bouye,* 688 F.2d 471 (7th Cir. 1982), the Court found no error in the exclusion of evidence in a bank robbery case that two witnesses would have identified the defendant as the man who robbed another bank, which was impossible since the defendant was in custody at the time the other bank was robbed. Although the evidence had little, if any, probative value in the instant case, we observe that had the *modus operandi* of the robberies been such that it was likely that one person committed both, the testimony would have been far more probative and probably would have been admitted. See also *United States v. Hyman,* 741 F.2d 906 (7th Cir. 1984) (in prosecution for possession of stolen goods, defendant's evidence as to prices of types of steel not involved in case properly rejected as irrelevant). In *United States v. Mancillas,* 580 F.2d 1301 (7th Cir.), *cert. denied,* 439 U.S. 958 (1978), the Court affirmed drug convictions, noting that although testimony concerning an informant's tip to law enforcement agents was not hearsay (because the statement was offered for the purpose of explaining how the enforcement agents determined to make an investigation), the tip was irrelevant because it did not matter why law enforcement officers conducted an investigation. Admission of the evidence was harmless, however.

United States v. Vue, 13 F.3d 1206 (8th Cir. 1994): The Court reversed the Hmong defendants' convictions for opium smuggling because a customs officer was permitted to

Irrelevant evidence — criminal cases (cont'd)

testify that much of the opium smuggling in the area involved Hmongs. In *United States v. Bear Ribs,* 722 F.2d 420 (8th Cir. 1983), the Court affirmed a conviction for assault with intent to commit rape, and upheld the exclusion of evidence that the victim, when intoxicated, routinely undressed and exposed herself. There was no evidence in this case that the defendant or any other witness saw the victim in a nude or semi-nude condition and the defendant denied seeing the victim at all. See also *United States v. Hollister,* 746 F.2d 420 (8th Cir. 1984) (accomplice's prior illegal activities, which were unknown to defendant, were irrelevant to duress defense to bank robbery charges). In *United States v. Eckmann,* 656 F.2d 308 (8th Cir. 1981), the Court reversed a conviction for receiving stolen merchandise, finding it was error to admit evidence showing that other prospective purchasers of the merchandise decided not to buy. This evidence was irrelevant to the appellant's intent and may have suggested to the jury that somehow he should be held to a standard of what others did rather than to a knowledge standard.

United States v. Robertson, 15 F.3d 862 (9th Cir.), *cert. granted,* 115 S. Ct. __ (1994): The Court held it was error (but harmless) to admit evidence that a drug dealer who had been trying to collect a debt from the defendant was never seen again after a car similar to the defendant's was observed at the drug dealer's house. The evidence, as well as evidence of the defendant's drug use and spousal abuse, did not tend to prove any material element of the cocaine distribution and RICO offenses charged. One Judge, specially concurring, noted that reversal might have been warranted in a closer case and that prosecutors should "focus their attention more carefully on prosecuting the defendant under charges appropriate to his crimes, and on distinguishing legitimate substantive evidence from evidence of bad acts that serves principally to prejudice the jurors." In *United States v. Dean,* 980 F.2d 1286 (9th Cir. 1992), the Court held that statements accusing the defendant of criminal activity, made to a police officer, were improperly admitted for the nonhearsay purpose of explaining why the officer went to the defendant's home to arrest him. The Court stated that the officer's reasons for going to the defendant's home "are not of consequence to the determination of the action, i.e., they do not bear on any issue involving the elements of the charged offense." In *United States v. Hernandez-Miranda,* 601 F.2d 1104 (9th Cir. 1979), the Court held it was error (but harmless) to admit evidence that a defendant charged with smuggling heroin in an auto had previously carried marijuana across the border in a backpack, since there was no logical basis to connect the two events. Unfortunately, the definition of relevance used by the Court was that it must be "more probable than not" that a person who has knowingly smuggled marijuana on his person will know of the presence of contraband concealed in a vehicle. This is the wrong test of relevance. The evidence would have been relevant if it had "any tendency" to make intent seem more likely than if there were no such evidence. Of course, a Rule 403 balancing analysis still might have warranted exclusion, but the Court never reached the stage of balancing in this case.

Reference to state law

McInnis v. A.M.F., Inc., 765 F.2d 240 (1st Cir. 1985): The Court reversed a judgment for a motorcycle manufacturer in an action by a motorcyclist injured when her cycle was struck by a car, but it sustained the admission of evidence that the plaintiff had been drinking prior to the accident. Although this was a diversity case and state courts required independent proof of intoxication other than evidence of drinking, the Court reasoned that the Federal Rules governed the question of relevance and possible prejudice.

Habecker v. Clark Equip. Co., 942 F.2d 210 (3d Cir. 1991): The Court reversed a judgment for the defendants in a product liability action arising out of a forklift accident because evidence had been admitted of what was known in the industry when the forklift was manufactured about the desirability of operating restraint systems. The Court believed that evidence of what was known at the time of manufacture about the desirability of a safety feature is irrelevant under the applicable Pennsylvania law in a crashworthiness case. In *Taylor v. Monette,* 564 F. Supp. 1 (E.D. Pa. 1982), the Court ruled *in limine* in a personal injury case held that undisputed evidence that the plaintiffs' medical expenses approximated $16,000 could not be used to prove the amount of the plaintiffs' pain and suffering. Although this was a diversity case and a state appellate court had held that medical expenses could be used to prove the amount of pain and suffering, the Court found that the dollar amount was irrelevant, and even if it could be marginally probative, it was more confusing than helpful.

Carter v. Massey-Ferguson, Inc., 716 F.2d 344 (5th Cir. 1983): The Court sustained a judgment for a woodcutter injured when a skidder manufactured by the defendant backed into him, concluding that Texas law, which governed this product liability case, made industry custom relevant and that it was error to exclude evidence of that custom. Exclusion was harmless error, however, where evidence of industry standards was admitted. In *Caldarera v. Eastern Airlines,* 705 F.2d 778 (5th Cir. 1983), a diversity action arising out of an airplane crash, the Court observed that state law barring evidence of remarriage on the question of damages was binding on a federal court. In response to the defendants' claim that the plaintiffs opened the door to the evidence by presenting evidence concerning the emotional problems arising from one plaintiff's loss of his mother, wife, and child, the Court found that there were other ways for the defendants to challenge this evidence and that it was not error to exclude evidence of the remarriage under Rule 403.

Barron v. Ford Motor Co. of Can. Ltd., 965 F.2d 195 (7th Cir.), *cert. denied,* 113 S. Ct. 605 (1992): In an action by an automobile passenger allegedly thrown through a defective sunroof in an accident, the Court held that the state rule barring evidence of seatbelt nonuse was a substantive rule to be applied in diversity cases, but that the rule covered only seatbelt evidence offered to prove the plaintiff's failure to exercise due care. In this case, the manufacturer was using the evidence only to show its reasonableness in not making the sunroof out of laminated glass, so it was admissible. In *In re Air Crash Disaster,* 803 F.2d 304 (7th Cir. 1986), the Court reversed a judgment for the plaintiffs in an action against an airplane manufacturer, holding that evidence of a decedent's income tax liability should have been admitted, since such evidence was relevant to the plaintiff's pecuniary damages under Arizona's wrongful death statute. It also held, however, that the jury should be instructed that its award would not be subject to federal income taxation, even though Arizona courts would not give such an instruction. The Court found a federal interest in preventing the jury from inflating an award as a result of an erroneous assumption concerning taxation. In a prior decision on interlocutory appeal from *in limine* rulings in the case, *In re Air Crash Disaster Near Chicago,* 701 F.2d 1189 (7th Cir.), *cert. denied,* 104 S. Ct. 204 (1983), the Court observed that a state's rule concerning evidence of damages may be so closely linked with the state's view of the proper measure of damages that the evidence rule may involve substantive rights and may be binding on federal courts under the *Erie* doctrine. But the Court also observed that a state's rule concerning proof of damages may represent a judgment concerning a jury's ability to handle evidence, in which case the Federal Rules would govern admissibility decisions in federal courts. The Court avoided a decision characterizing Illinois law, as it found that federal and state law were identical and that both permitted admission of income tax evidence. In *American Nat'l Bank & Trust Co. v. K-Mart Corp.,* 717 F.2d 394 (7th Cir. 1983), a suit by a tenant against a landlord for breach of a duty to keep premises in repair, state law permitted a tenant to sue a landlord who failed to keep premises in repair and to seek as damages the difference in the rental value of the premises in and out of repair. Since state law did not require that the tenant seek to sublet the premises, the Court held that an expert should have been permitted to give an opinion on the amount of the damages notwithstanding the fact that there was no sublease.

Potts v. Benjamin, 882 F.2d 1320 (8th Cir. 1989): In this personal injury and wrongful death action arising out of a car-truck collision, the Trial Judge excluded evidence that plaintiff's children were not in child restraint seats at the time of the accident on the ground that the governing Arkansas law made failure to use safety seats inadmissible. The Court held that although the Federal Rules govern admissibility and the state statute is phrased in procedural terms, it is clear that the statute establishes a substantive rule to be followed in a diversity action.

Adams v. Fuqua Indus., 820 F.2d 271 (10th Cir. 1987): The Court reversed a plaintiff's judgment in a product liability suit against the manufacturer of a lawn mower, holding that the defendant was improperly denied the opportunity to offer rebuttal evidence concerning the feasibility of safety features when the mower was made. It also held that state law should govern the question whether the jury should be told that a damage award would not be taxable to the plaintiff. In *Beacham v. Lee-Norse,* 714 F.2d 1010 (10th Cir. 1983), a product liability action, the Court excluded evidence of contributory negligence since state law recognized only unreasonable use, not contributory negligence, as a defense.

Relationship to other rules

United States v. Gonzalez-Lira, 936 F.2d 184 (5th Cir. 1991): At the trial of a defendant charged with smuggling marijuana into the United States in a tractor-trailer, the government introduced evidence that two years earlier a tractor-trailer owned by the defendant and driven by another man was stopped at the same border checkpoint and found to contain 2,000 pounds of marijuana. The Court held that even though the defendant was not charged in that incident, the evidence tended to show the thoroughness of the government's investigation, the defendant's awareness of means used to smuggle large quantities of marijuana, the defendant's awareness that his own rig had been used to smuggle marijuana, and the source of funds used to purchase the tractor involved in this case. The majority held that the evidence was not admissible under Rule 404(b), but was properly admitted under Rules 402 and 403; the concurring Judge believed that the evidence was admissible under Rule 404(b) to show knowledge and absence of mistake. In *Lubbock Feed Lots, Inc. v. Iowa Beef Processors, Inc.*, 630 F.2d 250 (5th Cir. 1980), an action for the unpaid price of cattle, the Court analyzed the relationship of Rules 401-403, which exclude irrelevant evidence totally and permit relevant evidence to be excluded, with Rule 105, which requires a limiting instruction upon request *after* it is decided that evidence is relevant and is to be admitted.

Douglass v. Eaton Corp., 956 F.2d 1339 (6th Cir. 1992): After a jury verdict for an employee who alleged she was discharged on racial grounds following an altercation, the Trial Judge ruled that evidence of discipline imposed on other employees for fighting had been improperly admitted. The Court reversed the grant of a new trial, holding that the evidence met the threshold test of relevance and it was error to find the other situations distinguishable based on an assessment of whether the employees had been aggressors or victims in the fights. The concurring Judge believed that the error was in treating the admissibility question under Rule 104(a) alone instead of as a conditional relevancy issue to be submitted to the jury under Rule 104(b). In *United States v. Williams*, 704 F.2d 315 (6th Cir.), *cert. denied*, 104 S. Ct. 481 (1983), evidence against the defendant, who was charged with attempted cocaine possession, included testimony that $3400 was confiscated from him when he was arrested, money the government claimed was to be used to make a cocaine purchase. The defendant offered testimony by an IRS employee that the defendant had stated that he owed $3300 in taxes and had expressed an intention to repay that amount if his mother sold a house and gave him the money. The defendant's statement to the witness qualified as a statement of a present intention to do a future act, but the statement was not probative and was inadmissible absent evidence that the mother had sold the house and given him money. Thus, the rule is that a statement of intent offered to prove subsequent conduct, while admissible under Rule 803(3), is nonetheless excluded if the subsequent conduct is conditioned on a fact as to which no evidence has been presented. This is simply a question of conditional relevance, governed by Rule 104(b).

United States v. Freeman, 816 F.2d 558 (10th Cir. 1987): Affirming a conviction for dealing in counterfeit notes, the Court held that testimony concerning agents' discussions with an informant were not hearsay, since they were offered to show steps taken in the investigation rather than the truth of any statements that were made. The Court observed, however, that "out-of-court statements by informants offered to explain the background of an investigation, like all evidence, must be evaluated under the criteria in Fed. R. Evid. Rules 401 and 403 for relevance and to prevent confusion or prejudice on the part of the jury."

Remote evidence

Sir Speedy, Inc. v. L & P Graphics, Inc., 957 F.2d 1033 (2d Cir. 1992): After a jury verdict in an action over breach of a franchise agreement, the Trial Judge ruled that income projections made by the franchisor should not have been admitted in proof of the franchisee's damages because they predated the applicable limitations period. The Court reversed the judgment n.o.v., holding it was error to exclude the documents, as the statute of limitations only bars stale claims and is not a rule of evidence. A suggestion that evidence is too old goes to its relevance and to its weight, which is a matter for the jury.

United States v. Morris, 957 F.2d 1391 (7th Cir.), *cert. denied,* 113 S. Ct. 380 (1992): The Court held, in a prosecution for conspiring to defraud the United States arising out of the purchase of a nursing home at an inflated price, that evidence of a 1980 partnership buyback valuation was relevant to the 1984 value of the nursing home partnership.

Similar circumstance evidence — accident and injury cases

Joy v. Bell Helicopter Textron, Inc., 999 F.2d 549 (D.C. Cir. 1993): In a suit by estates of helicopter crash victims against the manufacturer of an engine, the Court held that evidence of two other engine failures was properly admitted. The Court noted that other accidents need not have occurred in precisely the same manner to qualify as substantially similar, and the substantial similarity requirement is relaxed when unrelated incidents are offered for a purpose other than to prove that a product was unreasonably dangerous, e.g., to refute a suggestion that a helicopter part could not have been defective if made to a manufacturer's specifications. In *Brooks v. Chrysler Corp.,* 786 F.2d 1191 (D.C. Cir.), *cert. denied,* 107 S. Ct. 185 (1986), the Court affirmed a directed verdict for an auto manufacturer in an action claiming that an auto crashed into a telephone pole as a result of brake-piston seizure. Ruling *in limine,* the Trial Judge excluded five exhibits relating to a national highway safety administration investigation into brake-piston seizures and barred the plaintiffs' expert from relying on the exhibits. The exhibits were drawn from complaints by Chrysler's customers, correspondence between the government agency and Chrysler, internal Chrysler memoranda, and Chrysler correspondence with the Canadian government. The Court agreed that the exhibits were minimally probative and potentially prejudicial.

Grenier v. Dow Chem. Co., 628 F. Supp. 1529 (D. Me. 1986): In a product liability action against a herbicide manufacturer, the Court held that the plaintiff could introduce evidence that two of his six coworkers were suffering from the same neurological disease, as long as the plaintiff could establish that the coworkers' exposure to the defendant's product and their medical condition were substantially similar to the plaintiff's.

Seese v. Volkswagenwerk A.G., 648 F.2d 833 (3d Cir.), *cert. denied,* 454 U.S. 867 (1981): The Court upheld the introduction of information gathered as part of the Fatal Accident Reporting System operated under the auspices of the National Highway Traffic and Safety Administration in a suit arising from a single-car "roll over" accident. Although the data did not reveal much information about the other accidents, the Court said that missing details went to the weight to be given the evidence, not to its admissibility. In *DeMarines v. KLM Royal Dutch Airlines,* 580 F.2d 1193 (3d Cir. 1978), the Court reversed a judgment for the plaintiffs, who sued for an alleged airplane accident, on other grounds, and noted that the Trial Judge should not have excluded evidence that no other claims arose out of the same flight. The Court wrote:

> All of the evidence introduced by plaintiff on the issue of whether an "accident" had occurred bore upon the presence or absence of an injurious effect upon the passengers from the alleged accident. The plaintiff's own injury was the most probative evidence that an "accident" had occurred. The proffered proof of an absence of other claims tends to prove the absence of other injuries and is, therefore, comparably relevant. The possibility that persons may have sustained injuries without filing claims should not prevent the admission of pertinent evidence, and its negative aspect merely goes to the weakness and weight of such evidence rather than its admissibility. Rule 401 of the Federal Rules of Evidence states that evidence is relevant if it tends to make the existence of a fact more probable or less probable than it would be without the evidence. If other claims had been made against KLM, evidence of those claims would have been relevant to make the existence of an accident more probable. Proof of the absence of claims, though not carrying as much weight, makes the existence of the fact of the "accident" less probable than it would be without the evidence.

Johnson v. Ford Motor Co., 988 F.2d 573 (5th Cir. 1993): The Court held that evidence of other car accidents was inadmissible even for proving notice of a dangerous condition, since there was no reasonable similarity to the facts at issue. The other accidents involved different vehicle models or different years, and none involved the precise mechanical defect alleged in this case. In *Melton v. Deere & Co.,* 887 F.2d 1241 (5th Cir. 1989), the Court noted that evidence of similar accidents postdating manufacture of the machine causing the plaintiff's injuries could show that the machine design was more dangerous than users contemplated. See also *Jackson v. Firestone Tire & Rubber Co.,* 788 F.2d 1070 (5th Cir. 1986) (error to exclude evidence of similar wheel rim accidents); *Ramos v. Liberty Mut. Ins. Co.,* 615 F.2d 334 (5th Cir. 1980), *cert. denied,* 449 U.S. 1112 (1981) (error to exclude evidence of a prior, similar collapse of a mast of an offshore oil-drilling rig. In *Jackson v. Johns-Manville Sales Corp.,* 750 F.2d 1314 (5th Cir. 1985) (en banc), *modifying* 727 F.2d 506 (1984), an action by a former shipyard worker against manufacturers of asbestos, the Court held that letters written to and by the defendants were relevant on the question whether these defendants knew or should have known of the dangers of asbestos. Although the letters referred to other groups of workers, not to shipyard workers, the Court reasoned that "[a] study indicating that exposure to asbestos fibers is likely to cause harm to one group of workers is at least suggestive of the fact that other groups of workers who are also exposed to asbestos fibers face similar dangers." In *Dartez v. Fibreboard Corp.,* 765 F.2d 456 (5th Cir. 1985), another worker's suit against asbestos manufacturers, the Court held that a physician, who had worked for one manufacturer, could testify as to scientific studies linking exposure to asbestos and disease and the extent of dissemination of these studies throughout the asbestos industry. It concluded that one manufacturer's knowledge was a proper basis for concluding that other manufacturers should have had similar knowledge. In *McGonigal v. Gearhart Indus.,* 851 F.2d 774 (5th Cir. 1988), a personal injury suit

Similar circumstance evidence — accident and injury cases (cont'd)

against the manufacturer and assembler of a grenade that exploded prematurely, the Court held that evidence that another grenade manufactured by the defendant exploded prematurely was probative of the plaintiff's claim that the defendant was negligent in approving grenades with short fuses. The Court concluded, however, that it was error (but harmless) to admit evidence concerning explosions of grenades manufactured by others.

Engebretsen v. Fairchild Aircraft Corp., 21 F.3d 721 (6th Cir. 1994): In a product liability case, the Court upheld admission of expert testimony regarding postincident tests. Although the tests were not intended to duplicate the airplane landing that injured the plaintiff, the Court found they had probative value. In *Hines v. Joy Mfg. Co.*, 850 F.2d 1146 (6th Cir. 1988), the Court held that evidence of the lack of prior claims against the manufacturer of a mobile bridge unit was admissible to prove the absence of notice of any design defect in the unit. In *Rhodes v. Michelin Tire Corp.*, 542 F. Supp. 60 (E.D. Ky. 1982), a product liability case arising out of a tire blowout, the Court indicated that evidence of a tearing condition that developed in 200 flaps taken from the trucking company's fleet was relevant to prove a design defect and was more probative than prejudicial.

Bilski v. Scientific Atlanta, 964 F.2d 697 (7th Cir. 1992): The Court affirmed a judgment for the defendant in a product liability action for injuries suffered when the plaintiff slipped while cleaning snow and ice off a satellite dish, holding there was no abuse of discretion in admitting the defendant's records of injuries involving its products, which showed no prior accidents of this sort. Neither was there an abuse of discretion in excluding testimony by the plaintiff's witnesses about other falls from satellite dishes, as none had resulted in injuries reported to the defendant, so the testimony would have had little if any tendency to prove a risk foreseeable to the defendant. In *Nachtsheim v. Beech Aircraft Corp.*, 847 F.2d 1261 (7th Cir. 1988), the Court affirmed a judgment for a manufacturer whose plane crashed. Although it recognized broad discretion on the part of the Trial Judge to rule on the admissibility of other accident evidence, it also recognized that because direct evidence of causation disappears in airplane crash cases, a plaintiff may have a special need for other accident evidence. The Court concluded there was insufficient showing of substantial similarity between the crash involved in the instant case and another upon which the plaintiff relied and that admission of the evidence would have forced the defendant to litigate two crashes instead of one.

Burke v. Deere & Co., 6 F.3d 497 (8th Cir. 1993): The Court reversed (2-1) a judgment for the plaintiff, whose hand had been injured by an auger when he reached into a clean-out door on farm equipment manufactured by the defendant. Evidence of postsale accidents involving similar machines was admissible to prove defect, causation, and foreseeability of misuse, but in this case the evidence was impermissibly used on the issue of punitive damages. See also *R.W. Murray Co. v. Shatterproof Glass Corp.*, 758 F.2d 266 (8th Cir. 1985) (in suit for breach of warranty with respect to glass panels, Court upheld admission of evidence concerning other failures of similar panels); *Sturm v. Clark Equip. Co.*, 547 F. Supp. 144 (W.D. Mo. 1982), *aff'd*, 732 F.2d 161 (8th Cir. 1984) (evidence of the absence of prior accidents was admissible where it was limited to the same model of machine involved in the accident giving rise to the suit, so plaintiff's motion for a new trial following a jury verdict for the defendant in a product liability case denied). In *Harris v. Pacific Floor Mach. Mfg. Co.*, 856 F.2d 64 (8th Cir. 1988), a suit against the manufacturer of a floor buffer, the Court held that evidence of other lawsuits arising from accidents involving floor buffers made by other manufacturers was properly excluded in an action by a minor who was injured while using gasoline and a buffer to strip paint off a school floor. In *Hale v. Firestone Tire & Rubber Co.*, 756 F.2d 1322 (8th Cir. 1985), a product liability action against manufacturers of a tire rim that separated and struck one of the plaintiffs as he attempted to inflate a truck tire, the Court found it was an abuse of discretion to admit evidence concerning defects in a Firestone tire that was not involved in the case. In *Held v. Mitsubishi Aircraft Int'l, Inc.*, 672 F. Supp. 369 (D. Minn. 1987), a suit arising out of an airplane crash, the Judge ruled that an FAA report of an investigation of one model of aircraft made by a manufacturer was admissible in an action involving a different model. Most documents produced in connection with the investigation related to the model in question, and the FAA evaluated all of the manufacturer's models.

Wheeler v. John Deere Co., 862 F.2d 1404 (10th Cir. 1988): The Court held that it was not error to allow five witnesses, all of whom had lost limbs in past incidents, to testify as to their experiences with the defendant's defective machines, since their experiences were similar and tended to prove a defect. However, it was error to permit the plaintiff to question the manufacturer's expert about other accidents that had not been determined to involve similar circumstances. In *Ponder v. Warren Tool Corp.*, 834 F.2d 1553 (10th Cir. 1987), the Court observed that the decision whether to admit similar circumstance evidence of accidents depends on the theory urged in a case. It found no error in this case where the Trial Judge took a conservative approach and excluded evidence. In *Whiteley v. OKC Corp.*, 719 F.2d 1051 (10th Cir. 1983), the Court affirmed a judgment for the plaintiff in a breach of warranty action for personal injuries from defective propane, finding no error in the admission of evidence of a subsequent accident at the defendant's yard, since the accident was consistent with testimony that the defendant had been delivering adulterated gas. In *Johnson v. Colt Indus. Operating Corp.*, 609 F. Supp. 776 (D. Kan. 1985), *aff'd*, 797 F.2d 1530 (10th Cir. 1986), a personal injury action arising out of the discharge of an army revolver that had been dropped, the Court said that a judicial opinion in another case was admissible to prove the manufacturer's knowledge of similar accidents.

Borden, Inc. v. Florida E.C. Ry., 772 F.2d 750 (11th Cir. 1985): The Court reversed a judgment for a railroad because evidence of a prior incident of vandalism, similar to the one that resulted in the accident giving rise to this case, was improperly excluded. The evidence was relevant to show that the railroad had reason to know of a problem with its equipment. Exclusion was especially damaging because the railroad had argued that no similar vandalism had occurred previously.

Similar circumstance evidence — civil rights and discrimination cases

Outley v. City of New York, 837 F.2d 587 (2d Cir. 1988): The Court reversed a judgment for police officers in a civil rights case, holding that it was error to admit evidence of previous lawsuits by an arrestee and his wife against the City when there was no evidence that the suits were fraudulent.

Garraghty v. Jordan, 830 F.2d 1295 (4th Cir. 1987): In a civil rights action by a prison warden who sued following a five-day suspension without pay, the Court upheld the exclusion of evidence of disciplinary responses to actions by other employees.

Douglass v. Eaton Corp., 956 F.2d 1339 (6th Cir. 1992): After a jury verdict for an employee who alleged she was discharged on racial grounds following an altercation, the Trial Judge ruled that evidence of discipline imposed on other employees for fighting had been improperly admitted. The Court reversed the grant of a new trial, holding that the evidence met the threshold test of relevance and it was error to find the other situations distinguishable based on an assessment of whether the employees had been aggressors or victims in the fights. In *Schrand v. Federal Pac. Elec. Co.,* 851 F.2d 152 (6th Cir. 1988), the Court reversed a judgment for the plaintiff in an age discrimination action, because of the admission of testimony of two other discharged employees about statements made to them concerning their age. Since the person who made the decision to terminate the plaintiff was not involved in the termination decisions regarding the other two employees, who worked in a different region and division from the plaintiff, the Court reasoned that the evidence was irrelevant and prejudicial.

Iervolino v. Delta Air Lines, Inc., 796 F.2d 1408 (11th Cir. 1986), *cert. denied,* 479 U.S. 1090 (1987): The Court affirmed a judgment for an airline in an age discrimination suit by a former captain. It found no error in the admission of evidence concerning the medical condition of another former captain to show how age could affect a captain, and in the admission of a cockpit tape recording of an emergency aboard a flight to show the problems that might arise if a former captain served as a flight engineer. The Court found it was error to bar the plaintiff from revealing the names of other major airlines who would have permitted a captain to serve as a flight engineer, but a majority held the error was harmless. A dissenting Judge argued that the condition of the other captain was not shown to be representative of pilots over the age of 60 and that the tape recording amounted to theatrics designed to inflame the jury. See also *Smith v. Georgia,* 684 F.2d 729 (11th Cir. 1982) (remanding Title VII action, Court noted that Trial Judge did not indicate whether evidence of retaliation against other employees in similar circumstances was relevant). In *Murphy v. City of Flagler Beach,* 761 F.2d 622 (11th Cir. 1985), the Court granted a police officer, who claimed that he was fired in bad faith, a new trial because evidence that the police chief had engaged in and not criticized other officers for engaging in the same conduct used to justify the plaintiff's firing was erroneously excluded.

Similar circumstance evidence — other cases

Cibro Petroleum Prods. v. Sohio Alaska Petroleum Co., 602 F. Supp. 1520 (N.D.N.Y. 1985), *aff'd,* 798 F.2d 1421 (Temp. Emer. Ct. App.), *cert. dismissed,* 479 U.S. 979 (1986): In a suit by a refining company against a supplier for alleged breach of a crude oil supply contract, the Court held that evidence of the supplier's contracts with other parties was admissible to assist in interpreting the contract with the plaintiff, and that this was true irrespective of a trade usage or course of performance analysis.

Marathon LeTourneau Co. v. NLRB, 699 F.2d 248 (5th Cir. 1983): The Court enforced a Labor Board order based on a finding that an employer had engaged in unfair labor practices during an organizational campaign by discharging certain individuals. Although the Court noted that a summary prepared by the employer setting forth all discharges for a one-year period was admissible under Rule 1006 if it was relevant, it concluded that the Administrative Law Judge properly rejected the summary because it lacked probative value. The company claimed that the employees were fired because of their attendance records, but the summary failed to quantify the absenteeism or tardiness for which other employees were discharged and neglected to show whether explanations were considered and past violations tolerated.

Finch v. Monumental Life Ins. Co., 820 F.2d 1426 (6th Cir. 1987): Affirming a judgment holding an insurer liable on a life insurance policy, the Court held that testimony of another insured as to nonreceipt of a premium notice for the same month as that in which the plaintiff's deceased failed to make a payment was relevant and admissible.

SCNO Barge Lines, Inc. v. Anderson Clayton & Co., 745 F.2d 1188 (8th Cir. 1984): The Court affirmed a judgment for a lessor who claimed breach of an agreement to use the lessor's barges to transport soybean meal, holding that the Trial Judge properly excluded evidence of earlier contracts between the parties. The lessee's obligation under the earlier contracts shed no light on the dispute in the instant case.

Agristor Leasing v. Meuli, 865 F.2d 1150 (10th Cir. 1988): The Court held there was no error in excluding evidence pertaining to litigation over performance and marketing of a manufacturer's silos more than twenty years earlier, given the danger of confusing the jury with respect to differences between the older and newer experiences with silos.

Standard of care

Rolick v. Collins Pine Co., 975 F.2d 1009 (3d Cir. 1992), *cert. denied,* 113 S. Ct. 1417 (1993): In a diversity negligence action by a logger, the Court held it was error to exclude evidence of OSHA regulations as evidence of the defendant's standard of care, even though the OSHA law did not govern the relationship between the plaintiff and the defendant. Although the language of the OSHA standard was presented to the jury through evidence of an identical industry standard, the difference from a nationwide legal standard in the "quality" of the proof meant the error was not harmless. In *Josephs v. Harris Corp.,* 677 F.2d 985 (3d Cir. 1982), the Court, applying state law in a product liability case, held it was error to exclude evidence of standards or text materials used by an expert to support a conclusion that a product was defective. State law made the time of sale, not the time of manufacture, critical, so it was error to limit the evidence to material in existence at the time of manufacture. In *Seese v. Volkswagenwerk A.G.,* 648 F.2d 833 (3d Cir.), *cert. denied,* 454 U.S. 867 (1981), the Court approved the admission of a Federal Motor Vehicle Safety Standard which was not binding on the vehicle involved in the single-car "roll over" accident, but which was offered as evidence of what was reasonably necessary to make a window resistant to a "pop-out" crash.

Horne v. Owens-Corning Fiberglass Corp., 4 F.3d 276 (4th Cir. 1993): In a product liability case, the defendant introduced OSHA regulations requiring warnings to be placed on asbestos, to prove that it had issued even stronger warnings before being required to make any warnings under OSHA regulation. The Court found that the regulations were properly admitted as state-of-the-art evidence, even though they were promulgated many years after the plaintiff's exposure to asbestos. The Court stated that "state-of-the-art evidence, because it often is scientific in nature and results from a cumulative review of a field over time, should not be applied retroactively to *discredit* conduct at a given time prior to the culmination of the relevant research." But there was no such concern in this case because the defendant "was using subsequent findings and standards to *credit* prior conduct."

Dixon v. International Harvester Co., 754 F.2d 573 (5th Cir. 1985): The Court overturned a judgment n.o.v. for the defendant in a personal injury action against the manufacturer of a crawler tractor. The Court declined to decide whether OSHA standards should have been admitted to establish a standard of care where the standards were directed at employers and the defendant was a manufacturer, but it did hold that standards of the American National Standards Institute were admissible. In *Johnson v. Ford Motor Co.*, 988 F.2d 573 (5th Cir. 1993), the Court held that cautionary letters sent to Ford by the National Highway Traffic Safety Administration were properly excluded, since the letters were merely preliminary inquiries that did not result in action against Ford, and they concerned vehicle models different from that involved in the litigation.

Ross v. Black & Decker, Inc., 977 F.2d 1178 (7th Cir. 1992), *cert. denied*, 113 S. Ct. 1274 (1993): In a product liability action arising out of injuries caused by a circular saw, the Court held there was no abuse of discretion in admitting an Underwriters Laboratories standard for saw guards adopted after the saw was manufactured, as it was relevant to the dangerousness of the product.

Smith v. Firestone Tire & Rubber Co., 755 F.2d 129 (8th Cir. 1985): The Court held that it was not error to admit OSHA standards on behalf of a tire manufacturer as a response to the plaintiffs' claim that the manufacturer should have warned of defects in a rim. See also *Donovan v. General Motors*, 762 F.2d 701 (8th Cir. 1985) (OSHA standards should have been admitted as evidence of standard of care owed to plaintiff by his employer).

State of mind

United States v. Hanson, 994 F.2d 403 (7th Cir. 1993): In a fraud case, the defendant offered an out-of-court statement made to him, to the effect that he did not have to file a certain form. The Trial Judge excluded the statement as hearsay, but the Court held that the statement was not offered for its truth but rather for its impact on the defendant's state of mind. For this nonhearsay purpose, the evidence met the low threshold of relevance set forth in Rule 401. Erroneous exclusion of the statement was harmless, however. In *Wetherill v. University of Chicago*, 565 F. Supp. 1553 (N.D. Ill. 1983), a DES product liability action, the Court ruled that medical evidence concerning the relationship of DES to cancer could be admitted to prove the reasonableness of the plaintiffs' fears of contracting cancer as a result of exposure to the drug.

United States v. Castiglione, 876 F.2d 73 (9th Cir.), *cert. denied,* 110 S. Ct. 365 (1989): The Court affirmed a conviction for mailing a letter that threatened a Federal Judge, and held that the Judge's testimony regarding his knowledge of a prior assassination of a Federal Judge, and evidence of steps taken to protect him, showed his state of mind and was relevant to the essential issue of whether the letter could reasonably be read as containing a threat of injury.

Statute of limitations

Sir Speedy, Inc. v. L & P Graphics, Inc., 957 F.2d 1033 (2d Cir. 1992): After a jury verdict in an action over breach of a franchise agreement, the Trial Judge ruled that income projections made by the franchisor should not have been admitted in proof of the franchisee's damages because they predated the applicable limitations period. The Court reversed the judgment n.o.v., holding it was error to exclude the documents, as the statute of limitations only bars stale claims and is not a rule of evidence. A suggestion that evidence is too old goes to its relevance and to its weight, which is a matter for the jury.

D. LEGISLATIVE HISTORY

Advisory Committee's Note

Problems of relevancy call for an answer to the question whether an item of evidence, when tested by the processes of legal reasoning, possesses sufficient probative value to justify receiving it in evidence. Thus, assessment of the probative value of evidence that a person purchased a revolver shortly prior to a fatal shooting with which he is charged is a matter of analysis and reasoning.

The variety of relevancy problems is coextensive with the ingenuity of counsel in using circumstantial evidence as a means of proof. An enormous number of cases fall in no set pattern, and this rule is designed as a guide for handling them. On the other hand, some situations recur with sufficient frequency to create patterns susceptible of treatment by specific rules. Rule 404 and those following it are of that variety; they also serve as illustrations of the application of the present rule as limited by the exclusionary principles of Rule 403.

Passing mention should be made of so-called "conditional" relevancy. Morgan, Basic Problems of Evidence 45-46 (1962). In this situation, probative value depends not only upon satisfying the basic requirement of relevancy as described above but also upon the existence of some matter of fact. For example, if evidence of a spoken statement is relied upon to prove notice, probative value is lacking unless the person sought to be charged heard the statement. The problem is one of fact, and the only rules needed are for the purpose of determining the respective functions of judge and jury. See Rules 104(b) and 901. The discussion which follows in the present note is concerned with relevancy generally, not with any particular problem of conditional relevancy.

Relevancy is not an inherent characteristic of any item of evidence but exists only as a relation between an item of evidence and a matter properly provable in the case. Does the item of evidence tend to prove the matter sought to be proved? Whether the relationship exists depends upon principles evolved by experience or science, applied logically to the situation at hand. James, Relevancy, Probability and the Law, 29 Calif. L. Rev. 689, 696, n. 15 (1941), in Selected Writings on Evidence and Trial 610, 615, n. 15 (Fryer ed. 1957). The rule summarizes this relationship as a "tendency to make the existence" of the fact to be proved "more probable or less probable." Compare Uniform Rule 1(2) which states the crux of relevancy as "a tendency in reason," thus perhaps emphasizing unduly the logical process and ignoring the need to draw upon experience or science to validate the general principle upon which relevancy in a particular situation depends.

The standard of probability under the rule is "more ... probable than it would be without the evidence." Any more stringent requirement is unworkable and unrealistic. As McCormick § 152, p. 317, says, "[a] brick is not a wall," or, as Falknor, Extrinsic Policies Affecting Admissibility, 10 Rutgers L. Rev. 574, 576 (1956), quotes Professor McBaine, "it is not to be supposed that every witness can make a home run." Dealing with probability in the language of the rule has the added virtue of avoiding confusion between questions of admissibility and questions of the sufficiency of the evidence.

The rule uses the phrase "fact that is of consequence to the determination of the action" to describe the kind of fact to which proof may properly be directed. The language is that of California Evidence Code § 210; it has the advantage of avoiding the loosely used and ambiguous word "material." Tentative Recommendation and a Study Relating to the Uniform Rules of Evidence (Art. I. General Provisions), Cal. Law Revision Comm'n, Rep., Rec. & Studies, 10-11 (1964). The fact to be proved may be ultimate, intermediate, or evidentiary; it matters not, so long as it is of consequence in the determination of the action. Cf. Uniform Rule 1(2) which requires that the evidence relate to a "material" fact.

The fact to which the evidence is directed need not be in dispute. While situations will arise which call for the exclusion of evidence offered to prove a point conceded by the opponent, the ruling should be made on the basis of such considerations as waste of time and undue prejudice (see Rule 403), rather than under any general requirement that evidence is admissible only if directed to matters in dispute. Evidence which is essentially background in nature can scarcely be said to involve disputed matter, yet it is universally offered and admitted as an aid to understanding. Charts, photographs, views of real estate, murder weapons, and many other items of evidence fall in this category. A rule limiting admissibility to evidence directed to a controversial point would invite the exclusion of this helpful evidence, or at least the raising of endless questions over its admission. Cf. California Evidence Code § 210, defining relevant evidence in terms of tendency to prove a disputed fact.

RULE 402

A. OFFICIAL TEXT

Rule 402. Relevant Evidence Generally Admissible; Irrelevant Evidence Inadmissible

All relevant evidence is admissible, except as otherwise provided by the Constitution of the United States, by Act of Congress, by these rules, or by other rules prescribed by the Supreme Court pursuant to statutory authority. Evidence which is not relevant is not admissible.

B. EDITORIAL EXPLANATORY COMMENT

Relevant evidence admissible

Rule 402 makes clear that all relevant evidence is admissible, except as otherwise provided by the Constitution, federal statute, or valid Supreme Court-promulgated rules. All evidence that is not relevant is inadmissible. If evidence is relevant, it is up to the nonoffering party to invoke a specific rule, from the body of rules listed in Rule 402, which justifies exclusion of the evidence.

Sometimes it appears that Judges decide doubtful questions of relevance on the side of admissibility, at least where no strong cry of prejudice supports the relevance objection. In view of the rather undemanding standard of relevance that American Courts employ, this is perhaps not surprising. Fearing that evidence may tend to prove a fact in dispute in some hard-to-see way, Judges may be extraordinarily wary of exclusion.

The question arises whether, absent a specific claim of prejudice or confusion or a reasonable concern about undue consumption of time, Judges should worry about basic relevance objections. At first blush it may seem that the answer should be "no," since no harm is apparently done when general irrelevant evidence is introduced.

Harm comes in subtle forms, however, as well as in obvious ways. Irrelevant evidence by definition cannot help the trier of fact. It can only hurt. It must be apparent that in offering such evidence the proponent seeks some advantage from it. Whatever the advantage that is sought, it is an edge to which the proponent cannot properly lay claim. Yet the opponent may be helpless to identify the precise mischief at hand. Damage is not always demonstrable. For this reason, American Courts exclude irrelevant evidence without asking for a demonstration of harm. Even without the showing of damage, the fact remains that at best the evidence is useless, and at worst it is time-consuming as well as damaging in a way that evades proof. We prefer to err on the side of caution and to exclude anything that cannot satisfy even the low relevance threshold to admissibility.

Irrelevant evidence in response to irrelevant evidence

As a general proposition, it is correct to assert that irrelevant evidence is not admissible in litigation (assuming that a proper objection is made). There is one class of cases in which this general statement must be further refined — i.e., when one party offers evidence that is properly classified as irrelevant and the other party, after failing to object, offers to meet the irrelevant evidence with additional irrelevancies. The notion of "fighting fire with fire" (also called "curative admissibility") is an old one and the decision whether to admit irrelevant evidence in order to counter other irrelevant evidence seems to be the same under the Federal Rules of Evidence as at common law.[1]

The Trial Judge must decide whether the interests of justice are better served by penalizing the party who failed to object or by treating the party who began the parade of irrelevant evidence as being in no position to complain. Among the factors that the Trial Judge is likely to take into account in making a ruling are: the damage that can fairly be attributable to the initial offer of irrelevant evidence; whether the party who failed to object intentionally sat on his rights; whether a limiting instruction to disregard all of the irrelevant evidence is likely to work in the particular case; the amount of time that it would take to hear further irrelevant evidence; and the extent to which a failure of one party to respond to irrelevant evidence might mislead a jury untrained in evidence law to think that the irrelevant evidence was beyond challenge and therefore somewhat probative.

One thing, however, is clear: The doctrine of curative admissibility is only applicable where the adversary has already brought forth irrelevant or inadmissible evidence. It does not apply where the adversary's evidence was properly admitted in the first place. One cannot fight "fire with fire" if there was no "fire" to begin with.[2]

Sources of rules excluding relevant evidence

Rule 402 refers to four sources of possible exclusionary rules for relevant evidence: (1) the Constitution; (2) federal statutes; (3) the Federal Rules of Evidence; and (4) other Supreme Court rules, promulgated pursuant to statutory authority.

At the constitutional level, the most often invoked exclusionary rules are those excluding evidence obtained in violation of the Fourth Amendment right to be free from unreasonable search and seizure;[3] the Fifth Amendment right to be free from compelled

---

1. See generally Graham, *Waiver of Right to Object Other Than by Failure to Make Objection — The Concept of "Door Opening,"* 16 CRIM. L. BULL. 461 (1980).

2. See, e.g., United States v. Rosa, 11 F.3d 315 (2d Cir. 1993) (the doctrine of "curative admissibility" is only applicable where the adversary "has introduced inadmissible evidence" and when it is needed to rebut a false impression created: "Properly admitted evidence does not open the door to inadmissible evidence.").

3. Weeks v. United States, 232 U.S. 383 (1914).

self-incrimination;[4] the Fifth Amendment right to due process;[5] and the Sixth Amendment right to counsel.[6]

Recently, the constitutional basis of some of these exclusionary rules has been brought into question. The Supreme Court has held that the Fourth Amendment exclusionary rule is simply a court-made rule that is not itself required by the Constitution.[7] Similarly, the rule requiring exclusion of confessions obtained in violation of *Miranda v. Arizona* has been held to be court-made rather than constitutionally mandated.[8] It is a fair question whether such court-made rules fit within the prescribed sources of exclusion under Rule 402. Indeed, the Supreme Court has never discussed how these "court-made" exclusionary rules can be binding on the states, nor has it even located the source of power for these nonconstitutional rules. It has, however, distinguished the Fourth Amendment exclusionary rule from an exercise of a Federal Court's supervisory power — holding that while the Trial Court can invoke the exclusionary rule to exclude evidence obtained in violation of the Fourth Amendment, it cannot invoke its supervisory authority to exclude such evidence in situations where the exclusionary rule does not apply.[9]

Still, it is clear at this point that evidence obtained in violation of the Fourth Amendment or *Miranda* is excluded from a federal trial despite its relevance. Of course, there are certain exceptions to the exclusionary rule, as applied both to the Fourth Amendment and to *Miranda,* which must be noted by the practitioner.[10] Finally, application of the exclusionary rule is constitutionally required if the evidence is obtained in violation of the Due Process Clause or of the Sixth Amendment right to counsel.[11]

There are relatively few federal statutes that mandate exclusion of relevant evidence. The most often invoked example is the wiretapping statute, Title III of the Omnibus Crime Control and Safe Streets Act of 1968.[12] This Act requires the exclusion of evidence obtained through electronic surveillance in violation of the Act, despite the

---

4. Miranda v. Arizona, 384 U.S. 436 (1966).

5. Doyle v. Ohio, 426 U.S. 610 (1976) (Due Process Clause prohibits the prosecution from using defendant's post-*Miranda* warning silence).

6. Massiah v. United States, 377 U.S. 201 (1964) (confession excluded when obtained in violation of Sixth Amendment right to counsel); United States v. Wade, 388 U.S. 218 (1967) (postindictment identification excluded where it was obtained in violation of Sixth Amendment right to counsel).

7. See United States v. Calandra, 414 U.S. 338 (1974) (the exclusionary rule is "a judicially-created remedy designed to safeguard Fourth Amendment rights generally through its deterrent effect, rather than a personal constitutional right of the party aggrieved").

8. Oregon v. Elstad, 470 U.S. 298 (1985) (violation of *Miranda* is not itself a violation of the Constitution; therefore, the *Miranda* exclusionary rule is simply a court-made, prophylactic rule).

9. See United States v. Payner, 447 U.S. 727 (1980) (where exclusionary rule is inapplicable due to failure to satisfy standing requirements, the Trial Court cannot resort to supervisory power to exclude illegally obtained evidence).

10. For a thorough discussion of the exceptions to the Fourth Amendment and *Miranda* exclusionary rules, see Saltzburg, Capra & Hancock, BASIC CRIMINAL PROCEDURE 352-414, 469-84 (West 1994).

11. United States v. Kimball, 884 F.2d 1274 (9th Cir. 1989) (exclusion of evidence obtained in violation of the Sixth Amendment is constitutionally required); Brecht v. Abrahamson, 113 S. Ct. 1710 (1993) (exclusion of evidence obtained in violation of the Due Process Clause is constitutionally required).

12. 18 U.S.C.A. §§ 2510-20 (as modified by Title I of the 1986 Electronic Communications Privacy Act).

relevance of the information.[13] Other statutes have also been invoked to exclude relevant evidence from time to time.[14] Ordinarily, the statute must expressly provide for the exclusion of evidence; where Congress has not specifically provided for exclusion, the Courts have generally not imposed it as a remedy.[15]

The Federal Rules of Evidence contain many exclusionary rules. These rules can be usefully divided into two types: (1) rules that guard against prejudicial or untrustworthy evidence, such as Rules 403, 608, 609, 703, and the hearsay rule — the policy behind these rules is that even if evidence is relevant, its admission in certain cases could actually harm rather than advance the search for truth, due to the risk that the jury will be unfairly affected by prejudicial or unreliable evidence; and (2) rules that recognize that certain policies are more important than the need to admit all relevant evidence, such as Rules 407 through 412, the rules on privileges, and Rule 606.

As to other Supreme Court rules that may result in the exclusion of relevant evidence, the most important are those contained in the Federal Rules of Civil and Criminal Procedure, the Bankruptcy Rules and the Admiralty Rules. For example, Rule 37 of the Federal Rules of Civil Procedure provides that the Trial Judge can sanction a litigant who commits a discovery violation by precluding that litigant from introducing relevant evidence. As for the Federal Rules of Criminal Procedure, most of these rules do not specifically provide for exclusion of any evidence obtained in violation of the requirements set forth. Most Courts have held that in the absence of specific exclusionary language, a violation of a Federal Rule of Criminal Procedure does not result in exclusion of otherwise relevant evidence.[16] However, certain rules requiring notice or mandating discovery do permit a Trial Judge in the exercise of discretion to exclude evidence as a sanction. See, e.g., Federal Rules of Criminal Procedure 12.1(d), 12.2(d), 12.3(d), and 16(d)(2).

---

13. See, e.g., United States v. Wuliger, 981 F.2d 1497 (6th Cir. 1992) (tapes were made in violation of Title III, which criminalizes unauthorized, unconsensual wiretapping; Wuliger used the tapes to cross-examine a witness; Wuliger was indicted and convicted for disclosing the contents of the tape during the cross-examination; the Court rejected Wuliger's argument that he should not have been convicted because he only used the recordings for impeachment purposes; it refused to recognize an impeachment exception to the Wiretap Act, at least in the context of a civil proceeding, such as the divorce proceeding in which Wuliger used the recordings).

14. See, e.g., Lusby v. Union Pac. R.R. Co., 4 F.3d 639 (8th Cir. 1993) (admission of expert testimony was reversible error, because the expert, in formulating his opinion, considered materials which were prohibited under 23 U.S.C. § 409; Section 409 provides that reports, surveys and other materials compiled for the purpose of identifying, evaluating, or planning the safety of railway-highway crossings "shall not be admitted in Federal or State court or considered for any purposes in any action for damages arising from any occurrence at a location mentioned or addressed in such reports.").

15. See, e.g., United States v. Blue Diamond Coal Co., 667 F.2d 510 (6th Cir. 1981) (no suppression authorized for violation of statute requiring consent or administrative warrant for seizure of lawfully inspected records).

16. See, e.g., United States v. Schoenheit, 856 F.2d 74 (8th Cir. 1988) (violation of FED. R. CRIM. P. 41 requirements concerning nighttime execution of a warrant; exclusion is not required "unless the search would not have otherwise occurred or would not have been so abrasive if the rule had been followed, or there was evidence of an intentional and deliberate disregard" of the rule); United States v. Charles, 883 F.2d 355 (5th Cir. 1989) (violation of Rule 41 provision requiring officer to conduct a search with the warrant in hand does not require exclusion where the search would have occurred anyway).

Rules of professional responsibility

Federal Rule of Civil Procedure 83 provides authority for District Courts to promulgate local rules so long as they are not inconsistent with the Federal Rules. Pursuant to this rulemaking authority, every Federal District Court has promulgated local disciplinary rules for lawyers practicing in that Court. These rules are ordinarily, but not necessarily, identical to the rules applied at the state level in the state in which the Federal District Court sits.[17] The question arises whether evidence a lawyer obtains in violation of a District Court disciplinary rule can be excluded even though it is relevant. The most common situation is where the lawyer violates the disciplinary rule that prohibits contact with an adverse party whose counsel is not present.[18]

Neither the disciplinary rules nor the local rules incorporating them specifically provide for exclusion of evidence obtained from a violation. Nonetheless, some Courts, in the exercise of their supervisory power, have held that evidence obtained from the violation of a disciplinary rule must be excluded even though it is relevant.[19] But most courts have held that ethical breaches are properly remedied by professional sanctions against the offending attorney, not by the suppression of evidence or by other adverse rulings against the client.[20] As one Court stated: "The ethical rules were intended by their drafters to regulate the conduct of the profession, not to create actionable duties in favor of third parties."[21] Thus, the predominant view is that the appropriate remedy for a violation of a disciplinary rule is to sanction the lawyer, rather than to exclude the evidence obtained.

More fundamentally, a Court that excludes evidence obtained in violation of a disciplinary rule, where the rule itself does not provide for exclusion, is in effect exercising its supervisory power. Yet Rule 402 does not specify supervisory power as a proper basis of exclusion. The only permissible sources of power to exclude relevant evidence are the Constitution, federal statute, Federal Rules of Evidence, and Supreme Court rules prescribed pursuant to statutory authority. The doctrine of supervisory power is derived from the common law. Thus, a Court excluding relevant evidence on the basis of its supervisory power is, at the least, treading over unstable ground.

---

17. For a discussion of the various approaches of the Federal District Courts in promulgating disciplinary rules, see Burbank, *State Ethical Codes and Federal Practice: Emerging Conflicts and Suggestions for Reform,* 19 FORD. URB. L.J. 969 (1992).

18. See Model Code of Professional Responsibility DR 7-104; Model Rules of Professional Conduct 4.2 ("In representing a client, a lawyer shall not communicate about the subject of the representation with a party the lawyer knows to be represented by another lawyer in the matter, unless the lawyer has the consent of the other lawyer or is authorized by law to do so.").

19. See, e.g., United States v. Hammad, 846 F.2d 854, *reh'g denied,* 855 F.2d 36, *opinion revised,* 858 F.2d 834 (2d Cir. 1988) (where prosecutor obtains information from a defendant in the absence of defense counsel, in violation of DR 7-104, such evidence is subject to exclusion). For a discussion of *Hammad,* see Green, *A Prosecutor's Communications with Represented Suspects and Defendants: What Are the Limits?,* 24 CRIM. L. BULL. 283, 318-20 (1988).

20. See, e.g., Fund of Funds, Ltd. v. Arthur Andersen & Co., 567 F.2d 225, 236 (2d Cir. 1977).

21. Schatz v. Rosenberg, 943 F.2d 485 (4th Cir. 1991). See also W.T. Grant Co. v. Haines, 531 F.2d 671, 676-77 (2d Cir. 1976) ("The business of the court is to dispose of litigation and not to act as a general overseer of the ethics of those who practice here.").

State law

Rule 402, by negative inference, does not permit a Federal Court to exclude relevant evidence on the ground that it would be excluded in a state court; this is true even in a diversity case.[22] However, as the Commentary to Rule 401 indicates, the state law is controlling in a diversity case to the extent that it determines whether evidence relates to a matter in dispute. This is because the applicable substantive law determines the issues that are in dispute.[23] But once the disputed issues have been determined, the question of whether evidence is admissible to prove those issues is purely one of federal law.

It follows that in a federal criminal case, relevant evidence cannot be excluded merely because it was obtained in violation of state law.[24] The question of exclusion is one of federal law.[25]

C. ANNOTATED CASES

No significant decisions.

D. LEGISLATIVE HISTORY

Advisory Committee's Note

The provisions that all relevant evidence is admissible, with certain exceptions, and that evidence which is not relevant is not admissible are "a presupposition involved in the very conception of a rational system of evidence." Thayer, Preliminary Treatise on Evidence 264 (1898). They constitute the foundation upon which the structure of admission and exclusion rests. For similar provisions see California Evidence Code §§ 350, 351. Provisions that all relevant evidence is admissible are found in Uniform Rule 7(f); Kansas Code of Civil Procedure § 60-407(f); and New Jersey Evidence Rule 7(f); but the exclusion of evidence which is not relevant is left to implication.

Not all relevant evidence is admissible. The exclusion of relevant evidence occurs in a variety of situations and may be called for by these rules, by the Rules of Civil and Criminal Procedure, by Bankruptcy Rules, by act of Congress, or by constitutional considerations.

---

22. See, e.g., McInnis v. A.M.F., Inc., 765 F.2d 240 (1st Cir. 1985) (Trial Court properly admitted evidence of plaintiff's drinking on the day of the accident, despite state rule that would exclude such evidence in the absence of actual intoxication; Trial Court was "bound by the Federal Rules of Evidence rather than the state evidentiary rule judicially fashioned").

23. See, e.g., In re Air Crash Disaster near Chicago, 701 F.2d 1189 (7th Cir. 1983) (agreeing with the "many cases" that hold that state law cannot be invoked as a basis for excluding relevant evidence, but noting that "the relevance of the evidence is ascertainable only by reference to the substantive law of the state").

24. See United States v. Chavez-Vernaza, 844 F.2d 1368 (9th Cir. 1987) (evidence seized by state officials in compliance with federal law is admissible in federal court even though state law was violated); United States v. Sutherland, 929 F.2d 765 (1st Cir. 1991) ("Evidence obtained in violation of neither the Constitution nor federal law is admissible in federal court proceedings without regard to state law.").

25. See, e.g., United States v. Walker, 960 F.2d 409 (5th Cir. 1992) (evidence admissible even though it was obtained in violation of Texas law and would have been excluded in a Texas court: "the admissibility of evidence depends on the legality of the search and seizure under federal law").

Succeeding rules in the present article, in response to the demands of particular policies, require the exclusion of evidence despite its relevancy. In addition, Article V recognizes a number of privileges [ed. note: The Advisory Committee proposals on Article V were subsequently rejected by Congress]; Article VI imposes limitations upon witnesses and the manner of dealing with them; Article VII specifies requirements with respect to opinions and expert testimony; Article VIII excludes hearsay not falling within an exception; Article IX spells out the handling of authentication and identification; and Article X restricts the manner of proving the contents of writings and recordings.

The Rules of Civil and Criminal Procedure in some instances require the exclusion of relevant evidence. For example, Rules 30(b) and 32(a)(3) of the Rules of Civil Procedure, by imposing requirements of notice and unavailability of the deponent, place limits on the use of relevant depositions. Similarly, Rule 15 of the Rules of Criminal Procedure restricts the use of depositions in criminal cases, even though relevant. And the effective enforcement of the command, originally statutory and now found in Rule 5(a) of the Rules of Criminal Procedure, that an arrested person be taken without unnecessary delay before a commissioner or other similar officer is held to require the exclusion of statements elicited during detention in violation thereof. Mallory v. United States, 354 U.S. 449, 77 S. Ct. 1356, 1 L. Ed. 2d 1479 (1957); 18 U.S.C. § 3501(c).

While congressional enactments in the field of evidence have generally tended to expand admissibility beyond the scope of the common law rules, in some particular situations they have restricted the admissibility of relevant evidence. Most of this legislation has consisted of the formulation of a privilege or of a prohibition against disclosure. 8 U.S.C. § 1202(f), records of refusal of visas or permits to enter United States confidential, subject to discretion of Secretary of State to make available to court upon certification of need; 10 U.S.C. § 3693, replacement certificate of honorable discharge from Army not admissible in evidence; 10 U.S.C. § 8693, same as to Air Force; 11 U.S.C. § 25(a)(10), testimony given by bankrupt on his examination not admissible in criminal proceedings against him, except that given in hearing upon objection to discharge; 11 U.S.C. § 205(a), railroad reorganization petition, if dismissed, not admissible in evidence; 11 U.S.C. § 403(a), list of creditors filed with municipal composition plan not an admission; 13 U.S.C. § 9(a), census information confidential, retained copies of reports privileged; 47 U.S.C. § 605, interception and divulgence of wire or radio communications prohibited unless authorized by sender. These statutory provisions would remain undisturbed by the rules.

The rule recognizes but makes no attempt to spell out the constitutional considerations which impose basic limitations upon the admissibility of relevant evidence. Examples are evidence obtained by unlawful search and seizure, Weeks v. United States, 232 U.S. 383, 34 S. Ct. 341, 58 L. Ed. 652 (1914); Katz v. United States, 389 U.S. 347, 88 S. Ct. 507, 19 L. Ed. 2d 576 (1967); incriminating statement elicited from an accused in violation of right to counsel, Massiah v. United States, 377 U.S. 201, 84 S. Ct. 1199, 12 L. Ed. 2d 246 (1964).

House Subcommittee on Criminal Justice Notes

To accommodate the view that the Congress should not acquiesce in the Court's judgment that it has authority under the existing Rules Enabling Acts to promulgate Rules of Evidence, and the concern that the Congress must not affect adversely whatever authority the Court does have to promulgate rules, the Subcommittee amended "by other rules adopted by the Supreme Court" to read "by other rules prescribed by the Supreme Court pursuant to statutory authority" in this and other rules where the reference appears.

Report of the House Committee on the Judiciary

Rule 402 as submitted to the Congress contained the phrase "or by other rules adopted by the Supreme Court." To accommodate the view that the Congress should not appear to acquiesce in the Court's judgment that it has authority under the existing Rules Enabling Acts to promulgate Rules of Evidence, the Committee amended the above phrase to read "or by other rules prescribed by the Supreme Court pursuant to statutory authority" in this and other Rules where the reference appears.

RULE 403

A. OFFICIAL TEXT

Rule 403. Exclusion of Relevant Evidence on Grounds of Prejudice, Confusion, or Waste of Time

Although relevant, evidence may be excluded if its probative value is substantially outweighed by the danger of unfair prejudice, confusion of the issues, or misleading the jury, or by considerations of undue delay, waste of time, or needless presentation of cumulative evidence.

B. EDITORIAL EXPLANATORY COMMENT

Presumption of admissibility

This Rule codifies the common-law powers of the Trial Judge and states these powers as explicitly as they ever have been stated. Where the probative value of evidence is substantially outweighed by the danger of unfair prejudice, confusion, or undue consumption of time, the evidence may be excluded even though it is relevant. The drafters of the Rule provided that the probative value must be "substantially" outweighed by these other factors before evidence is excluded. "Substantially" is not defined and there is nothing in the Advisory Committee's Note or in the congressional material that indicates exactly what this word is intended to mean. But the policy of the Rule is that if the balance between probative value and countervailing factors is close, the Judge should admit the evidence. In other words, there is a presumption in favor of admitting relevant evidence. In order to overcome this presumption, the negative countervailing factors must be demonstrably greater than the probative value of the evidence.[1] The rationale is that exclusion amounts to a total deprivation of the offeror's probative evidence while admission may be accompanied by redaction, limiting instruction, or other safeguard by which both the objector and the offeror can ordinarily be accommodated.

Balancing standard

There has been some dispute as to the proper standard to be used in balancing probative value against prejudicial effect under Rule 403. Judge Weinstein and Professor Berger argue that the proper approach is to "give the evidence its maximum reasonable probative force and its minimum reasonable prejudicial value."[2] Disagreeing, Professor

---

1. See, e.g., United States v. Terzado-Madruga, 897 F.2d 1099 (11th Cir. 1990) (under Rule 403, the balance "should be struck in favor of admissibility"); United States v. Krenzelok, 874 F.2d 480 (7th Cir. 1989) (where both probative value and prejudicial effect are high, Rule 403 requires admission).

2. 1 Weinstein & Berger, WEINSTEIN'S EVIDENCE ¶ 403[03].

Dolan recommends that Courts "resolve all doubts concerning the balance between probative value and prejudice in favor of prejudice."[3]

We believe that the proper equation places on one side the maximum reasonable probative force of the offered evidence. Since parties must produce evidence in order to make a case, and since our evidence system allows juries to make all inferences reasonably deducible from the proof presented and allows the parties to argue about those inferences, it is evident to us that the maximum probative force of the evidence is properly viewed as the cost of excluding the evidence.

The other side of the equation should include the *likely* prejudicial impact of the evidence, rather than the minimum or maximum prejudicial effects. Few of us believe that juries will act perfectly in practice. In fact, Rule 403 assumes that juries cannot act this way. But there is no reason to assume that they will act as imperfectly as possible. We are confident that Trial Judges can identify the likely harm associated with probative evidence and can estimate its impact on the jury. Thus, the proper balance pits the maximum probative value of evidence against the likely prejudicial effect.[4]

Importance of the standard

Is the difference between these tests more than a semantic one? We think so. Consider, for example, *United States v. Brady*, 595 F.2d 359 (6th Cir.), *cert. denied*, 444 U.S. 862 (1979). This case represents a disappointing analysis under Rule 403. Two appellants complained that, in their trial on charges that they committed bank robbery in which deaths resulted, they were prejudiced by the admission of gruesome photographs of the victims. At trial the appellants stipulated that the deaths occurred by gunshot wounds to the head, but the Court of Appeals held that the Trial Court properly admitted the evidence because the stipulation did not state that the killings were in the course of a robbery. Had appellants been asked to so stipulate, they surely would have, since the bodies were on the floor of the bank that was robbed. Since the photos depicted three of the four victims lying on the floor in pools of their own blood, it is not even clear how this shows that the killings were part of a robbery. The only thing that is clear is that the photos might have had a tendency to inflame the passions of the jury. Perhaps the result that was reached is explained by the reliance on the Rule 403 approach that focuses on

---

3. Dolan, *Rule 403: The Prejudice Rule in Evidence*, 49 S. CAL. L. REV. 220 (1976).

4. Concerning special problems of balancing involved with protected speech, see Quint, *Toward First Amendment Limitations on the Introduction of Evidence: The Problem of United States v. Rosenberg*, 86 YALE L.J. 1622 (1977). The author argues that:

> to guard against the risk that expression protected by the First Amendment will be used impermissibly to penalize a criminal defendant, *evidence of a defendant's protected speech or association should be excluded, when offered by the government, unless the government can establish that the probative value of the evidence substantially outweighs its dangers.*

Id. at 1661-62 (emphasis in original). In connection with this article, see United States v. Giese, 597 F.2d 1170 (9th Cir. 1978), *cert. denied*, 444 U.S. 979 (1979).

the minimum possible prejudicial effect, rather than on the probable prejudicial effect as we recommend.

Evidence that Courts recognize to be dangerously prejudicial and presumptively improper in most cases may be accepted in cases in which it serves a special purpose and may be difficult to replace. See, e.g., *United States v. Bowers,* 567 F.2d 1309 (5th Cir. 1977), *cert. denied,* 435 U.S. 976 (1978). In that case, mug shots, which the Circuit Court had expressed concern about in *United States v. Rixner,* 548 F.2d 1224 (5th Cir.), *cert. denied,* 431 U.S. 932 (1977), were held properly admitted in response to a defendant's claim as to his appearance at an earlier time. Because the defendant refused to concede authenticity, the Trial Judge was unable to remove the indicia of a criminal record from the photographs.[5]

The meaning of "prejudice"

Evidence is not "prejudicial" merely because it is harmful to the adversary. After all, if it didn't harm the adversary, it wouldn't be relevant in the first place. Rather, the Rule refers to the negative consequence of "unfair" prejudice.[6] Unfair prejudice is that which could lead the jury to make an emotional or irrational decision, or to use the evidence in a manner not permitted by the rules of evidence. Professor Lempert, in *Modeling Relevance,* 75 MICH. L. REV. 1021 (1977), defines prejudicial evidence as "any evidence that influences jury verdicts without relating logically to the issue of guilt or innocence." We would prefer a slightly different definition: "prejudicial evidence is any evidence that affects the trier of fact in a manner not attributable to the permissible probative force of the evidence." This definition makes clear that evidence that strongly relates to the issue of guilt or liability might still be highly prejudicial, and also that evidence that is probative for a permissible use may nonetheless be prejudicial because the jury could use it for an impermissible purpose.

There are, of course, varying degrees of prejudice, and the Trial Court must take that into account when balancing under Rule 403. In a criminal case, any evidence of a defendant's prior criminal activity that is extremely similar to the charges is clearly on the high end of the prejudice scale. The degree of prejudice may well diminish if the evidence might permit some unsavory inferences, and yet does not clearly indicate

---

5. See also United States v. Oliver, 626 F.2d 254 (2d Cir. 1980) (approving use of mug-type shot as necessary).

6. See Ballou v. Henri Studios, 656 F.2d 1147 (5th Cir. 1981):

As this court has consistently held, unfair prejudice as used in Rule 403 is not to be equated with testimony simply adverse to the opposing party. Virtually all evidence is prejudicial or it isn't material. The prejudice must be unfair. Unfair prejudice within the context of Rule 403 means an undue tendency to suggest a decision on an improper basis, commonly, though not necessarily, an emotional one.

See also United States v. Russell, 919 F.2d 795 (1st Cir. 1990) (defendant was correct that proffered evidence was damaging, but evidence is not offered unless it is damaging; evidence is prejudicial within the meaning of the Rule "only where it is unfairly prejudicial.").

criminal or highly immoral activity. Thus, in *United States v. Thompson,* 990 F.2d 301 (7th Cir. 1993), the defendant was charged with being a felon in possession of a gun; the gun was found in an apartment in which he was sleeping. He argued that he neither knew of nor exercised control over the gun and was an infrequent guest at the apartment. The Trial Court permitted an agent to testify that officers found $13,000 cash, and expensive jewelry engraved with the defendant's first name, in the bedroom of the apartment. The defendant argued that this testimony should have been excluded under Rule 403, as it prejudiced the jury into thinking the defendant "was a bad guy." The Court of Appeals held that the evidence was properly admitted to show the defendant's control over the premises, and that the probative value was not substantially outweighed by the prejudicial effect because "it is not a crime to keep jewelry or cash in one's bedroom."

Less prejudicial alternatives

If other less prejudicial proof is available, or if the prejudice of the evidence could easily be minimized, the Trial Judge may decide to exclude evidence when the balance is close.[7] A Court should be more willing to exclude evidence when there are less prejudicial alternative means to prove the fact in issue.[8]

An example of this proposition is the case of *United States v. Torres-Flores,* 827 F.2d 1031 (5th Cir. 1987). Border Patrol Agent Rosario was chasing three suspected illegal aliens when one of them shot at him from a distance of fifty feet, then escaped across the border. Rosario filed a report of the incident, but no investigation was undertaken. Three months later, Rosario was sitting in the Border Patrol locker room, when he happened to look through a stack of nine photographs of men "suspected to be thiefs, smugglers, transvestites and the like," taken by Border Patrol agents when the suspects were in custody. He noticed a picture of a man who resembled the man who had shot at him. That man was Torres-Flores. At trial, when Rosario was questioned about the circumstances of his viewing the photographs, he stated that they were "pictures of various people we take, smugglers, transvestites." Eight of the nine photographs had descriptive material handwritten next to the individual's body, such as "robbery suspect," "in slammer for murder," "river bandit," "thief," and "transvestite." The defendant's photograph also had something written on it, but this was covered up by brown paper and tape when the picture was shown to the jury. There was no attempt to cover up the notations on the other photographs, which were also shown to the jury.

The Court of Appeals held that the Trial Court had committed reversible error in admitting the photographs and allowing them to be viewed by the jury. Of course, it was

---

7. See, e.g., United States v. Pace, 10 F.3d 1106 (5th Cir. 1993) *cert. denied,* 114 S. Ct. 2180 (1994) (in a narcotics case, the Court of Appeals held that the Trial Court erred when it permitted the prosecution to call the defendant's parole officer solely to establish the defendant's address; the testimony was prejudicial, since it informed the jury that the defendant had previously committed crimes; the probative value was minimal, since the defendant's address was not a major issue in dispute in the case; the Court emphasized the fact that the defendant's address could have been proven in a variety of less prejudicial ways).

8. See, e.g., Carter v. District of Columbia, 795 F.2d 116 (D.C. Cir. 1986) (prejudicial evidence excluded where "there were certainly other ways the evidence could have been admitted so that relevant aspects were retained and the prejudicial aspect minimized").

clear that the photographic array was relevant, since Rosario's identification was crucial to the case and thus the jury would have to be apprised of the circumstances of the prior identification. But the Court of Appeals reasoned as follows:

> While the photo-array was not without probative value, this value was substantially outweighed, Fed.R.Evid. 403, in the circumstances of this case, especially as the pictures could easily have been modified so as to avoid characteristics which would cause the jury to identify the defendant as having a prior record. The masking that was attempted was so inartful and incomplete as merely to invite the jury's attention to these prejudicial matters.[9]

The Court instructed that at a new trial, the government should "take more effective steps than mere taping to disguise the nature of the photographs." Of course, the reality is that the prejudice attendant to the photographs in *Torres-Flores* can never be completely rooted out. The jury would surely surmise that the photographs found by Rosario in the Border Patrol locker room were photographs of suspects with prior criminal contacts with the Border Patrol. Nobody would think that the photographs were culled from a pack of baseball cards or a family photo album. However, the Court in *Torres-Flores* did not require the government to eradicate all traces of prejudice before evidence could be admitted; it simply held that in a close case, Rule 403 may warrant exclusion if the offering party fails to take reasonable steps to control the prejudicial effect of the evidence.[10]

Demonstrative evidence

In order to explain or prove how a disputed event occurred, a party may find it helpful to demonstrate the event in court, or to provide a videotaped or even a computerized recreation of the disputed event. Such demonstrative evidence is regulated by the Trial Court under Rule 403. Obviously, a demonstration can never fully and accurately recreate a real-life event, and so there will be questions of probative value, jury confusion and prejudice; the degree to which the demonstration comes close to recreating a real-life event is crucial in determining admissibility.

Trial Courts have often exercised their discretion to admit demonstrations when relevant, so long as they do not create a serious misimpression as to how an event might

---

9. 827 F.2d at 1037 (quoting United States v. Fosher, 568 F.2d 207, 215 (1st Cir. 1978)).

10. See also Douglass v. Hustler Magazine, Inc., 769 F.2d 1128 (7th Cir. 1985) (damages claim for unauthorized publication of photos in a degrading magazine; the Trial Court abused its discretion by allowing plaintiff to present a slide show depicting the "worst of Hustler," which was offered to show the damages she suffered when her photos were published in the magazine: "To pick out the 128 worst pictures from many years of the magazine ... was to assail the senses and distract the mind .... The pictures apparently were selected with a view to highlighting the most offensive features of the magazine."); United States v. McManaman, 606 F.2d 919 (10th Cir. 1979) (evidence of conversation not admissible under Rule 403, even though parts of the conversation were relevant for impeachment; the government proffered the entire conversation, including inflammatory portions concerning murder plans: "the explosive portions were not excised, as can be done to avoid such dangers of prejudice").

have occurred.[11] However, Rule 403 does provide a limit on such demonstrations in egregious cases. A recent example is *United States v. Gaskell,* 985 F.2d 1056 (11th Cir. 1993). The defendant's daughter died from shaken baby syndrome, caused by the defendant's having shaken her. The dispositive question was whether the defendant intended to injure or to revive his daughter when he shook her. The Trial Judge allowed a defense expert to demonstrate shaken baby syndrome to the jury by shaking an infant mannequin used to practice CPR techniques. The expert shook the doll so forcefully that the head repeatedly swung back against the doll's back and then forward against the doll's chest. The expert testified that the neck of the CPR doll was stiffer than an infant's, and so greater force was required to produce the head movement associated with shaken baby syndrome.

The Court of Appeals held that the courtroom demonstration was reversible error, because the conditions of the demonstration "were not sufficiently similar to the alleged actions of the defendant to allow a fair comparison." While the demonstration did indicate how a baby's head would move during shaken baby syndrome, this could have been demonstrated in a less inflammatory manner by a direct manipulation of the doll's head. The Court concluded:

> The sight of an adult male repeatedly shaking a representation of an infant with the degree of force necessary to manipulate the doll's head in the required fashion was likely to form a strong impression upon the jury.... By displaying a greater degree of force than the level required to produce shaken baby syndrome in a seven month-old infant and by arbitrarily selecting a number of oscillations, the demonstration tended to implant a vision of Gaskell's actions in the jurors' minds that was not supported by any factual basis for the demonstration.

Thus, the Court found that the Trial Court had abused its discretion under Rule 403.[12]

---

11. See, e.g., Hale v. Firestone Tire & Rubber Co., 820 F.2d 928 (8th Cir. 1987) (no error to admit demonstration of mannequin hit by an exploding tire); Kehm v. Procter & Gamble Mfg. Co., 724 F.2d 613 (8th Cir. 1983) (in toxic shock syndrome case, there was no error in allowing plaintiff's expert to conduct experiment that purported to show how defendant's "Rely" component interacted with female enzyme; expert's testimony explained the difference between experimental conditions and those that would be found in the female body).

12. See also Four Corners Helicopters, Inc. v. Turbomeca, S.A., 979 F.2d 1434 (10th Cir. 1992) (in a case arising from a helicopter crash, the defendant claimed that the Trial Court erred in excluding evidence of an experiment conducted by their expert; although experiments purporting to simulate actual events are only admissible if made under substantially similar conditions, filmed evidence may be admitted to show relevant mechanical principles upon a lesser showing "that the experiment [was] conducted under conditions that were at least similar to those which existed at the time of the accident"; here, however, the experiment was not being offered simply to show physical principles but instead to demonstrate what the expert believed occurred in the helicopter engine; thus, substantial similarity was required and the Court held that the Trial Court did not abuse its discretion in excluding the experiment); Hinds v. General Motors Corp., 988 F.2d 1039 (10th Cir. 1993) (Trial Court did not abuse its discretion in excluding videotapes of automobile crash tests on grounds of unreliability and dissimilarity). But see Bonilla v. Yamaha Motors Corp., 955 F.2d 150 (1st Cir. 1992) (noting that generally dissimilarities between experimental and actual conditions affect the weight, not the admissibility, of the evidence and holding that the Trial Court did not abuse its discretion in determining that the conditions used by an expert in conducting tests were sufficiently alike).

Experts

In *Daubert v. Merrell Dow Pharmaceuticals, Inc.,* 113 S. Ct. 2786 (1993), the Supreme Court declared that expert testimony "can be both powerful and quite misleading because of the difficulty in evaluating it." The Court concluded that because of the heightened risks attendant to expert evidence, "the judge in weighing possible prejudice against probative force under Rule 403 ... exercises more control over experts than over lay witnesses." After *Daubert,* it can be expected that Trial Courts will use Rule 403 more aggressively to exclude the testimony of experts, especially where the testimony is based on questionable methodology or where it does not completely fit with the issues in the case.[13] *Daubert* is discussed extensively in the Editorial Explanatory Comment to Rule 702, *infra.*

Bench trials

Where the case is tried to a Judge, the risk of prejudice is not a proper ground for excluding evidence under Rule 403. It is nonsensical to ask the Judge to exclude evidence on the ground that it will prejudice her, since the Judge would have to be exposed to the evidence in order to make such a ruling.[14] Moreover, we can fairly presume that Trial Judges are unlikely to rule emotionally, or to misuse evidence, in the way that juries might.[15]

Similarly, an objection on the ground that evidence would be confusing has no place in a bench trial. Nor would it be a good idea even to suggest that the Trial Judge should exclude evidence because it would confuse him. Consequently, the only reason for excluding probative evidence under Rule 403 in a bench trial is that the evidence would be cumulative or a waste of time.

Relationship to other rules

When evidence is absolutely barred by some other Rule, Rule 403 does not give the Trial Judge the authority to admit evidence. The Rule is one of exclusion of otherwise admissible evidence.

---

13. See, e.g., Porter v. Whitehall Labs., 9 F.3d 607 (7th Cir. 1993) ("the suggested scientific testimony must fit the issue to which the expert is testifying"; expert testimony was properly excluded for lack of "fit" where the expert admitted that his conclusion was contingent upon ruling out certain alternative causes for plaintiff's medical condition, which could not in fact be ruled out).

14. See, e.g., Gulf States Utils. Co. v. Ecodyne Corp., 635 F.2d 517, 519 (5th Cir. 1981) (The portion of Rule 403 referring to prejudice "has no logical application in bench trials. Excluding relevant evidence in a bench trial because it is cumulative or a waste of time is clearly a proper exercise of the judge's power, but excluding relevant evidence on the basis of unfair prejudice is a useless procedure.").

15. Gulf States Utils. Co. v. Ecodyne Corp., 635 F.2d 517, 519 (5th Cir. 1981):

> Rule 403 assumes that a trial judge is able to discern and weigh the improper inferences that a jury might draw from certain evidence, then balance those improprieties against probative value and necessity. Certainly, in a bench trial, the same judge can also exclude those improper inferences from his mind in reaching a decision.

Some specific Rules may take precedence over this particular Rule. The clearest example is Rule 609, which provides that *crimen falsi* offenses are admissible for purposes of impeachment of a witness irrespective of the prejudicial impact of such evidence. See *Green v. Bock Laundry Mach. Co.,* 490 U.S. 504 (1989) (discussed in the Editorial Explanatory Comment to Rule 609), where the Supreme Court stated that the automatic admissibility provision of Rule 609(a)(2) permitted no judicial discretion to exclude evidence on Rule 403 grounds.[16] Also, for convictions not involving dishonesty or false statement, Rule 609(a)(1) provides a special balancing test for criminal defendants, whereby the prior conviction is excluded unless the probative value outweighs the prejudicial effect. Finally, Rule 609(b) provides for a special balancing test for all convictions as to which ten years have passed since conviction or confinement.

Where Rule 403 is not pre-empted by a specific Rule, the Trial Judge must apply it in tandem with other Federal Rules under which evidence would be admissible. This is particularly true with respect to other Rules that provide for permissible and impermissible purposes. So, for example, Rule 404(b) provides that prior bad acts cannot be used to prove the propensity of a person to commit an act, but that they can be used for other purposes. The Trial Court must then determine whether the probative value for the nonpropensity purpose is substantially outweighed by the risk that the jury will misuse the evidence for propensity. See the discussion in the Editorial Explanatory Comment to Rule 404.

Rule 403 has an interesting and complex relationship with Rule 801, the hearsay rule. The hearsay rule is purpose-specific in its exclusion; it operates only where the statement is offered for the truth of the matter asserted. When an out-of-court statement is offered for something other than its truth, then the Trial Court, upon appropriate objection, must balance the probative value and the prejudicial effect of the statement under Rule 403.

An example of the relationship between Rule 403 and the hearsay rule is provided in the case of *United States v. Harwood,* 998 F.2d 91 (2d Cir. 1993). Harwood was tried with McKee for possession and conspiracy to possess LSD with intent to distribute. The defendants were arrested after leaving an annual gathering of the "Rainbow Family" in Vermont. One undercover agent bought a small amount of LSD from McKee, who later drove away in a van. The van was driven by Harwood, who was subsequently found to be the owner. Police stopped the van, and a subsequent search uncovered LSD in the door panels, and a large amount of cash in the interior. Harwood claimed that he was not involved in drug activity, but rather was merely giving McKee a ride to and from the Rainbow Family gathering. McKee, his codefendant, claimed that the drugs were Harwood's and not McKee's. At trial, government agents were permitted to testify that through their "intelligence" sources they had learned that McKee was the main supplier of LSD at the Rainbow Family gathering.

The government argued that the "intelligence" testimony was not hearsay because it was not offered for its truth. Rather, it was merely offered as "background" evidence to explain the context of the police investigation. Specifically, the government stated that

---

16. See also United States v. Wong, 703 F.2d 65 (3d Cir. 1983) (Rule 609(a)(2) provides for automatic admissibility for convictions involving dishonesty or false statement: "the general balancing test of Fed.R.Evid. 403 is not applicable to impeachment by *crimen falsi* convictions under Fed.R.Evid. 609(a)(2)").

the "intelligence" testimony was offered only to explain why the undercover agents approached McKee — as opposed to anyone else at the Rainbow Family gathering — in order to obtain LSD. However, Judge McLaughlin saw through this artificial construction. He pointed out that if the "intelligence" evidence was really offered to explain the motivation of the undercover agents, then the evidence would have been irrelevant — or at least not sufficiently relevant to justify the risk that the jury would misuse the evidence for its truth. The motivation of the officers, and the need for the jury to understand the background of the investigation, was not a crucial issue in the context of the case. The risk that the jury would misuse the intelligence testimony for its truth substantially outweighed the probative value of the testimony in explaining "background."[17]

Unfortunately, there have been many instances in which the Courts have ignored the Rule 403 questions inherent in "background" evidence, and in which hearsay statements have been offered to "explain" events that are of minimal or no relevance. One example is *United States v. Norquay*, 987 F.2d 475 (8th Cir. 1993). Norquay was charged with rape, and witnesses testified that the victim told them that she had been raped. The Court of Appeals held that the statements were properly admitted as not hearsay, because they were offered not for the truth of their content but rather "to explain why the witnesses stopped on the highway late at night, took her to the police station, and sent her to be interviewed by the investigator." This analysis, however is misguided: the probative value of the statements for the articulated purpose was minimal, because the conduct of the *witnesses* at the time was only marginally relevant to the case. The prosecution really had no need to explain why the witnesses acted as they did, when there was no dispute as to their actions. In contrast, the prejudicial effect of the statement was obvious, because there was a strong likelihood that the jury would impermissibly use the statement for its truth — that the victim was actually raped. The Court in *Harwood* avoided this trap.[18]

Perhaps the *Norquay* Court would have avoided the trap as well had defense counsel specifically objected to the statements on Rule 403 grounds. It appears that defense counsel in *Norquay* made only a hearsay objection. Once the prosecution articulated a legitimate not-for-truth purpose, the hearsay objection was properly overruled, and it was

---

17. While the intelligence testimony was erroneously admitted, the *Harwood* Court found that the error was harmless.

18. For a result similar to *Harwood*, see United States v. Fountain, 2 F.3d 656 (6th Cir. 1993), where information on the defendant's criminal activity, offered not for its truth but rather to explain why the agents searched where they did, was held improperly admitted because the "reason Agent Primak searched the back bedroom simply was not a matter of dispute and was not in issue in this case." The Court stated that "because the agents' action needed no explanation, we can conclude only that Primak's information was offered to prove the truth of the matter asserted — that guns and narcotics were in the bedroom." See also United States v. Dean, 980 F.2d 1286 (9th Cir. 1992) (statements accusing the defendant of criminal activity, made to a police officer, were improperly admitted for the nonhearsay purpose of explaining why the officer went to the defendant's home to arrest him: the officer's reasons for going to the defendant's home "are not of consequence to the determination of the action, i.e., they do not bear on any issue involving the elements of the charged offense"); United States v. Hanson, 994 F.2d 403 (7th Cir. 1993) (statement made to the defendant, that he did not have to file a certain form, was not offered for its truth but rather for its impact on the defendant's state of mind, and it was relevant for this purpose; exclusion was error, but harmless).

incumbent on defense counsel to specifically argue that the prejudicial effect of the jury's misuse of the statement would substantially outweigh the minimal probative value of the statement for the purpose stated by the prosecution. If such an objection is not specifically made at trial, it ordinarily will not be entertained on appeal.[19]

Stipulations

Where a party is faced with evidence that is strongly probative and yet highly prejudicial, the party may find it prudent to stipulate to the fact that the evidence would prove. In this manner, the inflammatory effect of the evidence would be diminished if not eradicated; and while the stipulation may result in the concession of a point, the concession may be worth it in light of the probative value of the evidence that would have been proffered anyway.

But what happens where the adversary refuses to stipulate and insists on proving the point through the highly probative and yet highly prejudicial evidence? Most Courts hold that upon proper objection, the Trial Judge must factor the proffered stipulation into the Rule 403 balancing process.[20] The Advisory Committee's commentary to Rule 401 (defining relevant evidence) specifically states that "situations will arise which call for the exclusion of evidence offered to prove a point conceded by the opponent," and that a ruling excluding evidence in that situation can be justified under Rule 403. The Committee's reasoning is that if a point is undisputed, and evidence is nonetheless offered to prove the point, the probative value of that evidence is nonexistent because the proponent's case is not significantly advanced. And if the evidence used to prove the uncontested point is prejudicial, then it will almost always be the case that the probative value in proving an uncontested point is substantially outweighed by the risk of prejudice — rendering the evidence inadmissible under the explicit terms of Rule 403.

For example, in *United States v. Spletzer,* 535 F.2d 950 (5th Cir. 1976), the defendant was charged with escape from Federal custody. One element of that crime is that the defendant must have been in custody pursuant to a judgment or conviction. In order to prove this element, the government sought to introduce a certified copy of Spletzer's judgment of conviction for bank robbery. Spletzer objected on the ground that he had offered to stipulate to the conviction element of the crime. The Trial Court held that the government was not obligated to accept the proffered stipulation, and the conviction was admitted. The Court of Appeals reversed. It stated that "as a general rule a party may not preclude his adversary's proof by an admission or offer to stipulate." However, that general rule was subject to Rule 403, and under Rule 403, the probative

---

19. See, e.g., Lewis v. Kendrick, 944 F.2d 949 (1st Cir. 1991) (hearsay objection at trial did not specifically request the Trial Court to weigh the prejudicial nature of the evidence against its probative value; therefore the objection to the prejudicial nature of the evidence was not properly preserved for appeal).

20. See, e.g., United States v. Schwartz, 790 F.2d 1059 (3d Cir. 1986) (stipulation must be taken into account because "the presence or absence of genuine need for the questioned evidence is a legitimate part of the balancing analysis required by Rule 403"; evidence of prior drug crimes to prove intent to commit charged drug crime should have been excluded where the defendant "offered sweeping stipulations relieving the government of the need to prove anything other than that the substance possessed by [the buyer] when he was arrested had been obtained from the defendant").

value of proffered evidence is determined in part by the need for it; if a point is already proven, then there is little need for further evidence on that point, since it would be cumulative and lack probative value. In other words, the offering party can prove a point "as long as the probative value of the proof still exceeds the prejudicial effect, *taking into account the offer to stipulate.*" Under the facts of *Spletzer,* the Court found that the introduction of Spletzer's prior conviction violated Rule 403: Spletzer's proffered stipulation would have taken an entire element completely out of the case, and therefore any proof of that element would have little if any probative value. This minimal probative value was substantially outweighed by the prejudice Spletzer suffered when the jury found out he was a bank robber.[21]

It must be noted that some Courts have rejected the argument that a proffered stipulation has any bearing on the Rule 403 analysis. For example, in *United States v. Breitkreutz,* 8 F.3d 688 (9th Cir. 1993), the defendant was charged with being a felon in possession of a firearm. He offered to stipulate that he was a convicted felon. But the Trial Court held that the prosecution was not required to accept the stipulation and allowed the government to prove the unredacted felony conviction. The Court of Appeals held that this was not error, and stated flatly that a stipulation "has no place in the Rule 403 balancing process." The Court argued that a contrary position "would seriously undermine the rule that the prosecution has a right to refuse a stipulation." But this argument assumes that the prosecution has or should have such an absolute right. In our view, there is no such right if the stipulation carries as much probative value as the prosecution's evidence would carry; if that is so, then the only reason to reject the stipulation is an impermissible one, i.e., to bring prejudicial evidence before the jury.

All this is not to say that a stipulation will always suffice to take prejudicial evidence out of the case. It depends on whether the proffered evidence has probative value beyond the matter stipulated. Put another way, it depends on how well the stipulation disposes of the contested issue.[22] Thus, in *United States v. Peltier,* 585 F.2d 314 (8th Cir. 1978), the defendant took flight after several government agents were killed. The government offered evidence of flight to prove consciousness of guilt. In an attempt to preempt this evidence, the defendant offered to stipulate that he took flight. The prosecution rejected the offer, and the Court, correctly in our view, held that evidence of flight was properly

---

21. See also Silva v. Showcase Cinema Concessions, Inc., 736 F.2d 810 (1st Cir. 1984) (action arising from criminal attack on movie patron; defense sought to introduce the fact that the attacker had been convicted of manslaughter for the attack, as a means of proving that such an attack was not foreseeable by the defendant; it was not error to exclude evidence of a manslaughter conviction, where the plaintiffs were willing to stipulate that the assault was a "criminal act"; under these circumstances, there was no need to prove the conviction since the stipulation "should have made defendant's point"); Turner v. Allstate Ins. Co., 902 F.2d 1208 (6th Cir. 1990) (in wrongful termination action against insurer, the Trial Court properly excluded statistics indicating that the plaintiff granted too many discounts; the statistics were offered to show that the defendant had acted in good faith in terminating the plaintiff; but since the plaintiff stipulated that defendant had acted in good faith, and only contested the fact that he falsified documents, the statistical evidence was rendered irrelevant).

22. See, e.g., United States v. Dynalectric Co., 859 F.2d 1559 (11th Cir. 1988) (in prosecution for antitrust conspiracy, Trial Court did not commit error in admitting evidence of uncharged bid-rigging to prove intent; the defendants offered to stipulate that if the jury found that defendants agreed to fix bids, they would concede that they intended to restrain trade; this stipulation conceded nothing, and thus intent remained a contested issue in the case).

admitted despite the offer to stipulate. The Court noted that Peltier's flight was not simple, garden variety flight; Peltier had resorted to violence and mayhem in order to evade pursuing officers. Thus, a simple stipulation of "flight" would not be nearly as probative of consciousness of guilt as would the actual evidence of flight; the stipulation did not provide the jury with the full probative force of the proffered evidence.[23]

Surprise

If a claim of surprise is made, the Advisory Committee indicates a preference for a continuance, rather than exclusion, and post-Rules decisions support that view.[24] Of course, this does not mean that a party is entitled to a continuance by merely invoking the term "surprise." A claim of surprise will not be considered if the party has not diligently prepared for trial.

It also must be remembered that certain provisions of the Federal Rules of Civil and Criminal Procedure are designed to protect against unfair surprise. One example is a pretrial order entered pursuant to Rule 16 of the Federal Rules of Civil Procedure. This order controls the subsequent course of the action, and evidence and testimony may be disallowed to the extent that it is contrary to the order; exclusion is warranted without regard to Rule 403.

There are also notice provisions throughout the Federal Rules of Evidence, such as those found in Rules 404(b), 412, 803(24) and 804(b)(5). All these notice provisions are designed to protect against unfair surprise, and a failure to comply with these provisions warrants exclusion irrespective of Rule 403.

While surprise is not an independent ground for exclusion under Rule 403, it may, in some cases, bear upon the Rule 403 analysis. If a continuance is required to meet surprising evidence, there is a negative consequence of delay. If the surprising evidence is of marginal probative value, the Trial Judge may decide that the cost of delay substantially outweighs the probative value of the evidence and thus that exclusion is warranted under Rule 403.

---

23. See also United States v. Davis, 792 F.2d 1299 (5th Cir. 1986) (defendant charged with possession of firearms by a felon in interstate commerce; it was not error to admit evidence of previous uncharged possession of firearms, even though the defendant offered to stipulate to the interstate commerce element; an offer to stipulate is relevant under Rule 403, but not "necessarily decisive"; here, even after the stipulation, the uncharged misconduct remained relevant to prove when the charged possession occurred and to determine whether the defendant had made a gift of the firearms to his stepfather).

24. See, e.g., Le Maire v. United States, 826 F.2d 949 (10th Cir. 1987) (no error to admit physician's testimony despite plaintiff's objection that he was surprised by certain aspects of testimony that were different from pretrial statement; the remedy for coping with surprise is not to seek reversal after an unfavorable judgment, but rather to seek a continuance at the time the evidence is proffered); Conway v. Chemical Leaman Tank Lines, Inc., 687 F.2d 108 (5th Cir. 1982) ("the granting of a continuance is a generally more appropriate remedy than exclusion of evidence when claims of unfair surprise are raised").

Procedure for balancing

The practice in the Federal Courts since the adoption of Rule 403 leads us to conclude that rulings would probably be sounder at trial and more easily reviewed on appeal if trial counsel would take care to state their theories of relevance and claims of prejudice as clearly as possible before the Trial Judge rules. Along the same line, the Trial Judge would improve the record by stating, if only briefly, his or her reasons for a Rule 403 ruling.[25] Such reasons could be quickly dictated to the court reporter *outside* the presence of the jury *unless* the Trial Judge wishes to comment on the evidence that is admitted, in which case the reasons may be shared with the jury. If the Trial Court decides to exclude the evidence, a statement of reasons is especially necessary in order to provide counsel an opportunity to try to obviate the objection.[26]

Throughout this Manual, we note the utility of Trial Judges stating reasons on the record to explain their rulings.[27] Yet, we take exception to *United States v. Dolliole,* 597 F.2d 102 (7th Cir.), *cert. denied,* 442 U.S. 946 (1979). In the course of affirming the appellant's conviction as an accomplice to bank robbery, the Court of Appeals stated that the practice of entering a *written* finding as to the reasons for striking a balance under Rule 403 "should definitely be encouraged." Our position is that a statement for the record is as useful as a written statement, and that often it saves time during trial.[28]

Trial Court discretion

While the Rule 403 balancing process should be carefully conducted on the record, this is not to say that the Trial Judge's decision to admit or exclude evidence is itself strictly scrutinized. Rule 403 provides that evidence "may" be excluded, thus imparting significant discretion to the Trial Judge. The Appellate Court will not reverse a Rule 403 decision simply because the Appellate Judges would have ruled differently from the Trial

---

25. United States v. Sampson, 980 F.2d 883 (3d Cir. 1992) (abuse of discretion to admit prior bad acts of criminal defendant where Trial Court's determination of probative value was conclusory, and there was no statement in the record that indicated that the Trial Court had even performed the required Rule 403 balancing); United States v. Stovall, 823 F.2d 817 (5th Cir. 1987) (Trial Court's Rule 403 balancing would not be disturbed where there was an explicit, on-the-record determination that prejudice did not substantially outweigh probative value).

26. See, e.g., United States v. Jamil, 707 F.2d 638 (2d Cir. 1983) (Trial Court should provide a clear statement of its reasons for excluding evidence under Rule 403, so as to allow counsel to explain or to obviate the objection).

27. See, e.g., United States v. Collorafi, 876 F.2d 303 (2d Cir. 1989) (Trial Court making Rule 403 ruling should provide "a clear statement of its reasons" on the record); United States v. Robinson, 700 F.2d 205, 213 (5th Cir. 1983) ("In the absence of on-the-record findings ... we will be obliged to remand unless the factors upon which the probative value/prejudice evaluation were made are readily apparent from the record, and there is no substantial uncertainty about the correctness of the ruling.").

28. Another case suggesting that the finding should be written is United States v. Alessi, 638 F.2d 466 (7th Cir. 1980). See also United States v. Lavelle, 751 F.2d 1266 (D.C. Cir. 1985) (written findings "assist appellate courts in determining whether the proper analysis was employed"; however, failure to make written findings does not warrant reversal or remand where no request was made for such findings, or where the relevant factors are apparent and there is no uncertainty as to the correctness of the ruling).

Judge.[29] Error will only be found if the Trial Judge's decision cannot be supported by reasonable argument.[30] Appellate Courts recognize that the Trial Judge has a unique vantage point from which to detect and assess the negative factors that might arise from proffered evidence, and from which to balance these factors against the probative value of the evidence.[31] Essentially, Appellate Courts will check to see that a balancing process has been conducted; the result of a careful balancing process will not itself be second-guessed.[32] See the cases discussed in the Annotations under the heading "Appellate review standard."

On the other hand, the Trial Judge's discretion under Rule 403 is not unlimited. The following are some general limitations that have been imposed upon the Trial Judge's discretion:

(1) *Power to exclude is to be rarely invoked:* Because Rule 403 provides that the negative factors set forth in the Rule must *substantially* outweigh the probative value, it follows that the discretionary power to exclude should rarely be used.[33] Generally speaking, the Trial Court's decision to exclude evidence is more likely to be found an abuse of discretion than is the Trial Court's decision to admit evidence.[34]

---

29. See, e.g., United States v. Long, 574 F.2d 761, 767 (3d Cir. 1978) (Trial Court's Rule 403 ruling "should not be reversed simply because an appellate court believes that it would have decided the matter otherwise").

30. See, e.g., United States v. Coiro, 922 F.2d 1008 (2d Cir. 1991) (Rule 403 ruling can be set aside only if the Trial Judge acted "arbitrarily or irrationally"); United States v. York, 933 F.2d 1343 (7th Cir. 1991) (no error unless Trial Court's decision was "so unprincipled" as to amount to an abuse of discretion); United States v. Currier, 821 F.2d 52 (1st Cir. 1987) (the balance of probative value and prejudicial effect is "best left to the sound discretion of the trial judge" and Appellate Court will "impose our judgment only if a complaining party can demonstrate that the district court's ruling did not fall within the ambit of reasonable debate"); United States v. De Peri, 778 F.2d 963 (3d Cir. 1985) (Trial Judge's ruling under Rule 403 will only be reversed if it was "arbitrary or irrational").

31. See, e.g., C.A. Associates v. Dow Chem. Co., 918 F.2d 1485 (10th Cir. 1990) (Trial Judge is uniquely suited to balancing probative value against the harmful effects of proffered evidence, because of his or her familiarity with "the full array of the evidence"); United States v. Lau, 828 F.2d 871, 874 (1st Cir. 1987) (Trial Court is "more directly familiar than a court of appeals with the need for the evidence and its likely effect on the jury").

32. See, e.g., United States v. Beasley, 809 F.2d 1273 (7th Cir. 1987):

> [A]lthough appellate courts cannot often tell whether it was best, all things considered, to let in a given piece of evidence, it may be possible to tell whether the district court and the parties took the right things into account. A flaw in the process is easier to detect than is a flaw in the result....

See also McCarty v. Pheasant Run, Inc., 826 F.2d 1554 (7th Cir. 1987) (Trial Judge's exercise of discretion under Rule 403 will rarely be overturned where he "explains the reasoning process behind his conclusion").

33. See, e.g., Herrington v. Hiller, 883 F.2d 411 (5th Cir. 1989) (Trial Court's power to exclude relevant evidence should be used "sparingly"; abuse of discretion to exclude highly probative evidence where there was no strong indication that it would have been confusing or distracting).

34. See, e.g., United States v. Finestone, 816 F.2d 583, 585 (11th Cir. 1987) (Rule 403 provides extraordinary remedy that should be used only sparingly, and consequently the Trial Judge's discretion to exclude evidence is more limited than is the discretion to admit evidence).

(2) *Credibility questions are for the factfinder:* The Trial Judge may not invoke Rule 403 to exclude evidence merely because he or she finds it unbelievable.[35] Rather, the Trial Judge must assess the probative value of the evidence if believed by the jury, and balance that against the risk of prejudice, confusion and delay.[36]

(3) *Balancing process must be conducted:* As discussed above, a Trial Court that conducts a balancing process on the record is more likely to be affirmed than a Trial Court that excludes or admits evidence in a conclusory fashion; at a minimum, remand is a good possibility in the latter instance.[37]

(4) *Prejudice must be properly analyzed:* As discussed above, evidence is not prejudicial within the meaning of Rule 403 merely because it is harmful to the adversary's case. A Trial Court that excludes evidence as ''prejudicial'' merely because it is harmful — as opposed to unfair — runs a substantial risk of reversal.[38]

In limine rulings

When a party can anticipate the use of prejudicial evidence, it is often helpful to get a pretrial, *in limine* ruling on the Rule 403 question. Rule 103 is very general in setting forth the guidelines for offering and objecting to evidence. The Rule provides sufficient leeway when read in connection with Rule 403's direction to guard against undue prejudice to permit Trial Judges to rule on motions *in limine*. At the same time, it must be remembered that many motions under Rule 403 are particularly difficult to give final rulings on before trial, depending as they do on assessments of probative value and prejudicial effect that become manifest only in the trial itself. Therefore, it is extremely important that counsel wishing to admit or exclude evidence that has been subject to a Rule 403 *in limine* motion renew the offer of proof or objection at trial. For further discussion on this point, see the Editorial Explanatory Comment to Rule 103 under the heading ''Renewing an *in limine* objection at trial.''

---

35. See, e.g., Western Indus. v. Newcor Canada, Ltd., 739 F.2d 1198, 1202 (7th Cir. 1984) (Trial Judge ''does not have the right to prevent evidence from getting to the jury merely because he does not think it deserves to be given much weight''; error to exclude under Rule 403 merely because the Trial Court did not believe the witnesses); United States v. Thompson, 615 F.2d 329 (5th Cir. 1980) (''Rule 403 does not permit exclusion of evidence because the judge does not find it credible.'').

36. See, e.g., Bowden v. McKenna, 600 F.2d 282, 284 (1st Cir. 1979) (''Weighing probative value against unfair prejudice under Fed.R.Evid. 403 means probative value with respect to a material fact if the evidence is believed, not the degree the court finds it believable.'').

37. See, e.g., McQueeney v. Wilmington Trust Co., 779 F.2d 916, 922 (3d Cir. 1985) (where Trial Court ''did not articulate its reasons for its finding of prejudice'' and the evidence was not obviously prejudicial, remand was required).

38. See, e.g., Bordon, Inc. v. Florida E.C.R. Co., 772 F.2d 750 (11th Cir. 1985) (in property damage action arising from improper switching of a train after vandals had tampered with a switchbox, the Trial Court excluded a prior similar vandalization on the ground that it would be prejudicial to the railroad; this was error, because ''unfair prejudice as used in Rule 403 cannot be equated with evidence that is simply adverse to the opposing party'' and the evidence was not unfair simply because the railroad did not know the identities of the vandals in the prior incident).

231

Limiting instructions

As discussed in the Editorial Explanatory Comment to Rule 105, the impact of a limiting instruction in controlling prejudice must be considered by the Trial Court when balancing probative value and prejudice under Rule 403. The prejudice to be considered is that which remains after a limiting instruction is given; the Trial Judge must determine whether a limiting instruction is sufficient protection against the dangers addressed by this Rule to tip the scales in favor of admission.[39] Exclusion is warranted where the remaining prejudice — i.e., that which cannot be "instructed away" — substantially outweighs the probative value of the evidence.[40]

C. ANNOTATED CASES

Abuse of discretion — admission of evidence — association

United States v. Roark, 924 F.2d 1426 (8th Cir. 1991): The Court reversed the defendant's conviction for a conspiracy to manufacture methamphetamine because of government argument and two witnesses' testimony linking him to the Hell's Angels motorcycle club. Instructions to the jury at the conclusion of the trial to disregard the witnesses' testimony was completely insufficient to overcome the entire theme of the trial, which was "guilty by association."

Abuse of discretion — admission of evidence —
codefendant's conviction

United States v. Mitchell, 1 F.3d 235 (4th Cir. 1993): The Court reversed a conviction for a cocaine distribution conspiracy because the prosecutor referred to and emphasized that the defendant's brother had been convicted for participation in the conspiracy and the Trial Court gave no cautionary instructions. In *United States v. Blevins,* 960 F.2d 1252 (4th Cir. 1992), the Court held it was error, but harmless beyond a reasonable doubt, to permit mention that six nontestifying codefendants in the charged drug distribution conspiracy had pleaded guilty.

United States v. Leach, 918 F.2d 464 (5th Cir. 1990), *cert. denied,* 111 S. Ct. 2802 (1991): The defendant's conviction for a methamphetamine conspiracy was reversed in

---

39. See, e.g., United States v. Figueroa, 618 F.2d 934, 943 (2d Cir. 1980) (when balancing probative value and prejudicial effect under Rule 403, the Trial Judge "should carefully consider the likely effectiveness of a cautionary instruction that tries to limit the jury's consideration of the evidence to the purpose for which it is admissible"; the Trial Judge, "sensitive to the realities of the courtroom context as in all other trial rulings, must simply include a sound estimate of the likely force of limiting instructions in the overall Rule 403 determination").

40. See, e.g., Government of the Virgin Islands v. Pinney, 967 F.2d 912 (3d Cir. 1992) (in trial on rape charge, prior act of rape was unduly prejudicial, despite limiting instruction; a "realistic view of the capabilities of the human mind" requires Courts to acknowledge that in some situations there may be an unacceptable risk that jurors cannot follow limiting instructions).

part because of plain error in admitting prosecution evidence that a nontestifying coconspirator had pleaded guilty in the case.

United States v. De La Vega, 913 F.2d 861 (11th Cir. 1990), *cert. denied,* 111 S. Ct. 2011, 2012 (1991): During a trial on racketeering, narcotics, civil rights, and tax charges, evidence was elicited that a codefendant had been separately tried and convicted for his involvement in the case. The Court held that although the admission of guilty pleas or convictions of codefendants not subject to cross-examination is generally considered plain error because the jury may regard the issue of the remaining defendant's guilt as settled and the trial as a mere formality, in this case the error was harmless because of prompt and proper curative instructions. See also *United States v. Eason,* 920 F.2d 731 (11th Cir. 1990) (reversing conviction for defrauding the Farmers Home Administration because the government introduced evidence of a nontestifying coconspirator's prior conviction in the scheme).

Abuse of discretion — admission of evidence — confusing evidence

Adams v. Providence & Worcester Co., 721 F.2d 870 (1st Cir. 1983), *cert. denied,* 104 S. Ct. 2349 (1984): The Court held it was error in a FELA case to admit a letter to the plaintiff in which the general manager of the defendant railroad stated that he had been apprised by the plaintiff's lawyer that the plaintiff was incapacitated and that the defendant would remove the plaintiff from train-service for the protection of the public in light of the information supplied by the lawyer. During the trial it became clear that the plaintiff was not totally disabled and did not claim to be. The Court found that the letter must have confused the jury, since the question before it was whether the plaintiff had been "medically discharged," not whether he was able to work, and the letter was of little probative value on that issue.

Abuse of discretion — admission of evidence — criminal acts

United States v. Dockery, 955 F.2d 50 (D.C. Cir. 1992): The Court vacated and remanded convictions for drug trafficking and ex-felon firearms possession on the ground that evidence of prior convictions offered on the ex-felon count and on cross-examination of a defense witness had an unduly prejudicial effect as to the trafficking counts. In *Jordan v. Medley,* 711 F.2d 211 (D.C. Cir. 1983), the Court reversed a judgment for the plaintiffs in an action for assault and intentional infliction of emotional distress. The Court found that evidence that the defendant had been charged with criminal assault "went directly to the central issue of the case" and held that "where the evidence on that issue was closely balanced (as the hung jury in the first trial would suggest), we do not have the necessary assurance that the jury's judgment was not substantially swayed."

United States v. DiNome, 954 F.2d 839 (2d Cir.), *cert. denied,* 113 S. Ct. 94, 95 (1992): In a massive RICO prosecution, the Court held that evidence of certain crimes in which various defendants claimed no participation was relevant to prove the existence and nature of the RICO enterprise. Convictions of two defendants were reversed, however, because after RICO charges against them were dismissed, the evidence was irrelevant and highly prejudicial and their mistrial motions should have been granted.

United States v. Pace, 10 F.3d 1106 (5th Cir. 1993), *cert. denied,* 114 S. Ct. 2180 (1994): In a narcotics case, the Court held it was error (but harmless) for the prosecution to call the defendant's parole officer solely to establish the defendant's address. The testimony was prejudicial, since it informed the jury that the defendant had previously committed crimes; and the Court found the probative value to be minimal, since the defendant's address was not a major issue in dispute in the case, and since it could have been proved in a variety of less prejudicial ways.

United States v. Calhoun, 544 F.2d 291 (6th Cir. 1976): The Court held it was error to allow the defendant's parole officer to testify that he was the person shown in photographs of a bank robbery. Even if the government did not reveal the officer's relationship with the defendant, the defendant could not effectively cross-examine the witness without risking undue prejudice.

Wilson v. City of Chicago, 6 F.3d 1233 (7th Cir. 1993), *cert. denied,* 114 S. Ct. 1844 (1994): The plaintiff, who had shot and killed two policemen, brought a civil rights action alleging that police had tortured him in extracting a confession. Reversing a judgment for the individual defendants, the Court held that evidence of the killings was admissible, but that there had been an abuse of discretion in admitting evidence of the ugly details of the crimes. Arguments that the evidence was relevant to show the plaintiff's injuries were suffered while arrested or self-inflicted were not remotely plausible.

United States v. Fawbush, 900 F.2d 150 (8th Cir. 1990): The defendant's conviction for aggravated sexual abuse of two children was reversed, the Court holding that evidence the defendant sexually abused his daughters when they were children, even if relevant, was so inflammatory on its face as to divert the jury's attention from the material issues in the trial.

United States v. Breitkreutz, 8 F.3d 688 (9th Cir. 1993): Reversing the defendant's conviction for being a felon in possession of a firearm, the Court held that the government should not be precluded from offering proof of any prior felonies by the defendant's offer to stipulate that he was a convicted felon, but that it was an abuse of discretion to allow proof of three prior felonies. A concurring Judge believed that the government should only be permitted to prove the defendant's conviction, without mention of the underlying facts, and that a defendant should be able to stipulate as to his status (e.g., convicted felon) even though not to his actions or state of mind in committing the crime. In *United States v. Bland,* 908 F.2d 471 (9th Cir. 1990), the defendant, charged with being a felon in possession of a firearm, gave notice that his theory at trial would be that an officer planted the gun in order to justify shooting him in making an arrest. At the *voir dire* the Trial Judge told the jury not only that it was anticipated that the officer would testify he shot the defendant to prevent his escape and that he was aware of an outstanding warrant for the defendant, but also that the warrant was for the molestation, torture, and murder of a seven-year-old girl. The Court reversed the conviction because, although the existence of the warrant was relevant to show the officer did not have a motive to plant the gun, the members of the jury panel were not likely to forget details leading them to believe that acquitting the defendant might mean releasing an extremely dangerous child molester and killer into the community. See also

United States v. Echavarria-Olarte, 904 F.2d 1391 (9th Cir. 1990) (abuse of discretion (but harmless error) for DEA agent to give expert testimony on the operations of the Medellin drug cartel, which were unrelated to offenses with which defendant was charged).

United States v. Sullivan, 919 F.2d 1403 (10th Cir. 1990): The Court reversed convictions for offenses arising out of a conspiracy to manufacture amphetamine because the Trial Judge permitted a prosecutor to offer evidence despite rulings excluding it and denied a mistrial motion. Testimony that the arresting agents were heavily armed because of a fear that one of the defendants was acting as a sniper at the lab site, and that another defendant had previously participated in an unrelated amphetamine "cook" was more prejudicial than probative.

United States v. Hines, 955 F.2d 1449 (11th Cir. 1992): Reversing convictions for aggravated sexual assault, the Court held it was an abuse of discretion to admit photospreads from which the complainant had identified the defendants as her assailants, as there was no demonstrable need to introduce the photographs, the photos implied the defendants had prior criminal records, and the agent's testimony highlighted that the photos were of known criminals. In *United States v. Church,* 955 F.2d 688 (11th Cir.), *cert. denied,* 113 S. Ct. 233 (1992), a RICO prosecution for acts, including conspiracy to murder, committed in 1983 and 1984, the Court held it was harmless error to admit a tape recording of a 1979 conversation discussing a defendant's plan to kill a prosecutor.

Abuse of discretion — admission of evidence — flight

United States v. Kang, 934 F.2d 621 (5th Cir. 1991): In a prosecution for bribing an IRS agent, the defendant had stipulated to willful commission of the offense and asserted only an entrapment defense. The Court reversed his conviction, finding an abuse of discretion in admitting evidence of the defendant's flight, as it was not relevant to show his predisposition or the manner of the government's investigation. Thus, it was not only inadmissible under Rule 403 balancing because of the risk of prejudice, but it was also inadmissible under Rule 401 on relevancy grounds.

Abuse of discretion — admission of evidence — hearsay

United States v. Kang, 934 F.2d 621 (5th Cir. 1991): In a prosecution for bribing an IRS agent, the accused made an entrapment defense. The agent's testimony that his superiors had told him the defendant had violated liquor control commission regulations was admitted as evidence of the agent's state of mind, but the prosecutor argued in summation that it showed a predisposition to cheat on taxes. The Court reversed, as the prosecutor's attempt to exploit the testimony concerning out-of-court statements by linking it explicitly to impermissible propositions only aggravated the inherent prejudice of evidence having little probative value; the government's good faith, motive, or reasonableness is only of secondary significance, if relevant at all, in an entrapment case.

Abuse of discretion — admission of evidence —
less prejudicial alternative

Carter v. District of Columbia, 795 F.2d 116 (D.C. Cir. 1986): In a suit by arrestees asserting brutality claims against police, the Court held it was error for the plaintiffs to present detailed evidence of allegations of misconduct against narcotics officers contained in administrative complaints, pleadings in other cases, personnel files, and newspaper articles. The Court concluded that the plaintiffs could have elicited evidence that allegations were made and could have asked about the police department's response without exploring the alleged events in detail.

Wilk v. American Med. Ass'n, 719 F.2d 297 (7th Cir. 1983): Reversing on another ground a judgment for the defendants in an antitrust action by chiropractors, the Court indicated that it would have been obliged to reverse also because highly prejudicial evidence about one particular chiropractic school and one plaintiff's one-time arrangement with a furniture store to sell mattresses to his patients was admitted. The Court recognized that the evidence was relevant to the defendants' belief that "chiropractic is quackery," but it concluded that the defendants' beliefs could have been explored in a less prejudicial way with much less emphasis on alleged financial greed. In *United States v. Hansen,* 583 F.2d 325 (7th Cir.), *cert. denied,* 439 U.S. 912 (1978), the Court reversed a perjury conviction because the foreman of the grand jury that indicted a defendant was called to testify against him. The Court said that "[t]he [district] court and jury should be able to place the defendant's allegedly perjurious testimony in 'proper context' without help from the foreman of the grand jury." A transcript was to be preferred, because "when the foreman of the grand jury is called without any sufficient reason and in effect justifies the grand jury's actions and the resulting indictment, all precautions about the undue influence of the indictment are very likely for naught."

United States v. Bejar-Matrecios, 618 F.2d 81 (9th Cir. 1980): Reversing a conviction for illegally reentering the United States, the Court concluded it was error to admit a certified copy of a judgment showing that the appellant once pleaded guilty to the misdemeanor of illegal entry. Although the plea conclusively established that the appellant was an alien when he pleaded guilty, the jury was never told why the prior conviction was being used, the evidence was cumulative, and the jury might have used the evidence as proof of predisposition. In *United States v. Mejia,* 529 F.2d 995 (9th Cir. 1976), the Court reversed a heroin conviction because evidence that the defendant was supposed to report to jail on the day that he allegedly engaged in a narcotics transaction had been erroneously admitted to rebut his entrapment defense. This evidence was of little or no probative value on the issue of predisposition to commit the specific crimes charged and it was highly prejudicial. "Bluntly speaking, the government's introduction of the challenged evidence was an indulgence in prosecutorial pettifoggery."

United States v. Gaskell, 985 F.2d 1056 (11th Cir. 1993): The defendant's daughter died from shaken baby syndrome, caused by the defendant's shaking her. The dispositive question was whether defendant intended to injure or to revive his daughter when he shook her. The Trial Judge allowed an expert to demonstrate shaken baby syndrome to the jury by shaking an infant mannequin used to practice CPR techniques. The expert shook the doll so forcefully that the head repeatedly swung back against the doll's back and then forward against the doll's chest. The expert testified that the neck of the CPR doll was stiffer than an infant's, and so greater force was required to produce the head movement associated with shaken baby syndrome. The Court held that the courtroom demonstration was reversible error, because the conditions of the demonstration "were not sufficiently similar to the alleged actions of the defendant to allow a fair comparison.'' While the demonstration did indicate how a baby's head would move during shaken baby syndrome, this could have been demonstrated in a less inflammatory manner by a direct manipulation of the doll's head.

Abuse of discretion — admission of evidence — miscellaneous cases

LaPlante v. American Honda Motor Co., 27 F.3d 731 (1st Cir. 1994): In an action for injuries suffered while operating an All Terrain Vehicle, the plaintiff contended that Honda knew that its ATVs would fail to turn properly unless the rider shifted his or her weight in a counterintuitive manner. Over objection, the plaintiff introduced evidence that Honda had made $73,371,000 in profits from the sale of ATVs over a six-year period. The Court stated that the evidence of profits was somewhat probative of ''the credibility of Honda's explanation for its inaction''—that is, that the failure to provide adequate warnings about plowing may have resulted from greed rather than lack of knowledge. The Court ruled, however, that the risk of prejudice substantially outweighed the ''scant probative value'' of the evidence, and therefore that the Trial Court had ''miscalibrated its Rule 403 scales'' in admitting the evidence of profits.

Davidson v. Smith, 9 F.3d 4 (2d Cir. 1993): The Court reversed a judgment for the defendants in a prisoner's civil rights action because a defense witness violated an *in limine* order not to refer to the plaintiff's psychiatric history or his treatment at a state hospital for the criminally insane. Given the prejudicial effect of the evidence, the questionable efficacy of a curative instruction, and the relative strength of the plaintiff's case, it was error to deny the plaintiff's motion for a mistrial.

United States v. Copple, 24 F.3d 434 (3d Cir. 1994): In a mail fraud prosecution arising from a scheme to invest ''pre-need'' funds of funeral directors, the Court held that evidence of the extent of the victims' losses could be probative of the defendant's intent to convert the funds to his personal use, but the victims' testimony about the personal tragedies they suffered as a result of the fraud was unfairly prejudicial. The error in admitting the evidence was harmless, however.

United States v. Carter, 969 F.2d 197 (6th Cir. 1992): The Court reversed a conviction for selling cocaine to FBI agents, holding it was error to admit evidence of the defendant's purchase of household items, his two bank loan applications, and his failure to file tax returns. As this prosecution did not involve either a continuing criminal enterprise or an allegation that the defendant lacked a legitimate source of income to support an affluent lifestyle, the evidence was irrelevant and extremely prejudicial.

Buscaglia v. United States, 25 F.3d 530 (7th Cir. 1994): In a slip-and-fall case brought under the Federal Tort Claims Act, the Trial Court granted summary judgment after rejecting an affidavit from the plaintiff's expert which concluded that the tile on which the plaintiff slipped was unreasonably slippery for use in public buildings. The Trial Court reasoned that under Rule 403 the expert's testimony was only marginally probative, because the expert's conclusion was based on examining a tile sample that was dry and unwaxed, unlike the tile on which the defendant slipped. The Trial Court further found the proffered testimony unduly prejudicial because of the ''allure of scientific jargon and a witness with an advanced degree.'' But the Court of Appeals concluded that the Trial Court had committed "clear error on the basis of an incorrect weighing of the relevant factors." The Court noted that the tile sample tested by the expert had been provided by the defendant in response to a discovery request, and that the significance of the difference in the tiles was a question of weight. As to prejudice, the Court concluded that the Trial Court was in error because it had assumed that the case would be tried to a jury, whereas "the trier of fact in FTCA cases *is* the district court judge." Accordingly, the prejudice factor should weigh "far less heavily" than it would in a jury case. In *Fortino v. Quasar Co.,* 950 F.2d 389 (7th Cir. 1991), the Court reversed judgments for plaintiffs allegedly discharged because of national origin and age discrimination, holding that it was error to admit a videotaped speech by one of the defendant's executives that indicated age bias, as none of the plaintiffs was in the executive's group and he had no role in their discharge or in that of any other employee.

United States v. LaChapelle, 969 F.2d 632 (8th Cir. 1992): The defendant, charged with receiving child pornography through the mail, asserted an entrapment defense, and the government introduced a pornographic videotape seized from the defendant's home to show his knowledge of and intent to order child pornography. The Court held admission of the evidence was error (but harmless) because the possession was legal when the defendant first possessed the videotape. Evidence of predisposition to do what was once lawful is not by itself sufficient to show predisposition to do what is now illegal, so the slight probative value of the evidence was outweighed by its prejudicial effect.

Abuse of discretion — denial of continuance

Fenner v. Dependable Trucking Co., 716 F.2d 598 (9th Cir. 1983): The Court reversed a judgment for the plaintiff in a personal injury action, finding that the defendants were denied a fair trial when the Trial Judge refused to grant a continuance to permit the defendants' expert to testify. The Court reasoned that the Judge had lulled the defendants into thinking that the problem of their expert's unavailability would be worked out, and that the expert's testimony was material and not cumulative.

United States v. Russell, 717 F.2d 518 (11th Cir. 1983): The Court affirmed marijuana-related convictions, finding no error in the refusal to grant a recess late one afternoon so that a final defense witness could testify the next morning. Noting that "[t]he Federal Rules of Evidence discourage the admission of extrinsic evidence to prove or disprove issues which are collateral to the subject matter of the case," the Court concluded that the Trial Judge properly found the missing witness to be unimportant.

Abuse of discretion — exclusion of evidence — civil rights and employment discrimination cases

Zaken v. Boerer, 964 F.2d 1319 (2d Cir.), *cert. denied,* 113 S. Ct. 467 (1992): Reversing a judgment for the defendant, principal owner and executive of a company designing and selling women's clothing, in an action alleging employment discrimination based on pregnancy, the Court held that it was error to exclude a statement by the vice president for sales that the plaintiff's predecessor had been fired because she was pregnant. Where none of the plaintiff's three witnesses testified to the statement or gave objective direct evidence that pregnancy played a role in the defendant's employment decisions, the evidence should not have been excluded as cumulative.

Mullen v. Princess Anne Volunteer Fire Co., 853 F.2d 1130 (4th Cir. 1988): Although the Court affirmed a judgment for a fire company sued by a plaintiff who alleged discrimination in its membership policies, it stated that racial statements by a decision-maker are relevant to demonstrating racial animus and have great probative value. The Court recognized that "[t]estimony concerning racial remarks is certain to be emotionally charged," but reasoned that "[w]ords produce emotion as a result of the ideas that they represent," and "[t]he epithets involved here are offensive precisely because they convey the idea of racial bigotry." Error in excluding the remarks in this case was not prejudicial.

Plemer v. Parsons-Gilbane, 713 F.2d 1127 (5th Cir. 1983): The Court remanded an employment discrimination case for consideration of the plaintiff's statistical evidence, but indicated there was no error in excluding the plaintiff's evidence of an administrative settlement indicating that another woman had been paid discriminatorily, since this shed almost no light on whether the plaintiff's salary was discriminatory. The Court found, however, that the Trial Judge should not have excluded as irrelevant a letter written by a government contract compliance officer to the defendant that gave notice of deficiencies discovered in an on-site review. The letter might have shown widespread discrimination and thus would have tended to show that justifications for salary differences were pretextual.

Shahid v. City of Detroit, 889 F.2d 1543 (6th Cir. 1989): The Court reversed judgments for the defendants in a civil rights action, brought for alleged failure to provide medical care to a jail inmate prior to his death, because the Trial Judge had excluded black-and-white photographs of the decedent's body in his cell shortly after his death. By depicting paint dustings, bruises, and blood traces, the photos were relevant to whether he had sought assistance and the obviousness of his injuries, and the fact the body may have been moved before the photos were taken did not mean they were an inaccurate representation of what they depicted.

Estes v. Dick Smith Ford, Inc., 856 F.2d 1097 (8th Cir. 1988): The Court reversed a judgment in an employment discrimination case, finding that the plaintiff should have been permitted to introduce evidence of prior acts of discrimination against black customers by the service department for which he formerly worked. This evidence could have assisted the jury in resolving the issue of the employer's motive for discharging the plaintiff.

Baker v. Delta Air Lines, Inc., 6 F.3d 632 (9th Cir. 1993): In an age discrimination case, the Trial Judge excluded memos written in 1978 as having only attenuated relevance to the defendant's policy or practice in the period at issue. Reversing in part, the Court held that the memos were probative both of whether the defendants had a particular policy at that time (a fact put in issue by the defendants) and the motivation behind that policy (which was probative of the rationale for the policy later), and that this probative value outweighed the risks of jury confusion and time wasting. In *Miller v. Fairchild Indus.,* 885 F.2d 498 (9th Cir. 1989), *cert. denied,* 494 U.S. 1056 (1990), the plaintiffs, who alleged that they were discharged in retaliation for filing discrimination charges with the EEOC, were not permitted to introduce evidence of the defendant's hirings in other job categories after they were laid off, but the defendant was permitted to prove layoffs in other categories in order to show its economic condition. The Court held that excluding the plaintiffs' evidence was an abuse of discretion, but harmless because it would have provided only weak support for their contention that the defendant's economic condition was but a pretext for their layoffs.

Ross v. Buckeye Cellulose Corp., 980 F.2d 648 (11th Cir. 1993): In an employment discrimination action, evidence that managers who later worked at the plant had made racially derogatory remarks was excluded on the ground that it would open the door to further evidence about another of the defendant's plants, thereby substantially and unnecessarily prolonging the trial. The Court held that although the evidence may have been the "smoking gun" on the disparate treatment issue, there was no clear abuse of discretion where, even after the Trial Court indicated its willingness to admit the evidence if it were significant, plaintiffs' counsel did not highlight the significance of the evidence and only stated it was important to impeach testimony counsel had hoped unsuccessfully to elicit from another witness. In *Wilson v. City of Aliceville*, 779 F.2d 631 (11th Cir. 1986), the Court reversed a judgment for the City in an employment discrimination suit by a black officer who claimed that the City refused to hire him as police chief because of his race. It found clear error in the exclusion of evidence that the Mayor made a racial slur in a statement to the effect that the federal government would not tell him whom to hire. It rejected the Trial Judge's reliance on Rule 403, which it said should be used "sparingly," and concluded that reversal was proper, even though the case was tried to an advisory, not a regular, jury.

Abuse of discretion — exclusion of evidence — criminal defense

United States v. Morgan, 581 F.2d 933 (D.C. Cir. 1978): The defendant, charged with possession of narcotics with intent to distribute, attempted to introduce evidence that one of the occupants of an apartment in which drugs were found was involved in selling drugs and that the seized drugs belonged to this person, not the defendant. The Court, finding an abuse of discretion in the exclusion of this evidence, emphasized that the jury might have speculated in an improper way about the meaning of the drugs that were discovered unless it knew that there was some evidence that a person other than appellant might have been selling the drugs. In *United States v. Williams*, 561 F.2d 859 (D.C. Cir. 1977), the Court reversed a bank robbery conviction because the government introduced evidence of stolen money found in the appellant's sister's apartment, although it had almost no evidence that the appellant had access to the apartment and the jury was never told that the other inhabitant of the apartment had pleaded guilty to the robbery for which the appellant was charged. The Court emphasized the weak probative value of the evidence and the fact that without an instruction concerning the plea of guilty by the other inhabitant of the apartment the evidence was highly prejudicial. Justice Clark dissented, and four Circuit Judges, indicating they wanted to rehear the case *en banc*, believed that the defense would have objected to any mention of the fact that appellant's sister's roommate pleaded guilty.

United States v. Dwyer, 539 F.2d 924 (2d Cir. 1976): A defendant charged with various weapons violations pleaded not guilty by reason of insanity, but the principal psychiatric witness, who was making his first appearance in the courtroom as an expert witness, did not couch his testimony in the manner necessary to create a valid insanity defense. To bolster the psychiatric testimony, the defendant asked for permission to call a second expert. After a normal weekend recess, the second expert was called and was allowed to take the stand, but the government objected and the Trial Judge barred the testimony on the ground that it would not be helpful. Reversing, the Court emphasized the importance of the second psychiatric expert and stated that the probative value of the evidence was great and that it should not have been excluded "in the absence of a significant showing of unfair prejudice," which was lacking here.

United States v. Davis, 639 F.2d 239 (5th Cir. 1981): In reversing marijuana convictions, the Court found it was an abuse of discretion to exclude character evidence offered to impeach the key government witness. The Court warned that the exclusion of admissible evidence offered by defendants raises compulsory process problems and that an abuse of discretion is an error of constitutional dimension. In *United States v. Thompson,* 615 F.2d 329 (5th Cir. 1980), the Court reversed a conviction for violating federal election laws, holding it was error to dismiss a witness from the stand because the Court did not believe her testimony. "Rule 403 does not permit exclusion of evidence because the judge does not find it credible," said the Court, which added that the error also denied appellant his constitutional right to a fair trial. In *United States v. Riley,* 550 F.2d 233 (5th Cir. 1977), a former national bank examiner was convicted of misapplying bank funds by inducing the bank to issue cashier's checks for his remittance before he paid for them. These transactions differ from a customer's occasional overdraft, because a personal check does not require the bank to disburse any money that it does not have, while a cashier's check is a commitment by the bank to deliver cash to the payee. Reversing, the Court held it was error to exclude evidence of eighty other instances during the same time period in which the bank had issued cashier's checks without contemporaneous payment, which was offered to show that the transactions were regarded as informal loans or extensions of credit to bank officers. "Although the trial judge is traditionally accorded a wide range of discretion in the admission of evidence, ... it is axiomatic that such discretion does not extend to the exclusion of crucial relevant evidence establishing a valid defense."

United States v. Arthur, 949 F.2d 211 (6th Cir. 1991): The Court reversed a conviction for bank robbery, with one Judge considering it was an abuse of discretion to refuse to allow the defendant's brother, a codefendant who was trying to exculpate the defendant at trial, to put on a wig and baseball cap to demonstrate that with the disguise there was a close resemblance. The other Judges, concurring in the judgment, found no abuse of discretion, as all eyewitnesses except the codefendant testified that whoever robbed the bank was not wearing a wig.

United States v. Blaylock, 20 F.3d 1458 (9th Cir. 1994): The Court reversed a firearm conviction, holding it was error to exclude medical records of the defendant offered to show that he was receiving medical treatment for a bad back at the time of his arrest. These records might have cast doubt on police officers' testimony that they saw the defendant running with a gun in his hand. Further, there was no risk justifying exclusion under Rule 403 that a reasonable jury would be misled by the contents, even without expert interpretation, as the records were written in plain language.

United States v. Austin, 933 F.2d 833 (10th Cir. 1991): Reversing a conviction for resisting correctional officers, the Court held it was an abuse of discretion when the defense was mental illness to exclude records of prior hospitalizations on the ground solely of remoteness. The Court was unwilling to place a temporal limit on relevant proof of mental illness in view of its frequently long duration, its possible chronicity, and its recurrent manifestations.

United States v. Costa, 947 F.2d 919 (11th Cir. 1991), *cert. denied,* 112 S. Ct. 2289, 113 S. Ct. 360 (1992): Defendants charged with cocaine importation called a witness who would have testified that he had imported cocaine with three of the government witnesses but he had never known of the defendants in connection with his smuggling. The testimony was excluded on the ground that it related to a different conspiracy than the one alleged at trial and its admission would therefore tend to confuse the jury. The Court found no abuse of discretion, but expressed concern about the ruling, noting that applying the Rule in conspiracy cases to exclude potentially relevant evidence (regardless of who offers it) because it might cause jury confusion will usually be inconsistent with the general rule favoring the admission of such evidence and allowing the jury to decide if it relates to the indicted conspiracy.

Abuse of discretion — exclusion of evidence — miscellaneous cases

Swajian v. General Motors Corp., 916 F.2d 31 (1st Cir. 1990): The plaintiff in a product liability action alleged that his decedent was killed in a rollover accident caused by a defective axle in the vehicle she was driving. The Court reversed a judgment for the plaintiff, holding that the Trial Judge had not properly weighed probative value and prejudicial effect in excluding evidence relating to the decedent's alcohol consumption and blood alcohol level. In *Kassel v. Gannett Co.,* 875 F.2d 935 (1st Cir. 1989), the Court ordered a retrial on the damages issue in this defamation action by a Veterans Administration psychologist who alleged that defendant's libelous newspaper story led to the VA's reassigning him to a position where he had nothing to do. The Court held that a brief filed *pro se* by the plaintiff in a labor grievance proceeding protesting the reassignment should not have been excluded because his statements there that he had been transferred in reprisal for union activities and prior successful grievances were highly probative admissions directly contrary to his position at trial.

Blancha v. Raymark Indus., 972 F.2d 507 (3d Cir. 1992): In an asbestos case, the plaintiffs' theory was that all asbestos could cause the decedent's mesothelioma; the defendant's expert indicated that asbestos products containing chrysotile did not cause mesothelioma. After a verdict for the defendant, a new trial was granted, first on the ground that the expert's testimony was irrelevant without evidence that the defendant's product contained chrysotile, and later (on reconsideration) on the ground that the jury might have been confused by the expert testimony in the absence of evidence about the defendant's product. Reversing a judgment for the plaintiff on the new trial, the Court held that the expert's testimony was relevant, given the theory advanced and the plaintiffs' burden of proof on proximate causation, and that the danger of confusion did not so clearly outweigh the probative value of the expert's testimony as to justify exclusion. In *Herber v. Johns-Manville Corp.*, 785 F.2d 79 (3d Cir. 1986), the Court vacated a judgment for a worker who sued several asbestos suppliers but was awarded no damages by a jury. It held that the Trial Judge clearly erred in excluding under Rule 403 two types of evidence: relevant to damages compensable under state law: evidence that the plaintiff would have to undergo preventative monitoring for cancer in the future, and evidence of the plaintiff's fear of future cancer. In *United States v. Driggs*, 823 F.2d 52 (3d Cir. 1987), the Court found an abuse of discretion in a pretrial ruling in a Hobbs Act prosecution that the government could not introduce tape-recorded conversations of a union official in which he discussed payments to various officials other than the defendant. The Court concluded that the evidence was relevant to proving the intent of the official to make a gift to the defendant because he had been elected a judge. In our view, the Trial Judge was correct. The issue in this case was whether the defendant received a payment under color of official right. The evidence concerning the union official's intent did not establish that the judge had any idea of the official's purpose, and it tended to confuse the official's motive with the judge's.

Yarbrough v. Sturm, Ruger & Co., 964 F.2d 376 (5th Cir. 1992): The Court reversed a judgment against the defendant manufacturer in a product liability action for injuries suffered when a pistol stolen by the infant plaintiff accidentally discharged. Excluding evidence that the gun was stolen, which was probative because of the resulting tendency to carry it in a careless, concealed manner predictably increasing the risk of harm, unfairly prevented the defendant from fully making its contributory fault defense. In *Jackson v. Firestone Tire & Rubber Co.*, 788 F.2d 1070 (5th Cir. 1986), the Court reversed a part of a judgment against a wife whose husband was killed when a wheel rim exploded, finding that evidence of an alternative design, offered to demonstrate why the rim that caused the injury was defective, had been erroneously excluded. It also found that other evidence should have been admitted: evidence of other wheel components, which was relevant to the plaintiff's claim that a rim with several parts might end up mismatched; evidence of similar accidents; and evidence of various records of the defendants, even though some postdated the accident, since the records tended to show a long and continuous experience with certain tires and rims.

Laney v. Celotex Corp., 901 F.2d 1319 (6th Cir. 1990): In a worker's action for personal injuries arising from alleged asbestos exposure, the Court reversed a verdict for the plaintiff on the ground that evidence of his exposure to other asbestos products should have been admitted to support the defendant's argument that its asbestos was not a substantial factor in causing the plaintiff's injuries. In *Koloda v. General Motors Parts Div.*, 716 F.2d 373 (6th Cir. 1983), the Court reversed a judgment for an auto mechanic who sued for injuries allegedly arising out of his use of a lubricant and inhalation of its vapors. General Motors should have been permitted to offer evidence that there were no prior claims or accidents brought to its attention concerning the lubricant. The Court agreed with G.M. that the evidence was probative of its knowledge, which was important to the plaintiff's theory of a failure to warn, and it stated that it could see no reason why the evidence would have been unfairly prejudicial.

Western Indus. v. Newcor Canada, Ltd., 739 F.2d 1198 (7th Cir. 1984): In a suit arising out of a contract to purchase certain machines, the Court found it was reversible error to exclude three expert witnesses who would have testified about customary practice in the specialty welding machine trade. The Court said that a Judge may not listen to cross-examination of witnesses before their testimony is presented to the jury and forbid them to testify because the Judge disbelieves them.

SEC v. Peters, 978 F.2d 1162 (10th Cir. 1992): The Court reversed a judgment for the defendant in a civil action for insider trading violations, holding the SEC had been improperly precluded from asking the defendant and his character witnesses about allegations of other securities law violations, as the defendant had made his character and his unblemished history a very important part of his defense and the rulings deprived the jury of a fair and balanced opportunity to evaluate his character. The Trial Court had erroneously assigned the proposed evidence a probative value of "nil" and overemphasized its prejudicial effect and tendencies to raise collateral issues.

Johnson v. United States, 780 F.2d 902 (11th Cir. 1986): The Court remanded a wrongful death case brought by the parents of an infant who died after being taken to a military hospital, holding it was error to exclude as cumulative the testimony of a third expert witness who arguably had better credentials than the first two and whose analysis was somewhat different from the others'.

Abuse of discretion — exclusion of evidence — prosecution evidence

United States v. Blyden, 964 F.2d 1375 (3d Cir. 1992): The Court reversed a ruling *in limine* that evidence of an alleged assault for which the defendants had previously been acquitted could not be introduced in a prosecution for other offenses arising out of the same incident. The evidence was essential to the charge of gun possession during a crime of violence, so it was not "other crime" evidence and it had great probative value. In *United States v. Gatto,* 924 F.2d 491 (3d Cir. 1991), the Court reversed a ruling that granted a defendant's motion *in limine* to suppress a prospective eyewitness' trial testimony because the witness had allegedly been hypnotized during the criminal investigation. Even if the witness had been hypnotized, the probative value of his identification was substantial and could not be significantly discounted by the prejudice resulting from possibly suggestive police procedures.

United States v. Clifford, 704 F.2d 86 (3d Cir. 1983): The Trial Judge ruled that the government could not introduce correspondence in the defendant's handwriting to show stylistic similarities between it and threatening letters that allegedly were written by the defendant. The Court recognized the broad discretion that Rule 403 gives a Trial Judge, but found that the Trial Judge had misconstrued the government's offer of proof and confused the question of the sufficiency of the evidence to convict with the question of the admissibility of the correspondence. The Court saw no reason "why jurors cannot examine the documents for themselves and consider the similarities between the documents along with the rest of the evidence presented by the government."

United States v. Hans, 684 F.2d 343 (6th Cir. 1982): The government had obtained certain ledgers in which the defendant, a lawyer, had personally entered figures that the government claimed represented fees earned for workers' compensation services. To support its claim, the government secured the testimony of sixty of the defendant's clients, who indicated that they endorsed checks, which the defendant second-endorsed and cashed. The figures to the left of each client's name on the ledger coincided with the amounts that each client claimed had been paid to the lawyer. The government wanted to offer several hundred other checks that also had been second-endorsed by the defendant after being endorsed by clients whose names were in the ledger, but the Trial Judge excluded this evidence. The Court reversed, holding that the checks were relevant to prove gross receipts and that it could not be said that the evidence was substantially more prejudicial than probative.

Acquittals

United States v. Blyden, 964 F.2d 1375 (3d Cir. 1992): The Court reversed a ruling *in limine* that evidence of an alleged assault for which the defendants had previously been acquitted could not be introduced in a prosecution for other offenses arising out of the same incident. The evidence was essential to the charge of gun possession during a crime of violence, so it was not "other crime" evidence and it had great probative value. Any argument that it would be prejudicial essentially restates the double jeopardy and collateral estoppel claims previously rejected by the Court. It was, therefore, error to exclude the evidence on the possession count; rulings with respect to other counts for which the evidence was not essential must await the trial context.

Arizona v. Elmer, 21 F.3d 331 (9th Cir. 1994): In a state prosecution of a Border Patrol agent for shooting aliens crossing the Mexican border, the Court held it was not an abuse of discretion to exclude, on the defendant's *in limine* motion, evidence of a fatal shooting three months later for which the defendant had been charged and acquitted. The evidence was not relevant to any issue in the case and, while the record of balancing was not clearly articulated, the evidence would be extremely prejudicial, in all probability seizing and holding the jury's attention at trial. In *Borunda v. Richmond,* 885 F.2d 1384 (9th Cir. 1989), a civil rights action brought against the arresting officers after the plaintiffs had been acquitted of criminal charges, the plaintiffs introduced evidence of the acquittals solely to show the damages they had incurred. The Court said that, although it would have been inclined to exclude the evidence altogether because of its potential for prejudice and confusion, the Trial Court did not abuse its "very broad" discretion in admitting it with limiting instructions and instructions about the differing burdens of proof.

Appellate review standard

United States v. Akers, 702 F.2d 1145 (D.C. Cir. 1983): The Court affirmed a drug conviction, finding no error in the exclusion of photos of the crime area offered by the defense. The photos were excluded on the ground that they did not reflect the view of the officers who testified concerning their observations from a second-story view. Although the photos were admitted in a first trial in which the jury was unable to reach a verdict, the Court found no requirement that they must be admitted in a second trial. A concurring opinion suggested that when evidence admitted in one trial is excluded in a second trial, the Trial Judge should explain the reasoning carefully and the decision to exclude the evidence should be subjected to heightened judicial review.

United States v. Robinson, 560 F.2d 507 (2d Cir. 1977) (en banc), *vacating* 544 F.2d 611 (1976), *cert. denied,* 435 U.S. 905 (1978): The *en banc* decision of the Court referred to the "remarkable coincidence" of possession of a .38 caliber gun some weeks after a bank robbery and held that it was admissible to corroborate the government's chief witness and to show an opportunity to commit the robbery. Emphasizing the broad discretion afforded the Trial Judge in making Rule 403 rulings, the Court decided that it would be reluctant to reverse on the basis of a cold record unless it is convinced that the Trial Judge acted "arbitrarily or irrationally." Judge Oakes' dissenting opinion preferred a less deferential "abuse of discretion under the circumstances" standard. Judge Gurfein, who concurred in Judge Oakes' opinion, emphasized his view that the test of appellate review adopted by the majority was far too narrow. In *United States v. Schiff,* 612 F.2d 73 (2d Cir. 1979), the Court reversed a Trial Judge who admitted a videotape of a talk show in which negative comments about the defendant were made, but the Court reiterated the *Robinson* language. See also *United States v. Esdaille,* 769 F.2d 104 (2d Cir.), *cert. denied,* 474 U.S. 923 (1985) (Trial Judge's balancing will not be overturned unless arbitrary and irrational); *United States v. Khan,* 787 F.2d 28 (2d Cir. 1986) (no abuse of discretion where Trial Judge had not acted arbitrarily or irrationally in admitting evidence after a Rule 403 analysis).

Rovegno v. Geppert Bros., 677 F.2d 327 (3d Cir. 1982): The Court upheld the exclusion of evidence that the driver of a truck involved in an accident had a blood alcohol level that plaintiff's expert said rendered him unfit to drive, saying that its standard of review was "abuse of discretion" and it could find none. In our view, the evidence was obviously probative and it is difficult to see what unfair prejudice it would have worked to the defendant. The standard of abuse of discretion should be utilized so as to assure that a Trial Judge at least had a good reason for excluding evidence that on its face would seem important.

United States v. Johnson, 558 F.2d 744 (5th Cir. 1977), *cert. denied,* 434 U.S. 1065 (1978): Affirming convictions for making and subscribing false and fraudulent corporate income tax returns, the Court held that a Trial Judge's ruling balancing the probative value of evidence against its prejudicial effect may not be disturbed unless the decision was clearly erroneous.

United States v. Beasley, 809 F.2d 1273 (7th Cir. 1987): The Court held it was an abuse of discretion in a narcotics prosecution to admit evidence of the defendant's prior narcotics activity. Reversing, the Court observed:

> [A]lthough appellate courts cannot often tell whether it was best, all things considered, to let in a given piece of evidence, it may be possible to tell whether the district court and the parties took the right things into account. A flaw in the process is easier to detect than is a flaw in the result — and over the run of cases the consistent operation of process is more important, too....

The Court found that the pretrial hearing on the bad acts evidence was "perfunctory" and that the record indicated that the Trial Court had not carefully assessed whether the evidence would be probative for a permissible purpose; nor had it demonstrated "an effort to determine the likely effect of the evidence in poisoning Beasley's character."

The Court emphasized that it would probably not have reversed if the record indicated that the evidence was admitted after the Trial Judge carefully considered its probative value and prejudicial effect.

Borunda v. Richmond, 885 F.2d 1384 (9th Cir. 1989): In a civil rights action brought against the arresting officers after the plaintiffs had been acquitted of criminal charges, the plaintiffs introduced evidence of the acquittals solely to show the damages they had incurred. The Court said that, although it would have been inclined to exclude the evidence altogether because of its potential for prejudice and confusion, the Trial Court did not abuse its "very broad" discretion in admitting it with limiting instructions and instructions about the differing burdens of proof.

United States v. Terzado-Madruga, 897 F.2d 1099 (11th Cir. 1990): Rejecting the appellant's arguments that the government improperly introduced highly inflammatory evidence under the guise of other acts, the Court noted that the Trial Judge has broad discretion to admit evidence if it has any tendency to prove or disprove a fact in issue and only limited discretion to exclude it on grounds of unfair prejudice, so a decision to admit probative evidence will not be disturbed on appeal absent a clear showing of abuse of that discretion.

Balancing — bounds of discretion to exclude

Brown v. Trustees of Boston Univ., 891 F.2d 337 (1st Cir. 1989), *cert. denied,* 110 S. Ct. 3217 (1990): The plaintiff, suing for breach of contract and sexual discrimination after she was denied tenure, offered testimony of several professors comparing her qualifications with those of other faculty considered for tenure at the defendant University. The Court held that even though the professors' testimony was not in the file and thus not available to the University when it decided her case, it was relevant proof of pretext because it showed that the qualifications of others granted tenure were below the plaintiff's known qualifications. Because admitting such comparative evidence presents the risk of improperly substituting a judicial tenure decision, the evidence must be so compelling as to permit a reasonable finding of one-sidedness going beyond a mere difference in judgment, as in this case.

United States v. Mejia, 909 F.2d 242 (7th Cir. 1990): In affirming the defendant's conviction for conspiracy and possession of cocaine with intent to distribute, the Court noted that it is not reversible error to admit irrelevant details that have no probative value but do not prejudice a defendant.

K-B Trucking Co. v. Riss Int'l Co., 763 F.2d 1148 (10th Cir. 1985): Affirming the admission of a document in a suit alleging fraudulent misrepresentation, the Court observed that exclusion of evidence under Rule 403 is an extraordinary remedy that is to be used sparingly.

United States v. Terzado-Madruga, 897 F.2d 1099 (11th Cir. 1990): Rejecting the appellant's arguments that the government introduced highly inflammatory evidence under the guise of other acts, the Court noted that the Trial Judge has broad discretion to admit evidence if it has any tendency to prove or disprove a fact in issue and only limited discretion to exclude it on grounds of unfair prejudice, so a decision to admit probative evidence will not be disturbed on appeal absent a clear showing of abuse of that discretion. In *United States v. Betancourt,* 734 F.2d 750 (11th Cir.), *cert. denied,* 105 S. Ct. 440, 574 (1984), the Court noted that Rule 403 exclusion is an extraordinary remedy that should be used only sparingly.

Balancing — careful consideration required

United States v. Doe, 903 F.2d 16 (D.C. Cir. 1990): A black American and two Jamaicans were jointly charged with drug offenses. The Court reversed their convictions, in part because a detective was permitted to testify to the *modus operandi* of Jamaican drug dealers and how the market "has been taken over basically by Jamaicans." The Trial Judge had not balanced the severely prejudicial effect of the references, but had admitted the testimony solely because defense counsel had inquired on *voir dire* whether jurors would have greater difficulty affording Jamaicans a fair trial.

United States v. Delia, 944 F.2d 1010 (2d Cir. 1991): The Court held there was no abuse of discretion in admitting evidence that the defendant had told the principal prosecution witness he was a member of an organized crime family, as the careful balancing of the probative value of the evidence against its prejudicial effect, done only after the witnesses' cross-examination had been completed and her credibility vigorously challenged, warranted the decision to admit the evidence.

United States v. Beasley, 809 F.2d 1273 (7th Cir. 1987): The Court held it was an abuse of discretion in a narcotics prosecution to admit evidence of the defendant's prior narcotics activity. It found that the pretrial hearing on the bad acts evidence was "perfunctory" and that the record indicated that the Trial Court had not carefully assessed whether the evidence would be probative for a permissible purpose; nor had it demonstrated "an effort to determine the likely effect of the evidence in poisoning Beasley's character." The Court emphasized that it would probably not have reversed if the record indicated that the evidence was admitted after the Trial Judge carefully considered its probative value and prejudicial effect.

Balancing — factors to be considered

United States v. Pelullo, 14 F.3d 881 (3d Cir. 1994): In the second trial of a fraud and RICO case, the judgment of conviction on one of the fraud counts, which had been affirmed on appeal, was introduced to prove a predicate act. Reversing because the prior conviction was given preclusive effect, the Court noted that there had not been the required balancing of appropriate factors, such as the value of the conviction for the government, the relatively slight burden of re-proving the facts on which the conviction was based, and the potential prejudicial effect of admitting the judgment; on the remand, the Trial Court was directed to conduct a balancing analysis and state its reasons on the record for admitting or excluding the judgment of conviction.

United States v. Pizarro, 717 F.2d 336 (7th Cir. 1983), *cert. denied,* 471 U.S. 1139 (1985): The Court held that when a defendant raised an entrapment defense in a prosecution for selling heroin, the government was properly permitted to question him as to his supplier. Evidence that the defendant changed suppliers shed light on his disposition to commit the offense. The Court rejected an argument that the defendant should not have had to identify the supplier because he was afraid that a codefendant would seek reprisals against him. The Court noted that any dilemma in which the defendant found himself arose out of his own decision to become involved in illegal activities and was unsympathetic to the defendant's argument that his fear was a "prejudicial factor" to be weighed against the probative value of the answers sought by the government.

Balancing — generally

United States v. Bradshaw, 935 F.2d 295 (D.C. Cir. 1991): The Court affirmed a bank robbery conviction, noting that admission of prior convictions where sanity is the only issue presents different considerations from the usual case. Probativeness is generally unquestionable, since the insanity defense directly puts state of mind in issue, and a prior criminal record is highly relevant to the defendant's appreciation of the unacceptability of his conduct; there is no risk of primary prejudicial effect, since the defendant does not deny commission of the act; and there is a possibility that the evidence will prove prejudicial to the government by permitting the inference that the defendant is insane, since he continues to commit the same easily-detectable crime. Although the Trial Judge's ruling was terse, it appeared from the record as a whole that the relevant factors were considered.

Doty v. Sewall, 908 F.2d 1053 (1st Cir. 1990): In an action by a union member for mistreatment by union officials, the Court held that the emotional appeal of the plaintiff's Vietnam experience did not significantly outweigh its relevance on the issue of damages. It also found no abuse of discretion in allowing the plaintiff to testify he knew one of the defendants carried a gun to union meetings. The evidence made it less probable the plaintiff had assaulted the official, as the official contended.

Hurt v. Coyne Cylinder Co., 956 F.2d 1319 (6th Cir. 1992): In reversing a product liability judgment for the defendants on other grounds, the Court held there was no abuse of discretion in excluding a film offered by the plaintiffs. There was nothing improper in the Trial Judge's making a subjective determination that the film would be prejudicial, where there was no indication that the Judge's reaction was idiosyncratic and there is an obvious possibility of prejudice from a dramatic film that resembles but does not depict the accident in question.

United States v. McKinney, 954 F.2d 471 (7th Cir.), *cert. denied,* 113 S. Ct. 662 (1992): In a prosecution for murder in a prison, the government was permitted to introduce some evidence that the gang to which the defendant belonged had committed other murders. The Court held there was no abuse of discretion, as the government's theory was that the murder resulted from a gang contract; thus, how the gang operated was relevant to the charge, and the Trial Judge had been careful to limit the testimony about the gang and to preclude testimony implicating the defendant in any other murders.

Ross v. Buckeye Cellulose Corp., 980 F.2d 648 (11th Cir. 1993): In an employment discrimination action, evidence that managers who later worked at the plant had made racially derogatory remarks was excluded on the ground that it would open the door to further evidence about another of the defendant's plants, thereby substantially and unnecessarily prolonging the trial. The Court held that although the evidence may have been the "smoking gun" on the disparate treatment issue, there was no clear abuse of discretion where, even after the Trial Court indicated its willingness to admit the evidence if it were significant, plaintiffs' counsel did not highlight the significance of the evidence.

Balancing — requirement of record

United States v. Petrov, 747 F.2d 824 (2d Cir. 1984), *cert. denied,* 471 U.S. 1025 (1985): Reviewing obscenity convictions, the Court stated that, in assessing the community standards in an obscenity case, comparable material can be viewed as relevant under Rule 401. The Court emphasized, however, that Rule 403 should be used to carefully balance the value of comparable material against the dangers of admitting it. It added that "[e]ffective appellate review of such an issue requires the trial court to explain its decision. This is particularly so when the trial court decides an evidentiary question under Rule 403 . . . ."

United States v. Eufrasio, 935 F.2d 553 (3d Cir.), *cert. denied,* 112 S. Ct. 340 (1991): Appellants challenging RICO convictions asserted that Rule 403 objections to evidence of uncharged Mafia crimes had been made by motions *in limine* and that the Trial Judge had erred by not articulating the balance between probative value and prejudicial effect; the government asserted any Rule 403 errors had been waived by a failure to object explicitly when the evidence was introduced at trial. The Court held that the failure to articulate the balance was not per se reversible error. If the *in limine* motions did not constitute specific objections, the Trial Judge was not required to strike the balance on the record *sua sponte.* If the motions were the equivalent to a specific objection, the Appellate Court must decide whether the required balance was implicitly performed and, if not, must perform the balance itself. Repeating its injunction that Trial Judges should make the balancing explicit, the Court held there was no abuse of discretion in admitting the evidence in this case. See also *United States v. Long,* 574 F.2d 761 (3d Cir.), *cert. denied,* 439 U.S. 985 (1978), in which the Court likewise observed that "[w]here an objection does invoke Rule 403, the trial judge should record his balancing analysis to the extent that his exercise of discretion may be fairly reviewed on appeal. However, where Rule 403 is not invoked, the trial judge's balancing will be subsumed in his ruling." The Court emphasized the deference that should be paid the Trial Judge who sees the witnesses and hears live testimony and reiterated that the balancing under Rule 403 should take into account the probable effectiveness or ineffectiveness of a limiting instruction.

Bench trials

Schultz v. Butcher, 24 F.3d 626 (4th Cir. 1994): The Court reversed a judgment against the owner of a large boat in a personal injury action because evidence that the operators of the small boat in which the plaintiff was riding had been drinking was improperly excluded. In a bench trial, exclusion of unfairly prejudicial evidence is a useless procedure because the Judge is capable of rejecting any improper inferences; here, exclusion of the evidence prevented the large boat owner from fully developing a material issue.

Bodily exhibitions

Allen v. Seacoast Prods., Inc., 623 F.2d 355 (5th Cir. 1980): The Court upheld a ruling allowing an injured seaman to remove and replace his artificial eye in front of the jury.

Curry v. American Enka, Inc., 452 F. Supp. 178 (E.D. Tenn. 1977): In this personal injury action, the plaintiff moved *in limine* for permission to have each juror touch his burned hands in order to feel their hardness. The Court noted that the possibility of prejudice had to be weighed against the probative value of such a demonstration. Without making a final ruling, the Court suggested that plaintiff's testimony and that of his doctors might be adequate to prove the condition of the hands. The Court did decide that "any manual touching ... will be confined to those jurors who indicate to the Court a belief that such touching may enable them to understand and apply the evidence introduced in the ordinary manner." We believe that the Court's ruling should have been all-or-nothing. Otherwise, some jurors would become "witnesses" for other jurors.

Harris v. Illinois-California Express, Inc., 687 F.2d 1361 (10th Cir. 1982): In a wrongful death action, the Court indicated that it might have been improper for the Trial Court to permit physical identification of the decedent's daughter to the jury, but it found that any error was harmless. In *United States v. Lowe,* 569 F.2d 1113 (10th Cir.), *cert. denied,* 435 U.S. 932 (1978), a prosecution for kidnapping an infant, the Court held it was not an abuse of discretion to permit the government to bring the tiny infant into the courtroom for identification by the mother, despite the fact that the defendant offered to stipulate as to identity. Although we can appreciate the Court's desire to defer to the Trial Judge when Rule 403 balancing is undertaken, the opinion is unhelpful because it does not suggest what probative value the identification had after the defendant offered to take the issue of identity out of the case by stipulation. Certainly the prejudicial impact of mother and baby brought together before the eyes of the jury was obvious. This is among the cases in which the Appellate Court would be as well advised as a Trial Court to state its reasons for believing that evidence is more probative than prejudicial.

Civil rights and employment discrimination cases

Spain v. Gallegos, 26 F.3d 439 (3rd Cir. 1994): An EEOC employee brought a Title VII action, alleging that a sexually hostile work environment was created when rumors were circulated that she was having an affair with her supervisor. Plaintiff alleged that her supervisor demanded and received loans from her, in violation of Title VII employment rules, and that the private meetings between them gave rise to the rumors about an affair. The Trial Court prohibited plaintiff from introducing evidence about the loan transactions, and dismissed the case. But the Court of Appeals found that the Trial Court had abused its discretion, and reversed. The Court stated that the reason for the private meetings was relevant because it would demonstrate why the supervisor wanted to keep the meetings private, and why the meetings were so frequent. Moreover, the evidence would lend credibility to the plaintiff's assertion that the supervisor made no effort to stop the rumors, because doing so would have required the supervisor to "explain his conduct." The Court recognized the possibility "that the evidence would make the jury more likely to turn a breach of ethics into a finding of sexual harassment," and that as such the evidence was prejudicial. But it concluded that "vigorous cross-examination, presentation of contrary evidence, and careful instruction on the burden of proof are the traditional and appropriate means of attacking shaky but admissible evidence."

Cooley v. Carmike Cinemas, Inc., 25 F.3d 1325 (6th Cir. 1994): In an age discrimination case the Court held it was no abuse of discretion (or harmless error) to admit evidence that the plaintiff's supervisor had said two decades earlier, in his teen years, that he wanted to put older people in "a concentration camp," and that some years later he had said he did not want to go to a Thanksgiving Day dinner where his grandmother would be because he "[did not] like to be around old people." The comments were probative of the supervisor's state of mind and reflected a deep-rooted ongoing pattern that was anything but isolated; however, other evidence in the case meant that the jury did not need to hear the comments in order to believe the plaintiff's claim and to find that the defendant's explanations were pretextual.

Wilson v. Groaning, 25 F.3d 581 (7th Cir. 1994): Wilson was a prisoner who alleged that Groaning, a guard, used excessive force by punching him in the face in an attempt to return him to his cell. Groaning testified that Wilson spat on him and raised his arms as if to strike him, and that he responded by punching Wilson. Wilson argued that the evidence of spitting was irrelevant, because Groaning admitted that such an act would not justify the use of force, and that the evidence was extremely prejudicial. But the Court of Appeals found no error in the admission of the evidence of spitting. It held that "[l]eaving out this evidence would have left the jury with an unduly sanitized and incomplete version of the facts" and that "the evidence that Wilson spat on Groaning was relevant because it had tendency to make Groaning's claims that he felt threatened more probable." Also, the Court noted that "Rule 403 was never intended to exclude relevant evidence simply because it is detrimental to one party's case; rather, the relevant inquiry is whether any *unfair prejudice* from the evidence substantially outweighs its probative value." Finally, the Court agreed with Wilson that the Trial Court should not have allowed Groaning to testify that Wilson had sprayed him with a mixture of urine and fecal matter some hours after the punching incident. According to the Court, this evidence had no relevance to whether Groaning had previously used excessive force, and it was obviously prejudicial. However, the Court found that the Trial Judge immediately rectified the error through a limiting instruction, and therefore that a mistrial was not warranted.

Codefendant's guilty plea or immunity

United States v. Dworken, 855 F.2d 12 (1st Cir. 1988): The Court noted that a codefendant's plea may be elicited on direct to dampen the likely effects of an attack by a defendant, but cautioned that prosecutors may not use such a plea to support an inference of guilt on the part of other defendants. Although it found misconduct in the prosecutor's statements, reversal was not required.

United States v. Ramirez, 973 F.2d 102 (2d Cir. 1992): The Court reversed the defendant's conviction for narcotics and firearms offenses, holding it was error to refuse to instruct the jury that they should not consider a testifying codefendant's guilty plea as evidence of the defendant's guilt.

United States v. Thomas, 998 F.2d 1202 (3d Cir. 1993): The Court reversed the defendant's convictions for dealing in stolen property, holding that it was error to deny a defense motion to exclude the guilty pleas of coconspirators. Since the defendant pledged he would not elicit any information about the pleas and the only issue in dispute was intent, the majority reasoned that the government had no legitimate need for the evidence, and the effect of the pleas was to suggest that the defendant also was guilty. The dissenting Judge argued that the pleas were admissible for several reasons, one being that the credibility of the government's witnesses depended on the impression they created for the jury, and evidence of their pleas was relevant to creating that impression. In *United States v. Werme,* 939 F.2d 108 (3d Cir. 1991), *cert. denied,* 112 S. Ct. 1265 (1992), the Court affirmed a conviction for conspiracy to violate the Travel Act, noting that evidence of another party's guilty plea is not admissible to prove the defendant's guilt but may be admitted to show the witness' bias. The Court held it was error, but harmless, to fail to give a requested limiting instruction when a coconspirator's guilty plea was introduced. See also *Government of Virgin Islands v. Mujahid,* 990 F.2d 111 (3d Cir. 1993) (error, but harmless, merely to instruct jury to be cautious in evaluating cooperating witness without telling them witness' guilty plea could not be considered evidence of defendant's guilt); *United States v. Frankenberry,* 696 F.2d 239 (3d Cir. 1982), *cert. denied,* 103 S. Ct. 3544 (1983) (government may elicit on direct examination that a witness is in a protection program and has received substantial benefit, as long as it does not exploit any inference of threats by the defendant).

United States v. Countryman, 758 F.2d 574 (5th Cir. 1985): The Court held that it was permissible for the government to elicit on direct examination an alleged coconspirator's testimony concerning his guilty plea in order to blunt the impact of expected cross-examination, but it observed that the prosecutor may not attempt to use the plea as affirmative evidence of the defendant's guilt.

United States v. Odom, 13 F.3d 949 (6th Cir.), *cert. denied,* 114 S. Ct. 1859 (1994): The Court held that evidence of accomplices' convictions was relevant to the reliability of another accomplice's recantation of grand jury testimony regarding a conspiracy. In *United States v. Lochmondy,* 890 F.2d 817 (6th Cir. 1989), the Court held there was no error in admitting the guilty pleas of codefendants who testified at trial, not as evidence of the defendants' guilt, but as evidence of the witness' credibility after it had been attacked. In *United States v. Christian,* 786 F.2d 203 (6th Cir. 1986), the Court affirmed drug convictions, holding there was no plain error in the failure to give a limiting instruction *sua sponte* concerning a codefendant's guilty plea. After observing that a plea by a codefendant can be especially prejudicial, the Court reasoned that the potential for prejudice is greatly reduced where the codefendant testifies regarding the specific facts underlying the crimes in issue. In *United States v. Runnels,* 833 F.2d 1183 (6th Cir. 1987), the Court affirmed mail fraud convictions, but it observed that the government's revelation that a witness had entered a guilty plea "smack[ed] of sharp practice, at the least," since the only purpose for offering the evidence was to mislead the jury into thinking that the witness had no motive to be favorable to the government.

United States v. Sanders, 893 F.2d 133 (7th Cir.), *cert. denied,* 110 S. Ct. 2591 (1990): The Court held, in affirming the defendant's fraud convictions, that there was no abuse of discretion in admitting former codefendants' guilty pleas during the government's case-in-chief. The Court reasoned that the defendant's trial strategy was to imply that he was singled out while the former codefendant-witness went unpunished, which made admission of the plea evidence inevitable, and the jury was properly instructed not to consider the pleas as evidence against the defendant.

United States v. Smith, 893 F.2d 1269 (11th Cir. 1990): After the beginning of a trial of a drug conspiracy, two codefendants made a plea agreement and testified for the government. The Court held that evidence of the plea agreement was properly offered by the government to counter an anticipated contention of bias and that instructions made it clear that the evidence was not to be used as substantive evidence of guilt.

Collateral benefits

Hancock v. Dodson, 958 F.2d 1367 (6th Cir. 1992): In a civil rights action on behalf of an arrestee rendered incompetent allegedly as a result of the arrest, the Court held that there was no error in admitting evidence of an earlier no-fault lawsuit filed against an insurance company, as it was probative of whether the arrestee's condition was caused by a subsequent accident rather than the arrest and there was no showing it was unfairly prejudicial. A dissenting Judge believed that the evidence was not relevant because the claim against the insurer was not inconsistent with the theory that the accident aggravated a preexisting condition and it was prejudicial in suggesting that the plaintiff was making separate and inconsistent assertions regarding the cause of the injuries.

In re Air Crash Disaster, 803 F.2d 304 (7th Cir. 1986): In a suit against an aircraft manufacturer, the Court held that evidence of a widow's receipt of insurance benefits was properly excluded as unduly prejudicial, although it was relevant to her claim for nonpecuniary damages.

Cowens v. Siemens-Elema AB, 837 F.2d 817 (8th Cir. 1988): In a product liability action, the Court held that evidence that the plaintiff received worker's compensation benefits was properly admitted after the plaintiff testified about the financial stress he had undergone following the accident giving rise to the suit.

Collateral inquiries

Ramos-Melendez v. Valdejully, 960 F.2d 4 (1st Cir. 1992): In an employment civil rights case, the Court held there was no abuse of discretion in excluding testimony by the plaintiff's fellow employees, as they also had pending employment discrimination suits against the defendant and for their testimony to be significant it would be necessary in effect to try their cases as well as the plaintiff's.

United States v. LaRouche, 896 F.2d 815 (4th Cir.), *cert. denied,* 110 S. Ct. 2621 (1990): Affirming the defendants' convictions for fraud in obtaining loans they never intended to repay, the Court held that evidence of government intelligence and other activities directed at their organization was properly excluded, except as to unexpected actions frustrating their intent that lenders would be repaid, because any potential relevance was outweighed by the distraction that the inquiry into collateral issues would cause the jury.

Collateral matter to impeach

United States v. Tarantino, 846 F.2d 1384 (D.C. Cir.), *cert. denied*, 109 S. Ct. 108 (1988): Affirming drug conspiracy convictions, the Court held that the "specific contradiction" rule, which bars impeachment of a witness on a collateral issue, is a particular example of balancing under Rule 403 and may be invoked by a Trial Judge.

United States v. Beauchamp, 986 F.2d 1 (1st Cir. 1993): Affirming a forged check conviction, the Court held there was no error in precluding the defendant from calling a witness to testify that a government witness did not live at the address he testified to. Drawing an analogy to Rule 608(b)'s ban on extrinsic evidence, the Court reasoned that "[i]t is well established that a party may not present extrinsic evidence to impeach a witness by contradiction on a collateral matter." The Court concluded that the power to exclude evidence offered to impeach on a collateral matter is a particular example of the Trial Judge's authority to exclude evidence under Rule 403.

United States v. Benedetto, 571 F.2d 1246, 1250 (2d Cir. 1978): Reviewing a ruling that permitted other crimes evidence to be introduced in a public corruption case, the Court observed that "[o]nce a witness (especially a defendant-witness) testifies as to any specific fact on direct testimony, the trial judge has broad discretion to admit extrinsic evidence tending to contradict the specific statement, even if such statement concerns a collateral matter in the case." The Court cited both Rule 607 and Rule 403 and noted in a footnote that "Rule 607 appears to allow the continuation of federal practice in admitting extrinsic evidence to impeach specific errors or falsehoods in a witness' direct testimony, subject to Rule 403 considerations." In *United States v. King*, 560 F.2d 122 (2d Cir.), *cert. denied*, 434 U.S. 925 (1977), the Court affirmed fraud convictions, noting that under Rule 613 counsel is not required to confront a witness with a prior inconsistent statement before offering it. However, in some instances failure to elicit information from a witness about a prior inconsistent statement might lead to later exclusion of the evidence on the ground that it would take more time to present the evidence than is warranted under the circumstances.

United States v. Kozinski, 16 F.3d 795 (7th Cir. 1994): Affirming drug trafficking convictions, the Court held there was no abuse of discretion in excluding testimony by witnesses that would only contradict government witnesses on matters irrelevant to issues in the trial. In *Taylor v. National R.R. Passenger Corp.*, 920 F.2d 1372 (7th Cir. 1990), a jury verdict for the plaintiff in a FELA case was reversed because fourteen-year-old military medical records indicating complaints of back pain and a job application not mentioning back injuries had been erroneously admitted. The Court held that the records were irrelevant to the plaintiff's injury claim and were collateral extrinsic evidence inadmissible to impeach his testimony. See also *United States v. Rovetuso*, 768 F.2d 809 (7th Cir. 1985), *cert. denied*, 474 U.S. 1076 (1986) (Trial Judge properly excluded extrinsic evidence offered to impeach government witness on a collateral matter).

United States v. Grooms, 978 F.2d 425 (8th Cir. 1992): The Court affirmed the defendant's conviction for abusive sexual contact, holding there was no abuse of discretion in excluding extrinsic evidence of an alleged prior inconsistent statement offered to impeach a government witness, as the disputed statement related only to a collateral matter not affecting the substantive issues of the case.

Complex cases and evidence

United States v. International Business Machines Corp., 87 F.R.D. 411 (S.D.N.Y. 1980): In a protracted antitrust case the District Court denied permission to the defendant to call 124 witnesses not previously identified as part of its direct case. The Court observed that "[p]articularly in a protracted case, Rule 403 may serve as a predicate for imposition of blanket limits on a party's right to introduce evidence where the indicia of delay and cumulation are, generally, present." In *SCM Corp. v. Xerox Corp.*, 77 F.R.D. 10 (D. Conn. 1977), a complex antitrust case, the Trial Judge became concerned that the number of trial days was excessive, so he imposed a limit on the number of additional days available to the plaintiff to present its case. Although the Court recognized that Rule 403 "normally contemplates that the time-consuming nature of evidence will be determined as to each particular item of evidence offered," it concluded that "in a protracted case such as this, the purpose of the rule can best be achieved by considering time in the aggregate and leaving to counsel the initial responsibility for making individualized selections as to the relative degree of probative value from the mass of evidence available."

Confusing evidence

Kinan v. City of Brockton, 876 F.2d 1029 (1st Cir. 1989): The Court held, in a civil rights action for injuries received after being arrested as a result of an allegedly improper police broadcast, that evidence of two prior judgments against the defendants was properly excluded. The judgments were based on settlements rather than adjudications, and the prior claims involved excessive force rather than recklessly inaccurate police broadcasts, so their probative value on the adequacy of police training would be substantially outweighed by the risks of confusion and prejudice and the consumption of much unnecessary time in essentially retrying part or all of the two prior cases.

United States v. Thompson, 710 F.2d 915 (2d Cir. 1983), *cert. denied*, 104 S. Ct. 702 (1984): The Court affirmed the denial of a new trial motion by a former Congressman convicted in one of the ABSCAM prosecutions. It agreed with the Trial Judge that the dangers of confusion and delay, associated with evidence offered to prove that a government witness had duped another person, and therefore that it was more likely that he also duped Thompson, substantially outweighed its probative value and did not warrant a new trial.

Langer v. Monarch Life Ins. Co., 966 F.2d 786 (3d Cir. 1992): In an action by a physician against his employer and an insurer over disability insurance coverage, the physician and the insurer settled under a loan receipt agreement. The Court held there was no abuse of discretion in excluding evidence of the settlement from the trial of claims against the employer, as it may have confused the jury and misplaced their focus onto the subsidiary mitigation issue whether the settlement was a good deal rather than on the major issues in the case. In *Blancha v. Raymark Indus.*, 972 F.2d 507 (3d Cir. 1992), an asbestos case, the plaintiffs' theory was that all asbestos could cause the decedent's mesothelioma; the defendant's expert indicated that asbestos products containing chrysotile did not cause mesothelioma. After a verdict for the defendant, a new trial was granted, first on the ground that the expert's testimony was irrelevant without evidence that the defendant's product contained chrysotile, and later (on reconsideration) on the ground that the jury might have been confused by the expert testimony in the absence of evidence about the defendant's product. Reversing a judgment for the plaintiff on the new trial, the Court held that the expert's testimony was relevant, given the theory advanced and the plaintiffs' burden of proof on proximate causation, and that the danger of confusion did not so clearly outweigh the probative value of the expert's testimony as to justify exclusion. In *Bhaya v. Westinghouse Elec. Corp.*, 922 F.2d 184 (3d Cir. 1990), *cert. denied*, 111 S. Ct. 2827 (1991), the Court affirmed a judgment for the defendant in the second trial of an age discrimination case, holding there had been no error in granting a new trial after testimony indicating the defendant's management might be willing to "violat[e] ... the labor laws of their contract" or do "something illegal." The statements lacked any appreciable link to age discrimination or the ADEA, and they tended to confuse the jury by diverting attention from age discrimination to other unspecified illegality. One Judge dissented, arguing that the evidence was highly relevant to the employer's defense that it at all times tried to conform to the collective bargaining agreement. In *United States v. Driggs*, 823 F.2d 52 (3d Cir. 1987), the Court held it was an abuse of discretion to rule in a Hobbs Act prosecution that the government could not introduce a union official's tape-recorded conversations in which he discussed payments to various officials other than the defendant. The Court concluded that the evidence was relevant to proving the official's intent to make a gift to the defendant because he had been elected a judge. In our view, the Trial Judge was correct. The issue in this case was whether the defendant received a payment under color of official right. The evidence concerning the union official's intent did not establish that the judge had any idea of the official's purpose, and it tended to confuse the official's motive with the judge's.

    Tony Guiffre Distrib. Co. v. Washington Metropolitan Area Transit Auth., 740 F.2d 295 (4th Cir. 1984): The Court affirmed an inverse condemnation, finding that the Trial Judge properly excluded evidence concerning certain rents that were payable on property on the ground that the circumstances concerning the rents might confuse the jury. The Judge did permit experts to testify concerning the fair rental value of the property.

    United States v. Valencia, 957 F.2d 1189 (5th Cir.), *cert. denied*, 113 S. Ct. 254 (1992): In a drug prosecution, the government and defense joined in a request to play an authenticated tape recording of a conversation between Spanish-speaking conspirators, but the Trial Judge permitted only an English transcript that had been stipulated by the parties. In a careful opinion indicating some doubts about the ruling, the Court held there was no abuse of discretion, where two of the jurors could speak Spanish and hearing the tape might have been confusing. In *United States v. Moody*, 903 F.2d 321 (5th Cir. 1990), a mail and wire fraud prosecution, the defendant argued that absent coconspirators were especially adept at misleading people and that he was especially naive, so he sought to introduce extensive evidence of their character, organization, and practices. The Court held there was no abuse of discretion in excluding much of the evidence because it would shift the focus away from the defendant's culpability. In *Jackson v. Johns-Manville Sales Corp.*, 727 F.2d 506, *superseded*, 750 F.2d 1314 (5th Cir. 1985) (en banc), an action by a former shipyard worker for injuries allegedly caused by the defendants' failures to warn of the hazards of exposure to asbestos products, a panel of the Court found that twenty-five-year-old letters that were among the papers of the chairman of the board of one of the defendants should not have been admitted because they shed almost no light on the foreseeability of injury and would have confused and misled the jury. On rehearing *en banc,* the Court said the letters were not so remote in subject matter as to be devoid of probative value, and the Trial Court did not abuse its discretion when the letters were not inflammatory and the defendants had ample opportunity to make the jury aware of their remoteness.

City of Cleveland v. Cleveland Elec. Illuminating Co., 734 F.2d 1157 (6th Cir.), *cert. denied,* 469 U.S. 884 (1984): The Court affirmed a judgment for the utility in an antitrust action, holding there was no error in excluding a stipulation, entered into before the first of two trials, that the defendant utility had sponsored a taxpayer's suit that challenged a Federal Power Commission decision to require it to interconnect with the City's utility. The Court found that the stipulation was cumulative of other evidence concerning the defendant's attempts to eliminate competition and that it might have confused the jury by leading it to think that the taxpayer's suit was an anticompetitive act, which it was not. A dissenting Judge argued that sponsorship of the taxpayer suit, standing alone, might not have been anticompetitive, but the jury should have been permitted to consider the defendant's role in the suit as it might bear on a determination of whether the defendant was engaged in anticompetitive behavior.

United States v. Thomas, 11 F.3d 1392 (7th Cir. 1993): A defendant charged with bank robbery sought to prove she had been coerced into participation by her codefendant. The Court held there was no abuse of discretion in refusing to allow her to present evidence regarding each specific incident of abuse, as the marginal relevance of the evidence was clearly outweighed by the dangers of confusion of the issues, waste of time, and unnecessary presentation of evidence that would result if the defendant were allowed to conduct minitrials of each alleged incident.

Johnson v. Busby, 953 F.2d 349 (8th Cir. 1991): In a § 1983 action by a pretrial detainee, the Court held it was no abuse of discretion to exclude evidence of state minimum jail standards, as the standards, while helpful and relevant in some cases, do not represent minimum constitutional standards and would tend to mislead and confuse the jury as to the relevant standard of conduct. In *Stull v. Fuqua Indus.,* 906 F.2d 1271 (8th Cir. 1990), a product liability action for injuries suffered when the plaintiff's foot was caught beneath a riding mower, the Court held that a statement in a letter by the plaintiff's counsel to the CPSC that the plaintiff "tried to jump off the mower" was properly excluded under Rules 403 and 611(a) because the word "jump" is ambiguous, with meanings that could support each side's theory of the case. In *Ryan v. McDonough Power Equip. Co.,* 734 F.2d 385 (8th Cir. 1984), a product liability action brought on behalf of a child injured by a riding mower, the defendants were granted a new trial on the issue of liability. At the second trial, the Judge excluded the deposition of an expert who explained the nature of the girl's injury and the medical treatment she received. The Court affirmed, on the ground that the probative value of the deposition on the liability question was low and the possibility that the jury might be distracted by consideration of the extent of the damages was substantial.

Thurman Indus. v. Pay 'N Pak Stores, Inc., 875 F.2d 1369 (9th Cir. 1989): The plaintiff in an antitrust action offered, as evidence of anticompetitive conduct directed toward realizing monopoly power, testimony that the defendant, a competing chain of home improvement stores, attempted to coerce suppliers to refuse to sell home improvement products to competitors. The Court held the evidence was properly excluded, as the alleged conduct was only ambiguously anticompetitive, so it had little probative value, while it had a great potential to confuse or mislead the jury on the issue of specific intent to monopolize through predatory pricing.

Wheeler v. John Deere Co., 935 F.2d 1090 (10th Cir. 1991): Affirming a judgment for the plaintiff in an action for injuries suffered while servicing a combine, the Court rejected the manufacturer's contention that admitting design and product safety manuals diverted the jury's attention from reasonable consumer expectations to manufacturer's fault, which is irrelevant in a strict product liability action. Evidence of the defendant's knowledge of dangers is relevant in considering the adequacy of any warnings. In *United States v. Hairston*, 819 F.2d 971 (10th Cir. 1987), the Court affirmed convictions for willful failure to file tax returns, holding that the defendant's testimony concerning the impact that tax protest literature and seminars had on his understanding of tax law requirements was more probative than the literature itself and that there was no error in excluding the literature on the ground that it might confuse the jury.

United States v. Costa, 947 F.2d 919 (11th Cir. 1991), *cert. denied*, 112 S. Ct. 2289, 113 S. Ct. 360 (1992): Defendants charged with cocaine importation called a witness who would have testified that he had imported cocaine with three of the government witnesses but he had never known of the defendants in connection with his smuggling. The testimony was excluded on the ground that it related to a different conspiracy than the one alleged at trial, and its admission would therefore tend to confuse the jury. The Court found no abuse of discretion, but expressed concern about the ruling, noting that applying the Rule in conspiracy cases to exclude potentially relevant evidence (regardless of who offers it) because it might cause jury confusion will usually be inconsistent with the general rule favoring the admission of such evidence and allowing the jury to decide if it relates to the indicted conspiracy.

Mendenhall v. Cedarapids, Inc., 5 F.3d 1557 (Fed. Cir. 1993), *cert. denied*, 114 S. Ct. 1540 (1994): The Court held, in an action for patent infringement, that there was no abuse of discretion in excluding the judgment, opinion, and other evidence of an earlier proceeding in which patents at issue had been held valid. There was a high possibility of prejudice and confusion, since the opinion was not fact evidence on the myriad issues in the present case, and the jury may well have been confused by exposure to another Judge's statements on the law. The dissenting Judge believed that the prior holding of validity had substantial probative value and that the jury should be presumed to take its role seriously and to carry out its factfinding function competently and thoroughly.

Cumulative evidence

Miller v. Town of Hull, 878 F.2d 523 (1st Cir.), *cert. denied*, 110 S. Ct. 523 (1989): In this action by members of a town redevelopment authority alleging violation of First Amendment rights by the defendant Town and its Board of Selectmen in removing them, the Trial Court did not abuse its discretion in excluding the Board's ninety-five-page final decision. The Judge weighed the document's probative value against its prejudicial and cumulative effects and permitted the defendants to put the information it contained, which the plaintiffs were not attacking, before the jury through testimony.

Zaken v. Boerer, 964 F.2d 1319 (2d Cir.), *cert. denied,* 113 S. Ct. 467 (1992): Reversing a judgment for the defendant, principal owner and executive of a company designing and selling women's clothing, in an action alleging employment discrimination based on pregnancy, the Court held that it was error to exclude a statement by the vice president for sales that the plaintiff's predecessor had been fired because she was pregnant. Where none of the plaintiff's three witnesses testified to the statement or gave objective direct evidence that pregnancy played a role in the defendant's employment decisions, the evidence should not have been excluded as cumulative.

Pine Crest Preparatory School, Inc. v. Phelan, 557 F.2d 407 (4th Cir. 1977): The Court wisely held there was no error in permitting the introduction of a written document that was central to the dispute between the parties despite the fact that oral evidence had been received without objection concerning the language of the document. There was nothing unfair in placing in evidence the written contract and, in fact, it clarified the issue.

United States v. Crosby, 713 F.2d 1066 (5th Cir.), *cert. denied,* 104 S. Ct. 506 (1983): The Court affirmed convictions for kidnapping offenses, finding no error in the exclusion of out-of-court writings in a journal and oral statements by the defendant that were offered in support of his defense that he suffered posttraumatic stress syndrome as a result of his service in Vietnam. Expert witnesses were permitted to rely on this evidence and it was disclosed to the jury. Admission of additional testimony would have been cumulative. The Court also upheld the exclusion of records of a Veterans Outreach Center that contained opinions by counselors without training in psychiatry and were cumulative of testimony provided by experts for the defense. In *United States v. Edwards,* 702 F.2d 529 (5th Cir. 1983), the Court upheld extortion and mail fraud convictions, finding that a Trial Judge who admitted the testimony of five character witnesses for the defense did not abuse his discretion in refusing a continuance so that the defendant could present twenty-five additional character witnesses.

City of Cleveland v. Cleveland Elec. Illuminating Co., 734 F.2d 1157 (6th Cir.), *cert. denied,* 469 U.S. 884 (1984): The Court affirmed a judgment for the utility in an antitrust action, holding there was no error in excluding a stipulation, entered into before the first of two trials, that the defendant utility had sponsored a taxpayer's suit that challenged a Federal Power Commission decision to require it to interconnect with the City's utility. The Court found that the stipulation was cumulative of other evidence concerning the defendant's attempts to eliminate competition and that it might have confused the jury by leading it to think that the taxpayer's suit was an anticompetitive act, which it was not. A dissenting Judge argued that sponsorship of the taxpayer suit, standing alone, might not have been anticompetitive, but the jury should have been permitted to consider the defendant's role in the suit as it might bear on a determination of whether the defendant was engaged in anticompetitive behavior.

Wetherill v. University of Chicago, 565 F. Supp. 1553 (N.D. Ill. 1983): In a suit against University hospitals and a drug manufacturer, the Court ruled *in limine* that the defendants would be prevented from offering cumulative expert testimony.

United States v. Koessel, 706 F.2d 271 (8th Cir. 1983): The Court found no error in a cocaine possession case in the Trial Judge's limiting the defense to three character witnesses.

United States v. Ives, 609 F.2d 930 (9th Cir. 1979), *cert. denied,* 445 U.S. 919 (1980): The Court said that the Trial Judge erred (harmlessly, though) in rejecting defense evidence of past mental condition in support of an insanity defense and emphasized that Judges should not be quick to exclude (as cumulative) evidence of medical history that supports such a defense.

United States v. Shelton, 736 F.2d 1397 (10th Cir.), *cert. denied,* 105 S. Ct. 185 (1984): The Court held it was not an abuse of discretion to reduce the number of defense witnesses from seventy-eight to five where each witness would have said the same thing — i.e., the defendant did not ask for kickbacks and none were paid — even though the defendant was charged with 177 counts of mail fraud and extortion.

United States v. Johnson, 730 F.2d 683 (11th Cir.), *cert. denied,* 105 S. Ct. 186 (1984): Upholding convictions involving the filing of false statements with a federal agency, the Court affirmed a ruling that the defense could only present three character witnesses to testify as to a government witness' character for untruthfulness.

Defendant's exculpatory evidence

United States v. Spencer, 1 F.3d 742 (9th Cir. 1992, *amended* 1993): The defendant was charged with illegal possession of a firearm by a felon after a gun was found in a search of a car in which he was a passenger. When Miller, the owner of the car, was arrested five days later, a gun was found in the car he was driving. Pursuing a theory that the gun charged to him belonged to Miller, the defendant offered police reports of Miller's arrest to show that Miller possessed a gun similar to the one attributed to the defendant. A divided Court held there was no error in excluding the police reports under Rule 403. The dissenting Judge argued that the reports clearly were probative of mistaken identity and that there was no reason to believe that evidence relating to Miller would have confused the issues, misled the jury, or prejudiced the government, and that the Court was perpetuating "an increasingly common double-standard in criminal cases — a standard that allows prosecutors inordinate leeway with respect to the introduction of evidence harmful to the defendant while precluding defendants from introducing evidence that would tend to establish their innocence."

Drugs; drug and alcohol use

Swajian v. General Motors Corp., 916 F.2d 31 (1st Cir. 1990): The plaintiff in a product liability action alleged that his decedent was killed in a rollover accident caused by a defective axle in the vehicle she was driving. The Court reversed a judgment for the plaintiff, holding that the Trial Judge had not properly weighed probative value and prejudicial effect in excluding evidence relating to the decedent's alcohol consumption and blood alcohol level.

Conway v. Icahn & Co., 16 F.3d 504 (2d Cir. 1994): In an investor's action against his broker for selling securities to satisfy a margin call in October 1987, the defendant sought to introduce records that the plaintiff had been hospitalized in 1978, 1986, 1987, and 1988 for alcohol abuse, to show that he was incapable of making investment decisions during the relevant period. The Court held there was no abuse of discretion in admitting the 1987 records, since they related to hospitalization immediately after the relevant period, and in excluding the other records, which would have been more prejudicial than probative. In *United States v. Ruggiero,* 934 F.2d 440 (2d Cir. 1991), the Court affirmed convictions for conspiring to obstruct a grand jury investigation into the former whereabouts of a deceased narcotics fugitive, holding there had been no abuse of discretion when an FBI agent testified on redirect that many individuals, including the defendants, pictured at the fugitive's memorial service had been arrested for drug offenses. After defense counsel suggested repeatedly on cross-examination that the FBI acted improperly in observing the service, it was proper to correct this misimpression by testimony as to the reasons for the surveillance, including prior arrests. The Court also held that evidence of the fugitive's narcotics activities was relevant to the defendants' motives for conspiring to obstruct justice; it was not an abuse of discretion to determine that this probative value outweighed any possible prejudicial effect of guilt by association.

United Stated v. Carr, 25 F.3d 1194 (3d Cir. 1994): The Court held in a money laundering prosecution that evidence, including the reactions of drug-sniffing canines, was sufficient to show that the defendants knew the money involved was derived from illegal drug trafficking. One Judge believed that unrefuted studies indicating a trained dog will alert to all bundles of used currency, because a substantial portion of currency now in circulation is tainted with controlled substances, mean that it is not reasonable to infer that a person in possession of used currency bundles was a drug trafficker or associated with one, and that it is unfairly prejudicial to admit dog-alert evidence.

Estate of Larkins v. Farrell Lines, Inc., 806 F.2d 510 (4th Cir. 1986), *cert. denied,* 107 S. Ct. 1973 (1987): In an action by a sailor's estate against a shipowner, the Court held that evidence of the sailor's prior alcoholism was relevant to the cause, severity, and treatment of epileptic seizures, to his complaint of medical malpractice, and to the allegations of the shipowner's negligence in failing to take special precautions in his behalf.

Harless v. Boyle-Midway Div., 594 F.2d 1051 (5th Cir. 1979): In a wrongful death action resulting from a youth's death from inhaling a Freon propellant in a household product, the Court said that evidence that the youth used marijuana should not have been admitted on the issue of the value of the loss sustained by the mother, since it was more prejudicial than probative.

United States v. Blandina, 895 F.2d 293 (7th Cir. 1989): In a tax evasion prosecution, the government offered evidence of large marijuana transactions involving the defendant. The Court held that the evidence was clearly relevant in a "net worth" case, where the government was required to prove a likely source of income; the Trial Judge had made a finding that the witness was credible before allowing him to testify and had given a careful instruction about the limited purpose for the evidence, which abated any possible unfair prejudice.

Dillon v. Nissan Motor Co., 986 F.2d 263 (8th Cir. 1993): Affirming a judgment for the defendant in a product liability case brought by a passenger who was injured while riding in a vehicle manufactured by the defendant, the Court held that evidence of the plaintiff's cocaine and marijuana use was properly admitted as a possible cause for the aggressive and hostile behavior that the plaintiff attributed to the accident. In *O'Dell v. Hercules, Inc.,* 904 F.2d 1194 (8th Cir. 1990), an action for personal injuries from exposure to a toxic landfill, the defendant called one plaintiff as an adverse witness and asked about his use of marijuana and cocaine. The Court held there was no abuse of discretion, as the evidence had some tendency to indicate the plaintiff's attitude to risks from exposure to toxic chemicals, and in the circumstances was not harmfully prejudicial.

Fitzgerald v. McDaniel, 833 F.2d 1516 (11th Cir. 1987): Affirming a judgment for an arrestee in a suit alleging excessive force, the Court upheld the exclusion as unduly prejudicial of evidence of marijuana cultivation as well as threats allegedly made by the plaintiff to the arresting officer.

Hall v. General Motors Corp., 647 F.2d 175 (D.C. Cir. 1980): The Court affirmed a plaintiff's judgment in this product liability suit, upholding a ruling excluding some of the defendant's experimental test results as not having been conducted under circumstances sufficiently similar to the plaintiff's accident.

Experiments and demonstrations

Fusco v. General Motors Corp., 11 F.3d 259 (1st Cir. 1993): In a product liability action, the Trial Court granted the plaintiff's *in limine* motion to exclude a videotape in which the defendant purportedly demonstrated what would have happened had the product failed in the manner contended by the plaintiff. The Court held there was no abuse of discretion in excluding the tape, as the demonstration was rife with the risk of misunderstanding by the jury. In *Swajian v. General Motors Corp.,* 916 F.2d 31 (1st Cir. 1990), the plaintiff alleged that his decedent was killed in a rollover accident caused by a defective axle in the vehicle she was driving. The Court reversed a judgment for the plaintiff, but held there was no error in excluding a videotape demonstration prepared by the defendant, as it depicted an experienced test driver knowing what to expect in tests at controlled facilities involving axles that had been rigged to fracture. In *Lubanski v. Coleco Indus.,* 929 F.2d 42 (1st Cir. 1991), the Court affirmed a judgment for the defendant toy manufacturer in a product liability action brought by the mother of a child who was killed when struck by a car while riding on a three-wheeled riding apparatus, holding there was no error in admitting a series of photographic enlargements portraying a staged version of the accident scene. The Trial Court made the required preliminary determination that the photographs depicted a correct likeness and the plaintiff had not objected to the photographs in their original five-by-seven-inch form. In *Szeliga v. General Motors Corp.,* 728 F.2d 566 (1st Cir. 1984), the Court affirmed a judgment for an automobile manufacturer, holding there was no error in finding films — prepared by the manufacturer and offered to support its theory that a wheel fell off because of impact, not because of the loss of lug nuts — to be more probative than prejudicial. Dissimilarities between experimental and actual conditions went to the weight a jury might give the films, not admissibility.

United States v. Moreno, 897 F.2d 26 (2d Cir.), *cert. denied,* 110 S. Ct. 3250 (1990): In a drug distribution prosecution in which an issue was whether a warrantless seizure of a brick of cocaine wrapped in brown paper and tape came within the plain

Experiments and demonstrations (cont'd)

view doctrine, the Court held there was no error in denying a defendant's requests to make a physical demonstration with the brick and the bag from which it was seized, since the defense was accorded considerable leeway to explore their characteristics on cross-examination.

Chase v. General Motors Corp., 856 F.2d 17 (4th Cir. 1988): The Court reversed a judgment in a product liability case, finding that a videotape of braking tests performed by the National Highway Transportation Safety Administration should have been excluded. The conditions of the test were not similar to the conditions existing at the time of the accident. The Court also held that a videotape of braking tests made by the company's expert was properly excluded because of insufficient similarities between the test and accident conditions. Compare *Gladhill v. General Motors Corp.,* 743 F.2d 1049 (4th Cir. 1984), where the Court, after reversing a judgment for the defendants in a product liability suit on other grounds, said that a videotaped demonstration of an auto braking test, conducted by the defendant's test driver, should not be admitted in a second trial: "[T]he circumstances of the accident, as alleged, are so different from this test as to make the results largely irrelevant if not misleading." In *Slakan v. Porter,* 737 F.2d 368 (4th Cir. 1984), *cert. denied,* 470 U.S. 1035 (1985), the Court affirmed a judgment for an inmate against prison guards in a civil rights suit, finding no error in the admission of videotape evidence depicting a hose squirting water. The tape was properly used to demonstrate how the guards' actions could have injured an inmate; the water pressure and hose nozzle on the hose depicted were the same as those on the hose used against the plaintiff; and an expert was present to explain the tape.

Shipp v. General Motors Corp., 750 F.2d 418 (5th Cir. 1985): The Court affirmed a judgment against the defendant in an action by the owner-driver of a car injured in a rollover accident, holding that the Trial Judge properly admitted the plaintiff's film and photographs depicting an automobile similar to the one involved in the plaintiff's accident being dropped onto the driver's side of its roof from an elevation of one foot and also properly excluded the defendant's film illustrating unrestrained occupant movement in a rollover accident. The Court concluded that the plaintiff's film was relevant in that it obviously related to the kind of accident that occurred, while the defendant's involved a different vehicle with a substantially different roof and passenger compartment from the one involved in the accident. Moreover, the defendant's film portrayed multiple rollovers, rather than a single rollover such as that which occurred in the accident.

Hurt v. Coyne Cylinder Co., 956 F.2d 1319 (6th Cir. 1992): In reversing a product liability judgment for the defendants on other grounds, the Court held there was no abuse of discretion in excluding a film offered by the plaintiffs. There was nothing improper in the Trial Judge's making a subjective determination that the film would be prejudicial, where there was no indication that the Judge's reaction was idiosyncratic and there is an obvious possibility of prejudice from a dramatic film that resembles but does not depict the accident in question. In *United States v. Metzger,* 778 F.2d 1195 (6th Cir. 1985), *cert. denied,* 106 S. Ct. 3279 (1986), the Court affirmed a conviction for crimes relating to an automobile explosion that killed two people, and upheld the admission of a videotape of an experiment in which another car was destroyed by explosion. It stated that "the substantially similar standard is a flexible one which, even when construed strictly, does not require that all variables be controlled."

Nachtsheim v. Beech Aircraft Corp., 847 F.2d 1261 (7th Cir. 1988): Affirming a judgment for the manufacturer in an airplane crash case, the Court held that the defendant's videotape, which was used to demonstrate how ice accumulated and was removed from a plane, was admissible. Seventy-three hours of flight time went into the experiment, forty hours of that were taped, and a fifty-one-minute, edited film was made. The defendant argued that the plaintiffs did not promptly object to the tape or seek to have specific portions excised. The Court emphasized the Trial Judge's discretion and the fact that the tape was not offered to reenact the accident or to suggest that the experiment simulated actual events. In *Abernathy v. Superior Hardwoods, Inc.,* 704 F.2d 963 (7th Cir. 1983), a negligence action brought by a truckdriver against a forklift operator, the Court found no error in the decision to admit a videotape made by the defendant's president several years after the accident, which attempted to depict how logs are unloaded, in support of a contributory negligence claim. The Trial Judge permitted the film to be shown but did not allow the jury to hear the sound portion of the tape. Although the level of background noise was an issue in the case, the Court recognized that the microphone used to record the sound on the tape was not placed where the plaintiff had been and there was no indication that the courtroom volume control would have produced the same sound level as actually recorded. It commended the Judge "for not taking the easy way out, which would have been to let in all the minimally relevant nonprivileged evidence either party cared to offer."

Patterson v. F.W. Woolworth Co., 786 F.2d 874 (8th Cir. 1986): The Court affirmed a judgment for the defendants in an action alleging damage from an electric-fan fire, finding that expert testimony concerning experiments the witness conducted was properly admitted, since "[a]dmissibility ... does not depend on perfect identity between actual and experimental conditions." In *Hale v. Firestone Tire & Rubber Co.,* 820 F.2d 928 (8th Cir. 1987), an action for injuries caused by a wheel rim explosion, the Court held that a videotape of an explosion of a wheel rim striking a mannequin was properly admitted, even though the tire was inflated more than the tire involved in the explosion. The fact that the photographer did not retain a tape of six unsuccessful attempts to explode the tire was an issue for cross-examination, not a bar to admissibility. The Court had reversed a plaintiffs' judgment in the first trial of the action, 756 F.2d 1322 (8th Cir. 1985), because a film was admitted that involved substantially different conditions from those giving rise to the suit. In *Cowens v. Siemens-Elema AB,* 837 F.2d 817 (8th Cir. 1988), the Court affirmed a judgment for a manufacturer and distributor of an electronic lung ventilator. It held that evidence of experiments was properly excluded in the absence of proof that screens used in the experiment were manufactured at or near the time of the screen used in the ventilator. In *Borough v. Duluth, M. & I.R. Ry.,* 762 F.2d 66 (8th Cir. 1985), the Court affirmed a judgment for an injured railway worker, finding that the Trial Judge properly excluded the railroad's film, which demonstrated the proper way of stepping from a moving locomotive, as cumulative and as "carefully staged by the railroad for the purpose of this litigation." In *Randall v. Warnaco, Inc.,* 677 F.2d 1226 (8th Cir. 1982), a suit by a tent user injured by a fire in the tent, the Court said:

Experiments and demonstrations (cont'd)

> The admissibility of experimental evidence rests largely within the discretion of the trial court; the court's determination will not be overturned absent a showing of abuse of discretion. A court may properly admit experimental evidence if the tests were conducted under conditions substantially similar to the actual conditions. Admissibility, however, does not depend on perfect identity between actual and experimental conditions. Ordinarily, dissimilarities affect the weight of the evidence, not its admissibility.

The Court found no abuse of discretion in the admission of an experiment shown to the jury via videotape, but it warned that since the film duplicated the accident scene and almost reenacted the accident, it could have been deemed unduly prejudicial.

Robinson v. Missouri Pac. R.R., 16 F.3d 1083 (10th Cir. 1994): Affirming a judgment for the plaintiffs in a wrongful death action arising out of a train's collision with a car, the Court found that a video animation illustrating the plaintiff's expert's theory about how the collision had occurred presented a close question. The Court was not concerned that certain details were left out of the recreation, since they did not bear on the purpose of the exhibit, i.e., to illustrate the expert's testimony. It was bothered, however, with the tape's showing the car angling toward the approach of the train and rotating at impact and spinning off the tracks, since it was also possible that the train impaled the car on its front. On balance, the Court found no abuse of discretion, as the exhibit was entered for the limited purpose of illustrating expert testimony, a cautionary instruction was given, and the defendant was given opportunity for vigorous cross-examination. Furthermore, the verdict attributing some fault to the car's driver indicated that whatever undue prejudice might have arisen from this dramatic exhibit did not survive the entire trial. In a wrongful death action arising out of a helicopter crash, *Four Corners Helicopters, Inc. v. Turbomeca, S.A.,* 979 F.2d 1434 (10th Cir. 1992), the Court held there was no abuse of discretion in excluding videotape evidence of an experiment conducted by the defendant's expert, as there were substantial dissimilarities from the situation at issue. An experiment used simply to demonstrate the principles used in forming expert opinion need not strictly adhere to the facts, but this experiment was also used to demonstrate what the defendant believed occurred in the helicopter's engine. See also *Gilbert v. Cosco Inc.,* 989 F.2d 399 (10th Cir. 1993) (no abuse of discretion to admit "sled" tests of child restraint to illustrate scientific principles); *Hinds v. General Motors Corp.,* 988 F.2d 1039 (10th Cir. 1993) (no abuse of discretion in excluding defendant's crash test, where not substantially similar to accident in question and defendant proffered no articulable engineering principles test designed to demonstrate). In *Marsee v. United States Tobacco Co.,* 866 F.2d 319 (10th Cir. 1989), the Court affirmed a judgment for the defendant in a suit by a plaintiff who claimed that her son developed oral cancer from using snuff. It held there was no error in excluding a videotape deposition of a severely disfigured, postsurgical cancer patient whose case was similar to the son's in many respects. The proof of causation of injury was weak while the possibility of prejudice was great.

United States v. Gaskell, 985 F.2d 1056 (11th Cir. 1993): The Court reversed the defendant's conviction for involuntary manslaughter of his infant daughter, holding that an expert's demonstration of "shaken baby syndrome" using a rubber infant mannequin was not sufficiently similar to the circumstances of the infant's death to afford a fair comparison, and that the unfairly prejudicial nature of the demonstration outweighed any probative value. In *United States v. Rackley,* 742 F.2d 1266 (11th Cir. 1984), the Court affirmed a conviction for cocaine offenses, finding that the Trial Judge properly exercised his discretion to allow a demonstration of how a trained dog sniffed out narcotics after the defendant questioned the dog's ability to sniff out cocaine.

Experts

Sinai v. New England Tel. & Tel. Co., 3 F.3d 471 (1st Cir. 1993): Affirming a judgment for the plaintiff in an employment discrimination action, the Court held there was no abuse of discretion in permitting certain testimony by the plaintiff's psychologist. Prognosis evidence about the plaintiff's depression was very important to the damages issue, and the Trial Judge took care to ensure that the jury would not reach a verdict on improper grounds; evidence of the plaintiff's wife's own harassment and discrimination claims was proper on redirect in response to implications that the plaintiff's depression stemmed from preexisting marital difficulties. In *Pinkham v. Burgess,* 933 F.2d 1066 (1st Cir. 1991), the Court affirmed a judgment for the client in an attorney malpractice action, holding there was no abuse of discretion in excluding testimony by the defendant's psychological expert that a mental condition possibly existing years before the expert examined the defendant might have affected his ability to perceive the harm he was causing a client. The weak probative value of the evidence was substantially outweighed by the likelihood the jury would improperly consider it on the negligence issue. In *Nickerson v. G.D. Searle & Co.,* 900 F.2d 412 (1st Cir. 1990), the Court held in a product liability action arising out of injuries allegedly caused by an IUD that there was no abuse of discretion in prohibiting the plaintiff's counsel from cross-examining a defense expert witness about his experience in the abortion field, given the fierce emotional reaction engendered in many people by the subject.

United States v. Onumonu, 967 F.2d 782 (2d Cir. 1992): The defendant, charged with knowingly smuggling heroin from Nigeria in his alimentary canal, asserted he thought he was smuggling diamonds and offered an expert to testify to the feasibility and prevalence of smuggling diamonds in the same manner from Nigeria. The Court held it was error to exclude the testimony, as it was relevant to the defendant's subjective belief, did not fall under any of the Rule 403 exceptions to admissibility, and would have been helpful to a New York jury unlikely to be familiar with diamond smuggling out of Nigeria and even less so about the feasibility of smuggling diamonds by swallowing condoms.

Dixon v. CSX Transp., Inc., 990 F.2d 1440 (4th Cir.), *cert. denied,* 114 S. Ct. 305 (1993): In an FELA and state tort law action arising out of a train's collision with an automobile, the Court held it was reversible error to admit evidence from a human factors expert of an observational survey showing that 98 percent of motorists did not stop at the crossing and 64 percent did not look left. According to the Court, the evidence was wholly irrelevant to whether the plaintiff fulfilled the burden imposed by state law to act as a reasonably prudent person and, when taken with evidence that the plaintiff had looked left, it was prejudicial to the defendant because it strongly suggested the plaintiff was a more careful driver than most and could not be considered contributorily negligent. The dissenting Judge believed that because local custom is relevant to the duty of care, the evidence was properly admitted. In *Lohrmann v. Pittsburgh Corning Corp.*, 782 F.2d 1156 (4th Cir. 1986), the Court affirmed a judgment against a shipyard pipe fitter who claimed he contracted asbestosis from exposure to the defendants' products, holding that the Trial Judge properly ruled that the danger of unfair prejudice from mention of the plaintiff's fear of contracting cancer outweighed its probative value in light of the inability of the plaintiff's medical expert to state, with a reasonable degree of certainty, that the plaintiff would develop cancer.

United States v. Hartmann, 958 F.2d 774 (7th Cir. 1992): A man was murdered as part of a scheme by his wife and others to defraud life insurance companies. The Court held that even though only fraud was charged, it was not an abuse of discretion to admit expert testimony regarding the brutal manner in which the victim was slain, since the evidence provided corroboration and enhanced the credibility of conspirators' out-of-court admissions. In *Wallace v. Mulholland,* 957 F.2d 333 (7th Cir. 1992), a civil rights action for excessive force used by police in enforcing a commitment petition, the Court held there was no error in excluding evidence of the committed person's psychiatric history. Where the issue in the case was his actual behavior and how the officers responded to it, evidence about the general nature of his condition and the likelihood that someone with that condition would act aggressively was probably irrelevant and certainly prejudicial.

Rogers v. Raymark Indus., 922 F.2d 1426 (9th Cir. 1991): The Trial Judge had excluded testimony by one of the plaintiff's experts in a product liability wrongful death case arising out of World War II shipyard asbestos exposure as minimally probative, confusing, and cumulative. The Court found no abuse of discretion, rejecting the plaintiff's argument that she needed the testimony because it would be more articulate, eloquent, and clear than that from coworkers who had forgotten the details or were too unsophisticated to describe their working conditions accurately. In *United States v. Echavarria-Olarte,* 904 F.2d 1391 (9th Cir. 1990), the Court affirmed convictions for importing and distributing cocaine, holding it was an abuse of discretion (but harmless error) to permit a DEA agent to give expert testimony on the operations of the Medellin drug cartel, which were unrelated to the offenses with which the defendant was charged.

United States v. Gaskell, 985 F.2d 1056 (11th Cir. 1993): The Court reversed the defendant's conviction for involuntary manslaughter of his infant daughter, holding that it was an abuse of discretion to exclude expert testimony on the general lack of public awareness of the dangers of shaking an infant. Where the dispositive issue in the case was whether the defendant intended to revive the infant or to injure her, the evidence would be probative of his knowledge and intent, helpful to the trier, and not cumulative. In *Busby v. City of Orlando,* 931 F.2d 764 (11th Cir. 1991), the Court reversed in part a judgment against a discharged black employee of a city police department, holding that the plaintiff's expert witness should have been permitted to introduce testimony and a graph summarizing and explaining raw data introduced at trial in support of the plaintiff's claim of racial discrimination; without the witness' testimony there was no way for the jury to discern the meaning of the data accurately, so the evidence clearly was not cumulative. The witness, a psychological counselor, should also have been permitted to give testimony on the psychological impact of the termination, as it was directly relevant to the issue of damages and there was no other testimony regarding the psychological impact. In *Johnson v. United States,* 780 F.2d 902 (11th Cir. 1986), the Court remanded a wrongful death case brought by the parents of an infant who died after being taken to a military hospital, holding it was error to exclude as cumulative the testimony of a third expert witness who arguably had better credentials than the first two and whose analysis was somewhat different from the others'.

Flight, consciousness of guilt, suppression of evidence, etc.

United States v. Maravilla, 907 F.2d 216 (1st Cir. 1990): In affirming convictions of former Customs officers for robbery-related offenses in connection with the murder of a money courier, the Court held that there was no abuse of discretion in admitting evidence a defendant had tried to have the barrel on his gun changed. The effort to replace the barrel suggested an effort to eliminate features of the gun that might have linked it with a bullet found in or near the victim's body, which suggested a consciousness of guilt; there is no requirement that the prosecution introduce the much stronger evidence of the gun and the bullet, particularly since there was no showing that the government ever found such a bullet. In *United States v. Pina,* 844 F.2d 1 (1st Cir. 1988), the Court held that evidence of alleged threats made by the defendant to a witness after he testified was inadmissible. It reasoned that the inflammatory potential outweighed any probative value, since the witness had completed the testimony and could not be influenced by the threat. Admission of the evidence was harmless error, however.

United States v. Amuso, 21 F.3d 1251 (2d Cir.), *cert. denied,* 115 S. Ct. __ (1994): In 1990 the defendant mob boss went into hiding upon learning that he and fourteen others were to be indicted for RICO offenses and he remained a fugitive during that trial. After he was later arrested and convicted on RICO, murder, and other charges in a subsequent indictment, the Court held there was no abuse of discretion in admitting evidence of his flight, as a jury could as reasonably have found he fled out of consciousness of guilt as that he was concerned about spillover prejudice in being tried with fourteen others. However, it was error (but harmless) to instruct the jury that it could consider his "continued absence," where there was an insufficient factual predicate that he remained absent because of his consciousness of guilt with respect to the crimes charged. In *United States v. Perrone,* 936 F.2d 1403, *clarified,* 949 F.2d 36 (2d Cir. 1991), the Court reversed a defendant's conviction for conspiring to manufacture cocaine because there was insufficient evidence he knew the illegal purpose for listed chemicals he possessed, and it held that his false exculpatory statement was not usable as direct evidence of guilt when made in circumstances consistent with the innocent proposition that he felt the need to disassociate himself from criminal activity with which he surmised he was implicated. In *United States v. Bein,* 728 F.2d 107 (2d Cir.), *cert. denied,* 469 U.S. 837 (1984), the Court affirmed convictions for fraud and conspiracy growing out of a scheme to sell illegal commodity option contracts, upholding the admission of evidence that one defendant attacked a fellow corporate officer when the officer complained of an improper transfer of funds. The evidence was relevant to show consciousness of guilt.

269

United States v. Pungitore, 910 F.2d 1084 (3d Cir. 1990), *cert. denied,* 111 S. Ct. 2009, 2010 (1991): Affirming RICO convictions of Mafia members, the Court held that evidence of a defendant's flight soon after a coconspirator became a government informant was properly admitted, and a limiting instruction that the evidence be considered in connection with only one of the predicate acts, because the defendant was in custody at the time the RICO indictment was returned, had been properly rejected. In *United States v. Guerrero,* 803 F.2d 783 (3d Cir. 1986), the Court affirmed drug convictions, holding that evidence that a defendant threatened an alleged coconspirator to discourage him from testifying was properly admitted with an appropriate limiting instruction. Although threat evidence may be admitted to prove consciousness of guilt, it can be extremely prejudicial. The factors that should be weighed "include the importance and centrality to the ultimate issue in the case of the fact sought to be proved by the threat evidence, and the availability of other evidence to establish the fact sought to be proven by use of the threat evidence."

United States v. D'Anjou, 16 F.3d 604 (4th Cir.), *cert. denied,* 114 S. Ct. 2754 (1994): The Court held there was no abuse of discretion in admitting the defendant's false statements given to an agent of the Immigration and Naturalization Service after his arrest, as his lying was probative of consciousness of guilt of narcotics offenses.

United States v. Dillon, 870 F.2d 1125 (6th Cir. 1989): Affirming drug convictions, the Court found that the defendant's flight two years after the alleged crime and before the indictment was admissible, since it occurred within days of his learning of a codefendant's intent to implicate him in grand jury testimony.

Herry v. Deloney, 28 F.3d 608 (7th Cir. 1994): In a high school student's § 1983 action against a truant officer for nonconsensual sexual relations, the Court affirmed a judgment for the defendant, holding there was no error in precluding cross-examination of the defendant about a missing report. The evidence was totally out of the defendant's control shortly after he made it, and testimony about it would not so much support inferences that he was lying as simply invite conjecture. In *United States v. Fozo,* 904 F.2d 1166 (7th Cir. 1990), the Court held there was no abuse of discretion when a "script," written by one defendant for his codefendant's testimony in their trial for giving willfully false testimony to a grand jury, was admitted as evidence of consciousness of guilt. In *Empire Gas Corp. v. American Bakeries Co.,* 646 F. Supp. 269 (N.D. Ill. 1986), a breach of contract action, the buyer made a pretrial motion seeking permission to call a witness to testify that during discovery the seller willfully withheld documents containing statements regarding the merchantability of goods that were the subject of the contract. The Court distinguished the case from situations in which a party has suppressed evidence or offered perjured testimony, and held that since the buyer did receive the documents, the manner in which they were received was irrelevant. It also ruled that the proposed testimony would be unduly prejudicial, because jurors would not understand the way in which discovery works and the nature of discovery disputes.

United States v. Martinez, 681 F.2d 1248 (10th Cir. 1982): In a prosecution for sending explosives through the mail, the Court held it was error to exclude evidence of the defendant's flight. The Court suggested that flight evidence is often highly relevant, and commented that "[t]he fact that the accused may seek to rebut flight evidence in a way that would create new evidentiary problems is not a justification for excluding it, where, as here, it has highly probative value." But see *Hewitt v. City of Truth or Consequences,* 758 F.2d 1375 (10th Cir.), *cert. denied,* 474 U.S. 844 (1985) (evidence of officer's conduct after shooting the plaintiff's deceased properly excluded as unduly prejudicial when offered to prove state of mind at time of shooting).

United States v. Blakey, 960 F.2d 996 (11th Cir. 1992): In reversing the defendant's conviction for bank fraud and counterfeiting, the Court noted that there was no abuse of discretion in admitting evidence of his flight when FBI agents tried to arrest him. The flight occurred in the city where the crime had been committed when he was with a coconspirator he knew was being prosecuted for the crime, and there was some evidence he knew an indictment had been issued against him. One Judge dissented in part, believing that, on balance, admission of the flight evidence was reversible error. In *United States v. Borders,* 693 F.2d 1318 (11th Cir. 1982), *cert. denied,* 461 U.S. 905 (1983), the Court affirmed the conviction of a lawyer charged with involvement in an effort to bribe a federal judge, holding that evidence that the judge fled once he learned of the defendant's arrest was admissible to prove the judge's involvement in a conspiracy with the defendant.

Guilt by association

United States v. Johnson, 952 F.2d 565 (1st Cir. 1991), *cert. denied,* 113 S. Ct. 58 (1992): In a prosecution for violating arms export controls in connection with terrorist activities in Northern Ireland, the Court held there was no abuse of discretion in admitting evidence about the Provisional Irish Republican Army and the history of the Irish conflict. The evidence was probative of the indictment's characterization of the PIRA as a "body of insurgents" and, given the other evidence of the defendants' approval of and contribution to the methods and goals of the PIRA, presented at most a remote risk of guilt by association.

United States v. Ruggiero, 934 F.2d 440 (2d Cir. 1991): The Court affirmed convictions for conspiring to obstruct a grand jury investigation into the former whereabouts of a deceased narcotics fugitive, holding that evidence of the fugitive's narcotics activities was relevant to the defendants' motives for conspiring to obstruct justice; it was not an abuse of discretion to determine that this probative value outweighed any possible prejudicial effect of guilt by association.

United States v. Robinson, 978 F.2d 1554 (10th Cir. 1992), *cert. denied,* 113 S. Ct. 1855, 2938 (1993): Affirming convictions for cocaine base possession and conspiracy, the Court held that expert evidence tending to show that the defendants were active members of a gang whose main purpose was to sell cocaine was not impermissible "profile" evidence. Although the Trial Judge had admitted the evidence under Rule 404(b), a majority of the Court suggested that the evidence might not qualify under the Rule and concluded that the pertinent test is relevancy. The majority rejected the argument that evidence concerning gang membership tends only to show propensity and reasoned that "associational evidence may be directly relevant on the issues of formation, agreement and purpose of a conspiracy." The dissenting Judge believed that the government had impermissibly sought to prove that by exhibiting the characteristics of gang members, the defendants were members of a gang with criminal purposes and therefore were guilty of the charged conspiracy and underlying crimes; in any event, the gang affiliation evidence should have been inadmissible because it is inherently and unfairly prejudicial.

Hypnotized witness

United States v. Valdez, 722 F.2d 1196 (5th Cir. 1984): The Court reversed a conviction for extortion, finding that ''when, as here, a hypnotized subject identifies for the first time a person he has reason to know is already under suspicion, the post-hypnotic testimony is inadmissible whatever procedural safeguards were used to attempt to sanitize the hypnotic session.'' The Court found that the use of hypnosis in this context presented dangers of undue suggestiveness and that the resulting evidence was more prejudicial than probative. The Court went on to state that its holding did not make a hypnotized witness incompetent for all purposes and that ''[i]f a sufficiently reliable method exists for the witness to separate pre-hypnotic memory from post-hypnotic pseudomemory, such testimony may be admissible.'' It also observed that it was not adopting a per se rule excluding the use of hypnosis under all circumstances, since ''[i]n a particular case, the evidence favoring admissibility might make the probative value of the testimony outweigh its prejudicial effect.'' See also *United States v. Harrelson,* 754 F.2d 1153 (5th Cir.), *cert. denied,* 474 U.S. 908, 1034 (1985) (in a prosecution charging defendants with conspiring and killing a Federal Judge, the Court distinguished *Valdez* on the ground that two witnesses who made identifications had either identified or described a defendant prior to being hypnotized).

Sprynczynatyk v. General Motors Corp., 771 F.2d 1112 (8th Cir. 1985), *cert. denied,* 475 U.S. 1046 (1986): The Court reversed a judgment for a plaintiff who alleged product liability and negligence in the design of automobile brakes because the Trial Judge erred in admitting videotapes of a hypnotic session and rejecting the defendant's request for a limiting instruction explaining that the videotapes were admitted only to evaluate the opinions of an expert witness. The Court also rejected a *per se* rule barring the use of hypnosis to refresh the recollection of a witness. Instead, it held that hypnotically-refreshed testimony may be admitted if its proponent bears the burden of demonstrating that the procedures utilized were sufficient to guarantee reliability. The decision on admissibility is for the Trial Judge under Rule 104(a).

Illness or disease

Sinai v. New England Tel. & Tel. Co., 3 F.3d 471 (1st Cir. 1993): Affirming a judgment for the plaintiff in an employment discrimination action, the Court held there was no abuse of discretion in permitting certain testimony by the plaintiff's psychologist. Prognosis evidence about the plaintiff's depression was very important to the damages issue, and the Trial Judge took care to ensure that the jury would not reach a verdict on improper grounds; evidence of the plaintiff's wife's own harassment and discrimination claims was proper on redirect in response to implications that the plaintiff's depression stemmed from preexisting marital difficulties. In *Pinkham v. Burgess,* 933 F.2d 1066 (1st Cir. 1991), the Court affirmed a judgment for the client in an attorney malpractice action, holding there was no abuse of discretion in excluding testimony by the defendant's psychological expert that a mental condition possibly existing years before the expert examined the defendant might have affected his ability to perceive the harm he was causing a client. The weak probative value of the evidence was substantially outweighed by the likelihood the jury would improperly consider it on the negligence issue.

Davidson v. Smith, 9 F.3d 4 (2d Cir. 1993): The Court reversed a judgment for the defendants in a prisoner's civil rights action because a defense witness violated an *in limine* order not to refer to the plaintiff's psychiatric history or his treatment at a state hospital for the criminally insane. Given the prejudicial effect of the evidence, the questionable efficacy of a curative instruction, and the relative strength of the plaintiff's case, it was error to deny the plaintiff's motion for a mistrial.

Wallace v. Mulholland, 957 F.2d 333 (7th Cir. 1992): In a civil rights action for excessive force used by police in enforcing a commitment petition, the Court held there was no error in excluding evidence of the committed person's psychiatric history. Where the issue in the case was his actual behavior and how the officers responded to it, evidence about the general nature of his condition and the likelihood that someone with that condition would act aggressively was probably irrelevant and certainly prejudicial.

United States v. Ives, 609 F.2d 930 (9th Cir. 1979), *cert. denied,* 445 U.S. 919 (1980): The Court said that it was error (but harmless) to reject defense evidence of past mental condition in support of an insanity defense and emphasized that Trial Judges should not be quick to exclude (as cumulative) evidence of medical history that supports such a defense.

O'Banion v. Owens-Corning Fiberglas Corp., 968 F.2d 1011 (10th Cir. 1992): Affirming a judgment for the defendants in an action for asbestos-related disease, the Court held there was no abuse of discretion in prohibiting mention of the word "cancer" where the plaintiff offered no expert evidence that there was a reasonable medical probability of his developing cancer. In *United States v. Austin,* 933 F.2d 833 (10th Cir. 1991), the Court reversed a conviction for resisting correctional officers, holding it was an abuse of discretion when the defense was mental illness to exclude records of prior hospitalizations solely on the ground of remoteness. The Court was unwilling to place a temporal limit on relevant proof of mental illness in view of its frequently long duration, its possible chronicity, and its recurrent manifestations.

Wright v. Commercial Union Ins. Co., 818 F.2d 832 (11th Cir. 1987): Affirming a judgment for an insured who sued to recover on a policy covering business property, the Court held that evidence that the insured was suffering from terminal cancer when his building was damaged was admissible to rebut the defendant's claim that the insured had failed to comply with certain policy requirements.

Impeachment and rebuttal evidence

Vincent v. Louis Marx & Co., 874 F.2d 36 (1st Cir. 1989): The Court held that a District Court has discretion to balance probative value against prejudicial effect under Rule 403 before permitting a prior pleading filed on behalf of a party to be admitted under Rule 801(d)(2)(C). It remanded the case so that the balancing test could be applied. It also held that the District Court properly excluded evidence of a settlement in the earlier suit in which the pleading that was admitted in the instant case had been filed, noting that "[e]ven if the settlement amounts were relevant and had probative value, which is highly doubtful, Rule 403 is an exclusionary rule, not one providing for the admission of evidence."

Pitasi v. Stratton Corp., 968 F.2d 1558 (2d Cir. 1992): In a suit against a ski resort, the defendant offered testimony that it had never placed ropes between two trails where the plaintiff was injured. When the plaintiff recalled one of the defendant's employees, evidence that ropes had been placed between the trails the previous year was excluded on the grounds it was improper rebuttal and any probative value was outweighed by the prejudicial effect. The Court reversed, holding the evidence was both proper rebuttal, as not necessary to the plaintiff's *prima facie* case, and highly relevant to impeach the defendant's employee witnesses on the central issue of the defendant's negligence. In *United States v. Eisen,* 974 F.2d 246 (2d Cir. 1992), *cert. denied,* 113 S. Ct. 1619, 1840 (1993), the Court affirmed RICO convictions for a law firm's fraudulent conduct of personal injury litigation, holding there was no abuse of discretion in allowing the government to call witnesses that it had said "have refused to give up the lie." Where the government has called a witness whose corroborating testimony is instrumental in constructing its case, it has a right to question the witness, and to attempt to impeach him, about those aspects of his testimony that conflict with the government's account of the same events. The prejudicial effect of the impeachment in this case did not substantially outweigh the probative value of the evidence. In *United States v. Wallach,* 935 F.2d 445 (2d Cir. 1991), the prosecutor asked character witnesses for a defendant charged with racketeering about an incident where a state judge the defendant was promoting for appointment to the federal bench had approved a 60 percent legal fee for him in the settlement of a personal injury case. Reversing the convictions on other grounds, the Court noted that the government had a good faith basis for inquiring into the matter to challenge the basis for the character witnesses' opinions, but that the prosecutor argued the evidence to the jury in a manner well beyond the bounds of propriety and relevance. In *United States v. Harvey,* 547 F.2d 720 (2d Cir. 1976), the Court reversed a conviction for bank robbery on the ground that a key prosecution identification witness was improperly protected against evidence that the witness once had accused the appellant of fathering a child of hers. The Court emphasized that "bias of a witness is not a collateral issue and extrinsic evidence is admissible to prove that a witness has a motive to testify falsely," and said that "given the importance of ... biased testimony to the defense, whatever confusion or delay that may have resulted from its admission would have to have been overwhelming to satisfy Rule 403's balancing test."

United States v. Lehr, 562 F. Supp. 366 (E.D. Pa. 1983), *aff'd,* 727 F.2d 1100, 1101 (3d Cir. 1984): The Court denied postconviction motions by a defendant convicted of cocaine offenses, ruling that redirect examination of a government witness concerning a threat made by the defendant was permissible to rebut inferences the jury might have drawn as a result of cross-examination.

United States v. Ince, 21 F.3d 576 (4th Cir. 1994): The Court reversed a conviction for assault with a dangerous weapon, finding that "the United States' only apparent purpose for impeaching one of its own witnesses was to circumvent the hearsay rule and to expose the jury to otherwise inadmissible evidence of [the defendant]'s alleged confession.'' The Court noted that when the prosecution attempts to introduce a prior inconsistent statement to impeach its own witness, the statement's likely prejudicial impact often substantially outweighs its probative value for impeachment purposes because the jury may ignore limiting instructions and consider the ''impeachment'' testimony for substantive purposes.

Dollar v. Long Mfg., N.C., Inc., 561 F.2d 613 (5th Cir. 1977), *cert. denied,* 435 U.S. 996 (1978): The Court reversed a judgment for the defendant in a product liability action because of an erroneous ruling that a defense witness, who testified that the instrument used by the deceased was safe to operate, could not be impeached by a letter the witness sent to dealers selling the instrument warning them about its ''death-dealing propensities'' when used in the fashion it was used by the deceased. Although the District Court relied upon Rule 407, the Court concluded that the evidence was admissible under the last sentence of that Rule because it was offered for impeachment purposes. The Court stated that the evidence should not have been excluded under Rule 403 because there was no danger of *unfair* prejudice to the defendant.

United States v. Segines, 17 F.3d 847 (6th Cir. 1994): In a prosecution for cocaine distribution offenses, the Court held there was no abuse of discretion in admitting redirect testimony by a government witness that his apartment had been firebombed by friends of a defendant. Although the probative value of the evidence might have been outweighed by its prejudicial effect if offered on direct examination, here the defense opened the door by eliciting on cross-examination that the government had been supporting the witness for three months before the trial. The firebombing evidence addressed the witness' need for government support and protection and rebutted the suggestion that he was selling his testimony. In *United States v. Markarian,* 967 F.2d 1098 (6th Cir. 1992), *cert. denied,* 113 S. Ct. 1344 (1993), the Court affirmed a conviction for conspiracy to possess heroin with intent to distribute, holding there was no abuse of discretion in permitting rebuttal testimony about an incident connecting the defendant with drugs, as it was relevant to his knowledge or intent to deal and introduced in response to the defendant's sweeping statements (going far beyond the particular crimes charged) on direct examination concerning his experiences with drugs.

SEC v. Peters, 978 F.2d 1162 (10th Cir. 1992): The Court reversed a judgment for the defendant in a civil action for insider trading violations, holding the SEC had been improperly precluded from asking the defendant and his character witnesses about allegations of other securities law violations, as the defendant had made his character and his unblemished history a very important part of his defense and the rulings deprived the jury of a fair and balanced opportunity to evaluate his character. The Trial Court had erroneously assigned the proposed evidence a probative value of ''nil'' and overemphasized its prejudicial effect and tendencies to raise collateral issues.

In limine rulings

Zenith Radio Corp. v. Matsushita Elec. Indus. Co., 723 F.2d 238 (3d Cir. 1983), *rev'd on other grounds,* 475 U.S. 574 (1986): In a massive antitrust case in which the plaintiffs alleged that the defendants conspired to drive them out of the market for television receivers, the Court reversed most of the summary judgment entered by the

District Court. In the course of its opinion the Court expressed approval of the District Court's substantial use of *in limine* hearings on evidence questions "not only because the court's *in limine* consideration was far more efficient than if the rulings were deferred until the trial, with consequent interruptions, but also because the *in limine* procedure permitted more thorough briefing and argument than would have been likely had the rulings been deferred." Although the Court noted that there are "countervailing considerations, especially with respect to relevancy rulings under Rule 403 that may be made pre-trial without the benefit of the flavor of the record developed at trial," it found that the Trial Judge has discretion to make those rulings prior to trial and that the discretion was properly exercised in this case.

Invocation of privilege

United States v. Morris, 988 F.2d 1335 (4th Cir. 1993): The Court reversed an attorney's conviction for narcotics offenses because the prosecutor had been allowed to cross-examine the accused's wife about her invocation of the marital privilege before the grand jury. To permit the inference that she would have testified before the grand jury if she had something exculpatory to say would, in the Court's view, destroy the privilege.

Harrell v. DCS Equip. Leasing Corp., 951 F.2d 1453 (5th Cir. 1992): Affirming judgments in fraud suits arising out of a computer leasing program, the Court held there was no error in excluding evidence that a defendant had invoked his Fifth Amendment privilege at a deposition, although he subsequently complied with an order compelling him to answer. The evidence might have had some probative value on his credibility and the alleged fraud, but that was substantially outweighed by the potential prejudice because the jury might attach undue weight to the privilege claim or misunderstand the decision to invoke it.

United States v. Vandetti, 623 F.2d 1144 (6th Cir. 1980): After reversing a conviction for operating a gambling business on another ground, the Court discussed the difficulties that arise when codefendants, previously tried and convicted, are to be identified as part of the government's case, but have indicated that, if called, they will refuse to testify on self-incrimination grounds. If they assert the privilege in the presence of the jury, there is a danger of prejudice to the defendant. If, however, they do not testify at all once they are identified, the jury may wonder why they were not called. One suggestion by the Court was that the words "fifth amendment" not be used by the witnesses; instead, they simply could indicate before the jury that they will not testify.

Joint parties

United States v. Figueroa, 618 F.2d 934 (2d Cir. 1980): Three defendants — Acosta, Lebron, and Figueroa — were charged with conspiracy to possess and distribute heroin. At trial they suggested that the substance they had was not really heroin, but was brown sugar used to "rip off" a purchaser. The government responded by offering Acosta's prior conviction for selling heroin. The Court said that the prior conviction could not be used to show the identity of a substance in dispute. It also held that the government could not offer the conviction to show that Acosta intended to join a conspiracy between

Figueroa and Lebron, since Acosta's counsel clearly stated that he was not disputing the fact that Acosta was involved with the other two. The Court said the Trial Judge erred in not striking a proper Rule 403 balance not only as to Acosta, but also as to the two remaining defendants. Because the evidence concerning the nature of the substance the defendants had was the same as to all, the risk of prejudice to Figueroa and Lebron was almost the same as the risk to Acosta, and all three won reversal. In passing, the Court said that it was a close question whether, had the prior conviction been properly admitted against Acosta, a severance as to the others would have been required.

United States v. Bodden, 736 F.2d 142 (4th Cir. 1984): Affirming drug convictions, the Court upheld a ruling that barred one defendant from eliciting on cross-examination of a government agent a statement this defendant had made concerning the financial temptation of poor Colombians to engage in the smuggling business. The Court found that the statement would have been prejudicial to the Colombian defendants and that its value to the one defendant was not very great.

Gross v. Black & Decker, Inc., 695 F.2d 858 (5th Cir. 1983): An employee of a furniture company lost fingers while using a radial arm saw. She sued the manufacturer, and the manufacturer claimed that the injury was the result of the employer's failure to warn and to provide safety equipment. The Court held that evidence of the employer's activities was properly admitted. The probative value of the evidence, which was essential to the defendant's claim that it was the employer who was responsible for the accident, outweighed any prejudicial effects.

In re Beverly Hills Fire Litig., 695 F.2d 207 (6th Cir. 1982), *cert. denied,* 103 S. Ct. 2090 (1983): Although it reversed a judgment for defendant manufacturers of aluminum wiring alleged to be responsible for a supper club fire in which many persons died, the Court upheld a ruling that certain documents, which would have been admissions as to some defendants but hearsay as to others, should be excluded or redacted. The Court noted that the Trial Judge had severed the issue of causation from the question of liability and that the excluded evidence was cumulative on the causation issue. If the issues were combined, some of the evidence might be admitted with appropriate limiting instructions.

Judgments, court orders, and judicial opinions

Kinan v. City of Brockton, 876 F.2d 1029 (1st Cir. 1989): The Court held, in a civil rights action for injuries received after being arrested as a result of an allegedly improper police broadcast, that evidence of two prior judgments against the defendants was properly excluded. The judgments were based on settlements rather than adjudications, and the prior claims involved excessive force rather than recklessly inaccurate police broadcasts, so their probative value on the adequacy of police training would be substantially outweighed by the risks of confusion and prejudice and the consumption of much unnecessary time in essentially retrying part or all of the two prior cases. In *Silva v. Showcase Cinemas Concessions,* 736 F.2d 810 (1st Cir.), *cert. denied,* 105 S. Ct. 251 (1984), the Court upheld a judgment against a movie theater for the wrongful death of the plaintiff's son, who was killed in a parking lot after a movie, rejecting the defendant's argument that it should have been permitted to show that the assailant was convicted of manslaughter. Since the plaintiff stipulated that the killing was criminal, the manslaughter conviction was unnecessary to prove that it was an intentional act.

United States v. Ebner, 782 F.2d 1120 (2d Cir. 1986): The Court affirmed tax evasion convictions, upholding the admission of portions of a state court opinion revealing that the defendants had been given an authoritative statement that their bogus religion did not qualify for a tax exemption. The Trial Judge excluded portions of the opinion reciting facts and instructed the jury to consider the opinion only on the issue of intent.

United States v. Blood, 806 F.2d 1218 (4th Cir. 1986): Affirming an embezzlement conviction, the Court upheld permitting an IRS agent to support his expert opinion by reading portions of a prior Tax Court decision involving the defendant. The 1976 opinion involved similar issues and was relevant to proving that the defendant willfully violated the law in the instant case.

Harrell v. DCS Equip. Leasing Corp., 951 F.2d 1453 (5th Cir. 1992): Affirming judgments in fraud suits arising out of a computer leasing program, the Court held there was no error in excluding evidence of a nonfinal judgment in another case as proof of a predicate act under RICO, as the acting jury might give undue value to the previous determination. In *Brumley Estate v. Iowa Beef Processors, Inc.,* 704 F.2d 1351 (5th Cir. 1983), *cert. denied,* 104 S. Ct. 1288 (1984), the Court affirmed a judgment for the defendant in a suit for recovery of the unpaid purchase price of cattle. A jury found that the person who bought the cattle was not the defendant's agent. In two other cases, juries had found the same person to be an agent of the defendant, and in one other case a jury reached a no-agency conclusion as in this case. The Court held that no collateral estoppel effect would be given to the two findings of agency and the judgments entered pursuant to these findings were properly excluded under Rule 403, because they would have confused the jury. We suggest that the judgments also were inadmissible hearsay, not qualifying for admission under Rule 803(22). In *Rozier v. Ford Motor Co.,* 573 F.2d 1332 (5th Cir. 1978), a product liability action arising out of a fatal automobile accident, the Court held it was improper to admit evidence that the driver of the other car had pleaded guilty to involuntary manslaughter. Although it recognized that the convictions were admissible under Rule 803(22), the Court said that they should have been excluded under Rule 403. The admission of responsibility was made in the context of a criminal action to deter reckless driving and therefore "its relevance in a civil action based on a legal doctrine presumably intended to deter the negligent manufacture of automobiles is attenuated at best." The guilty plea would tend to confuse the jury into thinking that the manufacturer could not be the legal cause, in the civil action, of the plaintiff's decedent's death if the other driver was in the criminal action. See also *United States v. Cook,* 557 F.2d 1149 (5th Cir. 1977), *cert. denied,* 434 U.S. 1020 (1978) (reversing fraud conviction because an injunction order entered in another case was erroneously admitted).

United States v. Merklinger, 16 F.3d 670 (6th Cir. 1994): The defendant, charged with fraud, sought to introduce evidence that he had previously been acquitted of similar charges in a similar case. He argued that he made admissions to investigators in this case because he was despondent and that the previous acquittal was relevant to his state of mind. The Court held there was no abuse of discretion in granting a motion *in limine* to exclude the evidence, as there was no logical connection between the favorable verdict and the alleged despondency and evidence of the verdict could confuse the jury.

United States v. Bejar-Matrecios, 618 F.2d 81 (9th Cir. 1980): Reversing a conviction for illegally reentering the United States, the Court concluded it was error to admit a certified copy of a judgment showing that the appellant once pleaded guilty to the misdemeanor of illegal entry. Although the plea conclusively established that the appellant was an alien when he pleaded guilty, the jury was never told why the prior conviction was being used, the evidence was cumulative, and the jury might have used the evidence as proof of predisposition.

Johnson v. Colt Indus. Operating Corp., 797 F.2d 1530 (10th Cir. 1986): The Court upheld a judgment for the plaintiff against a manufacturer of a revolver that discharged when dropped. It found that a judicial opinion in another action was relevant to impeach the testimony of the manufacturer's officer that he was unaware of any other drop-fire lawsuits and also to show indifference toward known risk for punitive damage purposes. A majority of the Court held, however, that admission of the opinion was error (but harmless): The jury might have been confused by its relationship to the instant case, and the evidence of the accident giving rise to the other case and its results could have been accepted without using the opinion. A concurring Judge argued that admission of the full opinion was not error, since it had special probative value.

Mendenhall v. Cedarapids, Inc., 5 F.3d 1557 (Fed. Cir. 1993), *cert. denied,* 114 S. Ct. 1540 (1994): The Court held, in an action for patent infringement, that there was no abuse of discretion in excluding the judgment, opinion, and other evidence of an earlier proceeding in which patents at issue had been held valid. There was a high possibility of prejudice and confusion, since the opinion was not fact evidence on the myriad issues in the present case, and the jury may well have been confused by exposure to another Judge's statements on the law. The dissenting Judge believed that the prior holding of validity had substantial probative value and that the jury should be presumed to take its role seriously and to carry out its factfinding function competently and thoroughly.

Meaning of "prejudice"

Dollar v. Long Mfg., N.C., Inc., 561 F.2d 613 (5th Cir. 1977), *cert. denied,* 435 U.S. 996 (1978): The Court reversed a judgment for the defendant in a product liability action because of an erroneous ruling that a defense witness, who testified that the instrument used by the deceased was safe to operate, could not be impeached by a letter that the witness had sent to dealers selling the instrument warning them about its "death-dealing propensities" when used in the fashion it was used by the deceased. The Court stated that the evidence should not have been excluded under Rule 403 because there was no danger of *unfair* prejudice to the defendant. The Court said that "[o]f course, 'unfair prejudice' as used in Rule 403 is not to be equated with testimony simply adverse to the opposing party. Virtually all evidence is prejudicial or it isn't material. The prejudice must be 'unfair.'"

Nonevidentiary occurrences

Shu-Tao-Lin v. McDonnell Douglas Corp., 574 F. Supp. 1407 (S.D.N.Y. 1983), *rev'd in part,* 742 F.2d 45 (2d Cir. 1984): Granting a new trial for excessive damages in a suit for the wrongful death of an airline passenger, the Court noted that unavoidable nonevidentiary occurrences had tainted a damage award: The jury witnessed an emotional hallway meeting between a witness who saw the plane crash and the deceased's wife, during which both were in tears; and during the trial there were emotional displays by the deceased's widow and children.

Notice and knowledge

Exum v. General Elec. Co., 819 F.2d 1158 (D.C. Cir. 1987): In a product liability suit by an employee injured while using a french fryer, the Court held that it was error to exclude evidence concerning fifteen similar incidents. All but one occurred before the plaintiff was injured, and the Court reasoned that to prove notice, prior acts need not be as similar as they would have to be to prove the dangerousness of a product. Although the Court recognized that the incident arising after the plaintiff was injured could not prove notice, it concluded that it was so similar to the plaintiff's accident that it was probative of dangerousness.

Fiacco v. City of Rensselaer, 783 F.2d 319 (2d Cir. 1986), *cert. denied,* 480 U.S. 922 (1987): Affirming a judgment for an arrestee in a civil rights suit against a city and police officers, the Court stated that it had no doubt that, in the context of a claim that the City negligently supervised its officers in the use of force, evidence that a number of claims of brutality had been made by other persons was admissible. Even if the claims were invalid, the Court reasoned that the City was on notice of a possibility that its officers were using excessive force. In *United States v. Ebner,* 782 F.2d 1120 (2d Cir. 1986), the Court affirmed tax evasion convictions, upholding the admission of portions of a state court opinion revealing that the defendants had been given an authoritative statement that their bogus religion did not qualify for a tax exemption. The Trial Judge excluded portions of the opinion reciting facts and instructed the jury to consider the opinion only on the issue of intent.

Mills v. Beech Aircraft Corp., 886 F.2d 758 (5th Cir. 1989): A letter from the French aviation authorities to the defendant manufacturer warning of certain defects, was held properly excluded. The letter was offered to show the defendant's knowledge, but there was no showing that the letter applied to the type of airplane in issue and that the defect had manifested itself in circumstances substantially similar to the case at bar.

Koloda v. General Motors Parts Div., 716 F.2d 373 (6th Cir. 1983): The Court reversed a judgment for an auto mechanic who sued for injuries allegedly arising out of his use of a lubricant and inhalation of its vapors. General Motors should have been permitted to offer evidence that there were no prior claims or accidents brought to its attention concerning the lubricant. The Court agreed with G.M. that the evidence was probative of its knowledge, which was important to the plaintiff's theory of a failure to warn, and it stated that it could see no reason why the evidence would have been unfairly prejudicial.

McCarty v. Pheasant Run, Inc., 826 F.2d 1554 (7th Cir. 1987): Affirming a judgment for a hotel owner sued by a guest who was assaulted in her room, the Court held that the Trial Judge did not err in excluding evidence of criminal activity at the hotel that did not involve an entry like the one alleged in the instant case, while admitting evidence of prior similar entries.

Hale v. Firestone Tire & Rubber Co., 820 F.2d 928 (8th Cir. 1987): In a suit involving the explosion of a wheel rim, the Trial Judge admitted evidence of thirteen prior claims to prove notice of a defect, but excluded the defendant's evidence concerning the disposition of the claims, which was offered to demonstrate that the extent of the notice was exaggerated. Although the Court did not deem the limitation on the defendant's proof an abuse of discretion, it declared that "if this case is retried, the evidence should be admitted."

United States v. Navarro-Varelas, 541 F.2d 1331 (9th Cir. 1976), *cert. denied,* 429 U.S. 1045 (1977): The defendant, charged with knowingly importing cocaine, testified that he had no knowledge that cocaine was in a suitcase that he carried. He attempted to call a DEA agent to testify as an expert that narcotics smugglers commonly plant narcotics in secret compartments of suitcases and have an unwary traveler bring them into this country. Although the Court agreed with the Trial Judge that this evidence would have had no probative value in tending to disprove the defendant's guilt, we have some doubts. While it may be true that the defendant at trial had an opportunity to protest his innocence, a jury unschooled in narcotics traffic may find a story about planted drugs more incredible than it really is.

Hendrix v. Raybestos-Manhattan, Inc., 776 F.2d 1492 (11th Cir. 1985): Emphasizing the leeway afforded the Trial Judge in making Rule 403 rulings, the Court upheld the introduction of studies concerning asbestos dust exposure and asbestosis to prove knowledge of harm in personal injury actions. In *Worsham v. A.H. Robins Co.,* 734 F.2d 676 (11th Cir. 1984), the Court affirmed a judgment for the plaintiff in a product liability suit against the manufacturer of the Dalkon Shield IUD, finding no error in rulings admitting documents and permitting cross-examination that mentioned other litigation involving the Shield. The documents and cross-examination tended to show the kind of notice that the company had about problems caused by the Shield and the mention of the other litigation was not unduly prejudicial.

Official findings

Daigle v. Maine Med. Center, Inc., 14 F.3d 684 (1st Cir. 1994): The Trial Court in a diversity medical malpractice action ordered that the plaintiff present her case to a prelitigation screening panel as required by state law, and when the panel unanimously found no acts of negligence, followed the state law by admitting the findings into evidence without providing an opportunity for impeachment. Affirming a judgment for the defendant, the Court held that the federal evidence rules governing hearsay and impeachment do not seek to displace the state's substantive policy implemented by the screening panel procedure. Furthermore, the official seal of the state court and the court caption were redacted, to avoid unfairly prejudicial impact.

Black v. Ryder/P.I.E. Nationwide, Inc., 15 F.3d 573 (6th Cir. 1994): The Court held in an employee's action against his union for breach of the duty of fair representation that there was no abuse of discretion in excluding an NLRB decision refusing to issue a complaint in the case. Lacking any stated factual basis, the decision had almost no probative value, and the jury would be quite likely to assign it greater value than it was worth, given that it was the product only of an administrative investigation and not of an adjudicatory procedure.

Jetcraft Corp. v. Flight Safety Int'l, 16 F.3d 362 (10th Cir. 1993): In a negligence action arising out of a pilot-training accident, the Court held there was no error in excluding evidence of FAA enforcement actions taken against the defendants following the accident. The FAA's own characterization of the violation as a record-keeping omission undermined its relevance and the spectre of any regulatory violation, however collateral to the alleged violation, has a potential for prejudice or confusion.

Opening the door

Bender v. Brumley, 1 F.3d 271 (5th Cir. 1993): In a pretrial detainee's action against officers who allegedly beat him, the Court held there was no abuse of discretion in admitting inflammatory details of the murder for which the detainee had been arrested, as he had discussed the facts in great detail on direct examination.

Other claims

Raysor v. Port Auth., 768 F.2d 34 (2d Cir. 1985), *cert. denied,* 475 U.S. 1027 (1986): In a civil rights action for false arrest and malicious prosecution, the Court upheld the rejection of evidence concerning the plaintiff's litigiousness, since such evidence raised a substantial danger of jury bias.

Bunion v. Allstate Ins. Co., 502 F. Supp. 340 (E.D. Pa. 1980): The Court rejected evidence that the claimant was "claims-minded."

Bufford v. Rowan Cos., 994 F.2d 155 (5th Cir. 1993): When an employee sued for workplace injuries, the defendants contended that the action was fraudulent, copying a claim by the employee's former co-worker. In reversing a judgment for the defendants, the Court recognized it is a perfectly legitimate and valid defense to assert that a personal injury claim is fabricated or exaggerated, but it is not permissible to make an unsupported attack on the integrity of opposing counsel by relying on the identity of counsel in the two cases as a basis for contending the claim was fraudulent.

Photographs, movies, videotapes — events at issue

United States v. Weisz, 718 F.2d 413 (D.C. Cir. 1983), *cert. denied,* 104 S. Ct. 1285, 1305 (1984): The Court affirmed convictions involving conspiracy to commit bribery, as it found that videotape evidence showing a Congressman stuffing money in his pockets was properly admitted to prove the crime that the defendants were charged with committing. See also *United States v. Perry,* 731 F.2d 985 (D.C. Cir. 1984) (affirming Trial Judge who declined to edit audiotape containing one defendant's racially derogatory remark where defense tried to discredit tape and its totality was important).

United States v. Marvin, 687 F.2d 1221 (8th Cir. 1982), *cert. denied,* 460 U.S. 1081 (1983): Reviewing a conviction for food stamp offenses, the Court found no abuse of discretion in the Trial Judge's admission of a videotape that recorded only part of a transaction and that was ambiguous.

Photographs, movies, videotapes — generally

United States v. Schiff, 612 F.2d 73 (2d Cir. 1979): The Court reversed the conviction of a tax protestor who challenged the government's right to compel him to answer questions on a tax return and to pay his taxes because the Trial Judge admitted a videotape of a "talk show" appearance during which the host and a former assistant United States Attorney (who prosecuted tax cases) predicted with assurance that the defendant would be convicted and concluded that he ought to be. The Court found the evidence to be of limited probative value, since the defendant admitted nothing on the show, and concluded that there was a substantial chance of prejudice in the "fervid commentary that conveyed an air of incontestable truth." Compare *United States v. Tibbetts*, 646 F.2d 193 (5th Cir. 1981) (approving admission of videotape talk show in which taxpayer-defendant participated when there were no prejudicial remarks by anyone else on the tape).

Saturn Mfg. Co. v. Williams Patent Crusher & Pulverizing Co., 713 F.2d 1347 (8th Cir. 1983): In a patent infringement action, the Court upheld the admission of a motion picture of the plaintiff's device and the allegedly infringing product. The Court said that "[m]otion pictures of commercial devices are admissible to aid the jury in understanding the language of patent claims provided they are properly authenticated and are shown to have been made in substantial compliance with the teachings and claims of the patent alleged to be infringed." It also approved exclusion of the defendant's movie of another device, which was offered to show obviousness. This movie was not discovered until the second week of trial, and the Trial Judge had found that there was a danger of "ambush" sufficient to require a ruling that the risk of unfair prejudice outweighed the probative value of the film.

United States v. Binder, 769 F.2d 595 (9th Cir. 1985): The Court reversed a conviction for sexual offenses upon minor children, holding (2-1) that the Trial Judge erred in permitting the jury to replay during deliberations the videotaped testimony of the victims. The majority reasoned that the procedure unduly emphasized the victims' testimony and suggested that permitting the jury to replay the tape in an abridged fashion compounded the unfairness.

Durflinger v. Artiles, 727 F.2d 888 (10th Cir. 1984): The Court found no abuse of discretion when the Trial Judge, in a wrongful death action against doctors responsible for releasing a mental patient who killed his mother and brother, admitted a videotaped confession by the patient on the day of the murders to show the patient's state of mind near the time of the crimes. In discussing precedents on the use of videotapes, the Court observed that admissibility depends on the particular circumstances of each case.

Photographs, movies, videotapes — inflammatory depictions

Navarro de Cosme v. Hospital Pavia, 922 F.2d 926 (1st Cir. 1991): Affirming a judgment for the defendants in an action by the parents of a stillborn fetus, the Court held there was no error in excluding photographs of the fetus taken just before the autopsy, when it was already macerated and had begun to decompose. In *Lubanski v. Coleco Indus.,* 929 F.2d 42 (1st Cir. 1991), the Court affirmed a judgment for the defendant toy manufacturer in a product liability action brought by the mother of a child killed when struck by a car while riding on a three-wheeled riding apparatus. The Court found no error in admitting a series of photographic enlargements portraying a staged version of the accident scene. The Trial Court made the required preliminary determination that the photographs depicted a correct likeness and the plaintiff had not objected to the photographs in their original five-by-seven-inch form.

United States v. Whitfield, 715 F.2d 145 (4th Cir. 1983): The Court affirmed murder and robbery convictions, finding no error in admitting photographs of the murder victim that were used to show that a crescent wrench might have been used to strike the fatal blows. Originally, the Trial Judge excluded the photos, since the defendant stipulated that the victim was bludgeoned to death with a blunt instrument, but subsequently he admitted the evidence, and the Court found no abuse of discretion.

Walker v. Norris, 917 F.2d 1449 (6th Cir. 1990): Affirming a judgment for the plaintiff in a civil rights action against prison guards who failed to prevent an inmate's stabbing death, the Court held there was no abuse of discretion in admitting photographs of the inmate's body as evidence of conscious pain and suffering. In *Shahid v. City of Detroit,* 889 F.2d 1543 (6th Cir. 1989), the Court reversed judgments for the defendants in a civil rights action, brought for alleged failure to provide medical care to a jail inmate prior to his death, because the Trial Judge had excluded black-and-white photographs of the decedent's body in his cell shortly after his death. By depicting paint dustings, bruises, and blood traces, the photos were relevant to whether he had sought assistance and to the obviousness of his injuries. The fact the body may have been moved before the photos were taken did not mean they were an inaccurate representation of what they depicted.

United States v. Thomlinson, 897 F.2d 971 (8th Cir. 1990): The Court held there was no abuse of discretion in admitting in a drug prosecution evidence of the defendant's motorcycle club membership and photographs of his tattooed torso, as the evidence tended to prove his ownership of a briefcase discovered in his office, which contained notes of drug transactions, business cards for tattoo parlors, and a motorcycle club brochure.

United States v. Hitt, 981 F.2d 422 (9th Cir. 1992): Reversing a defendant's conviction for possessing a machine gun, the Court held it was reversible error to admit a photograph that showed a dozen weapons in addition to the one charged. Because the photo did not depict the weapon's mechanism, it was of marginal probative value, and it "could do no more than arouse irrational fears and prejudices." In *United States v. Carpenter,* 933 F.2d 748 (9th Cir. 1991), the Court affirmed convictions for killing migratory birds, holding there was no abuse of discretion in admitting an hour-and-a-half videotape showing federal agents digging up pits where the birds' bodies were buried and opening an incinerator containing charred bird parts, as the pictures, although gruesome, tended to refute the defenses that only a few hundred birds had been killed. The Court noted that discretion to admit evidence means freedom to reach a result an Appellate Court might not reach. In *United States v. Chambers,* 918 F.2d 1455 (9th Cir. 1990), the Court affirmed the defendant's conviction for possession of cocaine with intent to distribute, holding there was no abuse of discretion in admitting pictures of him wearing expensive clothing and gold jewelry. The photos were probative of his connection with another person in the case and it was highly unlikely that jurors would attach the same meaning to his dress as would a DEA agent, even though his dress may fit the agency's drug courier profile.

United States v. Naranjo, 710 F.2d 1465 (10th Cir. 1983): Affirming a murder conviction, the Court held that a photograph of the victim's head and torso, while gruesome, was properly admitted since it shed light on the pathologist's finding as to the cause of death and also was probative on the defense of accident. The Court said that "gruesomeness alone does not make photographs inadmissible" and emphasized that the photo "was not introduced solely for what prejudicial effect it could produce." See also *United States v. Soundingsides,* 819 F.2d 1529 (10th Cir. 1987) (autopsy photos with probative value in a murder case were properly admitted even though they were "undeniably gruesome").

United States v. Eyster, 948 F.2d 1196 (11th Cir. 1991): In the trial of a drug smuggling conspiracy, the government introduced a photograph of a plane crash involved in the conspiracy that clearly showed the torso of a burned body with an arm extending over a faceless head. The Court held that the photo was not probative of whether anyone else was willing to risk death to engage in smuggling, but there was not sufficient prejudice to find an abuse of discretion. The convictions were reversed on other grounds and the Trial Judge was urged to give greater focus to Rule 403 determinations. See also *United States v. De Parias,* 805 F.2d 1447 (11th Cir. 1986), *cert. denied,* 107 S. Ct. 3189 (1987) (photos of murder victim's badly decomposed body properly admitted to identify the victim, prove the means of death, and corroborate a crucial government witness.

Photographs, movies, videotapes — mug shots

Hygh v. Jacobs, 961 F.2d 359 (2d Cir. 1992): The Court reversed a damages award in a civil rights action by an arrestee who alleged that excessive force was used, because a mug shot photograph ostensibly offered to show the plaintiff was going through booking was irrelevant to false arrest damages. The photo related to events after arraignment and it prejudicially fastened the jury's attention on injuries for which the plaintiff had already been fully compensated.

United States v. Carrillo, 20 F.3d 617 (5th Cir.), *cert. denied,* 115 S. Ct. __ 1994): Affirming a conviction for distribution of cocaine and heroin, the Court held there was no abuse of discretion in admitting photographs of the defendant that were mug shots separated into front and side views and cropped and enlarged so that no identifying marks or measuring lines were visible. As altered, the photos minimized the implication that the defendant had a criminal record, and the manner of their introduction did not prejudicially draw attention to their source. See also *United States v. Torres-Flores,* 827 F.2d 1031 (5th Cir. 1987), discussed in the Editorial Explanatory Comment, where the Court reversed an assault conviction because mug shots of the defendant had been admitted. The Court observed that mug shots should only be admitted where the government has a genuine need for the evidence, the photos do not imply that the defendant has a prior criminal record, and the use at trial does not draw particular attention to the source or implications of the photos.

United States v. Hines, 955 F.2d 1449 (11th Cir. 1992): Reversing convictions for aggravated sexual assault, the Court held it was an abuse of discretion to admit photospreads from which the complainant had identified the defendants as her assailants, as there was no demonstrable need to introduce the photographs, the photos implied the defendants had prior criminal records, and the agent's testimony highlighted that the photos were of known criminals.

Photographs, movies, videotapes — surveillance and "day in the life" films

Grothusen v. National R.R. Passenger Corp., 603 F. Supp. 486 (E.D. Pa. 1984): The Court held that a surveillance film of the plaintiff, showing him without a limp, was properly admitted in an FELA case.

Bannister v. Town of Noble, 812 F.2d 1265 (10th Cir. 1987): The Court affirmed a judgment for a plaintiff injured in an automobile accident, upholding the admission of a "day in the life" film offered to prove how the plaintiff's paralysis adversely affected his daily life. The Court stated that a Trial Judge should examine a film outside the jury's presence to make a Rule 403 determination as to its admissibility. Here, such an examination had been made; the film accurately portrayed the plaintiff's daily routine and was not unduly prejudicial, even though it contained a couple of scenes that showed the plaintiff doing things he would not frequently do.

Physical evidence

United States v. Arango-Correa, 851 F.2d 54 (2d Cir. 1988): Affirming cocaine convictions, the Court held there was no error in permitting the government to display 500 pounds of cocaine to the jury. It observed that the Trial Judge carefully limited the duration of the display and that the cocaine was the principal physical evidence in the case.

United States v. MacDonald, 688 F.2d 224 (4th Cir. 1982), *cert. denied,* 459 U.S. 1103 (1983): In the prosecution of a former Army doctor for the murder of his wife and children, the Court found that the government proceeded properly in introducing the defendant's pajama top, which had been found draped over the wife's body, in order to show icepick wounds and to compare the pattern of the wounds with the pattern of wounds in the murdered wife's chest.

Braun v. Flynt, 726 F.2d 245 (5th Cir.), *cert. denied,* 105 S. Ct. 252 (1984): A novelty entertainer who performed an act with a swimming pig at an amusement park sued the publisher of *Chic Magazine,* a publication that emphasizes female nudity, alleging defamation and invasion of privacy. Although the Court vacated a judgment for the plaintiff and remanded for a new trial on damages, it upheld a ruling that the jury should see the entire magazine in which her picture appeared "so that the jury could, in effect, be placed in the position of the ordinary reader." The Court rejected an argument that the evidentiary impact of the other portions of the magazine was unfairly prejudicial.

United States v. Gonzalez, 933 F.2d 417 (7th Cir. 1991): The Court held there was no abuse of discretion in displaying for a few hours the 2,248 kilograms of cocaine seized from the defendants, as the evidence was relevant to establish the magnitude of the conspiracy and the likely purpose for possessing it, while the short period it was displayed and cautionary instructions regarding the purpose limited any prejudicial effect. In *United States v. Davis,* 838 F.2d 909 (7th Cir. 1988), a prosecution for conspiracy to distribute marijuana, the Court said that it could see no reason why the jury was permitted to examine a container filled with cash. The defendants did not challenge the fact that there was cash in the container, and the jury's examination added nothing to the case. The defendants' failure to object when the cash was tendered to the jury was not deemed plain error, however. In *Douglass v. Hustler Magazine, Inc.,* 769 F.2d 1128 (7th Cir. 1985), *cert. denied,* 106 S. Ct. 1489 (1986), the Court reversed an actress' judgment against a magazine for invasion of privacy, finding that it was error to permit an expert to show the jury the most offensive 128 photos from various years of the magazine, since the sample was not representative.

United States v. Thomlinson, 897 F.2d 971 (8th Cir. 1990): The Court held there was no abuse of discretion in admitting in a drug prosecution evidence of the defendant's motorcycle club membership and photographs of his tattooed torso, as the evidence tended to prove his ownership of a briefcase discovered in his office, which contained notes of drug transactions, business cards for tattoo parlors, and a motorcycle club brochure.

Polygraph and similar evidence

Dowd v. Calabrese, 585 F. Supp. 430 (D.D.C. 1984): In a libel action, the Court rejected the defendants' request that polygraph evidence supporting a reporter's claims concerning his interviews with the plaintiffs and confidential sources be admitted as evidence. The Court indicated that it was bound by precedent to exclude the evidence and also that, even if it had discretion to admit it, it would exclude the evidence on the ground that "the scientific reliability of such evidence is substantially outweighed by its confusing effect on the jury."

United States v. Lynn, 856 F.2d 430 (1st Cir. 1988): The Court reversed drug convictions, holding it was error to deny the defendant an opportunity to question a government witness concerning "inconclusive" answers on two polygraph tests. Since the government presented the plea agreement, which required that the defendant successfully complete a polygraph examination, the Court concluded that the defendant should have been permitted to demonstrate that the witness had a reason to curry favor with the government to avoid nullification of his agreement as a result of the tests. In *deVries v. St. Paul Fire & Marine Ins. Co.,* 716 F.2d 939 (1st Cir. 1983), affirming a judgment for the plaintiffs in a suit alleging bad faith denial of coverage under an insurance policy, the Court upheld a ruling excluding evidence that the plaintiffs refused to take a polygraph test. It reasoned that polygraph evidence has been deemed to be of dubious value by Federal Courts, and that any probative value that the evidence would have had on the question of the company's good faith was substantially outweighed by the prejudicial impact it might have had on the jury.

Polygraph and similar evidence (cont'd)

United States v. Rea, 958 F.2d 1206 (2d Cir. 1992): The Court held, in a prosecution for willful evasion of gasoline excise taxes, that there was no abuse of discretion in the denial of a defendant's motion *in limine* to introduce results of a polygraph examination to which he had voluntarily submitted. Even if such results are not per se inadmissible (as Circuit precedent intimates), there was no showing these results were sufficiently reliable or relevant to warrant admission.

United States v. A & S Council Oil Co., 947 F.2d 1128 (4th Cir. 1991): The principal government witness in a prosecution for false claims fraud had taken polygraph tests in which the government examiner concluded he was ''not truthful.'' A government motion *in limine* to exclude polygraph evidence was granted, and at trial the defense was not permitted to inquire about the tests while cross-examining a government expert whose report (entered in evidence) concluded that the key witness was competent. The Court reversed, holding that as a panel it could not overturn the Circuit's rule excluding polygraph evidence offered to prove the examinee's truthfulness, but that under Rule 705 the expert could be examined on the polygraph report he had considered in reaching his opinion on competency. In *United States v. Brevard,* 739 F.2d 180 (4th Cir. 1984), the Court reversed a bank robbery conviction because an FBI agent made statements while testifying that the jury might have interpreted as indicating that the defendant had failed a polygraph test. The Court found that the defendant's credibility was crucial and that the Trial Judge's instruction to the jury to disregard the agent's references was not sufficient protection against the possibility of prejudice.

Joubert v. Travelers Indem. Co., 736 F.2d 191 (5th Cir. 1984): The Court affirmed a judgment for the company, which alleged that an insured was responsible for setting two fires in his home, stating that the plaintiff's ''argument that the trial court erred in holding that a voice stress test was inadmissible is without merit.'' In *United States v. Martino,* 648 F.2d 367 (5th Cir. 1981), *cert. denied,* 456 U.S. 943, 949 (1982), the Court noted that the results of a polygraph exam are inadmissible.

United States v. Harris, 9 F.3d 493 (6th Cir. 1993): The Court held there was no abuse of discretion in excluding evidence that a defendant charged with cocaine offenses offered to take a polygraph examination. Because he did not agree to allow the results of any such examination, whatever they might be, to be admitted at a subsequent trial, the evidence was at best marginally relevant on the issue of credibility. In *United States v. Weiner,* 988 F.2d 629 (6th Cir.), *cert. denied,* 114 S. Ct. 142 (1993), the Court held there was no error in admitting evidence that the defendant in a fraud case had taken a polygraph examination, as it was offered only to show why he was no longer being used as an informant. In *United States v. Barger,* 931 F.2d 359 (6th Cir. 1991), the Court affirmed the conviction of a motorcycle gang member for arson and related offenses, holding there was no abuse of discretion in admitting evidence of a polygraph test given to an informant-witness, as it was relevant to his credibility and the test was part of his contract with the FBI, which the defense put in issue several times, and it was the defense rather than the government that elicited the results of the test. In *Wolfel v. Holbrook,* 823 F.2d 970 (6th Cir. 1987), *cert. denied,* 108 S. Ct. 1035 (1988), the Court reversed a judgment for an inmate who sued a corrections officer for an alleged beating. It observed that polygraph evidence is generally inadmissible absent a stipulation of the parties, although a party's willingness to take a polygraph might be admissible under limited circumstances. In this case, the Court held that it was error to admit evidence that the inmate was willing to take a lie detector test and to permit the inmate to interrogate a corrections officer concerning his refusal to submit to a polygraph examination regarding the alleged beating of another prisoner. In *Murphy v. Cincinnati Ins. Co.,* 772 F.2d 273 (6th Cir. 1985), the Court affirmed a judgment for an insured on a fire policy, holding that the Trial Judge did not err in permitting the plaintiff to testify about his willingness to take a lie detector test and to cooperate with the company. The Court found that the testimony was relevant both to his credibility and to the company's claim of good faith in rejecting a claim.

United States v. Dietrich, 854 F.2d 1056 (7th Cir. 1988): The Court affirmed convictions for dealing in counterfeit notes, observing that "[i]n this circuit, the admissibility of polygraph evidence is left to the discretion of the trial judge," and that "[d]istrict judges generally exercise their discretion in this area in favor of excluding polygraph evidence, because doubts about the probative value and reliability of this evidence are usually found to outweigh the risk of prejudice." In this case, the Trial Judge struck a witness' mention of having taken a polygraph test and admonished the jury to disregard the testimony. Although the defendant claimed that the Judge should have given a more elaborate instruction, he failed to request one and the instruction given was deemed adequate. In *United States v. Feldman,* 711 F.2d 758 (7th Cir.), *cert. denied,* 104 S. Ct. 352 (1983), the Court upheld mail and wire fraud convictions as it found that exclusion of evidence that the defendant passed a polygraph test four days before trial was properly excluded. The Court emphasized the discretion accorded the Trial Judge to admit or exclude such evidence and commented that the "eleventh hour, secret nature" of the test supported exclusion of the results. In *United States v. Williams,* 737 F.2d 594 (7th Cir. 1984), *cert. denied,* 470 U.S. 1003 (1985), a prosecution alleging a scheme to bribe a United States Senator at the expense of a Teamsters' pension fund, the Court held it was not an abuse of discretion to reject results of one defendant's polygraph tests. The Court did not hold that polygraph results are *per se* inadmissible, but it indicated that the Trial Judge has considerable discretion to exclude such results. See also *United States v. Tucker,* 773 F.2d 136 (7th Cir. 1985), *cert. denied,* 478 U.S. 1021, 1022 (1986) (no error for Trial Judge to exclude polygraph results where defendant refused to agree to admissibility of the results before taking the test).

United States v. Smith, 552 F.2d 257 (8th Cir. 1977): The Court ruled that polygraph evidence was properly rejected by the District Judge when the government objected to its admission. In *United States v. Oliver,* 525 F.2d 731 (8th Cir. 1975), *cert. denied,* 424 U.S. 973 (1976), a defendant was convicted of transporting the prosecutrix from Missouri to Kansas against her will for the purpose of sexual gratification. Affirming the conviction, the Court held that the defendant knowingly and willingly agreed to take a polygraph test and to have it admitted into evidence. Adopting a discretionary approach to the polygraph, the Court cited Rule 401 for the proposition that after proper authentication a polygraph could be admitted into evidence. Important to the foundation is the expert examiner. In fact, one polygraph examiner was barred from testifying for the defense partly because of inadequate credentials.

Polygraph and similar evidence (cont'd)

Brown v. Darcy, 783 F.2d 1389 (9th Cir. 1986): In a defamation suit, the Court held that polygraph evidence is inadmissible to establish the truth of statements made in a polygraph examination, absent a stipulation of the parties prior to the examination that the results will be admissible. It found that the admission of polygraph evidence required reversal. In *United States v. Bowen,* 857 F.2d 1337 (9th Cir. 1988), a prosecution for violating civil rights and conspiracy to defraud the government, the government alleged as overt acts one defendant's meeting with a polygrapher who prepared a false report. The Trial Judge ruled that evidence concerning the polygraphy would be excluded, even though it was offered to prove a conspiracy rather than to prove the falsity of statements made. The Court affirmed, finding that the evidence had the potential to confuse the jury, especially in light of defense evidence that the defendant whose report was allegedly falsified passed a second polygraph test. Moreover, the Court found that the prosecution had represented on numerous occasions that it would not seek admission of the evidence and that its change of heart was "beneath the standards we expect of our public prosecutors." In *United States v. Candoli,* 870 F.2d 496 (9th Cir. 1989), the Court found error (harmless, however) in a police agent's reference to asking an unindicted suspect in an arson case to take a lie detector test, since the jury might have improperly inferred that the suspect took a test, passed it, and was therefore properly eliminated as a suspect. In *United States v. Solomon,* 753 F.2d 1522 (9th Cir. 1985), the Court affirmed convictions, including two for first degree murder, as it found that the Trial Judge did not err in excluding a defense psychiatrist's testimony concerning narcoanalysis of one defendant. Since narcoanalysis does not reliably induce truthful statements, the Trial Judge had discretion to exclude the evidence as not being helpful and as being more prejudicial than probative. In *United States v. Falsia,* 724 F.2d 1339 (9th Cir. 1983), the Court sustained a defendant's cocaine conspiracy conviction and upheld the refusal to admit evidence of a polygraph test that was favorable to the defendant, reasoning that the Trial Judge could have concluded that the evidence might have been time-consuming, prejudicial, and confusing. In *United States v. Miller,* 874 F.2d 1255 (9th Cir. 1989), the Court held that a limiting instruction was insufficient to cure the erroneous admission of evidence that the defendant had made false statements on a polygraph test.

United States v. Soundingsides, 819 F.2d 1529 (10th Cir. 1987): The Court reversed a murder conviction on other grounds, but indicated that no reference should be made on retrial to a polygraph examination that appeared to indicate that a witness' statement to FBI agents that he saw the defendant beat the victim was true and his trial testimony to the contrary was false.

United States v. Piccinonna, 885 F.2d 1529 (11th Cir. 1989) (en banc): Overturning its prior rule holding polygraph evidence inadmissible *per se,* the Court *en banc* vacated a conviction for knowingly making false statements to a grand jury and held that polygraph evidence was now sufficiently accepted as reliable that it could be admitted on stipulation or for impeachment or corroboration under Rule 608 upon adequate notice and opportunity for the opponent also to conduct a polygraph examination, subject to the discretion of the Trial Judge. Three Judges dissented from the conclusion that polygraph evidence had gained acceptance in the scientific community as a reliable instrument for detecting lies.

Prejudice — duty to minimize

United States v. Dixon, 698 F.2d 445 (11th Cir. 1983): Appealing his conviction for income tax evasion and mail fraud, the defendant claimed he was exposed to unnecessary prejudice when the government established all items and expenses for two tax years in order to prove understatement of tax liability. The Court affirmed, saying that "there is no requirement that the government choose the least prejudicial method of proving its case." Although this statement is certainly true, it would be more accurate if it had these words added: "unless the Trial Judge requires the government to do so under Rule 403." If there are several ways to prove something and all are equally probative while one is highly prejudicial, a Court might well say that the prejudicial effect of the more inflammatory approach substantially outweighs its probative value.

Probation and parole officer testimony

United States v. Garrison, 849 F.2d 103 (4th Cir. 1988): The Court held it was proper to allow a probation officer to testify concerning the defendant's weight loss after the time of the robbery for which he was being tried. In *United States v. Allen,* 787 F.2d 933 (4th Cir. 1986), *vacated on other grounds,* 107 S. Ct. 1271 (1987), the Court upheld the admission of testimony by a police officer and a parole officer identifying two defendants from bank surveillance films. It concluded that "testimony by those who knew defendants over a period of time and in a variety of circumstances offers to the jury a perspective it could not acquire in its limited exposure to the defendants." No disclosure was made to the jury that the witnesses were law enforcement officers, but the defendants complained that they could not realistically cross-examine the witnesses concerning occupation and bias without eliciting testimony concerning the defendants' criminal activities. The Court found that "[n]othing in the Rules of Evidence or any other source is intended to relieve criminal defendants from difficult strategic choices," and praised the Trial Judge for carefully considering the approach to the two witnesses outside the hearing of the jury.

United States v. Pace, 10 F.3d 1106 (5th Cir. 1993), *cert. denied,* 114 S. Ct. 2810 (1994): In a narcotics case, the Court held that the Trial Court erred when it permitted the prosecution to call the defendant's parole officer solely to establish the defendant's address. The testimony was prejudicial, since it informed the jury that the defendant had previously committed crimes; and the Court found the probative value to be minimal, since the defendant's address was not a major issue in dispute in the case, and since it could have been proven in a variety of less prejudicial ways. The error was harmless, however.

United States v. Calhoun, 544 F.2d 291 (6th Cir. 1976): The Court reversed a conviction for armed bank robbery because the defendant's parole officer was permitted to testify that he was the person shown in photographs of the robbery. Although the government did not reveal the officer's relationship with the defendant, to avoid prejudicing the jury, the Court reasoned that the defendant could not effectively cross-examine the witness without risking undue prejudice. Note that cases from other Circuits have disapproved *Calhoun* to the extent that it implies "that a trial court's decision to allow a defendant's parole officer to testify against the defendant is a per se violation of

Rule 403.'' *United States v. Pace,* 10 F.3d 1106, 1115 (5th Cir. 1993) *(supra).* In most Circuits, the parole officer's testimony will be admissible if it is important to the case and if it cannot reasonably be provided by another person.

United States v. Stormer, 938 F.2d 759 (7th Cir. 1991): In the prosecution of a former police officer for bank robbery, the Court held there was no abuse of discretion in permitting other police officers to give opinion testimony as to the identity of the robber in the bank surveillance photographs. The testimony was helpful because the person pictured had made efforts to alter his appearance; this probative value was not substantially outweighed by the risk of disclosure of rumors of the defendant's alleged impropriety during the course of examining the witnesses as to their possible bias and prejudice.

United States v. Wright, 904 F.2d 403 (8th Cir. 1990): The Court held there was no abuse of discretion in admitting testimony from witnesses familiar with the defendant from his previous involvement in the criminal justice system, where that connection was not disclosed and the witnesses' contacts were extensive enough to be helpful in identifying the person depicted in surveillance films of bank robbery. The Court also held there was no confrontation violation where the failure to cross-examine the witnesses for bias resulted from a tactical decision, not a prohibition by the Trial Judge. In *United States v. Farnsworth,* 729 F.2d 1158 (8th Cir. 1984), the Court affirmed a bank robbery conviction, holding it was no abuse of discretion to admit testimony by parole officers who identified the defendant in surveillance films. The Court observed that the parole officers' status was not revealed nor was the defendant's prior record, and it suggested that the use of lay opinion identification by police or parole officers should only be used where no other adequate identification testimony is available, since the defendant obviously is severely restricted in cross-examining officers who might reveal a prior record.

United States v. LaPierre, 998 F.2d 1460 (9th Cir. 1993): In vacating the defendant's conviction for bank robbery and firearms offenses, the Court noted that it was an abuse of discretion to permit an investigating officer to give an opinion that the individual pictured in the bank surveillance photographs was the defendant. The testimony was unnecessary because the defendant's appearance had not changed, and it ran the risk of invading the province of the jury and prejudicing the defendant, especially because the officer had never seen the defendant in person. In *United States v. Butcher,* 557 F.2d 666 (9th Cir. 1977), two police officers and a parole officer were permitted to testify, because the defendant's appearance at the time of trial was slightly different from his appearance when arrested and prior to the robbery, that the defendant was the individual depicted in bank surveillance photographs. The Court upheld the opinions under Rule 701, but noted two problems: First, the witnesses were testifying on the basis of contact with the defendant at a time when his appearance was even less similar to the appearance of the person in the surveillance photos than it was at the time of trial, so it was arguable that the jury needed no help. More importantly, the use of police and parole officers could be prejudicial to the defendant by suggesting prior prolonged contact with law enforcement officials. The Court warned ''that use of lay opinion identification by policemen or parole officers is not to be encouraged, and should be used only if no other adequate identification testimony is available to the prosecution.''

"Profile" evidence

United States v. Simpson, 910 F.2d 154 (4th Cir. 1990): The Court reversed a conviction for unlawfully possessing a firearm and attempting to board an aircraft with a concealed weapon, holding it was an abuse of discretion to admit drug courier profile testimony. Even giving the evidence its maximum probative value and minimizing its prejudicial effect, the evidence had *de minimis* relevance but highly prejudicial impact in its insinuation of drug crimes in the trial.

United States v. Carter, 901 F.2d 683 (8th Cir. 1990): The Court held in a cocaine possession case that drug courier profiles are investigative tools, not evidence of guilt, and that their admission is inherently prejudicial, but that the error in admitting the evidence in this case, where there was no need to establish the validity of a search before the jury, was harmless. In *United States v. Wilson,* 930 F.2d 616 (8th Cir.), *cert. denied,* 112 S. Ct. 208 (1991), a drug trafficking prosecution, the Court held that introducing evidence of frequent flights, which was part of a drug courier profile, was relevant to rebut the defendant's argument he was ignorant of the contents of a package picked up from an airline; it was error (but harmless), however, for the prosecutor to argue in summation that the defendant fit the profile.

United States v. Lui, 941 F.2d 844 (9th Cir. 1991): The Court held it was an abuse of discretion, but harmless, to admit drug courier profile evidence to show *modus operandi,* where the defendant was caught red-handed with suitcases full of heroin and the government had no need to explain a complex criminal scheme. See also *United States v. Gomez-Norena,* 908 F.2d 497 (9th Cir.), *cert. denied,* 111 S. Ct. 363 (1990), (no plain error to admit drug courier profile testimony where it was not offered to prove that the defendant was guilty, and the jury was twice cautioned to consider it only as background material).

United States v. Robinson, 978 F.2d 1554 (10th Cir. 1992), *cert. denied,* 113 S. Ct. 1855, 2938 (1993): Affirming convictions for cocaine base possession and conspiracy, the Court held that expert evidence tending to show that the defendants were active members of a gang whose main purpose was to sell cocaine was not impermissible "profile" evidence. Profiles only help investigators decide whether to pursue a matter, but the expert in this case was explaining the physical evidence so as to connect the defendants to the charged crime. The dissenting Judge believed that the government had impermissibly sought to prove that by exhibiting the characteristics of gang members, the defendants were members of a gang with criminal purposes and therefore were guilty of the charged conspiracy and underlying crimes; in any event, the gang affiliation evidence should have been inadmissible because it is inherently and unfairly prejudicial.

Race and ancestry

United States v. Doe, 903 F.2d 16 (D.C. Cir. 1990): A black American and two Jamaicans were jointly charged with drug offenses. The Court reversed their convictions, in part because a detective was permitted to testify to the *modus operandi* of Jamaican drug dealers and how the market has been taken over basically by Jamaicans. The Trial Judge had not balanced the severely prejudicial effect of the references, but had admitted the testimony solely because defense counsel had inquired on *voir dire* whether jurors would have greater difficulty affording Jamaicans a fair trial.

United States v. Rodriguez Cortes, 949 F.2d 532 (1st Cir. 1991): The Court held it was reversible error to admit an unauthenticated Colombian identification card seized from a defendant charged with importing cocaine. In the majority's view, prosecution argument based on the card appealed to the jury to find the defendant guilty by reason of his national origin, inviting them to believe that if a person is born in Colombia he must be involved in drug trafficking. One Judge, concurring *dubitante,* agreed that the card's prejudicial effect substantially exceeded its probative value, but disagreed that the prosecutor's argument crossed the line.

United States v. Blackwood, 913 F.2d 139 (4th Cir. 1990): Affirming a conviction for possessing crack cocaine with intent to distribute, the Court held there was no abuse of discretion in admitting two Jamaican passports in the defendant's name found in one of the rooms where the drugs were located, as the value of the evidence in showing control of the room was not substantially outweighed by the risk that the passports would incite xenophobic hostility.

United States v. Vue, 13 F.3d 1206 (8th Cir. 1994): The Court reversed the Hmong defendants' convictions for opium smuggling because a customs officer was permitted to testify that much of the opium smuggling in the area involved Hmongs.

Relationship to other rules

United States v. Long, 917 F.2d 691 (2d Cir. 1990): In reversing RICO convictions, the Court held that an FBI agent had been improperly permitted under Rule 702 to testify about organized crime families, as the extensive descriptions had a highly prejudicial effect and only marginal relevance when the enterprise alleged was not a crime family and had only a single connection with organized crime.

United States v. Salmon, 944 F.2d 1106 (3d Cir. 1991), *cert. denied,* 112 S. Ct. 1213 (1992): A defendant charged with cocaine offenses was precluded from cross-examining a codefendant regarding the confidential informant's use of cocaine with them on the ground that it was extrinsic evidence inadmissible under Rule 608. The Court held that the evidence might have been relevant to the defendant's entrapment defense, but its probative value was at best slight and it was potentially prejudicial to the codefendant.

Cortes v. Maxus Exploration Co., 977 F.2d 195 (5th Cir. 1992): Affirming a judgment for the plaintiff in a Title VII sexual harassment action, the Court held there was no abuse of discretion in excluding the EEOC's determination of no probable cause for the charge. Although agency reports are presumptively admissible under Rule 803(8)(C), this report did not contain detailed evidentiary statements and findings of fact; rather, it was a conclusory determination that could have unfairly prejudiced the plaintiff's case.

Orth v. Emerson Elec. Co., 980 F.2d 632 (10th Cir. 1992): The Court affirmed a judgment for the plaintiffs in a product liability action arising out of a gas heater explosion, holding that there was no abuse of discretion in informing the jury that the plaintiffs had settled claims against the regulator manufacturer and instructing them to disregard any further reference to the settlement. Although mention of the settlement was not barred by Rule 408, the Court upheld the instruction because many of the same concerns about prejudice and deterrence to settlements exist regardless of the purposes for which the evidence is offered, and further reference to the settlement would tend to confuse the jury.

United States v. King, 713 F.2d 627 (11th Cir. 1983), *cert. denied*, 104 S. Ct. 1924 (1984): Reversing ruling that prior testimony of a key witness would be excluded in a retrial, the Court rejected the government's argument that the Trial Judge lacked authority to exclude evidence under Rule 403 that was admissible under Rule 804(b)(1), but it found that the Judge had reached an incorrect balancing ruling. The Court pointed out that evidence should be excluded only sparingly under Rule 403 and that the greater the need for the evidence the less likely it is to be excluded. The Court recognized the legitimacy of the Judge's concern that without seeing and hearing a key witness the jury might have trouble evaluating his credibility, but it concluded that the probative value of the testimony was extremely high and the risk of prejudice was low.

Relationship to Rule 404(b)

United States v. Currier, 836 F.2d 11 (1st Cir. 1987): Although the Court agreed with the government that a defendant charged with distributing Valium should have specifically objected under Rule 404(b) to a tape recording of a conversation that referred to the defendant's sale of weapons and other drugs, it found that the defendant's Rule 403 objection was sufficient to preserve the evidence question for appeal and concluded that the evidence was properly admitted as highly probative on the issue of intent. In *Bowden v. McKenna*, 600 F.2d 282 (1st Cir.), *cert. denied*, 444 U.S. 899 (1979), the Court reversed a judgment for the plaintiffs in a civil rights action arising out of an incident in which two policemen fatally shot a robbery suspect. The Court held that the defendants should have been permitted to offer identification testimony to establish that the suspect committed the robbery, as this might have established the suspect's motive to resist and thus might have corroborated the officers' story.

Government of Virgin Islands v. Pinney, 967 F.2d 912 (3d Cir. 1992): The Court reversed the defendant's conviction for rape of a seven-year-old girl, holding there was error in admitting evidence that the defendant had raped the victim's sister six years earlier. The two crimes were not parts of a single series of events or sufficiently distinctive to be probative on the perpetrator's identity (which was not contested, in any event), nor did the uncharged crime have sufficient utility in showing intent to outweigh the very real danger of being used for an improper purpose to the serious and unfair detriment of the defendant. In the absence of any explanation and of any justification apparent in the record, no deference could be given to the Trial Judge's reasoning in denying the defendant's Rule 403 motion; further, the cautionary advice given to the jury in its final instructions did not significantly reduce the risk of using this inflammatory evidence for an improper purpose.

United States v. Clark, 988 F.2d 1459 (6th Cir.) *cert. denied*, 114 S. Ct. 105 (1993): Affirming a conviction for murder to obstruct justice, the Court held that evidence of the defendant's plans to escape from prison, rob a race track, and set up a drug trade was neither probative of anything material to the charges nor prejudicial in light of voluminous admissible evidence of his automobile theft crimes.

United States v. Price, 617 F.2d 455 (7th Cir. 1980): Upholding a Hobbs Act conviction, the Court said that the Trial Judge should have stated reasons for permitting the government to offer Rule 404(b) evidence on the issue of intent following a Rule 403 objection, but that it would not presume error when the reason for balancing in favor of admission "was apparent."

United States v. Robertson, 15 F.3d 862 (9th Cir.), *cert. granted,* 115 S. Ct. __ (1994): The Court held it was error (but harmless) to admit evidence that a drug dealer who had been trying to collect a debt from the defendant was never seen again after a car similar to the defendant's was observed at the drug dealer's house. The evidence, as well as evidence of the defendant's drug use and spousal abuse, did not tend to prove any material element of the cocaine distribution and RICO offenses charged. One Judge, specially concurring, noted that reversal might have been warranted in a closer case and that prosecutors should "focus their attention more carefully on prosecuting the defendant under charges appropriate to his crimes, and on distinguishing legitimate substantive evidence from evidence of bad acts that serves principally to prejudice the jurors."

Samples v. City of Atlanta, 916 F.2d 1548 (11th Cir. 1990): The Court affirmed a summary judgment for the defendants in a § 1983 action by the parents of a youth fatally shot by a police officer, holding there was no abuse of discretion in admitting evidence the decedent's brother was in prison for murder, as the decedent had said he wanted to get locked up by a policeman so he could go see his brother and the evidence tended to show his motivation for threatening the officer.

Religious issues

United States v. Brandon, 17 F.3d 409 (1st Cir.), *cert. denied,* 115 S. Ct. __ (1994): After a witness in a bank fraud prosecution mentioned that two of the defendants were Jewish, defense counsel moved to dismiss and for a mistrial on the grounds that the testimony invited an impermissible inference that members of the same religion would be more likely to join a conspiracy and may have provoked anti-Semitic feelings. When the Trial Judge offered to try to ferret out any anti-Semitism on the jury, the counsel requested only dismissal, not further questioning of the jury, and expressed displeasure with the possibility of providing curative instructions that "would only magnify the problem." Affirming despite the possible inappropriateness of the testimony, the Court found that the level of prejudice, if any, was not sufficiently significant to overturn the decision to accept "the defendants' tactical choice to forgo more appropriate methods of addressing the potential prejudice in favor of the unrealistic and unnecessary solution of a dismissal or a new trial."

United States v. Moon, 718 F.2d 1210 (2d Cir. 1983), *cert. denied,* 104 S. Ct. 2344 (1984): The Court affirmed convictions arising from the filing of false tax returns, as it found that evidence of certain religious practices of the Unification Church was properly admitted on the central issue of whether stock and bank accounts belonged to the Church or to its leader personally.

Munn v. Algee, 924 F.2d 568 (5th Cir.), *cert. denied,* 112 S. Ct. 277 (1991): An automobile accident victim, following the tenets of her Jehovah's Witnesses faith, refused blood transfusions and died of her injuries. In the trial of the ensuing wrongful death action, her husband was asked about, *inter alia,* the Jehovah's Witnesses' refusal to "do service to their country'' and to salute the flag. One Judge concluded that admission of the evidence was an abuse of discretion under the Rule primarily because it was utterly irrelevant to how sincerely the victim and her husband adhered to the faith, but believed that the error did not affect the party's substantial rights. The concurring Judge disagreed that the evidence was irrelevant and said nothing about its prejudicial effect. The dissenting Judge considered that the calculated inflammatory effect of cross-examination regarding the views of other members of the faith had a prejudicial effect far beyond the probative value of the examination on the personal beliefs of the plaintiff-witness.

Remoteness

Jackson v. Johns-Manville Sales Corp., 750 F.2d 1314 (5th Cir. 1985) (en banc): In an action by a former shipyard worker for injuries allegedly caused by the defendants' failures to warn of the hazards of exposure to asbestos products, the Court affirmed admission of twenty-five-year-old letters that were among the papers of the chairman of the board of one of the defendants. The letters were not so remote in subject matter as to be devoid of probative value, they were not inflammatory, and the defendants had ample opportunity to make the jury aware of their remoteness.

Cooley v. Carmike Cinemas, Inc., 25 F.3d 1325 (6th Cir. 1994): In an age discrimination case the Court held it was no abuse of discretion (or harmless error) to admit evidence that the plaintiff's supervisor had said two decades earlier, in his teen years, that he wanted to put older people in "a concentration camp," and some years later that he did not want to go to a Thanksgiving Day dinner where his grandmother would be because he "[did not] like to be around old people." The comments were probative of the supervisor's state of mind and reflected a deep-rooted ongoing pattern that was anything but isolated; however, other evidence in the case meant that the jury did not need to hear the comments in order to believe the plaintiff's claim and to find that the defendant's explanations were pretextual.

United States v. Austin, 933 F.2d 833 (10th Cir. 1991): Reversing a conviction for resisting correctional officers, the Court held it was an abuse of discretion when the defense was mental illness to exclude records of prior hospitalizations on the ground solely of remoteness. The Court was unwilling to place a temporal limit on relevant proof of mental illness in view of its frequently long duration, its possible chronicity, and its recurrent manifestations.

Restricted admission of evidence

Clausen v. Sea-3, Inc., 21 F.3d 1181 (1st Cir. 1994): In an employee's action for personal injuries caused by a fall on a ramp, the Court found no plain error in admission of evidence that a defendant had replaced the ramp with steps three years later. The evidence was probative on the issue of which defendant controlled the premises, and the cautionary instruction sufficiently informed the jury as to the limited purpose for which it was admitted.

United States v. Reyes, 18 F.3d 65 (2d Cir. 1994): The Court reversed a conviction for conspiring to import narcotics, holding it was error to admit as nonhearsay a Customs agent's testimony regarding statements by two persons who implicated the defendant in the conspiracy, even though the declarants' exact words were not repeated. Although the jury was instructed that the statements were not admitted for their truth, the likelihood was sufficiently high that the jury would have treated the evidence for its truth anyway. The Court also rejected the argument that the evidence was properly admitted as "background" and observed that "contrary to the government's contention, the mere identification of a relevant non-hearsay use of such evidence is insufficient to justify its admission if the jury is likely to consider the statement for the truth of what was stated with significant resultant prejudice."

Morgan v. Woessner, 997 F.2d 1244 (9th Cir. 1993), *cert. dismissed,* 114 S. Ct. 671 (1994): In a civil rights action for false arrest, evidence of the plaintiff's character and reputation was admitted to show his damages, with the jury instructed not to consider it in deciding what the plaintiff had done. The Court, believing the issue a close one, held there was no abuse of discretion in admitting the evidence; although the jury may have been more inclined to believe the plaintiff once they heard of his good reputation, there was plenty of evidence that the defendant was the aggressor and the cautionary instruction blunted the improper impact of the testimony.

Self-serving statements

Healey v. Chelsea Resources Ltd., 947 F.2d 611 (2d Cir. 1991): In a securities fraud action, the Court held that the plaintiff's testimony regarding his reliance should not have been curtailed on the ground it was self-serving, as that goes to weight rather than admissibility, but the error was harmless because the ruling may only have prevented a cumulative summary.

Sexual activities

United States v. Harvey, 991 F.2d 981 (2d Cir. 1993): The Court reversed the defendant's conviction for knowingly receiving child pornography, holding that testimony concerning other pornography seized from his residence was irrelevant and so overwhelmingly prejudicial as to deny him a fair trial.

United States v. McMillon, 14 F.3d 948 (4th Cir. 1994): The Court held in a drug prosecution that it was not an abuse of discretion to preclude a defendant from cross-examining a cooperating coconspirator about the witness' use of drugs to force men to engage in sexual acts with him. Testimony regarding a witness' sexual life is not probative of his character for truthfulness; rather, it impairs the search for truth and harasses, annoys, or humiliates the witness in the process. In *United States v. Ham,* 998 F.2d 1247 (4th Cir. 1993), the Court reversed convictions for racketeering and mail fraud, holding that implications of child molestation, homosexuality, and abuse of women were unfairly prejudicial when they were not directly implicated in the crimes charged. In *United States v. Saunders,* 886 F.2d 56 (4th Cir. 1989), the Court affirmed a prisoner's assault conviction, but it rejected the government's argument that a prison evaluation report, which tended to prove the alleged victim's homosexual tendencies, should have been excluded under Rule 403. The report lent credence to the defendant's self-defense theory and bolstered his claim that the incident was sexually related. In *United States v. Kilbourne,* 559 F.2d 1263 (4th Cir.), *cert. denied,* 434 U.S. 873 (1977), the Court affirmed a murder conviction, holding that evidence of the defendant's sexual relations with the victim was relevant to show motive and that the probative value was not substantially outweighed by the danger of prejudice.

United States v. Davila, 704 F.2d 749 (5th Cir. 1983): The Court upheld convictions for depriving illegal aliens of their liberty by coercing sexual favors from them and for sexually abusing illegal aliens. It found that the Trial Judge did not abuse his discretion in excluding evidence that the complaining witnesses had previously engaged in prostitution: "[W]hatever probative value lay in the evidence as to possible prostitution was miniscule and the potential for confusion was substantial." In *United States v. Frick,* 588 F.2d 531 (5th Cir.), *cert. denied,* 441 U.S. 913 (1979), the Court reversed a defendant's conspiracy and fraud convictions on the ground that testimony concerning his sexual relations with a codefendant's secretary was highly prejudicial to him. The Court said that the government's contention that the evidence was properly admitted to show motive failed because there was no evidence that the defendant knew that the secretary had been instructed to make herself available to him. In *United States v. Grassi,* 602 F.2d 1192 (5th Cir. 1979), *vacated & remanded on other grounds,* 448 U.S. 902 (1980), a prosecution for interstate transportation of obscene material, defense counsel offered to stipulate that the films were obscene. The prosecutor objected, and the jury was shown three films that portrayed "homosexual acts of the most bizarre and repulsive nature." Rejecting both the argument that the government had an absolute right to refuse the stipulation and the counter-argument that the defendant had an absolute right to compel its acceptance, the Court said that a Rule 403 balancing analysis must be used and sustained the Trial Judge, finding that the films had probative value above and beyond the stipulation.

Herry v. Deloney, 28 F.3d 608 (7th Cir. 1994): A high school student brought a § 1983 action against a truant officer for nonconsensual sexual relations; the plaintiff's *in limine* motion to exclude evidence of her sexual activity with others was denied. Affirming a judgment for the defendant, the Court held there was no error in admitting evidence of other sexual activity and prior and subsequent abortions with instructions that it be considered solely on the issues of the amount of damages and whether alleged damages were attributable to the defendant. In *Campbell v. Ingersoll Milling Mach. Co.,* 893 F.2d 925 (7th Cir.), *cert. denied,* 111 S. Ct. 127 (1990), the Court affirmed a judgment n.o.v. for the defendant employer in a suit alleging race and sex discrimination in the plaintiff's termination, holding that evidence of an alleged sexual assault on the plaintiff by her supervisor was of little or no probative value on the motivation for her discharge or on her damages and was likely to lead the jury to a decision on an improper basis, such as sympathy.

Cummings v. Malone, 995 F.2d 817 (8th Cir. 1993): In a prisoner's civil rights action for excessive force during a prison investigation, the Trial Judge excluded evidence that the investigation centered on an allegation that the plaintiff had attempted to rape a prison employee. The Court agreed that this evidence was irrelevant and highly prejudicial. The Court also held that the Judge ruled properly in permitting defendants to show the plaintiff's possible bias because they had testified against him on felony charges but not permitting evidence that the charges were for attempted rape and assault arising out of the investigation incident. In *United States v. Ford,* 17 F.3d 1100 (8th Cir. 1994), the

Court held it was not an abuse of discretion to preclude evidence that the felony conviction of the prosecution's primary witness had been for a sex offense against a minor. Introduction of the specific felony could easily have distracted the jury without adding any real probative information. In *United States v. LaChapelle,* 969 F.2d 632 (8th Cir. 1992), the defendant, charged with receiving child pornography through the mail, asserted an entrapment defense and the government introduced a pornographic videotape seized from the defendant's home to show his knowledge of and intent to order child pornography. The Court held admission of the evidence was error (but harmless) because the possession was legal when the defendant first possessed the videotape. Evidence of predisposition to do what was once lawful is not by itself sufficient to show predisposition to do what is now illegal, so the slight probative value of the evidence was substantially outweighed by its prejudicial effect. In *United States v. Fawbush,* 900 F.2d 150 (8th Cir. 1990), a conviction for aggravated sexual abuse of children was reversed, the Court holding that evidence the defendant sexually abused his daughters when they were children, even if relevant, was so inflammatory on its face as to divert the jury's attention from the material issues in the trial. See also *United States v. Abodeely,* 801 F.2d 1020 (8th Cir. 1986) (probative value of evidence of the defendant's receipt of income from prostitution and of gambling activities outweighed any prejudicial effects in income tax evasion prosecution). In *United States v. One Feather,* 702 F.2d 736 (8th Cir. 1983), the Court upheld a rape conviction, finding no error in the Trial Judge's refusal to permit the defendant to ask the victim, who testified on direct examination that she was divorced and had an infant son, where her marriage and divorce took place. The defendant had been unable to find applicable records and believed that the witness had lied. Using Rule 412 as persuasive authority, the Court found that the Judge properly relied on Rule 403 to bar the questioning, since it would have prejudicially suggested that the victim had an illegitimate child.

United States v. Bland, 908 F.2d 471 (9th Cir. 1990): The defendant, charged with being a felon in possession of a firearm, gave notice that his theory at trial would be that an officer planted the gun in order to justify shooting him in making an arrest. At the *voir dire,* the Trial Judge told the jury not only that it was anticipated that the officer would testify he shot the defendant to prevent his escape and that he was aware of an outstanding warrant for the defendant, but also that the warrant was for the molestation, torture, and murder of a seven-year-old girl. The Court reversed the conviction because, although the existence of the warrant was relevant to show the officer did not have a motive to plant the gun, the members of the jury panel were not likely to forget details leading them to believe that acquitting the defendant might mean releasing an extremely dangerous child molester and killer into the community. In *United States v. Gillespie,* 852 F.2d 475 (9th Cir. 1988), the Court reversed a conviction for importing an alien for immoral purposes, holding it was error to admit evidence that the defendant had a homosexual relationship with the father who adopted him. This evidence was not relevant to any claim made by the defendant and was extremely prejudicial.

Stahl v. Sun Microsys., Inc., 19 F.3d 533 (10th Cir. 1994): In an action alleging sex discrimination in employment by means of a hostile work environment, the Court held there was no abuse of discretion in excluding evidence of a sexual relationship between the supervisor whose conduct was at issue and another defense witness. The evidence was not relevant to the merits, as there was no *quid pro quo* harassment claim, and its probative value as to the two witness' credibility was slight while its potential for unfair prejudice was obvious. In *United States v. Garot*, 801 F.2d 1241 (10th Cir. 1986), the Court affirmed convictions for mailing obscene matter and dealing in material exploiting minors, holding there was no error in admitting evidence of an envelope postmarked in Sweden that contained a brochure showing a color slide of explicit child pornography and a box containing hard-core films of child pornography. The evidence was relevant to prove scienter.

United States v. Lehder-Rivas, 955 F.2d 1510 (11th Cir.), *cert. denied*, 113 S. Ct. 347 (1992): The Court held that it was harmless error when the government suggested that the defendant in a cocaine importation conspiracy engaged in frequent "partying" and fathered an illegitimate child. In *Aetna Cas. & Sur. Co. v. Gosdin*, 803 F.2d 1153 (11th Cir. 1986), the Court reversed a judgment for the insurer in a dispute with its insured concerning the cause of a fire. Although it upheld the introduction of motive evidence that the insured had been charged with burglary and needed money to mount a defense, the Court held that evidence of pimping, pandering, and drug charges was unduly prejudicial.

Similar circumstances — civil rights and employment discrimination

Morris v. Washington Metropolitan Area Transit Auth., 702 F.2d 1037 (D.C. Cir. 1983): The plaintiff claimed that he was discharged as a transit police officer, *inter alia*, because of his criticism of racial discrimination by the Authority. Reversing a judgment for the defendant, the Court held that testimony by other employees offered to prove a custom or policy of retaliation by the Authority against employees who complained about the Authority's employment practices was improperly excluded. Likewise, it was error to exclude the plaintiff's testimony concerning disciplinary action against him following each of his complaints to the Authority. He should have been permitted "to testify to the discipline in a way that made evident the retaliatory motivation for the discipline."

Foley v. City of Lowell, Mass., 948 F.2d 10 (1st Cir. 1991): The Court held there was no abuse of discretion in admitting in an arrestee's civil rights case evidence of a particularly vile incident of police brutality six months later. Evidence of subsequent incidents can provide reliable insight into the policy in force at a previous time; the fact the later conduct was egregious is a hallmark of its probative value not its prejudicial effect, as the more outrageous the occurrences, the more probable that a policy of tolerance was in place. In *Brown v. Trustees of Boston Univ.*, 891 F.2d 337 (1st Cir. 1989), *cert. denied*, 110 S. Ct. 3217 (1990), the plaintiff, suing for breach of contract and sexual discrimination after she was denied tenure, offered testimony of several professors comparing her qualifications with those of other faculty considered for tenure at the defendant University. The Court held that, even though the professors' testimony was not in the file and thus was not available to the University when it decided her case, it was relevant proof of pretext because it showed that the qualifications of others granted tenure were below the plaintiff's known qualifications. Because admitting such comparative evidence presents the risk of improperly substituting a judicial tenure decision, the evidence must be so compelling as to permit a reasonable finding of one-sidedness going beyond a mere difference in judgment, as in this case.

Morgan v. City of Marmaduke, Ark., 958 F.2d 207 (8th Cir. 1992): In a civil rights suit alleging a police officer had used excessive force when making an arrest by intentionally colliding his patrol car with the plaintiff's motorcycle, the Court held it was error to admit evidence that the officer had three years earlier accidentally collided with a motorcycle whose driver he was attempting to arrest. Admitting evidence of the remote and dissimilar situation had a prejudicial effect against the officer. Evidence of another situation involving the officer's using his patrol car as a roadblock to stop a motorcyclist had been excluded; the Court held that although the circumstances were not entirely dissimilar from the plaintiff's case, exclusion was not an abuse of discretion.

Similar circumstances — generally

Davidson Oil Country Supply Co. v. Klockner, Inc., 908 F.2d 1238, *amended,* 917 F.2d 185 (5th Cir. 1990): In an action for breach of warranty against the distributor of well tubing, the Trial Judge granted the defendant's motion *in limine* excluding evidence that other substantially similar tubing made by the same manufacturer, but sold by other distributors, had failed in a similar manner. The Court reversed a judgment for the defendant, holding that the plaintiff should have been permitted to use the excluded evidence to show that the tubing had a latent manufacturing defect making it unmerchantable, that the defendant had knowledge of the defect, and that it had dealt with the plaintiff's claims in bad faith.

McCarty v. Pheasant Run, Inc., 826 F.2d 1554 (7th Cir. 1987): Affirming a judgment for a hotel owner sued by a guest who was assaulted in her room, the Court held that the Trial Judge did not err in excluding evidence of criminal activity at the hotel that did not involve an entry like the one alleged in the instant case, while admitting evidence of prior similar entries. In *Will v. Comprehensive Accounting Corp.,* 776 F.2d 665 (7th Cir. 1985), *cert. denied,* 475 U.S. 1129 (1986), the Court found no error in an antitrust-contracts case in the exclusion of evidence of how a franchisor acted with respect to twenty-two franchisees besides the plaintiff.

United States v. Soulard, 730 F.2d 1292 (9th Cir. 1984): Affirming convictions for subscribing false corporate income tax returns, the Court held that it was proper for the government to offer evidence comparing Soulard's gross receipts per gallon of ice cream mix with those of various subfranchisees. Although the Court stated that it might have been better to exclude this evidence, it declined to disturb the Trial Judge's ruling that its probative value outweighed the danger of jury confusion.

Similar circumstances — other accident cases

Edwards v. Consolidated Rail Corp., 567 F. Supp. 1087 (D.D.C. 1983), *aff'd,* 733 F.2d 966 (D.C. Cir.), *cert. denied,* 105 S. Ct. 252 (1984): Summary judgment was granted for the railroad in a suit brought by a child trespasser injured when he was exposed to high voltage lines. The Court found that evidence of other accidents, offered to show that the defendant should have known of the danger on its tracks, would be excluded as dissimilar and insufficiently probative to justify admission in light of its prejudicial aspects.

Amatucci v. Delaware & H. Ry., 745 F.2d 180 (2d Cir. 1984): The Court reversed an FELA judgment for an engineer who claimed that work conditions caused him to sustain a heart condition that rendered him unable to continue work. It found error in the admission of testimony that seven or eight other engineers had suffered heart attacks, since the circumstances and family histories concerning the other engineers was unknown.

Gardner v. Southern Ry., 675 F.2d 949 (7th Cir. 1982): In an action arising out of a truck-train collision, the Court found there was no abuse of discretion in excluding evidence of a prior collision between a train and truck since the prior accident was not similar enough to be of much probative value on the question whether the railroad was on notice of a dangerous condition. The Court noted that the Trial Judge admitted other, less prejudicial evidence that certain dangerous conditions had been evident for some time. See also *Kelsay v. Consolidated Rail Corp.,* 749 F.2d 437 (7th Cir. 1984) (judgment for railroad in train-car crash sustained, as Court held, 2-1, that there was no error in the exclusion of two accidents, twelve and thirty years earlier, at same crossing).

Hicks v. Six Flags Over Mid-America, 821 F.2d 1311 (8th Cir. 1987): The Court held that evidence of an accident six years before the plaintiff's was properly excluded.

Similar circumstances — product liability cases

Exum v. General Elec. Co., 819 F.2d 1158 (D.C. Cir. 1987): In a product liability suit by an employee injured while using a french fryer, the Court held that it was error to exclude evidence concerning fifteen similar incidents. All but one occurred before the plaintiff was injured, and the Court reasoned that to prove notice, prior acts need not be as similar as they would have to be to prove the dangerousness of a product. Although the Court recognized that the incident arising after the plaintiff was injured could not prove notice, it concluded that it was so similar to the plaintiff's accident that it was probative of dangerousness.

Harrison v. Sears, Roebuck & Co., 981 F.2d 25 (1st Cir. 1992): In a product liability suit involving a carpentry tool, the defendant's expert testified that the accident described by the plaintiff could not have occurred as alleged and that there had never been a similar complaint made to the manufacturer. The Court rejected an argument that the negative evidence was irrelevant on the issue of causation. In *Freund v. Fleetwood Enterprises,* 956 F.2d 354 (1st Cir. 1992), the Court affirmed a judgment for the defendant in a product liability action arising out of a fire in a recreational vehicle, holding there was no abuse of discretion in excluding recall documents tending to show that propane gas could leak from the vehicle's refrigerator. The probative value of the offered documents was undermined because the accidents they reported involved different brands of refrigerator, trailers rather than RVs, and different years and places of manufacture.

Gumbs v. International Harvester, Inc., 718 F.2d 88 (3d Cir. 1983): In a product liability action, the Court held that the plaintiff's evidence of other accidents involving similar bolts on trucks manufactured by the defendant was inadmissible, since there was no showing that the accidents took place under similar circumstances and some of the evidence involved vehicles with different parts. In *Wolf v. Procter & Gamble Co.,* 555

F. Supp. 613 (D.N.J. 1982), the Court ruled *in limine* in an action against the manufacturer and distributor of a tampon to recover for toxic shock syndrome that evidence of other injuries associated with the use of the tampon would be excluded. The other injuries were not similar enough to be helpful.

Alevromagiros v. Hechinger Co., 993 F.2d 417 (4th Cir. 1993): In a product liability action brought by a consumer injured by an allegedly defective ladder, the Court held there was no error in excluding evidence of a competing ladder with more safety features. The jury did not need to see examples of competing products to understand the nature of the product at issue and could easily have been misled or confused by the assumption that the competing product represented the relevant industry-wide standard.

Johnson v. Ford Motor Co., 988 F.2d 573 (5th Cir. 1993): The Court affirmed a judgment for a manufacturer in a product liability action, holding there was no abuse of discretion in excluding evidence of other accidents that did not involve the alleged mechanical defect relied upon by the plaintiff. See also *Mills v. Beech Aircraft Corp.,* 886 F.2d 758 (5th Cir. 1989) (letter from the French aviation authorities to defendant manufacturer warning of certain defects, offered to show the defendant's knowledge, properly excluded in absence of showing that letter applied to the type of airplane in issue and that the defect had manifested itself in circumstances substantially similar to case at bar); *Soden v. Freightliner Corp.,* 714 F.2d 498 (5th Cir. 1983) (upholding admission of evidence concerning other lawsuits brought against the manufacturer to show notice of a possible defect in the fuel tank of the truck).

Hurt v. Coyne Cylinder Co., 956 F.2d 1319 (6th Cir. 1992): In reversing a product liability judgment for the defendants on other grounds, the Court held there was no abuse of discretion in excluding a film offered by the plaintiffs. There was nothing improper in the Trial Judge's making a subjective determination that the film would be prejudicial, where there was no indication that the Judge's reaction was idiosyncratic and there is an obvious possibility of prejudice from a dramatic film that resembles but does not depict the accident in question.

Klonowski v. International Armament Corp., 17 F.3d 992 (7th Cir. 1994): The Court affirmed a judgment for the plaintiff in a diversity product liability action for injuries when a shotgun misfired, finding no abuse of discretion in excluding evidence that the defendant had imported 50,000 shotguns of the type involved in the accident without receiving any report of an accident, as there was no showing that all the guns imported had substantially identical trigger mechanisms. The Court also noted that negative evidence "is generally held inadmissible because of its insignificant probative qualities and its tendency to introduce a multitude of collateral inquiries." In *Ross v. Black & Decker, Inc.,* 977 F.2d 1178 (7th Cir. 1992), *cert. denied,* 113 S. Ct. 1274 (1993), a product liability action arising out of injuries caused by a circular saw, the Court held there was no abuse of discretion in admitting evidence of two other accidents involving the defendant's saw that occurred after the plaintiff's accident, as the circumstances were substantially similar and the fact the accidents occurred subsequently does not make them any less probative of the unreasonably dangerous design of the saw or the cause of the accident. In *Bilski v. Scientific Atlanta,* 964 F.2d 697 (7th Cir. 1992), the Court affirmed a judgment for the defendant in a product liability action for injuries suffered when the plaintiff slipped while cleaning snow and ice off a satellite dish, holding there was no abuse of discretion in admitting the defendant's records of injuries involving its products, which showed no prior accidents of this sort. Neither was there an abuse of discretion in excluding testimony by the plaintiff's witnesses about other falls from satellite dishes, as none had resulted in injuries reported to the defendant, so the testimony would have had little if any tendency to prove a risk foreseeable to the defendant. In *Estate of Carey v. Hy-Temp Mfg., Inc.,* 929 F.2d 1229 (7th Cir. 1991), the Court remanded a product liability action for a new trial, noting that "substantially similar" circumstances does not mean "identical," that the range between similar and identical is a matter to be addressed on cross-examination, and that the range is especially broadened when the similar events are offered to show notice as opposed to showing defect.

Drabik v. Stanley-Bostitch, Inc., 997 F.2d 496 (8th Cir. 1993): In a product liability action involving a pneumatic nailer, the Court held there was an abuse of discretion in admitting extensive evidence of dissimilar nailer accidents to impeach the defendant's expert. To hold that an expert who simply offers an opinion that the product is "generally safe" opens the door to all other accident evidence would create an exception swallowing the general rule requiring substantial similarity. In *Hale v. Firestone Tire & Rubber Co.,* 820 F.2d 928 (8th Cir. 1987), a suit involving the explosion of a wheel rim, the Trial Judge admitted evidence of thirteen prior claims to prove notice of a defect, but excluded the defendant's evidence concerning the disposition of the claims, which was offered to demonstrate that the extent of the notice was exaggerated. Although the Court did not deem the limitation on the defendant's proof an abuse of discretion, it declared that "if this case is retried, the evidence should be admitted."

Glover v. BIC Corp., 6 F.3d 1318 (9th Cir. 1993): In a product liability wrongful death action in which the defendant manufacturer of a cigarette lighter attempted to show that the decedent was the victim of a cooking accident, the Court held it was an abuse of discretion to exclude evidence of past fires in the victim's home. In *Cooper v. Firestone Tire & Rubber Co.,* 945 F.2d 1103 (9th Cir. 1991), a product liability action arising out of the explosion of a multipiece truck tire rim, the Court held there was no error in admitting evidence of dissimilar accidents involving the same type of rim. When an expert testifies that a product is generally safe, as the defendant's experts did, the witness' credibility can be undermined by showing that the witness had knowledge of prior accidents caused by the product, since evidence of other accidents, whether similar or not, tends to show the witness' claims of product safety are overstated and the witness therefore may not be reliable.

Gilbert v. Cosco Inc., 989 F.2d 399 (10th Cir. 1993): The Court held in a product liability action for injuries allegedly caused by a child restraint that there was no abuse of discretion in excluding memoranda of the defendant pertaining to child restraint models that were not the subject of the suit and that were mainly probative of "corporate mentality," which would be relevant only to punitive damages if liability were established. In *Four Corners Helicopters, Inc. v. Turbomeca, S.A.,* 979 F.2d 1434 (10th Cir. 1992), a wrongful death action arising out of a helicopter crash, the Court held there was no abuse of discretion in admitting evidence of other incidents involving defects in the manufacturer's helicopter engines, as there was sufficient similarity in the circumstances to be probative of defect, notice, and causation in this case. In *C.A. Assoc. v. Dow Chem. Co.,* 918 F.2d 1485 (10th Cir. 1990), a product liability action concerning an allegedly defective masonry mortar additive used on the plaintiff's building, the Trial Judge limited the plaintiff's proof regarding other buildings at which the mortar was used. The Court held there was no abuse of discretion, as the ruling was appropriate to avoid significant delay, confusion, and prejudice attendant on proof regarding numerous other buildings. In *Marsee v. United States Tobacco Co.,* 639 F. Supp. 466 (W.D. Okla. 1986), *aff'd,* 866 F.2d 319 (10th Cir. 1989), a suit by a plaintiff who claimed that her son developed oral cancer from using snuff, the Court held that testimony of another cancer victim who used snuff products would be excluded, given its weak probative value on the question of causation and the great possibility of prejudice.

Wilson v. Bicycle South, Inc., 915 F.2d 1503 (11th Cir. 1990): The Court affirmed judgments for the defendants in a product liability action, holding there was no abuse of discretion in excluding evidence of an allegedly similar accident because of the necessity for a considerable amount of extrinsic evidence to determine whether the incidents were sufficiently similar. In *Worsham v. A.H. Robins Co.,* 734 F.2d 676 (11th Cir. 1984), the Court affirmed a judgment for the plaintiff in a product liability suit against the manufacturer of the Dalkon Shield IUD, finding no error in rulings admitting documents and permitting cross-examination that mentioned other litigation involving the Shield. The documents and cross-examination tended to show the kind of notice that the company had about problems caused by the Shield and the mention of the other litigation was not unduly prejudicial.

Standard of conduct

Johnson v. Busby, 953 F.2d 349 (8th Cir. 1991): In a § 1983 action by a pretrial detainee, the Court held it was no abuse of discretion to exclude evidence of state minimum jail standards, as the standards, while helpful and relevant in some cases, do not represent minimum constitutional standards and would tend to mislead and confuse the jury as to the relevant standard of conduct.

Fulton v. St. Louis-S.F. Ry., 675 F.2d 1130 (10th Cir. 1982): In an FELA case, the Court held that the Trial Judge properly admitted evidence of a railroad association's loading rules, not as a legal standard of care but as evidence of the appropriate measure of caution required under certain circumstances.

United States v. Betancourt, 734 F.2d 750 (11th Cir.), *cert. denied,* 105 S. Ct. 440, 574 (1984): In a prosecution for illegally dispensing drugs, two doctors were properly permitted to testify for the government as to the applicable standard of conduct for medical practice.

State law

Croce v. Bromley Corp., 623 F.2d 1084 (5th Cir. 1980), *cert. denied,* 450 U.S. 981 (1981): A rock music star was killed in an airplane crash, and his family brought a wrongful death action. The Court upheld the introduction of evidence concerning future earnings, saying that admissibility of particular evidence should be determined as a matter of federal, not state, law.

Brown v. Royalty, 535 F.2d 1024 (8th Cir. 1976): Although it cited Rule 403 in this automobile collision case, the Court relied heavily on Missouri law in upholding the exclusion of evidence that the police failed to issue a traffic ticket to the defendant and that the plaintiff received payment from collateral sources. Although Rule 403 does not on its face require reference to state law, this case is a good example of one in which a Trial Judge can seek guidance from state law when no federal law is in point.

Romine v. Parman, 831 F.2d 944 (10th Cir. 1987): The Court held that federal law governed the determination whether evidence was too prejudicial to be admitted and that evidence of a driver's drinking of beer on the day of an accident and his payment of a fine resulting from a traffic citation was properly admitted. Although the Court was aware that payment of a traffic citation has been viewed as of little probative value, it found that the preferable approach was to admit the evidence and to permit the driver to explain why the fine was paid.

Stipulations — civil cases

Silva v. Showcase Cinemas Concessions, 736 F.2d 810 (1st Cir.), *cert. denied,* 105 S. Ct. 251 (1984): Upholding a judgment against a movie theater for the wrongful death of the plaintiff's son, who was killed in a parking lot after a movie, the Court rejected the defendant's argument that it should have been permitted to show that the assailant was convicted of manslaughter. Since the plaintiff stipulated that the killing was criminal, the manslaughter conviction was unnecessary to prove that it was an intentional act.

Heath v. Cast, 813 F.2d 254 (9th Cir.), *cert. denied,* 108 S. Ct. 147 (1987): The Court affirmed a judgment for police officers in a suit alleging illegal arrest and excessive use of force. Although the plaintiff offered to stipulate that he was biased against the police, the Trial Judge admitted evidence that the police had previously arrested the plaintiff and his brother. The Court affirmed, holding that the evidence was properly admitted to enable the jury to determine the extent of the bias.

Noel Shows, Inc. v. United States, 721 F.2d 327 (11th Cir. 1983): Affirming a judgment against a taxpayer seeking to recover an excise tax paid on a coin-activated amusement device, the Court upheld the exclusion of the plaintiff's patent on the device, which both parties had stipulated to be admissible. A majority of the Court held that the Trial Judge did not act unreasonably in determining that the patent might confuse the jury when it came to decide the only issue in dispute — i.e., whether the device involved a "substantial element of chance." A dissenting Judge noted that the stipulation had been approved by the Court and opined that the government, which objected to the evidence despite the stipulation, ought to be bound by its stipulations.

Stipulations — criminal cases — generally

United States v. Pedroza, 750 F.2d 187 (2d Cir. 1984), *cert. denied,* 479 U.S. 842 (1986): Reversing kidnapping convictions on another ground, the Court held that the admission of evidence concerning one defendant's involvement in a cocaine transaction, which explained the motive for the kidnapping, was proper. Although the defendants offered to stipulate that the ransom demanded for return of the kidnapped child was narcotics, the Court found that the stipulation "hardly sufficed to provide an understandable backdrop for the rather unusual theories offered to explain the events."

United States v. Grassi, 602 F.2d 1192 (5th Cir. 1979), *vacated & remanded on other grounds,* 448 U.S. 902 (1980), a prosecution for interstate transportation of obscene material, defense counsel offered to stipulate that the films were obscene. The prosecutor objected, and the jury was shown three films that portrayed "homosexual acts of the most bizarre and repulsive nature." Rejecting both the argument that the government had an absolute right to refuse the stipulation and the counter-argument that the defendant had an absolute right to compel its acceptance, the Court said that a Rule 403 balancing analysis must be used and sustained the Trial Judge, finding that the films had probative value above and beyond the stipulation.

United States v. Hiland, 909 F.2d 1114 (8th Cir. 1990): Affirming convictions related to unlawful sales of pharmaceuticals, the Court held that evidence regarding the drug's effects on premature infants was properly admitted despite the defendants' offered stipulation, because the stipulation reached only the drug's overall dangerousness, not its dangerousness when used as labelled, which was also part of the government's burden of proof. The Court also found that the evidence was not presented in an inflammatory manner and its use was carefully controlled. In *United States v. Bass,* 794 F.2d 1305 (8th Cir.), *cert. denied,* 107 S. Ct. 233 (1986), a defendant convicted for firearms violations claimed that the government should have been required to accept a stipulation as to identity and should have been barred from offering evidence of crimes committed by the defendants. Affirming, the Court observed that "a proper rule 403 balancing analysis will incorporate some assessment of the need for the allegedly prejudicial information in light of a valid stipulation," but found that the stipulation was insufficient where the crimes the government offered were interconnected with those charged and proved more than identity. See also *United States v. Ellison,* 793 F.2d 942 (8th Cir.), *cert. denied,* 107 S. Ct. 415 (1986) (government not bound to stipulate, but the general rule is subject to Rule 403, so that stipulation may be required where prejudicial effects of evidence substantially outweigh probative value).

Stipulations — criminal cases — mental elements

United States v. McDowell, 762 F.2d 1072 (D.C. Cir. 1985): In a drug prosecution, the Court upheld the admission of a bulletproof vest found in the defendant's closet to prove intent to sell drugs. It noted that the Trial Judge received no answer from defense counsel when she asked whether the defense would stipulate that the possessor of the drug intended to distribute it.

United States v. Garcia, 983 F.2d 1160 (1st Cir. 1993): In the course of affirming two defendants' convictions for possession of cocaine for distribution, the Court observed that

> [t]o prevent the admission of bad acts evidence, a defendant's offer to concede knowledge and/or intent issues must do two things. First, the offer must express a clear and unequivocal *intention* to remove the issues such that in effect if not in form, it constitutes an offer to stipulate. Second, notwithstanding the sincerity of

the defendant's offer, the concession must cover the necessary substantive ground to remove the issues from the case.

In this case, the Court found the defendant's offer stipulating to intent to distribute was insufficient where the evidence was also relevant to knowledge and intent to possess. It provided the following guidance to lower courts:

> We note, first of all, that a serious offer to concede or stipulate to issues of intent and/or knowledge should be explored by the district court. In the final analysis, however, whether such an offer is accepted remains in the sound discretion of the district judge. If the judge determines that the offer is acceptable, the judge should take steps to assure that the defendant is aware of the contents of the stipulation and of its implications before directing the jury that it may resolve the issue against the defendant. Second, from a survey of the circuits on stipulations in the area of 404(b) evidence, we have ascertained a preference for handling the matter before trial, or early in the trial process.

United States v. Mohel, 604 F.2d 748 (2d Cir. 1979): The Court overturned convictions on cocaine charges because the government unnecessarily presented other crimes evidence after the appellant unconditionally offered to stipulate that if he sold cocaine he did so with the requisite intent. The Court noted that the government would not have been unfairly treated, since the Judge could have informed the jury that intent was not a disputed issue in the case.

United States v. Jemal, 26 F.3d 1267 (3d Cir. 1994): Although generally evidence of a defendant's prior bad acts should not be admitted to show knowledge and intent when the defendant has proffered a comprehensive and unreserved stipulation that he possessed the requisite knowledge and intent, the Court held that the defendant's offer in this mail fraud case was not sufficiently comprehensive to remove those issues, so it was no abuse of discretion to admit evidence of his involvement in prior frauds.

United States v. Yeagin, 927 F.2d 798 (5th Cir. 1991): In order to exclude evidence of prior drug felony convictions, a defendant charged with possession of methamphetamine with intent to distribute and possession of a firearm as a convicted felon offered to stipulate both intent if the government proved possession and his prior felony convictions. Reversing and remanding, the Court held that admitting the convictions was prejudicial error, as the stipulations covered the elements to be proved by the evidence, the evidence was not necessary to an understanding of the full and real life context of the offense because the prior felonies had no relation to the factual circumstances of the present case, and the evidence must have had an extremely prejudicial effect on the jury. In *United States v. Kang,* 934 F.2d 621 (5th Cir. 1991), a prosecution for bribing an IRS agent, the defendant had stipulated to willful commission of the offense and asserted only an entrapment defense. The Court reversed his conviction, finding an abuse of discretion in admitting evidence of the defendant's flight, as it was not relevant to show his predisposition or the manner of the government's investigation; thus, it was not only arguably inadmissible under Rule 403 balancing because of the risk of prejudice, but it was also inadmissible under Rule 401 on relevancy grounds.

United States v. Zalman, 870 F.2d 1047 (6th Cir.), *cert. denied,* 109 S. Ct. 3248 (1989): In a prosecution of various offenses involving sham marriages, the Court held that the defendant could not complain about the introduction of testimony concerning his interrogating women about their willingness to enter into sham marriages. The Court found that the defendant had offered to stipulate to intent, but that his offer was conditioned on the government's acquiescence. It also found that the evidence was admitted to prove a common scheme or plan as well as to prove intent.

United States v. Washington, 17 F.3d 230 (8th Cir.), *cert. denied,* 115 S. Ct. __ (1994): The defendant, charged with being a felon in possession of a firearm after he used a shotgun in an armed robbery, offered to stipulate to knowing possession of a shotgun on that occasion. The Court noted that the government generally is not obligated to accept such an offer and that the probative value of the evidence on issues other than ones to which the defendant would stipulate is critical to the Rule 403 balancing, but found the way the evidence was admitted in this case was not unduly prejudicial.

United States v. Taylor, 17 F.3d 333 (11th Cir.), *cert. denied,* 115 S. Ct. __ (1994): The Court held that a defendant's offer to stipulate did not render evidence of his prior drug convictions inadmissible. First, his offer conceded only intent, while the government sought also to prove knowledge, motive, and absence of mistake. Second, the defendant agreed to stipulate that he had the intent to buy and sell drugs, but the government sought to prove he intended to join a conspiracy. In *United States v. Dynalectric Co.,* 859 F.2d 1559 (11th Cir. 1988), *cert. denied,* 490 U.S. 1006 (1989), the Court affirmed antitrust and mail fraud convictions, holding that the defendants' "offer to stipulate that if the defendants met and agreed to rig bids, they intended to restrain trade" was a tautology and was inadequate to bar the government from proving other evidence of bidrigging in order to establish an intent to engage in illegal conduct.

Stipulations — criminal cases — predicate convictions

United States v. Dockery, 955 F.2d 50 (D.C. Cir. 1992): The Court vacated and remanded convictions for drug trafficking and ex-felon firearms possession on the ground that evidence of prior convictions offered on the ex-felon count and on cross-examination of a defense witness had an unduly prejudicial effect as to the trafficking counts. Although the government had no obligation to accept the defendant's proposed stipulation regarding his prior convictions, its desire to offer live testimony simply factors into whether the ex-felon count should be severed for undue prejudice; the government has no right to both its proof and a joined trial.

United States v. Tavares, 21 F.3d 1 (1st Cir. 1994) (en banc): A defendant charged with being a felon in possession of a firearm offered to stipulate that he had a prior felony conviction, but the prosecutor refused to accept the stipulation and was permitted to prove the fact of the conviction and its nature, for larceny of a firearm. Vacating in a careful *en banc* opinion, the Court held it was an abuse of discretion to permit the government to reject the stipulation and to admit evidence beyond the fact of the prior conviction. The nature of the predicate felony is wholly unrelated to the crime charged and, except in unusual circumstances of which the Court could not conceive, the prejudice to the defendant substantially outweighs the probativeness of the facts surrounding the prior conviction. The Court noted that its decision was limited: The defendant may not keep the *fact* of the predicate felony from the jury by stipulation or other procedural device; the prosecution ordinarily cannot be forced to accept a stipulation if it prefers to introduce a judgment of conviction properly redacted; in some cases evidence concerning the nature of the prior conviction will be admissible for impeachment or other reasons; and a stipulation to a defendant's status as a felon is easily distinguishable from those relating to his actions or state of mind in committing the crime.

United States v. Gilliam, 994 F.2d 97 (2d Cir.), *cert. denied,* 114 S. Ct. 335 (1993): The defendant, charged with being a convicted felon in possession of a firearm, offered to concede the prior conviction element of the offense, so that the jury would not hear even the parties' stipulation regarding the conviction. The Court held there was no abuse of discretion in denying the request, as the jurors must have full knowledge of the nature of the crime if they are to speak for the people and exert their authority. The concurring Judge disagreed with the majority's assertion that mention of the prior conviction in the stipulation "is by definition not prejudicial," but would have found that the risk of unfair prejudice did not substantially outweigh the probative value of the stipulation.

United States v. Yeagin, 927 F.2d 798 (5th Cir. 1991): In order to exclude evidence of prior drug felony convictions, a defendant charged with possession of methamphetamine with intent to distribute and possession of a firearm as a convicted felon offered to stipulate both intent if the government proved possession and his prior felony convictions. Reversing and remanding, the Court held that admitting the convictions was prejudicial error, as the stipulations covered the elements to be proved by the evidence, the evidence was not necessary to an understanding of the full and real life context of the offense because the prior felonies had no relation to the factual circumstances of the present case, and the evidence must have had an extremely prejudicial effect on the jury.

United States v. Breitkreutz, 8 F.3d 688 (9th Cir. 1993): Reversing a conviction for being a felon in possession of a firearm, the Court held that the government should not be precluded from offering proof of any prior felonies by the defendant's offer to stipulate that he was a convicted felon, but that it was an abuse of discretion to allow proof of three prior felonies. A concurring Judge believed that the government should only be permitted to prove the defendant's conviction, without mention of the underlying facts, and that a defendant should be able to stipulate as to his status (e.g., convicted felon) even though not to his actions or state of mind in committing the crime.

United States v. O'Shea, 724 F.2d 1514 (11th Cir. 1984): The Court affirmed firearms and transporting a stolen vehicle convictions, finding no error in the admission of evidence that the defendant had previously been convicted of murder, although he offered to stipulate that he was a convicted felon. The Court noted that it had "declined to adopt a *per se* rule either for or against admission of evidence where the defendant offers to stipulate to an element of the offense," but it also stated that "[w]e have recognized ... that where the prior conviction is part of an offense and the defendant offers to stipulate to the prior conviction, it may constitute an abuse of discretion to allow the nature of the offense to be admitted." The Court sustained admission of the evidence because it found no error in the conclusion that evidence of the defendant's past was bound to come out through the witnesses that the government and other defendants indicated they would offer.

Surprise

Szeliga v. General Motors Corp., 728 F.2d 566 (1st Cir. 1984): The Court affirmed a judgment for an automobile manufacturer, holding there was no error in finding films — prepared by the manufacturer and offered to support its theory that a wheel fell off because of impact, not because of the loss of lug nuts — to be more probative than prejudicial. Although a question was raised as to whether the films should have been disclosed before trial pursuant to a pretrial order, the Trial Judge could have decided the question either way. The Court commented that "the remedy for coping with surprise is not to seek reversal after an unfavorable verdict, but a request for continuance at the time the surprise occurs."

United States v. DiPasquale, 740 F.2d 1282 (3d Cir. 1984), *cert. denied,* 105 S. Ct. 1226, 1227 (1985): The Court affirmed loansharking convictions, finding no error in the admission of evidence of overt acts in addition to those alleged in the indictment. The Court stated that "[g]enerally speaking, surprise is not a ground for the exclusion of evidence in a criminal trial."

Black v. J.I. Case Co., Inc., 22 F.3d 568 (5th Cir. 1994): In a product liability case, the plaintiffs objected to allowing Case to add a new defense on the first day of trial. The Court rejected the plaintiffs' claim that they were unfairly surprised, noting that the Trial Court offered the plaintiffs a continuance, which they declined, and that where a party claims unfair surprise, "the granting of a continuance is a more appropriate remedy than exclusion of the evidence." In *Conway v. Chemical Leaman Tank Lines, Inc.,* 687 F.2d 108 (5th Cir. 1982), a diversity case arising out of a crash between two trucks, the Court found there was no abuse of discretion in granting a new trial on the grounds of unfair surprise, after a witness called without any forewarning testified as to a new theory concerning asphalt marks on the highway. The Court said that the evidence was offered when the trial was almost completed and that "[a]lthough this Court has acknowledged that continuance is a preferable remedy for prejudicial error from unfair surprise, there is no ironclad rule requiring it."

Surveys and opinion polls

United States v. Local 560, 780 F.2d 267 (3d Cir. 1985), *cert. denied,* 106 S. Ct. 2247 (1986): In a civil RICO action, the Court held it was error to admit testimony concerning the violent reputation of the union's executive board that was based on interviews the witness had with 15 former and current members of the union, since no attempt at random selection was made; the witness had approached only persons known to be hostile to the leadership. In *Democratic Party v. National Conservative Political Action Comm'n,* 578 F. Supp. 797 (E.D. Pa. 1983), *aff'd in part and rev'd in part on other grounds,* 105 S. Ct. 1459 (1985), a three-judge Court held unconstitutional a section of the Presidential Election Campaign Fund Act. The Court found that the results of two nationwide telephone surveys were inadmissible because: (1) the plaintiffs failed to disclose the polls to the defendants sufficiently in advance of trial to enable the defendants to study their methodologies; and (2) the polls were irrelevant because they focused on distrust of political committees, not distrust of government officials, and they asked about contributions to candidates, not expenditures on behalf of candidates.

Lutheran Mut. Life Ins. Co. v. United States, 816 F.2d 376 (8th Cir. 1987): In a suit for an income tax refund, the Court held that a survey offered in an effort to establish the amount of time spent by the taxpayer's agents on policy loan servicing activities had not been conducted by an expert applying techniques assuring trustworthiness. In *Richardson v. Quik Trip Corp.,* 591 F. Supp. 1151 (S.D. Iowa 1984), a employee's action complaining that the employer's policy prohibiting beards had a racially discriminatory impact, the Court admitted a survey conducted on behalf of the defendant which purported to show customer concern regarding bearded convenience store personnel. The Court suggested that a party relying upon a survey that rests on subjective data has a special burden of showing reliability and it found that the survey was flawed in several ways, but it admitted the survey to show the basis for the employer's decision to discharge the plaintiff.

Time limits

SCM Corp. v. Xerox Corp., 77 F.R.D. 10 (D. Conn. 1977): In a complex antitrust case, the Trial Judge became concerned that the number of trial days was excessive, so he imposed a limit on the number of additional days available to the plaintiff to present its case. Although the Court recognized that Rule 403 "normally contemplates that the time-consuming nature of evidence will be determined as to each particular item of evidence offered," it concluded that "in a protracted case such as this, the purpose of the rule can best be achieved by considering time in the aggregate and leaving to counsel the initial responsibility for making individualized selections as to the relative degree of probative value from the mass of evidence available."

United States v. Reaves, 636 F. Supp. 1575 (E.D. Ky. 1986): In a tax fraud case, the government and the defendants challenged the Court's imposition of time limits on various stages of the trial, but the Court ruled that it had authority to impose limits in both criminal and civil cases.

MCI Communications Corp. v. American Tel. & Tel. Co., 708 F.2d 1081 (7th Cir.), *cert. denied,* 104 S. Ct. 234 (1983): In this complex antitrust case, the Court found no error in the Trial Judge's limiting each side to twenty-six days for presentation of its case-in-chief. The Court commented that

> [t]his exercise of discretion may be appropriate in protracted litigation provided that witnesses are not excluded on the basis of mere numbers.... Moreover, where the proffered testimony is presented to the court in the form of a general summary, the time limits should be sufficiently flexible to accommodate adjustment if it appears during trial that the court's initial assessment was too restrictive.

Johnson v. Ashby, 808 F.2d 676 (8th Cir. 1987): In a medical malpractice case, the Trial Judge imposed in advance of trial a strict time limit on the presentation of evidence.

The Court affirmed, noting that the unsuccessful plaintiff made no timely objection to the time limit. The Court observed, however, that "it may be an abuse of the trial court's discretion to exclude probative, noncumulative evidence simply because its introduction will cause delay, and any time limits formulated in advance of trial must be fashioned with this in mind." It disapproved of "rigid hour limits such as those initially suggested here," but found that there was no showing that the Trial Judge would not have extended the time if a proper objection had been made.

Waste of time

Stathos v. Bowden, 728 F.2d 15 (1st Cir. 1984): Affirming a judgment for the plaintiff in a sex discrimination suit, the Court upheld rulings that permitted the defendants' expert to offer three statistical studies regarding the raises and salaries given to men and women at the defendant commission, but refused to permit the expert to offer six other studies comparing the salaries at other lighting commissions. Any probative value of these studies, the Court found, would have been so tangential as to warrant exclusion as a "waste of time."

United States v. Thomas, 11 F.3d 1392 (7th Cir. 1993): A defendant charged with bank robbery sought to prove she had been coerced into participation by her codefendant. The Court held there was no abuse of discretion in refusing to allow her to present evidence regarding each specific incident of abuse, as the marginal relevance of the evidence was clearly outweighed by the dangers of confusion of the issues, waste of time, and unnecessary presentation of evidence that would result if the defendant were allowed to conduct mini-trials of each alleged incident. In *Scaggs v. Consolidated Rail Corp.,* 6 F.3d 1290 (7th Cir. 1993), the defendant in an employee's personal injury action had conducted surveillance of the plaintiff but found no indication of malingering that it wished to introduce as evidence. The Court held there was no error in granting the defendant's motion *in limine* barring mention of the defendant's surveillance practices, as evidence of no evidence was a waste of time and possibly prejudicial in this case.

United States v. Rewald, 889 F.2d 836 (9th Cir. 1989), *cert. denied,* 111 S. Ct. 64 (1990): The defendant in a fraud case claimed that he was a CIA agent who had been instructed to spend investor funds to cultivate foreign intelligence sources. The Court held there had been no abuse of discretion in excluding classified documents regarding his meetings with foreign businessmen and government officials, because they were of little probative value on whether he had been instructed to spend the money; presentation of the extensive evidence, and rebuttal to it, would have drawn out the proceedings and confused the jury.

Wealth

United States v. Weiss, 914 F.2d 1514 (2d Cir. 1990), *cert. denied,* 111 S. Ct. 2888 (1991): The Court held there was no error in a prosecution for Medicare and Medicaid fraud when the government presented evidence regarding a defendant's wealth and income, as the defendant sought to portray himself as virtually indigent and as not having profited from the alleged misconduct so not deserving punishment, and the Trial Judge twice instructed that the evidence was admitted only on credibility.

United States v. Zipkin, 729 F.2d 384 (6th Cir. 1984): After reversing the appellant's conviction for fraudulently appropriating for himself money belonging to an estate for which he was receiver, the Court strongly suggested that the Trial Judge should reconsider the decision to admit records from the appellant's divorce proceedings to prove that he committed the offense because he needed money. Although the Court did not find error in admitting the evidence, it reasoned that the evidence had little probative value and could prejudice a jury. It suggested that

> a trial court should be extremely cautious in admitting such evidence and the Government must have more than mere conjecture that impecuniosity was a motive, lest the poor be in position of being at greater suspicion of having committed a crime, even if a theft offense, because of the very fact of their impecuniosity.

D. LEGISLATIVE HISTORY

Advisory Committee's Note

The case law recognizes that certain circumstances call for the exclusion of evidence which is of unquestioned relevance. These circumstances entail risks which range all the way from inducing decision on a purely emotional basis, at one extreme, to nothing more harmful than merely wasting time, at the other extreme. Situations in this area call for balancing the probative value of and need for the evidence against the harm likely to result from its admission. Slough, Relevancy Unraveled, 5 Kan. L. Rev. 1, 12-15 (1956); Trautman, Logical or Legal Relevancy — A Conflict in Theory, 5 Van. L. Rev. 385, 392 (1952); McCormick § 152, pp. 319-21. The rules which follow in this Article are concrete applications evolved for particular situations. However, they reflect the policies underlying the present rule, which is designed as a guide for the handling of situations for which no specific rules have been formulated.

Exclusion for risk of unfair prejudice, confusion of issues, misleading the jury, or waste of time, all find ample support in the authorities. "Unfair prejudice" within its context means an undue tendency to suggest decision on an improper basis, commonly, though not necessarily, an emotional one.

The rule does not enumerate surprise as a ground for exclusion, in this respect following Wigmore's view of the common law. 6 Wigmore § 1849. Cf. McCormick § 152, p. 320, n. 29, listing unfair surprise as a ground for exclusion but stating that it is usually "coupled with the danger of prejudice and confusion of issues." While Uniform Rule 45 incorporates surprise as a ground and is followed in Kansas Code of Civil Procedure § 60-445, surprise is not included in California Evidence Code § 352 or New Jersey Rule 4, though both the latter otherwise substantially embody Uniform Rule 45. While it can scarcely be doubted that claims of unfair surprise may still be justified despite procedural requirements of notice and instrumentalities of discovery, the granting of a continuance is a more appropriate remedy than exclusion of the evidence. Tentative Recommendation and a Study Relating to the Uniform Rules of Evidence (Art. VI. Extrinsic Policies Affecting Admissibility), Cal. Law Revision Comm'n, Rep., Rec. & Studies, 612 (1964). Moreover, the impact of a rule excluding evidence on the ground of surprise would be difficult to estimate.

In reaching a decision whether to exclude on grounds of unfair prejudice, consideration should be given to the probable effectiveness or lack of effectiveness of a limiting instruction. See Rule 106 and Advisory Committee's Note thereunder. The availability of other means of proof may also be an appropriate factor.

RULE 404

A. OFFICIAL TEXT

Rule 404. Character Evidence Not Admissible to Prove Conduct; Exceptions; Other Crimes

(a) *Character evidence generally.* — Evidence of a person's character or a trait of character is not admissible for the purpose of proving action in conformity therewith on a particular occasion, except:

(1) Character of accused. — Evidence of a pertinent trait of character offered by an accused, or by the prosecution to rebut the same;

(2) Character of victim. — Evidence of a pertinent trait of character of the victim of the crime offered by an accused, or by the prosecution to rebut the same, or evidence of a character trait of peacefulness of the victim offered by the prosecution in a homicide case to rebut evidence that the victim was the first aggressor;

(3) Character of witness. — Evidence of the character of a witness, as provided in rules 607, 608, and 609.

(b) *Other crimes, wrongs, or acts.* — Evidence of other crimes, wrongs, or acts is not admissible to prove the character of a person in order to show action in conformity therewith. It may, however, be admissible for other purposes, such as proof of motive, opportunity, intent, preparation, plan, knowledge, identity, or absence of mistake or accident, provided that upon request by the accused, the prosecution in a criminal case shall provide reasonable notice in advance of trial, or during trial if the court excuses pretrial notice on good cause shown, of the general nature of any such evidence it intends to introduce at trial.

B. EDITORIAL EXPLANATORY COMMENT

Permissible and impermissible uses of character evidence

Character questions arise in two different ways in litigation. Character may be an element of a crime, a claim, or a defense. When this occurs, Courts say that character is "in issue." An example is the competency of a driver in an action for negligently entrusting a motor vehicle to an incompetent driver; another is an action for defamation of character in which the defendant referred to the plaintiff as a dishonest person. In such cases, it is clear that character evidence is relevant. In fact, it is more than relevant, because it is essential under the pertinent substantive law to prove character in order to prove the crime, claim, or defense. These cases are not covered by Rule 404. While not *explicitly* excluded, they are *implicitly* excluded by the definition of "the purpose" of offering evidence in subdivision (a). Rule 405(b) does cover these cases, however.

Sometimes character evidence is used for an entirely different purpose; it is used to demonstrate that because a person has a certain character trait, he or she acted on a specific occasion in conformity to this trait. In other words, this kind of character evidence is circumstantial evidence of a person's actions on a particular occasion. It is these cases that are covered by Rule 404(a). Subdivision (b) covers the use of particular acts of a person that may be indicative of the person's character.

The general rule and its exceptions

Subdivision (a) of the Rule states the general rule, which is that evidence of a person's character or trait of character is not admissible for the purpose of proving action in conformity therewith on a particular occasion. The rationale behind the general rule is set forth in the classic case of *Michelson v. United States,* 335 U.S. 469, 482 (1948). The discussion in *Michelson* is in the context of a criminal case, but its rationale is equally applicable to excluding evidence of character in a civil case:

> The [character] inquiry is not rejected because character is irrelevant; on the contrary, it is said to weigh too much with the jury and to so overpersuade them as to prejudge one with a bad general record and deny him a fair opportunity to defend against a particular charge. The overriding policy of excluding such evidence, despite its admitted probative value, is the practical experience that its disallowance tends to prevent confusion of issues, unfair surprise and undue prejudice.

But there are important exceptions to the general rule precluding character evidence where character is not "in issue." One is that a defendant in a criminal case is given the right to introduce evidence of his or her own pertinent character trait. Thus, in a fraud case the criminal defendant is permitted to call witnesses to testify that he is an honest person, in order to show that he was unlikely to have committed the dishonest act charged. The rationale for this is that the defendant deserves the benefit of all reasonable doubts and that good character may produce a reasonable doubt. This exception is covered in subdivision (a)(1) of the Rule.

For a similar reason, the accused is permitted to introduce evidence of a pertinent character trait of the victim of a crime; this exception is incorporated in subdivision (a)(2) of Rule 404. Rule 404(a)(2) provides that in a self-defense case, the door to character evidence is opened once any evidence that the victim was the first aggressor is offered. Since some evidence must be presented to warrant an instruction on self-defense, this subdivision may apply in every self-defense case. This subdivision is not applicable in rape and sexual assault cases; Rule 412 governs such cases.

Another common exception, also provided for in the Rule in subdivision (a)(3), is that when a witness is impeached (i.e., his credibility is attacked) or rehabilitated (i.e., his credibility is bolstered), this may be done by using character evidence. The forms of permissible and impermissible attack and rehabilitation are discussed under Rules 607, 608, 609, 610, and 613.

Character trait must be relevant

While the defendant has the option of introducing his character traits, or those of the victim, it is obvious that the character traits must be relevant to the case, or else they will be excluded under Rules 402 and 403. For example, in *United States v. Martinez,* 988 F.2d 685 (7th Cir. 1993), the defendants were charged with murder arising from a prison conflagration. Evidence of the violent character of the victims was held properly excluded as not relevant where there was no viable self-defense claim. The evidence showed that the victims were rendered defenseless and were repeatedly stabbed while lying motionless on the ground. The defendants argued that they were acting in self-defense at the beginning of the fight; but this was not relevant to the subsequent conduct that was at the heart of the murder charge.

"Law-abidingness"

Is "law-abidingness" a character trait? The government has often argued that "being prone to law-abiding conduct" is not an "actual" character trait but is rather a conclusion that must be drawn from other character traits such as honesty, reliability, and rectitude. However, the Courts have generally held that "character traits admissible under Rule 404(a)(1) need not constitute specific traits of character but may include general traits such as lawfulness and law-abidingness."[1]

This does not mean, however, that the defendant has unbounded freedom to define a character trait. For example, in *United States v. Diaz,* 961 F.2d 1417 (9th Cir. 1992), the defendant was charged with possession with intent to distribute more than 500 grams of cocaine. Defense counsel tried to ask a defense witness whether Diaz had a "character trait for being prone to large-scale drug dealing." However, the prosecution objected and the objection was sustained. The Court of Appeals found no error because a defendant's propensity (or lack thereof) to engage in large-scale drug-dealing "is not an admissible character trait." The proposed testimony was not the same as testimony that the defendant was law-abiding, because it was in effect too specific. The Court reasoned that an inquiry into a propensity to engage in large-scale drug-dealing

> would be misleading if addressed to a defendant with a record of criminal offenses other than drug-dealing: If answered in the negative [as the defendant in *Diaz,* of course, anticipated] the impression may be given that the defendant is a law-abiding person although he has a record of other crimes.[2]

---

1. United States v. Diaz, 961 F.2d 1417, 1419 (9th Cir. 1992). Indeed, the defendant in the landmark case of *Michelson* was permitted to prove his "law-abiding" character trait, and the Court held that a defendant may introduce favorable testimony concerning "the general estimate of his character." 335 U.S. at 476.

2. 961 F.2d at 1419.

Opening the door

The prosecution cannot, in the first instance, introduce character evidence to show that a person acted in accordance with a character trait. However, the prosecution can introduce character evidence responsively. As the *Michelson* Court put it: "The price a defendant must pay for attempting to prove his good name is to throw open the entire subject which the law has kept closed for his benefit and to make himself vulnerable where the law otherwise shields him."[3] Thus, defense counsel must consider whether introduction of character evidence is worth the risk.[4]

If defense counsel decides that the benefit of character evidence is not worth the cost of rebuttal, then counsel must guard against presenting any testimony that could be interpreted as character evidence. The character door can be deemed opened by means less obvious than calling a witness who testifies explicitly to a person's character trait. For example, in *United States v. Dahlin,* 734 F.2d 393, 395 (8th Cir. 1984), the defendant was charged with robbery; his alibi was that he was babysitting his sister's infant child at the time of the robbery. The prosecution argued that Dahlin could still have committed the robbery, by leaving the infant at home, unattended, for a period of time. Dahlin took the stand and testified that he was deeply devoted to his niece and that he never left the child alone. The prosecution rebutted this claim of Dahlin's family relations by questioning Dahlin about a knife fight that he had had with his father. The Court of Appeals held that Dahlin had opened the door to this evidence because he had "put at issue his reliability, responsibility and familial devotion, which were traits pertinent to the jury's appraisal of his defense."

We think that *Dahlin,* while a close case, was correctly decided. Certainly, a simple denial of guilt, or testimony in support of an alibi, cannot open the door to negative character evidence; if it could then the limitations in Rule 404(a) would be meaningless.[5] However, Dahlin did not simply deny that he left his niece unattended — he testified that he was too devoted to his niece to leave her unattended, and that he never did so. That is just another way of saying that he was "not the type of guy" to leave an infant unattended. Thus, Dahlin's testimony was far enough removed from the specific act at issue, and close enough to testimony about his personality and general conduct, to justify a ruling that he had opened the door to negative character evidence.

Of course, even if the defendant opens the character door, the prosecution's rebuttal is limited to that which is responsive. So, for example, if the defendant introduces evidence of a relevant character trait of the victim, the prosecution cannot respond with a negative character trait of the defendant — the door was never opened as to the

---

3. 375 U.S. at 492.

4. See, e.g., United States v. Gaertner, 705 F.2d 210 (7th Cir. 1983) (where defendant tried to depict himself as a "clean-liver," he opened the door to negative character evidence concerning drug involvement).

5. Compare United States v. Fountain, 768 F.2d 790 (7th Cir. 1985):

> To deny that one intended harm on a particular occasion is not to claim a generally peaceable character. And it cannot be right that merely by claiming self-defense ... a defendant puts his whole character in issue; that would make mincemeat of the limitations in Rule 404(a) on the use of character evidence.

defendant's character traits. Likewise, if the defendant introduces positive evidence concerning one of his character traits, the prosecution cannot respond with negative evidence concerning a different character trait.[6] Given these principles, it obviously makes sense for defense counsel to open the door as narrowly as is necessary to introduce favorable character evidence. While it is permissible, as discussed above, to introduce evidence that the defendant has a "law-abiding" character, this obviously opens the door about as broadly as it can be opened. Defense counsel might consider whether some subset of "law-abidingness" (such as honesty) would cover the favorable character evidence and yet limit the scope of rebuttal.

Character evidence "standing alone" instruction

Where a defendant introduces character evidence, the question arises whether the defendant is entitled to an instruction that positive character evidence, "standing alone," can be sufficient to create a reasonable doubt. The Federal Courts are in dispute about whether and when it is proper to give such a "standing alone" instruction. Some Courts have held that such an instruction is never necessary and often, if not always, is improper because it misleads the jury. As the Seventh Circuit put it in *United States v. Burke,* 781 F.2d 1234, 1239 (7th Cir. 1985):

> The "standing alone" instruction conveys to the jury the sense that even if it thinks the prosecution's case compelling, even if it thinks that defendant is a liar, if it also concludes that he has a good reputation this may be the "reasonable doubt" of which other instructions speak. A "standing alone" instruction invites attention to a single bit of evidence and suggests to jurors that they analyze this evidence all by itself. No instruction flags any other evidence for this analysis — not eyewitness evidence, not physical evidence, not even confessions. There is no good reason to consider *any* evidence "standing alone."[7]

Other Courts have stated that "standing alone" instructions are required where the defendant has presented character evidence.[8] Most Courts have held that while a defendant is never entitled to a "standing alone" instruction, it is ordinarily not an abuse of discretion to give one.[9]

We agree with the majority position that character evidence is rarely so probative or compelling as to require it to be considered apart from the other evidence in the case.

---

6. See, e.g., United States v. Fountain, 768 F.2d 790 (7th Cir. 1985) (while the door was opened for evidence concerning the defendant's credibility, the prosecution's reference to the defendant's violent character trait was not responsive: "Violent men are not necessary liars, and indeed one class of violent men consists of those with an exaggerated sense of honor.").

7. See also United States v. Winter, 663 F.2d 1120 (1st Cir. 1981) ("standing alone" instruction disapproved in all cases); Black v. United States, 309 F.2d 331 (8th Cir. 1962) (disapproved in all cases).

8. See, e.g., United States v. Lewis, 482 F.2d 632 (D.C. Cir. 1973) ("standing alone" instruction required where the defendant offers character evidence).

9. See, e.g., United States v. Pujana-Mena, 949 F.2d 24 (2d Cir. 1991), and the cases cited in note 2 of that case, 949 F.2d at 28.

This does not mean, however, that the giving of a "standing alone" charge should always be considered an abuse of discretion. We think that there could be some limited instances in which the evidence of good character is so central to the case, and so compelling, that the Trial Judge could consider a "standing alone" instruction to be an appropriate exercise of discretion. This is nothing more than an exercise of the Judge's power to comment on the evidence. We think that the danger of a "standing alone" instruction — that other evidence might be disregarded — can be tempered by reminding the jury that it must consider all the evidence in the case.[10] Of course, the jury should in all cases be informed of the limited purpose for which the character evidence is offered.[11]

Other crimes, wrongs, or acts

Subdivision (b) of this Rule provides that when evidence of other crimes or wrongs or acts (often referred to by the Courts as "uncharged misconduct" or "bad acts") is offered for some purpose other than to prove the character of a person in order to show action in conformity therewith, this Rule does not exclude the evidence. In a criminal case, for example, evidence of bad acts can be introduced to show identity through a distinctive *modus operandi*.[12]

It is no great surprise to find the second sentence of subdivision (b) receiving the most attention in the decided cases. While the second sentence is permissive and not mandatory, Courts have traditionally been very willing to let evidence of other crimes in, even when the prosecution's theory of relevance is quite weak.

Although the distinction between acts offered to prove propensity and acts offered for another purpose is not easily drawn, we think that it is helpful to consider whether the factfinder is asked to engage in a two-step reasoning process: to infer from behavior on

---

10. See the instruction approved by the Third Circuit in United States v. Logan, 717 F.2d 84, 92 (3d Cir. 1983):

> Where a defendant has offered evidence of good general reputation for truth and veracity, or honesty and integrity, or as a law-abiding citizen, the jury should consider such evidence along with all the other evidence in the case.
>
> Evidence of a defendant's reputation, inconsistent with those traits of character ordinarily involved in the commission of the crime charged may give rise to a reasonable doubt, since the jury may think it improbable that a person of good character in respect to those traits would commit such a crime.

Compare United States v. Pujana-Mena, 949 F.2d 24, 31 (2d Cir. 1991) ("standing alone" instruction is within Trial Judge's discretion so long as it is accompanied with a qualifying instruction that character evidence is to be considered together with the other evidence in the case; but "such a hybrid charge would be less than ideal in most cases" because it is "inherently confusing and contradictory").

11. See, e.g., United States v. Burke, 781 F.2d 1234 (7th Cir. 1985) (while a standing alone instruction is not permitted in this Circuit, the Trial Court should tell the jurors that they may use character evidence "to help evaluate the credibility of the innocent explanation" that the defendant offers for his acts).

12. See, e.g., United States v. Connelly, 874 F.2d 412 (7th Cir. 1989) (prior robbery admitted to prove identity due to distinctive *modus operandi,* in particular that "it is much more than coincidence that [duct] tape was used and applied in exactly the same manner as the prior crime"; similarities relied upon must be "sufficiently idiosyncratic to permit an inference of pattern for purposes of proof").

one occasion something about the nature of a person and then to infer from that how the person probably would have behaved on another occasion when the only connection between the two occasions is that the factfinder believes that people of a certain type would act the same way both times. If so, then the evidence is character evidence. If the factfinder can reason from one act about another without going through the first step, the evidence is not character evidence.[13]

There is nothing in this Rule that requires evidence of other crimes, wrongs, or acts to be admitted. Because Rule 403 applies to evidence even if it is ostensibly offered for a not-for-character purpose, the Judge must be very careful to balance the prejudicial effect of such evidence against its probative value. The Judge should also be careful to ensure that the purpose for which the evidence is offered is more than just a sham for introducing the evidence and using it in order to establish likely behavior on a particular occasion. In particular, Trial Judges should be wary when the proponent of bad act evidence cites a "laundry list" of possible purposes, without being able to articulate how the evidence is probative of those purposes or even that those matters are in issue in the case.[14] For example, in *United States v. Rivera,* 837 F.2d 906 (1988), *modified on other grounds en banc,* 874 F.2d 754 (10th Cir. 1989), the appellant's conviction was reversed after bad act evidence was admitted to show (according to the prosecutor) "four or five things, one of which is absence of mistake, motive, intent, identity, I forget what all, there are four or five." Neither the prosecutor nor the Judge articulated which if any of the elements were disputed in the case.[15] The Court of Appeals panel found an abuse of discretion, due to the Trial Court's failure to conduct an inquiry as to the appropriate (if any) not-for-character purpose for the evidence.

Prior bad acts offered by the defendant

The second sentence of Rule 404(b) is not confined to evidence offered by a prosecutor. A defense lawyer who claims that bad act evidence committed by a third party is probative of a not-for-character purpose should be able to take advantage of this

---

13. Kuhns, *The Propensity to Misunderstand the Character of Specific Act Evidence,* 66 IOWA L. REV. 777 (1981), is an excellent analysis of the problem of differentiating between acts offered to prove propensity and acts offered for another purpose.

14. See, e.g., United States v. Hogue, 827 F.2d 660 (10th Cir. 1987), in which a conviction was reversed where no proper purpose was articulated or evident for bad acts evidence:

> In demonstrating the relevance of proffered other acts evidence, the Government must articulate precisely the evidentiary hypothesis by which a fact of consequence may be inferred from the evidence of other acts. There must be a clear and logical connection between the alleged earlier offense or misconduct and the case being tried.

15. See also United States v. Harvey, 845 F.2d 760, 762 (8th Cir. 1988):

> Initially, we observe the district court's laundry list approach to Rule 404(b) is of little help to us. Rather than making a broad reference which merely restates the components of the rule, the district court should specify which components of the rule form the basis of its ruling and why. To that end the court should require the party invoking the rule to explain clearly its 404(b) analysis.

part of the Rule.[16] For a good example, see *Johnson v. Brewer,* 521 F.2d 556 (8th Cir. 1975). In that case, the Court held that exclusion of evidence of prior perjury offered to show the bias of a key prosecution witness denied the defendant a fair trial.[17]

A balancing test for other acts

Bad act evidence is not automatically admissible simply because the proponent has articulated a not-for-character purpose to which the evidence could be put. The Supreme Court, in *Huddleston v. United States,* 485 U.S. 681, 688 (1988), stated that the decision to admit evidence under Rule 404(b) depends as well on "whether the danger of unfair prejudice outweighs the probative value of the evidence in view of the availability of other means of proof and other factors appropriate for making decisions of this kind under Rule 403." Thus, the Court has recognized that exclusion is mandated if the probative value of the bad act, in proving the permissible, not-for-character purpose, is substantially outweighed by the risk that the jury would misuse the evidence as proof of bad character.

Most Courts have applied a four-part test in assessing bad acts evidence. As stated by the Court in *United States v. Rackstraw,* 7 F.3d 1476, 1479 (10th Cir. 1993), the test is as follows:

> (1) the evidence must be offered for a proper [not-for-character] purpose; (2) the evidence must be relevant [for that purpose]; (3) the trial court must make a Rule 403 determination of whether the probative value of the [bad] acts is substantially outweighed by its potential for unfair prejudice; and (4) pursuant to Fed.R.Evid. 105, the trial court shall, upon request, instruct the jury that the evidence of similar acts is to be considered only for the proper purpose for which it was admitted.[18]

---

16. See United States v. McClure, 546 F.2d 670 (5th Cir. 1977), discussed in Annotated Cases under "Use by defendant—bad acts by third party." United States v. Greschner, 647 F.2d 740 (7th Cir. 1981), is a useful illustration. One inmate, charged with stabbing another, offered evidence that the victim had previously stabbed someone else. This was offered to show that the victim was the first aggressor. Without reasoning that a person who stabbed someone once is the type of person who would stab another, the first incident is not helpful. This is character evidence and should only have been provable by reputation or opinion evidence (although the Court of Appeals apparently forgot this, perhaps because it does not appear the government argued it). If, however, the defendant claimed that he believed the victim was going to stab him when the victim pulled a knife, proof that the defendant had heard of the prior incident might be offered, not as character evidence about the victim, but to show why the defendant believed he was in danger.

17. See also United States v. Stevens, 935 F.2d 1380 (3d Cir. 1991) (reversible error to exclude other crimes committed by a third party in the same area in which the defendant was alleged to have committed similar crimes).

18. A slightly different four-pronged test is applied by some circuits. For example, the Court in United States v. Kern, 12 F.3d 122 (8th Cir. 1993), set forth the following test for assessing bad acts evidence offered under Rule 404(b):

> To properly admit Rule 404(b) evidence for purposes other than to prove propensity, it must (1) be relevant to a material issue raised at trial, (2) be similar in kind and close in time to the crime charged, (3) be supported by sufficient evidence to support a finding by a jury that the defendant

Under the Rule 403 test, evidence in a criminal case of serious criminal activity other than that charged should be examined very carefully. The more heinous the other acts by a defendant, the more likely the jury is to misuse the evidence and treat the defendant as a generally bad person, something the Rule does not permit.[19] Also, the more similar the bad act is to the act charged, the more likely the jury is to draw the impermissible inference that the defendant has a propensity to commit such acts.[20]

Under Rules 403 and 404(b), the decision should be made to allow the evidence to be introduced when the balance between probative value and prejudicial effect is close.[21] On the other hand, where the evidence is plainly prejudicial and is not very important to the government's case, it should be excluded.[22]

As discussed in the Editorial Explanatory Comment to Rule 403, the Trial Court must take into account whether the same point can be proven with evidence that does not refer to uncharged bad acts; the cost of admitting prejudicial evidence is unacceptable if equally probative and less prejudicial evidence is reasonably available. For example, it may be necessary in many cases to introduce the defendant's handwriting exemplar; but it is usually not necessary to do so by way of a document that refers to the defendant's uncharged crimes.[23]

It is very important that counsel make clear to the Trial Judge why other crimes evidence is being offered and why it is opposed so that the Judge is able to articulate for the record the reasons for reaching a certain balance. If both sides clearly state their reasons for offering and objecting to evidence, and if the Trial Judge makes a diligent attempt to weigh the competing concerns and to reach an appropriate balance, the correct

---

committed the other act, and (4) not have a prejudicial value that substantially outweighs its probative value.

19. See, e.g., United States v. Williams, 985 F.2d 634 (1st Cir. 1993) (evidence of prior murder was admitted solely for propensity; no attempt was made to link the murder to a plan of intimidation, which would have been relevant; nor was the murder admissible to show modus operandi, since the identity of the perpetrator of the charged crime was not in dispute); United States v. Bradley, 5 F.3d 1317 (9th Cir. 1993) (evidence of uncharged, unrelated murder is not probative of motive for attempted murder, where uncharged act occurred after the act charged; uncharged act only shows propensity).

20. See, e.g., Government of the Virgin Islands v. Pinney, 967 F.2d 912 (3d Cir. 1992) (in a rape case, evidence that defendant raped the complainant's sister six years earlier, while possibly probative of knowledge and intent, should have been excluded under Rule 403: "The obvious reason the government wanted Jamila's testimony before the jury was because of the substantial likelihood that one or more members of the jury would use this highly inflammatory evidence for exactly the purpose Rule 404(b) declared to be improper..."). Note that the result in *Pinney* would probably be changed under new Rules 413-415. See the Editorial Explanatory Comment to those Rules.

21. See, e.g., United States v. Clark, 988 F.2d 1459 (6th Cir. 1993) (where the defendant was charged with killing a witness to a crime the defendant committed, evidence of the underlying crime, even though highly prejudicial, is admissible under Rule 404(b) and Rule 403 to prove motive).

22. See, e.g., United States v. Gordon, 987 F.2d 902 (2d Cir. 1993) (prior minor drug transaction is not sufficiently probative of the defendant's participation in a major drug conspiracy; none of the alleged coconspirators were participants in the prior transaction; evidence should have been excluded under Rule 403).

23. See, e.g., United States v. Turquitt, 557 F.2d 464 (5th Cir. 1977) (reversible error to admit document referring to other crimes in order to authenticate defendant's handwriting, since "other known and less prejudicial specimens would have achieved the same result").

result will be reached in most cases. We think that this approach is basically what the Appellate Courts have been suggesting to their Trial Judges.

Stipulating intent

One of the not-for-character purposes listed in Rule 404(b) is intent. Often, the prosecution seeks to admit a bad act similar to that with which the defendant is charged, as proof that the defendant intended to commit the act charged.[24] Certainly, this can be probative evidence where the defendant disputes intent, for example by contending that he was duped, or mistaken, or that "it was an accident." But what if the defendant contends instead that he did not commit the crime, that he was never at the scene, that the witnesses are lying, that he was falsely identified, etc.? To what extent does the defendant's refusal to contest intent prevent the prosecution from proving it through uncharged misconduct?

The Supreme Court granted certiorari in *Hadley v. United States,* 112 S. Ct. 1261 (1992), to review the Ninth Circuit position that the defendant can never keep bad acts out of the case by way of stipulation. Hadley was charged with aggravated sexual abuse of a minor. Hadley's uncharged acts of sodomy with other minors were offered and admitted under Rule 404(b) to prove intent. He contended that the evidence was not relevant to intent, since his defense was a denial of participation in the charged sexual abuse, and at trial he offered not to argue the issue of intent. The Court of Appeals noted that where specific intent is an element of the crime, the prosecution must affirmatively prove intent beyond a reasonable doubt, and concluded that "this burden is not relieved by a defendant's promise to forgo argument on an issue." It stated that "Hadley's choice of defense did not relieve the government of its burden of proof and should not prevent the government from meeting this burden by an otherwise acceptable means."

The Supreme Court subsequently dismissed the writ of certiorari in *Hadley* as improvidently granted.[25] This dismissal leaves a split among Circuit Courts unresolved. The Second Circuit has adopted the most defendant-friendly solution to uncharged bad acts that are offered to prove intent. In *United States v. Figueroa,* 618 F.2d 934 (2d Cir. 1980), the Court stated that a defendant may completely forestall the admission of

---

24. See, e.g., United States v. Wynn, 987 F.2d 354 (6th Cir. 1993) (defendant's prior threats and acts of violence against his wife were properly admitted to prove intent to have his wife killed); United States v. Robichaux, 995 F.2d 565 (5th Cir. 1993) (prior fraudulent transaction properly admitted to rebut the defendant's claim that he did not know "what was going on" in the transaction for which he was charged); United States v. Arambula-Ruiz, 987 F.2d 599 (9th Cir. 1993) (prior conviction for possession of heroin with intent to distribute is probative of knowledge where defendant is charged with conspiring to possess heroin, and claims that he was an innocent bystander in the wrong place at the wrong time; however, prior arrests for being an undocumented alien and for illegal possession of a firearm "do not tend to prove a material issue of the drug conspiracy and possession charges" and were only offered to show the defendant's propensity to commit criminal acts). Compare United States v. DeVillio, 983 F.2d 1185 (2d Cir. 1993) (evidence that defendant possessed burglary tools "did not establish motive, intent, or opportunity to unlawfully transport a stolen vehicle or stolen goods which are the crimes charged against appellants"; it merely established that the defendant was a burglar, which is an impermissible purpose under Rule 404).

25. 113 S. Ct. 486 (1992).

uncharged misconduct on the issue of intent, simply by expressing a decision not to contest intent with "sufficient clarity." The defendant's decision is sufficiently clear if it justifies the Trial Court in precluding any subsequent cross-examination or argument that seeks to raise the issue, and in charging the jury that if they find all the other elements of the crime established beyond a reasonable doubt, they can resolve the intent issue against the defendant because it is not disputed.

The Second Circuit in *Figueroa* did not require a formal stipulation of intent from the defendant. It feared that a defendant might be reluctant to enter into a formal stipulation in these circumstances, since the conditional nature of the stipulation ("if you can prove I did it, I admit that I intended it") could be misunderstood by the jury. The *Figueroa* Court took a functional approach, stating that the issue of whether the defendant has not contested intent "depends not on the form of words used by counsel but on the consequences that the trial court may properly attach to those words." What this has come to mean is that if the defense proceeds solely on a theory that the defendant did not do the charged act at all, then bad acts are not admissible to prove intent; but if the defendant proceeds on a theory that he did the act innocently or mistakenly, an issue of intent is raised.[26] If the defendant simply denies guilt and does not put on a case, the issue of intent remains, and the prosecutor can prove it through probative acts of uncharged misconduct.[27] As applied to the facts of *Hadley,* the Second Circuit position would mean that Hadley's prior acts of sexual misconduct would not have been admissible to prove intent, since Hadley's defense was that he did not do the charged act at all.[28]

We think that the functional approach of the Second Circuit is too indeterminate. It requires the Trial Court to guess at what the defendant is doing. There is a risk of ambiguity, costly litigation, and gamesmanship by defense counsel — a risk that would be substantially diminished if the defendant were required to formally stipulate to intent. Another problem with the Second Circuit approach is that it can often not be determined

---

26. See, e.g., United States v. Colon, 880 F.2d 650 (2d Cir. 1989). The Eighth Circuit adopted the Second Circuit approach in United States v. Jenkins, 7 F.3d 803 (8th Cir. 1993) ("there is no issue of intent where the defendant claims he did not do the act at all, rather than simply asserting he did it either innocently or mistakenly").

27. See United States v. Colon, 880 F.2d 650 (2d Cir. 1989) ("Strictly speaking, Colon's plea of not guilty to the charge that he aided and abetted Alvarado's sale of heroin put his state of mind in dispute, as the government bore the burden of proving that Colon had the specific intent that his actions bring about the sale.").

28. The Second Circuit's functional approach has spawned litigation over whether a defendant has sufficiently expressed a decision not to contest intent. See United States v. Ortiz, 857 F.2d 900 (2d Cir. 1988), where the defendant was charged with possession of six glassine envelopes of heroin with intent to distribute. Ortiz put forth a mistaken identity defense at trial. Under the Second Circuit's view, this would have prohibited the introduction of uncharged misconduct to prove intent. But subsequently, defense counsel sought to argue that possession of six glassine envelopes of heroin was as consistent with personal use as with intent to distribute. The Second Circuit found no error in the Trial Court's ruling that the government would be allowed to rebut the personal use claim with evidence of Ortiz's uncharged narcotics transactions. Thus, *Ortiz* stands for the proposition that uncharged misconduct can be used to prove intent if the defendant explicitly or implicitly changes his mind and decides to argue the intent issue. As Judge Pierce stated in his concurring opinion in *Ortiz:* "Once a defendant has taken intent out of a case, that defendant cannot thereafter, without sufficient reason, attempt to renege on that waiver by reintroducing the issue of intent."

Stipulating intent (cont'd)

whether the defendant has contested intent until the close of the defendant's case. The consequence is that ordinarily, the prosecution is not permitted to prove intent through uncharged misconduct until rebuttal. This creates a problem if the defendant decides not to put on a case. In that situation, the prosecution must seek to reopen its case in order to introduce uncharged misconduct to prove intent. This procedure, to say the least, does not play well to the jury. As Professor Green states, the Second Circuit procedure results in an assortment of negative inferences to be suffered by the prosecution:

> The jury may well wonder why the prosecutor held back this obviously important [uncharged misconduct evidence] during the government's case-in-chief and may speculate that the prosecutor is withholding other, equally important evidence. The apparently belated introduction of this evidence may give rise to other adverse inferences. For example, it may lead a jury to speculate that the evidence was fabricated at the last moment. Belated introduction may also invite the argument that the government itself believed that its case was weak, and that is why it introduced this additional evidence as an apparent afterthought.[29]

The Second Circuit has held that any negative inferences suffered by the prosecution can be remedied by a jury instruction stating that "court procedure obliged the prosecution to defer its similar act evidence."[30] But we are not convinced that such a jury instruction would be sufficient to counter all the negative inferences that could be drawn.

Other Circuits, while agreeing with the Second Circuit that a defendant can prevent the use of uncharged acts to prove intent, have required the defendant to enter an explicit stipulation admitting intent, generally at the outset of the case.[31] For example, the Fifth Circuit, in *United States v. Merkt,* 794 F.2d 950 (5th Cir. 1986), held that it was permissible for the government to prove intent through acts of uncharged misconduct, even though Merkt's defense was mistaken identification. The Court held that the defendant had failed to make an "appropriate stipulation to avoid the introduction of extrinsic offense evidence."[32]

The Seventh Circuit and the Ninth Circuit, as seen in *Hadley,* take a different approach. These Courts hold that if the crime charged requires a showing of specific

---

29. Green, *"The Whole Truth?": How Rules of Evidence Make Lawyers Deceitful,* 25 LOY. L. REV. 699, 702 (1992).

30. United States v. Colon, 880 F.2d 650, 660 (2d Cir. 1989).

31. See, e.g., United States v. Manner, 887 F.2d 317 (D.C. Cir. 1989) (uncharged misconduct admissible to prove intent where there was no explicit offer to stipulate intent); United States v. Garcia, 983 F.2d 1160 (1st Cir. 1993) (a formal stipulation of intent is enough to keep bad acts bearing on intent out of the trial; however, a mere offer "not to argue" intent is an insufficient stipulation; whether an offer to stipulate sufficiently takes intent out of the case is a question within the sound discretion of the Trial Court).

32. Similarly, in United States v. Ferrer-Cruz, 899 F.2d 135 (1st Cir. 1990), the First Circuit held that uncharged misconduct was properly admitted to prove intent despite counsel's statement that he would not argue the issue of intent, and despite the fact that the defendant denied involvement in the crime; no formal stipulation had ever been offered.

intent, the defendant can *never* keep prior bad acts out of the case by stipulating to intent.[33] These Courts specifically reject the stipulation alternative on the ground that, "in effect, it allows the defendant to remove intent as an element of the crime charged."[34] But this is not so much a rationale for rejection as it is a simple description of the result reached under the formal stipulation alternative. Neither the Seventh nor the Ninth Circuit has ever explained why it is inappropriate for the defendant to alleviate the prosecution's burden of proving intent, or why, if the stipulation is sufficient, the prosecution has any legitimate need to introduce prejudicial bad acts evidence.[35]

We believe that if a stipulation is sufficiently clear to take intent out of a case, there is no legitimate reason to allow the prosecution to prove intent through the defendant's bad acts. The formal stipulation alternative is an effective compromise between the Second Circuit view, which is subject to exploitation by defendants, and the Seventh and Ninth Circuit view, which is subject to exploitation by the prosecution.

Of course, the fundamental premise of the stipulation alternative is that the stipulation given is sufficient to take intent out of the case; not every stipulation will do so. For example, in *United States v. Garcia,* 983 F.2d 1160 (1st Cir. 1993), the defendant was arrested while sleeping in an apartment in which a large quantity of drugs were found. He was charged with possession of narcotics with intent to distribute. In an attempt to keep his prior drug transactions out of the trial, he offered to stipulate to "intent to distribute" and to "knowledge about cocaine trafficking." The proffered stipulation was rejected and the prior drug transactions were admitted. The Court of Appeals found this to be error with respect to the element of intent to distribute, since in the First Circuit, a formal stipulation of intent is enough to keep bad acts bearing on intent out of the trial. However, the proffered stipulation of knowledge about cocaine trafficking was held properly rejected, because it would not have removed the entire element of knowledge from the case to which the bad acts would be relevant.[36] Stipulation to knowledge about

---

33. See, e.g., United States v. Kramer, 955 F.2d 479 (7th Cir. 1992) (Cudahy, J., concurring) ("the specific-intent exception of this circuit automatically precludes defendants charged with specific-intent crimes from *ever* removing intent as an issue in the case, even by stipulation"). Since the Supreme Court dismissed certiorari in *Hadley,* the Ninth Circuit has adhered to its view that even a formal stipulation does not prevent the prosecution from proving intent through bad acts. United States v. Breitkreutz, 8 F.3d 688 (9th Cir. 1993) (in felon-firearm possession case, the prosecution was not required to accept the defendant's stipulation that he was a convicted felon; stipulations have "no place in the Rule 403 balancing process").

34. United States v. Chaimson, 760 F.2d 798, 805 (7th Cir. 1985).

35. It should also be noted that the Seventh Circuit's rule is not without litigation costs, since there can be substantial ambiguity as to whether a crime is a specific-intent crime (for which intent cannot be stipulated away) or a general intent-crime (for which the defendant can keep uncharged misconduct evidence of intent out of the case). See, e.g., United States v. Gruttadauro, 818 F.2d 1323 (7th Cir. 1987) (crime requiring a showing of wilfulness is a general intent crime); United States v. Manganellis, 864 F.2d 528 (7th Cir. 1988) (stating that "purpose" corresponds with specific intent while "knowledge" corresponds with general intent).

36. The Court in *Garcia* also set forth four procedural guidelines for determining whether a defendant has sufficiently taken intent out of a case so as to render prior bad acts irrelevant to prove intent: (1) a mere offer "not to argue" intent is an insufficient stipulation; (2) whether an offer to stipulate sufficiently takes intent out of the case is a question within the sound discretion of the District Court; (3) the Trial Judge should make sure that the defendant is aware of the content and consequences of the stipulation; and (4) the matter should be handled before trial or early in the trial process, so as to avoid ambiguous, last-minute proffers by the defendant. 983 F.2d at 1163.

Stipulating intent (cont'd)

cocaine trafficking is not the same as stipulating to knowing possession of narcotics at the time of the arrest.[37]

Despite the arguments in favor of allowing the use of effective stipulations as a means of preempting bad act evidence, there may be some indication in the Supreme Court's opinion in *Estelle v. McGuire,* 112 S. Ct. 475 (1991), that the Court is prepared to allow expansive use of uncharged misconduct to prove intent in criminal cases. McGuire was charged and convicted in a state court of the murder of his infant daughter. His defense was that his wife had beaten the child, causing her death. The Trial Court admitted evidence that the infant had suffered extensive and serious injuries on many occasions before her death. Eventually the Ninth Circuit granted McGuire's habeas corpus petition, in part on the ground that the evidence of the infant's previous injuries had been improperly admitted. The Supreme Court reversed.

McGuire was a state case decided on constitutional grounds, so it did not deal directly with the Federal Rules of Evidence. However, the Court assumed, for argument's sake, that if the battered child evidence was irrelevant, the defendant's due process rights were violated and he was entitled to a writ of habeas corpus. The Court unanimously held that the battered child evidence was relevant even though McGuire had claimed that he did not commit the murder. Chief Justice Rehnquist reasoned that "the prosecution's burden to prove every element of the crime is not relieved by a defendant's tactical decision not to contest an essential element of the offense." While this is true, the fact is that McGuire did not merely plead guilty; he affirmatively argued that his wife had murdered the child. Under the Second Circuit's view, this affirmative argument would have rendered uncharged misconduct irrelevant to prove intent. So the result in *McGuire* represents an implicit rejection of the Second Circuit position.

It should be noted, however, that McGuire never formally offered to *stipulate* intent. Therefore, the reasoning in *McGuire* does not foreclose the Court, or any lower Court, from holding that a defendant who actually and effectively stipulates to intent can prevent the prosecution from proving intent through uncharged misconduct.[38]

When the defendant is permitted to stipulate to an element of the crime such as intent, the jury must still be made aware that the charged crime contains that element. The

---

37. See also United States v. Colon, 880 F.2d 650 (2d Cir. 1989) (the government alleged that Colon "steered" an undercover buyer to a drug source; Colon's defense was that he had merely responded to the buyer's request for drugs by innocently pointing to the general direction of drug activity down the street; Colon's counsel offered a stipulation that if the government proved that Colon knew the drug seller and was in fact directing the undercover buyer specifically to that drug seller, "then I will acknowledge that he intended to violate the federal narcotics law and intended to aid in the sale of drugs"; this stipulation was insufficient to take the issue of intent out of the case; the stipulation "conceded nothing" on the issue of intent, "as the government would still have had to prove that Colon meant to point the detective to [the drug seller] and not down the street").

38. Lower Courts have apparently not felt constrained by *McGuire*. See, e.g., United States v. Jenkins, 7 F.3d 803 (8th Cir. 1993) (adopting the Second Circuit's position — that the defendant's decision not to dispute intent precludes the use of bad acts to prove intent — without citing *McGuire*); United States v. Garcia, 983 F.2d 1160 (1st Cir. 1993) (adhering to prior law, that a formal stipulation by the defendant will preclude the use of bad acts to prove intent).

defendant is not entitled to recharacterize the crime with which he is charged. For example, in *United States v. Gilliam*, 994 F.2d 97 (2d Cir. 1993), the defendant was charged with being a felon in possession of a firearm. His proffered stipulation to the fact of his prior felony was accepted. But he also sought to stipulate to the element of the felony itself, so that the jury would be instructed that if it found that the defendant knowingly possessed the gun, it should find the defendant guilty. The Court held that such an instruction was inappropriate because it would deny the jury the right to know the crime for which it was convicting the defendant. The Court noted that "Gilliam is not charged with mere possession of a weapon, but with possession by a convicted felon. The jury speaks for the community in condemning such behavior, and it cannot condemn such behavior if it is unaware of the nature of the crime charged."

The *Gilliam* Court distinguished the cases discussed above that allow the defendant to stipulate to intent in order to keep prior bad acts out of the trial. In such cases, the jury is informed of the elements of the crime, but is also informed that one of the elements has been satisfied; the jury is thus made aware of the crime for which the defendant is convicted.

Standard of proof

In the early years of the Federal Rules, many courts required "clear and convincing evidence" that a criminal defendant committed an uncharged act before proof of the act could be admitted. But the Supreme Court rejected this standard as unduly stringent, and inconsistent with the language of Rule 104(b), in *Huddleston v. United States*, 485 U.S. 681 (1988). Huddleston was charged with selling stolen goods and possessing stolen property, charges relating to video cassette tapes. To prove the defendant's knowledge that the items were stolen, the government offered evidence concerning Huddleston's previous offer to sell new black and white television sets and a large quantity of home appliances. Huddleston challenged the admission of the evidence concerning the televisions, because the government's proof that these items were stolen was based solely upon the defendant's failure to produce a bill of sale and their low selling price.

In the lower Courts, Huddleston, the defendant had argued that the bad act evidence could not be admitted unless the government proved by clear and convincing evidence that the sets had been stolen. In the Supreme Court, however, he conceded that the clear and convincing evidence argument would fall in light of the Court's ruling in *Bourjaily v. United States* (discussed under Rules 104(a) and 801(d)(2)(E)). The defendant argued instead that the evidence could not have been properly admitted unless the Trial Judge found by at least a preponderance of the evidence that the sets were stolen. The Supreme Court unanimously rejected the argument.

Chief Justice Rehnquist's opinion for the Court reasoned that when evidence is offered for a proper purpose under Rule 404(b), "the evidence is subject only to general strictures limiting admissibility such as Rules 402 and 403." The Chief Justice wrote that no preliminary finding under Rule 104(a) is required when other act evidence is offered. Rather, the question of whether the defendant had committed the bad act was simply one of conditional relevancy — the relevancy of the bad act was conditioned on the defendant's having committed it. Questions of conditional relevancy are governed by Rule 104(b), under which the evidence is admitted if the proponent establishes enough

Standard of proof (cont'd)

evidence to support a finding of the conditional fact. As the Court put it in *Huddleston:* "The court simply examines all the evidence in the case and decides whether the jury could reasonably find the conditional fact — here, that the television sets were stolen — by a preponderance of the evidence." The Trial Court need not itself be convinced by a preponderance that the defendant committed the bad act. Responding to the defendant's argument that other act evidence might be unduly prejudicial, Chief Justice Rehnquist wrote as follows:

> We share petitioner's concern that unduly prejudicial evidence might be introduced under Rule 404(b).... We think, however, that the protection against such unfair prejudice emanates not from a requirement of preliminary factfinding by the trial court, but rather from four other sources: first, from the requirement of Rule 404(b) that the evidence be offered for a proper purpose; second, from the relevancy requirement of Rule 402 — as enforced through Rule 104(b); third, from the assessment the trial court must make under Rule 403 to determine whether the probative value of the similar acts evidence is substantially outweighed by its potential for unfair prejudice ...; and fourth, from Federal Rule of Evidence 105, which provides that the trial court shall, upon request, instruct the jury that the similar acts evidence is to be considered only for the proper purpose for which it was admitted....

(Citations and footnote omitted.)

The *Huddleston* decision establishes that the clear and convincing evidence test is no longer good law and that Rule 404(b) rulings fall within the conditional relevancy (subdivision (b)) rather than the preliminary factfinding (subdivision (a)) portion of Rule 104. It also highlights the importance of making Rule 403 objections when other act evidence is offered, and of explicitly seeking appellate review of Rule 403 objections that are overruled. The Court observed that the defendant had failed to explicitly seek such review in *Huddleston*.

The *Huddleston* Court implicitly recognized the problem with the clear and convincing evidence standard that was rarely noticed by the Courts adopting the requirement. The problem is that standards like clear and convincing evidence (or preponderance of the evidence, or even proof beyond a reasonable doubt), are selected to govern a decision by a trier of fact, Judge or jury, who is expected to take credibility into account. The standard represents a confidence level, not an abstract measure of the quantity or quality of evidence presented in any case. For example, a jury might convict a defendant — i.e., find him guilty beyond a reasonable doubt — on the basis of a single witness' testimony, despite contrary testimony by two defense witnesses. It may do so solely on the basis of a credibility determination. It may do so even if the Trial Judge would not have believed the single witness. The same is true of cases when clear and convincing evidence is the standard. A jury may believe evidence that the Judge would not believe. Because this is the case, the Judge generally is especially reluctant to reject evidence which, if believed by the jury, would be important to its decision.

This highlights the difficulty in asking the Trial Judge to admit other crimes evidence only when the Judge finds clear and convincing evidence supporting it. Is the Judge to decide credibility in this instance? Generally, the Courts have held that in making relevance and balancing types of decisions, the Trial Judge should not do so, for credibility determinations are the province of the jury. If Trial Judges may not determine credibility in order to decide whether to admit or exclude evidence under Rule 403, they still might ask whether the government's evidence of other crimes is strong enough for a jury to find the proof clear and convincing. In most cases a jury that could find the acts to be true could, if it believed the evidence, also find that it was clear and convincing. Thus, the clear and convincing standard represents a protection that is more apparent than real.

As the Court implied in *Huddleston,* we believe it is preferable for the Trial Judge to be aware of the prejudicial potential of bad acts evidence, to ensure that it is needed in a case, to inquire whether less prejudicial evidence is available to prove a point, and to carefully make a balancing decision using the standard we have suggested under Rule 403. This is the real protection in the long run for all litigants.

Under *Huddleston,* the prosecution must present evidence to support a finding by a preponderance that the bad act was committed and that the defendant was the actor. How, then, can the result in *Estelle v. McGuire,* 112 S. Ct. 475 (1991), be explained? As discussed above, the Court in *McGuire* was reviewing the constitutionality of a state decision, not an application of the Federal Rules of Evidence. Nonetheless, at least one of the issues in *McGuire* echoed the problem discussed in *Huddleston.* McGuire complained that the evidence of his infant daughter's prior injuries should not have been admitted in his murder trial, since the prosecution presented no evidence connecting him with those injuries. But Chief Justice Rehnquist, writing for the Court, reasoned that evidence of the daughter's previous injuries helped to prove that "the child died at the hands of another and not by falling off a couch, for example." That is, it tended to prove that the child did not die accidentally, and therefore that *somebody* inflicted the injuries with intent. The Court concluded that the evidence of prior injuries was probative on the question "of the intent with which the person who caused the injuries acted." For this purpose, it was probative whether linked to McGuire or not; it advanced the prosecution's case.

In *McGuire,* the prior injuries to the child were unconditionally relevant, since they proved that someone had intentionally harmed the child, and that factor itself was relevant. (Remember that McGuire made no formal offer to stipulate that the child was intentionally killed). In contrast, in *Huddleston,* the defendant was charged with knowing possession of stolen merchandise, and the uncharged misconduct concerned Huddleston's prior possession of stolen merchandise. In *Huddleston,* the mere fact that some other person previously possessed stolen merchandise would not have been relevant to Huddleston's knowledge. It was only relevant because Huddleston was that person; so the relevance of the previous possession was conditional upon it being connected to Huddleston. Thus, when the Court set forth its conditional relevance test in *Huddleston,* it did not consider the situation where a prior bad act could be relevant even though the defendant was not connected to the act. It met that situation in *McGuire.* In a case like *McGuire,* where the bad act is relevant whether or not the defendant committed it, the prosecution only needs to provide evidence sufficient to support a finding, by a preponderance of the evidence, that the act occurred.

Effect of prior acquittals

In *Dowling v. United States,* 110 S. Ct. 668 (1990), the Court strongly suggested that a prior bad act could be admissible under Rule 404(b) even though the defendant was acquitted of the act. Dowling was charged with bank robbery. The perpetrator wore a ski mask and carried a gun. The Trial Court allowed a witness to testify that Dowling and a man named Christian assaulted her two weeks after the bank robbery, and that during the assault Dowling was wearing a ski mask and carrying a handgun. Dowling was acquitted of charges arising from the assault; the government offered and the Trial Court admitted the assault victim's testimony to strengthen the identification of Dowling as the masked, gun-toting bank robber, and to link Dowling with Christian, who was the getaway driver for the bank robbery. The Third Circuit held that this was error (though harmless) because, among other things, Rule 404(b) could not apply to conduct for which the defendant had been acquitted.

The Rule 404(b) question was not raised in the Supreme Court in *Dowling*. Rather, Dowling argued that the collateral estoppel component of the Double Jeopardy Clause prohibited the proof of conduct for which he had been acquitted. In rejecting that claim, the Court relied heavily on the fact that the standard of proof governing the admissibility of Rule 404(b) evidence was considerably less than the beyond a reasonable doubt standard applied at a criminal trial. The Court noted that after *Huddleston,* the prosecution need only provide evidence sufficient to support a finding by a preponderance of the evidence that the defendant committed the prior bad act. Therefore, when the government offered evidence of the assault at the bank robbery trial, the government was not trying to relitigate the question of whether Dowling had committed the assault beyond a reasonable doubt: "Because a jury might reasonably conclude that Dowling was the masked man who entered Henry's home, even if it did not believe beyond a reasonable doubt that Dowling committed the crimes charged at the first trial, the collateral estoppel component of the Double Jeopardy Clause is inapposite." 110 S. Ct. at 672.

Dowling is not technically a Rule 404(b) case. But the Court's rationale leads to the conclusion that bad acts are not inadmissible under Rule 404(b) simply because the defendant has been acquitted of those acts. An acquittal is not dispositive given the significantly lower standard of proof applied to Rule 404(b) evidence after *Huddleston*. However, the defendant should be prepared to argue that the probative value of the bad act is diminished in light of the acquittal. As the Court stated in *Huddleston,* "the strength of the evidence establishing the similar act is one of the factors the court may consider when conducting the Rule 403 balancing."

Effect of prior arrests

If a bad act can be admitted even where the defendant has been acquitted of charges arising from the act, what should the result be if the defendant has simply been arrested for the act? A cogent answer was provided by the Court in *United States v. Robinson,* 978 F.2d 1554 (10th Cir. 1992). *Robinson* was a narcotics case, where conspiracy and intent were contested issues. The Trial Court admitted evidence that two of the defendants had been previously arrested for narcotics violations. The Court of Appeals held that the mere evidence of arrest, without any showing of the underlying act or circumstances, was not probative of intent, knowledge, or any other of the permissible purposes for bad act evidence under Rule 404(b). It concluded: "Rule 404(b) allows evidence concerning the prior activity of a particular defendant, not simply testimony that records indicate an arrest took place." Put another way, the mere fact of arrest did not show sufficiently, under *Huddleston*, that the bad act was committed and that the defendant committed it.

In contrast, officers in *Robinson* testified with respect to another defendant not merely about prior arrests but about specific acts of the defendant and the circumstances that culminated in the arrest (i.e., that drugs were found in the apartment and that the defendant was apprehended while trying to jump from a second story window). This evidence was found properly admitted because it was probative on the subject of intent and knowledge, and because the prosecution provided enough evidence to support a finding that the act was committed and that the defendant committed it.

Preliminary rulings

One way of avoiding problems at trial with bad act evidence is to seek a ruling by the Trial Judge before the bad acts are mentioned. One case recommending this is *Grimaldi v. United States,* 606 F.2d 332, 340 n.9 (1st Cir.), *cert. denied,* 444 U.S. 971 (1979). Of course, as discussed previously in the Editorial Explanatory Comment to Rule 103, an *in limine* ruling is ordinarily not definitive where admissibility is based on a balance of prejudice and probative value; it is rare that such a rule can be made conclusively before the trial unfolds and the evidence is proffered. Accordingly, it behooves counsel to renew an objection to evidence (or to reargue a decision to exclude it) previously considered by the Court in an *in limine* ruling.

Limiting instructions

Counsel, especially those representing criminal defendants, must be diligent if they are to limit the prejudicial effect of bad act evidence. If a Trial Judge is inclined to admit bad act evidence, defense counsel may want a limiting instruction. Although such an instruction may not work in some cases and even may be undesirable because it might call attention to the dangerous evidence, in other cases a caution to the jury from the judge may be beneficial. Unless the defendant requests a limiting instruction, it is unlikely that one will be given — though, as discussed in the Editorial Explanatory Comment to Rule 105, a Trial Judge may find it worthwhile in some cases to give a cautionary instruction *sua sponte* in order to protect against a reversal for plain error. If a proper request is made and the Trial Judge fails to give an instruction, an Appellate Court may well reverse.[39]

In some cases, the government can protect itself from possible reversal on appeal by using bad act evidence in a careful, restrained way.[40] But when the government is

---

39. See, e.g., United States v. Yopp, 577 F.2d 362 (6th Cir. 1978) (reversible error for failure to give instruction, upon request, that bad acts evidence could be used only as proof of intent, and not as a reflection on the defendant's character).

40. See, e.g., United States v. Free, 574 F.2d 1221 (5th Cir.), *cert. denied,* 439 U.S. 873 (1978) (Evidence of defendant's homosexuality was properly admitted because the government's allegation was that the defendant

unrestrained, defense counsel must ordinarily act if a defendant's rights are to be preserved.[41] It may be especially important for counsel to make clear that objections to bad act evidence are not abandoned when the defense tries to respond to the government's evidence after an objection is overruled.[42]

Also, counsel should seek to have bad act evidence objections resolved outside the hearing of the jury and should consider whether the Judge's cautionary instruction sometimes should be given before the jury hears the evidence.[43]

Trial Judges should be alert to the possible ineffectiveness of defense counsel; the failure to request a limiting instruction may be the result of negligence rather than considered strategy.[44] By asking whether defense counsel wants a limiting instruction in circumstances when one would seem desirable, Trial Judges might avoid plain error.[45]

---

was motivated to kill the victim because the victim refused to have homosexual relations with him: The Court of Appeals stated that the "record shows that the Government introduced the controverted evidence in a restrained and professional manner" and that in "carrying its burden of proof, the Government could not change the truth of the defendant's motivation.").

41. See, e.g., United States v. Levy, 578 F.2d 896 (2d Cir. 1978) (no error in referring to defendant's cooperation with the government in a previous case, where defense counsel "neither requested a curative instruction, nor accepted the trial judge's offer to give one").

42. See, e.g., United States v. Westbo, 576 F.2d 285 (10th Cir. 1978), where the Court was sympathetic to the defendant's "dilemma of having evidence of other crimes effectively before the jury but being unable to negate these inferences without waiving his objection to this inadmissible evidence."

43. See, e.g., United States v. Carleo, 576 F.2d 846 (10th Cir.), cert. denied, 439 U.S. 850 (1978):

> We are convinced that the trial court here acted with the sensitivity and caution that considerations of other crimes evidence require. The court called a recess in order carefully to consider the nature and purpose of the proffered evidence outside the presence of the jury before it was introduced. Moreover, the jury was instructed immediately prior to the introduction of the testimony that it was being received for the very limited purpose of shedding what light it may have, if any, on the motive and intent of the defendant.... We commend the trial court for the manner in which he handled the offer of proof and introduction of this evidence.

44. See, e.g., United States v. Bosch, 584 F.2d 1113, 1124 (1st Cir. 1978) (reversible error where defense counsel introduced an exhibit that made reference to defendant's prior crimes, and made no attempt to delete these crimes, which were not probative on any point in the case; Trial Judge should have known that defense counsel was incompetent because it was clear, based on statements defense counsel made in conference, that he had never even given any thought to deleting the references to prior crimes before admitting the exhibit:

> Although a court is entitled to rely to a great extent on the parties' attorneys to protect their own clients' interests, the court, too, has a duty to ensure that a criminal defendant receives a fair trial. Since the court should have become aware during the conference in chambers that counsel's performance was less than adequate, and since the jury was obviously prejudiced by its consideration of the references to the prior crimes, we find that the court by adhering to the invited error doctrine failed in the duty to ensure a fair trial.

45. See, e.g., United States v. Copelin, 996 F.2d 379 (D.C. Cir. 1993) (reversing a conviction for failure to give sua sponte limiting instruction and noting that there is a "huge presumption" of plain error where a Trial Judge omits a cautionary instruction when admitting impeachment evidence to which a jury could give substantive effect against a criminal defendant; that presumption was not overcome in this case, since evidence of defendant's prior drug activity could be used by the jury to draw a judgment about the crime charged).

"Back door" admission

Counsel should be especially careful not to let other crimes evidence squeeze in a back door when such crimes, if offered under Rule 404(b), would be rejected. For example, in *United States v. Williams,* 739 F.2d 297 (7th Cir. 1984), the prosecution called a police detective to testify about the investigation leading to the defendant's arrest. In the course of his testimony, the detective stated, over counsel's objection, that he knew the defendant by the sobriquet "Fast Eddie." The Court of Appeals found that this testimony constituted reversible error, because it was an impermissible reference to the defendant's character. The Court rejected the argument that "Fast Eddie" was a neutral name, concluding that it would "suggest to the jury that the defendant had some sort of history of or reputation for unsavory activity." The Court recognized that other cases had permitted evidence of a defendant's alias or nickname if it "aids in the identification of the defendant or in some other way directly relates to the proof of the acts charged in the indictment."[46] However, in this case, "the detective's testimony about the defendant's nickname was completely unrelated to any of the other proof against the defendant."[47] Counsel should be on guard against attempts such as that in *Williams* to sneak in references to other crimes.[48]

Acts that are inextricably intertwined with the crime charged

In a criminal case, Rule 404(b) operates to assure that the jury, when it convicts, does so for the offense charged, and not for general bad character. But it is sometimes difficult to determine which acts are part of the offense charged, and which are uncharged acts subject to Rule 404(b). The test used by the Courts is whether the acts that are the subject of the proof are "inextricably intertwined" with the basic elements of the crime charged. If so, Rule 404(b) is inapplicable and there is no need to articulate a "not-for-character" purpose for the evidence. Of course, Rule 403 will still apply to the evidence.[49] But it

---

46. See, e.g., United States v. Kalish, 690 F.2d 1144 (5th Cir. 1982), *cert. denied,* 459 U.S. 1108 (1983) (defendant's alias admissible where he had used it to conceal his identity from the arresting officer).

47. 739 F.2d at 300. See also United States v. Shelton, 628 F.2d 54 (D.C. Cir. 1980), where the Court reversed a conviction for assault on a federal officer because the defendant and a defense witness were cross-examined in a way that was intended to suggest that they "were members of the drug underworld involved in all sorts of skullduggery." The Court said that the conduct of the prosecutor "is not rendered more acceptable by the fact that it is less focused and more subtly addressed than traditional 'other crimes' evidence."

48. See also United States v. Vargas, 583 F.2d 380 (7th Cir. 1978):

> The fact that in this case the reference to other crimes came not from evidence but from the prosecutor's argument and his suggestions does not undermine the need for [Rule 404 and 403] protections but rather enhances it, since coming from the mouth of the representative of the United States, the statements carry much weight against the accused when they should properly carry none.

49. See United States v. Hilgeford, 7 F.3d 1340 (7th Cir. 1993):

> When deciding if the other acts evidence was admissible without reference to Rule 404(b), we must determine whether such evidence was intricately related to the facts of the case at hand. If we find the evidence is so related, the only limitation on the admission of such evidence is the balancing test

would be the rare case in which proof of an inextricably intertwined act could be considered so prejudicial as to justify exclusion under Rule 403.

One of the clearest cases of "intertwined" evidence arises in conspiracy cases where the government proffers evidence of an act committed during the course and in furtherance of a conspiracy. For example, in *United States v. Pace,* 981 F.2d 1123 (10th Cir. 1992), the Court held that Rule 404(b) did not prohibit the admission of evidence of the distribution of drugs by the defendant's coconspirator. The distribution occurred while the charged conspiracy was ongoing. The Court stated that "conduct during the life of the conspiracy that is evidence of the conspiracy is not Rule 404(b) evidence."[50]

A more difficult case is one such as *United States v. Hilgeford,* 7 F.3d 1340 (7th Cir. 1993). Hilgeford was charged with, among other things, willfully filing a false tax return. He claimed various deductions from two farms that he asserted were owned by him. However, these properties had been previously subject to foreclosure actions by a bank and by the United States, respectively. In the years prior to the challenged tax returns, Hilgeford had generated "a blizzard of complicated and groundless litigation, primarily involving his fruitless attempts to regain his two farms." Evidence of these frivolous proceedings was introduced at Hilgeford's trial. The Court of Appeals held that Rule 404(b) was not applicable to this evidence, because it was "intricately related to the fact of the case at hand." The Court explained as follows:

> The government argues that the record of defendant's failed litigation proves that he knew that the returns, premised as they are on his ownership of the property, were false.... Evidence demonstrating that a defendant knew he did not own certain property, when he submitted a tax return premised on a claim that he did own the property, goes directly to [the element of wilfulness].... The evidence of defendant's prior conduct is "intricately related" or "inextricably tied" to the facts in this case. It is therefore not subject to Rule 404(b).

On the Rule 403 question, the *Hilgeford* Court found no error in admitting the evidence of frivolous litigation, given the already-determined crucial nature of the evidence in proving wilfulness.

Cases such as *Hilgeford* are more difficult than the conspiracy cases discussed above, because the bad acts in *Hilgeford* did not occur in the time period covered by the indictment.[51] The fact that the act was probative of an element of the prosecution's case

---

required by Rule 403...

50. See also United States v. Royal, 972 F.2d 643 (5th Cir. 1992) (holding that background information concerning a conspiracy is not extrinsic evidence because it was "inextricably intertwined" with the crime charged); United States v. Stouffer, 986 F.2d 916 (10th Cir. 1993) (evidence relevant to establish the existence of a criminal enterprise is not extrinsic evidence).

51. A similarly problematic case is United States v. Simon, 767 F.2d 524 (8th Cir. 1985) (drug-related evidence was "closely and integrally related" to the charges concerning ownership and possession of firearms, even though no drug-related activity was included in the indictment).

does not distinguish it from bad act evidence covered by Rule 404(b); presumably all evidence offered by the prosecution in a criminal trial must be somehow probative of an element of the crime. The difference between the evidence in *Hilgeford* and that in *Huddleston,* where the Supreme Court held that Rule 404(b) was applicable when a prior act was offered to show the knowledge element as to the charged crime, is at best one of degree rather than of kind.

We note that there is no significant cost to requiring a Rule 404(b) analysis; all the prosecution must do is establish a not-for-character purpose for the bad acts evidence. Nor does avoiding Rule 404(b) absolve the Court of the duty, upon request, to provide a limiting instruction. Therefore, we suggest that Rule 404(b) should apply to all specific bad acts proffered by the prosecution, unless such acts occurred in the time period covered by the indictment and are substantively related to the charges.[52]

Purposes for bad acts evidence not listed in the Rule

Rule 404(b) provides a list of proper purposes for admitting bad acts evidence. This list is illustrative only; it is not intended to be exclusive.[53] A plain reading of Rule 404(b) indicates that it is satisfied whenever bad act evidence is offered for a purpose other than proving character.[54] Once the not-for-character purpose is articulated, it becomes a Rule 403 question — whether the probative value as to the not-for-character purpose is substantially outweighed by the risk that the jury will use the uncharged misconduct as evidence of bad character.

United States v. Reme, 738 F.2d 1156 (11th Cir. 1984), provides an interesting example of the "inclusiveness" of Rule 404(b). Reme and Pierrot were charged with transporting illegal aliens to the United States. The defendants, Haitian nationals, arrived by boat with eighty of their countrymen. Their defense was that they were merely passengers, and not transporters. The government called other occupants of the boat to testify that Pierrot made the passengers sing voodoo songs; that Pierrot made them submit to searches for valuables and black magic; that Pierrot conducted a voodoo ceremony that led to the dissappearance of two passengers; and that Reme beat the passengers. The Court of Appeals held that all this testimony was properly admitted under Rule 404(b) to show "control"; the Court was unconcerned that "control" was not specifically listed as a proper purpose in the Rule, because the Rule permits bad acts to be admitted for any not-for-character purpose — subject to Rule 403. On the Rule 403 question, the *Reme*

---

52. For an application of the "inextricably intertwined" test in accordance with our suggestion, see United States v. Stotts, 792 F.2d 1318 (5th Cir. 1986) (no error to compare handwriting exemplars with extortion letters written by the defendants; Rule 404(b) was not applicable because the extortion letters were specifically described in the indictment: "There was no crime not alleged in the indictment which was testified to by the handwriting expert.").

53. See, e.g., United States v. Simon, 767 F.2d 524 (8th Cir. 1985) ("Rule 404(b) is a rule of inclusion rather than exclusion and admits evidence of other crimes or acts relevant to any issue in the trial, unless it tends to prove only criminal disposition.").

54. See United States v. Copelin, 996 F.2d 379, 382 (D.C. Cir. 1993) ("Although it is not one of the listed permissible purposes, an attempt to impeach through contradiction is indisputably a legitimate reason to introduce evidence of other crimes or wrongs.").

Court found that the Trial Court had not abused its discretion, since control was a contested issue in the case, the evidence was strongly probative of the government's argument that the defendants controlled the boat, and the prejudice, though significant, did not substantially outweigh the probative value.

Civil cases

Civil litigants should remember that they too can use Rule 404(b).[55] For example, *Dillon v. Nissan Motor Co.,* 986 F.2d 263 (8th Cir. 1993), was a personal injury action, where the plaintiff claimed emotional injuries as a result of the accident. The plaintiff's drug use was held properly admitted for the not-for-character purpose of providing an alternative explanation for his emotional turmoil.[56] Other cases are set forth in the Annotated Cases, *infra.*

Notice

In 1991, Rule 404(b) was amended to require the prosecution, upon the defendant's request, to give notice in advance of trial of the "general nature" of any bad acts evidence it intends to introduce at trial. The purpose of the amendment is to prevent unfair surprise and to make it easier for the defendant to obtain a pretrial *in limine* ruling on bad acts evidence. The amendment plainly envisions that the notice requirement is to be flexibly applied. No specific time limits are set, and indeed the amendment permits notice to be given as late as during trial upon a showing of good cause. As to the substance of the notice, the prosecution need only disclose the "general nature" of the bad acts evidence.[57] There is no requirement that the notice be in writing. It can be expected that the notice provision will be applied as flexibly as the notice provisions contained in Rules 803(24) and 804(b)(5). See the Editorial Explanatory Comments to those Rules for a discussion of the notice provisions.

Note that the notice requirement applies solely to the prosecution. Thus, if the defendant wishes to admit bad acts evidence under Rule 404(b), there is no requirement of advance notification to the prosecution. Nor is there a notice requirement in civil cases, though other discovery provisions in the Federal Rules of Civil Procedure might well require pretrial disclosure.

---

55. See, e.g., West v. Love, 776 F.2d 170 (7th Cir. 1985) (inmate brought civil rights action alleging that he had been unreasonably attacked by prison guards; evidence that, before the attack, the plaintiff had been placed in an isolated ward due to his violent temper, was not impermissible character evidence; rather, it was offered to show the reasonableness of the guards' assessment of the danger presented by the plaintiff).

56. See also Eaves v. Penn, 587 F.2d 453 (10th Cir. 1978) (bad acts were admitted to show intent in a civil case involving a claim that a trustee breached a fiduciary duty).

57. See, e.g., United States v. Kern, 12 F.3d 122 (8th Cir. 1993) (notice provision complied with where defendant was given reports of bad acts evidence a week in advance of trial; the government had previously informed the defendant that it "might use evidence from some local robberies," and the government did not receive the reports of those robberies from state authorities until one week before trial).

C. ANNOTATED CASES

RULE 404(a) — CHARACTER EVIDENCE GENERALLY

Animals

Durst v. Newby, 685 F. Supp. 250 (S.D. Ga. 1988): The Judge denied a summary judgment motion by a defendant whose tractor-trailer collided with a cow, ruling that evidence of the wanderlust of cows is not character evidence excluded by Rule 404.

Character of criminal defendant — background

United States v. Paccione, 949 F.2d 1183 (2d Cir. 1991), *cert. denied,* 112 S. Ct. 3029 (1992): In affirming RICO convictions, the Court held there was no abuse of discretion in preventing a defendant from introducing evidence that his teenage son was born with cerebral palsy and he would never do anything to risk disabling himself from caring for the boy. The defendant had been allowed to present four character witnesses to his honesty and integrity, and testimony about the son, which had no bearing on those traits, could well influence the jury by sympathies having no bearing on the merits of the case. In *United States v. Blackwell,* 853 F.2d 86 (2d Cir. 1988), the Court ruled that a defendant may introduce evidence of a lack of prior convictions or arrests as background evidence rather than to prove good character, but that that the exclusion of such evidence in this case was harmless error.

United States v. Gillespie, 852 F.2d 475 (9th Cir. 1988): The Court reversed a conviction for importing an alien for immoral purposes, ruling that a defendant did not put his character in issue by offering limited background testimony concerning his childhood, and that it was error for the prosecution to call an expert to testify to the characteristics of child molesters.

Character of criminal defendant — defense evidence

United States v. Angelini, 678 F.2d 380 (1st Cir. 1982): Reversing a conviction for possession of methaqualone, the Court said that the defendant should have been permitted to offer character evidence that he was "a law-abiding person," since such evidence showed a pertinent trait of character. The Court equated "pertinent" with "relevant."

United States v. MacDonald, 688 F.2d 224 (4th Cir. 1982), *cert. denied,* 459 U.S. 1103 (1983): In the prosecution of a former Army doctor charged with killing his wife and children, the Court held there was no abuse of discretion in excluding the testimony of a forensic psychiatrist who would have testified that the defendant's personality configuration was inconsistent with an outrageous murder. Exclusion came after thirteen lay witnesses had vouched for the defendant's nonviolent character.

United States v. Roberts, 887 F.2d 534 (5th Cir. 1989): The Court held it was error, but harmless, to exclude testimony by a psychologist that the personality of a defendant charged with cocaine offenses was consistent with his claimed activity as a self-appointed vigilante. In *United States v. Hewitt,* 634 F.2d 277 (5th Cir. 1981), the Court held that a defendant always may offer evidence that he is a "law-abiding citizen" and is not limited to more specific character traits. In *United States v. Jackson,* 588 F.2d 1046 (5th Cir.), *cert. denied,* 442 U.S. 941 (1979), the Court held there was no error in barring evidence of a defendant's good character for truthfulness, since truthfulness "is not pertinent to the criminal charges of conspiracy to distribute heroin or possession of heroin."

United States v. Cylkouski, 556 F.2d 799 (6th Cir. 1977): The Court affirmed a conviction for conspiracy to facilitate an illegal gambling business. Discussing the relationship between Rules 404(a) and 608(a), the Court noted that the former Rule permits a criminal defendant (whether or not he testifies) to open the door to character evidence relating to substantive issues, while the latter permits a criminal defendant, like any other party, to rehabilitate any witness' credibility *only* after the witness is attacked. Thus, the defendant's credibility is treated like that of any other witness: only after he testifies and is impeached may it be rehabilitated. This case is a reminder of the importance of citing the correct evidentiary theory: defense counsel who cites Rule 608 as authority for offering character evidence faces that Rule's limitation on the use of the evidence, but the limitation can be avoided if Rule 404(a) can be utilized.

United States v. Staggs, 553 F.2d 1073 (7th Cir. 1977): The defendant's conviction for assaulting a federal officer was reversed because a psychologist was not permitted to testify that the defendant was more likely to hurt himself than to direct his aggressions toward others. Because Rule 404(a) permits an accused to introduce evidence of a pertinent character trait and the relevant federal statute required the government to prove a subjective intent to commit an assault, it was error to rule the psychologist's testimony irrelevant. In dictum, the Court seemed to approve the use of an expert opinion as to the character of a criminal defendant, which Rules 404(a) and 405 do not prohibit but which generally was not permissible at common law.

United States v. Diaz, 961 F.2d 1417 (9th Cir. 1992): In a prosecution for possession of cocaine with intent to distribute, the Court held it was error (but harmless) to preclude the defendant from asking his pastor about the defendant's "being prone to criminal conduct," as the inquiry was encompassed within permissible "law-abidingness." There was no error in precluding inquiry of his mother about his "being prone to large-scale drug dealing," as that specific propensity is not simply the converse of general "law-abidingness."

Character of criminal defendant — demeanor evidence

United States v. Cortez, 935 F.2d 135 (8th Cir. 1991), *cert. denied,* 112 S. Ct. 945 (1992): To help the jury understand the defendant's in-court testimony and the events surrounding his arrest and interrogation, the defense offered a psychologist to testify that the defendant had mental and emotional disorders manifested in an "inability to recall certain facts" and a withdrawn demeanor. The Court held there was no abuse of discretion in excluding the evidence, as it did not refer to a character trait encompassed by the Rule and it would not be helpful to the jury because those aspects of the defendant's personality would be readily apparent when he testified.

United States v. Schuler, 813 F.2d 978 (9th Cir. 1987): In a prosecution for threatening the life of the President, the prosecutor referred during closing argument to the nontestifying defendant's courtroom conduct — including laughing during testimony regarding his threats. Reversing, the Court held that the argument violated Rule 404(a) by "suggesting to the jury that Schuler's laughter was relevant apparently for the purpose of showing that he was of bad character because he considered the charges of threatening the life of the President to be a joke." One Judge dissented on the grounds that a defendant's courtroom demeanor is properly considered as evidence and that the laughter was evidence of mental state.

Character of criminal defendant — government evidence

United States v. Hans, 738 F.2d 88 (3d Cir. 1984): Reversing a bank robbery conviction on another ground, the Court ruled that it was error for the prosecution to elicit evidence concerning the government's focusing on the defendant as a suspect because agents in Detroit thought he was a likely suspect. The Court said that this testimony tended to establish only that the defendant was a known bank robber and that it was highly prejudicial to the defendant.

United States v. Tran Trong Cuong, 18 F.3d 1132 (4th Cir. 1994): Reversing a doctor's conviction for illegal distribution of controlled substances, the Court held it was error to permit the prosecutor to cross-examine a witness about the defendant's reputation for being an easy source of drugs, where the defendant had not offered any evidence of his good character.

United States v. Andrea, 538 F.2d 1255 (6th Cir. 1976): Affirming a conviction for bank robbery, the Court stated that the deliberate injection into the record by government witnesses of information pertaining to a defendant's incarceration on a different charge is offensive to the fair administration of justice; in this case, however, the error was harmless.

United States v. Williams, 739 F.2d 297 (7th Cir. 1984): The Court reversed a conviction for dealing in stolen motor vehicles on the ground that the government impermissibly elicited character evidence when a detective testified that he knew the defendant as "Fast Eddie."

United States v. Pavon, 561 F.2d 799 (9th Cir. 1977): The Court affirmed cocaine distribution convictions despite the fact that the government used a probation officer as a witness, apparently to establish the amount of income that the defendant was legally earning. The Court indicated that direct evidence of the defendant's criminal record could not have been admitted under Rule 404(b) or under Rule 404(a)(1), so evidence pointing to an inference to the same effect should also have been excluded. Although it found the error to be harmless, the Court issued a stern warning for future cases.

Character of victim

United States v. Bailey, 834 F.2d 218 (1st Cir. 1987): The Court held that a defendant convicted of corruptly endeavoring to influence a juror had no right to introduce evidence that, while serving on the jury, the juror spoke about the case to neighbors in violation of her oath. The Court rejected the defendant's analysis of the juror as a victim whose character could be explored by the defense, and found that the neighbor's testimony involved specific instances of extrinsic conduct that were barred under Rule 608.

United States v. Schatzle, 901 F.2d 252 (2d Cir. 1990): In the prosecution of a Secret Service agent for willfully depriving a citizen of his constitutional rights by subjecting him to excessive force, the defendant was permitted to prove that the victim had previously been arrested after an altercation with a police officer and, in order to rebut the victim's claim that failure to mention it on a bar application was inadvertent, to have the officer testify about the victim's attempt to have the charges dropped so as not to prejudice his bar application; however, the officer was not permitted to give details of the incident. The Court affirmed, holding that although Rule 404(a)(2) permits introduction of pertinent traits of a victim's character, the Trial Court did not abuse its discretion under Rule 403 to exclude evidence posing a genuine risk of focusing the jury upon the wrong event.

Mosser v. Fruehauf Corp., 940 F.2d 77 (4th Cir. 1991): In a product liability wrongful death action brought after a tractor-trailer overturned, the defendant offered the driver-decedent's personnel file, which showed that he had received citations for speeding, as evidence of habit or as proof of intent. The Court held that there was no error in declining to admit traffic citations unrelated to the incident in question against a dead man unable to defend himself.

United States v. Martinez, 988 F.2d 685 (7th Cir.), *cert. denied,* 114 S. Ct. 125, 127 (1993): Affirming three defendants' convictions for murder and assault in a prison, the Court held that, even if some evidence of the victims' past violent acts and racism was theoretically relevant to prove self-defense, exclusion was not prejudicial in this case, as there could not have been a rational finding of self-defense.

Civil cases

Rauh v. Coyne, 744 F. Supp. 1181 (D.D.C. 1990): In an action by a woman alleging sex and marital status discrimination in her discharge from employment, the Judge held she would not be permitted to give evidence of her performance at prior and subsequent jobs. Even though it would have a slight probative value on her performance for the defendants, it would be inadmissible character evidence vastly complicating the trial of the case.

Spell v. McDaniel, 604 F. Supp. 641 (E.D.N.C. 1985), *aff'd,* 824 F.2d 1380 (4th Cir. 1987): Ruling on posttrial motions by defendants held responsible for a police officer's unprovoked assault on the plaintiff, the Court held that evidence of other acts of brutality was admissible to prove the plaintiff's allegations that the officer's conduct resulted from the defendants' policies and practices.

Moorhead v. Mitsubishi Aircraft Int'l, Inc., 828 F.2d 278 (5th Cir. 1987): In a suit by survivors of passengers killed in an airplane crash, the Court held it was error to admit evidence of the pilot's records from a flight school refresher course and testimony of one of the instructors. This was inadmissible character evidence, but its admission was harmless since the Judge did not rely upon it in making findings in a bench trial. In *Carson v. Polley,* 689 F.2d 562 (5th Cir. 1982), a civil rights suit alleging that the defendants used excessive force in making an arrest, the Court said in dictum that the exceptions in Rule 404(a) to the ban on character evidence apply in quasi-criminal cases and that an assault and battery charge was quasi-criminal.

Ginter v. Northwestern Mut. Life Ins. Co., 576 F. Supp. 627 (E.D. Ky. 1984): In an action to recover on a life insurance policy, the company claimed that the deceased omitted material facts when he applied for insurance. The Court ruled *in limine* that the plaintiff could not offer testimony of witnesses "that the deceased was a man of good character who would be unlikely to submit a fraudulent or erroneous application," since "it is the intention of Rule 404(a) to exclude evidence of a character trait in civil cases, except where character itself is an element of the claim or defense, as in cases involving defamation."

McCluney v. Jos. Schlitz Brewing Co., 728 F.2d 924 (7th Cir. 1984): The plaintiff was fired after he threatened to resign if the secretary he had in North Carolina was not transferred to his new assignment in Wisconsin. In his civil rights employment action he claimed he was fired because he opposed the defendant's transfer policy on the ground that it discriminated against women. Affirming a judgment for the defendant, the Court held that evidence concerning other alleged discrimination against women and the plaintiff's sincere and honest concern for female employees was properly excluded as an attempt to establish the plaintiff's good character. If offered under Rule 404(b), the evidence would have consumed far too much time in light of its limited probative value.

Blake v. Cich, 79 F.R.D. 398 (D. Minn. 1978): Denying a new trial motion in a civil rights action against police officers, the District Court noted that character evidence proffered by plaintiffs to prove their own actions could not properly have been admitted because character evidence cannot be used circumstantially in a civil case.

Gates v. Rivera, 993 F.2d 697 (9th Cir. 1993): In a civil rights action against a police officer for using excessive force, the Court held it was harmless error for the defendant to testify that in his sixteen and a half years as a police officer, he had never shot anyone. The only issue in the case was whether the force used was excessive, not the officer's intent. In *Palmerin v. Riverside,* 794 F.2d 1409 (9th Cir. 1986), the Court held it was not error, in a civil rights case alleging that police officers used excessive force, to admit the plaintiffs' guilty pleas that admitted that they had used excessive force against the officers. The pleas were not character evidence, but were relevant to an assessment of the propriety of the officers' response to the plaintiffs' actions. In *Cohn v. Papke,* 655 F.2d 191 (9th Cir. 1981), a civil rights action brought against police officers who arrested the plaintiff and charged him with soliciting a homosexual act, the Court found that it was reversible error to have permitted an inquiry into whether the plaintiff was bisexual. The Court found that this was impermissible under Rule 404 and also that it was too prejudicial to be permitted under Rule 403.

Perrin v. Anderson, 784 F.2d 1040 (10th Cir. 1986): The Court affirmed a judgment for police officers sued by the estate of a man killed by police officers when they attempted to obtain information about a traffic accident. It reasoned that "[a]lthough the literal language of exceptions to Rule 404(a) applies only to criminal cases, we agree with the district court here that, when the central issue involved in a civil case is in nature criminal, the defendant may invoke the exceptions to Rule 404(a)." Since a judgment for the plaintiff would effectively have established that the officers killed the man without cause, the Court held that "[t]he resulting stigma warrants giving the same opportunity to present a defense that a criminal defendant could present.'' Thus, it concluded that reputation and opinion evidence, but not specific acts, could have been admitted. The error in admitting specific acts was harmless, however, in view of their admissibility as habit evidence. In *Rocky Mountain Helicopters, Inc. v. Bell Helicopters Textron*, 805 F.2d 907 (10th Cir. 1986), an action by a helicopter buyer and its insurer against a manufacturer, the Court affirmed a judgment based upon a jury verdict finding that the buyer and the seller were each negligent, holding there was no error in excluding evidence that the buyer had been warned that the pilot of its helicopter might be dangerous and that the pilot overloaded helicopters. Since the buyer stipulated that its helicopter was overloaded at the time of the crash, the Court reasoned that the Trial Judge properly determined that the excluded evidence might have been viewed as character evidence by the jury and thus misused. In *Hackbart v. Cincinnati Bengals, Inc.*, 601 F.2d 516 (10th Cir.), *cert. denied*, 444 U.S. 931 (1979), an action for injuries suffered by a professional football player during a game, the Trial Judge found for the defendants in a bench trial. The Court held, *inter alia*, that evidence of prior violent acts of the plaintiff during football games was not to be received merely to show that the plaintiff had violated rules in times past, but it suggested that the evidence might be received to show that the plaintiff was the first aggressor.

Jury instructions

United States v. Pujana-Mena, 949 F.2d 24 (2d Cir. 1991): Resolving apparently contradictory Circuit precedent and adopting the majority view, the Court held that under Rule 404(a)(1) the defendant may introduce evidence of good character to rebut an inference of guilt, but he is not entitled to an instruction that such evidence ''standing alone'' may be sufficient to create a reasonable doubt.

United States v. Logan, 717 F.2d 84 (3d Cir. 1983): The Court reversed a conspiracy conviction for the Trial Judge's plain error in failing to provide the jurors with any guidance or instructions concerning the proper consideration of character evidence during their deliberations. The defendant had requested a charge, albeit an erroneous one, and a majority of the Court concluded that the defendant's character was essential to the jury's evaluation of the case.

United States v. Borders, 693 F.2d 1318 (11th Cir. 1982), *cert. denied*, 461 U.S. 905 (1983): In the course of affirming a lawyer's conviction for involvement in a scheme to bribe a federal Judge, the Court discussed the appropriate instruction to the jury on the use of defense character evidence.

Pertinent traits

United States v. Nazzaro, 889 F.2d 1158 (1st Cir. 1989): In a mail fraud conspiracy prosecution, the Court held there was no error in excluding evidence of commendations received by the defendant police officer because, even if they were character evidence, the traits of bravery, attention to duty, and community spirit they purported to show were not pertinent to the crimes of which he was accused.

United States v. Jackson, 588 F.2d 1046 (5th Cir.), *cert. denied*, 442 U.S. 941 (1979): The Court held there was no error in barring evidence of a defendant's good character for truthfulness, since truthfulness "is not pertinent to the criminal charges of conspiracy to distribute heroin or possession of heroin."

Reputation in issue

United States v. Certain Real Prop. Known as 890 Noyac Rd., 945 F.2d 1252 (2d Cir. 1991): In reversing an order of forfeiture against a mother whose son allegedly used the property for drug dealing, the Court noted that the son's reputation as a supplier of drugs was relevant to the mother's knowledge. Because the son's reputation rather than his character was at issue, Rules 404 and 405 were inapplicable.

Witness' character

United States v. Lanza, 790 F.2d 1015 (2d Cir.), *cert. denied*, 107 S. Ct. 211 (1986): In a prosecution charging three defendants with wire fraud in a scheme to stage a fraudulent burglary at a jewelry store owned by the key prosecution witness, the Trial Judge prevented the defense from examining the witness concerning various loans and debts. The Court affirmed, finding that these were not bad acts under Rule 608(b), and that the evidence was not admissible under Rule 404(a) to show that the witness was the kind of person who borrowed money and did not repay it.

United States v. Bocra, 623 F.2d 281 (3d Cir.), *cert. denied*, 449 U.S. 875 (1980): The Court held that a defendant who wanted to ask an IRS agent questions about the agent's soliciting bribes in other tax cases to support his claim that the agent entrapped him was seeking to elicit only bad character evidence that was inadmissible.

RULE 404(b) — OTHER CRIMES, WRONGS, OR ACTS

Ability or opportunity

United States v. Carty, 993 F.2d 1005 (1st Cir. 1993): The Court held there was no abuse of discretion in admitting evidence of the defendant's prior purchase of cocaine, as it was probative of his opportunity to commit the charged offense of possession with intent to distribute. The dissenting Judge believed proof of the prior purchase was only improper propensity evidence, and even though the defendant was acquitted of the possession offense, the evidence could have led the jury to believe him a drug dealer and thus guilty of the charged firearms offenses. See also *United States v. Barrett*, 539 F.2d 244 (1st Cir. 1976) (reversing conviction on other grounds, Court approved introduction of evidence that appellant had knowledge of the workings of alarm systems, to show his ability to commit crimes related to stolen postage stamps).

United States v. Robinson, 560 F.2d 507 (2d Cir. 1977) (en banc), *vacating* 544 F.2d 611 (1976), *cert. denied*, 435 U.S. 905 (1978): The *en banc* decision of the Court of Appeals referred to the "remarkable coincidence" of possession of a .38 caliber gun some weeks after the charged bank robbery and held that it was admissible to corroborate the government's chief witness and to show an opportunity to commit the robbery. See also *United States v. Sliker*, 751 F.2d 477 (2d Cir. 1984), *cert. denied*, 105 S. Ct. 1772, 2679 (1985) (in bank fraud prosecution, testimony about a similar attempt to defraud explained defendant's ability to get phony checks).

United States v. Echeverri, 854 F.2d 638 (3d Cir. 1988): The Court held that a government witness' testimony that he had encountered the defendant one year before the charged conspiracy, when both went to a location to purchase substantial quantities of cocaine, was admissible to prove that the defendant had a source of such cocaine.

United States v. Covelli, 738 F.2d 847 (7th Cir.), *cert. denied,* 105 S. Ct. 211 (1984): Affirming convictions for crimes arising out of a shop robbery, the Court upheld the admission of testimony that one of the defendants had previously been in possession of a small caliber pistol, saying that "evidence of prior possession of a weapon can be used to prove opportunity and identification even where it cannot be directly identified as the weapon used in the crime." In *United States v. Fairchild,* 526 F.2d 185 (7th Cir. 1975), *cert. denied,* 425 U.S. 942 (1976), Judge (now Justice) Stevens upheld the introduction of evidence that the defendant possessed counterfeit money shortly after committing the charged crime of distributing counterfeit bills. Rules 401, 403, and 404(b) were cited to support the ruling, on the theory that the evidence showed an ability to distribute counterfeit notes and absence of accident or mistake. Trial Judges should, of course, be aware that when the defendant is not claiming accident or inability to distribute, evidence of other crimes such as was used in this case is dangerous and not very helpful.

United States v. Green, 648 F.2d 587 (9th Cir. 1981): The Court approved the introduction of evidence that the appellants were involved in certain past drug transactions on the ground that it established an opportunity for them to obstruct justice by attempting to frame others. Trial Judges were reminded, however, that they must carefully restrict the other crimes evidence to that which actually is probative and that they must be concerned about the prejudicial effect of other crimes evidence.

United States v. Garcia, 880 F.2d 1277 (11th Cir. 1989) (per curiam): In a prosecution for making false statements on a loan application, a former employee had been permitted to testify that, as a joke, the defendant had signed the employee's name to a paper purporting to sell the employee's apartment to the defendant and had then ripped up the paper. Affirming, the Court said the evidence was relevant to demonstrate the defendant's ability to prepare documents with faked signatures, it did not tend to show bad character, and the defendant was not prejudiced by proof of his tendency to make jokes.

Accident or mistake

United States v. Naylor, 705 F.2d 110 (4th Cir. 1983): The Court affirmed convictions for transporting a stolen car and other offenses, noting there was no error in an *in limine* ruling that a prior conviction for attempting to steal a car would be admitted if the defendant testified. The Court found that the Trial Judge relied on Rule 404, not Rule 609, and that the evidence was admissible to prove absence of mistake. The Court apparently construed the *in limine* ruling as providing that only if the defendant took the stand and claimed that he did not know that the vehicle was stolen, the prejudicial effect of the prior conviction would be outweighed by its probative value.

Dial v. Travelers Indem. Co., 780 F.2d 520 (5th Cir. 1986): The Court affirmed a judgment against insureds suing to collect on a fire insurance policy on their house. It upheld admission of evidence that the plaintiffs had been burned out of their previous home and that after the fire in this case two properties they occupied burned. The Court applied the same test it uses in criminal cases to conclude that the evidence was relevant since "the essential issue is the difference between an accident and an intended act."

United States v. Leight, 818 F.2d 1297 (7th Cir.), *cert. denied,* 108 S. Ct. 356 (1987): The Court affirmed a mother's conviction for murdering her infant son, finding no error in admitting evidence of injuries suffered by two other of the defendant's children to prove that the death was not an accident. See also *United States v. Wormick,* 709 F.2d 454 (7th Cir. 1983) (evidence of prior falsification of records properly admitted to prove the absence of mistake).

King v. Ahrens, 16 F.3d 265 (8th Cir. 1994): In a medical malpractice case, the Court held there was no abuse of discretion in excluding evidence that the defendant's medical license had been suspended eight years earlier, as any probative value the evidence had on the absence of mistake in failing to note critical information on the medical chart and on the doctor's credibility was substantially outweighed by its prejudicial effect, given the remoteness in time and the dissimilarity between the incidents.

United States v. Boise, 916 F.2d 497 (9th Cir. 1990), *cert. denied,* 111 S. Ct. 2057 (1991): Affirming a conviction for murder of a six-week-old child, the Court held that evidence of the victim's prior injuries when the defendant was the primary caretaker and of the victim's suffering from battered-child syndrome was properly admitted as evidence of intent and of the absence of accident.

United States v. Shannon, 836 F.2d 1125 (8th Cir.), *cert. denied,* 108 S. Ct. 2830 (1988): The Court held that other instances in which currency reports were not filed were admissible to negate lack of mistake with respect to the defendant's actions.

United States v. Cummings, 798 F.2d 413 (10th Cir. 1986): The Court affirmed a conviction for selling a stolen cab portion of a tractor-trailer, finding that evidence that the defendant was involved in a pattern or practice of dealing in stolen trucks and parts was admissible to prove intent and the absence of mistake.

Acquittals

Dowling v. United States, 110 S. Ct. 668 (1990), *aff'g* 855 F.2d 114 (3d Cir. 1988): To identify the perpetrator in a bank robbery case, the government offered evidence that the defendant had committed a house robbery two weeks later for which he had been charged and acquitted. The Court of Appeals held that the error in admitting the evidence was harmless; the Supreme Court held that there was no constitutional error. The Supreme Court's analysis is discussed in the Editorial Explanatory Comment, *supra.*

United States v. Blyden, 964 F.2d 1375 (3d Cir. 1992): The Court reversed a ruling *in limine* that evidence of an alleged assault for which the defendants had previously been acquitted could not be introduced in a prosecution for other offenses arising out of the same incident. The evidence was essential to the charge of gun possession during a crime of violence, so it was not "other crime" evidence and it had great probative value. Any argument that it would be prejudicial essentially restated the double jeopardy and collateral estoppel claims previously rejected by the Court. It was, therefore, error to exclude the evidence on the possession count; rulings with respect to other counts for which the evidence was not essential must await the trial context.

Arizona v. Elmer, 21 F.3d 331 (9th Cir. 1994): In a state prosecution of a Border Patrol agent for shooting aliens crossing the Mexican border, the Court held it was not an abuse of discretion to exclude, on the defendant's *in limine* motion, evidence of a fatal shooting three months later for which the defendant had been charged and acquitted. The evidence was not relevant to any issue in the case and, while the record of balancing was not clearly articulated, the evidence would be extremely prejudicial, in all probability seizing and holding the jury's attention at trial.

United States v. Guitierrez, 696 F.2d 753 (10th Cir. 1982), *cert. denied,* 461 U.S. 909 (1983): The Court affirmed bank robbery convictions, finding that the Trial Judge properly admitted evidence of a second bank robbery involving the two defendants. The Court said that the crime charged and the other crime possessed "signature quality" and were therefore proper evidence, even though one of the defendants had been acquitted on the other charge.

Acts charged

United States v. Parker, 699 F.2d 177 (4th Cir.), *cert. denied,* 104 S. Ct. 122 (1983): In a prosecution for impersonating an IRS agent, Brooks, the person to whom the impersonation was addressed, reported it to the IRS. A real IRS agent phoned the defendant, pretended to be Brooks and had a follow-up conversation in which the defendant again claimed to work for the IRS. Although the Court referred to this as other act evidence, it found that it was admissible. We believe that this was not evidence of an unrelated transaction, but was proof of the very impersonation charged and, as the Court ruled, was plainly admissible.

Carter v. United States, 549 F.2d 77 (8th Cir. 1977): Affirming a conviction for unlawfully receiving a firearm that had been transported in interstate commerce, the Court found no error in admitting a druggist's testimony that the defendant had presented him with a forged prescription for narcotic drugs, since that explained why the druggist was chasing the defendant at the time he abandoned the weapon on which the charges were based.

United States v. Montes-Cardenas, 746 F.2d 771 (11th Cir. 1984): A defendant's importation of cocaine formed part of a series of cocaine offenses with which he was charged.

Acts charged — acts inextricably interwoven, intrinsic, or part of single criminal episode

United States v. Levy, 731 F.2d 997 (2d Cir. 1984): Reversing a defendant's conviction for distribution of heroin and sustaining his conviction for possession of heroin with intent to distribute, the Court found it was error to admit evidence concerning a "sample transaction" in which the defendant supplied heroin to an informant earlier in the day on which he was charged with distribution. The Court reasoned that the words "inextricably intertwined" are not always applicable to transactions that are related to one another and that "it is not inconceivable that acts or crimes that occur almost contemporaneously with the indicted crime may be entirely unrelated to that crime." The Trial Judge erred in admitting the evidence of the other transaction without considering the government's explanation for its use and weighing its potential prejudicial effect against its probative value.

United States v. Adams, 759 F.2d 1099 (3d Cir.), *cert. denied,* 474 U.S. 906, 971 (1985): The Court held that weapons were properly introduced to show the scale of the charged narcotics conspiracy and the type of protection the defendants thought they needed.

United States v. Black, 692 F.2d 314 (4th Cir. 1982): The Court reversed a conviction for assaulting and impeding a correctional officer on another ground, but held that the Trial Judge properly admitted evidence that after the assault, the defendant returned to his cell and threw human feces at the victim. This was not another bad act, but proof of an act that arguably was committed to enable the defendant to conceal a knife. Thus, it was proof of the crime charged.

United States v. Ridlehuber, 11 F.3d 516 (5th Cir. 1993): In a prosecution for possession of a short-barreled shotgun, the Trial Court denied a motion *in limine* to exclude any evidence suggesting that the defendant had been engaged in drug manufacturing when the weapon was seized, and the government introduced considerable evidence of drug manufacturing over objection. The Court reversed the defendant's conviction because of the admission of the other crime evidence, rejecting the government's contention that the Rule was inapplicable because the evidence was not extrinsic. The drug manufacturing was not "inextricably intertwined" with the weapon possession in the sense that other acts furthering a conspiracy are. The drug manufacturing evidence did not arise out of the weapons charge; under the government's theory the opposite was true. Nor was the drug manufacturing part of a "single criminal episode," as the only episode proven was the weapon possession. As the Trial Court had not articulated its findings on the record, the Court reviewed the evidence and determined that there was insufficient proof the defendant had committed the extrinsic offense, and even if the proof had been sufficient, the prejudicial effect of the evidence that was offered substantially outweighed its probative value. One Judge dissented on the ground that the drug manufacturing evidence was intrinsic circumstantial evidence of knowledge and possession of the short-barreled shotgun. In *United States v. Maceo,* 947 F.2d 1191 (5th Cir. 1991), *cert. denied,* 112 S. Ct. 1510 (1992), the Court affirmed cocaine conspiracy convictions, holding that evidence of a defendant's personal use of cocaine and receipt of cocaine as legal fees was not extrinsic evidence but inextricably intertwined with the evidence used to prove the crimes charged, so was properly admitted to prove he knew about the drug trafficking conspiracy and knowingly participated in it. In *United States v. Torres,* 685 F.2d 921 (5th Cir. 1982), convictions for cocaine distribution were affirmed. The Court held that two "sample transactions" involving sales of cocaine were not extrinsic offenses and were properly admitted where they were "inextricably intertwined" with the crime charged. See also *United States v. Stovall,* 825 F.2d 817, *modified,* 833 F.2d 526 (5th Cir. 1987) (a purchase made with the money received from a loan was inextricably intertwined with the charge of receiving a benefit from the loan); *United States v. Tafoya,* 757 F.2d 1522 (5th Cir.), *cert. denied,* 474 U.S. 912 (1985) (evidence of defendant's assassination efforts admissible in tax prosecution to show that defendant earned money that he claimed was a gift).

United States v. Vincent, 681 F.2d 462 (6th Cir. 1982): In a prosecution for threatening the President, the Court held that, although it might have reached a different conclusion, there was no abuse of discretion in admitting additional threats made by the defendant at a psychiatric hospital after his arrest to educate the jury as to the entire setting of the case. See also *United States v. Reynolds,* 762 F.2d 489 (6th Cir. 1985) (videotape of defendant's conversation in which he mentioned future criminal activity in addition to the crime charged was admissible; statement involved intertwined events).

United States v. Menzer, 29 F.3d 1223 (7th Cir. 1994): The Court held, in a prosecution for arson resulting in the deaths of the defendant's two children, that evidence that the defendant was on probation for a 1986 conviction for sexual exploitation of a child was "intricately related" [*sic*] to the charged offense because it was the government's theory that the defendant burned down the house where his wife and children were sleeping in order to prevent their reporting his sexual abuse of the children which would result in revocation of his probation. In our view, this was other crime evidence admissible under the Rule to prove motive, and the Court's characterization of it as "intricately related" (and therefore outside the Rule) is confusing, especially with the conclusion that there was no abuse of discretion in admitting the evidence "because it was intricately related to the arson prosecution as probative evidence of Menzer's intent (motive)." The problem the Court was apparently trying to get around arises from its current test for admissibility under Rule 404(b), which requires that "the other act is similar enough and close enough in time to be relevant to the matter in issue." *United States v. Shackleford,* 738 F.2d 776, 779 (7th Cir. 1984). Similarity, however, is the measure of probative value for only some of the purposes listed in the Rule; rather than continue its confusing resort to "intricately related," the Court would be better off modifying its test to accommodate all the purposes permissible under the Rule. In *United States v. Roberts,* 933 F.2d 517 (7th Cir. 1991), the Court affirmed convictions for armed bank robbery and possession of a firearm by a convicted felon, holding there was no error in admitting evidence that the defendant was arrested two days after the robbery carrying a gun similar to the one used in the robbery. The evidence was not of extraneous other acts but rather "intricately connected" with the very crimes charged. See also *United States v. Vretta,* 790 F.2d 651 (7th Cir.), *cert. denied,* 107 S. Ct. 179 (1986) (evidence concerning the death of the victim's son was inextricably intertwined with the events leading to charged kidnapping).

United States v. Tate, 821 F.2d 1328 (8th Cir. 1987), *cert. denied,* 108 S. Ct. 712 (1988): In a prosecution for weapons violations, the Court held that the government properly proved that a defendant shot state troopers, since the shootings were intertwined with the weapons charges.

United States v. Warren, 25 F.3d 890 (9th Cir. 1994): The defendant stabbed two men in a fight; one victim died and the other recovered. The defendant was charged only with murder, and objected, under Rule 404(b), to evidence that he had stabbed another person in the fight. The Court of Appeals found no error in introducing this evidence. It held that the two acts of stabbing were "inextricably intertwined" because both were "part of a single course of action and occurred within moments of each other."

United States v. Veltmann, 6 F.3d 1483 (11th Cir. 1993): The defendants, charged with setting a fire in which their wife and mother (respectively) had died, alleged that the victim had committed suicide. The Court held that evidence of a prior fire on the defendants' property was properly admitted, as it was inextricably intertwined with the charged crime because both defendants had mentioned it in such a way as to direct the investigation toward another suspect. However, other evidence of fires on the defendants' property lacked similarity with the charged offense and thus failed to meet the threshold level of relevance for admissibility under the Rule. In *United States v. Leavitt,* 878 F.2d 1329 (11th Cir.), *cert. denied,* 110 S. Ct. 415 (1989), the Court held, in affirming convictions for offenses committed in a narcotics importation conspiracy, that evidence of a threatened kidnapping and illegal gun purchases not charged in the indictment was not extrinsic evidence under Rule 404(b) because it was inextricably intertwined with evidence of the charged offenses or necessary to complete the story of the charged offenses. See also *United States v. Martin,* 794 F.2d 1531 (11th Cir. 1986) (evidence of guns on a vessel carrying marijuana was direct evidence of crimes charged; no limiting instruction was required); *United States v. Cole,* 755 F.2d 748 (11th Cir. 1985) (videotaped conversations among conspirators admissible in drug prosecution despite references to money laundering, since the laundering was inextricably intertwined with the drug evidence).

Acts charged — conspiracy

United States v. Moosey, 735 F.2d 633 (1st Cir. 1984): In a drug prosecution charging a conspiracy and substantive offenses, the Court found no error in admission of specific acts not charged as substantive offenses to prove the conspiracy. It observed that the Trial Judge explained to the jury that the acts could be considered only on the conspiracy count.

United States v. Thai, 29 F.3d 785 (2d Cir. 1994): Affirming RICO convictions, the Court held that evidence of a beating administered to a member of the conspiracy, although it was uncharged, was not evidence of "other" crimes but was evidence as to the structure of the enterprise and the discipline imposed by the defendant leaders on the members.

United States v. Wooten, 688 F.2d 941 (4th Cir. 1982): In a marijuana importation case, the Court found that a prosecutor acted in good faith in asking a question concerning one defendant's possession of cocaine, where the defendant claimed to have withdrawn from a conspiracy and the question concerned the defendant's conduct at the time he claimed to have withdrawn.

United States v. Silva, 748 F.2d 262 (5th Cir. 1984): The Court held in a bank robbery conspiracy case that evidence that one conspirator kidnapped the bank president's wife and held her hostage was properly admitted to show the nature of the conspiracy and to connect the defendant to it. See also *United States v. Punch,* 722 F.2d 146 (5th Cir. 1983) (statements by a defendant concerning the seizure of a boat carrying marijuana properly admitted to show scope of the defendant's activities in a conspiracy case).

United States v. Mancari, 875 F.2d 103 (7th Cir. 1989), *cert. denied,* 499 U.S. 924 (1991): The government had offered other crimes evidence under Rule 404(b) rather than as proof of the conspiracy charged. Because the evidence was not offered to prove the conspiracy charged, the Court ultimately found insufficient evidence to support that charge and remanded with directions to acquit. It observed that the government might have avoided the problem by offering the evidence without restricting the offer to an extremely narrow theory.

United States v. Jones, 880 F.2d 55 (8th Cir. 1989): The Court held that evidence of one defendant's prior drug-related activities was properly admitted to show the existence of, and his participation in, the charged six-year drug enterprise.

United States v. Hill, 953 F.2d 452 (9th Cir. 1991): The defendant's conviction for conspiracy to distribute cocaine was reversed because a coconspirator had been permitted to testify to having used cocaine with the defendant five years previously. The Court held that the evidence was not probative of the background and development of, nor inextricably intertwined with, the conspiracy. Although it might have been relevant to the defendant's knowledge and intent, when admitted as direct evidence of the conspiracy it was given more weight than it deserved and its prejudicial and confusing effect substantially outweighed its probative value. In *United States v. Lai,* 944 F.2d 1434 (9th Cir. 1991), *cert. denied,* 112 S. Ct. 947 (1992), the Court held that evidence of drug transactions in late 1982 and around Thanksgiving 1985 were direct evidence of a drug conspiracy charging specific acts as early as July 1983 and "continuing to in or about October 1985." See also *United States v. Patterson,* 819 F.2d 1495 (9th Cir. 1987) (evidence of a shooting properly admitted in prosecution of narcotics distribution conspiracy, as it showed that the conspirators used violence to control the members of the conspiracy).

United States v. Robinson, 978 F.2d 1554 (10th Cir. 1992), *cert. denied,* 113 S. Ct. 1855, 2938 (1993): Affirming cocaine base possession convictions, the Court held that evidence of the defendants' membership in a gang was not barred by the Rule, but was directly relevant on the issues of formation, agreement, and purpose of the conspiracy. The dissenting Judge believed that the government had impermissibly sought to prove that by exhibiting the characteristics of gang members, the defendants were members of a gang with criminal purposes and therefore were guilty of the charged conspiracy and underlying crimes.

Acts charged — dealing

United States v. Giraldo, 822 F.2d 205 (2d Cir.), *cert. denied,* 108 S. Ct. 466 (1987): The Court held that tapes from the defendant's answering machine that contained orders for cocaine were admissible to prove the defendant's intent to distribute.

United States v. Masters, 622 F.2d 83 (4th Cir. 1980): In a prosecution for dealing in firearms without a license, the Court approved the admission of taped conversations between the defendant and undercover agents despite references to other sales and acts, since the evidence was necessary to complete the story of the crime charged and to prove that the defendant actually was "dealing."

Acts charged — fraud

United States v. Anzalone, 783 F.2d 10 (1st Cir. 1986): The Court affirmed a defendant's mail fraud convictions, finding that evidence of his prior dealings with insurance companies was admissible to prove the deception of the insurance companies that gave rise to the indictment.

United States v. Heinemann, 801 F.2d 86 (2d Cir. 1986), *cert. denied,* 479 U.S. 1094 (1987): Affirming convictions for conspiracy to defraud the United States in connection with the sale of "ministries" in purported tax-exempt churches, the Court found that evidence that a defendant had lied to a grand jury was proof of the conspiracy charged rather than an unrelated other act.

United States v. Brownlee, 890 F.2d 1036 (8th Cir. 1989): In affirming convictions for fraud offenses involving stolen and retitled automobiles, the Court held that proof the defendant used a false address when applying for a title to a stolen car was not other crimes evidence, but proof of part of the fraudulent scheme.

United States v. Soliman, 813 F.2d 277 (9th Cir. 1987): The Court upheld a conviction arising out of a scheme to forge death certificates and collect insurance proceeds, finding that a summary chart of 102 fraudulent insurance claims was direct evidence of the scheme alleged and not "other crimes" evidence. See also *United States v. Vaccaro,* 816 F.2d 443 (9th Cir.), *cert. denied,* 108 S. Ct. 262, 295 (1987) (evidence of specific uncharged jackpot cheating incidents was properly admitted to prove the conspiracy charged, i.e., to rig jackpots in hotels and casinos).

United States v. Roylance, 690 F.2d 164 (10th Cir. 1982): Affirming mail and securities fraud convictions, the Court found that evidence that certain investors were defrauded in intrastate transactions was admissible to prove the very scheme that the government alleged was also taking place in interstate transactions.

Acts charged — racketeering enterprise

United States v. Flynn, 852 F.2d 1045 (8th Cir.), *cert. denied,* 109 S. Ct. 511 (1988): In a racketeering case, the Court upheld the admission of evidence concerning the defendant's acts of retaliation against a family, since it demonstrated his relationship to the enterprise. It concluded, however, that discussions among members of the enterprise concerning contemplated murders was unduly prejudicial, and that "[t]he RICO statute has a tremendous potential for guilt by association." Error in admitting the evidence was harmless, however.

United States v. Rubio, 727 F.2d 786 (9th Cir. 1983, *amended* 1984): The Court affirmed a racketeering conviction, finding no error in the admission of evidence concerning the defendant's prior narcotics conviction despite the defense's stipulation concerning the conviction. The Court distinguished convictions used for impeachment purposes under Rule 609 and other crimes offered under Rule 404(b). Details concerning convictions used for impeachment rarely may be proved, but details concerning other crimes may be important — e.g., to prove a pattern of racketeering. The Court also found that evidence that the defendant possessed firearms in addition to those charged in the indictment was properly admitted, since the firearms were relevant to show involvement in the narcotics trade.

United States v. Finestone, 816 F.2d 583 (11th Cir.), *cert. denied,* 108 S. Ct. 338 (1987): The Court held that evidence of an execution-style murder was properly admitted in proving a pattern of racketeering activity.

Acts relevant to victim's state of mind

United States v. Miller, 895 F.2d 1431 (D.C. Cir.), *cert. denied*, 111 S. Ct. 79 (1990): The Court affirmed a conviction for bank fraud, holding it was error (but harmless) to admit a witness' testimony as to her knowledge that the defendant had recently been released from jail, ostensibly to show her innocent motivation in agreeing to cash a forged check for him, because her state of mind had not been made relevant in the case, and any probative value was greatly outweighed by the prejudicial effect.

United States v. DeVincent, 546 F.2d 452 (1st Cir. 1976), *cert. denied*, 431 U.S. 903 (1977): The Court, affirming loansharking convictions, held it was proper to allow testimony on the appellant's twenty-year-old conviction for armed robbery and his ten-year-old murder indictment. The evidence was not admitted to show that the appellant was a bad man, but to show that the debtor understood that any default on the loan would be punished with violence. The Court stated that it had "qualms still, for this testimony was remote and cumulative.... But the [trial] court, under these circumstances, may have reasoned that the testimony making these matters remote and cumulative also reduced their prejudicial impact."

United States v. Gigante, 729 F.2d 78 (2d Cir.), *cert. denied*, 104 S. Ct. 2390 (1984): The Court held that evidence that the debtor believed a loanshark had organized crime connections, and evidence of other credit transactions, was admissible to show the reasonableness of the debtor's fears.

United States v. Hattaway, 740 F.2d 1419 (7th Cir.), *cert. denied*, 105 S. Ct. 448, 599 (1984): The Court, upholding kidnapping convictions, found that evidence of the lifestyle of a motorcycle gang that held the woman victim was properly admitted to show how she was intimidated into remaining with the gang. See also *United States v. Blackwood*, 768 F.2d 131 (7th Cir.), *cert. denied*, 474 U.S 1020 (1985) (statements by judge concerning defendant's admission of past acts admissible in extortion case to prove why victim would believe that defendant was in position to exercise official power).

Appellate review

United States v. Gessa, 971 F.2d 1257 (6th Cir. 1992) (en banc): The Court said that it would apply a clearly erroneous standard of review to the factual determinations required by the Rule and an abuse-of-discretion standard to the required balancing of probative value and prejudicial effect, and held that evidence of other crimes was properly admitted in this case.

United States v. Beasley, 809 F.2d 1273 (7th Cir. 1987): The Court affirmed a conviction for attempting to obtain a controlled substance by misrepresenting the name of the person to appear on prescriptions, but reversed the defendant's convictions for obtaining the substance with the intent to distribute. The Court found that evidence that the defendant had acquired and distributed other drugs was erroneously admitted, since the other acts were not similar to the scheme alleged in the instant case. The Court observed that it might be better able "to tell whether the district court and the parties took the right things into account" than to decide whether a given piece of evidence should have been admitted. The Court added that "[d]iscretion, when exercised, will rarely be disturbed.'' It found that the record failed to demonstrate that the Trial Judge adequately considered the power of the bad act evidence to impugn the defendant's character.

Arrests

United States v. McCarthur, 6 F.3d 1270 (7th Cir. 1993): The Court held it was an abuse of discretion (but harmless error) to admit evidence that the defendant, who was charged with possessing three kilos of cocaine with intent to distribute, had previously been arrested for possession of a small amount of cocaine. Where the witness knew nothing of the circumstances of the arrest or the disposition of the charge, the arrest by itself did not establish any conduct by the defendant shedding any light on her intent or absence of mistake with respect to the charged offense.

United States v. Robinson, 978 F.2d 1554 (10th Cir. 1992), *cert. denied,* 113 S. Ct. 1855, 2938 (1993): The Court held it was error (but harmless) to admit evidence that two defendants charged with possession of cocaine base had previously been arrested, as the mere fact an arrest was made is not by itself an admissible ''prior bad act.'' With respect to a third defendant, the Court upheld evidence of arrests, supported by testimony about specific drug-related acts, which was offered to prove knowledge and intent.

Background — context events

United States v. Traitz, 871 F.2d 368 (3d Cir.), *cert. denied,* 110 S. Ct. 78 (1989): The Court held uncharged acts of violence were relevant to show the background of a conspiracy.

United States v. Percy, 765 F.2d 1199 (4th Cir. 1985): The Court held that evidence of prior drug activity was properly used to prove the background of subsequent activity. In *United States v. Martin,* 773 F.2d 579 (4th Cir. 1985), the Court affirmed a conviction for tax evasion, finding that evidence of the defendant's receipt of money from various activities, including bookmaking, was properly admitted to prove unreported income.

United States v. Shaw, 701 F.2d 367 (5th Cir. 1983), *cert. denied,* 104 S. Ct. 1419 (1984): Upholding convictions for murder and other offenses, the Court found that the prosecutor properly asked the defendant whether he had been drinking prior to the offenses charged and if he had become violent when drinking. This was not an attempt to establish character, but was a proper inquiry into whether intoxicants affected the defendant's behavior on the very night in question. On a petition for rehearing, 714 F.2d 544 (5th Cir. 1983), the Court observed that the evidence was relevant to show intent and to counter a defense of accident. See also *United States v. Tafoya,* 757 F.2d 1522 (5th Cir. 1985) (evidence of defendant's assassination efforts admissible in tax prosecution to show that the defendant had earned money that he claimed was a gift).

United States v. Jordan, 722 F.2d 353 (7th Cir. 1983): The Court held it was proper to refer to the defendant's acts that caused him to be barred from an airbase, to show the background for a subsequent charge of aggravated battery upon a security officer.

Williams v. Mensey, 785 F.2d 631 (8th Cir. 1986): Affirming a judgment against a prisoner who claimed he was assaulted in jail, the Court held that evidence that the plaintiff was involved in other fights was properly admitted to show his problems with other inmates before one of the defendants allegedly labeled him a "snitch." See also *United States v. Stumes,* 549 F.2d 831 (8th Cir. 1977) (in prosecution for mailing threatening letter, proper to admit testimony that recipient previously testified against appellant in a murder trial, where letter itself suggested the prior trial, and evidence was more probative than prejudicial).

United States v. O'Connor, 737 F.2d 814 (9th Cir. 1984), *cert. denied,* 469 U.S. 1218 (1985): The Court upheld the introduction of evidence concerning an aborted narcotics venture, which showed the background of subsequent cocaine activity that was the target of a government "sting" operation. See also *United States v. Nadler,* 698 F.2d 995 (9th Cir. 1983) (evidence of previous counterfeiting operation admissible in case charging counterfeiting offense to show background of conspiracy and common scheme); *United States v. McCown,* 711 F.2d 1441 (9th Cir. 1983) (evidence concerning meetings between undercover agents and defendant admissible to put cocaine transaction in context).

United States v. Harenberg, 732 F.2d 1507 (10th Cir. 1984): In a prosecution for misappropriation of bank funds, the Court held that evidence of the defendant's handling of other funds was admissible to show how the bank's funds were typically handled and who had authority to move funds.

United States v. Leichtman, 742 F.2d 598 (11th Cir. 1984): The Court held that where a kidnapping conspiracy grew out of a marijuana transaction, marijuana evidence was not extrinsic or "other crime" evidence. See also *United States v. Williford,* 764 F.2d 1493 (11th Cir. 1985) (evidence of cocaine transaction admissible to explain events in marijuana prosecution).

Background — generally

United States v. Childs, 598 F.2d 169 (D.C. Cir. 1979): The Court upheld a conviction for obstruction of mailed matter, but warned that it did not "subscribe to the broad proposition that evidence of other offenses may be introduced simply because it recounts events temporally related to the commission of a crime for which the accused is on trial."

United States v. Boykin, 679 F.2d 1240 (8th Cir. 1982): The Court upheld cross-examination of the defendant in a mail fraud case about his dating two women at the same time, as it showed the "blind trust" of one of them, which the defendant had exploited in his scheme.

United States v. Sullivan, 919 F.2d 1403 (10th Cir. 1990): The Court reversed convictions for offenses arising out of a conspiracy to manufacture amphetamine because the Trial Judge had permitted a prosecutor to offer evidence despite rulings excluding it and had refused to grant a mistrial motion. Testimony that the arresting agents were heavily armed because of a fear that one of the defendants was acting as a sniper at the lab site, and that another defendant had previously participated in an unrelated amphetamine "cook," was more prejudicial than probative. Although the prosecutor offered the latter evidence as "part of the history of the conspiracy," he made no effort to explain its probative purpose or to connect it to the charged crimes.

United States v. Chilcote, 724 F.2d 1498 (11th Cir.), *cert. denied,* 104 S. Ct. 2665 (1984): The Court upheld cocaine convictions, even though it found error in the admission of testimony by an undercover agent that the defendant had told him he had flown a plane to Colombia. The Court said that the agent's testimony would have been completely comprehensible without mention of the defendant's statement, which was totally unrelated to the crimes charged.

Background — relationship of participants

United States v. Morris, 700 F.2d 427 (1st Cir.), *cert. denied,* 461 U.S. 947 (1983): Affirming convictions on prostitution-related charges, the Court upheld the admission of a witness' testimony that one of the defendants had broken into her apartment, abducted her, and beaten her on different occasions, to show the relationship of the witness to the defendant and the purpose behind any interstate transportation.

United States v. Brennan, 798 F.2d 581 (2d Cir. 1986): The Court affirmed bribery and corruption convictions of a former state judge, finding that evidence of the alleged fixing of cases not charged in the indictment was properly admitted to prove the background of the defendant and another person. In *United States v. Bufalino,* 683 F.2d 639 (2d Cir. 1982), *cert. denied,* 459 U.S. 1104 (1983), the Court upheld a conviction for conspiracy to violate civil rights, finding that the government was properly permitted to question the defendant about organized crime connections to show that he might have prevailed upon a member of a crime organization to commit a murder as a matter of "professional courtesy."

United States v. Simmons, 679 F.2d 1042 (3d Cir. 1982), *cert. denied,* 103 S. Ct. 3117 (1983): In a prosecution for conspiracy to negotiate forged checks, the Court held that an unindicted coconspirator's testimony concerning acts of check forging before the period charged in the indictment was properly admitted to show the coconspirator's ongoing relationship with the defendants and to explain their scheme. See also *United States v. O'Leary,* 739 F.2d 135 (3d Cir. 1984), *cert. denied,* 105 S. Ct. 782 (1985) (testimony of defendant's coconspirator about numerous earlier purchases of cocaine from defendant was properly admitted to prove background of parties and their familiarity).

United States v. Fraser, 709 F.2d 1556 (6th Cir. 1983): Affirming a conviction for assisting an escaped felon, the Court held that evidence of occasions prior to the indictment when the defendant met with the escapee were properly admitted to show their relationship. See also *United States v. Ismail,* 756 F.2d 1253 (6th Cir. 1985) (prior hashish and cocaine transactions admissible in heroin prosecution to demonstrate relationship between defendant and another man and to demonstrate a scheme to import substances).

United States v. McKinney, 954 F.2d 471 (7th Cir.), *cert. denied,* 113 S. Ct. 662 (1992): In a prosecution for murder in a prison, the government was permitted to introduce some evidence that the gang to which the defendant belonged had committed other murders. The Court held there was no abuse of discretion, as the government's theory was that the murder resulted from a gang contract; thus, how the gang operated was relevant to the charge, and the Trial Judge had been careful to limit the testimony about the gang and to preclude testimony implicating the defendant in any other murders.

See also *United States v. Potts,* 840 F.2d 368 (7th Cir. 1987) (evidence of defendant's involvement in prison drug smuggling was admissible in prosecution for conspiracy to transport and present altered postal money orders, since the smuggling involved the same network of conspirators whose interests were intertwined); *United States v. Harding,* 525 F.2d 84 (7th Cir. 1975) (defendant's sale of narcotics on one occasion in the presence of an informant used to establish reason why defendant was willing to sell drugs on another occasion).

United States v. Horvath, 731 F.2d 557 (8th Cir. 1984): The Court affirmed tax evasion convictions, finding that evidence of one defendant's participation in a drug conspiracy was properly admitted to show that he had knowledge of and involvement in the concealment of other defendants' drug income. See also *United States v. DeLuna,* 763 F.2d 897 (8th Cir.), *cert. denied,* 474 U.S. 980 (1985) (various other crimes evidence admissible in prosecution for casino skimming conspiracy to show relationship of various people and interests in the casino).

United States v. Normandeau, 800 F.2d 953 (9th Cir. 1986): The Court held that evidence that defendants who imported marijuana in motor mounts had previously imported such mounts was admissible to show their prior relationship, whether or not it involved marijuana. See also *United States v. McKoy,* 771 F.2d 1207 (9th Cir. 1985) (evidence that a defendant charged with involvement in stolen goods previously bought stolen merchandise from a codefendant was admissible to prove background).

United States v. Neal, 718 F.2d 1505 (10th Cir. 1983), *cert. denied,* 105 S. Ct. 87 (1984): Evidence of the relationship between government witness and the defendant's relatives was properly admitted to show a scheme to defraud.

United States v. Alonso, 740 F.2d 862 (11th Cir. 1984), *cert. denied,* 105 S. Ct. 928 (1985): The defendants' personal use of cocaine was relevant to show why drug suppliers accepted the defendants' aid in criminal ventures. See also *United States v. Costa,* 691 F.2d 1358 (11th Cir. 1982) (permissible in drug prosecution to show that government witness had prior relationship with defendant involving cocaine where the evidence was "an integral and natural part" of the circumstances to which the witness testified); *United States v. Duff,* 707 F.2d 1315 (11th Cir. 1983) (admission of testimony that defendant and codefendant planned to take a trip together properly admitted in conspiracy and mail fraud prosecution to show their relationship).

Balancing — discretion to admit

United States v. Kramer, 955 F.2d 479 (7th Cir. 1992), *cert. denied,* 113 S. Ct. 595 (1993): Affirming convictions for conspiring to distribute marijuana as part of a continuing criminal enterprise that imported marijuana, the Court held that the Trial Judge exercised principled discretion in admitting evidence that one of the defendants had imported fifteen tons of marijuana in 1981, as the evidence showed specific intent, was not too remote to be relevant, and its prejudicial effect, if any, did not substantially outweigh its probative value. One Judge, concurring, expressed concern that the Circuit's rule that intent is "necessarily in issue" when a defendant is charged with a specific-intent crime had resulted in a great deal of prejudicial extrinsic evidence finding its way into many criminal trials. In *United States v. Chaverra-Cardona,* 879 F.2d 1551 (7th Cir.

1989), the Trial Judge properly admitted evidence of the underlying drug case and of the defendant's drug trafficking and finances to show motive, intent, and opportunity to carry out a charged conspiracy to murder a government attorney and a government witness. The Court held that details of most of the other acts were highly probative on those issues, so the value of the evidence was not significantly outweighed by the prejudicial effect of the image created of Colombian drug dealers; some of the minute details elicited regarding the investigation were not probative of the issues, but neither were they prejudicial.

United States v. Meester, 762 F.2d 867 (11th Cir.), *cert. denied,* 474 U.S. 1024 (1985): Affirming drug conspiracy convictions, the Court held there was no error in admitting evidence that certain conspirators killed a pilot who refused to return an airplane until he was paid, as the evidence tended to show a continuing conspiracy. In *United States v. Terebecki,* 692 F.2d 1345 (11th Cir. 1982), the Court affirmed a conviction for aiding and abetting wire fraud, finding no error in the admission of evidence concerning a questionable transaction that occurred some fifteen months after the charged fraud. The Court found that the testimony of a participant in the later transaction was enough for the jury to find that it actually occurred and held that the Trial Judge's decision to admit such evidence despite a claim of unfair prejudice under Rule 403 "will not be disturbed on appeal absent a clear showing of an abuse of discretion." See also *United States v. Messersmith,* 692 F.2d 1315 (11th Cir. 1982) (upholding, despite Rule 403 challenge, admission of evidence that defendant charged with unlawful possession and importation with intent to distribute methaqualone previously went out of the country to smuggle quaaludes).

Balancing — error to admit

United States v. Miller, 895 F.2d 1431 (D.C. Cir.), *cert. denied,* 111 S. Ct. 79 (1990): The Court affirmed a conviction for bank fraud, holding it was error (but harmless) to admit a witness' testimony as to her knowledge that the defendant had recently been released from jail, ostensibly to show her innocent motivation in agreeing to cash a forged check for him, because her state of mind had not been made relevant in the case, and any probative value was greatly outweighed by the prejudicial effect. In *United States v. James,* 555 F.2d 992 (D.C. Cir. 1977), the Court reversed a conviction for possession of heroin with intent to distribute on the ground that evidence of an arrest sixteen days before the charged offense was improperly admitted. After rejecting the argument that the defense opened the door to the evidence, the Court found that the probative value of the arrest, if offered on the issue of intent, was very weak, and in view of its lurid details, concluded that "we perceive no balance on which it properly could have been admitted."

United States v. Karas, 950 F.2d 31 (1st Cir. 1991): The Court held it was an abuse of discretion (but harmless) to admit evidence of the defendant's prior participation in a cocaine conspiracy during his trial on marijuana conspiracy charges. Where the defendant did not testify or put in any evidence, statements by defense counsel in the opening could not be the basis for admitting Rule 404(b) evidence on intent or knowledge regarding joining a conspiracy. The Court reversed a conviction for assault on a flight attendant in

Balancing — error to admit (cont'd)

United States v. Cortijo-Diaz, 875 F.2d 13 (1st Cir. 1989), finding that evidence of the defendant's earlier robbery conviction was likely to be used as propensity evidence and was not properly admitted under Rule 404(b). In *United States v. Ferreira,* 821 F.2d 1 (1st Cir. 1987), the Court reversed a bank robbery conviction, finding that it was not harmless error to admit evidence concerning weapons seized from the defendant upon his arrest. The evidence of firearms was irrelevant in a prosecution for an unarmed robbery in which there was no evidence that the defendant had a gun at the time of the robbery. In *United States v. Currier,* 821 F.2d 52 (1st Cir. 1987), a prosecution of a defendant for unlawful possession of a firearm, the Court found error (albeit harmless) in the admission of portions of a tape recording in which the defendant offered to sell Valium. The Court found that the prejudicial effect of the evidence outweighed its probative value.

United States v. Schwartz, 790 F.2d 1059 (3d Cir. 1986): The Court overturned a conviction for cocaine distribution because the Trial Judge erroneously admitted testimony from the person found in possession of cocaine on the date charged that the defendant had supplied him with cocaine on numerous other occasions. The Court noted great uncertainty as to the reasons for the admission of the evidence. Since the defendant "offered sweeping stipulations relieving the government of the need to prove anything other than that the substance possessed ... had been obtained from the defendant," the evidence should have been excluded under Rule 403, even if it tended to prove something other than general propensity.

United States v. Hernandez, 975 F.2d 1035 (4th Cir. 1992): The Court reversed a conviction for participation in a cocaine distribution conspiracy because a cooperating witness was permitted to testify during the government's direct case that the defendant had told him she had a special recipe for cooking crack because she "used to do that, sell that in New York." The relevance of the evidence to show intent was at best slight. The evidence was not necessary to show the context of the crime, and it was barely reliable. The Court held that, in any event, the balance of probative value and prejudicial effect was so one-sided that admission of the evidence was error. In *United States v. Melia,* 691 F.2d 672 (4th Cir. 1982), the Court found it was an abuse of discretion in a prosecution for receipt of stolen property to admit testimony that a government witness had been to the defendant's house on other occasions for illegal purposes. The Court emphasized that even though the defendant was tried for a "specific intent" crime, the other crime evidence offered against him was insufficiently probative to warrant admission in light of its prejudicial impact.

United States v. Hays, 872 F.2d 582 (5th Cir. 1989): In a prosecution for misapplication of savings and loan funds, the Court held that prejudicial error was committed when the government was permitted to introduce evidence concerning one defendant's allegedly improper activities during a time he was attempting to secure sufficient deposits to permit continued operation of another, provisionally chartered savings and loan association. The Court concluded that the evidence was cumulative, inflammatory and unduly prejudicial, and that it represented an effort to attack the character of the defendants. In *United States v. Fortenberry,* 860 F.2d 628 (5th Cir. 1988), the Court reversed convictions for offenses allegedly committed when the defendant placed a small explosive device on a car belonging to his ex-wife's father. It concluded that evidence of a series of attacks against the ex-wife, her attorney, her father, and others was improperly admitted for several reasons: The evidence concerned highly prejudicial acts, the government had no evidence that the defendant committed the acts, there was not even evidence that all were committed by the same person, and the so-called pattern did not appear to prove any fact in dispute in light of the defendant's concession of motive and opportunity to commit the charged crimes. In *United States v. Nichols,* 781 F.2d 483 (5th Cir. 1986), the defendant had previously been tried and convicted of two conspiracies arising out of the charged cocaine trafficking, and the Trial Judge admitted the conviction as evidence of intent and identity. The Court reversed, reasoning that "these convictions told the jury that Nichols had been found guilty of conspiring to commit the very crimes for which he was then on trial. The highly prejudicial nature of such evidence substantially outweighed its probative value for intent and identity." In *United States v. Shavers,* 615 F.2d 266 (5th Cir. 1980), an assault with a deadly weapon case, the Court found an abuse of discretion in the admission of ambiguous evidence regarding a prior act — making an arguably threatening statement while using a knife to slice a grapefruit — which "permitted the jury to infer that Shavers is a violent person with a propensity to use knives against people."

United States v. Zelinka, 862 F.2d 92 (6th Cir. 1988): The Court found an abuse of discretion in the admission of evidence that the defendant possessed cocaine at the time he was arrested, since the indictment charged a conspiracy that took place seventeen months earlier. The Court faulted the Trial Judge for not requiring the prosecutor to show the relevance of the evidence and the need for its use.

United States v. Beasley, 809 F.2d 1273 (7th Cir. 1987): The Court affirmed a conviction for attempting to obtain a controlled substance by misrepresenting the name of the person to appear on prescriptions, but reversed the defendant's convictions for obtaining the substance with the intent to distribute. The Court found that evidence that the defendant had acquired and distributed other drugs was erroneously admitted, since the other acts were not similar to the scheme alleged in the instant case. The Court observed that "[a]lmost any bad act evidence simultaneously condemns by besmirching character and by showing one or more" of the items listed in Rule 404(b). Therefore,

> [t]he district judge must both identify the exception that applies to the evidence in question and evaluate whether the evidence, although relevant and within the exception, is sufficiently probative to make tolerable the risk that jurors will act on the basis of emotion or an inference via the blackening of the defendant's character.

Adding that "[d]iscretion, when exercised, will rarely be disturbed," the Court found that the record failed to demonstrate that the Trial Judge adequately considered the power of the bad act evidence to impugn the defendant's character. See also *United States v. Hudson,* 843 F.2d 1062 (7th Cir. 1988) (convictions for entering a credit union with the intent to commit larceny reversed because some evidence of other crimes should not have been admitted; the Court noted that the Trial Judge did not engage in a careful on-the-record balancing of the relevant factors).

United States v. Harvey, 845 F.2d 760 (8th Cir. 1988): The Court reversed a conviction for avoiding payment of taxes relating to the sale of an airplane because the

Balancing — error to admit (cont'd)

government introduced evidence that ten years earlier the defendant made large sums of money from drug transactions. The Court criticized the Trial Judge's "laundry list" approach to admissibility, "which merely restates the components of the rule," and stated that "the district court should specify which components of the rule form the basis of its ruling and why." The Court added that federal prosecutors should never have offered this other crime evidence. In *United States v. Flynn,* 852 F.2d 1045 (8th Cir.), *cert. denied,* 109 S. Ct. 511 (1988), a racketeering case, the Court upheld the admission of evidence concerning the defendant's acts of retaliation against a family, since it demonstrated his relationship to the enterprise. It concluded, however, that discussions among members of the enterprise concerning contemplated murders was unduly prejudicial, and that "[t]he RICO statute has a tremendous potential for guilt by association." Error in admitting the evidence was harmless, however.

United States v. Robertson, 15 F.3d 862 (9th Cir.), *cert. granted,* 115 S. Ct. __ (1994): The Court held it was error (but harmless) to admit evidence that a drug dealer who had been trying to collect a debt from the defendant was never seen again after a car similar to the defendant's was observed at the drug dealer's house. The evidence, as well as evidence of the defendant's drug use and spousal abuse, did not tend to prove any material element of the cocaine distribution and RICO offenses charged. One Judge, specially concurring, noted that reversal might have been warranted in a closer case and that prosecutors should "focus their attention more carefully on prosecuting the defendant under charges appropriate to his crimes, and on distinguishing legitimate substantive evidence from evidence of bad acts that serves principally to prejudice the jurors." In *United States v. Bradley,* 5 F.3d 1317 (9th Cir. 1993), the Court reversed the defendants' convictions for conspiring and attempting to kill a witness scheduled to testify against one of their associates. Evidence of their involvement in another murder plot (in which a homicide actually occurred, although the wrong man was killed) had little probative value because the evidence connecting them with that murder was vague, the motivations in the two cases were dissimilar, and the evidence implicating their associate in the homicide was so weak that the testimony did little to advance the jurors' knowledge of the crucial relationship between the defendants and the associate. At the same time, the evidence was highly and unfairly prejudicial, especially in suggesting that the defendants were incompetent hired guns who could not even kill the right person. In *United States v. Brooke,* 4 F.3d 1480 (9th Cir. 1993), a conviction for offenses arising out of a pipe bombing was reversed for improper admission of evidence that the defendant had falsely claimed to friends to be suffering from terminal cancer. Extrinsic evidence was inadmissible to impeach the defendant's credibility, and any probative value the evidence had to show her efforts to gain help in disrupting the victim's relationship with the defendant's former boyfriend was substantially outweighed by the prejudicial effect of inducing resentment against one feigning cancer. In *United States v. Hill,* 953 F.2d 452 (9th Cir. 1991), a conviction for conspiracy to distribute cocaine was reversed because a coconspirator had been permitted to testify to having used cocaine with the defendant five years previously. The Court held that the evidence was not probative of the background and development of, nor inextricably intertwined with, the conspiracy. Although it might have been relevant to the defendant's knowledge and intent, when admitted as direct evidence of the conspiracy it was given more weight than it deserved and its prejudicial and confusing effect substantially outweighed its probative value. See also *United States v. Hodges,* 770 F.2d 1475 (9th Cir. 1985) (reversing a conviction for conspiracy to defraud lending institutions; evidence that approximately five months after the last alleged act of the conspiracy the defendant attempted to extort money from an alleged coconspirator to paint a favorable picture of her involvement was not highly probative of his state of mind at the time of the alleged conspiracy).

United States v. Sullivan, 919 F.2d 1403 (10th Cir. 1990): The Court reversed convictions for offenses arising out of a conspiracy to manufacture amphetamine because the Trial Judge had permitted a prosecutor to offer evidence despite rulings excluding it and had refused to grant a mistrial motion. Testimony that the arresting agents were heavily armed because of a fear that one of the defendants was acting as a sniper at the lab site, and that another defendant had previously participated in an unrelated amphetamine "cook," was more prejudicial than probative. Although the prosecutor offered the latter evidence as "part of the history of the conspiracy," he made no effort to explain its probative purpose or connect it to the charged crimes. In *United States v. Soundingsides,* 819 F.2d 1529 (10th Cir. 1987), the Court reversed a murder conviction, finding, *inter alia,* that the Trial Judge erroneously admitted testimony by the defendant's former girlfriend that he frequently beat her and caused her to lose her baby. The testimony involved five-year-old events, and the Court concluded that the evidence was of little probative value. There was no real dispute that whoever killed the victim in the instant case did so with malice, and the prior act evidence was extremely prejudicial. In *United States v. Shepherd,* 739 F.2d 510 (10th Cir. 1984), a conviction for transporting an explosive and conspiracy was overturned, as the Court found that a government witness who offered testimony concerning the defendant's actions relating to the crimes should not have been permitted to testify about the defendant's prior use of explosives. The Court concluded that the jury might have been led by the prior crime evidence to overlook the fact that the accomplice's uncorroborated testimony was the only evidence linking the defendant to the crime charged and to the prior crimes.

Balancing — generally

United States v. Bradshaw, 935 F.2d 295 (D.C. Cir. 1991): Affirming a bank robbery conviction, the Court noted that admission of prior convictions where sanity is the only issue presents different considerations from the usual case. Probativeness is generally unquestionable, since the insanity defense directly puts state of mind in issue, and a prior criminal record is highly relevant to the defendant's appreciation of the unacceptability of his conduct; there is no risk of primary prejudicial effect, since the defendant does not deny commission of the act; and there is a possibility that the evidence will prove not to the government's advantage, by permitting the inference that the defendant is insane, since he continues to commit the same easily-detectable crime. Although the Trial Judge's ruling was terse, it appeared from the record as a whole that the relevant factors were considered.

United States v. Siegel, 717 F.2d 9 (2d Cir. 1983): The Court found that evidence that one defendant arranged a bribe to assure peaceful union relations was not improperly admitted in a mail and wire fraud case. An important part of the government's case was using the $30,000 bribe to prove that a secret cash fund existed. The Court reasoned that "if the jury believed that the bribe money came from the fund, the evidence was damaging to the defendants' case; this, however, is not the type of unfair prejudice against which defendants are protected by Fed. R. Evid. 403." The Court emphasized that the jury was instructed that if it did not find that a payment was made from the alleged fund, it could not consider that payment.

United States v. Beasley, 809 F.2d 1273 (7th Cir. 1987): The Court affirmed a conviction for attempting to obtain a controlled substance by misrepresenting the name of the person to appear on prescriptions, but reversed the defendant's convictions for obtaining the substance with the intent to distribute. The Court found that evidence that the defendant had acquired and distributed other drugs was erroneously admitted, since the other acts were not similar to the scheme alleged in the instant case. Although "[s]ome language in the government's brief suggests that any commission of similar crimes is the sort of 'pattern' that permits the evidence to come in," "[u]nless something more than a pattern and temporal proximity is required, the fundamental rule is gone" and "a pattern is not itself a reason to admit the evidence." The Court observed that "[a]lmost any bad act evidence simultaneously condemns by besmirching character and by showing one or more" of the items listed in Rule 404(b). Therefore,

> [t]he district judge must both identify the exception that applies to the evidence in question and evaluate whether the evidence, although relevant and within the exception, is sufficiently probative to make tolerable the risk that jurors will act on the basis of emotion or an inference via the blackening of the defendant's character.

Adding that "[d]iscretion, when exercised, will rarely be disturbed," the Court found that the record failed to demonstrate that the Trial Judge adequately considered the power of the bad act evidence to impugn the defendant's character.

United States v. Meester, 762 F.2d 867 (11th Cir.), *cert. denied,* 474 U.S. 1024 (1985): Affirming drug conspiracy convictions, the Court stated that Rule 403 must be used in a "cautious and sparing" way:

> Its major function is limited to excluding matter of scant or cumulative probative force, dragged in by the heels for the sake of its prejudicial effect.... It is not designed to permit the court to "even out" the weight of the evidence, to mitigate a crime, or to make a contest where there is little or none.

Balancing — inclusionary approach

United States v. Benedetto, 571 F.2d 1246, 1248-50 (2d Cir. 1978): The Court indicated that it favored an "inclusionary" approach toward other crimes evidence, but noted the dangers of accepting such evidence. Referring to its past decisions, the Court wrote that "we have emphasized that admission of such strongly prejudicial evidence should normally await the conclusion of the defendant's case, since the court will then be in the best position to balance the probative worth of, and the Government's need for, such testimony against the prejudice to the defendant.''

United States v. Long, 574 F.2d 761 (3d Cir.), *cert. denied,* 439 U.S. 985 (1978): The Court indicated that it followed an ''inclusionary'' approach and, while recognizing the need for balancing probative value against prejudicial effect, concluded that ''[t]he draftsmen of Rule 404(b) ... intended to emphasize admissibility of 'other crime' evidence.'' Compare *United States v. Cook,* 538 F.2d 1000 (3d Cir. 1976) (requiring a careful balancing).

Balancing — requirement of record

United States v. Lavelle, 751 F.2d 1266 (D.C. Cir.), *cert. denied,* 474 U.S. 817 (1985): The Court upheld perjury and obstruction convictions of a former Assistant Administrator of the Environmental Protection Agency as it found that evidence of prior false statements by the defendant was properly admitted to prove intent. Although the Court expressed a preference for a statement of reasons by Trial Judges when admitting other act evidence over objection, it noted that the defendant made no request that the Judge state reasons on the record.

United States v. Rawle, 845 F.2d 1244 (4th Cir. 1988): The Court affirmed a marijuana conviction, even though the Trial Judge did not identify the reason for admitting evidence of prior acts by the defendant that involved transportation of marijuana. The Court stated that ''[w]hile an explicit ruling may be preferable and may indeed aid this Court in reviewing the record,'' it would not require such a ruling in every case.

United States v. Elwood, 993 F.2d 1146 (5th Cir. 1993): The Court remanded a conviction for drug trafficking offenses with instructions to make (as the defendant had requested *in limine*) record findings regarding the probative value/prejudicial effect of other crimes evidence. This was a close case and there was nothing in the record to reflect that the Trial Judge applied the correct test for admission of the evidence. On remand, the evidence was found admissible; that finding was affirmed, 999 F.2d 814 (5th Cir. 1993). In *United States v. Zabaneh,* 837 F.2d 1249 (5th Cir. 1988), the Court remanded a drug case for a determination whether other acts of the defendant should have been admitted. It stated that in the absence of balancing on the record ''we must remand unless the factors upon which the probative value/prejudice evaluation was made were readily apparent from the record and there was no substantial uncertainty about the correctness of the ruling.''

United States v. Acosta-Cazares, 878 F.2d 945 (6th Cir.), *cert. denied,* 110 S. Ct. 255 (1989): The Court held in a cocaine conspiracy prosecution that the failure to make findings on the record was not reversible error where counsel did not request any balancing and review of the record indicated that the probative value of other acts evidence was not substantially outweighed by its potential for prejudice.

United States v. Archer, 843 F.2d 1019 (7th Cir.), *cert. denied,* 488 U.S. 837 (1988): The Court observed that it was helpful for Trial Judges to state their balancing on the record in the course of admitting or excluding Rule 404(b) evidence, but affirmed a Judge who admitted other crimes evidence to prove intent in a prosecution of a prisoner for possessing objects with intent to escape.

United States v. Evans, 697 F.2d 240 (8th Cir.), *cert. denied,* 460 U.S. 1086 (1983): The Court recognized that an explicit finding by the Trial Judge would be helpful, but it declined to require one and assumed instead that the Judge who admitted evidence applied the correct standard. In this prosecution for conspiracy to possess marijuana, evidence of a witness's prior drug-related relationship with the appellant was offered to prove the appellant's motive and intention for meeting with the witness.

United States v. Dorsey, 819 F.2d 1055 (11th Cir. 1987), *cert. denied,* 108 S. Ct. 2002 (1988): The Court affirmed marijuana-related convictions, holding that a Trial Judge is not required to engage in on-the-record balancing in ruling on the admissibility of other act evidence.

Circumstances indicating criminality

United States v. Tafoya, 757 F.2d 1522 (5th Cir. 1985): The Court held that evidence of the defendant's assassination efforts was admissible in a tax prosecution to show that he earned money that he claimed was a gift.

United States v. Wood, 834 F.2d 1382 (8th Cir. 1987): The Court upheld admission of evidence that the defendant purchased an airplane for cash to prove he was engaged in drug trafficking.

United States v. Saintil, 753 F.2d 984 (11th Cir.), *cert. denied,* 472 U.S. 1012 (1985): Evidence that defendants charged with attempted smuggling of illegal aliens had murdered, battered, and starved illegal immigrants was relevant to prove that they were in control of a smuggling vessel.

Civil cases — civil rights and employment discrimination — generally

Miller v. Poretsky, 595 F.2d 780 (D.C. Cir. 1978): Although it affirmed a judgment for the defendant in a tenant's civil rights suit, the Court concluded that it was an abuse of discretion to exclude testimony that the landlord had similarly discriminated against other black tenants. As the landlord had been permitted to offer evidence that he had not discriminated against other tenants, the tenant should have been able to rebut this evidence. Judge Robinson, concurring, emphasized that whether or not the landlord had offered evidence concerning treatment of other tenants, the tenant should have been permitted to show discrimination against others. Citing Rule 404(b), he argued that discriminatory practices have grown more subtle and "victims may find it virtually impossible to prove [discriminatory purpose] unless permitted to introduce evidence that the defendant has engaged in one or more acts of discrimination against others." Thus, the tenant's evidence should not have been excluded under Rule 403. The Court's opinion indicated that the other Judges on the panel "concur in Judge Robinson's separate opinion."

Brown v. Trustees of Boston Univ., 891 F.2d 337 (1st Cir. 1989), *cert. denied,* 110 S. Ct. 3217 (1990): In an employment discrimination action brought after the plaintiff was denied tenure, the Court held that remarks derogatory to women made by the University's president were properly admitted as evidence of a discriminatory animus in making the tenure decision.

Commonwealth of Pa. v. Porter, 659 F.2d 306 (3d Cir. 1981) (en banc), *cert. denied,* 458 U.S. 1121 (1982): In a *parens patriae* civil rights action, the Court found that events occurring more than two years prior to the filing of the suit could be offered to show a pattern or practice of violating constitutional rights.

Johnson v. Hugo's Skateway, 974 F.2d 1408 (4th Cir. 1992) (en banc): The plaintiff in a civil rights action, alleging that he had been intimidated on racial grounds at a roller skating rink, introduced a prior consent decree in which the rink agreed to post signs of a nondiscriminatory policy and to instruct employees not to discriminate, as well as evidence that the rink had not complied with the decree. The Court held there was no error in admitting the decree, as it was not offered to prove that the rink had previously discriminated and was likely to do so again but to show, through the evidence of noncompliance, the rink's motive or intent on the present occasion.

Brown v. Miller, 631 F.2d 408 (5th Cir. 1980): In a civil rights action brought by a police chief against a town mayor, the Court reversed a punitive damage award on the ground that an independent bad act of the mayor was introduced as evidence.

Conklin v. Lovely, 834 F.2d 543 (6th Cir. 1987): In a suit by a discharged employee who claimed that the discharge was the result of protected political activity, the Court held that testimony by another employee that she was told she was being terminated because of her support for a former incumbent was admissible to prove intent on the part of the defendants, whether or not the other employee was one who could be fired on the basis of political affiliation.

Hunter v. Allis-Chalmers Corp., 797 F.2d 1417 (7th Cir. 1986): Affirming a judgment for the plaintiff in an employment discrimination action the Court upheld the admission of evidence that black workers other than the plaintiff had been harassed, as it found that the other acts tended to support the claim that the employer must have known that white workers were systematically harassing black workers. See also *Harris v. Harvey,* 605 F.2d 330 (7th Cir. 1979), *cert. denied,* 445 U.S. 938 (1980) (other acts admissible to show intent in discrimination case).

Hogan v. American Tel. & Tel. Co., 812 F.2d 409 (8th Cir. 1987): The Court, affirming a judgment for an employer in an employment discrimination case, noted that evidence of past acts of discrimination may be relevant to prove intent. It added, however, that such evidence may be excluded under Rule 403; it determined that any error in excluding evidence of prior acts of discrimination was harmless in this case, since the past acts involved facts substantially different from the demotion of the plaintiff.

Spulak v. K Mart Corp., 894 F.2d 1150 (10th Cir. 1990): The Court affirmed a judgment for the plaintiff in an age discrimination case, holding that testimony of other employees about their treatment by the defendant employer was relevant to the issue of the employer's discriminatory intent and that there was no abuse of discretion in finding the relevance of the evidence was not substantially outweighed by its prejudicial effect.

McWhorter v. City of Birmingham, 906 F.2d 674 (11th Cir. 1990): In a former police officer's civil rights suit for wrongful discharge, the plaintiff offered evidence that other officers were harassed and intimidated by the defendant police chief. The Court held that there was no abuse of discretion in excluding the evidence, as its admission could have led to a series of mini-trials regarding the other officers' grievances, and it did not rise to the level of a habit of harassing officers who exercised their First Amendment rights. In *Allen v. County of Montgomery*, 788 F.2d 1485 (11th Cir. 1986), the Court overturned a judgment for the defendants in a suit by a black female employee who claimed discrimination in employment because evidence of prior discrimination, which was important in proving intent, had been erroneously excluded. In *Phillips v. Smalley Maint. Servs.*, 711 F.2d 1524 (11th Cir. 1983), the Court affirmed a judgment for an employee on a Title VII claim and two pendent state claims, finding that the Trial Judge properly admitted testimony by another former employee that the defendant had subjected her to treatment similar to that experienced by the plaintiff. The evidence was admissible to show intent, motive or plan.

Civil cases — civil rights — prisoners and arrestees

Lewis v. District of Columbia, 793 F.2d 361 (D.C. Cir. 1986): In a civil rights action by a person who was shot by an arresting officer, the Court held that evidence of the plaintiff's prior arrests and drug use was properly admitted. The arrests were probative of whether the plaintiff ran from the officer because he thought the officer was a thief or because he wanted to avoid arrest. The drug use was relevant because it might have accounted for some of the injuries that the plaintiff attributed to the shooting.

Senra v. Cunningham, 9 F.3d 168 (1st Cir. 1993): In an action against police officers for using excessive force in arresting a man at his home after his auto struck a parked car, the defendants offered evidence of having previously responded to domestic disturbances resulting from the plaintiff's drunken and violent behavior, as well as evidence of the plaintiff's previous conviction for driving while intoxicated. The Court held there was no abuse of discretion in admitting evidence of the domestic disturbances, since it shed light on the reasonableness of the officers' responses. The prior conviction had been admitted to show the plaintiff's motivation for leaving the scene, but the Court reasoned that the arrest would have been justified merely because he had departed, so the evidence was of no probative value; the error was harmless, however. In a civil rights action against police officers, *Pittsley v. Warish*, 927 F.2d 3 (1st Cir.), *cert. denied*, 112 S. Ct. 226 (1991), the Court held that evidence of a plaintiff's prior arrest on gun-possession charges of which she was acquitted was properly admissible to show her motive and bias in bringing the lawsuit in light of one of the defendants' involvement in the prior proceeding. In *Gutierrez-Rodriguez v. Cartagena*, 882 F.2d 553 (1st Cir. 1989), a civil rights action for injuries suffered when the plaintiff was shot by plainclothes police officers, the Court held that evidence of past civilian complaints against one of the officers was properly admitted only to show gross lapses in supervising and disciplining the officer by defendant superior officers and that, particularly with the limiting instructions given, the probative value of the evidence was not significantly outweighed by its prejudicial effect. In *Wierstak v. Heffernan*, 789 F.2d 968 (1st Cir. 1986), a suit for use of excessive force in an arrest, the Court held there was no error in the exclusion of evidence concerning the plaintiff's involvement in a house-break and drug transaction earlier in the day of the arrest. Although the evidence was relevant to motive, it was unduly prejudicial. In *Lataille v. Ponte,* 754 F.2d 33 (1st Cir. 1985), the Court reversed a judgment for corrections officers in an action by a plaintiff who alleged that the officers had beaten him, because evidence of the plaintiff's disciplinary record was improperly admitted to prove that the plaintiff was a violent person and, therefore, probably was the first aggressor.

Berkovich v. Hicks, 922 F.2d 1018 (2d Cir. 1991): The Court held in an arrestee's civil rights action that there was no abuse of discretion in excluding evidence of seven prior civilian complaints against a defendant police officer, where the officer had been exonerated on all charges in six of the complaints and the seventh only involved using abusive language. In *O'Neill v. Krzeminski,* 839 F.2d 9 (2d Cir. 1988), the Court affirmed a finding that police officers used excessive force against an arrestee, but divided on the question whether a prior judgment against one officer for use of excessive force a month earlier should have been admitted. One Judge opined that the judgment was admissible to prove an aggravated state of mind, another opined that it was inadmissible but harmless, and the third found that it was harmless and did not offer an opinion on admissibility. Oddly, the Court focused only on Rule 404(b) and did not consider whether the judgment was inadmissible hearsay under Rule 803(22).

Carson v. Polley, 689 F.2d 562 (5th Cir. 1982): The Court reversed a judgment in favor of a sheriff and four deputies who allegedly used excessive force in making an arrest. It found error in the exclusion of a sheriff's department performance evaluation report on one deputy that stated that the deputy tended to get into arguments with inmates and let his temper flare up quickly. According to the Court, the report should have been admitted under Rule 404(b) to show the deputy's intent. In our view, this evidence was more akin to character evidence than to specific conduct that might tend to show intent. Thus it was properly excluded, although it might have been admitted to show that the sheriff was on notice of a problem regarding this deputy.

Wilson v. City of Chicago, 6 F.3d 1233 (7th Cir. 1993), *cert. denied,* 114 S. Ct. 1844 (1994): The plaintiff, who had shot and killed two policemen, sued, alleging police had tortured him in extracting a confession. Reversing a judgment for the individual defendants, the Court held that it was an abuse of discretion to exclude evidence that the officers had tortured two other suspects, since the other incidents tended to prove, *inter alia,* the defendants' intent and opportunity. In *Young v. Rabideau,* 821 F.2d 373 (7th Cir.), *cert. denied,* 108 S. Ct. 263 (1987), the Court affirmed a judgment for corrections officers sued for allegedly using excessive force against an inmate. The Court held that evidence of the inmate's disciplinary history was admissible to rebut the inmate's contention that he did not intend to poke an officer in the face or snatch a chain from the officer's hand. It also noted that past misconduct of the inmate, as reflected in his disciplinary history, was not admissible to show "bias" against authority, since this type of bias is too likely to be used as propensity evidence. In *Harris v. Davis,* 874 F.2d 461 (7th Cir. 1989), *cert. denied,* 493 U.S. 1027 (1990), the Court found it was error in a suit by a prisoner who alleged cruel and unusual punishment with respect to medical treatment to admit photographs of the prisoner that depicted him in suggestive poses and to admit evidence (ostensibly offered to show an alternative source of his injuries) concerning discipline for possession of moonshine. Two of the Judges deemed the errors harmless.

Parrish v. Luckie, 963 F.2d 201 (8th Cir. 1992): In a civil rights action by a woman claiming she had been falsely arrested and sexually assaulted by a police officer, the Court held that evidence of the officer's prior violent behavior was properly admitted as relevant to the police chief's knowledge of the officer's violent propensities. In *Tyler v. White*, 811 F.2d 1204 (8th Cir. 1987), a suit by prisoners alleging that guards injured them, the Court held that cross-examination of a defendant guard concerning his carrying brass knuckles after the incident was properly barred as calling for inadmissible character evidence. In *Lewis v. Sheriff's Dep't*, 817 F.2d 465 (8th Cir.), *cert. denied*, 108 S. Ct. 298 (1987), the Court held that defendants should not have been permitted to cross-examine the plaintiff concerning a prior fight with a deputy sheriff. The evidence appeared relevant only to create an impression that the plaintiff had a violent disposition. The error was harmless, however.

Hirst v. Gertzen, 676 F.2d 1252 (9th Cir. 1982): In a civil rights action brought after a Native American was found hanged in a jail cell, the Court upheld the Trial Judge's ruling excluding evidence that a deputy had engaged in violent and brutal conduct toward Native Americans on previous occasions. The Court found the evidence inadequate to establish identity of the victim's killer by *modus operandi* and concluded that the Judge properly could have excluded the evidence so that it would not be improperly used as character evidence.

Civil cases — generally

Jenkins v. TDC Mgmt. Corp., 21 F.3d 436 (D.C. Cir. 1994): The Court reversed a judgment for a plaintiff who claimed that a developer fraudulently induced him to enter into an employment contract and induced him to continue work by falsely promising to pay him fully for services rendered. The Court found error in the admission of testimony by three subcontractors that the developer had failed to pay them for their work. It noted that none of the subcontractors had indicated that their disputes with the developer were unusual in the construction industry, none indicated any indicia of fraud, and their disputes were remote in time from the plaintiff's. The Court observed that the line between inadmissible character evidence and evidence sufficient to show intent or a common scheme is imprecise, but reasoned that "when one must, in order to find similarity, define the character of the acts at such a high level of generality as here (greed, strategic behavior), and many of the events occur years after the conduct in dispute, we cannot find the conditions of admissibility under Rule 404(b) satisfied." In *Hemphill v. Washington Metro. Area Transit Auth.*, 982 F.2d 572 (D.C. Cir. 1993), the Court, in three separate opinions, held that a judgment for a defendant in an automobile accident case must be reversed, because the Magistrate Judge erroneously instructed the jury that it could consider whether the plaintiff, whose prior accidents were admitted as relevant to the cause of her injuries, "was merely unlucky or whether or not she is claims minded." The Magistrate Judge instructed the jury that it was entitled to take into consideration that it is unusual for a person not engaged in a hazardous activity to suffer negligent injuries within a short period of time at the hands of different persons. The Court unanimously agreed that when no charge of fabrication is made, it is improper to permit a jury to infer that a plaintiff is claims minded. In *Faison v. Nationwide Mtg.*

Corp., 839 F.2d 680 (D.C. Cir. 1987), *cert. denied,* 109 S. Ct. 70 (1988), a suit by debtors against, *inter alia,* a settlement attorney to recover for the loss of a home alleged to have resulted from fraud, the Court found error in the admission of prior acts involving members of the defendant's law firm, which were not clearly tied to the defendant. The error was harmless, however.

Veranda Beach Club L.P. v. Western Sur. Co., 936 F.2d 1364 (1st Cir. 1991): In an action by a partnership after its contract to purchase a resort fell through because of forgery by the defendant surety company's independent authorized agent, the Court held that evidence the agent's license had previously been suspended and that the defendant knew of the suspension was properly admitted under the Rule. Details of the event, including the fact that it arose from the agent's similar forgery, were properly excluded, as they would not have tended to show the agent's apparent authority or any other relevant fact. In *Doty v. Sewall,* 908 F.2d 1053 (1st Cir. 1990), an action by a union member alleging mistreatment by local union officials, the Court held there was no abuse of discretion in admitting evidence that other locals mistreated their members who were associated with the plaintiff, as the fact that the other locals' actions were communicated to the defendants might have had a tendency to show that mistreatment of the plaintiff was motivated by a desire to suppress dissent in the union. In *Jay Edwards, Inc. v. New England Toyota Distrib.,* 708 F.2d 814 (1st Cir.), *cert. denied,* 104 S. Ct. 241 (1983), an automobile dealership sued its distributor claiming that the distributor engaged in several bad faith actions against it. The Court found that evidence that the distributor engaged in harsh treatment against other dealers who had joined the plaintiff in forming an "Alliance" was properly admitted: "By suggesting a pattern of retaliatory practices against Alliance members, it was probative of NET's motive and intent, and its possible bad faith, in dealings with Edwards."

United States Football League v. National Football League, 842 F.2d 1335 (2d Cir. 1988): The Court affirmed a judgment awarding the plaintiff $1 in an antitrust action, holding that prior antitrust judgments against the defendant were properly excluded pursuant to Rule 403, even though "[p]rior antitrust violations and the history of competition in a market may, in appropriate cases, be admissible to establish market power and intent to monopolize." See also *Merrill Lynch Futures, Inc. v. Kelly,* 585 F. Supp. 1245 (S.D.N.Y. 1984) (evidence that two defendants conspired to foist upon the plaintiff a securities trade that it did not order was relied on as other act evidence tending to prove an alleged fraud in the execution of certain commodities sales).

Rothberg v. Bosenbloom, 771 F.2d 818 (3d Cir. 1985): In an action on promissory notes, the Court held that evidence concerning four other joint ventures was properly admitted since the defendants claimed an *in pari delicto* defense and the evidence was relevant to show knowledge and absence of mistake.

Mosser v. Fruehauf Corp., 940 F.2d 77 (4th Cir. 1991): In a product liability wrongful death action brought after a tractor-trailer overturned, the defendant offered the driver-decedent's personnel file, which showed that he had received citations for speeding, as evidence of habit or as proof of intent. The Court held that there was no error in declining to admit traffic citations unrelated to the incident in question against a dead man unable to defend himself. In *Morley v. Cohen,* 888 F.2d 1006 (4th Cir. 1989), a civil RICO action arising out of an allegedly fraudulent tax shelter, the Court held there had been no abuse of discretion in admitting evidence of the defendant's other business dealings, which were probative on the issue of intent.

Jones v. Southern Pac. R.R., 962 F.2d 447 (5th Cir. 1992): The Court held there was no error in excluding evidence of the defendant's engineer's prior safety infractions in a personal injury action arising out of a truck-train collision, as the evidence had slight probative value and would tend to distract the trier of fact from the main question of what actually happened. In *Dial v. Travelers Indem. Co.,* 780 F.2d 520 (5th Cir. 1986), the Court affirmed a judgment against insureds suing to collect on a fire insurance policy on their house. It upheld admission of evidence that the plaintiffs had been burned out of their previous home and that after the fire in this case two properties they occupied had burned. The Court applied the same test it uses in criminal cases to conclude that the evidence was relevant since "the essential issue is the difference between an accident and an intended act."

Blankenship & Assocs. v. NLRB, 999 F.2d 248 (7th Cir. 1993): The Court, enforcing the NLRB's cease-and-desist order against a consultant to an employer, held that the agency did not violate Rule 404(b) in taking notice of the facts of seven prior proceedings in which the consultant was involved although not named as a party. The Court said that the use of the previous decisions was "questionable," but emphasized that the consultant did not present any reason to the agency or to it to suggest that the earlier decisions contained erroneous findings of fact. See also *Chicago Coll. of Osteopathic Medicine v. George A. Fuller Co.,* 719 F.2d 1335 (7th Cir. 1983) (although the evidence could have been admitted, there was no error in excluding under Rule 403 evidence of defendant contractor's practices on other projects in this litigation involving disputes over various aspects of construction work on a medical clinic).

King v. Ahrens, 16 F.3d 265 (8th Cir. 1994): In a medical malpractice case, the Court held there was no abuse of discretion in excluding evidence that the defendant's medical license had been suspended eight years earlier, as any probative value the evidence had on the absence of mistake in failing to note critical information on the medical chart and on the doctor's credibility was substantially outweighed by its prejudicial effect, given the remoteness in time and the dissimilarity between the incidents. In *Monger v. Cessna Aircraft Co.,* 812 F.2d 402 (8th Cir. 1987), the Court affirmed a judgment for an aircraft manufacturer in a wrongful death case, holding that evidence of prior accidents is not admissible to prove that a party is accident prone and therefore likely to have been at fault. It also held that a letter from the FAA to the manufacturer reciting prior misconduct and containing a warning was properly excluded where it was unclear whether the letter related to the fuel system at issue in the case. In *Coast-to-Coast Stores, Inc. v. Womack-Bowers, Inc.,* 818 F.2d 1398 (8th Cir. 1987), the Court found no error in the exclusion of testimony by other franchise owners concerning complaints that were different in kind from those of franchisees involved in the instant suit. In *Jordan v. Clayton Brokerage Co.,* 861 F.2d 172 (8th Cir. 1988), *vacated on other grounds,* 499 U.S. 914 (1991), the Court affirmed a judgment for a commodities investor who sued his brokerage company. It held that evidence of a larger plan pursued by a trader for the company was properly admitted to show knowledge and absence of mistake on the part of the company. See also *Austin v. Loftsgaarden,* 675 F.2d 168 (8th

Cir. 1982) (no error to admit, in a securities fraud action, evidence of a prior fraud allegedly committed by the defendant, who denied any fraudulent intent).

Price v. Seydel, 961 F.2d 1470 (9th Cir. 1992): In a fraud action by the purchaser of a hotel, the plaintiff attempted to show that the defendant kept two sets of books, one accurate and the other showing greater income in order to induce purchase of the property. The Magistrate Judge excluded evidence of the first set, presuming they were kept for the purpose of defrauding the IRS, as impermissible evidence of other fraud. Reversing on other grounds, the Court noted that exclusion may well have been an abuse of discretion because the evidence was the linchpin of the plaintiff's misrepresentation theory.

Turley v. State Farm Mut. Auto. Ins. Co., 944 F.2d 669 (10th Cir. 1991): The Court reversed a judgment for the owner of an allegedly stolen automobile against the insurer following denial of coverage for damage to the car, holding it was error to exclude evidence offered by the defendant that the plaintiff and his coinsured had previously conspired to fake "slip-and-fall" accidents. The evidence was probative of whether the coinsured had an intent to defraud and whether there was collusion on the part of the plaintiff.

Hill v. Bache Halsey Stuart Shields Inc., 790 F.2d 817 (10th Cir. 1986): Reversing a judgment for a customer against a commodities futures broker, the Court held it was an abuse of discretion to exclude evidence of the plaintiff's trading five months after he closed his account with the defendant. The trading was similar to that done with the defendant, and the Court found that it was highly probative on the issue of whether the plaintiff authorized trades by the defendant. In *Bradbury v. Phillips Petroleum Co.,* 815 F.2d 1356 (10th Cir. 1987), the Court affirmed judgments for plaintiffs who sued a mineral exploration company for trespass, assault, and outrageous conduct. It found that evidence of other incidents in which the defendant trespassed or destroyed property was admissible to prove recklessness and to negate any claim of accident of mistake. Although the other incidents did not involve the same types of injuries as the plaintiffs alleged, they involved the same area, the same time period, and similar conduct.

Glados, Inc. v. Reliance Ins. Co., 888 F.2d 1309 (11th Cir. 1987, *modified,* 1989), *cert. denied,* 110 S. Ct. 3273 (1990): In an action by a restaurant owner on a fire insurance policy, the plaintiff attempted to rebut an arson defense by evidence that the prior owner had retained an interest as an insured party, and by showing similar fires at two other restaurants in which the prior owner had also retained a similar interest. The Court held that this evidence was properly admitted as relevant to whether the third party had a motive to set the fire.

Common plan or scheme

United States v. Lewis, 693 F.2d 189 (D.C. Cir. 1982): The Court upheld convictions on twenty counts of transporting forged securities, finding that evidence of other acts was properly admitted to prove a scheme.

United States v. Lau, 828 F.2d 871 (1st Cir. 1987), *cert. denied,* 108 S. Ct. 1729 (1988): The Court held that evidence of the defendants' prior importation of cocaine was admissible to establish ownership of a plane and a common scheme. In *United States v.*

Cepulonis, 530 F.2d 238 (1st Cir.), *cert. denied,* 426 U.S. 908, 922 (1976), the Court affirmed bank robbery convictions, upholding the admission of testimony that, in the course of their getaway after the robbery, the defendants fired at a police officer and a passing motorist, and of evidence of a shotgun not used in the robbery. The evidence was not admitted to show that the defendants were bad men, but to show that their plan was to distract the police by firing and that they had assembled weapons to be available for the task.

United States v. Levy, 865 F.2d 551 (3d Cir. 1989): The Court held that the use of a false passport was properly admitted to show common plan in a heroin distribution case.

United States v. Billups, 692 F.2d 320 (4th Cir. 1982), *cert. denied,* 104 S. Ct. 84 (1983): The Court affirmed convictions for violating the Hobbs Act, the Travel Act, and two criminal provisions in the Taft-Hartley Act. It found that evidence that the defendant had received other payoffs, which had been the subjects of counts dismissed by the Trial Judge, was admissible to show a common plan or scheme.

United States v. Krezdorn, 639 F.2d 1327 (5th Cir. 1981), *cert. denied,* 104 S. Ct. 1416 (1984): In a forgery case the Court found reversible error in the admission of thirty-two extrinsic forgeries, since the additional forgeries did not tend to establish a plan of which the charged forgeries were a smaller part. The Court noted also the possibility that a jury would be overwhelmed by the sheer numerosity of the offenses. See also *United States v. Colvin,* 614 F.2d 44 (5th Cir.), *cert. denied,* 446 U.S. 945 (1980) (where jury could conclude that defendant was responsible for injuries previously sustained by her infant daughter, evidence of prior injuries was admissible to show a pattern of abuse).

United States v. Hill, 898 F.2d 72 (7th Cir. 1990): The defendant was charged with conspiring to manufacture marijuana after he was arrested near a marijuana garden in July 1988. The Court held that evidence he was arrested in December 1987 with six pounds of marijuana seeds was probative of his plan and intent to grow marijuana in the spring of 1988. In *United States v. Beasley,* 809 F.2d 1273 (7th Cir. 1987), the Court affirmed a conviction for attempting to obtain a controlled substance by misrepresenting the name of the person to appear on prescriptions, but reversed the defendant's convictions for obtaining the substance with the intent to distribute. The Court found that evidence that the defendant had acquired and distributed other drugs was erroneously admitted, since the other acts were not similar to the scheme alleged in the instant case. Although "[s]ome language in the government's brief suggests that any commission of similar crimes is the sort of 'pattern' that permits the evidence to come in," "[u]nless something more than a pattern and temporal proximity is required, the fundamental rule is gone" and "a pattern is not itself a reason to admit the evidence." See also *United States v. Anderson,* 809 F.2d 1281 (7th Cir. 1987) (in prosecution for offenses relating to a scheme to fix cases involving driving under the influence, the Court held that evidence of a defendant's involvement in some bribery incidents could be used to prove a common plan involving another person).

United States v. Miller, 725 F.2d 462 (8th Cir. 1984): The Court affirmed convictions for offenses arising out of a fraudulent cattle transaction, finding that a transaction not charged in the indictment was part of a scheme or plan and helped to prove the intent of the defendants to defraud. See also *United States v. Thompson,* 730 F.2d 82 (8th Cir.), *cert. denied,* 469 U.S. 1024 (1984) (defendant's admission of prior involvement in counterfeiting activity admissible to show scheme or preparation); *United States v. Nabors,* 761 F.2d 465 (8th Cir.), *cert. denied,* 474 U.S. 851 (1985) (robberies of hospital pharmacies admissible to prove design, plan, and motive in drug case); *United States v. Calvert,* 523 F.2d 895 (8th Cir. 1975), *cert. denied,* 424 U.S. 911 (1976) (common plan evidence to prove scheme to collect on life insurance).

United States v. Jackson, 845 F.2d 880 (9th Cir.), *cert. denied,* 109 S. Ct. 149 (1988): The Court held that evidence that the defendant submitted a first set of false claims concerning checks that he had received was admissible to prove the charged scheme, which involved a second set of claims relating to the checks. In *United States v. Winters,* 729 F.2d 602 (9th Cir. 1984), a prosecution for kidnapping and transporting two women for immoral purposes, the Court held that evidence of the defendant's actions toward other women was properly admitted to show his common scheme of using physical force and threats to compel women to engage in acts of prostitution.

United States v. Primrose, 718 F.2d 1484 (10th Cir. 1983), *cert. denied,* 104 S. Ct. 2352 (1984): Affirming a defendant's convictions on thirteen of thirty-eight counts of mail fraud, the Court upheld the admission of evidence concerning forty-five kickbacks not charged in the indictment. It concluded that the fact that some of the kickbacks occurred beyond the statute of limitations did not require that they be excluded, since the indictment charged a scheme that began before the thirty-eight overt acts charged and the additional kickbacks were probative of that scheme. The Court noted that the jury was instructed on the proper use of the kickback evidence whenever it was admitted. See also *Lewis v. United States,* 771 F.2d 454 (10th Cir. 1985), *cert. denied,* 474 U.S 1024 (1985) (evidence of burglary of garage store admissible in prosecution for post office burglary to prove defendant's plan); *United States v. Parnell,* 581 F.2d 1374 (10th Cir. 1978), *cert. denied,* 439 U.S. 1076 (1979) (testimony about prior check kiting scheme that was direct precursor to scheme being prosecuted was admissible as proof of motive, intent, and the continuation of a common plan).

Connecting defendant with instrumentalities or fruits of crime

United States v. Moreno, 991 F.2d 943 (1st Cir. 1993): The Court affirmed a defendant's conviction for unlawful firearms possession, holding that evidence of gunshots heard prior to his companion's arrest and the companion's possession of a pistol when arrested made it more likely that the object the defendant was seen to pass along to a third companion was the sawed-off shotgun later found nearby. The dissenting Judge believed that the evidence at most showed the defendant's presence during the commission of other crimes by other persons, which is both irrelevant and highly prejudicial. In *United States v. Walters,* 904 F.2d 765 (1st Cir. 1990), the Court held that a photograph showing the defendant holding a weapon was properly admitted in his trial for using a firearm during drug trafficking to show the connection between him and guns that had been seized. In *United States v. D'Alora,* 585 F.2d 16 (1st Cir. 1978), the Court upheld the admission of evidence that the government gave marked money to a codefendant in connection with a drug sale several days before the purchase of larger amounts of drugs that it attributed to the appellant and the codefendant, and that the appellant ended up with some of the marked bills.

United States v. Miller, 688 F.2d 652 (9th Cir. 1982): In a prosecution for theft of a trailer, the Court found no error in admitting evidence that three conveyor belts, stolen from the trailer's owner, were in the defendant's possession. The evidence tended to establish that the trailer found with the defendant was the same trailer that had been stolen. See also *United States v. Calhoun,* 604 F.2d 1216 (9th Cir. 1979) (reversible error to admit evidence of "bait bills" taken in a bank robbery different from that charged in the instant case).

Consciousness of guilt

United States v. Boyle, 675 F.2d 430 (1st Cir. 1982): In an armed bank robbery case, the Court held evidence that the defendant used an alias and had false identification cards six days after the robbery was admissible to show consciousness of guilt.

United States v. Gatto, 995 F.2d 449 (3d Cir.) (en banc), *cert. denied,* 114 S. Ct. 391 (1993): Affirming racketeering convictions, the Court held there was no abuse of discretion in permitting the prosecutor to question a witness as to whether he had seen threatening looks from a courtroom spectator and the defendant. The government contended that these looks intimidated the witness and caused him to become hostile to the government and accommodating to the defense. Although testimony that a defendant looks unhappy during trial or appears irritated at someone testifying for the government will in many instances have little probative value and may be prejudicial, in this case the defendant did not ask for a Rule 403 ruling and the Trial Judge pointed out that the defendants had an opportunity to examine the witness with respect to any gestures or looks.

United States v. Kibler, 667 F.2d 452 (4th Cir.), *cert. denied,* 456 U.S. 961 (1982): Upholding a conviction for endeavoring to intimidate a witness, the Court found that evidence of an attempt by the appellant to persuade another witness to change testimony was properly admitted.

United States v. Rocha, 916 F.2d 219 (5th Cir. 1990), *cert. denied,* 111 S. Ct. 2057 (1991): Affirming convictions for kidnapping, extortion, and conspiracy, the Court held that evidence a defendant made a death threat against a government witness during the trial was probative of his guilt and of the validity of his duress defense.

United States v. Jackson, 886 F.2d 838 (7th Cir. 1989): The defendant, who was charged with fraudulently altering money orders, was ordered to provide handwriting exemplars but refused to do so. The Trial Judge granted the defendant's motion *in limine* against introducing evidence of his refusal. Affirming, on interlocutory review, the defendant's conviction of contempt for refusing to furnish the exemplars, the Court reversed the *in limine* ruling, holding that refusal to comply with a lawful order to provide exemplars was probative of the defendant's consciousness of guilt and not likely to produce an improper emotional decision by the jury.

Conspiracy — background evidence

United States v. Echeverri, 854 F.2d 638 (3d Cir. 1988): The Court held that a government witness' testimony that he had encountered the defendant one year before the charged conspiracy, when both went to a location to purchase substantial quantities of cocaine, was admissible to prove that the defendant had a source of such cocaine.

United States v. Nichols, 750 F.2d 1260 (5th Cir. 1985): Evidence of the defendants' previous involvement in transporting cocaine was admissible in a conspiracy prosecution to prove the way in which the conspiracy was established and carried out.

United States v. Passarella, 788 F.2d 377 (6th Cir. 1986): The Court affirmed counterfeiting and drug convictions, finding that testimony concerning prior drug deals was admissible to show the background and the development of the conspiracy charged.

United States v. Mora, 845 F.2d 233 (10th Cir.), *cert. denied,* 488 U.S. 995 (1988): The Court held that evidence of conspirator statements about an uncharged drug transaction one month before the charged transaction was admissible to explain how the conspiracy started. See also *United States v. Orr,* 864 F.2d 1505 (10th Cir. 1988) (evidence of other acts explained how conspiracy started).

Conspiracy — particular relevance and problems

United States v. Manner, 887 F.2d 317 (D.C. Cir. 1989), *cert. denied,* 493 U.S. 1062 (1990): The Court stated that a conspiracy charge "increases the probativeness of Rule 404(b) evidence," although it remanded for an on-the-record ruling under Rule 403. In *United States v. Moore,* 732 F.2d 983 (D.C. Cir. 1984), a majority of the Court affirmed convictions for conspiracy to sell cocaine, despite a vociferous dissent. The government's key witness, who had lived with one of the defendants, had set up a meeting for an undercover agent to purchase marijuana and cocaine. One defendant noticed that the agent's currency appeared to be marked, and no sale was actually made. The government arrested the defendants and charged them with conspiracy and a variety of substantive offenses. At trial, the witness detailed her former housemate's drug dealings. The majority found that the testimony was properly used to prove intent, especially since the defendants' theory was that the sale was a sham, not a real attempt to sell drugs, and the housemate raised an entrapment defense. The dissenting Judge observed that the witness could recall few specifics about any prior trafficking on the part of the housemate and expressed grave concern that the "vague and inferential bad acts testimony could not help but to aggravate the confusion, complexity and 'inherent dangers' that can be associated, even under the best of circumstances, with a conspiracy charge."

United States v. Tracy, 12 F.3d 1186 (2d Cir. 1993): In the prosecution of two leaders of a large drug trafficking conspiracy, the government introduced a copy of the complaint in the case that was annotated by one of the defendants with death threats against informant and agent sources of the allegations. The annotations had apparently been made after all the other conspirators had been arrested. The document was admitted against the conspirator making the annotations as evidence he had sufficient familiarity with the operation to identify the unnamed informants; the Trial Judge instructed that it was not binding on the other defendant on trial, but that acts and statements of coconspirators could be considered against any defendant in determining whether the government had proved the charges. The Court held that the annotated complaint should not have been admitted against the codefendant who did not make it because the statements were not made during and in furtherance of the conspiracy and that the instruction was insufficient to protect the codefendant from its use against him, but the error was harmless.

United States v. Dudek, 560 F.2d 1288 (6th Cir. 1977), *cert. denied,* 434 U.S. 1037 (1978): The Court upheld a ruling admitting evidence of crimes not charged in the indictment to show the appellant's intent. The Court suggested that in conspiracy cases, other crimes evidence might be "particularly probative" to show a system of criminal activity.

United States v. Grabiec, 563 F.2d 313 (7th Cir. 1977): In a prosecution for conspiracy to extort money under color of official right, the government offered evidence that on four other occasions the appellant's coconspirator accepted money in exchange for providing state licenses. The majority held that two of the occasions fell within the conspiracy charged, that the other two were properly admitted as a part of a pattern of conduct, and that instructions to the jury that the evidence of the four other occasions was admissible only to show the coconspirator's intent and was not to be used against the appellant were adequate. The dissenting Judge emphasized that there was no evidence that the appellant was involved on the other occasions or that they related in any way to the conduct that was at the heart of the charged conspiracy, that the evidence was not really probative on the intent issue, and that jury instructions in a conspiracy case were of little value.

United States v. Bronco, 597 F.2d 1300 (9th Cir. 1979): The Court reversed convictions of conspiracy to sell and possession and passing of counterfeit money, finding error in the refusal to grant a severance so that the conspiracy charge would be tried separately. The Court was concerned that evidence that the appellant was a violent man, admitted on the conspiracy charge, might have prejudiced the jury on the other charges.

United States v. Gamble, 541 F.2d 873 (10th Cir. 1976): The Court approved the introduction of other crimes evidence in a criminal prosecution, noting that "[s]uch evidence is particularly relevant in a conspiracy case."

United States v. Glen-Archila, 677 F.2d 809 (11th Cir.), *cert. denied,* 459 U.S. 874 (1982): Glen-Archila was a crew member of a ship found by the Coast Guard to be carrying marijuana in 1979. At his conspiracy trial, the government introduced evidence that he had been aboard a ship that the Coast Guard found carrying marijuana in 1976. According to the Court, "the government often has [difficulty] in proving intent in conspiracy cases," so there was no error in admitting the evidence. We question whether this balance gave sufficient weight to the possibility that a jury would misuse the evidence as character evidence.

Corroboration

United States v. Figueroa, 976 F.2d 1446 (1st Cir. 1992), *cert. denied,* 113 S. Ct. 1346 (1993): The Court held that evidence tending to show welfare fraud by defendants in a drug case was properly admitted as direct corroboration of significant conspiracy-related conversations with an informant.

United States v. Everett, 825 F.2d 658 (2d Cir. 1987), *cert. denied,* 108 S. Ct. 1035 (1988): Although the Court affirmed bank robbery convictions and the admission of testimony concerning a prior robbery, it indicated that when other crimes evidence is admitted for corroborative purposes, the corroboration must be "direct" and the matter corroborated must be "significant." In *United States v. Williams,* 577 F.2d 188 (2d Cir.), *cert. denied,* 439 U.S. 868 (1978), the Court affirmed a conviction for conspiracy to commit bank larceny, observing that other crimes evidence could be admitted to directly corroborate a significant matter in a case.

United States v. Hans, 738 F.2d 88 (3d Cir. 1984): The Court held that evidence seized from one codefendant was admissible against another, where the evidence corroborated a government witness' testimony about how the bank robbery occurred.

Foundation for other acts

Huddleston v. United States, 108 S. Ct. 1496 (1988): This important Supreme Court case holds that evidence offered under Rule 404(b) is to be assessed under Rule 104(b), the conditional relevance rule. The Court noted that the defendant was to be protected against undue prejudice according to Rule 403, not by the Trial Judge's application of a preponderance or clear and convincing standard under Rule 104. The case is discussed in the Editorial Explanatory Comment, *supra.*

United States v. Gilan, 967 F.2d 776 (2d Cir. 1992): The Court reversed a conviction for conspiring to steal a shipment of shoes, holding it was error to admit evidence of an earlier similar theft because there was no evidence linking the defendant to the earlier theft.

United States v. Kenny, 973 F.2d 339 (4th Cir. 1992): In a prosecution for obstructing a grand jury investigation, the Court held that testimony that a significant piece of paper had been taken in a burglary of a witness' apartment shortly after she appeared before the grand jury was not admissible under the Rule, as there was no evidence connecting the defendant to the break-in. The testimony was relevant and admissible, however, to explain the absence of the piece of paper at the trial. The Court also held it was an abuse of discretion (but harmless) to admit evidence that the defendant possessed checks made out to another, as there was no showing in the record that the checks were stolen or that the defendant was not authorized to endorse them.

United States v. Anderson, 933 F.2d 1261 (5th Cir. 1991): A conviction for arson of a furniture warehouse was reversed because the Trial Judge made no ruling that jurors could find by a preponderance that each of four previous fires involving the defendant's furniture factory had involved arson and that the defendant was involved. In *United States v. Fortenberry,* 860 F.2d 628 (5th Cir. 1988), the Court reversed convictions for offenses allegedly committed when the defendant placed a small explosive device on a car belonging to his ex-wife's father. It concluded that evidence of a series of attacks against the ex-wife, her attorney, her father, and others was improperly admitted because, *inter alia,* the government had no evidence that the defendant committed the acts and there was not even evidence that all were committed by the same person.

United States v. DeGeratto, 876 F.2d 576 (7th Cir. 1988): A conviction for transporting and receiving stolen truckloads of food products was reversed because the Trial Judge permitted the defendant to be cross-examined at length regarding a prostitution ring about which he denied any knowledge and in which there was no showing he had any involvement. In *United States v. Meeker*, 558 F.2d 387 (7th Cir. 1977), the Court reversed a conviction for failing to report income, holding that the prosecutor's questions, unsupported by evidence, that suggested prior misconduct on the part of the defendant and that the defendant was guilty of engaging in the very conduct for which he was being tried, required reversal.

United States v. Adediran, 26 F.3d 61 (8th Cir. 1994): In a prosecution for using false Social Security numbers in St. Louis as part of a check-kiting scheme, the Court held there was sufficient evidence connecting the defendant with uncharged crimes in Rockford, Ill., as checks issued in St. Louis were deposited in Rockford, false SSNs used at different banks in the two cities all began with the same first five digits, and there were similarities in identifications and in handwriting.

Identity generally — circumstances insufficiently probative

United States v. Pisari, 636 F.2d 855 (1st Cir. 1981): The Court reversed a conviction for committing a robbery with a knife because the government introduced a statement made by the defendant to a government agent admitting a prior robbery in which such a knife was used. The Court noted that there was no showing of identifying characteristics that would have worked to prove identity: There was no evidence of the kind of knives used, no proof of the timing of the other crime, and no similarity of motive. "The single fact that in committing a robbery, one invokes the threat of using a knife falls far short of a sufficient signature or trademark upon which to posit an inference of identity."

United States v. Neary, 733 F.2d 210 (2d Cir. 1984): The Court overturned a defendant's convictions for destroying his restaurant in 1981 with an explosive, finding that the Trial Judge improperly admitted evidence concerning two fires (1976 and 1977) at a tenement house he owned and another fire that destroyed his dry cleaning business (1980). The Court found that the question in the case was whether the defendant set fire to the building, since it was clear that someone had done so. It reiterated that prior acts used to prove identity must be more similar than acts offered for other purposes. Since the government had no evidence that the prior fires were incendiary in origin, the Court concluded that the acts were improperly used. The fact that the defendant might have collected insurance from the prior fires was not relevant to the question of identity; it is common knowledge that an insured can collect on a fire insurance policy covering property.

United States v. Carrillo, 981 F.2d 772 (5th Cir. 1993): The Court reversed a defendant's drug convictions, finding it was error to admit two other sales of controlled substances. The sales did not involve the kind of "signature" that would prove identity.

United States v. Wright, 901 F.2d 68 (7th Cir. 1990): The Court reversed a conviction for cocaine distribution because a tape-recorded telephone conversation in which the defendant claimed to be a wholesale drug dealer did not tend to show the identity of a perpetrator charged with a retail cocaine sale.

United States v. Luna, 21 F.3d 874 (9th Cir. 1994): The Court reversed bank robbery convictions, finding that the Trial Judge erred in admitting evidence of two subsequent bank robberies attributable to two of the defendants. The Court found that "the common features in this case were largely generic,'' since they involved use of guns, masks, gloves, and bags in a typical "takeover robbery," in which people are intimidated by loud entry, profanity, and abuse of bank employees. Differences in personnel among the robberies undermined the supposed distinctiveness of the crimes.

Identity generally — circumstances sufficiently probative

United States v. Ingraham, 832 F.2d 229 (1st Cir. 1987), *cert. denied,* 108 S. Ct. 1738 (1988): The Court upheld the admission of evidence of prior threatening phone calls to prove identity in a prosecution for threatening to kidnap or injure. In *United States v. Andiarena,* 823 F.2d 673 (1st Cir. 1987), the Court affirmed a drug conviction, holding that evidence of the defendant's prior involvement in a network was admissible to prove that he was the source of cocaine.

United States v. Cruz, 797 F.2d 90 (2d Cir. 1986), *cert. denied,* 107 S. Ct. 1631 (1987): Evidence that a defendant had thirteen vials of cocaine on the day after a sale was held properly admitted to prove that the defendant was the person who made the sale of similar vials. In *United States v. Gubelman,* 571 F.2d 1252 (2d Cir.), *cert. denied,* 436 U.S. 948 (1978), the Court held that evidence from others who had given the defendant bribes tended to make the defense argument of mistaken identity less likely.

United States v. Evans, 848 F.2d 1352, *modified on other grounds,* 854 F.2d 56 (5th Cir. 1988): The Court held that evidence that a firearm defendant had a gun, glasses, a wig, and false identification when she was arrested was properly admitted to prove, in connection with similar evidence found in an apartment, that the defendant was the person who illegally obtained firearms. The Court reasoned that there are proper ways to prove identity other than by proving a *modus operandi,* and that the similarity of the evidence in the instant case was probative of identity. In *United States v. Torres-Flores,* 827 F.2d 1031 (5th Cir. 1987), the Court reversed a conviction for assaulting a Border Patrol agent because of the improper use of mug shots, but it held that evidence that shortly after the assault the defendant had been apprehended at a point known for its high volume of illegal alien traffic was admissible to prove identity.

United States v. Monsour, 893 F.2d 126 (6th Cir. 1990) (per curiam): At the defendant's trial for bank robbery, a bank security guard was permitted to testify that the person in the robbery surveillance films was the same person whose car license number he secured eight days earlier after seeing him acting suspiciously at another nearby branch of the bank that was robbed. The Court held there was no error, stating that this was not prior bad act evidence, but was part of the investigative linkage that led the FBI to the defendant.

United States v. Chong Won Tai, 994 F.2d 1204 (7th Cir. 1993): Affirming a conviction for extortion, the Court held that evidence of the defendant's uncharged actions was relevant to prove identity and to prove that he intended to threaten by using the words he chose. This was not a case in which identity was proved by similar conduct, but rather by showing the defendant's connection with certain other individuals who were involved in the uncharged actions. In *United States v. Townsend,* 924 F.2d 1385 (7th Cir. 1991), the prosecution offered evidence that one defendant sold cocaine to an undercover agent before the charged conspiracy began. The Court held that the evidence was properly admitted as proof of identity because it demonstrated the defendant responded to a beeper number paged by another defendant during the conspiracy. In *United States v. Covelli,* 738 F.2d 847 (7th Cir.), *cert. denied,* 105 S. Ct. 211 (1984), the Court affirmed convictions for crimes arising out of the robbery of a shop and the disposition of stolen goods, upholding the admission of testimony that one of the defendants had previously been in possession of a small caliber pistol. It said that "evidence of prior possession of a weapon can be used to prove opportunity and identification even where it cannot be directly identified as the weapon used in the crime."

United States v. Jackson, 714 F.2d 809 (8th Cir. 1983): The Court approved the use of irregularities in invoices and time sheets to prove identity and lack of mistake in a prosecution for making false statements in federal invoices.

Identity — modus operandi

United States v. Medina, 761 F.2d 12 (1st Cir. 1985): The Court affirmed a conviction for conspiracy to commit extortion and actual extortion based upon a kidnapping, holding that evidence of a prior kidnapping involving the defendant was admissible to prove *modus operandi.*

United States v. Sanchez, 988 F.2d 1384 (5th Cir.), *cert. denied,* 114 S. Ct. 217 (1993): Stating, "It is well-settled that extraneous acts evidence offered to prove identity is admissible in the Fifth Circuit only if the circumstances of the extraneous act were so similar to the offense in question that they evince a signature quality," the Court concluded that evidence that the defendant acted with a second man in selling heroin in pink balloons was "not very compelling." However, evidence that the charged and uncharged transactions took place in the identical location and in the presence of the same car with the same license plate was "of signature quality." In an arson prosecution, *United States v. Scott,* 795 F.2d 1245 (5th Cir. 1986), the Court affirmed the admission of evidence of other acts of arson because the devices used to commit the acts established a "signature" that was identical to the devices used to commit the arson for which the defendants were charged. In *United States v. Myers,* 550 F.2d 1036 (5th Cir. 1977), *cert. denied,* 439 U.S. 847 (1978), a conviction for bank robbery was reversed because, *inter alia,* evidence of a subsequent bank robbery in another state was improperly admitted. The Court said that to prove *modus operandi,*

> it is not necessary that the charged crime and the other crimes be identical in every detail.... But they must possess a common feature or features.... The more unique each of the common features is, the smaller the number that is required for the probative value of the evidence to be significant.

The Court also said "a much greater degree of similarity between the charged crime and the uncharged crime is required when the evidence of the other crime is introduced to prove identity than when it is introduced to prove a state of mind."

United States v. Connelly, 874 F.2d 412 (7th Cir. 1989): The Court affirmed convictions relating to stolen goods, finding that evidence of a prior break-in to a home was properly admitted to prove *modus operandi* and to establish the identity of the defendant in the case.

Durns v. United States, 562 F.2d 542 (8th Cir.), *cert. denied*, 434 U.S. 959 (1977): The Court affirmed a kidnapping conviction, upholding as proper identity proof the introduction of evidence that the appellant unsuccessfully attempted to abduct another person in a similar manner.

United States v. Luna, 21 F.3d 874 (9th Cir. 1994): The Court reversed bank robbery convictions, finding that the Trial Judge erred in admitting evidence of two subsequent bank robberies attributable to two of the defendants. The Court found that "the common features in this case were largely generic," since they involved use of guns, masks, gloves, and bags in a typical "takeover robbery," in which people are intimidated by loud entry, profanity, and abuse of bank employees. Differences in personnel among the robberies undermined the supposed distinctiveness of the crimes. In *United States v. Johnson*, 820 F.2d 1065 (9th Cir. 1987), the Court affirmed convictions for two bank robberies, holding that evidence of a third bank robbery was properly admitted to prove identity by showing a *modus operandi*, i.e., orally asking for change and then demanding money. In *United States v. Andrini*, 685 F.2d 1094 (9th Cir. 1982), a prosecution for malicious destruction of a building, the Court upheld the introduction of testimony that during a camping trip the defendant had demonstrated his familiarity with techniques for starting fires. The demonstration bore sufficient similarity to the method of starting the fire that destroyed the building that it was admissible to prove the identity of the arsonist. In *United States v. Powell*, 587 F.2d 443 (9th Cir. 1978), the Court reversed a marijuana conspiracy conviction, in part because the Trial Judge admitted prior marijuana offenses against the defendant. The evidence was not admissible to show identity because the other offenses were not sufficiently distinctive.

United States v. McGuire, 27 F.3d 457 (10th Cir. 1994): Affirming a bank robbery conviction, the Court held there was no error in admitting evidence that the defendant, with one or both of the government's principal witnesses, had committed seven other robberies. Evidence that each involved traveling in a van to a medium-sized Midwest city, staying a day or two to purchase an inexpensive car and find a small bank with few employees close to a shopping area and interstate highway access, and committing the robbery when no customers were in the bank tended to show that the defendant was involved and that the charged robbery was part of a larger plan. A dissenting Judge agreed with the Rule 404(b) ruling, but believed the jury should have been cautioned about accepting uncorroborated accomplice testimony regarding the *modus operandi*. In *United States v. Patterson*, 20 F.3d 809 (10th Cir.), *cert. denied*, 115 S. Ct. __ (1994), the Court affirmed a conviction for aircraft piracy arising out of the hijacking of a small plane, holding that evidence of a similar hijacking by the defendant (see *United States v. Patterson*, 20 F.3d 801 (8th Cir. 1994)) was probative of identity where that issue was contested. In *United States v. Gutierrez*, 696 F.2d 753 (10th Cir. 1982), *cert. denied*, 461 U.S. 909, 910 (1983), the Court affirmed bank robbery convictions, finding that the Trial Judge properly admitted evidence of a second bank robbery involving the two defendants. The Court said that the crime charged and the other crime possessed "signature quality" and were therefore proper evidence, even though one of the defendants had been acquitted on the other charge.

United States v. Miller, 959 F.2d 1535 (11th Cir.) (en banc), *cert. denied,* 113 S. Ct. 382 (1992): The panel had reversed the defendant's conviction for cocaine trafficking on the ground that evidence of a second transaction was not sufficiently similar and distinctive to prove identity. 883 F.2d 1540 (11th Cir. 1989). The Court *en banc* affirmed the defendant's conviction, holding that the similarity of the two offenses, including the same supplier and same location, was sufficient to mark them as the handiwork of the accused. In *United States v. Lail,* 846 F.2d 1299 (11th Cir. 1988), the Court reversed a bank robbery conviction because evidence of an uncharged bank robbery was improperly admitted. Despite some similarities between the robberies — a lone gunman, use of a handgun, lack of disguise, proximity in time of occurrence — the Court concluded that the dissimilarities were so great that it was an abuse of discretion to admit the evidence. Compare *United States v. Stubbins,* 877 F.2d 42 (11th Cir.), *cert. denied,* 493 U.S. 940 (1989) (in prosecution for distributing "crack" cocaine, evidence of prior "crack" offense properly admitted on issue of identity, where both offenses occurred at same address and the defense had argued mistaken identity and had made much of the fact that the DEA agent's report had a different address from the one given in his testimony). In *United States v. Morano,* 697 F.2d 923 (11th Cir. 1983), the government claimed that Morano and another man burned the building containing Morano's business. The Court found no unfair prejudice to Morano in the admission of the other man's prior arson, as the prior arson was so similar to the one charged as to mark them as the work of the same individual.

Identity — names

United States v. Garcia-Rosa, 876 F.2d 209 (1st Cir. 1989), *cert. denied,* 493 U.S. 1030, *vacated on other grounds,* 498 U.S. 954 (1990): In this prosecution of a drug-importation conspiracy, the prosecutor and the witnesses referred to one of the defendants as "Guillo el Perro" and "Checo el Perro." After the defendant's witness testified the defendant was known by the former name, but he had a brother known by the latter, a prosecution witness testified that he had sold five kilos of cocaine to the defendant, whom he called "Checo el Perro." The Court reversed the defendant's conviction, holding that this evidence lacked the "highly distinctive quality" necessary when introducing other bad acts to show identity.

United States v. Aguirre Aguirre, 716 F.2d 293 (5th Cir. 1983): In a drug prosecution, an issue arose as to whether one defendant was referring to another when he used the name "Compadre" in conversations with an undercover agent. The defendant who used the name said that he and Compadre had been arrested in Chicago together. In the absence of the other defendant's willingness to stipulate that he was arrested in Chicago, the Court found that the government was properly permitted to prove that he was so arrested in order to show that he was Compadre.

United States v. Bowman, 798 F.2d 333 (8th Cir. 1986), *cert. denied,* 107 S. Ct. 906 (1987): Affirming a conviction arising out of the robbery of a pharmacist, the Court held that evidence that the defendant had documents in someone else's name was admissible to prove that he was the person identified by witnesses as having several different names.

Impeachment or rebuttal — contradiction

United States v. Johnson, 802 F.2d 1459 (D.C. Cir. 1986): Affirming a cocaine conviction, the Court found that a defendant opened the door to other crime rebuttal evidence when he presented evidence that he ran a legitimate business.

United States v. Fortes, 619 F.2d 108 (1st Cir. 1980): The defendant opened the door to other crimes evidence by claiming an innocent relationship with a codefendant.

United States v. Beverly, 5 F.3d 633 (2d Cir. 1993): A defendant charged with crack cocaine and firearms offenses testified that he had never possessed a gun in Albany, New York, had only very limited familiarity with guns, and was not in Albany on specified dates. Affirming, the Court held there was no abuse of discretion in permitting rebuttal evidence that he had committed two shootings on specified dates in Albany, although it noted "with distress" that the government overreached by including in its impeachment evidence the facts that the defendant had fired guns in Albany into a house, at a woman, and into the leg of a man. In *United States v. Bilzerian,* 926 F.2d 1285 (2d Cir.), *cert. denied,* 112 S. Ct. 63 (1991), a securities fraud prosecution centering on the defendant's characterization of funds used to purchase stock, the government elicited from an accountant who had prepared the defendant's tax returns that the defendant had stated the source was personal funds. On cross-examination, the defense sought to establish that the source was irrelevant for tax purposes and the tax returns were correct. The Court held that, although the deficiency was not relevant to the charges, there was no error in permitting the government to elicit on redirect that the defendant had underreported his income from the transaction by approximately $4 million, as the door had been opened to correct a false impression. One Judge, concurring in part and dissenting in part, considered that the cross-examination did not open the door, but that the error in the redirect was harmless. In *United States v. Pelusio,* 725 F.2d 161 (2d Cir. 1983), a prosecution for unlawful receipt of firearms, the Court found that the government properly cross-examined a defendant about prior instances in which he had been present in an auto with a shotgun, after he testified on direct examination that he was unaware of the presence of a gun in a car and would not have gotten in had he been aware. See also *United States v. Bari,* 750 F.2d 1169 (2d Cir. 1984), *cert. denied,* 472 U.S. 1019 (1985) (defendant in prosecution for escape opened door for evidence of previous and subsequent escape attempts by claiming that he was physically unable to make an escape attempt).

United States v. Rhodes, 779 F.2d 1019 (4th Cir. 1985), *cert. denied,* 106 S. Ct. 2916 (1986): The Court found that a defendant charged with drug offenses opened the door to evidence about prior convictions as a result of an opening statement and examination of witnesses that suggested that he was only a gambler, not a person involved with drugs. The convictions were used to support the government's claim of criminal intent. In *United States v. Dornhofer,* 859 F.2d 1195 (4th Cir. 1988), *cert. denied,* 109 S. Ct. 1639 (1989), the Court held that evidence of child pornography in the defendant's apartment was relevant to rebut his claim that material received in the mail was received by mistake. In *United States v. Brainard,* 745 F.2d 320 (4th Cir. 1984), *cert. denied,* 471 U.S. 1094 (1985), the Court held that evidence of a prior investment scheme was admissible to rebut the defendant's claim that he had been serving his client's

Impeachment or rebuttal — contradiction (cont'd)

interests in good faith. In *United States v. Tate,* 715 F.2d 864 (4th Cir. 1983), the Court reversed a conviction for receipt of a firearm by a convicted felon. The defendant, who was stopped by police while driving his wife's car, testified at trial that he did not know that two guns were in the trunk of the car. In rebuttal, the government offered evidence that the defendant had been seen in possession of some other gun at some earlier time. The Court found that the earlier possession could have shed no light on the state of the defendant's knowledge on the day he was stopped. In *United States v. Johnson,* 634 F.2d 735 (4th Cir. 1980), *cert. denied,* 451 U.S. 907 (1981), a doctor charged with tax evasion offered character evidence in her behalf, after which the government responded with evidence that her Medicaid billings reported four times as many services per patient as other Virginia doctors. A majority of the Court held that where a defendant has attempted to portray her character as being "completely at odds with the possession of a state of mind requisite to guilt," the government should be entitled to rebut this portrayal.

United States v. Carter, 953 F.2d 1449 (5th Cir.), *cert. denied,* 112 S. Ct. 2980 (1992): Affirming convictions for drug offenses, the Court held it was not error to introduce evidence that a defendant had been in prison for a misdemeanor, as the evidence was not used to impeach but to contradict his testimony that he had been continuously employed during that period. See also *United States v. Nichols,* 750 F.2d 1260 (5th Cir. 1985) (evidence of previous importation of marijuana admissible in cocaine conspiracy prosecution to rebut defendant's claim of lack of knowledge of illicit drug trade and denial of any previous trafficking); *United States v. Mortazavi,* 702 F.2d 526 (5th Cir. 1983) (after defendant testified that he had no intent to deliver drugs and had never been involved with drugs, evidence of drug transaction nine years earlier properly admitted). In *Croce v. Bromley Corp.,* 623 F.2d 1084 (5th Cir. 1980), *cert. denied,* 450 U.S. 981 (1981), a wrongful death action arising out of an airline crash, the Court held it was proper to allow the plaintiffs to offer evidence of the pilot's past conduct to rebut the defendant's various efforts to paint the pilot as a careful and safe operator. In *United States v. Johnson,* 542 F.2d 230 (5th Cir. 1976), the Court affirmed an escape conviction, holding that evidence of a previous felony conviction and the existence of an arrest warrant at the time of the offense was properly admitted to impeach the defendant's testimony that there was no reason he would not be carrying a gun other than the fact that he was not a law enforcement agent.

United States v. Acosta-Cazares, 878 F.2d 945 (6th Cir.), *cert. denied,* 110 S. Ct. 255 (1989): The Court held in a cocaine conspiracy prosecution that the defendant's counsel, by stating in his opening statement that his client was not involved in any conspiracy to distribute cocaine but was merely a "victim of circumstance," had opened the door to evidence during the prosecution's direct case of defendant's prior drug transactions. In *United States v. Dunn,* 805 F.2d 1275 (6th Cir. 1986), the Court held, 2-1, that it was error to admit evidence that the defendant, a contract egg producer charged with mail fraud involving insurance claims made following a fire, had previously stolen eggs. The evidence was irrelevant to rebut his claim that an egg wholesaler had a motive to burn his buildings; in fact, it tended to support the claim. Moreover, the Court found that the prosecutor argued to the jury that the evidence was character evidence. In *United States v. Czarnecki,* 552 F.2d 698 (6th Cir.), *cert. denied,* 431 U.S. 939 (1977), a government witness was asked whether he was paid by the defendant for efforts not involving collections. The Court upheld the question on the ground that the defendant had opened the door to proof of the employment relationship by claiming that someone else had hired the witness to extort payments.

United States v. Weisman, 736 F.2d 421 (7th Cir.), *cert. denied,* 105 S. Ct. 390 (1984): In a fraud prosecution, the Court held that the defendant's entry of a guilty plea on behalf of a corporation in 1980, the transcript of the plea proceeding, and other evidence concerning past investigations of the corporation and statements by the defendant regarding his fear of an FTC investigation were properly admitted to respond to the defendant's claim that he had no personal knowledge of any fraud committed by the corporation's employees. See also *United States v. Laughlin,* 772 F.2d 1382 (7th Cir. 1985) (photos of defendant in presence of cash and marijuana plants properly admitted to rebut defense theory that he was a recreational user, but photos of defendant using marijuana should have been excluded since they were consistent with the defense); *United States v. Fountain,* 768 F.2d 790 (7th Cir. 1985), *cert. denied,* 475 U.S. 1124 (1986) (defendant who made an issue of his purpose in having a knife in prison opened the door to evidence concerning his previous use of the knife); *United States v. Stump,* 735 F.2d 273 (7th Cir.), *cert. denied,* 105 S. Ct. 203 (1984) (evidence of improper prescriptions issued by defendant prior to date of crimes charged was admissible to show a continuing scheme and to rebut his claim that he never intended to act unlawfully); *United States v. Gaertner,* 705 F.2d 210 (7th Cir. 1983), *cert. denied,* 104 S. Ct. 979 (1984) (claim on direct examination by defendant charged with possession of cocaine with intent to distribute that he was not into "the drug thing" opened the door to rebuttal evidence of his prior convictions involving marijuana and tax evasion).

Williams v. Mensey, 785 F.2d 631 (8th Cir. 1986): Affirming a judgment against a prisoner who claimed he was assaulted in jail, the Court held that evidence that the plaintiff was involved in other fights was properly admitted to show his problems with other inmates before one of the defendants allegedly labeled him a "snitch." In *United States v. Burkett,* 821 F.2d 1306 (8th Cir. 1987), the Court held that after a defendant in a break-in testified that he had solved other burglaries for authorities, he opened the door to cross-examination concerning his involvement in other burglaries. See also *United States v. Lego,* 855 F.2d 542 (8th Cir. 1988) (evidence that defendant had previously been in possession of firearm admissible to negate his claim that he was carrying the weapon on the day charged only because of government inducements); *United States v. Bartley,* 855 F.2d 547 (8th Cir. 1988) (evidence of defendant's prior activity admissible to rebut his claim that he did not know two people who identified him). In *United States v. Gustafson,* 728 F.2d 1078 (8th Cir.), *cert. denied,* 105 S. Ct. 380 (1984), the Court held that a bank examiner's 1975 letter to the board of directors of a bank was properly admitted in a prosecution for a fraudulent check floating scheme that involved the bank in 1977 and 1978, since the letter put various defendants on notice of the problems with handling checks in certain ways and tended to rebut their defense that any improprieties were attributable to subordinates. See also *United States v. Vitale,* 728 F.2d 1090 (8th Cir.), *cert. denied,* 105 S. Ct. 103 (1984) (where defendant in drug case testified, his version of the facts was subject to rebuttal, even though the rebuttal might involve

Impeachment or rebuttal — contradiction (cont'd)

mention of possession of a stolen weapon); *United States v. Koessel,* 706 F.2d 271 (8th Cir. 1983) (permitting cross-examination of defendant concerning earlier cocaine conviction to rebut defense of a frame-up).

United States v. Lopez-Martinez, 725 F.2d 471 (9th Cir.), *cert. denied,* 469 U.S. 837 (1984): Reversing a conviction for importing heroin on other grounds, the Court ruled that evidence that the appellant was arrested in 1974 for possessing 600 pounds of marijuana and that he stated at the time that he was being paid $1,000 to haul the marijuana was admissible to rebut his claim that in the instant case he thought he was carrying marijuana rather than heroin. Since he received $1,000 for bringing a package weighing one and one-half pounds into the country, the Court reasoned that a jury could infer that he must have known he was carrying something worth more than marijuana. See also *United States v. Gering,* 716 F.2d 615 (9th Cir. 1983) (where defendant took stand and attempted to create a defense in a mail fraud prosecution, testimony could be offered to rebut the defense even though it might involve other acts); *United States v. Spetz,* 721 F.2d 1457 (9th Cir. 1983) (evidence that the defendant had written a book describing drug dealing and had shown it to his father was properly admitted to rebut the father's testimony that he had no knowledge that his son knew about such dealing); *United States v. Riggins,* 539 F.2d 682 (9th Cir. 1976), *cert. denied,* 429 U.S. 1045 (1977) (evidence of a fingerprint on other forged money orders admissible to rebut defense of a frame-up).

United States v. Lara, 956 F.2d 994 (10th Cir. 1992): The Court held there was no error in bringing out on cross-examination that the defendant in a construction fraud case was being prosecuted for an offense arising out of another construction project, as the defendant had opened the door by denying on direct examination that he had ever been prosecuted in any other case. In *United States v. Harris,* 903 F.2d 770 (10th Cir. 1990), the Court affirmed the defendant's conviction for marijuana trafficking, holding that failure to file reports of large cash transactions with the IRS was properly admitted to rebut his argument that the cash was derived from legitimate coin sales. In *United States v. Hogue,* 827 F.2d 660 (10th Cir. 1987), the Court reversed a conviction for voluntary manslaughter, holding that the defendant's assaults upon his girl friend and her children prior to and after the stabbing of the victim were not admissible to rebut the claim that the stabbing was accidental, but were impermissible propensity evidence. See also *United States v. Naranjo,* 710 F.2d 1465 (10th Cir. 1983) (defendant's previous batteries of murder victim admissible to rebut his testimony that the shooting was an accident, even though a gun had not been used in the previous batteries); *United States v. Dysart,* 705 F.2d 1247 (10th Cir.), *cert. denied,* 104 S. Ct. 339 (1983) (evidence of previous threats properly admitted to rebut a claim that defendant lacked the capacity to have an intent to commit the offense of threatening the President); *United States v. Lewis,* 700 F.2d 1328 (10th Cir.), *cert. denied,* 461 U.S. 947 (1983) (in marijuana importation case, evidence that defendant had been involved in similar, prior smuggling incident properly admitted to refute his claim that he had no prior experience in importing or selling drugs); *United States v. Pilling,* 721 F.2d 286 (10th Cir. 1983) (permissible for government to ask defendant, who testified that his sole interest in transactions leading to the prosecution was innocent, whether he had smoked marijuana and sniffed cocaine); *United States v. Harris,* 661 F.2d 138 (10th Cir. 1981) (when defendant charged with murdering his child claimed the death was accidental, permissible to admit evidence of injuries suffered by the child on other occasions).

United States v. Boon San Chong, 829 F.2d 1572 (11th Cir. 1987): The Court held in an extortion case that evidence that the defendant had previously invaded a home while armed to demand money was admissible, *inter alia,* to rebut the defendant's claim that he acted under duress in the instant case. In *United States v. Plotke,* 725 F.2d 1303 (11th Cir.), *cert. denied,* 105 S. Ct. 151 (1984), the Court found that when a defendant in a mail fraud and conspiracy case testified that he never had anything to do with burning his house or houses of others, the door had been opened to cross-examination asking the defendant whether he had been scarred at a fire at another person's house.

Impeachment or rebuttal — criminal defendant
opening the door to rebuttal

Government of Virgin Islands v. Martinez, 847 F.2d 125 (3d Cir. 1988): Although the Court affirmed a conviction for cocaine trafficking, it held that the defendant did not open the door to an inquiry into his prior drug transactions with an informant simply by cross-examining the informant regarding his own drug dealing.

United States v. Draiman, 784 F.2d 248 (7th Cir. 1986): Affirming a conviction arising from filing fraudulent insurance claims following a burglary, the Court upheld the admission of evidence that the defendant made prior fraudulent claims plus evidence concerning the defendant's possession of "hot" or "pirated" tapes. It found that the latter evidence was admissible because of the manner in which defense counsel cross-examined a government witness. The Court observed that " '[o]pening the door' is a risk even a skilled defense counsel, as in this case, assumed when a calculated effort is made to tiptoe over thin ice to gain some evidentiary advantage." In *United States v. Peco,* 784 F.2d 798 (7th Cir.), *cert. denied,* 106 S. Ct. 2281 (1986), the Court affirmed convictions of drug-related offenses, concluding that the Trial Judge carefully and properly ruled that the government could introduce evidence concerning death threats to an agent, since the defendant opened the door to the evidence by inquiring on cross-examination into the agent's promise of immunity to an informant and the evidence tended to explain the agent's reasons for promising. In *United States v. Wynn,* 845 F.2d 1439 (7th Cir. 1988), the Court held that a postal employee charged with embezzlement opened the door to questioning about other allegations made against him when he attempted to impeach a witness by questioning his motive for investigating the defendant. See also *United States v. Weston,* 708 F.2d 302 (7th Cir.), *cert. denied,* 464 U.S. 962 (1983) (defendants, who were convicted of involvement with stolen property taken from couple who were murdered, opened the door to mention of the murders by cross-examining a government witness to demonstrate that she did not tell the FBI everything she knew immediately after the murders and robbery).

United States v. Womochil, 778 F.2d 1311 (8th Cir. 1985): The Court affirmed cocaine convictions, finding that the government was properly permitted to elicit on redirect examination of an agent testimony concerning other information that had been obtained relating to the defendant's activities; after the defendant's cross-examination had left the misleading impression that the defendant had never been under suspicion. See also *United States v. Large,* 729 F.2d 636 (8th Cir. 1984) (government's reference to money found in defendant's suitcase as fruit of prior drug transaction permissible where defense counsel brought out the prior transaction in cross-examining a government witness).

United States v. Wales, 977 F.2d 1323 (9th Cir. 1992): The Court affirmed the defendant's conviction for making a false declaration to Customs about the amount of currency he was carrying, holding there was no error in admitting evidence that the defendant was carrying false drivers' licenses after he had offered evidence his passport and other documents were legitimate. One Judge concurred in the judgment on this point, but noted there is no authority in the Rules for this "opening the door" doctrine; further, the doctrine as announced provides neither a clear rule nor a basis for extrapolating a rule by analogy, which is not fair to lawyers and judges.

United States v. Johnson, 730 F.2d 683 (11th Cir.), *cert. denied,* 469 U.S. 857, 867 (1984): The Court held that defense cross-examination of a government witness opened the door to extrinsic evidence, since the cross-examination might have created a false impression of one defendant's relationship to another. See also *United States v. Bent,* 707 F.2d 1190 (11th Cir. 1983), *cert. denied,* 104 S. Ct. 2174 (1984) (defendant, who testified on direct examination that his previous voyages to the United States were for legitimate reasons, could be asked on cross-examination about prior involvement in drug smuggling scheme); *United States v. Killingsworth,* 719 F.2d 1130 (11th Cir. 1983), *cert. denied,* 104 S. Ct. 1311 (1984) (in prosecution of defendant for conspiracy to defraud the government, evidence that employees whom defendant was to train were actually conducting training in another program was properly admitted to rebut defendant's claim of unawareness of training requirement as condition of government funding).

Impeachment or rebuttal — government or civil party opening the door to rebuttal

United States v. Simpson, 992 F.2d 1224 (D.C. Cir.), *cert. denied,* 114 S. Ct. 286 (1993): The Court held it was plain error to permit "impeachment" of the defendant's denial on cross-examination that he knew how dilaudid was packaged with evidence of his prior arrest for possession of dilaudid, as the only issue in the present case was his possession of dilaudid and neither his knowledge of how it was packaged nor his prior possession was relevant to that issue.

Bonilla v. Yamaha Motors Corp., 955 F.2d 150 (1st Cir. 1992): Reversing a judgment for the defendant in a product liability action arising out of a motorcycle accident, the Court held that it was error to cross-examine the plaintiff about speeding violations inadmissible under Rule 404(b) simply in the hope that he would deny them, thus opening up the "red herring" for impeachment. See also *United States v. Ruiz-Batista,* 956 F.2d 351 (1st Cir.), *cert. denied,* 113 S. Ct. 105 (1992) (strongly condemning government procedure of asking defendant whether he had possessed cocaine on other occasions and, after receiving a denial, seeking to show such occasions for purpose of impeachment).

United States v. Warledo, 557 F.2d 721 (10th Cir. 1977): Convictions for conspiracy to set fire to a railroad bridge, conspiracy to obstruct interstate commerce, and possession of an incendiary bomb were reversed because the government was improperly permitted to ask one of the defendants whether he possessed a rifle found in his automobile and to introduce the rifle together with a clip and bullets to rebut his denial of possession. The Court properly refused to permit the government to open the door for this dangerous form of impeachment on an irrelevant matter, and it reversed all the defendants' convictions because the conspiracy charges made it likely that the evidence would have affected all of them.

Impeachment or rebuttal — specific acts to impeach

United States v. Copelin, 996 F.2d 379 (D.C. Cir. 1993): The Court reversed a cocaine distribution conviction, concluding that although the prosecution was properly permitted to ask the defendant about testing positive on drug tests to impeach his statements that he had only seen drugs advertised on television, the failure to instruct the jury on the permissible use of the defendant's positive tests was plain error. In *United States v. Simpson,* 992 F.2d 1224 (D.C. Cir.), *cert. denied,* 114 S. Ct. 286 (1993), the Court held it was plain error to permit ''impeachment'' of the defendant's denial that he knew how dilaudid was packaged with evidence of his prior arrest for possession of dilaudid, as the only issue in the present case was his possession of dilaudid and neither his knowledge of how it was packaged nor his prior possession was relevant to that issue. In *United States v. Eaton,* 808 F.2d 72 (D.C. Cir. 1987), testimony by a defendant that he lacked knowledge of or familiarity with drugs opened the door to cross-examination as to the defendant's prior conviction and drug use.

United States v. McFadyen-Snider, 552 F.2d 1178 (6th Cir. 1977), *cert. denied,* 435 U.S. 995 (1978): The Court reversed bank fraud convictions, holding that the prosecutor improperly attempted to impeach the appellant with proof of her sexual conduct, which the Court said was irrelevant, ''especially ... where the conduct does not involve a substantive issue of the case.''

United States v. Pacione, 950 F.2d 1348 (7th Cir. 1991), *cert. denied,* 112 S. Ct. 3054 (1992): The Court affirmed a conviction for threatening a revenue officer, holding there was no abuse of discretion in permitting rebuttal witnesses to testify about the defendant's reputation for untruthfulness and their opinions of his untruthfulness. Although he had been convicted in connection with the business out of which their knowledge arose, it was defense counsel who brought out his prior bad acts.

United States v. Brooke, 4 F.3d 1480 (9th Cir. 1993): The defendant was convicted of offenses arising out of a pipe bombing directed at a companion of her former boyfriend. The conviction was reversed for improper admission of evidence that the defendant had falsely claimed to friends to be suffering from terminal cancer. The Court noted that the evidence was relevant to show that the defendant had made extraordinary efforts to gain help in disrupting the victim's relationship with the former boyfriend, but the probative value was substantially outweighed by the prejudicial effect of inducing resentment against one feigning cancer.

393

"Inadvertent" disclosure

United States v. Terry, 729 F.2d 1063 (6th Cir. 1984): Although it affirmed two appellants' conspiracy convictions arising out of their involvement with stolen vehicles, the Court expressed concern about law enforcement officers making "inadvertent" remarks about a defendant's criminal history. It opined that "if the government took appropriate caution to instruct its witnesses before trial, these types of remarks would occur with less frequency."

United States v. Gray, 730 F.2d 733 (11th Cir. 1984): The Court held that reversal was not required where a prosecutor, relying on a ruling in a prior trial of the case, mentioned in an opening statement that the defendant was behind on payments to a probation officer in order to show a motive for robbery; the Trial Judge subsequently decided not to admit any evidence regarding the probation officer.

Insanity defense

United States v. Bradshaw, 935 F.2d 295 (D.C. Cir. 1991): Affirming a bank robbery conviction, the Court noted that admission of prior convictions where sanity is the only issue presents different considerations from the usual case. Probativeness is generally unquestionable, since the insanity defense directly puts state of mind in issue, and a prior criminal record is highly relevant to the defendant's appreciation of the unacceptability of his conduct; there is no risk of primary prejudicial effect, since the defendant does not deny commission of the act; and there is a possibility that the evidence will prove not to the government's advantage, by permitting the inference that the defendant is insane, since he continues to commit the same easily-detectable crime. Although the Trial Judge's ruling was terse, it appeared from the record as a whole that the relevant factors were considered.

United States v. Emery, 682 F.2d 493 (5th Cir.), *cert. denied,* 459 U.S. 1044 (1982): The defendant in a bank robbery case conceded the robbery, but claimed he was insane at the time. The Court upheld the introduction of evidence that he had robbed another bank a month previously, on the ground that the evidence helped to explain a psychiatrist's diagnosis that the defendant had the capacity to conform his conduct to legal requirements.

United States v. Brown, 785 F.2d 587 (7th Cir. 1986): Affirming a conviction for failure to appear at sentencing, the Court upheld admission of evidence of the defendant's fraud upon two trucking companies after the date of the sentencing hearing. The evidence was properly admitted to respond to the defendant's insanity defense.

United States v. Ruster, 712 F.2d 409 (9th Cir. 1983): The Court upheld the introduction of evidence, offered to rebut an insanity defense, that the defendant, who was charged with filing false and fraudulent Social Security claims, had previously submitted false claims and engaged in break-ins. The Court found that the evidence shed light on his mental state.

Intent — assault, homicide, abuse, etc.

United States v. Cortijo-Diaz, 875 F.2d 13 (1st Cir. 1989): The Court vacated a conviction for interfering with a flight attendant because evidence that the defendant had been convicted of attempted robbery and sentenced as a predicate violent felon had been erroneously admitted. It was not relevant, other than to show propensity, to the defendant's argument that he did not intend to interfere. The Court criticized the Trial Judge's rote restatement of the Rule 404(b) exceptions and once again stated that the Rule excludes other acts relevant only to show criminal propensity.

United States v. Sanders, 964 F.2d 295 (4th Cir. 1992): The Court reversed a conviction for assault with a dangerous weapon in a prison, holding it was error to admit evidence of the defendant's prior convictions for inmate assault and contraband possession. As the defendant admitted the stabbing and claimed only self-defense, the only issue was whether that was the reason for the admitted act; the prior offenses had no probative value on his intent and could show only his general criminal disposition. The dissenting Judge thought that the defendant's admission did not eliminate the need for determining whether self-defense provided the motive, as the defendant claimed, or the stabbing was accompanied by assaultive intent, as the government claimed.

United States v. Levario Quiroz, 854 F.2d 69 (5th Cir. 1988): The Court held that admission of evidence of a separate and unrelated shooting was plain error in a prosecution for assault of a federal officer with a deadly weapon. The case turned on the credibility of the defendant and a Border Patrol Agent, and the defendant suffered several disadvantages, including his difficulty in speaking English and the fact that evidence indicated that he was being sought by the sheriff for a crime.

United States v. Pirovolos, 844 F.2d 415 (7th Cir.), *cert. denied,* 109 S. Ct. 147 (1988): The Court held that evidence that defendant had guns on other occasions was admissible to show intent, after the defendant claimed self-defense. See also *United States v. Shoffner,* 826 F.2d 619 (7th Cir.), *cert. denied,* 108 S. Ct. 356 (1987) (evidence that defendant had made one threat against his wife to discourage her testimony was admissible to disprove his claim that a second threat was a joke).

United States v. Burk, 912 F.2d 225 (8th Cir. 1990): The Court affirmed a conviction for assaulting an IRS officer, holding that evidence the defendant had been convicted in 1982 of threatening to assault a police officer was properly admitted, after the defendant's counsel said in his opening statement that the defendant had no intention of hurting the officer. See also *United States v. Engleman,* 648 F.2d 473 (8th Cir. 1981) (in prosecution for a plot to kill a man in order to collect insurance proceeds, evidence was admitted concerning another killing in which one defendant was involved some thirteen years earlier that also involved an attempt to obtain insurance money).

United States v. Boise, 916 F.2d 497 (9th Cir. 1990), *cert. denied,* 111 S. Ct. 2057 (1991): The Court affirmed the defendant's conviction for murder of a six-week-old child, holding that evidence of the victim's prior injuries when the defendant was the primary caretaker and of the victim's suffering from battered-child syndrome was properly admitted as evidence of intent and of the absence of accident. See also *United States v. Lewis,* 837 F.2d 415 (9th Cir.), *cert. denied,* 109 S. Ct. 304 (1988) (evidence that defendant charged with murdering his stepson severely punished the stepson six weeks before the child's death was properly admitted to prove intent); *United States v. Bettencourt,* 614 F.2d 214 (9th Cir. 1980) (error to admit evidence that the defendant, an attorney charged with interfering with a federal officer, was arrested for interfering with local officers twenty-one months earlier because "except to prove Bettencourt's propensity to resort to self-help, a commentary on his character, there is no rational connection between the two occurrences," especially since there was no proof of intent on the prior occasion).

United States v. Soundingsides, 819 F.2d 1529 (10th Cir. 1987): The Court reversed a murder conviction, finding, *inter alia,* that it was error to admit testimony by the defendant's former girl friend that he frequently beat her and caused her to lose her baby. The testimony involved five-year-old events, and the Court concluded that the evidence was of little probative value. There was no real dispute that whoever killed the victim in the instant case did so with malice, and the prior act evidence was extremely prejudicial.

United States v. Church, 955 F.2d 688 (11th Cir.), *cert. denied,* 113 S. Ct. 233 (1992): In a RICO prosecution for acts, including conspiracy to murder, committed in 1983 and 1984, the Court held it was harmless error to admit a tape recording of a 1979 conversation discussing a defendant's plan to kill a prosecutor. Any probative value the evidence might have had on the defendant's intent was diminished by the remoteness of the conversation and was substantially outweighed by the likelihood that the jury would draw prejudicially impermissible inferences about the defendant's character. In *United States v. Williams,* 816 F.2d 1527 (11th Cir. 1987), the Court affirmed a conviction for assault with a dangerous weapon, holding that evidence of two prior rapes was properly admitted to prove the defendant's intent, since the facts surrounding the rapes were "strikingly similar" to those surrounding the assaults. The Court stated that "[t]he rule in this circuit is that extrinsic evidence of similar acts will possess great probative value if the defendant's intent is in issue and if the government lacks other strong evidence of defendant's intent." The Court concluded that the rape evidence was probative and that the possibility of prejudice was not too great to permit the evidence to be introduced.

Intent — civil rights cases

Brown v. Trustees of Boston Univ., 891 F.2d 337 (1st Cir. 1989), *cert. denied,* 110 S. Ct. 3217 (1990): In an employment discrimination action brought after the plaintiff was denied tenure, the Court held that remarks derogatory to women made by the University's president were properly admitted as evidence of a discriminatory animus in making the tenure decision.

United States v. Dise, 763 F.2d 586 (3d Cir. 1985), *cert. denied,* 474 U.S. 982 (1985): In a civil rights prosecution of a hospital aide, the Court held that evidence of other instances in which he abused inmates was properly admitted to show willfulness and intent.

United States v. Ebens, 800 F.2d 1422 (6th Cir. 1986): The Court reversed a conviction for interfering with the civil rights of a citizen of Chinese descent. It found that evidence that a man who might have been the defendant had made a derogatory remark about a black man some eight years earlier should have been excluded. There was a danger that the jury would use the evidence as character evidence, it was remote in time, and the showing that it was the defendant who made the statement was weak.

Intent — drug cases

United States v. Payne, 805 F.2d 1062 (D.C. Cir. 1986): The Court affirmed a defendant's conviction for possession of marijuana with intent to distribute, finding that evidence of guns found in the defendant's apartment was properly admitted to prove intent to distribute. See also *United States v. Manner,* 887 F.2d 317 (D.C. Cir. 1989) (evidence that defendant sold drugs after the crimes with which he was charged was admissible), *cert. denied,* 493 U.S. 1062 (1990). In *United States v. Foskey,* 636 F.2d 517 (D.C. Cir. 1980), the Court reversed a drug conviction after the government introduced evidence that two years previously the defendant was arrested for possession of similar drugs. After noting that the only purpose for which the evidence might have been offered permissibly was to show intent, the Court found that there was insufficient similarity between the two events to justify admission of the evidence and that even if it were relevant, the evidence should have been excluded under Rule 403. The Court said:

> Rules 403 and 404(b) are not obstacles to be cleared at all costs, even by cutting around corners whenever it is possible to do so. These rules were designed to ensure a defendant a fair and just trial.... The district court, required to make on-the-spot decisions, does not have the luxury of engaging in the type of careful balancing we have undertaken here.... There is a large measure of responsibility in the prosecutor to weigh the evidence independently.

United States v. Karas, 950 F.2d 31 (1st Cir. 1991): The Court held it was an abuse of discretion (but harmless) to admit evidence of the defendant's prior participation in a cocaine conspiracy during his trial on marijuana conspiracy charges. Where the defendant did not testify or put in any evidence, statements by defense counsel in the opening could not be the basis for admitting Rule 404(b) evidence on intent or knowledge regarding joining a conspiracy. In *United States v. Ferrer-Cruz,* 899 F.2d 135 (1st Cir. 1990), the defendant, convicted of aiding and abetting possession of cocaine with intent to distribute, argued that evidence of prior convictions for possessing cocaine and marijuana were inadmissible because he defended on the ground of mistaken identity. The Court held that the mistaken identity defense did not necessarily remove the issues of knowledge or intent, that the defendant did not clearly stipulate to remove those issues, and that the defendant did in fact argue "mere presence" in a car with cocaine. The dissenting Judge expressed concern about the Circuit's inclusionary approach to the Rule, considered that the defendant had raised "mere presence" only in the grand jury and not at trial, and concluded that the evidence was being used only to show propensity. In *United States v. Rubio-Estrada,* 857 F.2d 845 (1st Cir. 1988), a majority held that evidence of a prior drug conviction was admissible to prove knowledge and intent in a prosecution for possession of cocaine with intent to distribute. A dissenting Judge argued that the prior conviction was improperly admitted, constituted character evidence, and was more prejudicial than probative. See also *United States v. Munson,* 819 F.2d 337 (1st Cir. 1987) (evidence of drug transactions other than those charged were admissible to prove intent to conspire); *United States v. Molinares Charris,* 822 F.2d 1213 (1st Cir. 1987) (defendant's prior smuggling admissible to prove intent to transport marijuana). The Court reversed drug convictions in *United States v. Lynn,* 856 F.2d 430 (1st Cir. 1988), finding that a 1974 marijuana conviction should not have been admitted to prove a 1985 charge of drug smuggling, since there was no evidence connecting the earlier conviction to the later charges and the defendant claimed that the government witnesses were lying about his participation, not that he lacked intent.

Intent — drug cases (cont'd)

United States v. Colon, 880 F.2d 650 (2d Cir. 1989): The defendant was prosecuted for aiding a heroin sale, after he told an undercover agent who asked to buy drugs to "wait over there" by a man who made the sale. The Court reversed his conviction on the ground that evidence of two prior heroin sales, offered to show intent and knowledge, had been improperly admitted, because his defense that he had no recollection of the drug transaction at all meant that intent had been stipulated out of the case, even though no formal stipulation was offered.

United States v. Hernandez, 975 F.2d 1035 (4th Cir. 1992): The Court reversed a conviction for participation in a cocaine distribution conspiracy because a cooperating witness was permitted to testify during the government's direct case that the defendant had told him she had a special recipe for cooking crack because she "used to do that, sell that in New York." The relevance of the evidence to show intent was at best slight. The evidence was not necessary to show the context of the crime, and it was barely reliable. The Court held that, in any event, the balance of probative value and prejudicial effect was so one-sided that admission of the evidence was error. See also *United States v. Tedder,* 801 F.2d 1437 (4th Cir. 1986), *cert. denied,* 480 U.S. 938 (1987) (prior drug transactions with codefendant admissible to prove knowledge and intent in marijuana prosecution); *United States v. Hines,* 717 F.2d 1481 (4th Cir. 1983), *cert. denied,* 104 S. Ct. 2656, 2668 (1984) (affirming drug-related convictions; evidence of certain transactions relating to counts that had been severed prior to trial were properly admitted to show intent). But see *United States v. Davis,* 657 F.2d 637 (4th Cir. 1981) (Trial Judge erred, in a case charging conspiracy to distribute heroin, in admitting evidence that a defendant was involved in selling heroin six years earlier; evidence did not tend to prove intent and was not part of a common plan or scheme, but error was harmless).

United States v. Gadison, 8 F.3d 186 (5th Cir. 1993): Affirming convictions for conspiracy to distribute cocaine base, the Court held there was no error in admitting a defendant's prior conviction for cocaine possession because he put his intent in issue by entering a not guilty plea to the conspiracy charge. In *United States v. Williams,* 900 F.2d 823 (5th Cir. 1990), a prosecution for using the mails to facilitate drug trafficking, the Trial Judge granted the defendant's motion *in limine* to exclude evidence of nineteen prior similar mailings from fictitious Los Angeles addresses. The Court reversed, holding that the evidence, which was connected to the defendant, tended to show knowledge and intent, even if the packages did not contain drugs, because they might have been used as test deliveries; so long as it is not suggested to the jury that there were twenty deliveries of cocaine, there would be little danger that the probative value of the evidence on knowledge and intent would cause unfair prejudice or confusion.

United States v. Elkins, 732 F.2d 1280 (6th Cir. 1984): The Court upheld admission of prior cocaine transactions to prove intent in a cocaine prosecution.

United States v. McCarthur, 6 F.3d 1270 (7th Cir. 1993): The Court held it was an abuse of discretion (but harmless error) to admit evidence that the defendant, who was charged with possessing three kilos of cocaine with intent to distribute, had previously been arrested for possession of a small amount of cocaine. Where the witness knew nothing of the circumstances of the arrest or the disposition of the charge, the arrest by itself did not establish any conduct by the defendant shedding any light on her intent or absence of mistake with respect to the charged offense. In *United States v. Kramer,* 955 F.2d 479 (7th Cir. 1992), *cert. denied,* 113 S. Ct. 595, 596 (1993), the Court affirmed convictions for conspiring to distribute marijuana as part of a continuing criminal enterprise that imported marijuana, holding that the Trial Judge exercised principled discretion in admitting evidence that one of the defendants had imported fifteen tons of marijuana in 1981. The evidence showed specific intent, it was not too remote to be relevant, and its prejudicial effect, if any, did not substantially outweigh its probative value. One Judge, concurring, expressed concern that the Circuit's rule that intent is "necessarily in issue" when a defendant is charged with a specific-intent crime had resulted in a great deal of prejudicial extrinsic evidence finding its way into many criminal trials. In *United States v. Mazzanti,* 888 F.2d 1165 (7th Cir. 1989), *cert. denied,* 110 S. Ct. 2167 (1990), the Court affirmed a conviction of conspiracy to distribute cocaine, holding that after the defendant made a blanket denial of wrongdoing the government could, in rebuttal, overcome the denial and reestablish the element of intent by offering evidence of the defendant's other cocaine transactions.

United States v. Jenkins, 7 F.3d 803 (8th Cir. 1993): The defendant's conviction for distributing LSD was reversed because evidence that he previously sold marijuana was improperly admitted. The Court held that where the defendant unequivocally denied committing the acts charged, evidence of other crimes that might be probative of intent or knowledge was inadmissible. In *United States v. Norton,* 846 F.2d 521 (8th Cir. 1988), the Court rejected a defendant's claim that his prior cocaine transactions were improperly admitted to prove intent in a drug prosecution, since his only defense was that he was coerced into engaging in the charged acts. The Court stated that "the government is not limited in its proof of its case by a defendant's representations of what his defense will be after the government rests," and that intent was an element that the government was required to prove. See also *United States v. Nichols,* 808 F.2d 660 (8th Cir.), *cert. denied,* 107 S. Ct. 1976 (1987) (error, but harmless, to admit evidence of prior unrelated cocaine transactions in prosecution for cocaine distribution).

United States v. Jones, 982 F.2d 380 (9th Cir. 1992, *amended* 1993): In a prosecution for conspiring to import marijuana, the Court held that evidence of the defendant's involvement in prior marijuana smuggling operations was not made irrelevant by the defendant's complete denial of participation in the crime. Intent is an element of the charged crimes, and the fact that he did not contest those particular elements did not relieve the government of its burden of proving them beyond a reasonable doubt, which it was entitled to do by probative evidence. In *United States v. Adrian,* 978 F.2d 486 (9th Cir. 1992), the Court held, on an interlocutory appeal of an *in limine* ruling to exclude evidence of prior narcotics convictions in a drug case on the ground they were not probative of anything but propensity, that prior possession and sale of narcotics may be probative of intent to distribute; the case was remanded to allow the government to develop the record and to permit the Trial Court an opportunity to weigh the danger of unfair prejudice against the probative force of the evidence. In *United States v. Mehrmanesh,* 689 F.2d 822 (9th Cir. 1982), the Court affirmed a conviction for importing heroin and possessing it with intent to distribute. It analyzed several kinds of other crimes evidence and pointed out that the government had failed to articulate the hypotheses that justified the introduction of the evidence. Nevertheless, it held that the

Intent — drug cases (cont'd)

defendant's prior conviction for smuggling hashish five years earlier was admissible on the issue of intent to distribute. Drug use paraphernalia seized at the defendant's residence should not have been admitted, since it was propensity evidence. Finally, the Court held that evidence establishing that large quantities of other drugs were seized at the residence was properly admitted to demonstrate an intent to distribute.

Fitzgerald v. United States, 719 F.2d 1069 (10th Cir. 1983): The Court held that evidence of drugs belonging to one defendant was properly admitted against another defendant where there was concerted action and the evidence was probative of intent to distribute. See also *United States v. Johnson,* 734 F.2d 503 (10th Cir. 1984) (witness' testimony about defendant's prior cocaine transactions and amounts were admissible to prove intent to distribute).

United States v. Cardenas, 895 F.2d 1338 (11th Cir. 1990): The Trial Judge admitted evidence at the defendant's trial on drug conspiracy and possession charges of his prior drug usage and dealings to prove his knowledge of cocaine and intent to possess it. Rejecting the defendant's argument that knowledge and intent were not at issue and that the sole issue was identity, the Court held that intent is an issue whenever the defendant enters a not guilty plea to a conspiracy charge without taking affirmative steps to remove the issue of intent from the case. The dissenting Judge would not require affirmative steps to remove the intent issue when the substantive act is charged along with the conspiracy, as proof of the substantive act necessarily carries with it proof of intent. The dissenter also believed there was an abuse of discretion because the evidence was minimally probative and highly prejudicial on identity, which was the central issue of the case. In *United States v. Pollock,* 926 F.2d 1044 (11th Cir.), *cert. denied,* 112 S. Ct. 593 (1991), the Court upheld admission of the defendant's prior conviction for conspiracy to import marijuana in a cocaine conspiracy prosecution, noting that if the government can do without other crimes evidence in proving intent, it should, but if the evidence is essential to obtain a conviction, it may come in. "This may seem like a 'heads I win; tails you lose' proposition, but it is presently the law." In this case, because of the limited evidence of conspiratorial intent, the prior convictions were that much more probative.

Intent — extortion

United States v. Zeuli, 725 F.2d 813 (1st Cir. 1984): Another extortion transaction was held properly admitted to prove intent in a prosecution for conspiracy to extort.

United States v. Wilkes, 685 F.2d 135 (5th Cir. 1982): In a prosecution for extortion against a justice of the peace who used his official stationery to threaten arrest of those who did not respond to his letters, the Court upheld the introduction of proof of prior unlawful collection practices. Even though the defendant offered to stipulate that the letters were sent with the intent to collect payment of debts, the Court found that the issue of intent to extort remained in the case, and that the evidence was appropriately received on that issue.

United States v. Benton, 852 F.2d 1456 (6th Cir.), *cert. denied,* 109 S. Ct. 555 (1988): The Court upheld the admission of evidence that a defendant previously received kickbacks for ignoring bootlegging violations to establish his intent with respect to receipt of money from cocaine dealers. The defendant had claimed that he was investigating the dealers, and the prior act evidence tended to establish a plan of extortion. See also *United States v. Davis,* 707 F.2d 880 (6th Cir. 1983) (testimony by a witness that he was coerced into performing work at a sheriff's residence was properly admitted into the sheriff's RICO and Hobbs Act trial to show sheriff's intent to extort similar labor from his deputies).

United States v. Schweihs, 971 F.2d 1302 (7th Cir. 1992): The Court affirmed extortion convictions, holding there was no abuse of discretion in admitting other act evidence during the government's case-in-chief where there was ample reason to believe that the defendant would raise intent or knowledge as an issue, even though the Hobbs Act does not necessarily involve specific intent. In *United States v. Shackleford,* 738 F.2d 776 (7th Cir. 1984), the Court reversed an extortion conviction on the ground that the Trial Judge erred in admitting evidence of a similar instance of misconduct and in telling the jury that it could consider the evidence for the purposes permitted by Rule 404(b). Since the defendant's intent could be inferred from his threats and he never suggested he would raise lack of intent as a defense, the Court concluded that the similar act evidence should not have been admitted. See also *United States v. Tuchow,* 768 F.2d 855 (7th Cir. 1985) (other act evidence admissible to prove intent in extortion case).

United States v. Haskins, 737 F.2d 844 (10th Cir. 1984): The Court held that evidence of kickbacks outside the period covered by the indictment was admissible to prove intent in an extortion prosecution.

Intent — firearms cases

United States v. Swiatek, 819 F.2d 721 (7th Cir.), *cert. denied,* 108 S. Ct. 245 (1987): The Court found harmless error in the admission of a defendant's willingness to deal in stolen property and cars in a prosecution for firearms offenses.

United States v. Hooton, 662 F.2d 628 (9th Cir. 1981), *cert. denied,* 455 U.S. 1004 (1982): The Court held it was proper for the government to use other acts to show the defendant's intent to engage in a business of dealing in firearms as opposed an intent to enhance his gun collection.

United States v. Mittleider, 835 F.2d 769 (10th Cir. 1987), *cert. denied,* 108 S. Ct. 1279 (1988): Evidence of the defendant's subsequent conversation with an undercover agent concerning a gun purchase was admissible to show intent and absence of mistake in a prosecution for firearms violations.

Intent — fraud, forgery, counterfeiting, false statements, etc.

United States v. Nicely, 922 F.2d 850 (D.C. Cir. 1991): The Court reversed the defendants' convictions because a conspiracy involving a scheme to defraud a seller of computers into offering money to secure contracts and a separate conspiracy to launder money were improperly joined. The misjoinder was prejudicial because evidence of one scheme would be inadmissible in proving the other; it was not probative of intent and could not have survived a Rule 403 balancing. See also *United States v. Oppon,* 863 F.2d 141 (1st Cir. 1988) (evidence of other occasions when defendant falsely represented his citizenship admissible to prove intent in instant case); *United States v. McNeill*, 728 F.2d 5 (1st Cir. 1984) (evidence that defendant in mail fraud case gave a false address to the city retirement board from whom he sought disability benefits was admissible to show intent to defraud); *United States v. Cardillo*, 708 F.2d 29 (1st Cir.), *cert. denied*, 104 S. Ct. 531 (1983) (defendant's efforts to sell counterfeit coins held admissible in a prosecution for possession of counterfeit coins with intent to defraud).

United States v. Caputo, 808 F.2d 963 (2d Cir. 1987): The Court held evidence of previous credit card schemes admissible to prove intent in a prosecution for possession of an unauthorized credit card. See also *United States v. Smith*, 727 F.2d 214 (2d Cir. 1984) (similar act evidence could be used to prove intent to commit fraud in securities and wire fraud case, especially since defendant claimed that he was the victim of other brokers and of market forces).

United States v. Whaley, 786 F.2d 1229 (4th Cir. 1986): Affirming a conviction for making false statements on a loan application, the Court held that evidence concerning a similar transaction (in which the defendant used his status as a retired FBI agent to obtain special treatment from a car rental agency) three months after the application as well as evidence of conduct prior to the application was admissible to prove intent. In *United States v. Greenwood*, 796 F.2d 49 (4th Cir. 1986), the Court affirmed a defendant's convictions for submitting false vouchers to his employer, the FBI. It held that two prior acts of bank loan misstatements and meal reimbursement cover-up were properly admitted to prove the absence of mistake. See also *United States v. Bice-Bey*, 701 F.2d 1086 (4th Cir.), *cert. denied*, 464 U.S. 837 (1983) (upholding a conviction for credit card fraud involving a telephone order for electronic equipment, and finding that evidence of earlier calls was admissible to prove intent).

United States v. Campbell, 845 F.2d 1374 (6th Cir.), *cert. denied*, 109 S. Ct. 259 (1988): The Court held evidence regarding the billing of other patients was admissible to prove an intent to defraud Medicare. See also *United States v. Crachy*, 800 F.2d 83 (6th Cir. 1986), *cert. denied*, 479 U.S. 1042 (1987) (evidence of prior acts relating to counterfeit bills admissible to prove intent); *United States v. Hamilton*, 684 F.2d 380 (6th Cir.), *cert. denied*, 459 U.S. 976 (1982) (in prosecution for uttering altered obligations of the United States, evidence of previously passing a $2 bill altered to look like a $20 bill was properly admitted to prove intent and identity).

United States v. Macey, 8 F.3d 462 (7th Cir. 1993): The Court held it was error (but harmless) to admit evidence in a fraud trial that the defendant had previously changed an employee's records in an attempt to avoid paying compensation owed. The evidence did not so much show the defendant's intent as his willingness to break the law in a pinch, which is exactly what the Rule precludes. In *United States v. Draiman*, 784 F.2d 248 (7th Cir. 1986), the Court affirmed a mail fraud conviction arising from the defendant's filing false insurance claims after a burglary. Upholding the admission of evidence of prior fraudulent claims, it reasoned that mail fraud requires proof of specific intent and that a defendant cannot unilaterally remove intent as an element. The Court cautioned, however, that the government should not be permitted to "flood the courtroom" with other crimes evidence merely because specific intent must be proved. See also *United States v. Neely*, 980 F.2d 1074 (7th Cir. 1992) (no abuse of discretion in admitting evidence of defendant's participation in false-theft insurance fraud scheme as bearing on his state of mind in charged staged-collision insurance fraud scheme); *United States v. Taggatz,* 831 F.2d 1355 (7th Cir. 1987) (evidence of prior check-kiting scheme admissible to show intent, scheme and absence of mistake); *United States v. Chaimson,* 760 F.2d 798 (7th Cir. 1985) (admission of prior bribe payments to a county assessor upheld in a mail fraud prosecution involving bribery of officials as part of a scheme to fraudulently reduce real estate assessments).

United States v. Fitterer, 710 F.2d 1328 (8th Cir.), *cert. denied,* 104 S. Ct. 165 (1983): The Court held that evidence of an earlier insurance fraud was probative of intent in a mail fraud case. See also *United States v. Hardrich,* 707 F.2d 992 (8th Cir.), *cert. denied,* 104 S. Ct. 481 (1983) (evidence of prior conviction for uttering a forged instrument properly admitted to show intent in prosecution for uttering forged treasury checks).

United States v. Faust, 850 F.2d 575 (9th Cir. 1988): Evidence that the defendant forged a letter was held admissible to prove an intent to forge checks.

United States v. Cook, 745 F.2d 1311 (10th Cir. 1984): The defendant's false identification and attempts to evade identification were admitted to show knowledge and intent in a prosecution for making false representations in a currency transaction report.

United States v. Simon, 839 F.2d 1461 (11th Cir.), *cert. denied,* 108 S. Ct. 2883, 109 S. Ct. 158 (1988): The Court held that evidence that salespersons charged with fraud worked at other companies and that some were instrumental in accomplishing a fraud was admissible to prove intent. See also *United States v. Jackson,* 761 F.2d 1541 (11th Cir. 1985) (in prosecution of physician for using mails to effectuate a scheme to defraud insurance companies, evidence that defendant had accepted money for providing fraudulent medical excuses for employees to document absences was admissible to prove fraudulent intent); *United States v. Parr,* 716 F.2d 796 (11th Cir. 1983) (in a counterfeiting and conspiracy case, a tape recording of a conversation between one defendant who was selling counterfeit bills, a prospective purchaser, and an undercover informant was admissible); *United States v. Scott,* 701 F.2d 1340 (11th Cir.), *cert. denied,* 464 U.S. 856 (1983) (instances in which defendant used a name other than his own to obtain credit admissible to demonstrate intent in making false statements to banks and misusing the mails).

Intent — generally

United States v. O'Connor, 580 F.2d 38 (2d Cir. 1978): The Court reversed a conviction of a government inspector for taking money from meatpacking companies in connection with his official duties, finding that evidence of other bribes allegedly received by the defendant was improperly received as evidence of intent, since there really was no issue of intent in the case. In dealing with Rule 404(b) problems, the Court stated that, although other crimes evidence may be admitted, "caution and judgment are called for, and a Trial Judge faced with an other crimes evidence problem should require the Government to explain why the evidence is relevant and necessary."

Sparks v. Gilley Trucking Co., 992 F.2d 50 (4th Cir. 1993): The defendant in a personal injury action arising out of a car-truck collision introduced evidence of the plaintiff's prior speeding convictions "to show intent, preparation, plan or motive to race

Intent — generally (cont'd)

or speed on the day in question.'' The Court reversed a judgment for the defendant, holding that intent was not relevant to the contributory negligence defense being asserted and that there was no foundation for any theory of "plan," "motive," or "preparation." The dissenting Judge considered intent relevant to the defendant's attempt to prove the plaintiff had been racing.

United States v. Prati, 861 F.2d 82 (5th Cir. 1988): The Court said that "in a conspiracy case the mere entry of a not guilty plea raises the issue of intent sufficiently to justify the admissibility of extrinsic offense evidence." See also *United States v. Rubio,* 834 F.2d 442 (5th Cir. 1987) (prior evidence of child pornography admissible in child pornography prosecution to prove defendant's intent to receive items through the mail); *United States v. Westmoreland,* 841 F.2d 572 (5th Cir.), *cert. denied,* 109 S. Ct. 62 (1988) (testimony concerning defendant's financial records in prior term as judge admissible to prove intent with respect to receipt of money while serving as county supervisor); *United States v. Wilson,* 732 F.2d 404 (5th Cir.), *cert. denied,* 105 S. Ct. 609 (1984) (extraneous acts of terrorism properly admitted to show intent where defendant denied intent and claimed he was working for the CIA); *United States v. Roberts,* 619 F.2d 379 (5th Cir. 1980) (defendant's prior conviction for a gambling offense properly admitted to prove that he intended to join a conspiracy).

United States v. Beechum, 582 F.2d 898 (5th Cir. 1978) (en banc), *rev'g* 555 F.2d 487 (5th Cir. 1977), *cert. denied,* 440 U.S. 920 (1979): In this leading case, the crucial question at trial was whether the defendant took a silver dollar from the mail with the intent to keep it or whether he was planning to turn the coin in to postal authorities. On the issue of intent, the government offered evidence that the defendant had two Sears credit cards in his pocket which were not issued to him and which were unsigned. The *en banc* Court held that Rule 404(b) requires a two-part analysis:

> First, it must be determined that the extrinsic offense evidence is relevant to an issue other than the defendant's character. Second, the evidence must possess probative value that is not substantially outweighed by its undue prejudice and must meet the other requirements of rule 403.

In the first step of the analysis, "the task for the trial judge is to determine whether there is sufficient evidence for the jury to find that the defendant in fact committed the extrinsic offense," and whether the charged offense and the other crime are similar. How similar the offenses must be depends upon the theory of admissibility urged: identity, for example, would require much greater similarity than intent. Regarding the balancing step, the Court noted that there is grave danger of prejudice when other crimes evidence is offered and that "[t]his danger is particularly great where, as here, the extrinsic activity was not the subject of a conviction; the jury may feel that the defendant should be punished for that activity even if he is not guilty of the offense charged." Abjuring mechanical solutions, the Court called "for a commonsense assessment of all the circumstances surrounding the extrinsic offense." Among the factors noted were the extent to which intent was an issue, the need of the government to use the evidence, the similarity of the charged and other offense, the temporal relationship between the charged and other offense, the nature of the criminal activity charged, and the probable effectiveness of a limiting instruction. The Court indicated that its analysis governed extrinsic offense evidence whether the extrinsic offense occurred before or after the offense charged, and that its analysis "applies whenever the extrinsic activity reflects adversely on the character of the defendant, regardless whether that activity might give rise to criminal liability." Five dissenters argued that the majority's approach tended to admit propensity evidence despite the first sentence of subdivision (b), that its approach was inconsistent with the restrictions found in Rules 608 and 609, and that other Circuits utilized tests that were more protective of criminal defendants and more likely to produce fairer trials. But the principal difference between the majority and the dissent was that on the issue of intent the majority did not require the extrinsic offense to include the same essential physical elements as the charged offense; it was enough that the government's evidence was sufficient to convince a jury that the defendant had the same state of mind when committing both offenses. The dissenters favored an objective test of similarity of the elements of both offenses.

United States v. Kramer, 955 F.2d 479 (7th Cir. 1992), *cert. denied,* 113 S. Ct. 595 (1993): The Court affirmed convictions for conspiring to distribute marijuana as part of a continuing criminal enterprise that imported marijuana, holding that the Trial Judge exercised principled discretion in admitting evidence that one of the defendants had imported fifteen tons of marijuana in 1981, as the evidence showed specific intent, was not too remote to be relevant, and its prejudicial effect, if any, did not substantially outweigh its probative value. One Judge, concurring, expressed concern that the Circuit's rule that intent is "necessarily in issue" when a defendant is charged with a specific-intent crime had resulted in a great deal of prejudicial extrinsic evidence finding its way into many criminal trials. In *United States v. Gruttadauro,* 818 F.2d 1323 (7th Cir. 1987), the Court held that it was error to admit evidence of prior contacts between an employer and a union business agent charged with willfully receiving money from the employer. After holding that "the mental state of wilfulness is not similar to a specific intent crime," the Court found that the defendant had not placed his mental state in issue and that the admission of the other act evidence was erroneous, although harmless. See also *United States v. Arnold,* 773 F.2d 823 (7th Cir. 1985) (taped conversation discussing prior unsuccessful attempt to bribe witness admissible to prove specific intent to obstruct grand jury investigation); *United States v. Radseck,* 718 F.2d 233 (7th Cir. 1983), *cert. denied,* 104 S. Ct. 1291 (1984) (prior acts of defendant in soliciting kickbacks in return for insurance business admissible to prove intent).

United States v. Miller, 874 F.2d 1255 (9th Cir. 1989): The Court held that evidence that the defendant, an FBI agent, had previously sold information to an FBI informant was not sufficiently similar to the charged espionage conspiracy to be admissible as proof of intent.

United States v. Cardenas, 895 F.2d 1338 (11th Cir. 1990): The Trial Judge admitted evidence at the defendant's trial on drug conspiracy and possession charges of his prior drug usage and dealings to prove his knowledge of cocaine and intent to possess it. Rejecting the defendant's argument that knowledge and intent were not at issue and that the sole issue was identity, the Court held that intent is an issue whenever the defendant enters a not guilty plea to a conspiracy charge without taking affirmative steps to remove

Intent — generally (cont'd)

the issue of intent from the case. After reviewing the *Beechum* factors (*United States v. Beechum,* 582 F.2d 898 (5th Cir. 1978) (en banc), *cert. denied,* 440 U.S. 920 (1979) (*supra*)), the Court concluded there was no error in admitting the evidence. The dissenting Judge would not require affirmative steps to remove the intent issue when the substantive act is charged along with the conspiracy, as proof of the substantive act necessarily carries with it proof of intent. The dissenter also believed there was abuse of discretion because the evidence was minimally probative and highly prejudicial on identity, which was the central issue of the case. In *United States v. Pollock,* 926 F.2d 1044 (11th Cir.), *cert. denied,* 112 S. Ct. 593 (1991), the Court upheld admission of the defendant's prior conviction for conspiracy to import marijuana in a cocaine conspiracy prosecution, noting that if the government can do without other crimes evidence in proving intent, it should, but if the evidence is essential to obtain a conviction, it may come in. "This may seem like a 'heads I win; tails you lose' proposition, but it is presently the law." In this case, because of the limited evidence of conspiratorial intent, the prior convictions were that much more probative. See also *United States v. Hurley,* 755 F.2d 788 (11th Cir. 1985) (evidence that defendant was with husband after escape admissible to prove intent to help him escape).

Intent — tax cases

United States v. Johnson, 893 F.2d 451 (1st Cir. 1990): The Court held that evidence of filing blatantly false tax exemption claims and failing to file an income tax return in 1987 was admissible to negate a defense to charged tax evasion in 1982-86 that the defendant had relied in good faith on the advice of others in filing false returns for those years.

United States v. Tarricone, 996 F.2d 1414 (2d Cir. 1993): The Court affirmed a defendant's convictions arising from participation in a scheme to evade gasoline excise taxes, holding there was no error in admitting evidence that the defendant controlled New York City's bootleg gas operations, where the defendant did not clearly indicate that he was not disputing knowledge or intent. In a prosecution for tax evasion, *United States v. Collorafi,* 876 F.2d 303 (2d Cir. 1989), the Court reversed *in limine* orders excluding memorandum decisions dismissing the defendant's earlier civil challenges to the income tax laws as meritless and frivolous, holding they were admissible on the issue of the defendant's knowledge and wrongful intent and their probative value was not substantially outweighed by any dangers of prejudice or confusion.

United States v. McClain, 934 F.2d 822 (7th Cir. 1991): In a public corruption case, the Court held that any error was harmless when the government introduced evidence of illegal taps on gas lines as probative of intent to evade taxes. See also *United States v. Micke,* 859 F.2d 473 (7th Cir. 1988) (evidence that defendant offered to backdate documents to support fraudulent tax claims admissible to prove intent with respect to other taxpayers); *United States v. Birkenstock,* 823 F.2d 1026 (7th Cir. 1987) (upholding admission of evidence regarding the defendant's earlier tax returns as bearing upon his intent in a willful failure to file prosecution).

United States v. Richards, 723 F.2d 646 (8th Cir. 1983): The defendant's communications with the IRS concerning 1983 taxes were admissible in a prosecution involving his 1981 return.

United States v. Bergman, 813 F.2d 1027 (9th Cir.), *cert. denied,* 108 S. Ct. 154 (1987): The Court held that a defendant's W-2 and W-4 forms were properly admitted to show willfulness in a prosecution for failure to file a tax return.

United States v. Rothbart, 723 F.2d 752 (10th Cir. 1983): Evidence that the defendant previously filed late personal tax returns was held admissible to show intent in a prosecution for failure to file timely quarterly employer's returns.

United States v. Dixon, 698 F.2d 445 (11th Cir. 1983): The Court affirmed, using evidence that tax liability was understated in 1977 as evidence of an intent to evade taxes in 1975 and 1976.

Intent — theft, robbery, and stolen property offenses

United States v. Blood, 806 F.2d 1218 (4th Cir. 1986): The Court held that a prior Tax Court decision involving the defendant was admissible to support an expert's opinion and relevant to prove the defendant willfully violated the law in an embezzlement case.

United States v. Beechum, 582 F.2d 898 (5th Cir. 1978) (en banc), *rev'g* 555 F.2d 487 (5th Cir. 1977), *cert. denied,* 440 U.S. 920 (1979): In this leading case, the crucial question at trial was whether the appellant took a silver dollar from the mail with the intent to keep it, or whether he was planning to turn the coin in to postal authorities. The Court held there was no error when the government offered evidence on the intent issue that the defendant had two Sears credit cards in his pocket which were not issued to him and which were unsigned.

United States v. Mothershed, 859 F.2d 585 (8th Cir. 1988): The Court reversed a conviction for aiding and abetting a bank robbery, because the Trial Judge admitted evidence of a previous conviction for possession of stolen bank money. The Court rejected the Trial Judge's ruling that the prior act was relevant with respect to intent, since there was no showing that the defendant intended at the time of his earlier crime that a bank be robbed. In *United States v. Krapp,* 815 F.2d 1183 (8th Cir.), *cert. denied,* 108 S. Ct. 174 (1987), the Court held that evidence of other violations of postal regulations was relevant to prove an intent to defraud or mislead on the part of a postmaster who claimed that she was not properly instructed on the correct procedures for reporting shortages. See also *United States v. Burkett,* 821 F.2d 1306 (8th Cir. 1987) (evidence of unrelated burglaries properly admitted to prove intent in prosecution for break-in at post office, even though defendant had indicated he intended to rely solely on alibi).

United States v. McCollum, 732 F.2d 1419 (9th Cir.), *cert. denied,* 105 S. Ct. 301 (1984): The Court upheld a defendant's conviction for attempting a 1982 bank robbery, finding that a 1970 conviction for armed robbery, admitted under Rule 609, was admissible under Rule 404(b) to prove intent, where the defendant claimed that he committed the instant crime under the influence of hypnosis. A dissenting Judge argued that it was inappropriate to sustain admission of evidence on a theory never argued to the Trial Court and that the prejudicial effect of the evidence outweighed its probative value.

In *United States v. Albuquerque,* 538 F.2d 277 (9th Cir. 1976), a prosecution for interstate transportation of a vehicle knowing it to be stolen, the Court concluded that "hotwiring" tools, admitted on the theory that they demonstrated the defendants' intent, were not relevant to any element in the case; they did not demonstrate defendants' knowledge that the automobile was, in fact, stolen.

United States v. Cummings, 798 F.2d 413 (10th Cir. 1986): The Court affirmed a conviction for selling a stolen cab portion of a tractor-trailer, finding that evidence that the defendant was involved in a pattern or practice of dealing in stolen trucks and parts was admissible to prove intent and the absence of mistake.

Joinder of claims

United States v. Holloway, 1 F.3d 307 (5th Cir. 1993): The Court reversed a defendant's robbery conviction because his motion to sever a charge for being a convicted felon in possession of a weapon (arising out of his possession when arrested two months after the latest robbery) had been denied. Had the weapons charge not been improperly joined, he could have precluded evidence that he was a convicted felon who had a weapon when arrested by not testifying, and even if he did testify, it is unlikely the fact of his prior conviction would be repeated to the jury or the fact of his gun possession would be admissible.

Joint defendants

United States v. Hernandez, 780 F.2d 113 (D.C. Cir. 1986): The Court held that evidence that one of two defendants was involved in a fight hours before being arrested for possession of a firearm was relevant to prove motive. It also found, however, that there was insufficient evidence to conclude that the other defendant was involved in the fight. Thus, the admission of the evidence against him was prejudicial error.

United States v. David, 940 F.2d 722 (1st Cir.), *cert. denied,* 112 S. Ct. 605, 908, 1298, 2301 (1991): The Court affirmed convictions in connection with a drug conspiracy, holding that evidence of violence by one member of the conspiracy was properly admitted. The Rule 404(b) objection by the defendant was properly rejected, because the challenged evidence was independently admissible as proof that he ran a continuing criminal enterprise and thus was not "other crimes" evidence. Other defendants lacked standing to raise Rule 404(b) objections to evidence of conduct not attributable to them, and the evidence did not have a prejudicial spillover effect.

United States v. Danzey, 594 F.2d 905 (2d Cir.), *cert. denied,* 441 U.S. 951 (1979): One of two defendants convicted of bank robbery confessed to fifteen bank robberies, and the evidence "was so plainly relevant as to be classic similar act evidence admissible under the rule ... to show a *modus operandi.*" The Court concluded, however, that an inadequately redacted form, which included the word "Blank" as a substitute for the name of the accomplice identified by the defendant who confessed, required reversal as to the codefendant, because of possible spillover effects. Compare *United States v. Rosenwasser,* 550 F.2d 806 (2d Cir.), *cert. denied,* 434 U.S. 825 (1977), where the appellant was not permitted to cross-examine an FBI agent who testified that he had arrested the codefendant for a similar offense three weeks after the charged hijacking. The jury was instructed that the other crimes evidence was admissible only against the codefendant and not against the appellant. Because the other crime involved a building in which the defendant conducted his business, however, the case presented "a close question," but the Court concluded that the limiting instruction was sufficiently strong to protect the appellant. One Judge dissented.

United States v. Johnson, 610 F.2d 194 (4th Cir. 1979), *cert. denied,* 446 U.S. 911 (1980): One defendant's cross-examination of a government witness brought out inadmissible other crimes evidence about a codefendant. The Court held (2-1) that, since the evidence did not carry the imprimatur of the government and was the subject of a cautionary instruction, its admission was not prejudicial error. See also *United States v. Smith Grading & Paving, Inc.,* 760 F.2d 527 (4th Cir. 1985), *cert. denied,* 474 U.S 1005 (1985) (in prosecution for conspiracy to rig bids, introduction of one defendant's previous bidrigging to prove knowledge and intent to enter a conspiracy was more probative than it was prejudicial upon other defendants).

United States v. Salomon, 609 F.2d 1172 (5th Cir. 1980): The Court found it was error not to grant a severance when a codefendant testified about other crimes involving the defendant.

United States v. Phillips, 599 F.2d 134 (6th Cir. 1979): The Court reversed a bank robbery conviction because an unindicted accomplice was permitted to testify that the defendant was involved in three other bank robberies. The Court recognized that it might be probative on the issue of identity that a defendant committed three other crimes with the same person, if this person were also charged with the fourth crime, but it found no "necessariness of association" in the instant case.

United States v. Cardall, 885 F.2d 656 (10th Cir. 1989): In reversing one defendant's fraud conviction, the Court held that there was insufficient evidence the defendant was actually involved in bad acts of codefendants that the government offered against him and the others. In *United States v. Warledo,* 557 F.2d 721 (10th Cir. 1977), convictions for conspiracy to set fire to a railroad bridge, conspiracy to obstruct interstate commerce, and possession of an incendiary bomb were reversed because the government was improperly permitted to ask one of the defendants whether he possessed a rifle found in his automobile and to introduce the rifle together with a clip and bullets to rebut his denial of possession. The Court rejected the government's opening of the door for this dangerous form of impeachment on an irrelevant matter, and it reversed all the appellants' convictions because the conspiracy charges made it likely that the evidence would have affected all of them.

United States v. Bovain, 708 F.2d 606 (11th Cir.), *cert. denied,* 464 U.S. 898, 997, 1018 (1983): The Court affirmed heroin convictions, finding no spillover prejudice in the admission of evidence offered by one defendant that he had been convicted of another offense and was serving time during the early part of the conspiracy alleged by the government. The Court emphasized that the Trial Judge took "great pains" to advise the jury as to the proper use of the prior conviction.

Jury instructions

United States v. Sampson, 980 F.2d 883 (3d Cir. 1992): The Court reversed a conviction for marijuana possession because evidence of prior drug crimes had been admitted without the government articulating, and without the Trial Court putting into the record and instructing the jury as to, the permissible inferences. Where the government has not clearly stated reasons why the evidence is relevant to any legitimate purpose, there is no basis to believe the jury will cull the proper inferences from the evidence, and by simply repeating the entire litany of permissible theories under the Rule, the Trial Judge's instruction gave the jury inadequate guidance.

United States v. Gordon, 780 F.2d 1165 (5th Cir. 1986): The Court affirmed conspiracy and fraud convictions arising from a scheme to file a false theft claim with respect to a truck, holding there was no error in admitting evidence that the defendant had previously defrauded an insurance company. The evidence was relevant and not unduly prejudicial in a fraud case. The Court added that the Trial Judge's limiting instruction cured any possible problem with the admission of the evidence.

United States v. Steele, 727 F.2d 580 (6th Cir.), *cert. denied,* 104 S. Ct. 2396 (1984): Where a government witness stated that one of the defendants in a narcotics case had previously spent time in a South American jail and the Trial Judge immediately instructed the jury to disregard the statement, the Court found that the defendant's rights were protected and that no mistrial was required.

United States v. Townsend, 924 F.2d 1385 (7th Cir. 1991): In a drug distribution conspiracy trial, the prosecution offered evidence that one defendant sold cocaine to an undercover agent before the charged conspiracy began. The Court held that the evidence was properly admitted as proof of identity because it demonstrated the defendant responded to a beeper number paged by another defendant during the conspiracy. The jury should not have been instructed it could consider the evidence as proof of intent or knowledge, however, but the error was harmless.

United States v. Gonzalez, 975 F.2d 1514 (11th Cir. 1992): The defendant was charged with conspiring to conduct money laundering and with money laundering on or about July 27. The Court reversed the defendant's conviction on the latter count because the Trial Judge had erroneously refused to give an instruction that limited use of evidence of money laundering in May and June to showing the defendant's intent and guilty knowledge.

Knowledge — assault, homicide, abuse, etc.

United States v. Sanders, 964 F.2d 295 (4th Cir. 1992): Reversing a conviction for assault with a dangerous weapon in a prison, the Court held it was error to admit evidence of the defendant's prior convictions for inmate assault and contraband possession. As assault is not the kind of crime in which knowledge is even implicitly in issue, the evidence was not probative of anything except criminal propensity. In *United States v. Fleming,* 739 F.2d 945 (4th Cir. 1984), *cert. denied,* 105 S. Ct. 970 (1985), the Court affirmed a murder conviction arising from an automobile collision, finding that evidence of the defendant's previous convictions for driving while intoxicated was properly admitted to show "that defendant had grounds to be aware of the risk his drinking and driving while intoxicated presented to others."

Knowledge — civil rights cases

United States v. White, 788 F.2d 390 (6th Cir. 1986): The Court affirmed a conviction for conspiring and aiding and abetting in violating the housing rights of a black family, holding that evidence of a fire at a codefendant's home prior to the burning of the victimized family's house was relevant to the defendant's knowledge of his codefendant's propensity to engage in arson and was admissible to prove why the defendant went to the codefendant for help. The Court also held that evidence of a subsequent arson by the codefendant should not have been admitted even if the defendant learned of it, since later knowledge did not prove what the defendant knew at the time of the relevant acts.

United States v. Sellers, 906 F.2d 597 (11th Cir. 1990): In affirming convictions for violating a theft suspect's civil rights by allowing a codefendant to beat him, the Court held there was no abuse of discretion in admitting evidence of the codefendant's violent acts and reputation for violence, as it supported the government's theory that the defendants knew of the codefendant's violent proclivities and intended to use him to beat a confession out of the suspect.

Knowledge — drug cases

United States v. Arias-Montoya, 967 F.2d 708 (1st Cir. 1992): The Court held it was error (but harmless) to admit the defendant's ten-year-old conviction for cocaine possession to negate his assertion that he had no knowledge of the cocaine packaged for distribution that was found in the trunk of the car he was driving, as the evidence had no probative value for that purpose. One Judge concurred in the result, on the ground that the Rule bars other crimes evidence to show action in conformity with character, but not to prove intent and knowledge. In *United States v. Ferrer-Cruz,* 899 F.2d 135 (1st Cir. 1990), the defendant, convicted of aiding and abetting possession of cocaine with intent to distribute, argued that evidence of prior convictions for possessing cocaine and marijuana were inadmissible because he defended on the ground of mistaken identity. The Court held that the mistaken identity defense did not necessarily remove the issues of knowledge or intent, that the defendant did not clearly stipulate to remove those issues, and that the defendant did in fact argue "mere presence" in a car with cocaine. The dissenting Judge expressed concern about the Circuit's inclusionary approach to the Rule, considered that the defendant had raised "mere presence" only in the grand jury and not at trial, and concluded that the evidence was being used only to show propensity. In *United States v. Garcia-Rosa,* 876 F.2d 209 (1st Cir. 1989), *cert. denied,* 493 U.S. 1030, *vacated on other grounds,* 498 U.S. 954 (1990), the Court reversed a conviction for offenses in connection with a drug-importation conspiracy, holding that evidence of drugs found in the defendant's home at the time of his arrest, sixteen months after the events in issue, was not admissible because he had never put his knowledge of drugs at issue, so it could not be used to rebut implications that he "knew nothing about drugs";

it was not probative to imply his knowledge that a loan given at the earlier time was to be used for an illegal drug-related purpose; and the prejudicial effect of the evidence far exceeded any probative value it might have. In *United States v. Moccia,* 681 F.2d 61 (1st Cir. 1982), a prosecution for possession of marijuana and diethylpropion with intent to distribute, the Court upheld the admission of evidence of a state court conviction to prove knowledge. The drugs were found buried under some dog food in the freezer room of a farmhouse where the defendant lived. Although the defendant offered to stipulate that whatever he did was done knowingly and intentionally, the Court said that the prior conviction might have helped the jury because a prior marijuana user might have been more likely to spot marijuana and more likely to associate with those who use it. In our view, the prior conviction had little, if any, probative value, given the stipulation, and its similarity to the crime charged should have required exclusion.

United States v. Gordon, 987 F.2d 902 (2d Cir. 1993): The Court reversed a conviction for cocaine offenses arising out of the defendant's arrival at an airport to pick up a person who was carrying cocaine and marijuana, holding that his arrest a year earlier while in possession of crack cocaine did virtually nothing to prove what he knew at the airport and that the evidence was clearly prejudicial. The dissenting Judge thought there was sufficient similarity to show knowledge of drug dealing activity and it was unnecessary to show specific knowledge of importation. See also *United States v. Arango-Correa,* 851 F.2d 54 (2d Cir. 1988) (records obtained in searches of defendant's car and apartment admissible to prove knowledge of contents of a shipment); *United States v. Da Silva,* 725 F.2d 828 (2d Cir. 1983) (evidence of similar importation of drugs admissible to show knowledge).

United States v. Gonzalez-Lira, 936 F.2d 184 (5th Cir. 1991): At the trial of a defendant charged with smuggling marijuana into the United States in a tractor-trailer, the government introduced evidence that two years earlier a tractor-trailer owned by the defendant and driven by another man was stopped at the same border checkpoint and found to contain 2,000 pounds of marijuana. The Court held that even though the defendant was not charged in that incident, the evidence tended to show the thoroughness of the government's investigation, the defendant's awareness of means used to smuggle large quantities of marijuana, the defendant's awareness that his own rig had been used to smuggle marijuana, and the source of funds used to purchase the tractor involved in this case. The majority held that the evidence was not admissible under Rule 404(b), but was properly admitted under Rules 402 and 403; the concurring Judge believed that the evidence was admissible under 404(b) to show knowledge and absence of mistake. In *United States v. McDonald,* 905 F.2d 871 (5th Cir.), *cert. denied,* 111 S. Ct. 566 (1990), the Court held it was error (but harmless) to cross-examine a defendant charged with importing marijuana about his prior use of speed and cocaine, as that would not lead to an inference that he knew his car contained marijuana when he was arrested and would only be probative of his character as a drug user. See also *United States v. Nichols,* 750 F.2d 1260 (5th Cir. 1985) (evidence of previous importation of marijuana admissible in cocaine conspiracy prosecution to rebut defendant's claim of lack of knowledge of illicit drug trade and denial of any previous trafficking); *United States v. Contreras,* 602 F.2d 1237 (5th Cir.), *cert. denied,* 444 U.S. 971 (1979) (evidence of defendant's drug use subsequent to charged events admissible to show knowledge at the relevant time).

United States v. Hitow, 889 F.2d 1573 (6th Cir. 1989): The Court held that evidence a defendant had previously purchased several thousand pounds of marijuana was relevant to show his knowledgeable participation in the charged conspiracy to possess more than 1,000 pounds of marijuana with intent to distribute.

United States v. Davis, 838 F.2d 909 (7th Cir. 1988): The Court held that other drug transactions were admissible to prove knowledge of a conspiracy.

United States v. O'Connell, 841 F.2d 1408 (8th Cir.), *cert. denied,* 108 S. Ct. 2857 (1988), 109 S. Ct. 799 (1989): The Court held other acts admissible in a drug prosecution to prove a knowing contribution to the conspiracy.

United States v. Mayans, 17 F.3d 1174 (9th Cir. 1994): The Court reversed cocaine convictions, finding, *inter alia,* that it was error to admit evidence of an earlier drug deal to show the defendant's knowledge without requiring the government to demonstrate a logical connection between involvement in the prior acts and the knowledge alleged in the instant case. The Court observed that the Judge "was satisfied with information of the crudest sort," had declined to undertake the required Rule 403 balancing, and had erroneously admitted the prior act both as Rule 404(b) evidence and as evidence of an additional overt act, which meant that the defendant could not obtain a limiting instruction. In *United States v. Garcia-Orozco,* 997 F.2d 1302 (9th Cir. 1993), the Court reversed convictions for importing and possessing marijuana, holding that evidence of the defendant's prior arrest for possession with intent to distribute heroin, which arose from an incident when he was riding as a passenger in a car that contained drugs, was irrelevant. Although the defendant was arrested while driving a car in the instant case, the Court reasoned that was no logical basis to infer that he knew that drugs were in his vehicle simply because previously drugs were found in a car in which he was a passenger, especially where the defendant was convicted on the earlier occasion only of resisting arrest, and there was no demonstrated connection between the drugs and him. In *United States v. Bibo-Rodriguez,* 922 F.2d 1398 (9th Cir.), *cert. denied,* 111 S. Ct. 2861 (1991), the Court affirmed the defendant's conviction for importing cocaine, holding there was no error in admitting evidence he imported marijuana in a similar manner nine weeks later to prove that the charged importation was knowing.

United States v. Kendall, 766 F.2d 1426 (10th Cir. 1985), *cert. denied,* 474 U.S. 1081 (1986): The Court held that other act evidence was properly used to show knowledge and absence of mistake in a drug prosecution.

United States v. Edwards, 696 F.2d 1277 (11th Cir.), *cert. denied,* 461 U.S. 909 (1983): The Court affirmed convictions arising out of a drug importation conspiracy. It found that one defendant's statements concerning his involvement in prior drug smuggling were admissible to prove knowledge of importation and distribution.

Knowledge — firearms cases

United States v. Flores Perez, 849 F.2d 1 (1st Cir. 1988): The Court reversed a conviction for aiding and abetting a firearms transaction, finding that evidence of the defendant's pending firearm charges in Puerto Rico was erroneously admitted. There was no evidence, aside from the fact that charges were brought, that the Puerto Rico case involved an unlicensed or stolen weapon. The Court held that the jury should not have been told that the defendant had been charged with the other offenses, and expressed doubt as to whether the other charges were relevant to a case in which the firearms offense involved an obliterated serial number.

United States v. Teague, 737 F.2d 378 (4th Cir. 1984), *cert. denied,* 105 S. Ct. 913 (1985): The Court held that the defendant's prior offer to sell a gun was admissible to prove knowledge and intent in case in which he denied knowing that a pistol was in his car.

United States v. Johnson, 562 F.2d 515 (8th Cir. 1977): The Court upheld using the defendant's previous possession of weapons to show knowledge on a firearms charge.

United States v. Kindred, 931 F.2d 609 (9th Cir. 1991): The Court reversed a conviction for possession of an unregistered firearm, an inoperable World War I German machine gun, holding it was an abuse of discretion to admit evidence of an eleven-year-old misdemeanor conviction for failing to register a handgun. General knowledge of a requirement that firearms must be registered was not a material element of the offense charged, which required the defendant's specific knowledge that he possessed a dangerous device of a type that would alert one to the likelihood of regulation.

United States v. Shomo, 786 F.2d 981 (10th Cir. 1986): The Court reversed a conviction for possession of a firearm by an ex-felon. It found that evidence that a rifle had been confiscated within two weeks of the crime charged in this case was improperly admitted to show the defendant's knowledge that it was illegal for him to possess a firearm, since knowledge was not an element of the offense. The Court observed that the government had ample evidence and "tried this case on the theory of 'Give a dog an ill name and hang him.'"

United States v. Pearson, 746 F.2d 787 (11th Cir. 1984): Evidence of the large number of guns found in the defendant's residence was admitted to prove that the defendant, charged with violating a firearms statute, must have known that the weapons were on the premises.

Knowledge — fraud, forgery, counterfeiting, false statements, etc.

United States v. Rhodes, 886 F.2d 375 (D.C. Cir. 1989): In reversing a conviction for bank fraud and forgery, the Court held it was plain error to admit evidence of other fraudulent activity, since because it was not sufficiently connected with defendant it did not undermine his defense that he did not know that check he presented was bad.

United States v. Crocker, 788 F.2d 802 (1st Cir. 1986): The Court affirmed a conviction for conspiracy to commit bank theft, holding that the fact that a defendant had previously been arrested while riding in a car with a codefendant and counterfeit checks was highly probative of the defendant's knowledge in a prosecution arising out of the transportation of the codefendant to a bank to cash the counterfeit checks.

United States v. Wiley, 846 F.2d 150 (2d Cir. 1988): The Court held that it was error, but harmless, in a prosecution for a scheme to defraud potential distributors of home security and energy saving devices to admit a document that indicated that a state court had enjoined the mastermind of the scheme (who testified for the government) and one of the defendants from doing business because of their false statements in the course of selling other distributorships. The Court reasoned that even a cautionary instruction could not remove the risk that the jury would treat the evidence as proof of a propensity. See also *United States v. Nemes,* 555 F.2d 51 (2d Cir. 1977) (similar transactions after the charged events properly introduced to show knowledge and intent in prosecution for Medicare and Medicaid fraud).

United States v. Brainard, 745 F.2d 320 (4th Cir. 1984), *cert. denied,* 471 U.S. 1099 (1985): The Court held that evidence of a prior investment scheme was admissible to rebut the defendant's claim that he had been serving his client's interests in good faith.

United States v. York, 888 F.2d 1050 (5th Cir. 1989): In a complex fraud prosecution, the defendant suggested that he was unaware of the details of certain transactions and that another man was really the key player and decisionmaker. The Court held that evidence the defendant received a million-dollar check from the other man was admissible to show the defendant's knowledge of the transactions and to rebut the suggestion he was merely a pawn in the scheme.

United States v. Studley, 892 F.2d 518 (7th Cir. 1989): In a prosecution for knowingly disposing of farm equipment pledged by another farmer to the Farmers Home Administration, the Trial Judge denied a motion *in limine* to exclude evidence that the defendant had previously sold grain through a third person in order to bypass the requirement of obtaining an FHA endorsement on the check received for sale of the grain. The Court held that the other acts were sufficiently similar to the crime charged to be probative on the defendant's knowledge of the practice of selling property through third parties to avoid having to get FHA releases and of how to dispose of pledged property without detection, and that the prejudicial effect, if any, of the evidence was limited by "clear and appropriate" cautionary instructions to the jury to consider the other acts "only on the question of motive, intent, knowledge and absence of mistake or accident." In a fraud prosecution, *United States v. Weisman,* 736 F.2d 421 (7th Cir.), *cert. denied,* 105 S. Ct. 390 (1984), the Court found that the defendant's entry of a guilty plea on behalf of a corporation in 1980, the transcript of the plea proceeding, and other evidence concerning past investigations of the corporation and statements by the defendant regarding his fear of an FTC investigation were properly admitted to respond to the defendant's claim that he had no personal knowledge of any fraud committed by the corporation's employees.

United States v. Anderson, 879 F.2d 369 (8th Cir.), *cert. denied,* 493 U.S. 982 (1989): In a public-contract fraud prosecution, evidence that the defendants had previously confessed to state antitrust charges of collusive and noncompetitive bidding for public construction projects was properly admitted to show the defendants had knowledge of each other's activities and had acted in accordance with each other's actions. In *United States v. Popow,* 821 F.2d 483 (8th Cir. 1987), the Court held that a prior deportation was admissible to prove knowledge in a prosecution for making false representations to the INS and for misrepresenting identity at the border. See also *United States v. Hutchings,* 751 F.2d 230 (8th Cir. 1984), *cert. denied,* 474 U.S. 829 (1985) (permissible to present evidence in fraud case of defendant's previous acts showing that he had knowledge of proper procedure regarding disclosure to insurance premium finance company of fees charged).

Knowledge — generally

United States v. Sutton, 801 F.2d 1346 (D.C. Cir. 1986): In a prosecution arising out of a conspiracy to bribe federal officials, the Court reasoned that convictions for obstruction of justice and conspiracy to obstruct justice that involved events that took place 18 months before the charged conspiracy were relevant to prove the defendant's knowledge that transfers of money he had authorized were used to bribe federal officials.

United States v. Walker, 710 F.2d 1062 (5th Cir. 1983), *cert. denied,* 104 S. Ct. 995 (1984): The Court upheld a conviction for conspiracy to intimidate a grand jury witness, holding that evidence of the defendant's boasts to a fellow conspirator concerning prior violent acts was admissible to show his knowledge of the purposes of the conspiracy and that the probative value of the evidence exceeded any prejudicial effects.

United States v. Marshall, 683 F.2d 1212 (8th Cir. 1982): The Court approved a ruling that two reports by Department of Agriculture employees concerning visits to the defendant's grocery store in 1976 and 1978, which suggested that he might have been violating federal law concerning redemption of food stamps, could be used in a prosecution for food stamp improprieties that took place in 1981. The dissenting Judge found that the reports did not establish clearly enough that any violations had occurred in the earlier years and that they were unduly prejudicial. In our view, the preferable procedure would have been to redact the reports, admitting only those portions indicating that the defendant had been informed of certain requirements of federal law. Reference to past violations was not needed to prove knowledge.

United States v. Thomas, 893 F.2d 1066 (9th Cir.), *cert. denied,* 111 S. Ct. 80 (1990): The Court held that previous convictions for molesting young girls were properly admitted to show that a defendant charged with child pornography knew that the girl pictured with him performing sex acts was a minor.

Knowledge — illegal aliens

United States v. Rubio-Gonzalez, 674 F.2d 1067 (5th Cir. 1982): The Court held that records of the appellant's prior illegal entries into the country were properly admitted to show his knowledge and state of mind and were more probative than prejudicial. See also *United States v. Ortega-Chavez,* 682 F.2d 1086 (5th Cir. 1982) (evidence that defendant, charged with involvement in smuggling aliens into United States, went to Mexico on other occasions for smuggling purposes admissible to show knowledge and intent).

United States v. Eufracio-Torres, 890 F.2d 266 (10th Cir. 1989), *cert. denied,* 110 S. Ct. 1306 (1990): The Court affirmed a conviction for transporting illegal aliens, holding that evidence of the defendant's prior conviction of illegally entering the United States was probative of his requisite knowledge that the aliens he transported were in this country illegally and that the prejudicial effect of the evidence was minimal, since the jury was already aware that he had entered the country illegally from his presentation of evidence regarding participation in the amnesty program.

United States v. Saldivar, 710 F.2d 699 (11th Cir. 1983): The Court held that evidence that a father and son charged with aiding and abetting transportation of illegal aliens repeatedly paid for transportation knowing their illegal status was admissible as probative of knowledge.

Knowledge — tax cases

United States v. Verkuilen, 690 F.2d 648 (7th Cir. 1982): The Court affirmed convictions for failing to file income tax returns for 1976 and 1977, upholding the admission of evidence that in 1974 the appellant had filed a form indicating the correct number of withholding allowances, but that in 1976 his withholding form claimed more allowances than he was entitled to. The Court found that the evidence tended to show knowledge of what was required and supported the government's claim that the failures to file were willful. See also *United States v. Serlin,* 707 F.2d 953 (7th Cir. 1983) (defendant's failure to file 1979 tax return admissible in prosecution for willful failure to file returns in 1976 and 1977).

Knowledge — theft and stolen property offenses

United States v. Hadaway, 681 F.2d 214 (4th Cir. 1982): The Court, in a prosecution for aiding and abetting theft from an interstate shipment, upheld the admission of testimony about other occasions when the defendant was involved in similar situations as tending to establish that the defendant knew he was dealing with stolen goods. The evidence was admissible even though it involved acts that occurred eighteen months after the crime charged. A dissent charged that the evidence was unnecessary and that it was little more than propensity evidence.

United States v. Falco, 727 F.2d 659 (7th Cir. 1984): The Court, although it recognized the closeness of the question, upheld a ruling that four prior interstate theft convictions (two in 1952, one in 1962, and one in 1978) could be used to prove knowledge in a prosecution for a similar offense. The Trial Judge was not clearly wrong in reasoning that a person involved in prior similar offenses would have recognized a shipment of stolen goods. The Court observed that the defendant could have brought out at an *in limine* hearing any differences between the prior events and the crime charged, and agreed with the Trial Judge that the pattern of conduct, rather than the age of the convictions, was significant. One Judge dissented, arguing that the balance between probative value and unfair prejudice was "so lop-sided in the direction of unfair prejudice" that reversal was required. See also *United States v. Hyman,* 741 F.2d 906 (7th Cir. 1984) (evidence that defendant had discussed ways of manipulating paperwork to make purchases of stolen steel look legitimate was admissible to prove knowledge).

United States v. Estabrook, 774 F.2d 284 (8th Cir. 1985): The Court upheld a conviction for receiving stolen property, holding it was not error to admit other acts tending to show knowledge on the part of the defendant as part of the government's case-in-chief, where the defendant had indicated from the outset that knowledge would be disputed.

United States v. Daly, 716 F.2d 1499 (9th Cir. 1983), *cert. dismissed,* 104 S. Ct. 1456 (1984): Evidence that the defendant sold a stolen car, although not charged in the indictment, was admissible to show the defendant's knowledge in a prosecution alleging a car theft scheme. In *United States v. Albuquerque*, 538 F.2d 277 (9th Cir. 1976), a prosecution for interstate transportation of a vehicle knowing it to be stolen, the Court concluded that "hotwiring" tools, admitted on the theory that they demonstrated the defendants' intent, were not relevant to any element in the case; they did not demonstrate defendants' knowledge that the automobile was in fact stolen.

United States v. Robinson, 687 F.2d 359 (11th Cir. 1982): The Court held that testimony of two convicted silver burglars concerning their use of the appellant as a "fence" was properly admitted to prove knowledge, intent, and *modus operandi* in a prosecution for transporting stolen goods.

Litany of purposes

United States v. Cortijo-Diaz, 875 F.2d 13 (1st Cir. 1989): The Court reversed a conviction for assault on a flight attendant, finding that evidence of the defendant's earlier robbery conviction was likely to be used as propensity evidence and was not properly admitted under Rule 404(b). It added that the laundry-list instruction given to the jury by the Trial Judge was undecipherable, and that the supplementary instructions were worse.

United States v. Sampson, 980 F.2d 883 (3d Cir. 1992): The Court reversed a conviction for marijuana possession because evidence of prior drug crimes had been admitted without the government articulating, and without the Trial Court putting into the record and instructing the jury as to, the permissible inferences. Where the government has not clearly stated reasons why the evidence is relevant to any legitimate purpose, there is no basis to believe the jury will cull the proper inferences from the evidence, and by simply repeating the entire litany of permissible theories under the Rule, the Trial Judge's instruction gave the jury inadequate guidance.

Sparks v. Gilley Trucking Co., 992 F.2d 52 (4th Cir. 1993): The defendant in a personal injury action arising out of a car-truck collision introduced evidence of the plaintiff's prior speeding convictions "to show intent, preparation, plan or motive to race or speed on the day in question." The Court reversed a judgment for the defendant, holding that intent was not relevant to the contributory negligence defense being asserted and that there was no foundation for any theory of "plan," "motive," or "preparation." The dissenting Judge considered intent relevant to the defendant's attempt to prove the plaintiff had been racing.

United States v. Studley, 892 F.2d 518 (7th Cir. 1989): In a prosecution for knowingly disposing of farm equipment pledged by another farmer to the Farmers Home Administration, the Trial Judge denied a motion *in limine* to exclude evidence that the defendant had previously sold grain through a third person in order to bypass the requirement of obtaining an FHA endorsement on the check received for sale of the grain. The Court held that the other acts were sufficiently similar to the crime charged to be probative on the defendant's knowledge of the practice of selling property through third parties to avoid having to get FHA releases and of how to dispose of pledged property without detection, and that the prejudicial effect, if any, of the evidence was limited by "clear and appropriate" cautionary instructions to the jury to consider the other acts "only on the question of motive, intent, knowledge and absence of mistake or accident."

United States v. Kern, 12 F.3d 122 (8th Cir. 1993): Affirming bank robbery convictions, the Court held that evidence of a prior robbery was properly admitted on the issue of intent to conspire, but noted that it "[did] not countenance the district court's use of this virtual laundry list of permissible Rule 404(b) purposes." In *United States v. Harvey,* 845 F.2d 760 (8th Cir. 1988), the Court reversed a conviction for avoiding payment of taxes relating to the sale of an airplane because the government introduced evidence that ten years earlier the defendant made large sums of money from drug transactions. The Court criticized the Trial Judge's "laundry list" approach to admissibility, "which merely restates the components of the rule," and stated that "the district court should specify which components of the rule form the basis of its ruling and why." In *United States v. Mothershed,* 859 F.2d 585 (8th Cir. 1988), the Court observed that "[w]e have not been aided in our review of the relevancy issue in this case by the 'laundry list' approach taken at trial."

United States v. Rivera, 837 F.2d 906 (10th Cir. 1988): A panel of the Court reversed a defendant's drug-related convictions, finding that the government improperly used evidence of two substantial drug offenses not charged in the indictment. It concluded that the government failed to articulate precisely its 404(b) analysis and that the Trial Judge failed to identify the specific purpose for which the evidence was admitted. The Court reasoned that the government must do more than "parrot the list of elements in Rule 404(b)," and it found that the limiting instruction given by the Judge was erroneous. On rehearing *en banc,* the Court was equally divided, so this part of the panel opinion was withdrawn. 874 F.2d 754, *clarified,* 900 F.2d 1462 (10th Cir. 1989) (en banc). See also *United States v. Doran,* 882 F.2d 1511 (10th Cir. 1989) ("laundry list" not the best way to proceed, but defendant did not object and instruction not plain error). In *United States v. Morales-Quinones,* 812 F.2d 604 (10th Cir. 1987), the Court affirmed a conviction for transporting illegal aliens, observing that before admitting evidence of other criminal acts, "the trial court must specifically identify the purpose for which such evidence is offered; a broad statement merely invoking or restating Rule 404(b) will not suffice." Although the Trial Judge's ruling in this case was somewhat general, the Court found that the defendant's prior acts were admissible to prove the absence of mistake or accident in the defendant's actions.

Modus operandi

United States v. Williams, 985 F.2d 634 (1st Cir. 1993): After arguing at sidebar that the evidence showed "how bad [defendant and a coconspirator] are," the government introduced evidence that the defendant had told a witness that "he had killed a couple of people." On appeal of convictions for cocaine distribution offenses, the government argued that the evidence showed the defendant's *modus operandi* of intimidation. Concluding that the impermissible propensity ground first asserted was the only justification supported in the record, the Court found admission of the evidence error (but harmless). *Modus operandi* evidence is admissible to prove identity, but identity was not disputed; moreover, the evidence was not placed into any context, other than temporal, related to the development or operation of the conspiracy. One Judge, concurring, wrote separately "simply to express my exasperation at the repeated abuse of Rule 404(b) by government prosecutors."

United States v. Montoya, 891 F.2d 1273 (7th Cir. 1989): A defendant was charged in a drug conspiracy after he and another had been stopped in a car in which $44,000 was discovered hidden in the trunk. To rebut his claim that he had no knowledge of the money, and thus lacked requisite intent to be a participant in the conspiracy, the government offered evidence that the two men had earlier been arrested traveling together and heroin had been found hidden in the other man's shoes. The Court held that the similarities between the events established a *modus operandi* for transporting contraband and proceeds from the sale thereof, and that the Trial Judge's instructions mitigated the unfair prejudicial effect, if any, of the evidence.

United States v. Miller, 959 F.2d 1535 (11th Cir.) (en banc), *cert. denied,* 113 S. Ct. 382 (1992): The panel had reversed the defendant's conviction for cocaine trafficking on the ground that evidence of a second transaction was not sufficiently similar and distinctive to prove identity. 883 F.2d 1540 (11th Cir. 1989). The Court *en banc* affirmed the defendant's conviction, holding that the similarity of the two offenses, including the same supplier and same location, was sufficient to mark them as the handiwork of the accused.

Motive — civil rights cases

Bowden v. McKenna, 600 F.2d 282 (1st Cir.), *cert. denied,* 444 U.S. 899 (1979): The Court reversed a judgment for the plaintiffs in a civil rights action arising out of an incident in which two policemen fatally shot a robbery suspect, holding that the defendants should have been permitted to offer identification testimony to establish that the suspect committed the robbery, as this might have established the suspect's motive to resist and thus might have corroborated the officers' story.

United States v. Bufalino, 683 F.2d 639 (2d Cir. 1982), *cert. denied,* 459 U.S. 1104 (1983): The Court upheld a conviction for conspiracy to violate civil rights, finding that the Trial Judge properly admitted a tape recording of an extortion attempt for which the defendant had previously been convicted where the victim was the person whose civil rights the defendant was charged with conspiring to violate and the tape tended to show a motive for the conspiracy.

Hernandez v. Cepeda, 860 F.2d 260 (7th Cir. 1988): In an arrestee's civil rights action against police officers, the Court held that evidence that the arrest was for rape and aggravated kidnapping was admissible to prove the plaintiff's motive to resist arrest.

United States v. Franklin, 704 F.2d 1183 (10th Cir.), *cert. denied,* 104 S. Ct. 146 (1983): The Court affirmed a conviction for killing two black men for using a public facility, holding that a prior racial incident involving the defendant was properly admitted to prove a racial motive for the killings.

Motive for arson

Underwood v. Colonial Penn Ins. Co., 888 F.2d 588 (8th Cir. 1989): The Court held in an action on a fire policy that a sheriff was properly permitted to testify that the insured refused to take a polygraph test in connection with a claim that personal property had been stolen, as the sheriff's suspicions implicit in the request may have provided a motive for arson and the evidence impeached the insured's testimony that he had cooperated and had no reason not to cooperate in the theft investigation.

United States v. Buchanan, 787 F.2d 477 (10th Cir. 1986): The Court affirmed a conviction for unregistered firearm possession and conspiracy, finding that evidence of the defendant's prior hostility toward the victim of an arson was relevant to prove motive.

Glados, Inc. v. Reliance Ins. Co., 888 F.2d 1309 (11th Cir. 1987, *modified,* 1989), *cert. denied,* 110 S. Ct. 3273 (1990): In an action by a restaurant owner on a fire insurance policy, the plaintiff attempted to rebut an arson defense by evidence that the prior owner had retained an interest as an insured party and by showing similar fires at two other restaurants in which the prior owner had also retained a similar interest. The Court held that this evidence was properly admitted as relevant to whether the third party had a motive to set the fire. In *Aetna Cas. & Sur. Co. v. Gosdin,* 803 F.2d 1153 (11th Cir. 1986), the Court reversed a judgment for the insurer in a dispute with its insured concerning the cause of a fire. Although it upheld the introduction of motive evidence that the insured had been charged with burglary and needed money to mount a defense, the Court held that evidence of pimping, pandering, and drug charges was unduly prejudicial. In *United States v. Kerr,* 778 F.2d 690 (11th Cir. 1985), the Court affirmed fraud convictions arising out of a scheme to burn two businesses to collect insurance. It found that evidence that one defendant, a pharmacist, engaged in irregular activities in the dispensing of drugs was admissible to prove a motive for the scheme. A strong dissent argued that the other act evidence was probative only of character and should have been excluded.

Motive for assault, homicide, kidnapping, etc.

United States v. Bufalino, 683 F.2d 639 (2d Cir. 1982), *cert. denied,* 459 U.S. 1104 (1983): The Court upheld a conviction for conspiracy to violate civil rights, finding that the Trial Judge properly admitted a tape recording of an extortion attempt for which the defendant had previously been convicted where the victim was the person whose civil rights the defendant was charged with conspiring to violate and the tape tended to show a motive for the conspiracy.

United States v. Russell, 971 F.2d 1098 (4th Cir. 1992), *cert. denied,* 113 S. Ct. 1013 (1993): Affirming a murder conviction in a case in which no body or murder weapon was ever found, the Court held there was no abuse of discretion in admitting evidence of the defendant's less than honorable discharge from the Marine Corps and his extramarital affairs, as the defendant may have seen the victim, his ex-wife and a Marine officer, as a symbol of an institution he had come to resent. In *United States v. Lewis,* 780 F.2d 1140 (4th Cir. 1986), the Court affirmed a hospital patient's conviction for assaulting a fellow patient, holding that evidence of a prior altercation between the two patients was admissible as motive evidence. In *Roshan v. Fard,* 705 F.2d 102 (4th Cir. 1983), the Court reversed a judgment for a plaintiff suing for injuries suffered in a fight.

The defendant's evidence establishing that he had been an informant for the government and had supplied information that led to the conviction of the plaintiff should have been admitted to show a motive for the plaintiff to attack him, since it could not be said that the prejudicial effect of the evidence substantially outweighed its probative value.

United States v. Benton, 637 F.2d 1052 (5th Cir. 1981): In a prosecution charging the defendant with involvement in killing a fellow prison inmate, the Court upheld the admission of evidence that the defendant was involved in several murders of which the victim allegedly had knowledge.

United States v. Vance, 871 F.2d 572 (6th Cir.), *cert. denied,* 110 S. Ct. 323 (1989): The Court held that prior bad acts by the defendant were admissible to show a motive to assist the wife of a convicted drug dealer in the murder of a state prosecutor.

United States v. Menzer, 29 F.3d 1223 (7th Cir. 1994): The Court held, in a prosecution for arson resulting in the deaths of the defendant's two children, that evidence that the defendant was on probation for a 1986 conviction for sexual exploitation of a child was "intricately related" [*sic*] to the charged offense because it was the government's theory that the defendant burned down the house where his wife and children were sleeping in order to prevent their reporting his sexual abuse of the children which would result in revocation of his probation. In our view, this was other crime evidence admissible under the Rule to prove motive, and the Court's characterization of it as "intricately related" (and therefore outside the Rule) is unnecessarily confusing, especially given the Court's conclusion that there was no abuse of discretion in admitting the evidence "because it was intricately related to the arson prosecution as probative evidence of Menzer's intent (motive)." In *United States v. Hattaway,* 740 F.2d 1419 (7th Cir.), *cert. denied,* 105 S. Ct. 448, 599 (1984), the court, upholding kidnapping convictions, found that evidence of the murder of the victim's boyfriend was properly admitted to show a motive for the abduction.

Cerro Gordo Charity v. Fireman's Fund Am. Life Ins. Co., 819 F.2d 1471 (8th Cir. 1987): In an action to recover the proceeds of life insurance policies, the company defended on the theory that the insured's brother killed him after arranging the policies on his life. The Court affirmed the admission of evidence of numerous other life insurance policies covering the insured as tending to show a motive for murder. In *United States v. Turpin,* 707 F.2d 332 (8th Cir. 1983), the Court affirmed a conviction for attempting to make railroad facilities hazardous. It found that evidence that the defendant had killed a man was properly admitted, since the government alleged that the defendant placed the man's body in a car at a railroad crossing in the hope that the car would be demolished and the cause of the man's death hidden. See also *United States v. Wagoner,* 713 F.2d 1371 (8th Cir. 1983) (evidence of involvement in auto theft ring properly admitted to show motive for participation in scheme to bomb state trooper's car); *United States v. Gomez,* 733 F.2d 69 (8th Cir. 1984) (proof that defendant, convicted of aiding and abetting a kidnapping, asked the kidnapper to commit another violent act, admissible as evidence of defendant's motive to gain custody of his son from his estranged wife).

United States v. Brown, 880 F.2d 1012 (9th Cir. 1989): The Court reversed murder and firearm convictions, finding that evidence of the defendant's attempt seven years earlier to recover his property at gunpoint and his shooting into a home was inadmissible in a prosecution for shooting a mail carrier as she delivered mail to his parents' home.

The government had said the evidence showed that the motive behind the killing was the defendant's desire to obtain the thrill he received from creating violence. In *United States v. Bowman,* 720 F.2d 1103 (9th Cir. 1983), the Court sustained a conviction for assault, finding that evidence of the defendant's earlier assault conviction was properly admitted to show his motive for attacking the victim in this case. The government contended that the defendant believed that the victim was responsible for his earlier conviction. See also *United States v. Bradshaw,* 690 F.2d 704 (9th Cir. 1982), *cert. denied,* 463 U.S. 1210 (1983) (upholding kidnapping conviction, and finding that evidence as to defendant's sexual activity with the kidnapped child was relevant to show a motive for the kidnapping).

United States v. Buchanan, 787 F.2d 477 (10th Cir. 1986): The Court affirmed a conviction for unregistered firearm possession and conspiracy, finding that evidence of the defendant's prior hostility toward the victim of an arson was relevant to prove motive. In *United States v. Franklin,* 704 F.2d 1183 (10th Cir.), *cert. denied,* 104 S. Ct. 146 (1983), the Court affirmed a conviction for killing two black men for using a public facility, holding that a prior racial incident involving the defendant was properly admitted to prove a racial motive for the killings.

Motive for drug activity

United States v. Masse, 816 F.2d 805 (1st Cir. 1987): The Court affirmed a cocaine distribution conviction, holding that evidence that the defendant was in possession of cocaine while on bail for the charges on which he was convicted in this case was properly admitted to prove a drug habit and to establish a motive for distributing drugs. See also *United States v. Kadouh,* 768 F.2d 20 (1st Cir. 1985) (defendant's use of cocaine admissible to show motive for him to become involved in drug activity).

United States v. Galyen, 798 F.2d 331 (8th Cir. 1986): The Court affirmed a conviction for obtaining a controlled substance by misrepresentation and for possession with intent to distribute, holding that evidence suggesting that the defendant was involved in drug dealing was admissible to prove a motive for using misrepresentations to obtain controlled substances.

United States v. Palmer, 3 F.3d 300 (9th Cir. 1993), *cert. denied,* 114 S. Ct. 1120 (1994): Affirming a conviction for manufacturing marijuana plants, the Court held it was error (but harmless) to admit the defendant's postarraignment statement to law enforcement officials that ''I don't want any deals. I have been through this before. I just want to get it behind me.'' The Court rejected the government's argument that the statement, which tended to prove prior acts, was admissible to prove motive, since motive did not establish a material element of any offense charged. In *United States v. Saniti,* 604 F.2d 603 (9th Cir.), *cert. denied,* 444 U.S. 969 (1979), the Court held that evidence that a bank robbery defendant had a $250 a day drug habit was properly admitted to show his motive for robbery.

United States v. Harrell, 737 F.2d 971 (11th Cir. 1984), *cert. denied,* 105 S. Ct. 923, 1392 (1985): The Court found that evidence concerning a motorcycle club's way of life was admissible to prove the motive and object of a drug-trafficking conspiracy.

Motive for firearms offenses

United States v. Pelusio, 725 F.2d 161 (2d Cir. 1983): In a prosecution for unlawful receipt of firearms, the Court found that the government properly cross-examined a defendant about whether the defendant's brother had been shot by someone connected with organized crime, whether the defendant had been involved in gambling, and whether he had heard there was a contract out on him. The questions were relevant to proving a motive for receiving a firearm.

United States v. Hatfield, 815 F.2d 1068 (6th Cir. 1987): The Court upheld the admission of evidence of burglary paraphernalia seized from a defendant charged with being a felon in possession of a firearm. The defendant had denied knowledge of the presence of the gun, and the Court found that the burglary evidence was relevant to show that the defendant had a motive to possess a gun.

United States v. Troop, 890 F.2d 1393 (7th Cir. 1989): To show the defendant's motive to participate in the charged conspiracy to sell cocaine, the Court held there was no error in admitting evidence that he previously worked at a drug house where he skimmed cocaine for his personal use off large amounts of the drug before they were sold. In *United States v. Taylor,* 728 F.2d 864 (7th Cir. 1984), a prosecution for possession of an unregistered machine gun and silencer, the Court found that other evidence discovered in a search of the appellant's residence — cocaine, other weapons, stereo and video equipment without serial numbers, and fur and leather jackets without labels — was properly admitted to show a motive for possession of the machine gun and silencer.

United States v. Jordan, 893 F.2d 182 (8th Cir.), *vacated on other grounds,* 110 S. Ct. 2581, *reaff'd on reconsideration,* 913 F.2d 1286 (1990), *cert. denied,* 111 S. Ct. 2247 (1991): The Court affirmed a conviction of being a felon in possession of a firearm, holding that there was no abuse of discretion in admitting evidence that the defendant possessed $3,900 at the time of his arrest, as it was probative of motive for possession of a weapon, which the government had to prove. In *United States v. Moore,* 735 F.2d 289 (8th Cir. 1984), the Court noted that it was improper for the prosecutor to argue in closing that a defendant, charged with illegal possession of firearms, had shotguns in his possession because he was involved with drugs. "The fact that the defendant possessed drugs does not necessarily make it likely that the guns found during the raid were his."

Motive for fraud, false statements, etc.

United States v. Birney, 686 F.2d 102 (2d Cir. 1982): The Court upheld a conviction for making false entries in bank records, finding that evidence that the defendant had embezzled money was properly admitted to show a motive for the falsification. See also *United States v. Sliker,* 751 F.2d 477 (2d Cir. 1984), *cert. denied,* 105 S. Ct. 1772, 2679 (1985) (evidence of defendant's loansharking admissible to show motive for defrauding bank).

United States v. Cordell, 912 F.2d 769 (5th Cir. 1990): The Court held that evidence that the defendant bank official had previously violated lending limits was properly admitted in a prosecution for making false entries in bank records to show his motivation for concealing the lending violations involved in the case.

United States v. Mullins, 22 F.3d 1365 (6th Cir. 1994): In a prosecution for obstruction of justice arising from the alteration of logbooks for police aircraft that had been subpoenaed by the grand jury, the Court held that evidence of kickbacks and unauthorized use of the airplanes was relevant to the defendant's motive to suppress information. In *United States v. Tager,* 788 F.2d 349 (6th Cir. 1986), the Court affirmed fraud convictions arising out of securities transactions, holding that evidence of an unpaid tax judgment against the defendant exceeding $500,000 was properly admitted to prove motive.

United States v. Shriver, 842 F.2d 968 (7th Cir. 1988): In a prosecution for making false statements to a bank, the Court held that evidence that the defendant defaulted on a franchise agreement was properly admitted to prove a motive for making the false statements. The Court noted that "similarity is not an appropriate requirement" for other acts used to prove motive.

United States v. Conners, 894 F.2d 987 (8th Cir. 1990): Affirming the defendant's convictions for bank fraud and embezzlement, the Court held there was no abuse of discretion in admitting evidence of frauds against another bank, as the circumstances were probative of motive because they showed his need for a large amount of money. In *United States v. Gaylen,* 798 F.2d 331 (8th Cir. 1986), the Court affirmed a conviction for obtaining a controlled substance by misrepresentation and for possession with intent to distribute, holding that evidence suggesting that the defendant was involved in drug dealing was admissible to prove a motive for using misrepresentations to obtain controlled substances. See also *United States v. Poston,* 727 F.2d 734 (8th Cir.), *cert. denied,* 104 S. Ct. 2179 (1984) (evidence of a "check kite" scheme was admissible in prosecution for misapplication of federally insured funds as tending to prove motive; the misapplication would have covered the amount of the "kited" check).

United States v. Wales, 977 F.2d 1323 (9th Cir. 1992): The Court affirmed the defendant's conviction for making a false declaration to Customs about the amount of currency he was carrying, holding that evidence he attempted after his arrest to clean out his safe deposit box before the government could examine its contents was clearly an attempt to conceal the $150,000 in gold coins there, which was consistent with the government's theory that he had as a motive for submitting a false declaration concealing his assets and avoiding an explanation of their source. See also *United States v. Conners,* 825 F.2d 1384 (9th Cir. 1987) (in prosecution for currency violations, defendant's cocaine activities tended to supply motive for concealing money). In *United States v. Brown,* 912 F.2d 1040 (9th Cir. 1990), a bank fraud prosecution, the Court held that evidence that the recipient of funds illegally channeled through a defendant shortly thereafter served as a similar illegal conduit of funds to the defendant was properly admitted as tending to show why the defendant participated in the charged transaction.

United States v. Kerr, 778 F.2d 690 (11th Cir. 1985): The Court affirmed fraud convictions arising out of a scheme to burn two businesses to collect insurance. It found that evidence that one defendant, a pharmacist, engaged in irregular activities in the dispensing of drugs was admissible to prove a motive for the scheme. A strong dissent argued that the other act evidence was probative only of character and should have been excluded.

Motive for obstruction of justice or perjury

United States v. Willoughby, 860 F.2d 15 (2d Cir. 1988), *cert. denied,* 109 S. Ct. 846 (1989): Affirming convictions for conspiracy to obstruct justice and witness tampering, the Court held that evidence of a robbery by the defendants demonstrated a motive to prevent witnesses from testifying at the robbery trial. In *United States v. Bufalino,* 683 F.2d 639 (2d Cir. 1982), *cert. denied,* 459 U.S. 1104 (1983), the Court upheld a conviction for conspiracy to violate civil rights, finding that the Trial Judge properly admitted a tape recording of an extortion attempt for which the defendant had previously been convicted where the victim was the person whose civil rights the defendant was charged with conspiring to violate and the tape tended to show a motive for the conspiracy.

United States v. Boone, 759 F.2d 345 (4th Cir.), *cert. denied,* 474 U.S. 861 (1985): The Court held that evidence of other crimes was admissible to prove the motive for the defendant's perjury.

United States v. Maggitt, 784 F.2d 590 (5th Cir. 1986): The Court affirmed witness-tampering convictions as it found that one defendant's prior incarceration was admissible to prove a motive to threaten a witness. See also *United States v. Chagra,* 754 F.2d 1186 (5th Cir.), *cert. denied,* 474 U.S. 922 (1985) (charges of conspiracy to obstruct justice and to possess marijuana with intent to distribute were properly joined with charges involving murder of Federal Judge, since they related to the defendant's motive to kill the Judge and efforts to finance a jail break following the murder); *United States v. Barron,* 707 F.2d 125 (5th Cir. 1983) (evidence of tax evasion scheme admissible as proof of motive behind charged perjury).

United States v. Vance, 871 F.2d 572 (6th Cir.), *cert. denied,* 110 S. Ct. 323 (1989): The Court held that prior bad acts by the defendant were admissible to show a motive to assist the wife of a convicted drug dealer in the murder of a state prosecutor.

United States v. Wagoner, 713 F.2d 1371 (8th Cir. 1983): The Court held that evidence of the defendant's involvement in an auto theft ring was properly admitted to show a motive for participating in the charged scheme to bomb a state trooper's car.

Motive for theft, robbery, and stolen property offenses

United States v. Lamberty, 778 F.2d 59 (1st Cir. 1985): The Court reversed a postmaster's conviction for opening the package of another, finding that the government improperly elicited testimony that the postmaster was suspected of taking packages from the post office. The motive of the investigators was not relevant to the prosecution's case.

United States v. Smith, 605 F.2d 839 (5th Cir. 1979): The Court held that evidence of prior convictions and an impending prison sentence were properly introduced to show a defendant's motive in dealing with cars with the intent not to pay for them.

United States v. Holt, 817 F.2d 1264 (7th Cir. 1987): The Court affirmed a defendant's convictions for masterminding a bank robbery. It found that evidence of his thefts of checks was admissible to prove financial problems that provided a motive for the robbery. In *United States v. Cyphers,* 553 F.2d 1064 (7th Cir.), *cert. denied,* 434 U.S. 843 (1977), a bank robbery case, the Court held it was proper to admit testimony that a defendant asked a government informer to purchase $1,000 worth of heroin for him shortly after a robbery occurred, since the testimony was offered to show the defendant's motive for the robbery.

United States v. Mays, 822 F.2d 793 (8th Cir. 1987): The Court upheld the introduction in a bank robbery case of evidence of another bank robbery as part of proving a motive for the crime charged. It also held, however, that it was error (but harmless) to admit evidence of a subsequent breaking and entering.

United States v. Feldman, 788 F.2d 544 (9th Cir. 1986), *cert. denied,* 107 S. Ct. 955 (1987): Affirming a bank robbery conviction, the Court upheld the admission of testimony offered to prove motive that a defendant was living beyond his means and owed money.

Motive — generally

United States v. Lamberty, 778 F.2d 59 (1st Cir. 1985): The Court reversed a postmaster's conviction for opening the package of another, finding that the government improperly elicited testimony that the postmaster was suspected of taking packages from the post office. The motive of the investigators was not relevant to the prosecution's case.

United States v. Fakhoury, 819 F.2d 1415 (7th Cir. 1987), *cert. denied,* 108 S. Ct. 749 (1988): The Court found a prosecutor's closing argument to have been "reprehensible" (but not plain error) in its prejudicial and inflammatory use of other act evidence that had been admitted to prove motive. Rather than arguing simply about motive, the prosecutor made broadside attacks on the defendant's character.

United States v. Palmer, 3 F.3d 300 (9th Cir. 1993), *cert. denied,* 114 S. Ct. 1120 (1994): Affirming a conviction for manufacturing marijuana plants, the Court held it was error (but harmless) to admit the defendant's postarraignment statement to law enforcement officials that "I don't want any deals. I have been through this before. I just want to get it behind me." The Court rejected the government's argument that the statement, which tended to prove prior acts, was admissible to prove motive, since motive did not establish a material element of any offense charged.

United States v. Martinez, 890 F.2d 1088 (10th Cir. 1989), *cert. denied,* 110 S. Ct. 1532 (1990): The Court held, in a prosecution for knowingly failing to surrender for service of sentence, that evidence of the defendant's prior conviction and subsequent indictment for cocaine trafficking was relevant to his motive to commit the offense and that an instruction to consider it only for that purpose meant that the potential prejudice did not substantially outweigh the probative value of the evidence.

United States v. Vance, 730 F.2d 736 (11th Cir. 1984): The Court held that evidence that the defendant had substantial income in several tax years was admissible to prove that he had a motive to fail to file returns.

Notice

United States v. Tuesta-Toro, 29 F.3d 771 (1st Cir. 1994): The Court affirmed a drug trafficking conviction, holding that the defendant had not made a cognizable Rule 404(b) request with a motion calling for "confessions, admissions and statements ... that in any way exculpate, inculpate or refer to the defendant." At a minimum the defense must present a timely request sufficiently clear and particular to fairly alert the prosecution that the defense is invoking its specific right to pretrial notification of the general nature of all Rule 404(b) evidence the prosecution intends to introduce.

United States v. French, 974 F.2d 687 (6th Cir. 1992), *cert. denied,* 113 S. Ct. 1012, 1431, 2403 (1993): Affirming convictions for marijuana offenses, the Court rejected a defendant's objection that counsel was not timely notified of other crimes evidence, as counsel was told a week before trial, there was ample opportunity to prepare for the damaging consequences of the evidence, and there was no motion to continue.

United States v. Kern, 12 F.3d 122 (8th Cir. 1993): Affirming bank robbery convictions, the Court held there was adequate notice of a prior robbery where the government informed the defendants at a hearing before the Magistrate Judge more than two weeks before the trial that it might use evidence from some local robberies and provided the defendants with state reports concerning these robberies approximately a week before trial.

Predisposition

United States v. Armendariz-Mata, 949 F.2d 151 (5th Cir. 1991), *cert. denied,* 112 S. Ct. 2288 (1992): Where a defendant charged with cocaine possession claimed entrapment, the Court held that evidence of his association with a drug trafficker was properly admitted to prove his predisposition.

United States v. Nolan, 910 F.2d 1553 (7th Cir. 1990), *cert. denied,* 111 S. Ct. 1402 (1991): The Court held it was error, but harmless in the circumstances, for the Trial Judge to instruct that evidence of a bank robbery defendant's prior bank robberies could be considered on his "predisposition," as well as on identity and intent. Mention of that purpose in the pattern jury instruction is proper only when the defendant puts the matter in issue, as in an entrapment defense.

United States v. LaChapelle, 969 F.2d 632 (8th Cir. 1992): The defendant, charged with receiving child pornography through the mail, asserted an entrapment defense and the government introduced a pornographic videotape seized from the defendant's home to show his knowledge of and intent to order child pornography. The Court held admission of the evidence was error (but harmless) because the possession was legal when the defendant first possessed the videotape. Evidence of predisposition to do what was once lawful is not very probative of whether there is a predisposition to do what is now illegal; the Court concluded that the slight probative value of the evidence was outweighed by its prejudicial effect. In *United States v. Thomas,* 964 F.2d 836 (8th Cir.), *cert. denied,* 113 S. Ct. 265 (1992), a prosecution for weapons possession in connection with drug trafficking, evidence of the defendant's possession of a weapon in another drug deal was introduced to show that presence of a firearm "was no mistake or accident because defendant had a predisposition toward possessing" firearms during drug trafficking. The Court declined to rule on the admissibility of the evidence, but cautioned prosecutors to avoid creating issues on appeal by offering redundant evidence when presenting a case as airtight as this one.

Preparation

United States v. Sliker, 751 F.2d 477 (2d Cir. 1984), *cert. denied,* 105 S. Ct. 1772, 2679 (1985): The Court held in a bank fraud prosecution that testimony about a similar attempt to defraud explained the defendant's ability to get phony checks in preparation for the charged fraud.

United States v. Gano, 560 F.2d 990 (10th Cir. 1977): The defendant, employed as a social worker at a Veterans Hospital, had sexual relations with the wife of a patient and subsequently with her daughter. In a prosecution for having carnal knowledge of a female under the age of sixteen, the Court upheld admission of evidence that the defendant sold marijuana to the mother and gave it to the child himself, as the evidence showed preparation for the crime — i.e., lowering the child's resistance. The Court also commented that evidence of the defendant's sexual relations with the mother was admissible because of its close connection with the criminal conduct involving the child.

Remoteness

United States v. DeFiore, 720 F.2d 757 (2d Cir. 1983), *cert. denied,* 104 S. Ct. 1684, 3511 (1984): In a prosecution charging a scheme to defraud city and state tax officials, the Court rejected a defendant's claim that evidence of other acts should not have been used to prove intent because the acts were outside the five-year limitations period for the offenses charged.

United States v. Arnold, 890 F.2d 825 (6th Cir. 1989): Affirming a conviction for conspiracy to distribute marijuana, the Court held that although it was a close question, there was no abuse of discretion in permitting the defendant's alibi witness to be asked about a minor marijuana transaction with the defendant eighteen years previously, as it was unlikely the witness or the defendant was seriously or unfairly prejudiced, especially considering the government's strong evidence of the defendant's involvement in the charged offense.

United States v. Gometz, 879 F.2d 256 (7th Cir. 1989), *cert. denied,* 493 U.S. 1033 (1990): Evidence that the defendant in this prosecution for assault and possessing dangerous weapons in prison had been convicted of abetting the murder of a prison guard in 1983 was too remote in time, and there was no showing the acts were similar, to be admissible on defendant's intent in this case. The error was harmless, however.

King v. Ahrens, 16 F.3d 265 (8th Cir. 1994): In a medical malpractice case, the Court held there was no abuse of discretion in excluding evidence that the defendant's medical license had been suspended eight years earlier, as any probative value the evidence had on the absence of mistake in failing to note critical information on the medical chart and on the doctor's credibility was substantially outweighed by its prejudicial effect, given the remoteness in time and the dissimilarity between the incidents. In *United States v. Johnson,* 879 F.2d 331 (8th Cir. 1989), the Court held that evidence that the defendant in this murder prosecution had previously threatened his aunt with a knife could be relevant to his awareness of the risk his actions posed to the victim, thus tending to show the required element of malice, but the threat six years previously was too remote from the defendant's state of mind at the time of the offense. The error was harmless, however.

United States v. Simtob, 901 F.2d 799 (9th Cir. 1990): The defendant's conviction of distribution of cocaine was affirmed, the Court finding no abuse of discretion in admitting evidence of a 1973 conviction of LSD distribution and a 1974 conviction of marijuana distribution to show predisposition rebutting an entrapment defense. In *United States v. Spillone,* 879 F.2d 514 (9th Cir. 1989), *cert. denied,* 498 U.S. 864, 878 (1990), there was no abuse of discretion in admitting evidence of the defendant's 1971 conviction of a similar crime to show intent in a loansharking prosecution. Rejecting an inflexible rule with respect to the remoteness of other acts, the Court held that given the similarity of the offenses, the prior conviction was not so remote as to require its exclusion.

United States v. Hernandez, 896 F.2d 513 (11th Cir.), *cert. denied,* 111 S. Ct. 159 (1990): The Court held that evidence of a six-year-old conviction otherwise admissible under the Rule might carry far less probative weight due to its temporal remoteness were it not for the fact the defendant spent much of the interim period in prison and was still on probation when arrested.

Stipulations — criminal cases — generally

United States v. Garcia, 983 F.2d 1160 (1st Cir. 1993): In the course of affirming convictions for possession of cocaine for distribution, the Court observed that

> [t]o prevent the admission of bad acts evidence, a defendant's offer to concede knowledge and/or intent issues must do two things. First, the offer must express a clear and unequivocal *intention* to remove the issues such that, in effect if not in form, it constitutes an offer to stipulate. Second, notwithstanding the sincerity of the defendant's offer, the concession must cover the necessary substantive ground to remove the issues from the case.

In this case, the Court found a defendant's offer stipulating to intent to distribute was insufficient where the evidence was also relevant to knowledge and intent to possess. It provided the following guidance to lower courts:

> We note, first of all, that a serious offer to concede or stipulate to issues of intent and/or knowledge should be explored by the district court. In the final analysis, however, whether such an offer is accepted remains in the sound discretion of the district judge. If the judge determines that the offer is acceptable, the judge should take steps to assure that the defendant is aware of the contents of the stipulation and of its implications before directing the jury that it may resolve the issue against the defendant. Second, from a survey of the circuits on stipulations in the area of 404(b) evidence, we have ascertained a preference for handling the matter before trial, or early in the trial process.

In *United States v. Ferrer-Cruz,* 899 F.2d 135 (1st Cir. 1990), the defendant, convicted of aiding and abetting possession of cocaine with intent to distribute, argued that evidence of prior convictions for possessing cocaine and marijuana were inadmissible because he defended on the ground of mistaken identity. The Court held that the mistaken identity defense did not necessarily remove the issues of knowledge or intent, that the defendant did not clearly stipulate to remove those issues, and that the defendant did in fact argue "mere presence" in a car with cocaine. The dissenting Judge expressed concern about the Circuit's inclusionary approach to the Rule, considered that the defendant had raised "mere presence" only in the grand jury and not at trial, and concluded that the evidence was being used only to show propensity.

United States v. Colon, 880 F.2d 650 (2d Cir. 1989): In reversing a conviction of aiding a heroin sale because prior sales were improperly admitted after the defendant had in effect stipulated intent out of the case, the Court noted that the prosecutor should have waited until it was clear what theory the defense was asserting before introducing the other acts evidence.

United States v. Yeagin, 927 F.2d 798 (5th Cir. 1991): In order to exclude evidence of prior drug felony convictions, a defendant charged with possession of methamphetamine with intent to distribute and possession of a firearm as a convicted felon offered to stipulate both intent if the government proved possession and his prior felony convictions. Reversing and remanding, the Court held that admitting the convictions was prejudicial error, as the stipulations covered the elements to be proved by the evidence, it was not necessary to an understanding of the full and real life context of the offense because the prior felonies had no relation to the factual circumstances of the present case, and the evidence must have had an extremely prejudicial effect on the jury.

United States v. Hebeka, 25 F.3d 287 (6th Cir. 1994): Defendant, a grocer, was charged with food stamp fraud. He had been previously convicted for food stamp fraud, and banned for life from participating as a grocer in the food stamp program. The main factual dispute at trial was whether the defendant had actually sold his grocery store after his first conviction — so that the subsequently charged food stamp fraud could not be attributed to him — or whether the sale was a sham. The government introduced the defendant's prior food stamp conviction at trial, as relevant to his motivation, intent, and plan in setting up a sham transfer of the grocery store. The defendant objected and offered to stipulate that he had been disqualified from the food stamp program; he argued that in light of the stipulation, the actual conviction was irrelevant. The Court of Appeals rejected this argument, stating that "the defendant has no right to selectively stipulate to particular elements of the offense." Accordingly, the prior conviction was relevant to motive and was properly admitted.

Stipulations — criminal cases — intent

United States v. Williams, 577 F.2d 188 (2d Cir.), *cert. denied,* 439 U.S. 868 (1978): The Court affirmed a conviction for conspiracy to commit bank larceny, observing that "other crimes evidence is inadmissible when that issue [intent] is not really in dispute" and that intent "will usually not be in issue if the defendant takes the stand and, as his sole defense, claims that he did not commit the alleged acts at all." But the Court went on to hold that, because "the testimony linking appellant to the conspiracy was subject to an innocent interpretation and appellant . . . did not affirmatively take the issue of intent out of the case,'' there was no error in admitting other crimes evidence.

United States v. Jemal, 26 F.3d 1267 (3d Cir. 1994): Although the Circuit's general rule is that evidence of a defendant's prior bad acts should not be admitted to show knowledge and intent when the defendant has proffered a comprehensive and unreserved stipulation that he possessed the requisite knowledge and intent, the Court held that the defendant's offer in this mail fraud case was not sufficiently comprehensive to remove those issues, so it was no abuse of discretion to admit evidence of his involvement in prior frauds.

United States v. Yeagin, 927 F.2d 798 (5th Cir. 1991): This case is discussed *supra* under ''Stipulations — criminal cases — generally.''

United States v. Taylor, 17 F.3d 333 (11th Cir.), *cert. denied,* 115 S. Ct. __ (1994): The Court held that a defendant's offer to stipulate did not render evidence of his prior drug convictions inadmissible. First, his offer conceded only intent, while the government sought also to prove knowledge, motive, and absence of mistake. Second, the defendant agreed to stipulate that he had the intent to buy and sell drugs, but the government sought to prove he intended to join a conspiracy.

Stipulations — criminal cases — predicate convictions

United States v. Yeagin, 927 F.2d 798 (5th Cir. 1991): This case is discussed *supra* under ''Stipulations — criminal cases — generally.''

Subsequent acts — generally

United States v. Watson, 894 F.2d 1345 (D.C. Cir. 1990): The Court affirmed a conviction for cocaine possession, holding that evidence that the defendant participated in a cocaine transaction three months after the charged offense was relevant to his knowledge and intent on the occasion in question. The Court rejected the argument that Rule 404(b) automatically barred evidence of subsequent acts, but noted that the temporal (as well as the logical) relationship between a later act and a defendant's earlier state of mind attenuates the relevance of such proof.

United States v. Rodriguez-Cardona, 924 F.2d 1148 (1st Cir.), *cert. denied,* 112 S. Ct. 54 (1991): Evidence that an informant tried to buy cocaine from the defendant four months after the sales charged in the indictment was erroneously admitted as probative of pattern, mode of operation, lack of surprise and mistake, and intent. Because none of those issues was specifically disputed, the primary, if not the only, purpose of the evidence was to show propensity. The error was harmless, however.

United States v. Ramirez, 894 F.2d 565 (2d Cir. 1990): In affirming a conviction for cocaine offenses, the Court rejected any per se rule that subsequent similar act evidence inherently lacks relevancy and held that evidence of the defendant's participation in a cocaine sale in September 1988 was relevant to establish his knowledge and mental state at the time of the charged offense in December 1987.

United States v. Echeverri, 854 F.2d 638 (3d Cir. 1988): The Court held that evidence of cocaine in the defendant's apartment eighteen months after the termination of the alleged conspiracy was not probative, but its admission was harmless error.

United States v. Bakke, 942 F.2d 977 (6th Cir. 1991): The Court reversed a defendant's conviction for participation in a drug conspiracy ending in October 1987 because evidence had been admitted that he pleaded guilty to possessing drugs in April 1988, and there was no showing of any relationship between the charged conspiracy and subsequent drug transactions. The government's argument that he must have "learned the ropes" of the marijuana trade by participating in the earlier conspiracy would be mere speculation.

United States v. Betts, 16 F.3d 748 (7th Cir. 1994): The Court held it was error (but harmless) to admit evidence of sixteen pounds of marijuana and related paraphernalia seized at defendants' home eighteen months after the end of the charged marijuana distribution conspiracy, since it had little or no probative worth in establishing knowledge or intent regarding the conspiracy. The concurring Judge suggested the evidence may have shown the defendants were in the drug business on a continuing basis and thus were more likely to have participated in the charged conspiracy, but the majority rejected a distinction between proof of a propensity to commit drug offenses (clearly inadmissible under the Rule) and proof that drug trafficking was a person's occupation. We note that proof of a continuing business may be probative in showing knowledge or intent, but that in this case acts eighteen months apart with nothing to connect them would not be probative of a continuing business.

United States v. Fischel, 693 F.2d 800 (8th Cir. 1982): In a prosecution for possession of methamphetamine with intent to distribute and for conspiracy, the Court upheld the introduction of evidence showing that two months after the conspiracy ended the defendant provided the drug at a party. The evidence was used to rebut a suggestion that another person was the real drug dealer, not the defendant.

United States v. Hodges, 770 F.2d 1475 (9th Cir. 1985): The Court reversed a conviction for conspiracy to defraud lending institutions, finding error in the admission of testimony that approximately five months after the last alleged act of the conspiracy the defendant attempted to extort money from an alleged coconspirator to paint a favorable picture of her involvement. The Court reasoned that the defendant's state of mind five months later was not highly probative of his state of mind at the time of the alleged conspiracy.

Hill v. Bache Halsey Stuart Shields Inc., 790 F.2d 817 (10th Cir. 1986): Reversing a judgment for a customer against a commodities futures broker, the Court held it was an abuse of discretion to exclude evidence of the plaintiff's trading five months after he closed his account with the defendant. The trading was similar to that done with the defendant, and the Court found that it was highly probative on the issue of whether the plaintiff authorized trades by the defendant. See also *United States v. Mittleider,* 835 F.2d 769 (10th Cir. 1987), *cert. denied,* 108 S. Ct. 1279 (1988) (evidence of defendant's subsequent conversation with undercover agent concerning gun purchase admissible to show intent and absence of mistake in prosecution for firearms violations).

United States v. Miller, 959 F.2d 1535 (11th Cir.) (en banc), *cert. denied,* 113 S. Ct. 382 (1992): The panel had reversed the defendant's conviction for cocaine trafficking on the ground that evidence of a second transaction nine months later was not sufficiently similar and distinctive to prove identity. 883 F.2d 1540 (11th Cir. 1989). The Court *en banc* affirmed the defendant's conviction, holding that the similarity of the two offenses, including the same supplier and same location, was sufficient to mark them as the handiwork of the accused. In *United States v. Terebecki,* 692 F.2d 1345 (11th Cir. 1982), the Court affirmed a conviction for aiding and abetting wire fraud, finding no error in the admission of evidence concerning a questionable transaction that occurred some fifteen months after the charged fraud. The Court found that the testimony of a participant in the later transaction was enough for the jury to find that it actually occurred and held that the Trial Judge's decision to admit such evidence despite a claim of unfair prejudice under Rule 403 "will not be disturbed on appeal absent a clear showing of an abuse of discretion."

Subsequent acts — intent

United States v. Brown, 16 F.3d 423 (D.C. Cir.), *cert. denied,* 115 S. Ct. __ (1994): Rejecting the defendant's argument that it was error to join counts related to drug and firearms possession in November 1990 with counts related to similar possession in February 1991, the Court held that a pager and firearms seized in February were relevant to show intent, knowledge, or absence of mistake with respect to the November offenses. One Judge dissented on the ground that there was insufficient temporal nexus between the two events for the latter to shed significant light on the defendant's intent at the earlier time and there were no circumstances suggesting the subsequent acts were materially connected with the prior event.

United States v. Nemes, 555 F.2d 51 (2d Cir. 1977): In a prosecution for Medicare and Medicaid fraud, the Court held that similar transactions that took place after the events giving rise to the instant case were properly introduced to show knowledge and intent.

United States v. Boyd, 595 F.2d 120 (3d Cir. 1978): The Court reversed convictions on conspiracy and substantive drug counts, holding it was error to admit proof of postconspiracy actions by two defendants. The Court found that the later actions shed no light on the defendants' intent at an earlier time.

United States v. Whaley, 786 F.2d 1229 (4th Cir. 1986): Affirming a conviction for making false statements on a loan application, the Court held that evidence concerning a similar transaction (in which the defendant used his status as a retired FBI agent to obtain special treatment from a car rental agency) three months after the application, as well as evidence of conduct prior to the application, was admissible to prove intent.

United States v. Johnson, 934 F.2d 936 (8th Cir. 1991): The Court affirmed convictions for aiding and abetting in heroin distribution, holding that evidence of the defendant's participation in subsequent drug transactions was admissible to prove his prior knowledge and intent.

United States v. Ayers, 924 F.2d 1468 (9th Cir. 1991): The Court affirmed convictions for a 1985 tax evasion conspiracy, holding that evidence one defendant submitted a customs declaration in 1987 falsely denying possession of more than $10,000 in currency was highly probative of his intent to defraud the government.

United States v. Mittleider, 835 F.2d 769 (10th Cir. 1987), *cert. denied,* 108 S. Ct. 1279 (1988): Evidence of the defendant's subsequent conversation with an undercover agent concerning a gun purchase was admissible to show intent and absence of mistake in a prosecution for firearms violations.

Subsequent acts — knowledge

United States v. Garcia-Rosa, 876 F.2d 209 (1st Cir. 1989), *cert. denied,* 493 U.S. 1030, *vacated on other grounds,* 498 U.S. 954 (1990): The Court held, in reversing a conviction for offenses in connection with a drug-importation conspiracy, that evidence of drugs found in the defendant's home at the time of his arrest, sixteen months after the events in issue, was not admissible because he had never put his knowledge of drugs at issue, so it could not be used to rebut implications that he "knew nothing about drugs"; it was not probative to imply his knowledge that a loan given at the earlier time was to be used for an illegal drug-related purpose; and the prejudicial effect of the evidence far exceeded any probative value it might have.

United States v. Ramirez, 894 F.2d 565 (2d Cir. 1990): In affirming a conviction for cocaine offenses, the Court rejected any per se rule that subsequent similar act evidence inherently lacks relevancy and held that evidence of the defendant's participation in a cocaine sale in September 1988 was relevant to establish his knowledge and mental state at the time of the charged offense in December 1987. See also *United States v. Nemes,* 555 F.2d 51 (2d Cir. 1977) (similar transactions after the charged events properly introduced to show knowledge and intent in prosecution for Medicare and Medicaid fraud).

United States v. Hadaway, 681 F.2d 214 (4th Cir. 1982): The Court, in a prosecution for aiding and abetting theft from an interstate shipment, upheld the admission of testimony about other occasions when the defendant was involved in similar situations as tending to establish that the defendant knew he was dealing with stolen goods. The evidence was admissible even though it involved acts that occurred eighteen months after the crime charged. A dissent charged that the evidence was unnecessary and that it was little more than propensity evidence.

United States v. Contreras, 602 F.2d 1237 (5th Cir.), *cert. denied,* 444 U.S. 971 (1979): The Court held that evidence of the defendant's drug use subsequent to the charged events was admissible to show knowledge at the relevant time.

United States v. White, 788 F.2d 390 (6th Cir. 1986): The Court affirmed a conviction for conspiring and aiding and abetting in violating the housing rights of a black family, holding that evidence of a fire at a codefendant's home prior to the burning of the victimized family's house was relevant to the defendant's knowledge of his codefendant's propensity to engage in arson and was admissible to prove why the defendant went to the codefendant for help. The Court also held that evidence of a subsequent arson by the codefendant should not have been admitted even if the defendant learned of it, since later knowledge did not prove what the defendant knew at the time of the relevant acts.

United States v. Johnson, 934 F.2d 936 (8th Cir. 1991): The Court affirmed convictions for aiding and abetting in heroin distribution, holding that evidence of the defendant's participation in subsequent drug transactions was admissible to prove his prior knowledge and intent.

United States v. Bibo-Rodriguez, 922 F.2d 1398 (9th Cir.), *cert. denied,* 111 S. Ct. 2861 (1991): The Court affirmed the defendant's conviction for importing cocaine, holding there was no error in admitting evidence that he imported marijuana in a similar manner nine weeks later to prove that the charged importation was knowing.

Timing for introduction

United States v. Colon, 880 F.2d 650 (2d Cir. 1989): In reversing a defendant's conviction of aiding a heroin sale for improper admission of prior sales after the defendant had in effect stipulated intent out of the case, the Court noted that the prosecutor should have waited until it was clear what theory the defense was asserting before introducing the other acts evidence. In *United States v. Benedetto,* 571 F.2d 1246, 1248-50 (2d Cir. 1978), the Court indicated that it favored an "inclusionary" approach toward other crimes evidence, but noted the dangers of accepting such evidence. Referring to its past decisions, the Court wrote that "we have emphasized that admission of such strongly prejudicial evidence should normally await the conclusion of the defendant's case, since the court will then be in the best position to balance the probative worth of, and the Government's need for, such testimony against the prejudice to the defendant." See also *United States v. Danzey,* 594 F.2d 905 (2d Cir.), *cert. denied,* 441 U.S. 951 (1979) (suggesting that other crimes evidence offered to prove intent should be reserved for rebuttal, since intent may be inferred from the act proved by the government).

United States v. Smith Grading & Paving, Inc., 760 F.2d 527 (4th Cir.), *cert. denied,* 474 U.S. 1005 (1985): In a prosecution for a conspiracy to rig bids, the Court upheld the introduction of one defendant's previous bidrigging to prove knowledge and intent to enter a conspiracy. It held that extrinsic evidence may be properly admitted under Rule 404(b) even though it could not be used under Rule 608(b), but it suggested that "the better practice is for the prosecutor to introduce this type of evidence in his or her case in chief" rather than on rebuttal in an effort "to have the last say through evidence of a defendant's prior misconduct."

United States v. Schweihs, 971 F.2d 1302 (7th Cir. 1992): The Court affirmed extortion convictions, holding there was no abuse of discretion in admitting other act evidence during the government's case-in-chief where there was ample reason to believe that the defendant would raise intent or knowledge as an issue, even though the Hobbs Act does not necessarily involve specific intent.

United States v. Southwest Bus Sales, Inc., 20 F.3d 1449 (8th Cir. 1994): In a prosecution for conspiring to suppress competition in school bus sales and mail fraud, the Trial Court excluded evidence of an earlier Sherman Act conspiracy and false bid bonds during the government's case-in-chief and admitted it only during the government's rebuttal, on the ground that the defendants' testimony had put in issue the questions of intent to conspire, motive and opportunity, lack of mistake, and knowledge. Affirming, the Court found no abuse of discretion, but noted that the government should have been allowed to introduce the other acts in its case-in-chief, since intent was an element of the charges and thus an issue relevant to the government's burden of proving its case. In *United States v. Olsen,* 589 F.2d 351 (8th Cir. 1978), *cert. denied,* 440 U.S. 917 (1979), the Court held that because counsel's opening statement raised lack of knowledge as a defense, the government could offer Rule 404(b) evidence in its case-in-chief.

United States v. Hearst, 563 F.2d 1331 (9th Cir. 1977), *cert. denied,* 435 U.S. 1000 (1978): The Court affirmed admission of other crimes evidence to show intent, observing that the government justified its introduction of the evidence as part of its case-in-chief on the ground that it was clear from the outset of the trial that the appellant would raise a duress defense, and there was no basis for assuming any undue prejudice from the timing of the government's proof.

Unfair use

United States v. Sauseda, 24 F.3d 97 (10th Cir. 1994): In a prosecution for possession of marijuana with intent to distribute and for using a firearm during a drug transaction, the government introduced the fact that the defendant was carrying a small amount of cocaine when he was arrested. The Trial Court admitted the cocaine into evidence on the ground that "whatever he's got on him when he's arrested, the Government can go into that." In an opinion by Retired Supreme Court Justice White, sitting by designation, the Court of Appeals held that the Trial Judge's reasoning was "inadequate." Justice White stated that Rule 404(b) nowhere suggests that evidence of uncharged crimes are admissible "solely because that evidence is found on the body of the person when arrested." However, the Court found any error to be harmless, and accordingly refused to consider whether the evidence might have been admissible on grounds consistent with Rule 404(b).

United States v. Crutchfield, 26 F.3d 1098 (11th Cir. 1994): In a prosecution of a married couple for illegal importation of Figi banded iguanas, the Court held that pervasive prosecutorial misconduct required reversal of the conviction. The Court mentioned, as one of the most egregious acts of misconduct, the questioning of a prosecution witness about the fact that the female defendant "was pregnant with another man's child" before she married the male defendant. The Court stated that "the prosecutor's decision to place the sexual character of Penny Crutchfield before the jury in a case involving the importation of iguanas is simply inexcusable." In *United States v. Philibert,* 947 F.2d 1467 (11th Cir. 1991), the Court held that the defendant, charged with making a threatening telephone call, had been deprived of a fair trial by the admission of evidence that he had purchased certain firearms two months before the call, as the weapons were entirely unrelated to the call. Although the purchases may have been additional evidence of his paranoid schizophrenia, such use is barred by the Rule; the error was exacerbated because the only weapon displayed was the one he never had in his possession.

Use by defendant — bad acts by third party

United States v. Wright, 783 F.2d 1091 (D.C. Cir. 1986): In a kidnapping case, the Court held that the Trial Judge properly prevented one defendant from cross-examining

Use by defendant — bad acts by third party (cont'd)

another concerning his pulling a gun on a business partner. Although the Court referred to this as character evidence, it appears that the defendant who sought to cross-examine was doing so in support of a duress defense. Knowledge of the other defendant's previous act with a gun might have been relevant to prove the reasonableness of fear on the part of the cross-examining defendant. It does not appear, however, that this theory was advanced in the case. In *United States v. Sampol,* 636 F.2d 621 (D.C. Cir. 1980), the Court reversed convictions for assassinating a former Chilean Ambassador to the United States on another ground, but held it was proper to exclude *modus operandi* evidence offered to show that the key government witness, a participant in the assassination, had carried out other acts working alone. The Court noted that *modus operandi* evidence can be offered by the defense, but observed that the link between the government witness and other acts was tenuous, the other acts were not done in the same manner, and the witness had not yet met the defendants when the other acts took place.

United States v. Aboumoussallem, 726 F.2d 906 (2d Cir. 1984): To support a defense that he had been unwittingly duped by relatives into carrying heroin from Lebanon into the United States, the defendant offered testimony concerning another instance in which his relatives smuggled hashish oil into an innocent woman's suitcase. The Court stated that "the standard of admissibility when a criminal defendant offers similar acts evidence as a shield need not be as restrictive as when a prosecutor uses such evidence as a sword," since "risks of prejudice are normally absent when the defendant offers similar acts evidence of a third party to prove some fact pertinent to the offense." But the Court found no abuse of discretion in the Trial Judge's ruling that the probative value of evidence about the other incident was insufficient in light of the confusion and delay that would result were the evidence admitted.

United States v. Stevens, 935 F.2d 1380 (3d Cir. 1991): A defendant charged with robbery and sexual assault tried to introduce testimony by the victim of a similar crime three days later that the defendant was not the assailant. The two crimes took place within a few hundred yards of one another and were otherwise so similar that the investigators initially believed that the same person had committed both crimes. Moreover, the fruits of the robberies, which occurred in New Jersey, both surfaced near Ft. Meade, Maryland. Reversing, the Court held that it was error to exclude this "reverse 404(b)" evidence, as its probative value was not substantially outweighed by the prospect of undue delay or confusion of the issues.

United States v. Reeves, 892 F.2d 1223 (5th Cir. 1990): In affirming a conviction for extortion, the Court held there was no abuse of discretion in excluding evidence, offered on an entrapment defense, of a government witness' remote and unrelated contact with State officials, as it was not pertinent to the defendants' predisposition to commit the crimes charged, nor was it evidence of the sort of "systematic campaign of threats and intimidation" held admissible in *United States v. McClure,* 546 F.2d 670 (5th Cir. 1977). In *McClure,* the Court reversed convictions for selling heroin for erroneous exclusion of evidence that the same government informant who allegedly coerced the defendant into making the sales of heroin resulting in his prosecution subsequently coerced three other individuals into making narcotics sales. Noting that Rule 404(b) is generally used by the government to introduce evidence, the Court indicated that in this case the defendant should have been able to take advantage of it and to have introduced evidence of the informant's scheme because "a jury could not properly convict him absent the opportunity to hear the proffered testimony bearing upon his theory of defense and weigh its credibility along with the other evidence in the case."

United States v. Perez, 870 F.2d 1222 (7th Cir.), *cert. denied,* 110 S. Ct. 136 (1989): The Court upheld exclusion of defense evidence concerning an arrest of a government witness, since the defendant did not make a showing that the witness was the source of narcotics on the earlier occasion and did not support an argument that she was the "head" of the drug operation.

United States v. Spencer, 1 F.3d 742 (9th Cir. 1992, *amended* 1993): The defendant was charged with illegal possession of a firearm by a felon after a gun was found in a search of a car in which he was a passenger. When Miller, the owner of the car, was arrested five days later, a gun was found in the car he was driving. Pursuing a theory that the gun charged to him belonged to Miller, the defendant offered police reports of Miller's arrest to show that Miller possessed a gun similar to the one attributed to the defendant. A divided Court held there was no error in excluding the police reports under Rule 403. The majority conceded in its amended opinion that defendants could use Rule 404(b), but said that because hiding a gun under a car seat is not a distinctive crime, the evidence would not be probative on the issue of identity and would otherwise be time-wasting and confusing. The dissenting Judge argued that the reports clearly were probative of mistaken identity and that there was no reason to believe that evidence relating to Miller would have wasted time, confused the issues, or prejudiced the government, and that the Court was perpetuating "an increasingly common double-standard in criminal cases — a standard that allows prosecutors inordinate leeway with respect to the introduction of evidence harmful to the defendant while precluding defendants from introducing evidence that would tend to establish their innocence." In *United States v. Perkins,* 937 F.2d 1397 (9th Cir. 1991), the Court held it was not an abuse of discretion in a bank robbery prosecution to exclude evidence offered by the defendant of three bank robbery counts that had been dismissed, which he argued would tend to show that the same person committed all four robberies, as the *modus operandi* of the dismissed counts was not sufficiently similar to the charged offense to support an inference of identity. In *United States v. McCourt,* 925 F.2d 1229 (9th Cir.), *cert. denied,* 112 S. Ct. 121 (1991), the defendant, charged with filing false tax returns, offered evidence that a prior occupant of his house had a criminal record. The Court held there was no error in excluding the evidence, as its only relevance would be to show the former resident's propensity to act in conformity with the prior acts, which the Rule prohibits as to both defendants and third parties.

United States v. Puckett, 692 F.2d 663 (10th Cir.), *cert. denied,* 459 U.S. 1091 (1982), 460 U.S. 1024 (1983): Affirming convictions arising out of a scheme to defraud banks, the Court held there was no error in excluding testimony offered by one defendant that would have established that a codefendant had conned others. The testimony was intended to bolster a claim that the codefendant conned the defendant into taking certain actions. The Court found that the excluded testimony concerned acts that were unrelated and dissimilar to the crimes charged.

Use by defendant — bad acts by third party (cont'd)

United States v. Cohen, 888 F.2d 770 (11th Cir. 1989): The Court reversed convictions for fraud and tax evasion because the defendants were not permitted to show that the government's primary witness, who pleaded guilty in connection with the scheme, had previously participated in a similar scheme, which would have shown his ability to concoct and conduct such a scheme without aid from the defendants. In *United States v. Rodriguez*, 917 F.2d 1286 (1990) (per curiam), *vacated in part on other grounds*, 935 F.2d 194 (11th Cir. 1991) (per curiam), *cert. denied*, 112 S. Ct. 911 (1992), the Court affirmed convictions for drug-related offenses, holding there was no abuse of discretion in excluding evidence offered by the defendants in support of an entrapment defense that government agents and an informant in the undercover operation had "hounded" another man into smuggling marijuana on another occasion. The defendants provided no specifics; moreover, the other man had pleaded guilty and denied any enticements had been offered by the agents.

Use by defendant — good acts by defendant

United States v. Reifsteck, 841 F.2d 701 (6th Cir. 1988): Affirming a conviction for conspiring to unlawfully use electronic devices, the Court recognized that a defendant might be able to offer evidence of good conduct under Rule 404(b) to rebut an allegation of illicit intent, but it found that the exclusion of other act evidence offered by the defense was not reversible error because it was cumulative of evidence that was admitted.

United States v. Burke, 781 F.2d 1234 (7th Cir. 1985): The Court affirmed extortion convictions relating to a defendant's scheme to get victims to pay him money that he claimed he would give to the FBI, which was investigating the victims. The defendant offered not only character evidence, but also his own testimony that he had planned to squeal on his clients and that he had given tips and leads to law enforcement officers in the past. Since the defendant's intent was in dispute and the government asked him about whether he had ever misled law enforcement officers, the Court was troubled by the exclusion of the evidence but found no abuse of discretion. In our view, the evidence should have been admitted to negate the intent alleged, pursuant to Rule 404(b). In *United States v. Payne*, 635 F.2d 643 (7th Cir. 1980), *cert. denied*, 451 U.S. 972 (1981), defense evidence that the defendant had bought cars in Detroit below "redbook value" was deemed properly excluded in a prosecution for conspiracy to transport stolen motor vehicles as having only dubious relevance to prices of cars coming to Indiana from Kentucky and as having a tendency to confuse the issues.

United States v. Garvin, 565 F.2d 519 (8th Cir. 1977): A conviction for mail fraud was reversed in part because the Court concluded that the appellant was unfairly denied an opportunity to introduce evidence of truthful responses to questions on insurance applications to rebut the government's theory that his false answers on some applications represented a scheme to defraud.

Witness' credibility

United States v. Miller, 895 F.2d 1431 (D.C. Cir.), *cert. denied*, 111 S. Ct. 79 (1990): The Court affirmed a conviction for bank fraud, holding that evidence that a witness who participated in the defendant's check-forging scheme knew of his prior robbery conviction was admitted not to show his propensity but to lend credence to the witness' claim that she feared for her safety if she did not comply with his demands, a state of mind relevant to her credibility.

United States v. Everett, 825 F.2d 658 (2d Cir. 1987), *cert. denied,* 108 S. Ct. 1035 (1988): Although the Court affirmed bank robbery convictions and the admission of testimony concerning a prior robbery, it indicated that when other crimes evidence is admitted for corroborative purposes, the corroboration must be "direct" and the matter corroborated must be "significant."

United States v. Scarfo, 850 F.2d 1015 (3d Cir.), *cert. denied,* 109 S. Ct. 263 (1988): The Court affirmed an extortion and conspiracy conviction, holding it was proper to admit evidence of the defendant's involvement in various murders. Two cooperating witnesses had been granted immunity from prosecution with respect to these murders, and evidence of the defendant's involvement was important for fair jury consideration of their credibility. See also *United States v. Hans,* 738 F.2d 88 (3d Cir. 1984) (evidence seized from one codefendant admissible against another where the evidence corroborated government witness' testimony about how bank robbery occurred).

United States v. Bratton, 875 F.2d 439 (5th Cir.), *cert. denied,* 110 S. Ct. 340 (1989): The Court held, in affirming a conviction for aiding and abetting commission of wire fraud and possession of stolen property, that it was not an abuse of discretion to allow the government to cross-examine the defendant's wife regarding past physical abuse by him against her, because that tended to show a motivation to falsify or fabricate her testimony. The Trial Judge gave a limiting instruction that the evidence could be considered only in assessing the witness' credibility.

United States v. Serlin, 538 F.2d 737 (7th Cir. 1976): The Court concluded that testimony regarding other acts by the defendant was necessary to prepare the Court and jury for the witness' very damaging testimony that he acted as a "set-up man" for the defendant in luring new customers into the fraudulent scheme.

D. LEGISLATIVE HISTORY

Advisory Committee's Note

Subdivision (a). This subdivision deals with the basic question whether character evidence should be admitted. Once the admissibility of character evidence in some form is established under this rule, reference must then be made to Rule 405, which follows, in order to determine the appropriate method of proof. If the character is that of a witness, see Rules 608 and 610 for methods of proof.

Character questions arise in two fundamentally different ways. (1) Character may itself be an element of a crime, claim, or defense. A situation of this kind is commonly referred to as "character in issue." Illustrations are: the chastity of the victim under a statute specifying her chastity as an element of the crime of seduction, or the competency of the driver in an action for negligently entrusting a motor vehicle to an incompetent driver. No problem of the general relevancy of character evidence is involved, and the present rule therefore has no provision on the subject. The only question relates to allowable methods of proof, as to which see Rule 405, immediately following. (2) Character evidence is susceptible of being used for the purpose of suggesting an inference that the person acted on the occasion in question consistently with his character. This use of character is often described as "circumstantial." Illustrations are: evidence of a violent disposition to prove that the person was the aggressor in an affray, or evidence of honesty in disproof of a charge of theft. This circumstantial use of character evidence raises questions of relevancy as well as questions of allowable methods of proof.

In most jurisdictions today, the circumstantial use of character is rejected but with important exceptions: (1) an accused may introduce pertinent evidence of good character (often misleadingly described as "putting his character in issue"), in which event the prosecution may rebut with evidence of bad character; (2) an accused may introduce pertinent evidence of the character of the victim, as in support of a claim of self-defense to a charge of homicide or consent in a case of rape, and the prosecution may introduce similar evidence in rebuttal of the character evidence, or, in a homicide case, to rebut a claim that deceased was the first aggressor, however proved; and (3) the character of a witness may be gone into as bearing on his credibility. McCormick §§ 155-161. This pattern is incorporated in the rule. While its basis lies more in history and experience than in logic, an underlying justification can fairly be found in terms of the relative presence and absence of prejudice in the various situations. Falknor, Extrinsic Policies Affecting Admissibility, 10 Rutgers L. Rev. 574, 584 (1956); McCormick § 157. In any event, the criminal rule is so deeply imbedded in our jurisprudence as to assume almost constitutional proportions and to override doubts of the basic relevancy of the evidence.

The limitation to pertinent traits of character, rather than character generally, in paragraphs (1) and (2) is in accordance with the prevailing view. McCormick § 158, p. 334. A similar provision in Rule 608, to which reference is made in paragraph (3), limits character evidence respecting witnesses to the trait of truthfulness or untruthfulness.

The argument is made that circumstantial use of character ought to be allowed in civil cases to the same extent as in criminal cases, i.e., evidence of good (nonprejudicial) character would be admissible in the first instance, subject to rebuttal by evidence of bad character. Falknor, Extrinsic Policies Affecting Admissibility, 10 Rutgers L. Rev. 574, 581-583 (1956); Tentative Recommendation and a Study Relating to the Uniform Rules of Evidence (Art. VI. Extrinsic Policies Affecting Admissibility), Cal. Law Revision Comm'n, Rep., Rec. & Studies, 657-658 (1964). Uniform Rule 47 goes farther, in that it assumes that character evidence in general satisfies the conditions of relevancy, except as provided in Uniform Rule 48. The difficulty with expanding the use of character evidence in civil cases is set forth by the California Law Revision Commission in its ultimate rejection of Uniform Rule 47, *id.*, 615:

> Character evidence is of slight probative value and may be very prejudicial. It tends to distract the trier of fact from the main question of what actually happened on the particular occasion. It subtly permits the trier of fact to reward the good man and to punish the bad man because of their respective characters despite what the evidence in the case shows actually happened.

Much of the force of the position of those favoring greater use of character evidence in civil cases is dissipated by their support of Uniform Rule 48 which excludes the evidence in negligence cases, where it could be expected to achieve its maximum usefulness. Moreover, expanding concepts of "character," which seem of necessity to extend into such areas as psychiatric evaluation and psychological testing, coupled with expanded admissibility, would open up such vistas of mental examinations as caused the Court concern in Schlagenhauf v. Holder, 379 U.S. 104, 85 S. Ct. 234, 13 L. Ed. 2d 152 (1964). It is believed that those espousing change have not met the burden of persuasion.

Subdivision (b) deals with a specialized but important application of the general rule excluding circumstantial use of character evidence. Consistently with that rule, evidence of other crimes, wrongs, or acts is not admissible to prove character as a basis for suggesting the inference that conduct on a particular occasion was in conformity with it. However, the evidence may be offered for another purpose, such as proof of motive, opportunity, and so on, which does not fall within the prohibition. In this situation the rule does not require that the evidence be excluded. No mechanical solution is offered. The determination must be made whether the danger of undue prejudice outweighs the probative value of the evidence, in view of the availability of other means of proof and other factors appropriate for making decisions of this kind under Rule 403. Slough and Knightly, Other Vices, Other Crimes, 41 Iowa L. Rev. 325 (1956).

1987 Amendment

The entire Advisory Committee Note accompanying the gender-neutralizing changes effective October 1, 1987 is as follows: "The amendments are technical. No substantive change is intended."

1991 Amendment

The Advisory Committee Note accompanying the 1991 amendment to subdivision (b) reads as follows:

> Rule 404(b) has emerged as one of the most cited Rules in the Rules of Evidence. In many criminal cases evidence of an accused's extrinsic acts is viewed as an important asset in the prosecution's case against an accused. Although there are a few reported decisions on use of such evidence by the defense, *see, e.g., United States v. McClure,* 546 F.2d 670 (5th Cir. 1990) (acts of informant offered in entrapment defense), the overwhelming number of cases involve introduction of that evidence by the prosecution.
>
> The amendment to Rule 404(b) adds a pretrial notice requirement in criminal cases and is intended to reduce surprise and promote early resolution of the issue of admissibility. The notice requirement thus places Rule 404(b) in the mainstream with notice and disclosure provisions in other rules of evidence. *See, e.g.,* Rule 412 (written notice of intent to offer evidence under rule), Rule 609 (written notice of intent to offer conviction older than 10 years), Rule 803(24) and 804(b)(5) (notice of intent to use residual hearsay exceptions).
>
> The Rule expects that counsel for both the defense and the prosecution will submit the necessary request and information in a reasonable and timely fashion. Other than requiring pretrial notice, no specific time limits are stated in recognition that what constitutes a reasonable request or disclosure will depend largely on the circumstances of each case. *Compare* Fla.Stat.Ann. § 90.404(2)(b) (notice must be given at least 10 days before trial) *with* Tex.R.Evid. 404(b) (no time limit).
>
> Likewise, no specific form of notice is required. The Committee considered and rejected a requirement that the notice satisfy the particularity requirements normally required of language used in a charging instrument. *Cf.* Fla.Stat.Ann. § 90.404(2)(b) (written disclosure must describe uncharged misconduct with particularity required of an indictment or information). Instead, the Committee opted for a generalized notice provision which requires the prosecution to apprise the defense of the general nature of the evidence of extrinsic acts. The Committee does not intend that the amendment will supercede other rules of admissibility or disclosure, such as the Jencks Act, 18 U.S.C. § 3500, et. seq. nor require the prosecution to disclose directly or indirectly the names and addresses of its witnesses, something it is currently not required to do under Federal Rule of Criminal Procedure 16.
>
> The amendment requires the prosecution to provide notice, regardless of how it intends to use the extrinsic act evidence at trial, i.e., during its case-in-chief, for impeachment, or

for possible rebuttal. The court in its discretion may, under the facts, decide that the particular request or notice was not reasonable, either because of the lack of timeliness or completeness. Because the notice requirement serves as condition precedent to admissibility of 404(b) evidence, the offered evidence is inadmissible if the court decides that the notice requirement has not been met.

Nothing in the amendment precludes the court from requiring the government to provide it with an opportunity to rule *in limine* on 404(b) evidence before it is offered or even mentioned during trial. When ruling *in limine*, the court may require the government to disclose to it the specifics of such evidence which the court must consider in determining admissibility.

The amendment does not extend to evidence of acts which are "intrinsic" to the charged offense, *see United States v. Williams,* 900 F.2d 823 (5th Cir. 1990) (noting distinction between 404(b) evidence and intrinsic offense evidence). Nor is the amendment intended to redefine what evidence would otherwise be admissible under Rule 404(b). Finally, the Committee does not intend through the amendment to affect the role of the court and the jury in considering such evidence. *See United States v. Huddleston,* __ U.S. __, 108 S.Ct. 1496 (1988).

House Subcommittee on Criminal Justice Notes

In the March 1971 draft the second sentence of (b) began "It may, however, be admissible for other purposes...." The Subcommittee preferred the 1971 formulation as placing greater emphasis on admissibility than did the final Court version.

Report of the House Committee on the Judiciary

The second sentence of Rule 404(b) as submitted to the Congress began with the words "This subdivision does not exclude the evidence when offered." The Committee amended this language to read "It may, however, be admissible," the words used in the 1971 Advisory Committee draft, on the ground that this formulation properly placed greater emphasis on admissibility than did the final Court version.

Report of the Senate Committee on the Judiciary

This rule provides that evidence of other crimes, wrongs, or acts is not admissible to prove character but may be admissible for other specified purposes such as proof of motive.

Although your committee sees no necessity in amending the rule itself, it anticipates that the use of the discretionary word "may" with respect to the admissibility of evidence of crimes, wrongs, or acts is not intended to confer any arbitrary discretion on the trial judge. Rather, it is anticipated that with respect to permissible uses for such evidence, the trial judge may exclude it only on the basis of those considerations set forth in Rule 403, i.e., prejudice, confusion or waste of time.

Citations to Hearings and Debates

Letter from Edward W. Cleary to Herbert E. Hoffman, April 13, 1973, in Supp. to Hearings on Proposed Rules of Evidence Before the Subcomm. on Criminal Justice of the House Comm. on the Judiciary, 93rd Cong., 1st Sess., at 21-22 (1973).

Letter from W. Vincent Rakestraw to Hon. James O. Eastland, June 14, 1974, in Hearings on H.R. 5463 (Federal Rules of Evidence) Before the Senate Comm. on the Judiciary, 93rd Cong., 2d Sess., at 121, 123, 126 (1974).

RULE 405

A. OFFICIAL TEXT

Rule 405. Methods of Proving Character

(a) *Reputation or opinion.* — In all cases in which evidence of character or a trait of character of a person is admissible, proof may be made by testimony as to reputation or by testimony in the form of an opinion. On cross-examination, inquiry is allowable into relevant specific instances of conduct.

(b) *Specific instances of conduct.* — In cases in which character or a trait of character of a person is an essential element of a charge, claim, or defense, proof may also be made of specific instances of that person's conduct.

B. EDITORIAL EXPLANATORY COMMENT

Different uses of character evidence

The Editorial Explanatory Comment accompanying Rule 404 discussed two different uses of character evidence: In some cases, character is itself in issue, and character evidence is necessary if an issue is to be correctly decided. In other cases, character evidence is introduced as circumstantial evidence of conduct on a particular occasion and is generally barred, except that the defendant is given the right to open an inquiry into character in a criminal case, special provision is made for criminal cases where the defendant claims self-defense, and character evidence may be used to impeach or support the credibility of a witness (a matter governed by Rules 607, 608, and 609). Rule 404 deals only with the circumstantial use of character evidence, while the instant Rule is not so limited.

Reputation evidence

The Rule provides that when evidence of a character trait is permitted, proof may be made by testimony as to reputation. Reputation evidence is usually presented by calling a witness to the stand who is familiar with the reputation of the person whose character is to be proved, and asking the witness to state what the reputation is in the community where the person lives. The foundation for such testimony comes in the form of establishing that the witness has sufficient familiarity with the people in the community so that the witness can make a valid attempt at assessing reputation.[1]

---

1. See, e.g., United States v. Perry, 643 F.2d 38 (2d Cir. 1981) (no error to exclude testimony by private investigator as to defendant's good reputation in the community, where the witness was "merely going to testify as to a few conversations he had with one of Perry's coworkers at the barbershop, with the minister of Perry's church, and with a laundry proprietor"; character witness "must be able to demonstrate his own familiarity

There is a growing trend to permit testimony as to the person's reputation where he works or commonly associates, as well as where he lives. The Federal Rule does not indicate the scope of reputation evidence, but Courts have considered themselves free to develop the law of reputation testimony much as they were doing prior to the adoption of the Rules.[2] Common-law requirements as to requisite experience in the community and knowledge of community talk have been carried forward. Hearsay exceptions found in Rule 803(19) and (21) suggest that associates in a community are qualified to give reputation evidence.

Opinion evidence

The provision of Rule 405(a) permitting opinion evidence spawned great controversy. Opinion evidence was generally not permitted in common-law jurisdictions, and the House Committee on the Judiciary deleted the language about the admissibility of opinion evidence in its proposed draft of the Rules. The Committee indicated its concern that opinion testimony might turn a trial into a swearing contest between conflicting character witnesses. But during House debate, the Advisory Committee's language was reinstated, and the Senate concurred in the reinstatement. The Rule now permits the use of opinion evidence to prove character. As with reputation witnesses, a foundation must be laid for opinion witnesses; the proponent must establish that the witness is sufficiently familiar with the witness whose character is being proved.

Most commentators applaud the expansion of the definition of admissible character evidence to include opinion evidence. We find ourselves less sanguine about the benefits of this expansion of the Rule, because we fear that many people who harbor grudges against litigants may too freely express negative opinions as to character. Cross-examination demonstrating bias may be some protection, but is it sufficient? There is no way to know for sure. We are also a little concerned about the ability of some influential citizens to command "popular" character witnesses to offer favorable opinions that will be perhaps unduly influential with a jury. The old common-law rule may have been a little bit wooden and a rather imperfect screen against opinion,[3] but it did symbolize a general distrust of character evidence and a specific distrust of personalized character evidence that we may well seek to reconsider in the future.

Another cause for concern exists: Is it wise to expand the scope of opinion evidence to cover psychiatric opinion and other expert opinion, as the last two sentences of the Advisory Committee's Note state that this Rule does? Arguably, the answer is "yes," because such evidence is more meaningful than lay opinion evidence. On the other hand, character evidence is suspect because it threatens to turn trials away from an inquiry into the facts and toward an inquiry into the moral worth of individuals. Expert character testimony seems likely only to accentuate that threat. Nonetheless, the Rule contemplates

---

with the defendant's reputation and his competence to speak for the community'').

2. See, e.g., United States v. Oliver, 492 F.2d 943, 946 (8th Cir. 1974) (''courts have readily extended the concept of community to include the community in which one works, as well as where one lives'').

3. See Government of the Virgin Islands v. Petersen, 553 F.2d 324, 328 (3d Cir. 1977) (Rule 405 ''reflects the reality that reputation evidence has been largely opinion in disguise'').

the use of experts as character witnesses, and some Courts have so applied the Rule.[4] Of course, the proffered expert testimony must satisfy the standards for expert witnesses set forth in Rules 702 through 704,[5] as well as the standards of Rule 403.[6]

Specific evidence

Where character is not "in issue," it may be directly proved only through reputation or opinion. Proof by way of specific acts is not permitted.[7] However, counsel can inquire into relevant specific acts while cross-examining character witnesses. The Rule permits inquiry into specific acts in order to test the knowledge and, thus, the qualification and credibility of the character witness.[8] For example, a character witness who testifies to the defendant's good reputation for peaceableness may be asked: "Have you heard that the defendant committed a murder three years ago?" If the witness has not heard of it, then an implication is created that he is not sufficiently qualified to attest to the defendant's reputation in the community. If the witness has heard about the specific act, and still testifies to the defendant's good reputation in the community, then an implication is created that the community itself is suspect, or that the witness is lying about the good reputation. Similarly, if the witness expresses his opinion that the defendant is a peaceloving person, he can be asked whether he knows about the previous murder. If he did not know, then the basis for his opinion is suspect. If he did know, and yet still had a favorable opinion about the defendant, then the witness himself is suspect.

While ostensibly the Rule permits the use of specific acts only to test character witnesses, the cross-examination permitted by the Rule can be a powerful prosecution

---

4. See, e.g., United States v. Roberts, 887 F.2d 534 (5th Cir. 1989) (Trial Court erred in excluding expert testimony that the defendant's naive and autocratic personality traits were consistent with his claimed activity as a self-appointed vigilante).

5. See, e.g., United States v. Webb, 625 F.2d 709 (5th Cir. 1980) (expert testimony that defendant was nonviolent held properly excluded as unhelpful, since such a character trait is a proper subject of lay testimony).

6. See, e.g., United States v. MacDonald, 688 F.2d 224 (4th Cir. 1982) (Trial Court did not commit error in excluding proffered expert testimony that the defendant had a "personality configuration inconsistent with the outrageous and senseless murders of his family"; the testimony was properly excluded under Rule 403, since it would be confusing to the jury, it was cumulative of testimony from lay witnesses, and it would foster a battle of the experts).

7. See, e.g., United States v. Talamante, 981 F.2d 1153 (10th Cir. 1992) (in a self-defense case, the defendant could not offer specific acts to prove the defendant's character trait for aggressiveness; the victim's character was not "in issue" in the strict sense, and where character is not in issue, it can only be proved through reputation and opinion evidence); United States v. Camejo, 929 F.2d 610 (11th Cir. 1991) (specific acts of good conduct cannot be introduced by positive character witnesses).

8. See, e.g., United States v. Glass, 709 F.2d 669 (11th Cir. 1983) (defendant in a drug case was a sheriff, who called favorable character witnesses; it was proper to question these witnesses as to whether they were aware that the defendant had accepted a bribe to dispose of a drug case pending in court: "In bringing forth character witnesses, Glass initiated the subject of his character and good name; government counsel merely attempted to test the credibility of the witnesses by asking them about specific instances of misconduct going to the nature of their character testimony.").

weapon in a criminal case, allowing the jury to consider specific bad acts that might not otherwise have been admissible.[9]

Defense counsel may wish to note, however, that sometimes the damage done on cross-examination may be repaired on redirect. For example, if a reputation witness is asked whether he had heard "that the defendant had previously been charged with an assault," defense counsel may, if the facts support it, ask the character witness: "Have you also heard that charges were dropped against the defendant for lack of evidence?"[10]

Good faith proof of specific acts

While a party may cross-examine a character witness with relevant specific acts, the party may not prove that these acts occurred, if the only purpose is to test the character witness. Subdivision (a) provides that "inquiry is allowable" into relevant specific instances of conduct. This language does not permit extrinsic proof of the conduct. The rationale is that the probative value of proof of such a collateral matter is substantially outweighed by the risk of prejudice, confusion, and delay; after all, the bad act is only probative in these circumstances to test the knowledge of the character witness. It is not worth it, under the circumstances, to prove to the jury that the act occurred.

Nonetheless, counsel must have some proof in hand that the act occurred, before the act can be used to test the witness on cross-examination. There would be an obvious risk of abuse if a party were permitted to inquire about specific acts with no proof that the acts even occurred. Consequently, Courts have required that the "alleged bad act must have a good faith basis in fact."[11] Upon request by the opposing party, the Trial Court should require the cross-examiner to lay a foundation out of the presence of the jury before asking the character witness about specific acts.[12]

The "good faith basis" test is not a strenuous one; it does not require that proof of the specific act be admissible under the rules of evidence. Consequently, the good faith

---

9. See, e.g., United States v. Apfelbaum, 621 F.2d 62 (3d Cir. 1980) (character witnesses not called because of threatened impeachment with defendant's bad acts); United States v. Davenport, 753 F.2d 1460, 1463 (9th Cir. 1985) ("The danger in such a situation is that the prosecution will use the question to waft an unwarranted innuendo into the jury box.").

10. See generally Note, *Have You Heard? Cross-Examination of a Criminal Defendant's Good Character Witness: A Proposal for Reform,* 9 U.C. DAVIS L. REV. 365 (1976). The Note makes a useful suggestion that Trial Judges should feel free to exercise the discretionary authority to exclude evidence provided by Rule 403 in dealing with cross-examination of character witnesses. See the discussion on Rule 403 *infra* in this Editorial Explanatory Comment.

11. United States v. Nixon, 777 F.2d 958, 970 (5th Cir. 1985). See also United States v. Adair, 951 F.2d 316, 319 (11th Cir. 1992) (reputation witness may be asked on cross-examination whether he has heard about relevant bad conduct by the defendant, but "the government must have a good faith factual basis for the incidents").

12. See, e.g., United States v. Davenport, 753 F.2d 1460, 1464 (9th Cir. 1985) (government must have "a good faith belief in the misconduct of the defendant which was the subject of the question. If mistrial is to be avoided, this good faith must be established to the satisfaction of the court, outside the presence of the jury, before the question is asked."); United States v. Reese, 568 F.2d 1246 (6th Cir. 1977) (better practice is for Trial Judge to conduct voir dire to determine good faith basis as to alleged bad acts, before allowing prosecutor to cross-examine defense witnesses).

basis test has often been met through hearsay statements of law enforcement officers, implicating the defendant in criminal activity.[13] Still, it is clear that such questions cannot be asked if there is no proof at all that the act occurred.[14]

Permissible cross-examination

Ostensibly, a witness who gives an opinion, rather than testimony as to the person's reputation, is testifying to what he knows about the person, rather than what he has heard. But it is not as clear as the Advisory Committee suggests that the "have you heard" question is inappropriate for opinion character witnesses. What a witness has heard about the defendant (or the victim) is probably relevant to the witness' opinion. Thus, the questioner should in most cases be permitted to ask an opinion witness either a "do you know" or a "have you heard" question, or both.[15] Likewise, since testimony as to reputation is often thinly disguised opinion testimony, and since one's knowledge of reputation may be affected by specific acts that one has heard about, the Trial Court should be flexible in permitting the use of "do you know" questions on cross-examination of reputation witnesses.[16]

Relationship to Rule 607

One of the confusing aspects of the Rules is their loose use of the words "impeachment" and "cross-examination." Rule 607 provides that any party can attack the credibility of any witness. But Rules 405(a) and 608(b)(2) only provide for an inquiry into specific instances of conduct on the *cross-examination* of a character witness — i.e., a witness testifying as to the character of a defendant or a victim. It is sensible to distinguish between the impeachment needs on direct and cross-examination of character witnesses. The cross-examiner is entitled to probe the knowledge of the witness by asking about specific events. But the direct examiner is barred from such an inquiry lest "impeachment" of one's own witness becomes an excuse for using specific acts instead of the required reputation or opinion evidence to prove character. This is one of those special places where the impeachment needs of the parties are not the same. Because the

---

13. See, e.g., United States v. Nixon, 777 F.2d 958 (5th Cir. 1985) (good faith basis found where prosecutor relied on hearsay statements of police officers, implicating the defendant in drug activity); United States v. Bright, 588 F.2d 504 (5th Cir. 1979) (government's proffer of a letter of reprimand for stipulation and its willingness to reopen the case in order to prove the fact of defendant's reprimand by a Judge, demonstrated the necessary good faith factual basis for cross-examination of defense witness concerning the reprimand).

14. See, e.g., United States v. Davenport, 753 F.2d 1460, 1464 (9th Cir. 1985) (abuse of discretion where prosecutor was permitted to inquire about a bad act without establishing any basis in fact that the act occurred).

15. See, e.g., United States v. Collins, 779 F.2d 1520 (11th Cir. 1986) (opinion witness could be asked whether he had heard of defendant's arrests and convictions).

16. See SEC v. Peters, 978 F.2d 1162, 1172 (10th Cir. 1992) (Rule 405 "dismantled the distinction" between reputation and opinion testimony, and therefore opinion and reputation witnesses should be treated similarly on cross-examination).

direct examiner usually has a choice of character witnesses, this form of "testing" the witness is seldom necessary during direct examination.

Character in issue

When a character trait is an essential element of one party's case, greater freedom to inquire into specific instances of conduct is permitted by subdivision (b).[17] The rationale is that substantive law has recognized the trait as important and the most probative evidence should be utilized. In some instances, proof of specific acts may not merely be permitted, but it may even be required — e.g., to prove the incompetence of an employee in a negligent entrustment case. Special proof requirements find their roots in the underlying substantive law.

A complicated question of whether character is "in issue" arises when a criminal defendant puts forth an entrapment defense. For example, in *United States v. Donoho*, 575 F.2d 718 (9th Cir.), *vacated*, 439 U.S. 811, *new trial ordered*, 586 F.2d 682 (1978), the Court held that there was no error in excluding defense evidence of specific acts of good conduct when it was offered in support of the defendant's entrapment defense. The Court indicated its confusion when it first stated that an entrapment defense puts the defendant's predisposition "in issue," but then concluded that an entrapment defense did not involve the character of a defendant. The Court explained that conclusion by saying that "predisposition" refers only to the defendant's state of mind at the time of the act and that evidence of the defendant's character is only one means of proving (circumstantially) that state of mind. Most authorities, however, treat "predisposition" and "character" as equivalent terms.[18] Under that view, an entrapment defense may present an issue of whether the defendant possessed a certain kind of character: If the government seeks to rebut the defense by showing the defendant's predisposition (i.e., character), the parties should be able to offer specific act evidence under Rule 405. On the other hand, if the government only denies that the allegedly entrapping events took place, predisposition is not in dispute and specific act evidence should be inadmissible on simple grounds of relevance. Probably, a judicious use of Rule 403 will be necessary to balance the government's right to prove predisposition when the defendant claims entrapment against the danger of prejudice that accounts for Rule 404(b). In the unusual case such as *Donoho*, in which the defendant offers the specific act evidence, the danger of prejudice may be lessened, but the probative value of the evidence will depend on whether the government has focused on predisposition as part of its case.

Jury instructions

The Supreme Court recognized in *Michelson v. United States*, 335 U.S. 469 (1948), that the evidence rules on character testimony are not as logical as one might wish them

---

17. See, e.g., Meiners v. Moriarty, 563 F.2d 343 (7th Cir. 1977) (specific acts admissible where relevant to plaintiff's character in an action for defamation).

18. See, e.g., Unites States v. Mazza, 792 F.2d 1210 (1st Cir. 1986), *cert. denied*, 107 S. Ct. 1290 (1987) (probative specific acts can be offered to rebut an entrapment defense because such a defense puts the defendant's character "in issue").

to be. It is reasonable for juries to wonder why they hear about reputation and opinion, but not about details to back up the more general testimony. Rarely are juries told the reason for the absence of specific evidence.

More troublesome is the occasional failure to give a jury instruction concerning the proper use of questions put on cross-examination to a character witness. If a cross-examiner asks a "have you heard" or "do you know" question and the witness answers "yes," there is not much to worry about. The "yes" answer will either be explained or the witness' testimony will be weakened by the force of the cross-examination. But if the witness answers "no," what is the jury to do with the answer? The cross-examiner is not allowed to prove that the act asked about actually occurred. And if the witness denies hearing or knowing about it, how can the jury conclude that the witness' answer weakens testimony unless it knows that the act actually happened? Now, if some character witnesses answer "yes," while others answer "no," this may be helpful in assessing the credibility of those who respond in the negative. Still, a problem of prejudice and confusion remains when all of the witnesses answer "no" or where there is only one character witness.[19] Perhaps the demeanor of the witnesses in answering will be important, but it is also true that the question is not evidence.

To help jurors understand the character rules, the following instruction has been proposed for use in Alaska. Although it refers to a witness' character for truthfulness, it can easily be modified to cover any pertinent character trait of a defendant.

> Do not be surprised that these witnesses limit their testimony to reputation and opinion and do not describe the specific acts of the witness that they know or have heard about. The law does not allow them to testify about the specific past actions of a witness. It would take too long for us to consider all the good and bad things that a witness may ever have done.
>
> However, a person who testifies about a witness' reputation for truthfulness or who gives his opinion about a witness' truthfulness may be asked whether he has heard or knows specific things about the witness. If he answers "yes," he may be asked to explain how these things have affected the reputation or his opinion of the witness. If he answers "no," you may consider how this answer bears on what he has said, remembering that what is stated in a question is not evidence and should not be assumed to be true.[20]

Relationship to Rule 403

Trial Judges must keep in mind that Rule 403 governs the offer of impeachment evidence under the instant rule as under virtually all of the Federal Rules of Evidence

---

19. See, e.g., United States v. Davenport, 753 F.2d 1460, 1463 (9th Cir. 1985) (witness' denial leaves "uncontroverted the insinuation that the defendant had planned to engage in additional bank robberies. The prejudice to the defendant was, thus, created by the question itself rather than by the testimony given in response.").

20. See also United States v. Birney, 686 F.2d 102, 108 (2d Cir. 1982) (cross-examination of character witnesses, by asking about bad acts committed by the defendant, was proper where the Trial Court instructed the jury that the cross-examination was directed solely at the weight that should be given to the testimony of the character witness, and not to prove that the defendant was a bad person or that the acts really occurred).

with the exception of some parts of Rule 412 and Rule 609 (and, perhaps, Rules 413-415). There is no more reason to allow one party to obtain an unfair advantage through cross-examination than through direct examination.

In *United States v. Dawson,* 556 F. Supp. 418 (E.D. Pa. 1982), *aff'd,* 727 F.2d 1099, 1100, 1101 (3d Cir. 1984), the Court held that the government properly asked one defendant's character witness whether he knew that the defendant had been convicted of murder, even though the conviction had been reversed on appeal. The Court reasoned that since a witness could have been asked about an arrest not followed by a conviction, the witness also could be asked about a conviction that had been overturned. This reasoning is logical, but fails to consider the prejudice that might arise from the mention of a conviction. One would expect character witnesses for the defendant to answer questions about the conviction by saying that it had little or no effect on reputation or opinion because it had been declared invalid. Such answers would suggest that the conviction has little probative value when used to impeach the character witnesses. Its prejudicial effect on a jury might well be great however, since the jury may assume, no matter what instructions the judge gives, that the defendant is a murderer who escaped on a technicality. The admissibility question is close. Defense counsel should seek an *in limine* ruling on the scope of cross-examination before offering character witnesses to testify on behalf of a defendant whose conviction has been reversed on appeal.

Guilt-assuming questions

The qualification and credibility of a witness who testifies to the defendant's good character can be tested by inquiring into the defendant's relevant specific acts. But a more difficult question is whether the witness can be tested by an assumption of the defendant's guilt as to the crime charged. For example, in *United States v. Wilson,* 983 F.2d 221 (11th Cir. 1993), the defendant was convicted of bank fraud and possessing and selling unauthorized credit card numbers. At trial, he admitted the sale of the numbers, but denied fraudulent intent. He called character witnesses who testified to their good opinion of his honesty and integrity. On cross-examination, the witnesses were asked whether their opinion would change if they knew that Wilson had sold credit card numbers to an undercover agent. The Court found that these questions were proper.

Most Courts have found it to be impermissible to ask guilt-assuming hypothetical questions of any witnesses who have testified about the defendant's good character.[21] The rationale is that "[s]ince character evidence is admitted only as bearing upon guilt or innocence, an opinion based upon the assumption that the defendant is guilty cannot have any probative value in deciding that issue."[22] And, of course, the defendant is

---

21. See, e.g., United States v. Mason, 985 F.2d 147 (4th Cir. 1993) (hypothetical questions to character witnesses assuming defendant's guilt are impermissible); United States v. Oshatz, 912 F.2d 534 (2d Cir. 1990) (same).

22. United States v. Morgan, 554 F.2d 31 (2d Cir.), *cert. denied,* 434 U.S. 965 (1977) (Mansfield, J., concurring).

likely to suffer prejudice if guilt is assumed, albeit hypothetically, by the prosecution and by the defense witness.[23]

In our view, the cross-examiner already has sufficient ways to examine character witnesses concerning things they have heard or know about the defendant. There is no reason to allow hypothetical questions to be based on the facts of the case being tried. Such a hypothetical comes perilously close to treading on the presumption of innocence.

However, the limitation on guilt-assuming hypotheticals is only triggered if the question put to the character witness actually presumes guilt. The Court in *Wilson* held that the questions put by the prosecutor did not assume guilt because "the witnesses were asked about nothing more than Wilson already had admitted during his time on the stand: he sold credit card numbers to an undercover Secret Service agent." The question did not assume the issue that was in dispute, i.e., whether Wilson sold the credit cards with fraudulent intent.[24]

Relationship to Rule 412

As we did with the Comment to Rule 404(a), we emphasize here that proof of sexual activity on the part of a rape victim is now covered by Rule 412, and not by this Rule.

C. ANNOTATED CASES

RULE 405(a) — REPUTATION OR OPINION

Cross-examination — generally

United States v. Martorano, 557 F.2d 1 (1st Cir. 1977), *cert. denied,* 435 U.S. 922 (1978): In a prosecution for loansharking, one witness was permitted to testify concerning the appellant's reputation for collection practices. Although recognizing that many Courts have permitted questioning a reputation witness as to the specific persons who served as his sources of information, the Court upheld a ruling barring such questions in the instant case. The Court noted that the cross-examiner would be bound by the answers of the witness, that there was evidence to suggest that the witness could have answered the questions to the detriment of the examiner, and that a number of traditionally accepted devices were available to cast doubt upon the reasonableness of the reputation testimony — e.g., asking the witness to specify the rumors that he had heard and the number of people from whom he had heard them. Especially important to the Court was the danger to third parties if their names were disclosed.

---

23. One Circuit has distinguished between opinion witnesses, where guilt-assuming questions may be permissible, and reputation witnesses, where they are not. See United States v. White, 887 F.2d 267 (D.C. Cir. 1989). The rationale for such a distinction is obscure.

24. See also United States v. Velasquez, 980 F.2d 1275 (9th Cir. 1992) (in a prosecution for bank robbery, it was proper to ask character witnesses whether their opinion would change if it were established that the defendant had taken a grenade into a bank and inquired about money; defendant admitted this act, and merely denied that he had the intent to rob the bank).

United States v. Beros, 833 F.2d 455 (3d Cir. 1987): The Court held that the Trial Judge properly permitted the government to cross-examine defense character witnesses in a prosecution for conversion of union funds concerning their knowledge of the defendant's false swearing on a marriage license application.

United States v. Ochoa, 609 F.2d 198 (5th Cir. 1980): A defendant's conviction on a heroin charge was reversed because the government had been permitted to cross-examine her about the prior bad conduct of her relatives. The Court noted that although she had offered two character witnesses, the government should have been restricted to rebutting their testimony about *her* character.

United States v. Jordan, 722 F.2d 353 (7th Cir. 1983): In a prosecution for aggravated battery, the Court found it was proper for the government to ask a witness, who testified that the defendant's character for law-abidingness was good, whether he had heard of the defendant's prior arrest.

United States v. Adair, 951 F.2d 316 (11th Cir. 1992): In a Hobbs Act prosecution of a former police chief for protecting cocaine and illegal liquor sales, the Court held there was no abuse of discretion in an *in limine* ruling permitting character witnesses to be cross-examined about their knowledge of the defendant's prior conviction for hindering the apprehension of a felon. The prosecution had a good faith basis for the questions, they would have tested the witnesses' knowledge of the defendant's reputation, and they were relevant to the character traits raised at trial. See also *United States v. Glass,* 709 F.2d 669 (11th Cir. 1983) (prosecutor properly permitted to ask defense character witnesses in drug case whether they knew that defendant, a sheriff, had accepted money to dispose of a pending drug case and whether they knew about his ticket fixing).

Cross-examination — good faith basis

United States v. Wallach, 935 F.2d 445 (2d Cir. 1991): The prosecutor asked character witnesses for a defendant charged with racketeering about an incident in which a state judge, whom the defendant was promoting for appointment to the federal bench, had approved a 60 percent legal fee for him in the settlement of a personal injury case. Reversing the convictions on other grounds, the Court noted that the government had a good faith basis for inquiring into the matter to challenge the basis for the character witnesses' opinions, but that the prosecutor argued the evidence to the jury in a manner well beyond the bounds of propriety and relevance. In *United States v. Bermudez,* 526 F.2d 89 (2d Cir. 1975), *cert. denied,* 425 U.S. 970 (1976), the Court affirmed convictions for conspiracy to distribute cocaine, holding that it was proper to permit cross-examination of character witnesses for a defendant by asking them whether they had heard that he was arrested on a marijuana charge in 1974. Before cross-examining the witnesses, the prosecutor had informed the Judge of the proposed line of inquiry and supplied documentary proof of the arrest.

United States v. Luffred, 911 F.2d 1011 (5th Cir. 1990): In reversing the defendant's bank fraud convictions on other grounds, the Court noted that error was also committed when the government was permitted to impeach character witnesses by questions referring to other crimes for which no factual basis had been laid.

United States v. Reese, 568 F.2d 1246 (6th Cir. 1977): The Court, affirming a conviction for receiving stolen property, suggested that before character witnesses who testify as to a defendant's reputation are asked about community rumors, the Trial Judge should have "a voir dire examination to determine whether there were actually such rumors before permitting the cross-examination. This would have avoided any random shots to the prejudice of the appellant."

United States v. Finley, 934 F.2d 837 (7th Cir. 1991): In the RICO and Hobbs Act prosecution of a state court clerk, a government witness testified on cross-examination to his opinion that the defendant was an honest and dedicated public servant. The Court held there was no abuse of discretion when the witness was asked on redirect whether he had previously said the defendant lost his position on an election ticket because of an extortion incident. Because the prosecutor asked what the witness had said, not what the witness had heard, the question had a factual basis, even if the extortion incident was only unsubstantiated rumor. In *United States v. Alvarez,* 860 F.2d 801 (1988), *adhered to on reh'g,* 868 F.2d 201 (7th Cir.), *cert. denied,* 493 U.S. 829 (1989), a narcotics prosecution, the Court upheld cross-examination of two defense character witnesses about certain events, since the defendant had spoken about these events to the witnesses and the government had a good faith basis for its questions.

Cross-examination — guilt-assuming hypotheticals

United States v. White, 887 F.2d 267 (D.C. Cir. 1989): Although the Court reversed a defendant's bribery conviction, it held there had been no error in permitting cross-examination of a character witness with hypotheticals that assumed the defendant was guilty of the crimes for which he was on trial. The Court noted that it may be improper to cross-examine a witness testifying only to community reputation with hypotheticals, but that is not true for witnesses expressing their own opinion of the defendant's character.

United States v. Oshatz, 912 F.2d 534 (2d Cir. 1990), *cert. denied,* 111 S. Ct. 1695 (1991): After the defendant in a tax fraud case elicited favorable opinion testimony regarding his character, the prosecutor asked the witnesses whether their opinions would change if they knew the defendant had committed the charged crimes. The Court reaffirmed the prohibition of *United States v. Morgan,* 554 F.2d 31 (2d Cir.), *cert. denied,* 434 U.S. 965 (1977) (see Editorial Explanatory Comment), on guilt-assuming hypothetical questions of lay character witnesses, noting that any probative value is greatly outweighed by the risk of impairing the presumption of innocence. The error was harmless, however. One Judge, concurring in the result, disagreed on the grounds that such questions are extremely helpful in probing the witness' bias and standards and that the risks of prejudice cited by the majority are nonexistent or overstated.

United States v. Curtis, 644 F.2d 263 (3d Cir. 1981), *cert. denied,* 459 U.S. 1018 (1982): When a defendant charged with narcotics offenses claimed entrapment and offered reputation evidence through character witnesses, the prosecution responded by asking the witnesses how their opinions of the defendant's character would be affected by an admission by the defendant of participation in the narcotics activity. The Court held it was error to permit the government's examination because a reputation witness should be impeached only on matters relating to reputation.

United States v. Mason, 993 F.2d 406 (4th Cir. 1993): The Court reversed convictions for cocaine offenses, finding that the prosecutor improperly questioned defense character witnesses by asking them whether their opinion of the defendant would change if they believed he distributed drugs. The Court reasoned that "an opinion elicited by a question that assumes that the defendant is guilty can have only negligible probative value as it bears on the central issue of guilt," and that "adherence to a basic concept of our justice system, the presumption of innocence, is not served by this line of questioning."

United States v. Candelaria-Gonzalez, 547 F.2d 291 (5th Cir. 1977): The Court reversed convictions for narcotics violations on the ground, *inter alia,* that character witnesses who testified on behalf of one defendant were improperly impeached. Although the Trial Judge did not permit asking whether the indictment would affect the witness' opinion of the defendant, the government was permitted to ask whether the defendant's reputation would be affected if he were convicted of trafficking in narcotics. The Court concluded that the "hypothetical questions struck at the very heart of the presumption of innocence which is fundamental to Anglo-Saxon concepts of fair trial." In the same vein, the Court held that the government improperly destroyed the presumption of innocence accorded an accused when it asked a character witness whether it would be inconsistent with his knowledge of the defendant *if* a DEA agent testified that the defendant was known as a major narcotics trafficker.

United States v. McGuire, 744 F.2d 1197 (6th Cir. 1984), *cert. denied,* 471 U.S. 1004 (1985): The Court affirmed convictions for offenses involving false entries in bank records, holding that after character witnesses gave their opinions of one defendant and his reputation, they were properly asked whether they knew of a pending civil suit against him charging that he and others had engaged in unfair trade practices. The Court observed, however, that "it would be error to allow the prosecution to ask the character witness to assume defendant's guilt of the offenses for which he is then on trial."

United States v. Williams, 738 F.2d 172 (7th Cir. 1984): The Court found error (harmless, however) in the government's cross-examining defense character witnesses by asking them whether their opinions would change if it were shown the defendant were guilty.

United States v. Barta, 888 F.2d 1220 (8th Cir. 1989): The Court held it was error, but harmless, to ask a witness who testified in a tax evasion case to the defendant's reputation for high character and trustworthiness whether his opinion of that reputation would change if the defendant had acted as charged; such a question undermined the presumption of innocence.

United States v. James, 728 F.2d 465 (10th Cir.), *cert. denied,* 469 U.S. 826 (1984): The Court affirmed convictions for fraud and extortion, but found error in the prosecution's redirect examination of a witness who had been asked on cross-examination by the defense about the defendant's reputation. The prosecutor asked whether the reputation would be as good if its charges were true, and the Court said that it was improper to have asked the witness to assume the guilt of the defendant. See also *United States v. Primrose,* 718 F.2d 1484 (10th Cir. 1983) (guilt-assuming hypothetical on cross-examination of reputation witness harmless error), *cert. denied,* 104 S. Ct. 2352 (1984);

United States v. Polsinelli, 649 F.2d 793 (10th Cir. 1981) (drug convictions reversed because the prosecutor improperly asked defense character witnesses what their opinions would be if they assumed the defendant was guilty of the acts charged by the government).

United States v. Wilson, 983 F.2d 221 (11th Cir. 1993): The Court held there was no error in a prosecution for bank fraud and unauthorized use of credit card numbers in asking the defendant's character witnesses whether their favorable opinions would change if they knew he had sold credit card numbers, as the defendant had already admitted the act and was only denying fraudulent intent. Because the questions were therefore not guilt-assuming, there was no need to decide when, or whether, guilt-assuming hypotheticals would be permissible.

Cross-examination — remote specific acts

United States v. Edwards, 549 F.2d 362 (5th Cir.), *cert. denied,* 434 U.S. 828 (1977): The Court noted that in questioning a character witness, a cross-examiner attempting to test whether the character witness is credible can ask the witness about events that are more than ten years old, because the ten-year limitation of Rule 609(b) has no application to such questioning.

United States v. Alvarez, 860 F.2d 801 (1988), *adhered to on reh'g,* 868 F.2d 201 (7th Cir.), *cert. denied,* 493 U.S. 829 (1989): In a narcotics prosecution, the Court upheld cross-examination of two defense character witnesses about events occurring in and before 1973. It observed that the government allegations of continuing violations of the immigration laws included the earlier time period.

Cross-examination — reputation and opinion witnesses distinguished

United States v. Curtis, 644 F.2d 263 (3d Cir. 1981), *cert. denied,* 459 U.S. 1018 (1982): When a defendant charged with narcotics offenses claimed entrapment and offered reputation evidence through character witnesses, the prosecution responded by asking the witnesses how their opinions of the defendant's character would be affected by an admission by the defendant of participation in the narcotics activity. The Court held it was error to permit the government's examination because a reputation witness should be impeached only on matters relating to reputation.

United States v. Frost, 914 F.2d 756 (6th Cir. 1990): The Court affirmed convictions for banking offenses, holding there was no abuse of discretion in permitting character witnesses, who testified to the defendants' community reputations, to be asked on cross-examination whether their opinions of those reputations would change if they had heard of specific acts of conduct. Describing the situation as a textbook application of the Rule, the Court rejected the defendants' argument that, because only reputation evidence had been elicited, cross-examination could mention only acts likely to have been known in the community.

United States v. Manos, 848 F.2d 1427 (7th Cir. 1988): The Court affirmed a defendant's racketeering and extortion convictions, as it found that defense character witnesses were properly cross-examined about specific instances of conduct. It concluded that both reputation and opinion witnesses may be cross-examined about specific instances.

SEC v. Peters, 978 F.2d 1162 (10th Cir. 1992): The Court reversed a judgment for the defendant in a civil action for insider trading violations, holding the SEC had been improperly precluded from asking the defendant's opinion character witnesses whether they had heard of other securities law claims made against him. "Have you heard" questions are as relevant to opinion as to reputation character testimony, and it is clear that the Rule intends to treat the two types similarly.

Defendant's testimony

United States v. Giese, 597 F.2d 1170 (9th Cir.), *cert. denied,* 444 U.S. 979 (1979): Affirming (2-1) the defendant's conviction for conspiring to bomb military bases to dramatize opposition to the Vietnam War, the Court upheld cross-examination of the defendant about the contents of a book entitled *From the Movement Toward Revolution,* which had been admitted because it bore his fingerprints and thus connected him to the conspiracy. The majority said he had opened the door to the cross-examination by testifying about eighteen books that he said were representative of his views. The majority observed that, unlike a character witness, a "defendant-witness may cite specific instances of conduct as proof that he possesses a relevant character trait such as peaceableness." That statement is not true under Rule 405(a), although we note that the case was tried before the effective date of the Rules. In our view, it is questionable whether in a situation like this the government may say the defendant has "opened the door" after it has failed to object to specific-acts character evidence.

United States v. Solomon, 686 F.2d 863 (11th Cir. 1982): The Court affirmed convictions for a truck hijacking conspiracy, holding that the Trial Judge properly sustained objections to defense attempts to have a defendant answer questions about the composition of his family and his service in the military. The answers would not have amounted to reputation or opinion evidence, which is the exclusive means of proving good character.

Expert testimony

United States v. Oshatz, 912 F.2d 534 (2d Cir. 1990), *cert. denied,* 111 S. Ct. 1695 (1991): In ruling that guilt-assuming hypothetical questions of lay character witnesses are improper, the Court left open the possibility that they might be asked on cross-examination of expert character witnesses. One Judge, concurring only in the judgment, said that expert character testimony is one of those ideas whose time has not yet come, and with common sense and a modicum of luck never will.

United States v. Hill, 655 F.2d 512 (3d Cir. 1981), *cert. denied,* 464 U.S. 1039 (1984): The Court reversed drug convictions because the Trial Judge excluded a psychologist's expert testimony, offered to support an entrapment defense, that the defendant was uniquely susceptible to government inducements. Citing its prior decision in *United States v. Curtis,* 644 F.2d 263 (3d Cir. 1981), *cert. denied,* 459 U.S. 1018

(1982), the Court said that Rule 405(a) permits "two kinds of character evidence, now allowing testimony by an expert witness on traits of character which may be substantively relevant."

United States v. Webb, 625 F.2d 709 (5th Cir. 1980): The Court held, in a prosecution for shooting at a flying helicopter, that there was no error in excluding expert testimony that the defendant lacked "propensity to commit a violent act," as that was a character trait plainly within the ken of lay jurors.

Extrinsic specific act evidence to rebut character testimony

United States v. Benedetto, 571 F.2d 1246 (2d Cir. 1978): Citing Rule 405, the Court observed in dictum that the fact "[t]hat the defense improperly attempted to establish defendant's good character by reference to specific good acts did not justify the prosecution's use of testimony [extrinsic evidence] concerning bad acts either in its direct case or in rebuttal."

United States v. Reed, 700 F.2d 638 (11th Cir. 1983): The Court reversed convictions for embezzlement and unlawful possession and obstruction of the mail because the prosecutor asked the defendant on cross-examination whether he recalled being in possession of marijuana at the time of arrest and making a statement regarding marijuana use, and the prosecutor then presented testimony to contradict the defendant's answers. The government claimed that the defendant opened the door to negative character evidence by offering character witnesses who testified as to his general reputation and his reputation for truth and veracity. The Court noted that the government could have offered evidence that would have rebutted the defendant's evidence of good character for honesty and truthfulness, but that possession of marijuana was not such evidence. We would also observe that the government may respond to defense character evidence by asking the character witnesses if they have heard or know of specific acts of bad character, but it may not introduce extrinsic evidence to prove the acts.

Jury instructions

United States v. Benally, 756 F.2d 773 (10th Cir. 1985): Reversing a defendant's conviction for vehicular homicide, the Court held it was error to give an instruction on other crimes evidence when the only mention of prior arrests and convictions came in the prosecution's cross-examination of a defense character witness. Since the jury was not to assume that the facts stated in questions were true, the instruction, which stated that testimony of other acts, wrongs, or crimes had been introduced, was incorrect.

Relevant community

United States v. Mandel, 591 F.2d 1347, *vacated,* 602 F.2d 653 (4th Cir. 1979) (*en banc*), *cert. denied,* 445 U.S. 959, 961 (1980): Although it overturned mail fraud and racketeering convictions on other grounds, the Court of Appeals panel cited this Manual and indicated to Trial Judges that character evidence offered to impeach a witness (or to respond to impeachment evidence) could take the form of reputation or opinion based in the locality where a witness worked as well as the locality where the witness lives. An equally divided *en banc* Court reinstated the convictions, but did not comment on this point.

Religious beliefs

Government of Virgin Islands v. Petersen, 553 F.2d 324 (3d Cir. 1977): Affirming a murder conviction, the Court held there was no error in prohibiting the defendant from introducing testimony regarding his religious affiliation to demonstrate that he rejected violence. Recognizing that the defendant's religious beliefs rejecting violence would "be logically probative of the proposition that defendant acted in conformity with his belief on the night of the homicide," the Court nevertheless held that the testimony was properly excluded. "A person may or may not act in accordance with a professed belief; it is the observation of the defendant's *behavior* over a length of time which is the recognized basis for both reputation and opinion testimony." Because Rule 405(a) "reflects an accommodation between logical relevance on the one hand and the desire to avoid prejudice, confusion, surprise and consumption of trial time on the other," the Court held "that the appropriate means to elicit opinion testimony under the rule is to inquire directly as to the witness' opinion concerning the relevant character trait of the accused."

Specific good acts

United States v. Barry, 814 F.2d 1400 (9th Cir. 1987): The Court affirmed convictions for unauthorized sale of government property. It found no error in the exclusion of defense evidence of an FBI rap sheet showing only one prior arrest, which ended in dismissal of charges, and two commendation letters written twelve years prior to the unauthorized sales. The Court cited *Government of Virgin Islands v. Grant,* 775 F.2d 508 (3d Cir. 1985), for the proposition that testimony of multiple instances of good conduct appears to violate a strict reading of Rule 405 and is generally less probative than reputation or opinion evidence. The Court left open the question of whether specific acts of good conduct might be admissible under Rule 404(b) to support an entrapment defense.

United States v. Russell, 703 F.2d 1243 (11th Cir. 1983): The Court affirmed convictions in a marijuana conspiracy case, finding that evidence of specific good acts offered on behalf of a defendant was properly excluded, since evidence of other noncriminal conduct is generally not probative of whether a defendant committed the acts charged.

Testimony about victim

United States v. Piche, 981 F.2d 706 (4th Cir. 1992), *cert. denied,* 113 S. Ct. 2356 (1993): In a prosecution for conspiring to violate civil rights of Asian-Americans, the Court held that, even though evidence of two victims' character was admissible to prove that they were predisposed to participate in violent acts, character was not in dispute and only reputation or opinion evidence could have been admitted.

United States v. Kills Ree, 691 F.2d 412 (8th Cir. 1982): The Court upheld a conviction for involuntary manslaughter, finding that the Trial Judge properly excluded evidence concerning specific instances in which one victim allegedly beat another. This was not reputation or opinion evidence.

United States v. Talamante, 981 F.2d 1153 (10th Cir.), *cert. denied,* 113 S. Ct. 1876 (1993): The Court upheld a defendant's conviction for assault, finding that the Trial Judge ruled correctly in excluding specific acts offered by the defense to prove that the victim was the first aggressor. Since the defendant was attempting to prove the victim's character, which was not in issue, the defendant was limited to reputation and opinion evidence.

RULE 405(b) — SPECIFIC INSTANCES OF CONDUCT

Competency of employee

Webb v. City of Chester, 813 F.2d 824 (7th Cir. 1987): Affirming a plaintiff's judgment in a sex discrimination suit arising out of her discharge from a police department, the Court upheld exclusion of evidence that two years after her discharge the plaintiff demonstrated incompetence while employed as a part-time officer in another city. Although the plaintiff's competence was an issue in the case, the Court concluded that the Trial Judge did not err in finding that the evidence was too remote in time and too prejudicial. In *Crawford v. Yellow Cab Co.,* 572 F. Supp. 1205 (N.D. Ill. 1983), a passenger injured in one of the defendant's cabs claimed that the company willfully and wantonly entrusted the cab to the driver. The Court ruled that evidence of the driving record of the plaintiff's driver was admissible, since it was used to show an element of the claim, incompetency, rather than as circumstantial character evidence.

In re Aircrash, 684 F.2d 1301 (9th Cir. 1982): In a suit by survivors of passengers killed in an airplane crash, the Court held that training records of a pilot were admissible to prove that he was incompetent to fly and that the airline was on notice of this before the accident. Once the competency of an employee is in issue, specific instances of conduct are permissible to prove incompetency; indeed, it may be the only proof available.

Defamation

Meiners v. Moriarity, 563 F.2d 343 (7th Cir. 1977): In a defamation action, reputation evidence was held to be relevant at least as to damages, and the Court found error in the Trial Judge's refusal to permit questions of those persons claiming injury to reputation about events that might have injured their reputations. Although the Court cited Rule 405, it appeared to have confused reputation as a matter in issue and reputation used to prove character. Reputation was not used in this case to show a person's character, because character was not in issue and it could not be used circumstantially to prove consistent conduct. In any event, specific acts could not have been used to prove character. Rather, reputation was in issue as an element of damages and specific acts were probative of what kind of reputation the claimants were likely to have had.

Entrapment

United States v. Mazza, 792 F.2d 1210 (1st Cir. 1986), *cert. denied,* 107 S. Ct. 1290 (1987): The Court affirmed cocaine convictions, finding that evidence of one defendant's prior cocaine purchases was admissible to rebut an entrapment defense.

United States v. Toner, 728 F.2d 115 (2d Cir. 1984): Affirming convictions for firearms offenses, the Court found there was no error in excluding evidence, offered to support an entrapment defense, that a defendant had twice rejected an informant's proposals to engage in firearms transactions. Since the defendant's evidence showed only that he lacked funds necessary to pursue the informant's proposals, the Court found that it was not probative of a predisposition not to commit firearms offenses. In *United States v. Williams,* 705 F.2d 603 (2d Cir.), *cert. denied,* 104 S. Ct. 524 (1983), the ABSCAM prosecution of a former United States Senator, the Court held that the Trial Judge properly permitted the government to respond to an entrapment defense with evidence that the Senator used his influence on behalf of himself and his wife even when no government agent asked him to. This evidence tended to establish his predisposition. See also *United States v. Miah,* 433 F. Supp. 259 (E.D. Pa. 1977) (government permitted to ask defendant about heroin transactions after charged crimes, to rebut entrapment defense), *aff'd,* 571 F.2d 573 (3d Cir. 1978).

United States v. Manzella, 782 F.2d 533 (5th Cir.), *cert. denied,* 106 S. Ct. 1991, 107 S. Ct. 457 (1986): Affirming racketeering convictions, the Court found that extrinsic evidence of a defendant's prior crimes was admissible to show predisposition in response to an entrapment defense. In *United States v. Parrish,* 736 F.2d 152 (5th Cir. 1984), the Court held that evidence of a prior drug offense conviction was admissible in a drug prosecution to prove predisposition once a defendant raised an entrapment defense.

United States v. Faymore, 736 F.2d 328 (6th Cir.), *cert. denied,* 105 S. Ct. 213 (1984): Affirming a conviction for narcotics offenses, the Court held that an entrapment defense permits the government to use proof of a defendant's character to prove predisposition to commit the crime.

United States v. Swiatek, 819 F.2d 721 (7th Cir.), *cert. denied,* 108 S. Ct. 245 (1987): The Court held that the government should not have been permitted to introduce evidence that the defendant was willing to deal in stolen jewelry and cars to rebut an entrapment defense in a prosecution for firearms offenses. It stated that such evidence was only minimally relevant to a predisposition to sell firearms. The error was deemed harmless, however. In *United States v. Moschiano,* 695 F.2d 236 (7th Cir. 1982), *cert. denied,* 104 S. Ct. 110 (1983), the Court affirmed convictions for drug-related offenses, holding that evidence of *subsequent* similar acts could be admitted to prove predisposition in response to an entrapment claim. In the instant case, the Court found that one defendant's attempt to purchase large amounts of Preludin three months after the events leading to heroin charges was relevant to the entrapment defense offered against those charges.

United States v. McGuire, 808 F.2d 694 (8th Cir. 1987): Although the Court found it was error to permit the government to introduce evidence in its case-in-chief to rebut an anticipated entrapment defense, it held that the error was harmless and was attributable to the defendant's approval of the Judge's instructions to the jury during voir dire concerning the defense of entrapment.

United States v. Barry, 814 F.2d 1400 (9th Cir. 1987): The Court affirmed a defendant's convictions, finding no abuse of discretion in the exclusion of evidence offered in support of an entrapment defense. It reasoned that even if the evidence could properly be admitted as specific good act evidence, it was hearsay and remote. In *United States v. Donoho,* 575 F.2d 718 (9th Cir.), *vacated,* 439 U.S. 811, *new trial ordered,* 586 F.2d 682 (1978) (see Editorial Explanatory Comment), the Court affirmed a firearms conviction, holding there was no error in excluding defense evidence of specific instances of good conduct offered to support an entrapment defense. The Court took the unusual position that even though an entrapment defense puts the defendant's predisposition in issue, it does not involve the character of a defendant. See also *United States v. Bramble,* 641 F.2d 681 (9th Cir. 1981), *cert. denied,* 459 U.S. 1072 (1982) (possession of marijuana not probative of predisposition to sell cocaine).

United States v. Badolato, 710 F.2d 1509 (11th Cir. 1983): Where a defendant charged with involvement in cocaine trafficking urged in his opening statement that he was entrapped by government agents, the Court found that a videotape of a meeting between the defendant and government agents in which marijuana was discussed was admissible to show predisposition. See also *United States v. Roper,* 874 F.2d 782 (11th Cir.) (other crimes evidence admissible to rebut entrapment), *cert. denied,* 110 S. Ct. 189, 369 (1989).

Specific acts giving rise to liability

Silkwood v. Kerr-McGee Corp., 485 F. Supp. 566 (W.D. Okla. 1979), *modified on other grounds,* 667 F.2d 908 (10th Cir. 1981), *rev'd on other grounds,* 464 U.S. 238 (1984): In an action for personal injuries allegedly caused through the escape of plutonium from the defendant's facility, the District Court held that evidence of the defendant's negligent or reckless handling of plutonium was admissible, because it tended to prove that the very harm alleged in the case was caused by the defendant's actions.

D. LEGISLATIVE HISTORY

Advisory Committee's Note

The rule deals only with allowable methods of proving character, not with the admissibility of character evidence, which is covered in Rule 404.

Of the three methods of proving character provided by the rule, evidence of specific instances of conduct is the most convincing. At the same time it possesses the greatest capacity to arouse prejudice, to confuse, to surprise, and to consume time. Consequently the rule confines the use of evidence of this kind to cases in which character is, in the strict sense, in issue and hence deserving of a searching inquiry. When character is used circumstantially and hence occupies a lesser status in the case, proof may be only by reputation and opinion. These latter methods are also available when character is in issue. This treatment is, with respect to specific instances of conduct and reputation, conventional contemporary common law doctrine. McCormick § 153.

In recognizing opinion as a means of proving character, the rule departs from usual contemporary practice in favor of that of an earlier day. See 7 Wigmore § 1986, pointing out that the earlier practice permitted opinion and arguing strongly for evidence based on personal knowledge and belief as contrasted with "the secondhand, irresponsible product of multiplied guesses and gossip which we term 'reputation.'" It seems likely that the persistence of reputation evidence is due to its largely being opinion in disguise. Traditionally character has been regarded primarily in moral overtones of good and bad: chaste, peaceable, truthful, honest. Nevertheless, on occasion nonmoral considerations crop up, as in the case of the incompetent driver, and this seems bound to happen increasingly. If character is defined as the kind of person one is, then account must be taken of varying ways of arriving at the estimate. These may range from the opinion of the employer who has found the man honest to the opinion of the psychiatrist based upon examination and testing. No effective dividing line exists between character and mental capacity, and the latter traditionally has been provable by opinion.

According to the great majority of cases, on cross-examination inquiry is allowable as to whether the reputation witness has heard of particular instances of conduct pertinent to the trait in question. Michelson v. United States, 335 U.S. 469, 69 S. Ct. 213, 93 L. Ed. 168 (1948); Annot., 47 A.L.R.2d 1258. The theory is that, since the reputation witness relates what he has heard, the inquiry tends to shed light on the accuracy of his hearing and reporting. Accordingly, the opinion witness would be asked whether he knew, as well as whether he had heard. The fact is, of course, that these distinctions are of slight if any practical significance, and the second sentence of subdivision (a) eliminates them as a factor in formulating questions. This recognition of the propriety of inquiring into specific instances of conduct does not circumscribe inquiry otherwise into the bases of opinion and reputation testimony.

The express allowance of inquiry into specific instances of conduct on cross-examination in subdivision (a) and the express allowance of it as part of a case-in-chief when character is actually in issue in subdivision (b) contemplate that testimony of specific instances is not generally permissible on the direct examination of an ordinary opinion witness to character. Similarly as to witnesses to the character of witnesses under Rule 608(b). Opinion testimony on direct in these situations ought in general to correspond to reputation testimony as now given, i.e., be confined to the nature and extent of observation and acquaintance upon which the opinion is based. See Rule 701.

1987 Amendment

[The entire Advisory Committee Note accompanying the gender-neutralizing changes effective October 1, 1987 is as follows: "The amendment is technical. No substantive change is intended."]

House Subcommittee on Criminal Justice Notes

June 28, 1973

The Subcommittee approved subdivision (b) as proposed by the Court, with the specific understanding that the Rule applies only in those relatively rare situations where character is truly an issue in the case.

October 10, 1973

The Court's version of subdivision (a) had proposed to change existing law by allowing evidence of character in the form of opinion as well as reputation testimony. Predicated in part on the view that wholesale allowance of opinion testimony might tend to turn a trial into a swearing contest between conflicting character witnesses the Subcommittee decided to delete from this Rule, as well as from Rule 608, reference to opinion testimony. [This deletion was subsequently reinstated in the Rule as ultimately passed].

Report of the House Committee on the Judiciary

Rule 405(a) as submitted proposed to change existing law by allowing evidence of character in the form of opinion as well as reputation testimony. Fearing, among other reasons, that wholesale allowance of opinion testimony might tend to turn a trial into a swearing contest between conflicting character witnesses, the Committee decided to delete from this Rule, as well as from Rule 608(a) which involves a related problem, reference to opinion testimony. [This deletion was subsequently reinstated in the Rule as ultimately passed].

Report of the House and Senate Conferees

The Senate makes two language changes in the nature of conforming amendments. The Conference adopts the Senate amendments.

Citations to Hearings and Debates

Letter from Edward W. Cleary to Herbert E. Hoffman, April 13, 1973, in Supp. to Hearings on Proposed Rules of Evidence Before the Subcomm. on Criminal Justice of the House Comm. on the Judiciary, 93rd Cong., 1st Sess., at 21-22 (1973).

Letter from Edward W. Cleary to Herbert E. Hoffman, April 17, 1973, and accompanying material, in Supp. to Hearings on Proposed Rules of Evidence Before the Subcomm. on Criminal Justice of the House Comm. on the Judiciary, 93rd Cong., 1st Sess., at 40-41 (1973).

Debate in the House of Representatives, 120 Cong. Rec. H546-H549 (daily ed. February 6, 1974).

Letter from W. Vincent Rakestraw to Hon. James O. Eastland, June 14, 1974, in Hearings on H.R. 5463 (Federal Rules of Evidence) Before the Senate Comm. on the Judiciary, 93rd Cong., 2d Sess., at 121, 123-24, 126 (1974).

RULE 406

A. OFFICIAL TEXT

Rule 406. Habit; Routine Practice

Evidence of the habit of a person or of the routine practice of an organization, whether corroborated or not and regardless of the presence of eyewitnesses, is relevant to prove that the conduct of the person or organization on a particular occasion was in conformity with the habit or routine practice.

B. EDITORIAL EXPLANATORY COMMENT

Rule and rationale

As discussed in the Editorial Explanatory Comment to Rule 404, character evidence is ordinarily inadmissible when offered to prove the conduct of a person on a particular occasion. In contrast, Rule 406 provides that evidence of a habit of a person is ordinarily admissible to prove that the conduct of the person on a particular occasion was in conformity with the habit. The Rule also provides admissibility for "organizational" practice: Evidence of the routine practice of a business organization is admissible to show that the organization acted on a particular occasion in conformity with its routine practice.

The rationale for admitting evidence of habit and not of character is based mostly on a differentiation of probative value. It is not always, or even often, the case that a person acts in accordance with a character trait. Violent people, for example, do not act violently on every conceivable occasion. In contrast, the specificity and consistency attendant to habit give increased confidence that a person acted in accordance with habit on a specific occasion.[1] If a person has a habit of wearing a seatbelt, for example, this is much more probative evidence of his wearing a seatbelt on a certain occasion than is evidence that he is generally a safety-oriented person.

Character distinguished

Courts have generally proceeded cautiously in permitting the admission of a pattern of conduct as habit, "because it necessarily engenders the very real possibility that such evidence will be used to establish a party's propensity to act in conformity with its general character, thereby thwarting Rule 404's prohibition against the use of character

---

1. See Jones v. Southern Pac. R.R., 962 F.2d 447, 449 (5th Cir. 1992) ("Habit evidence is superior to character evidence because the uniformity of one's response to habit is far greater than the consistency with which one's conduct conforms to character.").

evidence except for narrowly prescribed purposes."[2] That is, Courts are concerned that the rule admitting evidence as habit will swallow the rule that excludes character evidence.[3]

Although it is difficult to delineate the difference between character and habit,[4] generally it may be said that the more particular and the more regular the performance of an act, the more likely it is to be regarded as habit. In other words, the easier it is to describe with particularity what it is that someone does and the more routine the action, the more likely a Court is to hold the activity to be a habit.

One Court has recently stated the test for habit as follows: "To offer evidence of a habit, a party must at least demonstrate a regular practice of meeting a particular kind of situation with a specific type of response."[5] Another Court has added that "habit refers to the type of non-volitional activity that occurs with invariable regularity. It is the non-volitional character of habit evidence that makes it probative."[6] Thus, activity that is extremely complicated is unlikely to be considered habit, since such activity would ordinarily be dependent on a significant thought process, and a number of contingencies, and all of this is inconsistent with the notion of habit as reflexive and semiautomatic.[7] Also, activity that is dependent on cooperation from other individuals, or that is dependent on a number of instrumentalities, is unlikely to be considered as habit, because the circumstances will ordinarily be subject to too much variation.[8]

---

2. Simplex, Inc. v. Diversified Energy Sys., 847 F.2d 1290, 1293 (7th Cir. 1988).

3. See, e.g., United States v. Mascio, 774 F.2d 219 (7th Cir. 1985) (there is no such thing as a habit of committing insurance fraud, because evidence of such "habits" "would be identical to the kind of evidence that is the target of the general rule against character evidence").

4. See, e.g., Perrin v. Anderson, 784 F.2d 1040 (10th Cir. 1986) ("Character and habit are closely akin."). In *Perrin,* the Court held there was no error in a finding that the plaintiff's previously violent encounters with police officers evidenced a habit, rather than a character trait for violence.

5. Jones v. Southern Pac. R.R., 962 F.2d 447, 449 (5th Cir. 1992).

6. Weil v. Seitzer, 873 F.2d 1453, 1460 (D.C. Cir. 1989). See also United States v. Rangel-Arreola, 991 F.2d 1519 (10th Cir. 1993) (defendant was a trucker; a large amount of marijuana was found in his fuel tank; he objected to exclusion of evidence that it was common practice for truck drivers to accept jobs without checking the fuel tanks; the Court holds that the common practice did not constitute habit, since the behavior of truck drivers upon the acceptance of a job is volitional and "not of the reflexive nature or consistency required" to constitute habit).

7. See, e.g., United States v. Troutman, 814 F.2d 1428 (10th Cir. 1987) (evidence of past official conduct not admissible as habit because "extortion or refraining from extortion is not a semi-automatic act and does not constitute habit"); Weil v. Seitzer, 873 F.2d 1453 (D.C. Cir. 1989) (testimony that doctor had prescribed steroids to other patients held not admissible as habit because it is "not of the non-volitional, habitual type that ensures its probative value").

8. See, e.g., Halloran v. Virginia Chemicals Inc., 41 N.Y.2d 386, 393 N.Y.S.2d 341 (1977) ("On no view ... can conduct involving not only oneself but particularly other persons or independently controlled instrumentalities produce a regular usage because of the likely variation of the circumstances in which such conduct will be indulged.") In *Halloran,* the plaintiff, a car mechanic, was injured when a can of Freon exploded while he was servicing an automobile's air conditioning unit. The Court in *Halloran* held that evidence of the plaintiff's "usual practice" of using an immersion coil to heat the water in which he then placed the Freon was admissible as habit evidence, to show that the plaintiff followed this (dangerous) practice on the day he was injured. The Court noted that the plaintiff was in "complete control" of the circumstances attendant to the act.

Routine organizational practice

With respect to a business or other type of organization, greater emphasis is placed on the routine nature of the activity than on its particularity; there is not the same problem of drawing a line between general and specific qualities that exists with natural persons. Because the line between habit and character is not so problematic with respect to organizations, Courts admit routine organizational practice more liberally, noting that there is significant probative value in the routinized aspects of organizational activity.[9] However, in order to invoke the more liberal admissibility requirements attendant to organizational activity, the proponent must show that the activity is that of a structured organization; a loose-knit, ad hoc alliance of individuals does not give rise to the same inference of routinized activity.[10]

Eyewitnesses and corroboration

Note that habit evidence is admissible even though there may be eyewitnesses to an event. This reflects the drafters' view that habit can indeed be highly probative evidence. In fact, since habit evidence need not be corroborated, the Rule recognizes that in some cases it may be decisive.[11]

Proof of habit

Although the draft of Rule 406 approved by the Supreme Court provided that habit or routine practice could be proved by testimony in the form of an opinion or by specific instances of conduct sufficient in number to warrant a finding that a habit existed or that a practice was routine, this provision was deleted in the Congress. Apparently, Congress wished to allow Courts to develop and consider methods of proof on a case-by-case basis. One would suspect that the best proof of a habit is that someone acted in a particular way at specific and frequent instances, and also that the person did not act otherwise at other

---

9. See, e.g., Rosenburg v. Lincoln Am. Life Ins. Co., 883 F.2d 1328 (7th Cir. 1989) (evidence that insurance company waived certain standard conditions when issuing a policy was admissible as evidence of routine practice); Garvey v. Dickinson College, 763 F. Supp. 799 (M.D. Pa. 1991) (in Title VII action, evidence of a college's routine procedures for screening faculty applicants, processing applications and reviewing candidates for tenure were admissible under Rule 406).

10. See, e.g., United States v. Rangel-Arreola, 991 F.2d 1519 (10th Cir. 1993) (defendant was a trucker who was found with a large amount of marijuana in the fuel tank of the truck he was driving; he objected to exclusion of evidence that it was common practice for truck drivers to accept jobs without checking the fuel tanks; the Court holds that Rule 406 was not applicable because a loose-knit group such as freelance truck drivers did not form a cohesive organization with a structure and routinized practice).

11. See, e.g., Loughan v. Firestone Tire & Rubber Co., 749 F.2d 1519, 1523 (11th Cir. 1985) ("Evidence of habit or routine is to be weighed and considered by the trier of fact in the same manner as any other type of direct or circumstantial evidence.").

similar instances.[12] Probably the best testimony will be by a witness who has personal knowledge of the conduct of the relevant actor on numerous separate occasions.

Whatever the mode of proof, the touchstone of admissibility is to provide an "adequacy of sampling and uniformity of response" in specific circumstances.[13] The burden of proving habit is on the proponent of the evidence.[14] So, if only a few instances are shown, and the conduct has occurred over the course of a long period of time, it is unlikely that sufficient evidence of habit will be found; and this is especially so if the instances of conduct are not exactly identical in detail.[15] Conversely, habit is more likely to be found if the proponent can provide multiple instances of specific, identical conduct over a relatively short period of time.

Relationship to other rules

Since character evidence is generally excluded, and only habit evidence is admitted, the Judge will probably want to ensure that she is indeed dealing with a habit and not general character before permitting any evidence to be introduced. It is likely, therefore, that the Judge will look to Rule 104 and decide to make a preliminary determination that a habit exists before permitting the evidence to be introduced.

Several respected lawyers have suggested that the acceptance of habit evidence in Rule 406 is a mistake. Their theory is that habit and character evidence are so closely related that character evidence barred at the front door, under Rule 404, will come in the back door, under Rule 406. Without disparaging this concern, we believe that the line between character and habit, while admittedly hazy, is a line worth drawing. Habit evidence, properly administered, can be powerful circumstantial proof as to conduct. The more particular the conduct and the more frequent its occurrence, the more powerful the evidence and the less danger that some people will be penalized or rewarded because they are "good" or "bad" human beings.

---

12. See, e.g., Simplex, Inc. v. Diversified Energy Sys., 847 F.2d 1290, 1294 (7th Cir. 1988) (the Rule 406 inquiry "necessitates some comparison of the number of instances in which any such conduct occurs with the number in which no such conduct took place"; evidence of late performance of contracts was not admissible under Rule 406 where the proponent made no attempt at "a comparison of the number of late and defectively performed contracts relative to those without such inadequacies").

13. McWhorter v. City of Birmingham, 906 F.2d 674, 679 (11th Cir. 1990) (evidence of harrassment did not constitute habit where only a few instances were shown).

14. See, e.g., Weil v. Seltzer, 873 F.2d 1453 (D.C. Cir. 1989) (fact that evidence of specific instances was uncontradicted held not dispositive, since "the admissibility of habit evidence under Rule 406 does not hinge on the ability of the party seeking exclusion of the evidence to disprove the habitual character of the evidence. Rather, the burden of establishing the habitual nature of the evidence rests on the proponent of the evidence.").

15. See, e.g., Jones v. Southern Pac. R.R., 962 F.2d 447 (5th Cir. 1992) (in a negligence action arising out of a train accident, plaintiff offered evidence of prior safety infractions of the conductor; these were not admissible as habit evidence because the plaintiff had not demonstrated a regular practice of meeting a particular kind of situation with a specific type of conduct; the conductor was cited for nine safety infractions over a twenty-nine-year period, and the infractions were varied).

Rule 403 should be kept in mind by the conscientious Trial Judge.[16] When the habit to be proved is likely to be used by a jury as an indication of moral worth, the Judge may exclude proof of habit if its value in the case is substantially outweighed by its potential to distort the jury's factfinding function. In drawing the line between character and habit, it may be wise for the Trial Judge to make the difficult, but useful, attempt to establish a sliding scale for conduct evidence, with totally neutral evidence at one end and highly charged evidence at the other. Evidence falling close to the former may be deemed habit in close cases, and evidence falling close to the latter should be treated as character evidence in close cases.

In attempting to authenticate evidence, the careful lawyer will notice the relationship that potentially exists between Rule 406 and Rule 901(b)(4). One of the ways that evidence can be identified is to show that a particular person or organization habitually produces similar evidence. For example, in a case in which a particular document inadvertently has been removed from its place in a business' records, authentication might be accomplished by showing that the business routinely records certain information, that the information usually recorded is of the same type that appears in the questioned document, and that the record that would usually exist is missing. The habit evidence might be enough to get the document before the trier of fact.

C. ANNOTATED CASES

Customs of an industry or business

United States v. Seelig, 622 F.2d 207 (6th Cir.), *cert. denied,* 449 U.S. 869 (1980): One ground given for reversing pharmacists' convictions for improperly dispensing controlled drugs was that the defendants were erroneously denied an opportunity to offer expert testimony "as to the custom of pharmacists regarding the sales of over-the-counter exempt drugs."

Anderson v. Malloy, 700 F.2d 1208 (8th Cir. 1983): A rape victim sued the owners and operators of a motel claiming they did not take adequate measures to protect motel guests. The Court reversed a judgment for the defendants, partly because the Trial Judge erred in excluding evidence of the custom and practice of other area hotels and motels.

United States v. Rangel-Arreola, 991 F.2d 1519 (10th Cir. 1993): The defendant, charged with importing marijuana after it was found in his truck's fuel tanks, sought to support his defense that he had no knowledge of the marijuana by offering evidence that it was common practice for truck drivers to accept jobs without checking the fuel tanks. The Court held the evidence was not admissible under the Rule because it neither showed the defendant's conduct nor that of an organization from which consistent conduct might be inferred. Furthermore, the defendant was not offering to show a regular practice of meeting a particular situation with essentially reflexive behavior.

---

16. See, e.g., United States v. Brechtel, 997 F.2d 1108 (5th Cir. 1993) (evidence of routine business practice properly excluded under Rule 403, where the habit was of "tenuous relevance" to the issues, and where "the chain of analogies required to ground relevance of this evidence might well have rendered it confusing to the jury").

Custom or practice of a particular organization

Weil v. Seltzer, 873 F.2d 1453 (D.C. Cir. 1989): Vacating a judgment for the plaintiff in a malpractice suit, the Court held that the plaintiff failed to justify as habit evidence proof that the defendant had prescribed steroids to five other allergy patients while representing the drugs to be something else. The evidence was not of the "nonvolitional, habitual type that assures its probative value."

United States Football League v. National Football League, 842 F.2d 1335 (2d Cir. 1988): Affirming a judgment awarding $1 to the plaintiff in this antitrust action, the Court held that evidence of three or four antitrust judgments against a defendant over a twenty-year period was not admissible as habit evidence. In *United States v. Angelilli,* 660 F.2d 23 (2d Cir. 1981), *cert. denied,* 455 U.S. 910, 945 (1982), the Court discussed the relationship among Rule 404(b) evidence offered to prove a continuing scheme, evidence offered as conspiratorial acts, and habit evidence offered to show conformity to a habit. The Court counseled some caution in jumping from the fact that someone has done similar acts to the conclusion that the person has a habit of doing such acts and concluded that special care is needed to prevent evidence of past practice of some members of an organization from being used to show how others acted at different times. In *United States v. General Foods Corp.,* 446 F. Supp. 740 (N.D.N.Y.), *aff'd,* 491 F.2d 1322 (2d Cir. 1978), the FDA brought an action alleging that adulterated food was introduced into interstate commerce by defendants. The Court held that to refute the allegations defendants could introduce evidence of routine business practices involving cleanup, sanitation, and maintenance.

Wilson v. Volkswagen of Am., Inc., 561 F.2d 494 (4th Cir. 1977), *cert. denied,* 434 U.S. 1020 (1978): The Court reversed a default judgment on the issue of liability for an automobile accident after finding willful failure to comply with a discovery order. The Court was critical of the District Judge's finding that the defendants in the instant case and in other cases demonstrated a habit or pattern of conduct designed to avoid discovery. The Court stated that "habit or pattern of conduct is never to be lightly established, and evidence of examples, for purpose of establishing such habit, is to be carefully scrutinized before admission." It also noted that in evaluating the frequency and the number of actions by a person that are alleged to constitute a habit, the District Judge must keep in mind that the key criteria are adequacy of sampling and uniformity of response. "[R]egularity of conduct such as that charged against defendants requires some comparison of the number of instances in which any such conduct occurs with the number in which no such conduct took place."

United States v. West, 22 F.3d 586 (5th Cir. 1994): In a bankruptcy fraud prosecution, the Trial Court excluded evidence that in the 1980s it was the routine practice of the FDIC to sell notes held by a failed institution at a discount and that the FDIC routinely allowed parties to purchase their own discounted notes through "straw" purchasers. The Court of Appeals found no error, concluding that "the evidence proffered by West to prove the FDIC's routine practice, when considered in light of the FDIC's dealings with literally thousands of debtors during the mid- to late-1980s, falls far short of the adequacy of sampling and uniformity of response which are the controlling considerations governing admissibility" under Rule 406. The Court also held that evidence of FDIC policies, as distinct from routine practice, could not be introduced under the terms of Rule 406, though it expressed no opinion on whether the policies could be introduced under some other Rule such as Rule 401.

Simplex, Inc. v. Diversified Energy Sys., 847 F.2d 1290 (7th Cir. 1988): Affirming a judgment for a supplier who sued a purchaser for breach of contract, the Court held that evidence of the supplier's conduct with respect to other contracts was not admissible to prove a routine practice of late deliveries and defective performance. Not only did the Court doubt whether the evidence "approaches the level of specificity to be considered semi-automatic conduct," but it also reasoned that the defendant failed to compare the number of late or defective contract performances with the number of adequate performances. In *Rosenburg v. Lincoln Am. Life Ins. Co.,* 883 F.2d 1328 (7th Cir. 1989), the defendant disputed coverage under a group life insurance policy on the ground that 40 percent of the group had not enrolled. The Court held that evidence that defendant's agents had a habit of selling conditional insurance, waiving such conditions, and later asserting them as defenses was admissible as routine practice evidence relevant to whether defendant had waived the conditions. In *Wetherill v. University of Chicago,* 570 F. Supp. 1124 (N.D. Ill. 1983), the Court, ruling *in limine* in an action by two plaintiffs who claimed injuries as a result of their mothers' receiving a drug as part of a study conducted in the defendant's hospitals, held that the defendants could introduce evidence of a routine practice of obtaining consent by participants in the study. The Court found that the evidence of specific instances in which patient consent had been obtained was sufficient to warrant a finding that there was a routine practice.

Maynard v. Sayles, 817 F.2d 50 (8th Cir.), *vacated,* 831 F.2d 173 (1987) (*en banc*): A panel of the Court reversed a judgment dismissing a civil rights suit against police officers who allegedly abused the plaintiff when arresting him. It held that the Trial Judge erred in excluding the testimony of a former police officer who worked for three years in the same department and with three of the defendants. The witness would have testified that when a fellow officer has used excessive force during an arrest, other officers will not discuss the incident except to corroborate the fellow officer's version of the arrest. The plaintiff's failure to produce more than one witness to testify to the "code of silence" did not render the testimony inadmissible. On rehearing *en banc,* the panel opinion was vacated and the decision below was affirmed by an equally-divided Court.

Meyer v. United States, 464 F. Supp. 317 (D. Colo. 1979), *aff'd,* 638 F.2d 155 (1980): Finding for the government in a Tort Claims Act case, the District Court relied on a dentist's habit and custom to find that the dentist properly warned a patient as to the risks of a surgical procedure.

United States v. Sheffield, 992 F.2d 1164 (11th Cir. 1993): Reversing a conviction for embezzling Air Force property, the Court held that the defendant was wrongly denied his right to introduce evidence that it was the custom of the air base to produce authorized retirement gifts for high-ranking employees. Evidence of the custom was relevant to the defendant's state of mind in ordering the production of certain items. In *G.M. Brod & Co. v. U.S. Home Corp.,* 759 F.2d 1526 (11th Cir. 1985), an action by a management company against a condominium developer, the Court held that it was error (but harmless) to admit testimony on behalf of the management company concerning an alleged practice of breaching contracts with small businesses. It found that the number of specific instances, when compared with the thousands of contractual dealings of the developer with small businesses, failed to establish a habit.

Habits of individuals — drinking

Reyes v. Missouri Pac. R.R., 589 F.2d 791 (5th Cir. 1979): Reversing a judgment for the defendant in a diversity action for damages suffered by a plaintiff run over by a train, the Court found "that four prior convictions for public intoxication spanning a three and one-half year period are of insufficient regularity to rise to the level of 'habit' evidence."

Keltner v. Ford Motor Co., 748 F.2d 1265 (8th Cir. 1984): In an action by a motorist alleging enhancement of injuries following an accident as a result of the doors of his van jamming, the Court sustained a judgment for the manufacturer. It found no error in the admission of testimony concerning the plaintiff's drinking habit — i.e., he regularly drank a six-pack of beer four nights a week — especially in view of the fact that there was evidence that the plaintiff smelled of alcohol after the accident and the plaintiff testified that he could not remember if he had been drinking on the night of the accident.

United States v. Pinto, 755 F.2d 150 (10th Cir. 1985): The Court affirmed a defendant's convictions for burglary and assault with intent to rape. It held that the Trial Judge did not err in excluding evidence concerning four instances of conduct over an eight-year period in which the defendant entered premises uninvited on the ground that it was insufficient to establish a habit of wandering into wrong houses while intoxicated.

Loughan v. Firestone Tire & Rubber Co., 749 F.2d 1519 (11th Cir. 1985): Affirming a manufacturer's judgment in a product liability action brought by a tire mechanic injured when parts of a rim-wheel assembly separated while being remounted, the Court upheld the admission of testimony concerning the mechanic's routine practice of drinking. There was no direct testimony that he had been drinking on the day of the accident, but the Court reasoned that proof of habit may be presented through indirect evidence. The Court stressed that habit and pattern evidence is never to be lightly established and admitted, and that the key criteria are "adequacy of sampling and uniformity of response of ratio of reactions to situations."

Habits of individuals — financial matters

Utility Control Corp. v. Prince William Constr. Co., 558 F.2d 716 (4th Cir. 1977): The Court reversed a judgment against a defendant held liable as a guarantor of a contract on the ground that the District Judge improperly admitted evidence that on a previous occasion the person acted as a guarantor for the defendant company.

> Proof of something done in [sic] a single occasion is hardly proof of a habit. Particularly is this so when proof is lacking that the occasion on which the habit was supposedly formed and the occasion on which it is claimed that the habit was followed are related or even similar.

Habits of individuals — use of force or coercion

United States v. Callahan, 551 F.2d 733 (6th Cir. 1977): In a Hobbs Act prosecution charging extortion by a union official from a construction contractor, the defendant was not permitted to cross-examine the government's principal witness about past confrontations with union representatives. The Court reversed the convictions on the ground that the evidence might have established under Rule 406 a routine practice of paying off local unions for the sake of expediency and might have established that there was no fear involved.

Perrin v. Anderson, 784 F.2d 1040 (10th Cir. 1986): The Court affirmed a judgment for police officers sued by the estate of a man killed when the officers attempted to obtain information about a traffic accident. It held that testimony by four officers concerning five violent acts by the deceased against police officers was admissible, even though five events would ordinarily not establish a habit. The defendants had made an offer of proof that eight officers would testify as to numerous incidents, and the Trial Judge limited the proof to four witnesses in order to avoid undue prejudice. In *United States v. Troutman,* 814 F.2d 1428 (10th Cir. 1987), the Court affirmed a conviction for conspiracy to commit extortion, finding no error in exclusion of evidence that the defendant had not previously conditioned an award of state business upon the making of political contributions. The Court reasoned that "[e]xtortion or refraining from extortion is not a semi-automatic act and does not constitute habit."

United States v. Holman, 680 F.2d 1340 (11th Cir. 1982): In a prosecution arising out of marijuana smuggling, one of the defendants testified that his son, a government witness, coerced him into participating. The Court held that the Trial Judge properly excluded evidence that on another occasion the son, while serving as a crew member on a ship, tried to persuade his captain to take marijuana aboard. According to the Court, this was not evidence sufficient to establish a habit on the part of the son to force people to smuggle drugs.

Sufficient number of instances

United States v. Newman, 982 F.2d 665 (1st Cir. 1992), *cert. denied,* 114 S. Ct. 59 (1993): The Court affirmed a conviction of a correctional officer for violating the civil rights of an inmate, holding that the Trial Judge had properly excluded the testimony of another correctional officer concerning how prisoners were handcuffed to cell bars. Although the witness would have testified that he had seen between seventy-five and one hundred inmates handcuffed to certain cell bars, there was no indication as to the total number of instances in which handcuffing took place. Thus, there was no way for the Judge to determine whether the witness was testifying to a virtually invariable practice.

Utility Control Corp. v. Prince William Constr. Co., 558 F.2d 716 (4th Cir. 1977): The Court reversed a judgment against a defendant held liable as a guarantor of a contract on the ground that the District Judge improperly admitted evidence that on a previous occasion the person acted as a guarantor for the defendant company.

> Proof of something done in [sic] a single occasion is hardly proof of a habit. Particularly is this so when proof is lacking that the occasion on which the habit was supposedly formed and the occasion on which it is claimed that the habit was followed are related or even similar.

Reyes v. Missouri Pac. R.R., 589 F.2d 791 (5th Cir. 1979): Reversing a judgment for the defendant in a diversity action for damages suffered by a plaintiff run over by a train, the Court found "that four prior convictions for public intoxication spanning a three and one-half year period are of insufficient regularity to rise to the level of 'habit' evidence."

Perrin v. Anderson, 784 F.2d 1040 (10th Cir. 1986): The Court affirmed a judgment for police officers sued by the estate of a man killed when the officers attempted to obtain information about a traffic accident. It held that testimony by four officers concerning five violent acts by the deceased against police officers was admissible, even though five events would ordinarily not establish a habit. The defendants had made an offer of proof that eight officers would testify as to numerous incidents, and the Trial Judge limited the proof to four witnesses in order to avoid undue prejudice. In *United States v. Pinto,* 755 F.2d 150 (10th Cir. 1985), the Court affirmed a conviction for burglary and assault with intent to rape. It held that the Trial Judge did not err in excluding evidence concerning four instances of conduct over an eight-year period in which the defendant entered premises uninvited on the ground that it was insufficient to establish a habit of wandering into wrong houses while intoxicated.

G.M. Brod & Co. v. U.S. Home Corp., 759 F.2d 1526 (11th Cir. 1985): In an action by a management company against a condominium developer, the Court held that it was error (but harmless) to admit testimony on behalf of the management company concerning an alleged practice of breaching contracts with small businesses. It found that the number of specific instances, when compared with the thousands of contractual dealings of the developer with small businesses, failed to establish a habit.

Uniform response

Jones v. Southern Pac. R.R., 962 F.2d 447 (5th Cir. 1992): The Court held there was no error in excluding evidence of the defendant's engineer's prior safety infractions in a personal injury action arising out of a truck-train collision, as the evidence, of several incidents over a long career, could hardly be characterized as a habit.

D. LEGISLATIVE HISTORY

Advisory Committee's Note

Subdivision (a). [As proposed by the Advisory Committee, Rule 406 contained two subdivisions; subdivision (b) was deleted by Congress.] An oft-quoted paragraph, McCormick § 162, p. 340, describes habit in terms effectively contrasting it with character.

> Character and habit are close akin. Character is a generalized description of one's disposition, or of one's disposition in respect to a general trait, such as honesty, temperance, or peacefulness. "Habit," in modern usage, both lay and psychological, is more specific. It describes one's regular response to a repeated specific situation. If we speak of character for care, we think of the person's tendency to act prudently in all the varying situations of life, in business, family life, in handling automobiles and in walking across the street. A habit, on the other hand, is the person's regular practice of meeting

a particular kind of situation with a specific type of conduct, such as the habit of going down a particular stairway two stairs at a time, or of giving the hand-signal for a left turn, or of alighting from railway cars while they are moving. The doing of the habitual acts may become semi-automatic.

Equivalent behavior on the part of a group is designated "routine practice of an organization" in the rule.

Agreement is general that habit evidence is highly persuasive as proof of conduct on a particular occasion. Again quoting McCormick § 162, p. 341:

> Character may be thought of as the sum of one's habits though doubtless it is more than this. But unquestionably the uniformity of one's response to habit is far greater than the consistency with which one's conduct conforms to character or disposition. Even though character comes in only exceptionally as evidence of an act, surely any sensible man in investigating whether X did a particular act would be greatly helped in his inquiry by evidence as to whether he was in the habit of doing it.

When disagreement has appeared, its focus has been upon the question what constitutes habit, and the reason for this is readily apparent. The extent to which instances must be multiplied and consistency of behavior maintained in order to rise to the status of habit inevitably gives rise to differences of opinion. Lewan, Rationale of Habit Evidence, 16 Syracuse L. Rev. 39, 49 (1964). While adequacy of sampling and uniformity of response are key factors, precise standards for measuring their sufficiency for evidence purposes cannot be formulated.

The rule is consistent with prevailing views. Much evidence is excluded simply because of failure to achieve the status of habit. Thus, evidence of intemperate "habits" is generally excluded when offered as proof of drunkenness in accident cases, Annot., 46 A.L.R.2d 103, and evidence of other assaults is inadmissible to prove the instant one in a civil assault action, Annot., 66 A.L.R.2d 806. In Levin v. United States, 119 U.S. App. D.C. 156, 338 F.2d 265 (1964), testimony as to the religious "habits" of the accused, offered as tending to prove that he was at home observing the Sabbath rather than out obtaining money through larceny by trick, was held properly excluded:

> It seems apparent to us that an individual's religious practices would not be the type of activities which would lend themselves to the characterization of "invariable regularity." [1 Wigmore 520.] Certainly the very volitional basis of the activity raises serious questions as to its invariable nature and hence its probative value.

Id. at 272.

These rulings are not inconsistent with the trend towards admitting evidence of business transactions between one of the parties and a third person as tending to prove that he made the same bargain or proposal in the litigated situation. Slough, Relevancy Unraveled, 6 Kan. L. Rev. 38-41 (1957). Nor are they inconsistent with such cases as Whittemore v. Lockheed Aircraft Corp., 65 Cal. App. 2d 737, 151 P.2d 670 (1944), upholding the admission of evidence that plaintiff's intestate had on four other occasions flown planes from defendant's factory for delivery to his employer airline, offered to prove that he was piloting rather than a guest on a plane which crashed and killed all on board while en route for delivery.

A considerable body of authority has required that evidence of the routine practice of an organization be corroborated as a condition precedent to its admission in evidence. Slough, Relevancy Unraveled, 5 Kan. L. Rev. 404-49 (1957). This requirement is specifically rejected by the rule on the ground that it relates to the sufficiency of the evidence rather than admissibility.

A similar position is taken in New Jersey Rule 49. The rule also rejects the requirement of the absence of eyewitnesses, sometimes encountered with respect to admitting habit evidence to prove freedom from contributory negligence in wrongful death cases. For comment critical of the requirements see Frank, J., in Cereste v. New York, N.H. & H.R. Co., 231 F.2d 50 (2d Cir. 1956), *cert. denied,* 351 U.S. 951, 76 S. Ct. 848, 100 L. Ed. 1475, 10 Vand. L. Rev. 447 (1957); McCormick § 162, p. 342. The omission of the requirement from the California Evidence Code is said to have effected its elimination. Comment, California Evidence Code § 1105.

Subdivision (b). [This subdivision was deleted by Congress.] Permissible methods of proving habit or routine conduct include opinion and specific instances sufficient in number to warrant a finding that the habit or routine practice in fact existed. Opinion evidence must be "rationally based on the perception of the witness" and helpful, under the provisions of Rule 701. Proof by specific instances may be controlled by the overriding provisions of Rule 403 for exclusion on grounds of prejudice, confusion, misleading the jury, or waste of time. Thus the illustrations following A.L.I. Model Code of Evidence Rule 307 suggest the possibility of admitting testimony by *W* that on numerous occasions he had been with *X* when *X* crossed a railroad track and that on each occasion *X* had first stopped and looked in both directions, but discretion to exclude offers of 10 witnesses, each testifying to a different occasion.

Similar provisions for proof by opinion or specific instances are found in Uniform Rule 50 and Kansas Code of Civil Procedure § 60-450. New Jersey Rule 50 provides for proof by specific instances but is silent as to opinion. The California Evidence Code is silent as to methods of proving habit, presumably proceeding on the theory that any method is relevant and all relevant evidence is admissible unless otherwise provided. Tentative Recommendation and a Study Relating to the Uniform Rules of Evidence (Art. VI. Extrinsic Policies Affecting Admissibility), Rep., Rec. & Study, Cal. Law Rev. Comm'n, 620 (1964).

House Subcommittee on Criminal Justice Notes

June 28, 1973

This rule was approved as proposed by the Court, although the Subcommittee was aware of the comments submitted to the Advisory Committee when the 1969 and 1971 drafts were circulated. The comments brought to the Subcommittee's attention were excerpted by the Reporter from reports of the following:

Association of the Bar of the City of New York, Second Circuit Conference Committee on Trial Practice and Technique, New York County Lawyers Association Committee on Federal Courts, Arizona State Bar Trial Practice Section, Washington State Bar Association Committee, American College of Trial Lawyers Committee, Florida State Bar Federal Rules Committee, Department of Justice, South Carolina Chapter of the American College of Trial Lawyers, the Virginia Trial Lawyers Association, the District of Columbia Judicial Conference Special Committee, and the American Bar Association Special Committees on Federal Rules of Procedure and Uniform Rules of Evidence for Federal Courts.

The subheading "(a) Admissibility" was dropped from the Rule for purposes of consistency of style in view of the Subcommittee's deletion of subsection (b).

The Subcommittee was also of the view that the method of proof of habit and routine practice should be left to the courts on a case by case basis and so struck out subdivision (b).

Citations to Hearing and Debates

Letter from Edward W. Cleary to Herbert E. Hoffman, May 18, 1973, and accompanying material, in Supp. to Hearings on Proposed Rules of Evidence Before the Subcomm. on Criminal Justice of the House Comm. on the Judiciary, 93rd Cong., 1st Sess., at 84-87 (1973).

Letter from Edward W. Cleary to Herbert E. Hoffman, May 29, 1973, in Supp. to Hearings on Proposed Rules of Evidence Before the Subcomm. on Criminal Justice of the House Comm. on the Judiciary, 93rd Cong., 1st Sess., at 96-97 (1973).

Letter from James F. Schaeffer to Hon. William L. Hungate, June 5, 1973, and accompanying material, in Supp. to Hearings on Proposed Rules of Evidence Before the Subcomm. on Criminal Justice of the House Comm. on the Judiciary, 93rd Cong., 1st Sess., at 100-04 (1973).

RULE 407

A. OFFICIAL TEXT

Rule 407. Subsequent Remedial Measures

When, after an event, measures are taken which, if taken previously, would have made the event less likely to occur, evidence of the subsequent measures is not admissible to prove negligence or culpable conduct in connection with the event. This rule does not require the exclusion of evidence of subsequent measures when offered for another purpose, such as proving ownership, control, or feasibility of precautionary measures, if controverted, or impeachment.

B. EDITORIAL EXPLANATORY COMMENT

Subsequent repairs and remedial measures

Judges and lawyers are perhaps most familiar with this Rule when it is expressed in the following terms: If someone makes repairs after an accident, those repairs are not admissible against the person making them to prove that person was negligent prior to or at the time of the accident. Rule 407 is written in slightly more inclusive language, however. It provides that any measures that are taken after an event, which if they had been taken previously would have made the event less likely to occur, cannot be introduced as evidence to prove negligence or culpable conduct in connection with the event. This expansion beyond evidence of subsequent repairs includes such evidence as subsequent installation of safety devices, a change in company rules, and discharge of employees.[1]

However, in order to qualify for exclusion under Rule 407, the action taken by the defendant must at least have been a ''measure.'' For example, in *Prentiss & Carlisle v. Koehring-Waterous,* 972 F.2d 6 (1st Cir. 1992), the plaintiff was injured when a product manufactured by the defendant caught fire. Defendant sent employees to the site of the accident to investigate. These investigations resulted in reports concerning the cause of the fire. The Court held that the reports were not subject to exclusion under Rule 407, because they did not constitute remedial measures. According to the Court, it ''would strain the spirit of the remedial measure prohibition in Rule 407 to extend its shield to evidence contained in post-event tests or reports.'' While a product analysis or

---

1. See, e.g., Specht v. Jensen, 863 F.2d 700 (10th Cir. 1988) (civil rights action for damages resulting from allegedly illegal search; city press release announcing that disciplinary action would be taken against offending officer held properly excluded as evidence of a subsequent remedial measure).

postaccident report might lead to the taking of remedial measures, it does not mean that the report or analysis itself is excluded under the Rule.[2]

The social policy basis of the Rule

The principal argument in favor of the Rule is a social policy argument: that without the Rule, remedial measures would not be taken after an accident, for fear that such measures could be used as an admission of fault or culpability on the part of the defendant. The conclusion is that the absence of a rule such as Rule 407 would put the public safety at risk. As Judge Posner has put it: "A major purpose of Rule 407 is to promote safety by removing the disincentive to make repairs (or take other safety measures) after an accident that would exist if the accident victim could use those measures as evidence of the defendant's liability."[3] Thus, the Rule is based on the deleterious social consequences that would arise in the *absence* of an exclusionary rule.

Yet, a strong argument can be made that the articulated social policy does not justify the Rule. The policy argument presumes that a person or organization would know that there is no exclusionary rule for subsequent remedial measures in the relevant jurisdiction, and would also know that in the absence of such a rule, a subsequent remedial measure could constitute an admission of fault. If a defendant has that kind of knowledge of the rules of evidence, that defendant would also know that the failure to correct a situation in which an accident occurred could be admissible as well, with far more serious consequences to the defendant. That is, if a remedial action is not undertaken, and *another* accident occurs, the well-informed defendant would know that there would be a strong case of gross negligence or recklessness, and possible liability for punitive damages. Thus, such a defendant, even in the absence of a rule such as Rule 407, would be very likely to take corrective measures in order to avoid more serious liability for future accidents. Since the defendant is highly likely to take corrective measures even in the absence of Rule 407, it follows that the social policy argument behind Rule 407 is flawed. If the policy of promoting safety were the only basis for the Rule, then Rule 407 would be nothing more than a windfall for defendants, who would probably take corrective action even in the absence of any exclusionary Rule.

Judge Posner, however, disagrees with this analysis. He argues as follows:

---

2. See also Dow Chem. Corp. v. Weevil-Cide Co., 897 F.2d 481 (10th Cir. 1990) (internal memorandum of defendant, concluding that defendant should remain in a line of business without conducting further product research, could not be excluded as evidence of a subsequent remedial measure, because the report did nothing that would have made the harm less likely to occur: "Remedial measures are those actions taken to remedy any flaws or failures."); Rocky Mountain Helicopters v. Bell Helicopters, 805 F.2d 907 (10th Cir. 1986):

> It would strain the spirit of the remedial measure prohibition in Rule 407 to extend its shield to evidence contained in post-event tests or reports.... [S]uch tests are usually conducted for the purpose of investigating the occurrence to discover what might have gone wrong or right. Remedial measures are those actions taken to remedy any flaws or failures indicated by the test.

3. Flaminio v. Honda Motor Co., 733 F.2d 463, 467 (7th Cir. 1984).

One might think it not only immoral but reckless for an injurer, having been alerted by the accident to the existence of danger, not to take steps to correct the danger. But accidents are low-probability events. The probability of another accident may be much smaller than the probability that the victim of the accident that has already occurred will sue the injurer and, if permitted, will make devastating use at trial of any measures that the injurer may have taken since the accident to reduce the danger.[4]

We think that most defendants, having become aware of a dangerous condition after an accident, would not be as easily persuaded as Judge Posner that a future accident is a low-probability event. More importantly, even if a future accident is considered unlikely, we think that most defendants would conclude that the risk of substantially higher liability resulting from an uncorrected condition would be too great to bear, should the low-probability event ever come to pass. In other words, most defendants would correct a dangerous condition after an accident, even if Rule 407 did not exist.

Yet, despite the weakness of the social policy argument, both the Advisory Committee comments and the subsequent cases rely on social policy as the principal rationale for the Rule.[5] This is important to remember, because a subsequent remedial measure may then be admissible in situations where the "no disincentive to repair" rationale is clearly inapplicable. See the discussion of permissible purposes, below.

The relevance basis of the Rule

The more persuasive basis for the Rule is that subsequent remedial measures are of marginal relevance in assessing the defendant's culpability or fault, and that this marginal relevance is almost always substantially outweighed by the risk of jury confusion created by the introduction of a subsequent remedial measure.[6] The balance so often favors

---

4. *Id.* at 470.

5. For a somewhat different view of the social policy underpinning of Rule 407, see LEMPERT & SALTZBURG, A MODERN APPROACH TO EVIDENCE 194 (2d ed. 1982). The authors analyze the social policy argument as follows:

> There is another possible rationale for the rule, one which courts rarely articulate, but which seems to make more sense than the instrumental explanation. This is that people who take post-accident safety measures are doing exactly what good citizens should do. In these circumstances, so long as the relevance of the activity is not great, courts do not wish to sanction procedures which appear to punish praiseworthy behavior. Perhaps courts do not articulate this reason because they are reluctant to rationalize their decisions on the basis of what truly motivates them, namely a subjective sense of the decent thing to do. They prefer instead to rest their decision on its efficacy in promoting behavior which all agree is desirable, even if they must assert by fiat an efficacy which appears unlikely.

6. See, e.g., Grenada Steel Indus. v. Alabama Oxygen Co., 695 F.2d 883 (5th Cir. 1983) (in a product liability case, the Court reasoned that "evidence of subsequent repair or change has little relevance to whether the product in question was defective at some previous time," and that such evidence "threatens to confuse the jury by diverting its attention from whether the product was defective at the relevant time to what was done later").

exclusion that it makes sense to impose a generalized rule of exclusion rather than to rely initially on a case-by-case approach under Rule 403.

We believe that to understand Rule 407 it is imperative to focus on why a lawyer would want to offer subsequent remedial measures following an event in order to argue that this evidence proves negligence or culpable conduct. The only reason is to make an argument something like the following one:

> Ladies and gentlemen of the jury, you have heard that the defendant in this case actually repaired his (insert property) following the accident. Now what does this mean to you? It must mean that he thought the (insert property) was inadequate in the condition it was in at the time of the accident. Now, I ask you, if it was in need of repair after the accident, what about at the time of the accident? If this defendant indicated by making his repair after the accident that repair was needed, have you any doubt that it was also needed before the accident took place? Well, no repair was made at that time. And I tell you that you are therefore justified in finding the failure to make the repair that was made later before this tragedy occurred to be negligence.

The problem with this argument is that negligence is properly assessed according to what the defendant knew or should have known prior to the accident, not what he knew as a result of the accident. But it is extraordinarily difficult for a jury to draw this distinction. The very fact of an accident is likely to influence the jury to think that the repair should have been made earlier. What Rule 407 does is to keep the jury's attention on the defendant's information and conduct at the relevant time — i.e., prior to the accident.[7]

Permissible uses of evidence of subsequent remedial measures

The Rule specifically provides that the evidence need not be excluded if it is offered for some purpose other than showing prior negligence or culpability, such as proving ownership or control, or the feasibility of precautionary measures, where those issues are controverted by the defendant. If, for example, D is driving a vehicle that collides with the car of P, and P brings an action for damages against D, to determine whether evidence of subsequent remedial measures will be admitted it is necessary to look to the purpose for which the evidence is offered. Assume that P contends that D was driving a car with unsafe brakes. If P wants to introduce the fact that after the accident D had the brakes repaired, and the purpose for offering the evidence is to show that prior to the accident D failed to exercise reasonable care to inspect the brakes, the evidence will be excluded. If, however, D defends against P and urges that he had no control over the car and no opportunity to check the brakes since the car belonged to someone else, P may very well be able to introduce the fact that after the accident it was D who had the brakes repaired in order to show that D had control of the vehicle.

---

7. See, e.g., Cook v. McDonough Power Equip., Inc., 720 F.2d 829 (5th Cir. 1983) (function of Rule 407 is to "focus the evidence to that most relevant" to proving liability at the time of the accident).

Issues in controversy

In cases where a party wants to introduce evidence of subsequent remedial measures ostensibly for a purpose other than to prove negligence or culpability, the Judge should make certain that the evidence is offered to prove a point that is actually in controversy. If, for example, control is not controverted, there is no reason to allow evidence to come in on that issue; it is not relevant, because it is cumulative in proving control.[8] Because evidence of subsequent remedial measures might be used by a jury as an admission of fault no matter what sort of limiting instruction the Trial Judge gives, the Judge should attempt to ensure that the purpose for which such evidence is offered is a valid one. This is what the Rule means when it sets forth permissible purposes for evidence of subsequent remedial measures, "if controverted." On the other hand, if an issue such as control is truly placed in controversy, then the jury can profit from knowing that repairs were made by the defendant after an accident. There is little danger that the jury will misuse the evidence by focusing on the wrong time period when these issues are raised by the defendant.

Permissible purposes — product liability cases

The concept of "product liability" includes many different kinds of actions. It becomes clearer all the time that proving that a design was defective is not much different in many jurisdictions from proving negligence and that design changes made years after a product is sold are not very probative on the state of the earlier art.

At this point, almost all Federal Courts have held that Rule 407 is fully applicable to product liability cases. Proof of "product liability" is not a permissible purpose, despite the language of the Rule, which designates only two impermissible purposes — negligence or culpable conduct. Nor do the Courts distinguish between manufacturing defect cases, defective design cases or failure to warn cases. If a claim falls under the rubric of "product liability," then Rule 407 applies regardless of the specific theory advanced.[9]

---

8. See, e.g., Hull v. Chevron U.S.A., Inc., 812 F.2d 584 (10th Cir. 1987) (subsequent remedial measure not admissible to prove defendant controlled a forklift, where defendant "acknowledged not only that its employees operated the forklift, but also its responsibility for hiring and firing" the employees who worked the forklift; thus, the proffered evidence "would be either cumulative or trespass inferentially into the Rule 407 prohibited terrain of proof of culpable conduct.").

9. See, e.g., Kelly v. Crown Equip. Co., 970 F.2d 1273 (3d Cir. 1992) ("The reasons for refusing to differentiate between negligence actions and strict liability claims apply with equal force to the more subtle differences between failure to warn and design defect theories"; Rule 407 applies "to products liability actions generally regardless of the specific theory advanced."). But see Herndon v. Seven Bar Flying Serv., 716 F.2d 1322 (10th Cir. 1983) (refusing to apply Rule 407 in a product liability case).

Most of the Courts reason that the social policy basis of the Rule is as applicable to defendants in product liability cases as it is in negligence cases.[10] While this is true, the policy itself is suspect even in negligence cases, as discussed above.

Other Courts reason, more persuasively, that the relevance-based aspects of the Rule are equally applicable to strict liability cases and negligence cases. As the Fifth Circuit has stated:

> The real question is whether the product or design was defective at the time the product was sold. The jury's attention should be directed to whether the product was reasonably safe at the time it was manufactured.... The introduction of evidence about subsequent changes in the product or its design threatens to confuse the jury by diverting its attention from whether the product was defective at the relevant time to what was done later. Interpreted to require the evidence to focus on the time when the product was sold, Rule 407 would conform to the policy expressed in Rule 403, the exclusion of relevant information if its probative value is substantially outweighed by the danger of confusion.[11]

In a product liability case, if the issue in dispute concerns the design of a product, and if liability is to be measured on the basis of the state of the art when the product was made, there is a danger that introduction of subsequent design changes will confuse the jury with respect to the knowledge they are to require of the defendant, in much the same way that a jury might be confused by subsequent repair evidence in a negligence case. It seems to us that a jury would have difficulty in understanding that what a defendant learned as a result of an accident or from new information in an industry is not probative of whether the defendant was negligent before the accident, or whether a product was defective in design when it was made.[12]

---

10. See, e.g., Flaminio v. Honda Motor Co., 733 F.2d 463, 473 (7th Cir. 1984):

> [W]e agree with the majority view that the rule does apply to strict liability cases... The analysis is not fundamentally affected by whether the basis of liability is the defendant's negligence or his product's defectiveness or inherent dangerousness. In either case, if evidence of subsequent remedial measures is admissible to prove liability, the incentive to take such measures will be reduced.

See also Gauthier v. AMF, Inc., 788 F.2d 634 (9th Cir. 1986), noting that most Courts have held that

> there is no practical difference between strict liability and negligence in defective design cases and the public policy rationale to encourage remedial measures remains the same.... [I]t is precisely the large manufacturers who are defendants in many product liability suits who are most likely to know about Rule 407 and be affected by the decision whether to apply it.

11. Grenada Steel Indus. v. Alabama Oxygen Co., 695 F.2d 883, 888 (5th Cir. 1983).

12. A similar analysis is offered in Henderson, *Product Liability and Admissibility of Subsequent Remedial Measures; Resolving the Conflict by Recognizing the Difference Between Negligence and Strict Tort Liability*, 64 NEB. L. REV. 1 (1985).

Permissible purposes — feasibility

Rule 407 by its terms is not applicable if feasibility is controverted. For example, assume that the plaintiff has been injured by a product and claims that it was defectively designed. Ordinarily, to prove defective design, the plaintiff will have to suggest some alternative design that would have made the product less dangerous. If the defendant claims that the alternative suggested was not feasible — either because it would have been prohibitively expensive, or that it was not within the state of the art at the time of manufacture — then feasibility is controverted and the Rule does not prevent the admission of subsequent remedial measures, offered solely to prove feasibility. Of course, the defendant is entitled to a limiting instruction as to the permissible use of the evidence; and in rare cases, the probative value of the subsequent remedial measure as proof of feasibility might be substantially outweighed by the risk of prejudice and confusion, so that the evidence could still be excluded under Rule 403.[13]

The feasibility "exception" to Rule 407 is rarely applicable, however, because feasibility is a weak defense where the defendant has in fact undertaken a subsequent remedial measure. It is difficult to argue that a suggested change was prohibitively expensive or beyond the state of the art, when the change was in fact made after the accident. Consequently, most defendants concede feasibility when subsequent remedial measures have been taken. Such a concession prevents the plaintiff from arguing that feasibility is in controversy, and therefore precludes the use of subsequent remedial measures on that point.[14] The defendant remains free to defend on the ground that the suggested change, while feasible, would not have made the condition significantly safer, or would have resulted in other disadvantages such that the defendant's original conduct was reasonable. As one Court has put it, "where a defendant argues about the trade-offs involved in taking precautionary measures, it is not placing *feasibility* in issue."[15]

---

13. This would be rare because the defendant is affirmatively contesting feasibility, and the plaintiff is simply providing a fair response.

14. See, e.g., Mills v. Beech Aircraft Corp., 886 F.2d 758, 764 (5th Cir. 1989) (revised manual, offered to show the feasibility of providing a better installation instruction, held properly excluded under Rule 407: "The feasibility exception to Rule 407 does not apply when feasibility is not in controversy. The defendants in the present case did not contest the feasibility of a better installation instruction, but rather maintained that the instructions in the [original] manual were acceptable."); Middleton v. Harris Press & Shear, Inc., 796 F.2d 747 (5th Cir. 1986) (product liability suit where plaintiff claims that product was defectively designed by failing to include a circuit interrupt device; design change by defendant to include such a device was not admissible to prove feasability: "Though Harris contended that circuit interrupt devices were unreliable and not a safety device of first choice, the feasibility of installing them was not called into dispute," since the defendant stipulated that the change was feasible "in the sense of being physically possible"); Probus v. K-Mart, Inc., 794 F.2d 1207, 1210 (7th Cir. 1986) (subsequent remedial measures held not admissible to prove feasibility where "the plaintiff does not contend that the defendants testified that the material used in the end cap was either the best material available or that the use of another material would not have been feasible").

15. Gauthier v. AMF, Inc., 788 F.2d 634, 638 (9th Cir. 1986):

In this case, AMF conceded that the safety devices were technologically and economically feasible but then argued that they concluded that the safety problem was not great enough to warrant the trade-off of consumer frustration, increased complexity of the product, and risk of consumer efforts to disconnect the safety device.

Permissible purpose — impeachment

Impeachment of witnesses is specifically listed as a permissible purpose for admitting subsequent remedial measures. Presumably, the mode of impeachment contemplated is that of contradiction — the subsequent remedial measure may be relevant to contradict testimony from the defendant's witness, thus making that witness less credible before the jury.

The problem is that almost any testimony given by defense witnesses could be contradicted at least in some minimal way by a subsequent remedial measure. If the defendant's expert testifies that the product was safe, a subsequent remedial measure could be seen as contradicting that testimony. If the defendant is asked on cross-examination whether he thinks that he had taken all reasonable safety precautions, and answers in the affirmative, then a subsequent remedial measure can be seen as contradicting that testimony.

If "impeachment" means simple contradiction, then the impeachment exception to Rule 407 would threaten to swallow the Rule itself.[16] Accordingly, most Courts have held that a subsequent remedial measure is not admissible for impeachment if it is offered for simple contradiction of a defense witness' testimony.[17]

On the other hand, if the defendant's witnesses testify in superlatives — e.g., "this is the safest product on the market" — then the evidence of a subsequent remedial measure provides more than simple contradiction. It shows that the witness puffed and exaggerated while on the stand. As such, the remedial measure provides a more direct and probative form of impeachment, which justifies a limited exception to the Rule.[18] Likewise, if defense witnesses testify that the product or condition has not been changed

---

See also Fish v. Georgia-Pacific Corp., 779 F.2d 836, 840 (2d Cir. 1985):

> Nor was the evidence of the warning admissible on the limited issue of the feasibility of providing a warning in 1977. Georgia-Pacific states that it was willing to admit the feasibility of providing a warning in 1977; it simply contended that it did not have a legal duty to do so.

16. See, e.g., Harrison v. Sears, Roebuck & Co., 981 F.2d 25 (1st Cir. 1992) ("Rule 407's impeachment exception must not be used as a subterfuge to prove negligence or culpability"; a desire merely to undercut an expert's qualifications cannot be sufficient to trigger the impeachment exception, or else the exception could swallow the rule of exclusion).

17. See, e.g., Kelly v. Crown Equip. Corp., 970 F.2d 1273 (3d Cir. 1992) (impeachment exception does not apply merely because the expert testified that the product was of an excellent and proper design; if impeachment exception applied to simple contradiction, the exception would swallow the rule); Flaminio v. Honda Motor Co., 733 F.2d 463 (7th Cir. 1984) (no impeachment with subsequent remedial measures where defense witnesses merely testified to the safety of the product under normal circumstances).

18. See, e.g., Muzyka v. Remington Arms Co., 774 F.2d 1309 (5th Cir. 1985) (subsequent remedial measures, offered for impeachment purposes, were improperly excluded where defense witnesses testified that the product "embodied the ultimate in gun safety" and that it was "*the* best and *the* safest rifle of its kind on the market"; the jury was improperly denied "evidence in impeachment of the experts who spoke in those superlatives").

since the accident, then evidence of subsequent remedial measures provides a more direct and probative, and hence a permissible, form of impeachment.[19]

Measures taken by third parties

Is a subsequent remedial measure excluded by Rule 407 if the action is taken by someone other than the defendant? For example, in *Dixon v. International Harvester Co.,* 754 F.2d 573 (5th Cir. 1985), the plaintiff was injured while working on a tractor, after an object entered the tractor cab through an open area between the support bar and the dashboard. After the accident, the owner of the tractor added screening and a metal plate to close off this open area of the tractor cab. The plaintiff sued International Harvester, alleging defective design. Harvester sought to exclude the tractor owner's remedial measure, but the Court held that Rule 407 was inapplicable. The Court relied on the policy basis for the Rule, which is "to avoid discouraging defendants from making necessary repairs or changes to products or dangerous conditions." It concluded that since the remedial measure "was made by a non-defendant, Rule 407 does not bar the evidence."

The reasoning of *Dixon* is questionable insofar as it is based on policy arguments. If, as we have argued, the policy basis of Rule 407 is flawed, and the Rule is more justifiably based on relevance grounds, then a strong argument can be made that *Dixon* is wrongly decided. If the probative value of a defendant's own change is generally substantially outweighed by the risk of jury confusion, then this should *a fortiori* be true with respect to a third party's change.

Two further arguments can be made against the result in *Dixon:*

(1) There is nothing in the language of Rule 407 that distinguishes between measures taken by defendants and nondefendants. The Rule excludes *any* measure which, if taken, would have made the event less likely to occur, if offered to show negligence or culpability (or strict liability, in the view of most Courts).

(2) Even if the policy basis for the Rule is accepted, the Rule should not distinguish between defendants and nondefendants. The owner of the tractor in *Dixon* had no way of knowing whether he would be a defendant or not. Indeed, there was a good probability, at the time the repair was made, that the owner would be included as a defendant in any subsequent lawsuit. The distinction in *Dixon* between defendants and nondefendants is thus improperly based on a factor that arises well after the point at which one would seek to encourage remedial conduct.

Despite these arguments, the Courts have uniformly held that Rule 407 is inapplicable to changes made by third parties.[20]

---

19. See, e.g., Harrison v. Sears, Roebuck & Co., 981 F.2d 25, 31 (1st Cir. 1992) ("A more direct impeachment use of subsequent remedial measure evidence would exist if Appellees' witness stated that he did not change the product after the alleged accident was brought to his employer's attention.").

20. See the cases cited in the Annotated Cases under the heading "Third party repairs."

Preaccident remedial measures

Suppose the plaintiff bought a snowblower in January 1991. Then, in November 1991, the defendant changed the design of the snowblower. Then, in January 1992, the plaintiff was injured when using his (unmodified) snowblower. Is the defendant's preaccident design change excluded by Rule 407?

Rule 407 applies only to measures taken "after an event" that would have made the event less likely to occur. A defendant who made a preaccident design change is therefore forced to argue that the "event" to which the Rule applies must be the manufacture or sale of the original product, and not the subsequent accident. But this is an odd construction of the Rule. It makes no sense to focus on measures that would have made the sale or manufacture of a product less likely to occur. A fair reading of the Rule thus indicates that preaccident remedial measures are not covered. As one Court has stated: "In the first sentence of the Rule, the plain meaning of the phrase 'would have made the event likely to occur,' suggests reference to the accident or injury, not manufacture."[21]

Even the articulated social policy basis for the Rule is not implicated by preaccident remedial measures. A manufacturer will not be deterred from making safety improvements before an accident has even occurred. If the defendant is concerned about the use of a remedial measure in some hypothetical future case, then it can "limit its liability by recalling the unimproved product."[22]

Relationship to Rule 403

On its face, Rule 407 provides that evidence of subsequent remedial measures is admissible if offered for certain purposes other than to show negligence or culpable conduct. The Rule does not say, however, that when evidence is offered for another purpose it must be admitted. In deciding whether or not to admit evidence of remedial measures taken after an accident, the Trial Judge must weigh the probative value of the evidence on the issue for which it is offered against the possibility that the jury will misuse the evidence as an implicit admission of culpability.[23] It is important for the Trial Court first to assure itself that the issue on which the subsequent remedial evidence is offered is actually in dispute; then it must make a Rule 403 balancing judgment.

---

21. Huffman v. Caterpillar Tractor Co., 908 F.2d 1470, 1482 (10th Cir. 1990) (en banc). But see Kelly v. Crown Equip. Co., 970 F.2d 1273 (3d Cir. 1992) (while convinced that the language of the Rule does not cover preaccident measures, the Court is constrained by prior precedent in the Circuit to hold that Rule 407 does apply to such measures).

22. Traylor v. Husqvarna Motor Co., 988 F.2d 729, 733 (7th Cir. 1993) (expressing "doubt that a producer will often be deflected from making improvements by fear about the consequences to his litigating position in hypothetical future cases — cases especially hypothetical because no accident has yet occurred.").

23. See, e.g, Middleton v. Harris Press & Shear, Inc., 796 F.2d 747 (5th Cir. 1986) (remedial measure not excluded under Rule 407 because it was made by someone other than the defendant; however, exclusion of the evidence was proper under Rule 403 due to its tendency to divert the jury's attention away from the defendant's conduct at the time of manufacture).

Unusual cases

The Rule can occasionally have significance outside of the typical negligence and product liability cases. See, e.g., *World Boxing Council v. Cosell*, 715 F. Supp. 1259 (S.D.N.Y. 1989) (barring proof that allegedly defamatory language was altered in subsequent edition of book); *Vander Missen v. Kellogg-Citizens Nat'l Bank*, 481 F. Supp. 742 (E.D. Wis. 1979) (barring proof that defendant took steps to prevent future acts of discrimination).

Erie concerns

Most cases in which Rule 407 is applicable are personal injury cases that are brought in Federal Court under the diversity jurisdiction. But not all states have a rule identical to Rule 407. For example, Rule 407 of the Maine Rules of Evidence states that evidence of subsequent remedial measures "is admissible," while Hawaii Rule 407 permits subsequent remedial measures in product liability cases.[24] Where the State and Federal rules on subsequent remedial measures are in conflict, which rule should apply?

Whether Rule 407 presents an *Erie* problem depends to some extent on what is the driving force behind the Rule. If the Rule is based on the social policy of encouraging repairs, then an argument can be made that it is "substantive" under *Erie* because the Rule would be designed to control primary conduct rather than courtroom procedure. Thus, one Circuit has held that state law should govern in a conflict with Rule 407, on the ground that the Rule is based "on policy considerations rather than relevancy or truthseeking," and that these policy considerations are a fundamental part of the state law of tort liability.[25]

The foregoing analysis, however, assumes that Rule 407 is based primarily on a social policy of encouraging repairs. As discussed above, the social policy basis of the Rule is questionable, and the Rule is more properly justified on relevance grounds. If the Rule is actually relevance-based, then it is undoubtedly procedural in *Erie* terms. As one Court put it: "Congress's judgment that juries are apt to give too much weight to [subsequent remedial measures] evidence is a procedural judgment, that is, a judgment concerning procedures designed to enhance accuracy or reduce expense in the adjudicative process."[26]

Remember that the Federal Rules are "presumptively procedural" after *Hanna v. Plumer*, 380 U.S. 460, 472 (1965) (finding no *Erie* violation as to Federal Rules covering "matters which, though falling within the uncertain area between substance and procedure, are rationally capable of classification as either"). At a minimum, there is a sufficient relevancy basis in the Rule to justify it as "procedural" after *Hanna*. Consequently, most Courts see no *Erie* violation in applying Rule 407 where a state rule

---

24. On the state versions of Rule 407, see generally G. JOSEPH & S. SALTZBURG, EVIDENCE IN AMERICA, ch. 17.

25. Moe v. Avions Marcel Dassault-Breguet Aviation, 727 F.2d 917 (10th Cir. 1984).

26. Flaminio v. Honda Motor Co., 733 F.2d 463, 471 (7th Cir. 1984).

is in conflict.[27] And this is so, for the most part, even in those Courts that remain enamored of the social policy basis for the Rule. Even if the social policy is predominant, the relevance basis for the Rule is at least a subsidiary purpose, sufficient to qualify the Rule as procedural after *Hanna*.[28]

C. ANNOTATED CASES

Admiralty case

Hall v. American Steamship Co., 688 F.2d 1062 (6th Cir. 1982): In a personal injury action by a seaman claiming unseaworthiness as a result of being injured when he was not told to leave the deck in rough weather, evidence was admitted concerning changes in the procedures that he was undertaking at the time he was injured. Reversing a judgment for the plaintiff, the Court found that "[s]ince there was no dispute as to the physical and weather conditions at the time Hall was injured, even if the change of policy were relevant as proof of these prior conditions, the policy change could not, under the terms of Rule 407, be admitted for such purpose." The Court reasoned that the evidence had been offered to prove culpable conduct, something not permitted by the Rule.

Antitrust case

Noble v. McClatchy Newspapers, 533 F.2d 1081 (9th Cir. 1975), *vacated on other grounds*, 433 U.S. 904, *cert. denied*, 433 U.S. 908 (1977): One of the issues raised by the plaintiffs was whether certain provisions in distributorship contracts violated the antitrust laws. The District Court refused to admit evidence that after the termination of plaintiffs' distributorship the defendants deleted the provisions in the lease that were objected to by the plaintiffs. Citing Rule 407, the Court approved this ruling, saying that "it is well settled that evidence of subsequent remedial measures is not admissible to prove culpability of prior conduct."

Balancing probative value against prejudicial effect

Friedman v. National Presto Indus., 566 F. Supp. 762 (E.D.N.Y. 1983): In an action based on negligence and strict liability theories against the manufacturer of a pressure

---

27. See, e.g., Kelly v. Crown Equip. Co., 970 F.2d 1273 (3d Cir. 1992) (Rule 407 is "arguably procedural" because it "operates on the presumption that undue prejudice is likely in certain situations, expressing a distrust of a jury's ability to draw the proper inferences from the evidence"); Rioux v. Daniel Int'l Corp., 582 F. Supp. 620 (D. Me. 1984) (concluding that it was up to Congress to determine when to defer to State law, and noting that Congress had deferred to the States in other rules such as Rule 501).

28. See Flaminio v. Honda Motor Co., 733 F.2d 463, 472 (7th Cir. 1984):

> Rule 407 is not based on substantive considerations only. An important though not the primary reason for the rules was distrust of juries' ability to draw correct inferences from evidence of subsequent remedial measures. Although it was a mild distrust, as shown by the exceptions built into the rule, it is enough to establish the rule's constitutionality in diversity cases.

cooker, the Court found that New York law on product liability focuses on "unreasonable danger," a concept akin to negligence. It indicated that evidence of a design change could not be offered so long as the manufacturer did not dispute that an alternative design was feasible when the plaintiff's pressure cooker was manufactured. If feasibility were disputed, the Court said it would have to decide whether a 1979 design is sufficiently probative of feasibility in 1970, when the plaintiff bought her cooker, to be admitted over a Rule 403 objection.

Rockwood Ins. Co. v. Clark Equip. Co., 713 F.2d 577 (10th Cir. 1983): The Court affirmed a judgment for an insurer against the bailee of a logging machine for the amount paid to its insured for the loss of the machine by fire. An expert for the insurance company originally concluded that the design of the machine was not defective. He changed his opinion, however, when he received a letter from the manufacturer after the fire suggesting certain design modifications. The manufacturer succeeded in excluding the evidence and it was dismissed as a defendant. The Court reasoned that there was no evidence concerning the manufacturer's motivation in sending the letter or the exact date when the letter was sent. It upheld the exclusion of the evidence under Rule 403, since the evidence against the bailee was strong.

Stallworth v. Illinois Cent. Gulf R.R., 690 F.2d 858 (11th Cir. 1982): Although the Court reversed a judgment for the railroad in an action brought by a motorist injured at a crossing at night, it upheld the Trial Judge's ruling excluding evidence that the railroad placed flares at the crossing immediately following the collision. The Court said that even though the plaintiff urged that the evidence tended to show feasibility of repair and to impeach, the Trial Judge "has broad discretion under Rule 403."

Control

Clausen v. Sea-3, Inc., 21 F.3d 1181 (1st Cir. 1994): In an employee's action for personal injuries caused by a fall on a ramp, the Court found no plain error in admission of evidence that a defendant had replaced the ramp with steps three years later. The evidence was probative on the issue of which defendant controlled the premises, and the cautionary instruction sufficiently informed the jury as to the limited purpose for which it was admitted.

Hull v. Chevron U.S.A., Inc., 812 F.2d 584 (10th Cir. 1987): The Court affirmed a judgment for a drilling company employee injured in a forklift accident. It held that evidence that after the accident the drilling company discharged the employee who had operated the forklift and changed its operating procedures was inadmissible against the company as a subsequent remedial measure. Although another defendant offered the evidence ostensibly to prove that the company had the right to control the forklift, the Court held that this was an undisputed fact so that the evidence was not needed to prove control.

Disciplinary proceedings

Maddox v. City of Los Angeles, 792 F.2d 1408 (9th Cir. 1986): In a civil rights suit against police officers and the City growing out of the death of an arrestee, the Court held there was no error in excluding evidence that a defendant officer admitted during a disciplinary proceeding that he violated City policy with respect to a choke hold. The Court reasoned that the disciplinary proceeding was a subsequent remedial measure by the City, and that the evidence would have been unduly prejudicial if offered against the officer since the jury might have inferred that the officer was guilty of wrongdoing simply because there was a proceeding. Evidence of the City policy was admitted for the jury's consideration.

Specht v. Jensen, 863 F.2d 700 (10th Cir. 1988): In a civil rights suit arising out of searches of the plaintiff's home and office, the Court held that the Trial Judge properly excluded a press release issued by city officials which stated that officers exercised poor judgment in failing to read a "writ of assistance" thoroughly and that disciplinary action would be taken.

Feasibility

In re Joint E.D. & S.D. Asbestos Litig., 995 F.2d 343 (2d Cir. 1993): The Court held that, since feasibility was not contested, it was error to admit evidence that a manufacturer placed warnings on its product after a worker's last exposure to asbestos. "'Feasibility' is not an open sesame whose mere invocation parts Rule 407 and ushers in evidence of subsequent repairs and remedies."

Whitehead v. St. Joe Lead Co., 729 F.2d 238 (3d Cir. 1984): In an opinion reversing a summary judgment for the defendant in a product liability action, the Court observed that warnings to users of products containing lead that were included with products manufactured after the plaintiff was exposed to lead during her employment could be considered on the question of whether warnings were feasible at a reasonable cost. See also *Cumberland County Utils. Auth. v. M/T Delbar,* 604 F. Supp. 383 (D.N.J. 1985) (evidence of subsequent repairs not admissible where feasibility not controverted).

Albrecht v. Baltimore & O.R.R., 808 F.2d 329 (4th Cir. 1987): The Court reversed a judgment for an employee in an FELA case, holding it was error to admit evidence that after the accident that injured the plaintiff the railroad made improvements to the area in which the accident occurred. It concluded that the feasibility of repairs was stipulated by the railroad, and that the plaintiff was the one who attempted to make it appear that feasibility was disputed while examining a railroad employee. In *Doyle v. United States,* 441 F. Supp. 701 (D.S.C. 1977), a wrongful death action arising out of a motor boat collision with the guide cable for a ferry, the plaintiff was permitted to introduce evidence of subsequent remedial measures to rebut the United States' claim that the measures were not feasible.

Reese v. Mercury Marine Div., 793 F.2d 1416 (5th Cir. 1986): Affirming a judgment for the plaintiffs in a wrongful death action against the manufacturer of an outboard motor, the Court held that a manual containing warnings about the absence of a switch, published a year after the accident giving rise to the suit, was admissible to prove feasibility. The manufacturer had offered evidence that only a retailer could properly instruct the consumer with respect to such a switch. In *Middleton v. Harris Press & Shear, Inc.,* 796 F.2d 747 (5th Cir. 1986), the Court affirmed a judgment for a manufacturer in a product liability case, finding that evidence of remedial modifications to a machine was properly excluded where feasibility was not disputed. See also *Grenada*

Steel Indus. v. Alabama Oxygen Co., 695 F.2d 883 (5th Cir. 1983) (where feasibility was not controverted in product liability case, evidence of subsequent repairs was properly excluded). In *Gardner v. Chevron U.S.A., Inc.*, 675 F.2d 658 (5th Cir. 1982), the Court affirmed an employer's judgment in a wrongful death action, concluding it was not error to exclude evidence that a broken pipe was replaced with a heavier grade of pipe following the accident that gave rise to the litigation, even though the employer's foreman testified that he would have used the original size of pipe if he were constructing a well like the one involved in this case. The Court said that because the employer never contested that a larger sized pipe could feasibly have been used, the evidence was inadmissible to controvert feasibility.

Probus v. K-Mart, Inc., 794 F.2d 1207 (7th Cir. 1986): In a suit by a plaintiff who fell from a ladder, the Court held it was proper to exclude evidence that after the accident the manufacturer strengthened a cap on the ladder. Although the manufacturer claimed that the cap used on the plaintiff's ladder was adequate, the evidence was not admissible to controvert that claim, since the manufacturer was not contending that a stronger cap would not have been feasible. In *Wetherill v. University of Chicago*, 565 F. Supp. 1553 (N.D. Ill. 1983), the Court ruled *in limine,* in an action by two plaintiffs claiming injuries from exposure *in utero* to a drug (DES) administered to their mothers, that evidence of the manufacturer's publications concerning DES after the plaintiffs were born would be excluded if offered to show the feasibility of giving warnings in connection with DES use. Feasibility was not a disputed issue in the case.

Anderson v. Malloy, 700 F.2d 1208 (8th Cir. 1983): The Court reversed judgment for the defendants in an action by a rape victim against the owners and operators of a motel. It held that the defendants disputed the feasibility of installing "peep hole and safety chains" and that the plaintiff should have been permitted to show that they were installed after she was raped. A dissenting Judge argued that the defendant had questioned only the necessity of further precautions, not their feasibility. This case demonstrates how a broad view of "feasibility" can effectively remove the protection that Rule 407 is intended to provide. A defendant is entitled to claim that he acted with reasonable care without putting in issue the feasibility of additional repairs. If, however, a defendant claims that it would have been impossible (or infeasible) to do more than was done, then subsequent measures may be used to contradict the assertion.

Transgo, Inc. v. Ajac Transmission Parts Corp., 768 F.2d 1001 (9th Cir. 1985), *cert. denied*, 474 U.S. 1059 (1986): The Court affirmed a trademark and copyright infringement judgment for the plaintiff, finding that the plaintiff properly introduced evidence of revised instruction sheets distributed by the defendant in connection with a kit. The evidence rebutted the defendant's claim that it was not feasible to produce instructions that differed from the plaintiff's.

Impeachment or rebuttal

Harrison v. Sears, Roebuck & Co., 981 F.2d 25 (1st Cir. 1992): In a product liability suit involving a carpentry tool, the defendant's expert testified that the accident described by the plaintiff could not have occurred as alleged and that there had never been a similar complaint made to the manufacturer. The Court held there was no error in excluding evidence, including the expert's statement that he had worked on design changes for the tool, offered to impeach him, since the danger that the jury would misuse the evidence as proof of negligence outweighed the impeachment value of the evidence.

Pitasi v. Stratton Corp., 968 F.2d 1558 (2d Cir. 1992): In a personal injury action against a ski resort, the plaintiff alleged the defendant had been negligent in failing to rope off the side entrances to a closed trail. The Court held it was error to exclude evidence the defendant closed off the side entrance after the plaintiff's accident, as it tended to rebut the defense that the plaintiff had been contributorily negligent in entering an area where the dangerous conditions were so obvious that warnings or ropes were unnecessary. This decision illustrates the thin line separating inadmissible subsequent remedial measure evidence from admissible impeachment evidence. In our view, had the resort limited its evidence to testimony that the risks were sufficiently obvious that no warning devices were needed, the subsequent remedial measures would not have been admissible, since there really would be no "impeachment"; in reality, the evidence would have served no purpose other than to suggest that the defendant's denial of negligence was inconsistent with taking subsequent remedial measures, and the Rule prohibits such evidence. But, in asserting that the plaintiff was so careless that no reasonable person would have failed to appreciate the risk, the defendant opened the door to impeachment.

Petree v. Victor Fluid Power, Inc., 887 F.2d 34 (3d Cir. 1989): On trial following remand of his strict product liability action (see 831 F.2d 1191 (3d Cir. 1987), discussed *infra*), the plaintiff alleged that defective warnings on a press manufactured in 1959 led to his injuries in 1983, and offered evidence that defendant had begun placing a warning decal on all its new presses in 1980. The Court held that the evidence was admissible to impeach the defendant's expert's testimony that there was no need to warn because the particular risk had been designed out of the machine, and that the Trial Judge erroneously assessed the effect of the decision in the first trial when balancing prejudicial effect against probative value. In *Kenny v. Southeastern Pa. Transp. Auth.,* 581 F.2d 351 (3d Cir. 1978), *cert. denied,* 439 U.S. 1073 (1979), the Court set aside a j.n.o.v. for the defendant, concluding that a plaintiff, who alleged negligence on the part of a transit system after she was raped in a station, offered sufficient evidence to support a jury verdict when she showed deficient lighting on the station platform and insufficient attention to conditions by the only employee on the premises. The Court held there was no error in allowing testimony that new lighting had been installed on the platform a few days after the attack against the plaintiff. Citing this Manual, the Court held that "when the defendant opens up the issue by claiming that all reasonable care was being exercised at the time, then the plaintiff may attack that contention by showing later repairs which are inconsistent with it." This is another reminder that simply claiming that the conduct of a defendant was not negligent and was reasonable under the circumstances does not open the door to subsequent repair evidence, while claiming that all reasonable care was being taken opens the door to such evidence.

Kerr-McGee Corp. v. Ma-Ju Marine Servs., 830 F.2d 1332 (5th Cir. 1987): A worker suing her employer and a vessel owner elicited testimony from a supervisor called as an adverse witness that a handrail was not necessary to make the deck safe and then sought to impeach the witness with evidence that a handrail was added to the deck after the plaintiff's accident. The Court upheld exclusion of the evidence, as there was no showing that the supervisor had ordered the addition of the rail, and the risk of confusion and prejudice might well have substantially outweighed its probative value. In *Jones v. Benefit Trust Life Ins. Co.*, 800 F.2d 1397 (5th Cir. 1986), an action by an insured alleging tortious breach of a disability insurance contract, the Court held that evidence of the defendant's policy with a different insured was properly admitted to impeach the claim of the defendant's witnesses that the plaintiff's policy was ambiguous. In *Muzyka v. Remington Arms Co.*, 774 F.2d 1309 (5th Cir. 1985), the Court held it was error to exclude evidence of a design change in a rifle several months after an accident, since the manufacturer claimed that the design was the best and safest at the time of the accident. In *Bickerstaff v. South Cent. Bell Tel. Co.*, 676 F.2d 163 (5th Cir. 1982), a personal injury action by a telephone customer who sued the company for failing to give warnings against the use of a telephone during an electrical storm, the plaintiff argued that evidence that the defendant put a warning in its monthly note to subscribers should have been admitted to impeach two witnesses who said that a warning was not advisable and that it was unnecessary since everyone was aware of the danger. Although the Court observed that the impeachment exception to Rule 407, if applied broadly, may swallow up the basic limitation on the use of subsequent repair evidence found in the Rule, it concluded that the impeachment probably should have been permitted. The error was harmless, however. In *Dollar v. Long Mfg., N.C., Inc.*, 561 F.2d 613 (5th Cir. 1977), *cert. denied*, 435 U.S. 996 (1978), the Court reversed a judgment for the defendant in a product liability action. A defense witness testified that the instrument used by the deceased was safe to operate; the plaintiff should have been permitted to impeach with a letter sent by the witness to dealers selling the instrument, warning them about its "death-dealing propensities" when used in the fashion it was used by the deceased. Although the Trial Judge relied upon Rule 407, the Court concluded that the evidence was admissible under the last sentence of the Rule because it was offered for impeachment purposes. The Court stated that the evidence should not have been excluded under Rule 403 because there was no danger of *unfair* prejudice to the defendant.

Patrick v. South Cent. Bell Tel. Co., 641 F.2d 1192 (6th Cir. 1980): The Court held that postaccident repairs could be offered to rebut a claim that there was no need for improvement in the situation.

Jaeger v. Hennsison, Durham & Richardson, Inc., 714 F.2d 773 (8th Cir. 1983): Affirming a plaintiff's judgment in a personal injury action against an architectural firm resulting from a construction site accident, the Court upheld the introduction of photographs of a portion of a stairway that was involved in the accident. Although the photographs showed that the portion involved in the accident had been replaced, the Court reasoned that they were properly used to impeach defense witnesses who testified concerning the specifications for the stairway.

Transgo, Inc. v. Ajac Transmission Parts Corp., 751 F.2d 1040 (9th Cir. 1985): In a trademark and copyright infringement action, the Court held that the evidence of the defendant's changed instruction sheet was properly admitted to impeach or rebut its claim that it could not have modified its sheet to make it look different from the plaintiff's.

Rimkus v. Northwest Colorado Ski Corp., 706 F.2d 1060 (10th Cir. 1983): An injured skier, claiming that a ski resort was negligent in failing to mark an outcropping of rock onto which he fell, introduced evidence (including photos) showing that the resort set up bamboo poles above the outcropping after the accident. The jury was instructed that it could not consider the evidence on the question of negligence. The Court affirmed, reasoning that although "[t]he trial judge might well have excluded the evidence," it was not an abuse of discretion to admit it to undermine the testimony of a defense witness who claimed that the plaintiff, an experienced instructor, was contributorily negligent in not seeing the rocks, which were visible.

Wilkinson v. Carnival Cruise Lines, Inc., 920 F.2d 1560 (11th Cir. 1991): The Court reversed a judgment for the plaintiff in an action brought for injuries suffered when an automatic sliding glass door ran over her foot. Evidence the door was left open for the remainder of the cruise was improperly admitted, as it did not impeach testimony that the door was in normal operating condition at the time of the accident. Citing this Manual, the Court noted that the witness had not asserted that the defendants had exercised "all reasonable care" in maintaining the door, nor had he represented that it was in the "safest" or "best" condition.

Libel case

World Boxing Council v. Cosell, 715 F. Supp. 1259 (S.D.N.Y. 1989): In this libel action, the Court held that evidence that language in the contested passage had been altered in a subsequent paperback edition of the book was inadmissible under the policy of the Rule, because elimination of defamatory language in a subsequent edition limits the extent of damage to an individual's reputation by keeping injurious material from the eyes of new readers.

Plaintiff's repairs

Public Service Co. v. Bath Iron Works Corp., 773 F.2d 783 (7th Cir. 1985): Reversing a judgment for plaintiffs who sued a manufacturer for damages resulting from the failure of a device purchased from the manufacturer in 1979, the Court found it was error to exclude evidence concerning a similar device manufactured in the 1950s, since the evidence was relevant to proving that the defendant had complied with the plaintiffs' instructions in manufacturing the device that failed. The Court also found error in the exclusion of evidence of the plaintiffs' 1983 plans for the device. Observing that it is unclear whether the exclusionary policy of Rule 407 applies when a plaintiff's remedial measures are offered to refute allegations that a defendant was negligent, since a "party who is not in danger of being sued may be less likely to be deterred from making subsequent improvements by the possibility that the improvements will be used against it," the Court did not reach the question since the subsequent improvements in the instant case were admissible to impeach the plaintiffs' claim that the directions to the defendant in 1979 were adequate.

Product liability cases

McFarlane v. Caterpillar, Inc., 974 F.2d 176 (D.C. Cir. 1992): In a product liability action arising out of the alleged brake failure of a bulldozer, the Court held it was error to exclude as a subsequent remedial measure a postaccident service report containing a statement that indicated a spool in the hydraulic system did not meet manufacturing

Product liability cases (cont'd)

specifications, as that portion of the report reflected only the unaltered state of the spool at the time it was inspected. Exclusion of the report was not error, however, because no sufficient business record foundation had been laid. In *Prentiss & Carlisle Co. v. Koehring-Waterous Div.*, 972 F.2d 6 (1st Cir. 1992), the Court affirmed a judgment for the purchaser of a timber harvesting machine that caught fire, holding there was no error in admitting an interoffice memo from the defendant analyzing the cause of the accident, since even though remedial measures followed, the analysis itself was not a remedial measure of the sort excluded by the Rule. In *Raymond v. Raymond Corp.*, 938 F.2d 1518 (1st Cir. 1991), a strict product liability action arising out of a fatal accident involving a sideloader, the Court held that the Rule applies to strict liability cases. Because the design changes offered in evidence had been ordered before the accident, however, they were not excludable under the Rule; but there was no abuse of discretion in excluding them under Rule 403.

Fish v. Georgia-Pacific Corp., 779 F.2d 836 (2d Cir. 1985): The Court reversed a judgment for homeowners who sued a manufacturer of particle board, alleging that it failed to warn them of hazards associated with a floor used to build their home. The Court concluded it was error to admit evidence that the defendant issued warnings six or seven years after the plaintiffs built their home. In *Lindsay v. Ortho Pharmaceutical Corp.*, 637 F.2d 87 (2d Cir. 1980), the Court reversed a judgment against a manufacturer of oral contraceptives, concluding that changes on warning labels to patients should not have been admitted against the manufacturer when the changes were largely attributable to FDA requirements. The Court appeared to favor the manufacturer's analogy to Rule 407 when it concluded that under Rule 403 the evidence was too prejudicial to have been admitted.

Kelly v. Crown Equip. Co., 970 F.2d 1273 (3d Cir. 1992): In an action arising out of a worker's injuries on a forklift, the Court held that evidence of subsequent changes was inadmissible, regardless of whether the plaintiff's theory was failure to warn or design defect.

Werner v. Upjohn Co., 628 F.2d 848 (4th Cir. 1980), *cert. denied*, 449 U.S. 1080 (1981): Reversing a plaintiff's judgment in an action against an ophthalmologist and drug manufacturer, the Court held it was error to admit evidence of a revised warning issued by the manufacturer the year after the plaintiff visited the defendant doctor. Feasibility, said the Court, was not a disputed issue. The Court went on to decide that there should be no difference in the treatment of negligence and strict liability cases, especially when the issues raised by the two theories overlap.

Hardy v. Chemetron Corp., 870 F.2d 1007 (5th Cir. 1989): The Court affirmed a judgment for a manufacturer who was sued by a worker injured while cleaning a machine, and held that Rule 407 applies in product liability cases. The Court added that "[e]vidence of subsequent measures [is] no more admissible to rebut a claim of non-negligence than it is to prove negligence directly." In the Fifth Circuit's first appellate decision on whether Rule 407 applies in product liability cases, *Grenada Steel Indus. v. Alabama Oxygen Co.*, 695 F.2d 883 (5th Cir. 1983), the Court affirmed a judgment for the defendants, holding that the Trial Judge properly excluded evidence that a defendant had manufactured a differently designed valve after the accident. The Court reasoned that voluntary changes intended to improve products should be encouraged and that they might be discouraged if Rule 407 were inapplicable to product liability cases; even more important, "evidence of subsequent repair or change has little relevance to whether the product in question was defective at some previous time." The Court added that

> [t]he jury's attention should be directed to whether the product was reasonably safe at the time it was manufactured.... The introduction of evidence about subsequent changes in the product or its design threatens to confuse the jury by diverting its attention from whether the product was defective at the relevant time to what was done later.

Traylor v. Husqvarna Motor, 988 F.2d 729 (7th Cir. 1993): Reversing a judgment for a manufacturer of a maul in a suit by a bystander who was injured when a metal chip from the maul struck his eye, the Court observed that it had previously understood "culpable conduct" to include the creation of a product defect. In the instant case, the manufacturer made changes in the specifications for its product after the maul that injured the plaintiff was sold but before the accident occurred. The Court expressed doubts about whether manufacturers would hesitate to make improvements because of a fear for its litigation position in hypothetical future cases when no accident had yet occurred. It did not decide the meaning of "after the event," however, because it concluded that, even if the Magistrate Judge had been correct in reading Rule 407 to cover preaccident changes, the evidence in the instant case was clearly admissible for impeachment. In *Ross v. Black & Decker, Inc.,* 977 F.2d 1178 (7th Cir. 1992), *cert. denied,* 113 S. Ct. 1274 (1993), a product liability action arising out of injuries caused by a circular saw, the Court held there was no abuse of discretion in admitting evidence of design changes made after the saw was manufactured, as the defendant had not stipulated to the feasibility of the remedial measures it took nor had it made any objection when the Trial Judge ruled that the measures would be admitted because the defendant contested feasibility. In *Flaminio v. Honda Motor Co.,* 733 F.2d 463 (7th Cir. 1984), the Court affirmed judgments for a Japanese manufacturer and an American distributor in an action brought by a plaintiff who suffered severe injuries in a motorcycle accident, aligning with other Courts holding that Rule 407 applies in product liability cases. It observed that the concept "strict liability" is something of a misnomer and may tend to suggest a greater difference between product liability and negligence actions than really exists. Looking at the purposes of the Rule — promoting safety measures and preventing juror confusion and misuse of evidence — the Court found that the Rule served the same purpose in product liability cases as it does in negligence cases.

Bizzle v. McKesson Corp., 961 F.2d 719 (8th Cir. 1992): The Court, affirming a judgment for the defendants in an action for injuries allegedly suffered because of a defective walking cane, held that evidence that a defendant recalled a particular model of cane should not have been excluded under the Circuit's interpretation of the Rule, but there was no error because the probative value of the evidence, given the minimal showing that the model recalled was the same as that involved in the litigation, was easily outweighed by the dangers of unfair prejudice and of misleading the jury. In *DeLurya v. Winthrop Labs,* 697 F.2d 222 (8th Cir. 1983), a product liability action against a drug

Product liability cases (cont'd)

manufacturer, the Court held it was improper to admit evidence that the defendant changed its package insert after the plaintiff used the drug. In prior decisions — *Robbins v. Farmers Union Grain Term. Ass'n,* 552 F.2d 788 (8th Cir. 1977); *Farner v. Paccar, Inc.,* 562 F.2d 518 (8th Cir. 1977); *Unterburger v. Snow Co.,* 630 F.2d 599 (8th Cir. 1980) — the Court had held that "the rule against admitting evidence of subsequent remedial measures does not apply to actions based on strict liability," but it found that the prior decisions did not apply in this case where the governing law focused on whether the manufacturer distributed its drug without reasonable and adequate warnings of dangers inherent and reasonably foreseeable in the proper use of the drug. The Court found this to be almost identical to a negligence standard and concluded that the exclusionary rule must be applied. In *Kehm v. Procter & Gamble Mfg. Co.,* 724 F.2d 613 (8th Cir. 1983), the Court held there was no error in refusing to instruct the jury in a toxic shock syndrome case that withdrawal of a tampon from the market could only be considered as background evidence, not as evidence of culpable conduct. The majority agreed with and would follow *DeLuryea,* but concluded that since the manufacturer had been the one to offer the evidence and had attempted to suggest that it had voluntarily withdrawn the product and thus to demonstrate good faith, and the voluntariness of the withdrawal was hotly contested, the requested instruction might have obscured the issues and would not have been very useful to the manufacturer. The Court distinguished *Kehm* and *DeLuryea* in *Roth v. Black & Decker, Inc.,* 737 F.2d 779 (8th Cir. 1984), as it reiterated its prior holdings that Rule 407 is inapplicable to actions based in strict liability in tort. It stated that the Rule does apply in a case involving a duty to warn. The Court found that Rule 407 did not bar evidence of subsequent remedial measures in *R.W. Murray Co. v. Shatterproof Glass Corp.,* 758 F.2d 266 (8th Cir. 1985), a suit against a glass company for breach of warranty in connection with panels that it installed in a building.

Gauthier v. AMF, Inc., 788 F.2d 634, *amended,* 805 F.2d 337 (9th Cir. 1986): The Court reversed a judgment for the plaintiff in a product liability action against the manufacturer of a snow thrower. It held that Rule 407 applies to product liability cases and concluded that admitting evidence of design changes by the defendant and by the industry after the accident was prejudicial error. The defendant conceded that safety devices were feasible, but argued that the safety problem was not great enough to warrant the trade-off of consumer frustration, increased complexity of the product, and risk of consumer efforts to disconnect the safety device. The Court held that this was not an attack on feasibility, but was an argument that the design was reasonable at the time. In its opinion denying rehearing, the Court added that the evidence should have been excluded under Rule 403.

Herndon v. Seven Bar Flying Serv., Inc., 716 F.2d 1322 (10th Cir. 1983), *cert. denied,* 104 S. Ct. 2170 (1984): The Court affirmed a judgment for the plaintiffs in a product liability action arising out of an airplane crash, holding it was proper to admit a service bulletin, issued by the defendant more than a year after the accident, indicating that a switch in the plane needed to be modified. The Court suggested that unless a manufacturer expressly concedes that at the time of an accident a product could have been made safer, feasibility of design modifications is an issue in dispute, but declined to base its decision in this case (where there was no express concession) on the narrow ground that the evidence was properly admitted on the feasibility issue. Rather, it concluded that Rule 407 should not bar evidence of subsequent remedial measures in an action that is based on strict liability and indicated that when negligence and strict liability theories are combined, a limiting instruction as to the proper use of the evidence should be given when it is requested by a defendant. The Court also ruled that FAA Airworthiness Directives could be admitted, on the rationale that

> [w]here a superior authority requires a tort feasor to make post-accident repairs, the policy of encouraging voluntary repairs which underlies Rule 407 has no force — a tort feasor cannot be discouraged from voluntarily making repairs if he *must* make repairs in any case.

This reasoning does respond to one of the policies underlying Rule 407. And if strict liability means liability for any injuries caused by a product whether or not it was unreasonably dangerous or negligently manufactured, the argument is sound. If some form of culpable conduct must be shown, and if our argument is accepted that one danger in admitting evidence of subsequent repairs is that it tends to confuse the pre- and post-accident settings, then it is not so clear that FAA and similar directives should be admitted in all cases. In *Meller v. Heil Co.,* 745 F.2d 1297 (10th Cir.), *cert. denied,* 467 U.S. 1206 (1984), the Court held that evidence of subsequent design changes in a dump bed assembly for a dump truck was properly admitted to show feasibility of alternative designs and that the evidence, accompanied by a limiting instruction, was not unduly prejudicial. The Court noted that product modifications may be relevant to factual issues that are related to the question of dangerousness and that the Rule does not exclude evidence offered on such factual issues, but observed that "evidence of subsequent product changes will usually be irrelevant as direct proof of the ultimate contention that the product is unreasonably dangerous," since "[p]roducts are modified for a host of reasons unrelated to safety, and therefore the modification itself typically does not have any tendency to make more probable the past dangerousness of the product." In *Kloepfer v. Honda Motor Co.,* 898 F.2d 1452 (10th Cir. 1990), an action arising out of the death of a passenger on an all-terrain vehicle (ATV), the Court held that a consent decree relating to ATV safety entered between the United States and major ATV manufacturers (including the defendant) two years after the accident in question was properly excluded as irrelevant to the case. In *Dow Chem. Corp. v. Weevil-Cide Co.,* 897 F.2d 481 (10th Cir. 1990), an equitable subrogation action brought by the manufacturer of a grain fumigant against the marketer after settlement of product liability claims, the Court held that an internal report on the question whether the manufacturer should withdraw from the market should not have been excluded as evidence of subsequent remedial measures, because the conclusion of the report was that the company should remain in the business, and thus there was nothing in the report to make the harm less likely to occur.

Reference to state law

Rioux v. Daniel Int'l Corp., 582 F. Supp. 620 (D. Me. 1984): In a wrongful death action arising from maintenance of a vertical concrete piping system, the defendant moved *in limine* to bar the introduction of evidence that it changed the method by which it secured the concrete piping after the accident in suit. The District Judge observed that Maine admits evidence of subsequent remedial measures to prove negligence whereas Rule 407 excludes the evidence. After pointing out that Congress indicated the state evidence rules to which it wanted Federal Courts to defer — Rules 302, 501, and 601 — the Court concluded that Rule 407 would govern the action and barred the use of the evidence of a changed method to prove negligence.

Kelly v. Crown Equip. Co., 970 F.2d 1273 (3d Cir. 1992): In a diversity action arising out of a worker's injuries on a forklift, the Court held that evidence of subsequent changes was inadmissible, regardless of allegedly conflicting state law, as the Rule is "arguably procedural" and therefore governs.

Flaminio v. Honda Motor Co., 733 F.2d 463 (7th Cir. 1984): The Court decided that Rule 407 properly was applied in a product liability action arising under Wisconsin law, even though Wisconsin state courts might have admitted subsequent remedial measure evidence. The Court suggested that there is less difference between product liability and negligence actions in many instances than their labels might indicate, and it found that Rule 407 serves the same purpose in both kinds of actions. Although the Court recognized that there is a substantive aspect to the Rule, it concluded that substantive and procedural concerns both support exclusion of subsequent remedial measure evidence and that "[a]n important — reason for the rule was distrust of juries' ability to draw correct inferences from evidence of subsequent remedial measures."

Monger v. Cessna Aircraft Co., 812 F.2d 402 (8th Cir. 1987): In the course of affirming a judgment for an aircraft manufacturer in a wrongful death case, the Court observed that it is unclear whether federal or state law should govern the admissibility of subsequent remedial measures in a diversity case. It found that any error in the admission of such evidence was harmless in the instant case.

Moe v. Avions Marcel Dassault-Breguet Aviation, 727 F.2d 917 (10th Cir.), *cert. denied,* 105 S. Ct. 176 (1984): The Court affirmed judgments for defendants in a wrongful death action arising out of a plane crash, but it disagreed with the analysis used by the Trial Judge in ruling on subsequent remedial measure evidence. The Judge had ruled that a circular published by the airplane's manufacturer following the crash was inadmissible under Rule 407. The Court held, however, that in a diversity case when there is a conflict between Rule 407 and state law, state law should govern "because Rule 407 is based primarily on policy considerations rather than relevancy or truth seeking," and the policy considerations are a fundamental part of the state's law of liability. Nonetheless, there was no error in excluding the circular, since negligence and product liability theories were both involved in the case, and state law only permitted the use of the evidence on the latter theory. Thus, Rule 403 would have permitted exclusion, especially since the plaintiffs were permitted to paraphrase the circular in cross-examining the defendants' pilot-experts. One Judge would not have resolved the state-federal controversy, since it was unnecessary to do so in this case. The decision relies heavily on the idea that Rule 407 and similar state rules are intended to promote repairs; we suggest, however, that they rest mostly on relevance grounds, which calls the Court's reasoning into question. In *Wheeler v. John Deere Co.,* 862 F.2d 1404 (10th Cir. 1988), the Court reiterated that in diversity strict liability cases the admissibility of subsequent remedial measures is governed by state law, and held that it was error to admit evidence to prove feasibility after it had been stipulated.

Repairs before accident

Rollins v. Board of Govs. for Higher Educ., 761 F. Supp. 939 (D.R.I. 1991): In a wrongful death action arising out of an electrocution while working on ship-to-shore power cables, the Court held that all evidence of pre-accident discussions, drafts, and deliberations, and of actual alterations or repairs regarding the hardware or procedures involved would be admitted, but evidence of actual repairs made after the date of the accident were inadmissible to show the defendant's culpability.

Petree v. Victor Fluid Power, Inc., 831 F.2d 1191 (3d Cir. 1987): The plaintiff was injured in a 1983 accident involving a press manufactured in 1949. The Trial Judge excluded the plaintiff's evidence that the defendant manufacturer put warning decals on new presses beginning in 1980. The Court affirmed, holding that in strict product liability actions Rule 407 bars not only evidence of remedial measures after the date of the accident, but also after the date of sale, as of which date state law measures the defective nature of the product. *Petree* was followed, but questioned in light of the Rule's language, in *Kelly v. Crown Equip.*, 970 F.2d 1273 (3d Cir. 1992).

City of Richmond v. Madison Mgt. Group, Inc., 918 F.2d 438 (4th Cir. 1990): In an action for fraud and breach of contract brought by the City against the successor to the manufacturer of a concrete water pipe that burst, the Court held that a change made after the sale in the kind of reinforcing wire used in that type of pipe was properly admitted, as the relevant event for purposes of the Rule was the bursting of the pipe, not its sale to the City.

Cates v. Sears, Roebuck & Co., 928 F.2d 679 (5th Cir. 1991): In a product liability action by a consumer injured while operating a radial arm saw, the plaintiff offered evidence that changes in warning labels on that model were authorized before, but implemented after, he bought the saw. The Court held that exclusion of the evidence was error (but harmless) because, although the focus of a product liability case is on the dangers inherent in the product as it leaves the manufacturer, the relevant time under the Rule is the accident, which occurred after implementation. In *Roberts v. Harnischfeger Corp.*, 901 F.2d 42 (5th Cir. 1989), the Court affirmed a plaintiff's judgment against the manufacturer of a hydraulic crane, noting that Rule 407 would not exclude evidence that subsequent to manufacturing the crane involved, but before the plaintiff was injured, the defendant had made a protective device standard equipment on that type of crane. The evidence was held irrelevant under Rules 402 and 403 to the reasonableness of the design at the time of manufacture, however.

Traylor v. Husqvarna Motor, 988 F.2d 729 (7th Cir. 1993): Reversing a judgment for a manufacturer of a maul in a suit by a bystander who was injured when a metal chip from a maul struck his eye, the Court observed that it had previously understood "culpable conduct" to include the creation of a product defect. In the instant case, the manufacturer made changes in the specifications for its product after the maul that injured the plaintiff was sold but before the accident occurred. The Court expressed doubts about whether manufacturers would hesitate to make improvements because of a fear for its litigation position in hypothetical future cases when no accident had yet occurred. It did not decide the meaning of "after the event," however, because it concluded that, even if the Magistrate Judge had been correct in reading Rule 407 to cover pre-accident changes, the evidence in the instant case was clearly admissible for impeachment.

Burke v. Deere & Co., 6 F.3d 497 (8th Cir. 1993): The Court reversed (2-1) a judgment for the plaintiff, whose hand had been injured by an auger when he reached into a clean-out door on farm equipment manufactured by the defendant. Post-sale, pre-accident evidence that the defendant had installed warning decals and modified similar equipment was admissible to prove the existence of a dangerous defect in the product, but in this case the evidence was impermissibly admitted as ostensibly relevant to punitive damages.

Huffman v. Caterpillar Tractor Co., 908 F.2d 1470 (10th Cir. 1990): In a product liability wrongful death action involving a pipelayer, the Court held that the relevant "event" under the Rule was the fatal injury, not manufacture of the machine, so that a design change implemented by the defendant manufacturer before the accident would not be excluded even if the Circuit did view the Rule as inapplicable to strict product liability cases.

Repairs ordered before accident

Raymond v. Raymond Corp., 938 F.2d 1518 (1st Cir. 1991): In a strict product liability action arising out of a fatal accident involving a sideloader, the Court held that the design changes offered in evidence were not excludable under Rule 407 because they had been ordered before the accident. However, the Court found there was no abuse of discretion in excluding them under Rule 403.

Kaczmarek v. Allied Chem. Corp., 836 F.2d 1055 (7th Cir. 1987): In an action by a truck driver who was doused while unloading sulphuric acid, the Court declined to create an exception to Rule 407 for remedial measures ordered before but implemented following an accident.

Kociemba v. G.D. Searle & Co., 683 F. Supp. 1579 (D. Minn. 1988): In an action for injuries from an intrauterine device received in June 1977, the defendants moved *in limine* to exclude mention of a November 1977 warning issued pursuant to the Food & Drug Administration's May 1977 regulation. The motion was denied, both because the defendant knew in May that a warning would be required and the policy of the Rule "is inapplicable when the determination to make the change is made prior to a plaintiff's injury," and because the policy is inapplicable when the remedial measure is mandated rather than voluntary.

Repairs required by law

Villari v. Terminix Int'l, Inc., 692 F. Supp. 568 (E.D. Pa. 1988): In a homeowner's action against an exterminator alleging that the defendant contaminated a house, the Court held that evidence that the defendant discontinued use of termiticides was inadmissible. The discontinuation took place at the same time the EPA was negotiating with the primary manufacturer to discontinue their sale. Although the plaintiff argued that the discontinuance was involuntary and that exclusion of evidence of involuntary measures cannot promote safety measures, the Judge observed that the strong policy justification for Rule 407 counseled against exceptions that might deter efforts to remove potential hazards and concluded that voluntariness of a measure should be presumed absent a clear showing of coercion. In this case, the defendant stopped using the products at a time when they could lawfully be used. Thus, the discontinuance was a voluntary subsequent remedial measure.

Chase v. General Motors Corp., 856 F.2d 17 (4th Cir. 1988): The Court reversed a judgment in a product liability case, finding, *inter alia,* that evidence of a recall following an accident should not have been admitted.

Rozier v. Ford Motor Co., 573 F.2d 1332 (5th Cir. 1978): In a wrongful death action alleging the defendant's negligent design of a fuel tank, the Court reversed a judgment for the defendant because the defendant had withheld an engineer's report that should have been disclosed in discovery. The Court said that the report, which discussed alternative fuel tank designs in an apparent effort to anticipate a revised National Highway Traffic Safety Administration standard, would not have been excluded by Rule 407 and that to invoke the exclusionary rule "here is particularly inappropriate since the estimate was prepared not out of a sense of social responsibility but because the remedial measure was to be required in any event by a superior authority."

Kociemba v. G.D. Searle & Co., 683 F. Supp. 1579 (D. Minn. 1988): In an action for injuries from an intrauterine device received in June 1977, the defendants moved *in limine* to exclude mention of a November 1977 warning issued pursuant to the Food & Drug Administration's May 1977 regulation. The motion was denied, because the policy of the Rule is inapplicable when the remedial measure is mandated rather than voluntary.

Reports recommending repairs

Alimenta (U.S.A.), Inc. v. Stauffer, 598 F. Supp. 934 (N.D. Ga. 1984): In an action by a commodities firm alleging a conspiracy to defraud by a former employee and another person, the Court ruled *in limine* that a report on the firm's business practices by an outside consultant, made after the employee left the firm, would be excluded under Rule 407 and also under Rule 403. We wonder whether the contents of the report can be a subsequent remedial measure absent some showing that any recommendations were carried out. If not, the Judge's alternative reliance on Rule 403 appears to be wise.

Rocky Mountain Helicopters, Inc. v. Bell Helicopters Textron, 805 F.2d 907 (10th Cir. 1986): The Court affirmed a judgment in a suit by a helicopter buyer and its insurer against a manufacturer that was based upon a jury verdict finding that the buyer and the seller were each negligent. It found that evidence that the manufacturer had conducted a stress study after the accident giving rise to the suit was properly admitted, since Rule 407 "does not read so broadly as to exclude post-accident tests or reports" and "[i]t would strain the spirit of the remedial measure prohibition in Rule 407 to extend its shield to evidence contained in post-event tests or reports."

Third party repairs

Raymond v. Raymond Corp., 938 F.2d 1518 (1st Cir. 1991): In a strict product liability action against the manufacturer arising out of a fatal accident involving a sideloader, the Court held that subsequent repairs undertaken by the defendant's employer were not excluded by the Rule, but there was no abuse of discretion in excluding the evidence under Rule 403.

Herrington v. Hiller, 883 F.2d 411 (5th Cir. 1989): In an action for birth injuries allegedly caused by the defendant hospital's failure to provide twenty-four-hour anesthesia services, the Court held it was an abuse of discretion under Rule 403 to exclude evidence that the third-party provider of anesthesia services had refused to provide such services because of hospital policy regarding nurses administering anesthesia, but that twenty-four-hour services were provided two years after the accident. Furthermore, the evidence was not barred by Rule 407 because the changes were made by the third party. In *Myers v. Pennzoil Co.,* 889 F.2d 1457 (5th Cir. 1989), the Court held there was no error in excluding evidence offered by the defendant of postaccident remedial measures by the plaintiff's employer. Although Rule 407 does not apply to measures by nonparties, the ruling was not an abuse of discretion because under the applicable law the employer was immune from tort liability, so the employer's fault was immaterial to the determination of liability. In *Koonce v. Quaker Safety Prods. & Mfg. Co.,* 798 F.2d 700 (5th Cir. 1986), an action by surviving family members of an employee killed in a flash fire at an ammunitions plant against the manufacturer and supplier of a safety suit, the Court found that a memo written soon after the accident by the employer was not excluded by Rule 407 where the employer was not a party. The memorandum was inadmissible hearsay, however. In *Dixon v. International Harvester Co.,* 754 F.2d 573 (5th Cir. 1985), the Court overturned a judgment n.o.v. for the manufacturer of a "crawler tractor" in a suit for damages occurring when a pine sapling entered the cab of the tractor. The Court held that changes in the tractor made after the accident by the employer, rather than the manufacturer, were not excluded by Rule 407.

Pau v. Yosemite Park & Curry Co., 928 F.2d 880 (9th Cir. 1991): The Court reversed a judgment for the defendant bicycle rental company in a wrongful death action arising out of an accident in a national park, holding it was error to exclude evidence that the Park Service erected warning signs at the site after the accident. The Rule does not bar evidence of remedial measures by third parties, and the evidence was relevant to express warranty claims against the defendant. In *In re Aircrash in Bali, Indonesia,* 871 F.2d 812 (9th Cir.), *cert. denied,* 110 S. Ct. 277 (1989), the Court held that an FAA report after an accident was not a subsequent remedial measure, since it was not a repair by the defendant airline.

D. LEGISLATIVE HISTORY

Advisory Committee's Note

The rule incorporates conventional doctrine which excludes evidence of subsequent remedial measures as proof of an admission of fault. The rule rests on two grounds. (1) The conduct is not in fact an admission, since the conduct is equally consistent with injury by mere accident or through contributory negligence. Or, as Baron Bramwell put it, the rule rejects the notion that "because the world gets wiser as it gets older, therefore it was foolish before." Hart v. Lancashire & Yorkshire Ry. Co., 21 L.T.R.N.S. 261, 263 (1869). Under a liberal theory of relevancy this ground alone would not support exclusion as the inference is still a possible one. (2) The other, and more impressive, ground for exclusion rests on a social policy of encouraging people to take, or at least not discouraging them from taking, steps in furtherance of added safety. The courts have applied this principle to exclude evidence of subsequent repairs, installation of safety devices, changes in company rules, and discharge of employees, and the language of the present rule is broad enough to encompass all of them. See Falknor, Extrinsic Policies Affecting Admissibility, 10 Rutgers L. Rev. 574, 590 (1956).

The second sentence of the rule directs attention to the limitations of the rule. Exclusion is called. for only when the evidence of subsequent remedial measures is offered as proof of negligence or culpable conduct. In effect it rejects the suggested inference that fault is admitted. Other purposes are, however, allowable, including ownership or control, existence of duty, and feasibility of precautionary measures, if controverted, and impeachment. 2 Wigmore § 283; Annot., 64 A.L.R.2d 1296. Two recent federal cases are illustrative. Boeing Airplane Co. v. Brown, 291 F.2d 310 (9th Cir. 1961), an action against an airplane manufacturer for using an allegedly defectively designed alternator shaft which caused a plane crash, upheld the admission of evidence of subsequent design modification for the purpose of showing that design changes and safeguards were feasible. And Powers v. J. B. Michael & Co., 329 F.2d 674 (6th Cir. 1964), an action against a road contractor for negligent failure to put out warning signs, sustained the admission of evidence that defendant subsequently put out signs to show that the portion of the road in question was under defendant's control. The requirement that the other purpose be controverted calls for automatic exclusion unless a genuine issue be present and allows the opposing party to lay the groundwork for exclusion by making an admission. Otherwise the factors of undue prejudice, confusion of issues, misleading the jury, and waste of time remain for consideration under Rule 403.

For comparable rules, see Uniform Rule 51; California Evidence Code § 1151; Kansas Code of Civil Procedure § 60-451; New Jersey Evidence Rule 51.

RULE 408

A. OFFICIAL TEXT

Rule 408. Compromise and Offers to Compromise

Evidence of (1) furnishing or offering or promising to furnish, or (2) accepting or offering or promising to accept, a valuable consideration in compromising or attempting to compromise a claim which was disputed as to either validity or amount, is not admissible to prove liability for or invalidity of the claim or its amount. Evidence of conduct or statements made in compromise negotiations is likewise not admissible. This rule does not require the exclusion of any evidence otherwise discoverable merely because it is presented in the course of compromise negotiations. This rule also does not require exclusion when the evidence is offered for another purpose, such as proving bias or prejudice of a witness, negativing a contention of undue delay, or proving an effort to obstruct a criminal investigation or prosecution.

B. EDITORIAL EXPLANATORY COMMENT

Rationale

It has long been the policy of the law to promote settlements. The Federal Rule codifies the common law, at least with respect to the general exclusion of offers of settlement. The Federal Rule also recognizes, as a subsidiary rationale, that compromise evidence often has little or no probative value when used to prove the validity or amount of a claim. An offer to compromise may well represent a desire to buy peace rather than an admission of liability. At least this is so if the offer is significantly less than the claim.[1]

At common law, a line was drawn between offers to settle and admissions of fact made during settlement negotiations. Factual admissions could be introduced against the party making the admissions unless they were inextricably bound up with offers to settle. As a result, negotiations were often couched in hypothetical form, purely to avoid factual admissions. This created a trap for the unwary. It also impeded the free-flowing, informal discussion that is often necessary for effective settlement negotiations. The

---

1. See Martin, *Offers of Settlement,* N.Y. L.J. Aug. 14, 1992, p. 3, col. 1.

Federal Rule avoids these problems by excluding statements made in settlement negotiations when offered to prove the validity or amount of a claim.[2]

Facts revealed during settlement negotiations

It was the Advisory Committee that first recommended that statements or conduct made or taking place in the course of settlement negotiations be excluded. Its intent was to allow free and open bargaining in which the parties could make concessions for bargaining purposes that they would not have to later explain. The House of Representatives liked the basic idea and substituted a Rule designed to exclude admissions of liability and opinions, but clearly providing: "Evidence of facts disclosed during compromise negotiations, however, is not inadmissible by virtue of having been first disclosed in those negotiations."

One of the concerns of the House was that if facts revealed during negotiations could not be introduced against the party revealing them, those parties dealing with government agencies would be reluctant to furnish factual information at preliminary meetings and would wait until the negotiation stage in order to obtain some sort of immunity with respect to the facts. But the Senate believed, and with some justification, that the House misread the intentions of the Advisory Committee. The Senate viewed the Advisory Committee's recommendation as disabling the government from introducing specific evidence obtained in the course of negotiations, but not from proving facts disclosed during the quest for settlement by evidence obtained elsewhere. The Senate also may have been concerned that under the House draft, Courts might have difficulty differentiating admissions of liability from evidence of facts and distinguishing opinion from fact, especially in light of Rule 701.

The Senate restored the language of the Rule approved by the Supreme Court. This language provided that factual admissions made during settlement negotiations are inadmissible under the Rule. But the Senate added a sentence to ensure that evidence, such as documents, is not rendered inadmissible merely because presented in the course of compromise negotiations if the evidence is discoverable otherwise. The philosophy of the addition is that a party should not be able to immunize from admissibility documents otherwise discoverable merely by offering them in compromise negotiations. This is the same philosophy underlying the House changes. The Senate version prevailed. In sum, settlement negotiations cannot be used as proof of facts relating to a claim or its amount, but facts revealed during settlement negotiations are provable by evidence other than conduct or statements that make up compromise negotiations.

Otherwise discoverable evidence

Preexisting documents — i.e., those made outside of negotiations — do not fall within the exclusionary language of the Rule, since they are not "made in compromise

---

2. See Fiberglass Insulators, Inc. v. Dupuy, 856 F.2d 652, 654 (4th Cir. 1988) ("The Federal Rule of Evidence is broader than the common law exclusionary rule in many jurisdictions and excludes from evidence all statements made in the course of settlement negotiations.").

negotiations.'' Thus, they always are discoverable. But there is an ambiguity in Rule 408 that is attributable to a compromise between the House and Senate versions of the bill. The Rule provides that statements made in compromise negotiations are inadmissible. This is the basic exclusionary thrust of the Rule. But Rule 408 also provides that it ''does not require the exclusion of any evidence otherwise discoverable'' because it is presented during compromise discussions. Since any party can be asked to make admissions under Rules 30 (Depositions), 33 (Interrogatories), and 36 (Request for Admissions) of the Federal Rules of Civil Procedure, it could be argued that any admission, always being discoverable, is always admissible. Such a reading would, however, destroy the utility of the Rule. The answer lies in reading Rule 408 as permitting the introduction of any admissions *actually obtained during discovery,* even though the same admissions may also have been made in settlement negotiations. This protects the sanctity of the bargaining table without providing an immunity for any and all evidence voluntarily disclosed during bargaining. It should satisfy the concerns of both houses of Congress.

Scope of the Rule

Five general points can be made about the scope of the Rule:

(1) Compromise evidence is only inadmissible when offered to prove liability for or invalidity of a claim or its amount. It is not inadmissible under the Rule when offered for some other purpose, such as proving the bias or prejudice of a witness.[3] Of course, the evidence still might be excludible under Rule 403. See the discussion of relationship to other Rules, *infra*.

(2) If the ''other purpose'' is really an issue that bears ultimately on an element of liability, then the rule of exclusion will apply. For example, in *Trebor Sportswear Co. v. The Limited Stores, Inc.,* 865 F.2d 506 (2d Cir. 1989), the defendant interposed a statute of frauds defense to plaintiffs' breach of contract claim. In response, plaintiffs offered a proposed draft agreement written by the defendant after the dispute between the parties had already arisen. The draft agreement was sent to ''resolve the current issues and allow us to go forward with our business relationship,'' and legal action was threatened if the plaintiffs did not sign the agreement. The plaintiffs argued that the draft agreement was admissible despite Rule 408, since it was offered not to prove the validity of the claim, but only in order to meet the statute of frauds defense. But the Court rejected this argument, on the ground that ''satisfying the statute of frauds was the first step to proving, ultimately, the validity of [the] claims of breach of contract.'' The Court concluded that ''since the two questions were so closely intertwined, admission of the documents even initially for the purpose of meeting the statute of frauds requirement

---

3. See, e.g., Bituminous Constr., Inc. v. Rucker Enters., 816 F.2d 965 (4th Cir. 1987) (letters containing settlement offers were properly admitted to show defendant's understanding of its obligations under a joint check agreement); Reichenbach v. Smith, 526 F.2d 1072 (5th Cir. 1976) (evidence of ''Mary Carter'' settlement agreements between the plaintiff and other defendants should have been admitted to show the bias of the witness). See also Martin, *Offers of Settlement,* N.Y. L.J. Aug. 14, 1992, p. 3, col. 1 (''[W]hile FRE 408 may appear at first to be a stringent prohibition on admissibility, in truth it bars evidence only when offered for relatively narrow purposes and otherwise leaves the door open for a trial judge to admit relevant evidence at his or her discretion.'').

would, under the circumstances of this case, militate against the public policy considerations which favor settlement negotiations and which underlie Rule 408.''

(3) Compromise negotiations are only excluded under the Rule when they relate to a claim that was disputed as to either validity or amount. If there was no such dispute, then the Rule does not apply. For example, where a debtor admits the validity and amount of a debt, and simply tries to negotiate for a lesser payment, the statements made pursuant to such negotiations are not protected by the Rule.[4] See the fourth paragraph of the Advisory Committee's Note, *infra*. Similarly, statements or conduct occurring before a controversy has even arisen are not excluded by the Rule.[5]

(4) Rule 408 applies even if the settlement is between a party to the litigation and a nonparty. Thus, the fact that a party settled a litigation with another is not admissible to prove the validity or amount of the claim currently before the Court. The Rule is drafted to provide every incentive for compromise, and without such a broad Rule of exclusion, litigants would be deterred from settling where multiple suits have been or might be brought.[6] Similarly, when the parties to a suit have engaged in settlement negotiations in previous related litigation between themselves, the compromise evidence is excluded when offered to prove the validity or amount of the claim currently before the Court.[7]

(5) Offers to furnish or to accept valuable consideration are protected, not other offers.

Evaluative reports

In some cases, parties in the course of settlement negotiations mutually retain the services of a consultant, who is commissioned to prepare an independent evaluative report designed to facilitate the settlement process. For example, in a suit arising from a complex securities transaction, the parties might commission an independent accountant to determine whether generally accepted accounting methods were used in the preparation of an important financial statement. The purpose would be to determine the strength of the plaintiff's claim that improper accounting methods were used. In these circumstances, the resulting report should be as protected under Rule 408 as is any statement made by the parties in settlement negotiations. This is because such a report is used by all parties

---

4. See, e.g., In re B.D. Int'l Discount Corp., 701 F.2d 1071 (2d Cir. 1983) (statements made before bankruptcy, by which the bankrupt sought to arrive at a mutually satisfactory schedule of repayments, were not excluded under Rule 408, since at the time the statements were made the bankrupt did not dispute the debts, but "was simply endeavoring to get more time in which to pay").

5. See, e.g., Deere & Co. v. International Harvester Co., 710 F.2d 1551 (Fed. Cir. 1983) ("Rule 408, on its face, is limited to actual disputes over existing claims and, accordingly, cannot be applicable to an offer, albeit one ultimately rejected, to license an, as yet, uncontested patent.").

6. See, e.g., Branch v. Fidelity & Cas. Co. of N.Y., 783 F.2d 1289, 1294 (5th Cir. 1986) ("The spectre of a subsequent use to prejudice a separate and discrete claim is a disincentive which Rule 408 seeks to prevent."); United States v. Contra Costa County Water Dist., 678 F.2d 90 (9th Cir. 1982) (settlement by the plaintiff with another defendant, of a closely related but separate claim, held inadmissible under Rule 408).

7. See, e.g., Fiberglass Insulators, Inc. v. Dupuy, 856 F.2d 652 (4th Cir. 1988) (prior settlement negotiations in related litigation between the parties held inadmissible under Rule 408 in current litigation).

to determine the appropriate settlement, if any. As one Court put it, such a report is "intended to be part of the negotiations toward compromise."[8]

Impeachment

The Rule appears to provide that statements made during compromise negotiations should be admissible to impeach the person making the statements whose testimony at trial is inconsistent with his settlement posture, even if the prior statement is not probative of bias. We suggest that the Rule not be applied so broadly, however. Admission for impeachment should depend on whether the person who made the statement is a party to the present action, or rather is merely a witness.

Our proposed distinction can be illustrated by the following example: An injured automobile driver, *P*, sues the manufacturer of another driver's, *D's*, car for damages resulting from a collision between the two; *P* and *D* have settled *P's* claims against *D* following *D's* admission during settlement negotiations that he was drunk at the time of the accident; the manufacturer discovers *D's* settlement statements, and uses them to impeach *D's* trial testimony that he was sober at the time of the accident, wholly aside from whether a claim of bias can be established.

In this circumstance, the impeachment should be allowed. The basic policy of the Rule is to protect the party making the admission from suffering at trial because of it. When *D* is not a party and has no financial stake in the *P v. Manufacturer* litigation, *D* is not treated unfairly if he is impeached by statements made during settlement negotiations. Since *P* never could control *D's* tongue and bore the risk that *D* would make inconsistent statements before testifying, *P* is not treated unfairly either. The one legitimate concern is that the jury will misuse the evidence and give it substantive value. But the jury is almost certain to be told of any settlement between *P* and *D* anyway because it suggests bias. Thus, the prejudicial effect of *D's* statements does not substantially outweigh the probative value of the evidence for impeachment purposes.

The argument could be made with respect to this hypothetical case that the impeachment of *D* in the litigation brought by *P* against the manufacturer should not be permitted, because the manufacturer really is attempting to show that *D* was responsible for the accident, and the impeachment evidence is being used to undercut *D's* version that he was not culpable. It is true in this instance that the line between impeachment and an attempt to prove that *D* was culpable is a very thin one, and perhaps for some it does not exist. But the evidence is highly probative; *D* personally is not disadvantaged by its offer; and *D's* statement is not being offered to prove the invalidity of any claim made by *D*. Thus we think that the best reading of the Rule is to admit the evidence for impeachment purposes.

But it is entirely a different matter to allow *D* to be impeached by settlement statements if settlement has not been achieved and *D* is the defendant at trial. In most

---

8. Blu-J, Inc., v. Kemper C.P.A. Group, 916 F.2d 637, 639 (11th Cir. 1990) (report by independent accountant concerning an important financial statement was protected by Rule 408, since the parties, while engaged in settlement negotiations, commissioned the accountant to prepare the report in order to determine whether the plaintiff "had a case").

cases we think that the Court should decide against admitting statements made during settlement negotiations as impeachment evidence when they are used to impeach a party who tried to settle a case but failed. The philosophy of the Rule is to allow the parties to drop their guard and to talk freely and loosely without fear that a concession made to advance negotiations will be used against them at trial.[9] Opening the door to impeachment evidence on a regular basis may well result in more restricted negotiations.

We do not think that this encourages perjury. Rather, it permits parties to bargain without fear that any concession made for bargaining purposes will be used as evidence. A choice must be made between allowing free bargaining where parties can let their hair down and try to reach settlement in a variety of ways and requiring parties and their agents to cast all factual statements either in hypothetical form or pursuant to an explicit agreement that the statements are offered for bargaining purposes only. A Rule cannot have it both ways. We believe that Rule 408 opts to promote free-wheeling bargaining and that use of statements for impeachment purposes every time that bargaining breaks down would undercut the Rule.

It should be noted that nothing in our reading of the Rule would prevent a perjury prosecution, in which the statements made in negotiation could be used as proof; in these circumstances, the statements would not be offered as proof of validity or amount of a claim. Nor would our view prevent a fraud action arising out of a settlement fraudulently obtained. Also, we note that each party to bargaining has reason to distrust the other's statement of the facts, so free discussion is unlikely to mislead anybody. If impeachment is to be permitted whenever bargaining breaks down, it is probable that most lawyers will waste their client's time with hypothetical versions of facts that could be stated directly. Such inefficiency ought not to be encouraged.

Relationship to other rules and statutes

Another reason to read Rule 408 as we do is to make it consistent with Rule 410, which covers bargaining in criminal cases and which does not allow statements made in bargaining to be used for impeachment. Since some bargaining may involve both civil and criminal liability, a uniform approach to the Rules would be helpful.

Note that (as with subsequent remedial measures under Rule 407) the mere fact that compromise evidence is offered for a "not-for-validity-of-the-claim" purpose (such as bias) does not mean that it is automatically admissible. The Trial Court still has discretion under Rule 403 if the probative value of the evidence for the permissible purpose is substantially outweighed by the risk that the jury will use the compromise evidence as proof of the validity or amount of the claim.[10]

---

9. See Fiberglass Insulators, Inc. v. Dupuy, 856 F.2d 652, 654 (4th Cir. 1988) ("The public policy of favoring and encouraging settlement makes necessary the inadmissibility of settlement negotiations in order to foster frank discussions.").

10. See, e.g., Meyer v. Pennzoil Co., 889 F.2d 1457 (5th Cir. 1989) (Trial Judge did not abuse his discretion in excluding compromise evidence offered to impeach witnesses for bias, where Trial Judge determined that the probative value of the evidence as to bias was substantially outweighed by the risk of prejudice and confusion); Williams v. Chevron U.S.A., Inc., 875 F.2d 501 (5th Cir. 1989) (no error to exclude plaintiff's settlement with a third party, even where it was offered to impeach plaintiff's testimony that he lacked

It should be noted that some statutes bar disclosure of settlement-type evidence. These statutes may be more protective than Rule 408, since they may control discovery as well as trial use of evidence. One such statute, 42 U.S.C. § 2000e-5(b) (covering EEOC conciliation efforts), is discussed in *Branch v. Phillips Petroleum Co.,* 638 F.2d 873 (5th Cir. 1981).[11]

Use by party making settlement offer

The policy behind Rule 408 is to assure that statements and offers made in settlement negotiations do not come back to haunt the party who made them. But what if the party who makes a settlement offer wants to use it as evidence at trial? This problem was encountered by the Second Circuit in *Pierce v. F.R. Tripler & Co.,* 955 F.2d 820 (2d Cir. 1992). *Pierce* was an employment discrimination suit arising out of the elimination of the plaintiff's position. The employer sought to introduce the fact that it had offered to settle the case by giving the plaintiff a job in a different subsidiary. The purpose for introducing the offer was to prove the employer's lack of intent to discriminate, and to show that the plaintiff, who rejected the offer, had failed to mitigate damages. The employer argued that the exclusion mandated by Rule 408 was inapplicable because it was designed to protect those who *made* offers of settlement, not those who received them; since the employer was the offeror in this case and did not want the protection of Rule 408, it contended that the Rule was inapplicable.

Despite the inapplicability of the public policy for the Rule in this circumstance, the *Pierce* Court held that settlement offers are subject to Rule 408 even if it is the offeror who seeks to admit them. The Court noted that the plain language of the Rule offers no distinction between offerors and offerees.[12]

The *Pierce* Court also relied on an alternative policy ground to reject a rule that would allow more liberal use of settlement agreements. The Court noted that settlement negotiations are almost always between and among opposing attorneys, and that these attorneys are likely to have different interpretations of the seriousness of offers and negotiations, and are also likely to disagree on what terms were set forth in any proposed settlement. These disputes of fact would have to be resolved by the factfinder, probably through testimony of the attorneys themselves. The Court was thus concerned that the "widespread admissibility of the substance of settlement offers could bring with it a rash of motions for disqualification of a party's chosen counsel who would likely become a witness at trial." The Court concluded that "we prefer to apply Rule 408 as written and exclude evidence of settlement offers to prove liability for or the amount of a claim regardless of which party attempts to offer the evidence."

---

financial means to pay for a surgical procedure; the jury might have "confused" this purpose with the one prohibited by Rule 408, and this risk of confusion justified exclusion under Rule 403).

11. See also 42 U.S.C. § 3610(a) (in connection with disputes under the Fair Housing Act, statements made in informal resolution proceedings are not admissible in subsequent proceedings, without written consent of the parties).

12. The Supreme Court has consistently applied the plain meaning rule to the Federal Rules of Evidence. See Capra, *Salerno, Plain Meaning, and the Supreme Court,* N.Y. L.J. July 17, 1992, p. 3, col. 1.

Of course, the concern of the Court in *Pierce* about disqualification of counsel loses its force when the settlement offer is in writing. In such a situation, there is often no need for the attorney to testify because the document speaks for itself. Similarly, negotiations conducted without counsel pose no problems of attorney disqualification.

More importantly, the *Pierce* approach to the Rule is problematic because it will often leave employers and other defendants without any good evidence on mitigation of damages. Even the *Pierce* Court recognized that the principal policy of the Rule — to encourage settlements — is not at stake where the party who made the offer wants to introduce it to prove lack of mitigation. In our view, the party who makes a settlement offer should be able to introduce it on the question of mitigation, at least where there is no equally probative alternative evidence reasonably available.

C. ANNOTATED CASES

Ambiguity of "settlement"

Winchester Packaging, Inc. v. Mobil Chem. Co., 14 F.3d 316 (7th Cir. 1994): Where use of the term "settlement" in correspondence between parties to a contract dispute was ambiguous between "to pay a bill" and "to compromise a legal dispute," the Court held there was no abuse of discretion under the circumstances in excluding the correspondence.

Appellate review of factfinding

Trans Union Credit Information Co. v. Associated Credit Servs., 805 F.2d 188 (6th Cir. 1986): In a suit by a computer service company seeking specific performance of an agreement with a credit bureau, the Court, applying the clearly erroneous standard, upheld exclusion of evidence concerning an alleged oral repudiation of the agreement as settlement negotiations.

Bad faith insurance denial

Lampliter Dinner Theater v. Liberty Mut. Ins. Co., 792 F.2d 1036 (11th Cir. 1986): Affirming dismissal of a claim by an insured that the defendant acted in bad faith in denying coverage in two suits against the insured, the Court held that evidence could not be admitted that the defendant ultimately settled the two suits, since such evidence was barred by Rule 408. Moreover, the Court concluded that "an eventual settlement does not indicate that an initial denial of coverage was in bad faith."

Bias and impeachment evidence

Estate of Spinosa, 621 F.2d 1154 (1st Cir. 1980): In a wrongful death and personal injury action arising out of an automobile accident, the Court said that it was not error to exclude a settlement agreement in an earlier suit against a family member alleging negligent maintenance of the vehicle that was involved in the accident, since the family member was asked at trial whether he had been sued in state court. We believe that in most cases, the fact of settlement is better evidence of possible bias than the fact of suit. In this case, however, we suspect that the settlement was arrived at by an insurance carrier, so the probative value of the evidence on the witness' bias probably was low; in addition, any rehabilitation evidence might have gone into the insurance and reminded the jury that the defendant may have been insured.

John McShain, Inc. v. Cessna Aircraft Co., 563 F.2d 632 (3d Cir. 1977): In an action arising out of two accidents involving a plane purchased by the plaintiff from the defendant, the Court held there was no error in admitting evidence of the plaintiff's entering into a compromise with a company that repaired the plane. The settlement evidence properly showed the bias of an expert witness called by the plaintiff, since a sister corporation of the witness' employer entered into the settlement in exchange for the expert testimony.

Myers v. Pennzoil Co., 889 F.2d 1457 (5th Cir. 1989): The defendant in this product liability action sought to impeach witnesses called by the plaintiff by showing they had originally been named as defendants and had settled with the plaintiff. The Court held there was no error in excluding the evidence, as it could have led to jury confusion and the defendant was otherwise given wide latitude in bringing out the witnesses' possible bias. In *United States Aviation Underwriters, Inc. v. Olympia Wings, Inc.,* 896 F.2d 949 (5th Cir. 1990), a declaratory judgment action by an insurer to determine whether coverage applied to an accident involving its insured's aircraft, the Court held that evidence the insurer had settled fraud claims against the insured's mechanic was admissible to show that the mechanic, whose testimony had been impeached on cross-examination by showing inconsistencies with his previous deposition, was at trial a more neutral, unbiased witness. In *Williams v. Chevron U.S.A., Inc.,* 875 F.2d 501 (5th Cir. 1989), the Court held that evidence of an employee's settlement with a contractor could be excluded on grounds of likely jury confusion in a suit by the employee against the owner of the platform, even though the evidence was offered to rebut testimony by the employee that he did not have the financial means to pay for a recommended surgical procedure. In *Reichenbach v. Smith,* 528 F.2d 1072 (5th Cir. 1976), a pre-Rules case citing Rule 408 as persuasive authority, the Court held that the Rule would not bar use of a "Mary Carter" settlement for impeachment purposes, but emphasized that the Trial Judge had discretion to determine whether the probative value was substantially outweighed by the prejudicial effect.

Bachenski v. Malnati, 809 F. Supp. 610 (N.D. Ill.), *aff'd,* 11 F.3d 1371 (7th Cir. 1993): In an action by a taxicab passenger against the driver of an auto that struck the cab, the Court held inadmissible evidence that the driver and taxicab company had settled a third-party claim against the company with an agreement that the company would pay 90 percent of any judgment rendered against the driver. The driver was not told of the settlement, thus making it of little value to show bias, and the Trial Judge reasoned that the potential prejudice from the evidence was enormous.

Hudspeth v. Commissioner, 914 F.2d 1207 (9th Cir. 1990): Reversing an income tax deficiency finding, the Court held that evidence the Commissioner's expert had given significantly different values to similar timber in a case that was settled was inadmissible on the proper value of the timber in this case but was admissible to show bias on the part of the expert. In *Brocklesby v. United States,* 767 F.2d 1288 (9th Cir. 1985), *cert. denied,* 474 U.S. 1101 (1986), the Court affirmed a judgment against the manufacturer of an approach chart in a case arising out of an airline crash, holding there was no error in admitting evidence of a compromise settlement between the manufacturer and the United States to attack the credibility of witnesses for the manufacturer and the government.

Consent decrees

Crouse-Hinds Co. v. Internorth, Inc., 518 F. Supp. 413 (N.D.N.Y. 1980): In an action by a corporation to block a takeover as being anticompetitive, the Court decided to admit evidence that the defendant entered *nolo* pleas to antitrust charges more than twenty years earlier and that it agreed to a consent judgment in another antitrust action ten years earlier. According to the Court, the plaintiff's need for evidence of anticompetitive tendencies outweighed the social policy benefits of rules like Rule 408. In our view, rules like Rules 410 and 408 encourage *nolo* pleas, consent judgments, and other settlements by assuring that, once accepted, they will not be used as if they were confessions. Certainly, there would be no prohibition on discovery by a plaintiff concerning earlier anticompetitive practices. This should provide useful evidence without threatening the policy of encouraging settlement.

Zenith Radio Corp. v. Matsushita Elec. Indus. Co., 723 F.2d 238 (3d Cir. 1983), *rev'd on other grounds,* 475 U.S. 574 (1986): In a massive antitrust case in which the plaintiffs alleged that the defendants conspired to drive them out of the market for television receivers, the Court reversed most of the summary judgment for the defendants. As part of its decision, the Court held that findings by the Japanese Fair Trade Commission were admissible under Rule 803(8). A majority of the Court found evidence of reliability in the fact that the defendants had entered into a consent agreement based on the findings. Although the agreement was not itself admissible, it could be relied upon under Rule 104 in deciding the admissibility of hearsay evidence.

Johnson v. Hugo's Skateway, 974 F.2d 1408 (4th Cir. 1992) (en banc): The plaintiff in a civil rights action, alleging that he had been intimidated on racial grounds at a roller skating rink, introduced a prior consent decree in which the rink agreed to post signs of a nondiscriminatory policy and to instruct employees not to discriminate, as well as evidence that the rink had not complied with the decree. The Court held the consent decree was not inadmissible evidence of a compromise, as it was not offered to prove that the rink had previously discriminated but to show, through the evidence of noncompliance, the rink's motive or intent on the present occasion.

United States v. Cohen, 946 F.2d 430 (6th Cir. 1991): In a prosecution for making and selling pirated videotapes, the Court held there was no error in admitting a consent judgment from the companion civil copyright infringement suit. The judgment was the defendant's personal admission agreeing to be enjoined permanently from infringing the plaintiffs' copyrights. The dissenting Judge noted that the consent judgment did not contain an admission of liability or wrongdoing and would have characterized it as a settlement agreement offered only to prove liability and therefore inadmissible under Rule 408.

Kerr v. First Commodity Corp., 735 F.2d 281 (8th Cir. 1984): Affirming the plaintiff's judgment in an action alleging fraud in the sale of commodities, the Court found that a consent decree that the defendant had entered into with the Commodity Futures Trading Commission in 1976 was properly admitted to show knowledge and intent to commit fraud in 1977 and 1978, and that a 1980 consent decree was also properly admitted to impeach testimony by the defense suggesting that all problems identified in the 1976 decree had been solved at the time of the decree.

Kloepfer v. Honda Motor Co., 898 F.2d 1452 (10th Cir. 1990): In a product liability action arising out of the death of a passenger on an all-terrain vehicle (ATV), the Court held that a consent decree relating to ATV safety entered between the United States and major ATV manufacturers (including the defendant) two years after the accident in question was properly excluded as irrelevant to the case. In *Wegerer v. First Commodity Corp.,* 744 F.2d 719 (10th Cir. 1984), a successful fraud action by investors against a commodity option brokerage firm and its principals, the Court upheld the admission of a 1976 consent decree between the defendants and the Commodity Futures Trading Commission, which was used to show the defendants' knowledge and intent to defraud.

Criminal cases

United States v. Baker, 926 F.2d 179 (2d Cir. 1991) (per curiam): Reviewing a conviction for possession of stolen goods, the Court held that because Rule 408 applies only to civil litigation, there was no error in admitting evidence of the defendant's prearrest attempts to "make a deal" with investigating officers. In *United States v. Gonzalez,* 748 F.2d 74 (2d Cir. 1984), a prosecution for wire and mail fraud, the Court upheld the admission of statements by the defendant, made while negotiating a settlement to a potential civil claim, that a promissory note issued to a Portuguese bank was a forgery and that he was liable on the note. The Court reasoned that the statements were not used to establish the validity or invalidity of the civil claim and thus could be admitted under Rule 408. It found no policy reason for excluding the evidence in a criminal case.

United States v. Peed, 714 F.2d 7 (4th Cir. 1983): The Court affirmed convictions for mail fraud and making false statements to the government, finding that recorded statements in which the defendant attempted to get a complainant to drop charges against her were not part of an offer to settle a disputed claim, but were part of an effort to obstruct a criminal investigation and were admissible.

United States v. Hays, 872 F.2d 582 (5th Cir. 1989): The Court held that the erroneous admission of evidence regarding a settlement between defendants charged with conspiracy and misapplication of funds and their savings and loan association was prejudicial. It concluded that the government's offer of the evidence to assist the jury in understanding the breadth of the alleged conspiracy "stands at direct odds with the clear mandates of Rule 408."

Damage issues

Branch v. Fidelity & Cas. Co., 783 F.2d 1289 (5th Cir. 1986): In litigation arising from an offshore platform accident, the Court held it was error (but harmless) to admit evidence of a settlement agreement between the families of workers who were killed and one of the parties to an indemnity agreement. In *Belton v. Fibreboard Corp.,* 724 F.2d 500 (5th Cir. 1984), the Court reversed a plaintiffs' judgment in a products liability suit because the Trial Judge told the jury when it returned its verdict that the amount awarded was less than the amount of the settlement with other defendants, so that the plaintiffs would receive nothing as a result of the verdict, and then permitted the jury to deliberate further and return another verdict. The Trial Judge violated Rule 408 by permitting the jury to consider the plaintiffs' settlements with other defendants as part of the proof of the amount of the claim. In *McHann v. Firestone Tire & Rubber Co.,* 713 F.2d 161 (5th Cir. 1983), the Court reversed a judgment for a tire manufacturer in a personal injury action, holding it was error to admit evidence of a settlement between the plaintiff and the service station where he was injured, since the jury might have erroneously concluded that the service station would not have settled unless it was at fault in the accident. Rather than admit the settlement, the Court suggested that the Trial Judge should deduct the amount of the settlement from any recovery the plaintiff might obtain.

United States v. Contra Costa County Water Dist., 678 F.2d 90 (9th Cir. 1982): The United States supplied the water needs of the District. After an adjoining landowner did work on his land that imperiled a canal system, the United States sued him and the District for the cost of repair. Ultimately, the landowner settled with the government. The settlement took the following form: The landowner paid $30,000 and received an offset in the amount of $45,000 for the diminution in the value of his property. The District claimed that the total of $75,000 should be a credit in its dispute with the government, whereas the government only permitted a credit of $30,000. The Court held that Rule 408 barred evidence of settlement negotiations. In our view, this is a misreading of the Rule. In this case, which arose on cross-motions for summary judgment, the only question was a legal one: What portion, if any, of the amount paid by the landowner ought to be credited to the District? The settlement with the landowner was a fact. If the District was entitled to a credit, it should have been entitled to show the settlement as evidence of the proper amount of the credit.

Foreign law

Morris v. LTV Corp., 725 F.2d 1024 (5th Cir. 1984): The Court affirmed a judgment for the defendant in an action by a real estate broker to recover a commission on the sale of a hotel located in Mexico. It upheld the exclusion of a letter from the corporation to the plaintiff offering a settlement, finding that federal evidence law, not Mexican law, governed the admissibility ruling.

Instructions concerning missing parties

Kennon v. Slipstreamer, Inc., 794 F.2d 1067 (5th Cir. 1986): The Court reversed a judgment for a moped rider against a windshield manufacturer, finding that the Trial Judge erred in telling the jury that the plaintiff had settled with other defendants for the nominal sum of ten dollars. The Court reasoned that "[i]n a case such as this one, where the absence of defendants previously in court might confuse the jury, the district court may, in its discretion, inform the jury of the settlement in order to avoid confusion.'' But it found that ''disclosing the amount of the settlement serves no such purpose,'' and that it might have prejudiced the remaining defendant by suggesting that the others were not liable and that the plaintiff would receive compensation, if any, only from the remaining defendant.

Arhart v. Micro Switch Mfg. Co., 798 F.2d 291 (8th Cir. 1986): In a product liability suit, various defendants sought indemnity and contribution under state law. The Court described various approaches used in state courts in dealing with settling and nonsettling tortfeasors. It upheld the Trial Judge's telling the jury that various defendants who had started the case had settled, so that the jury would understand their absence.

Mitigation of damages

Urico v. Parnell Oil Co., 708 F.2d 852 (1st Cir. 1983): Plaintiffs sued for the loss of use of a truck damaged in a collision with a truck owned by the defendants. The Court upheld a jury verdict for the plaintiffs, finding that testimony that evidence of detailed settlement discussions between the plaintiffs' attorney and the defendants' insurance company was properly admitted to show an excuse for the plaintiffs' failure to mitigate their damages.

Pierce v. F.R. Tripler & Co., 955 F.2d 820 (2d Cir. 1992): To show a failure to mitigate damages in an age discrimination action, the defendant proffered evidence that the plaintiff had been offered another job after he was denied a promotion. Affirming a judgment for the plaintiff, the Court held the evidence was properly excluded as it went to the amount of the claim and the job offer was an attempt to compromise the claim. In the Court's view, to admit such settlement offers, even at the instance of the offeror, could inhibit settlement discussions and interfere with the effective administration of justice by often necessitating that counsel become witnesses at trial.

Notice and knowledge

Fidelity & Deposit Co. v. Hudson United Bank, 493 F. Supp. 434 (D.N.J. 1980), *rev'd on other grounds,* 653 F.2d 766 (3d Cir. 1981): In an action by an insurer to rescind a banker's blanket bond on the ground that it had been procured by fraud, the Court ruled that Rule 408 barred the use of evidence that the bank had accepted money in settlement of a previous action against an insurance company on a claimed loss that the plaintiff alleged had been discovered, but not revealed, before the plaintiff issued the bond. In our view, the settlement was probably irrelevant or at least not very probative, but the fact that the prior suit was filed is extremely powerful evidence, perhaps conclusive on the facts of this case, that the defendant had knowledge of the loss before the bond was issued.

Spell v. McDaniel, 824 F.2d 1380 (4th Cir. 1987), *cert. denied,* 108 S. Ct. 752 (1988): The Court affirmed a jury's verdict finding both an officer and the City liable for use of excessive force in making an arrest. It held that evidence of a prior settlement by the City of another brutality claim brought by a different plaintiff, and of arrest quotas, was properly admitted to prove that the City was aware of a practice and that it fostered an atmosphere of aggressive and lawless behavior.

Bradbury v. Phillips Petroleum Co., 815 F.2d 1356 (10th Cir. 1987): Affirming judgments for plaintiffs who sued a mineral exploration company for trespass, assault and outrageous conduct, the Court held that evidence that the defendant had settled with other landowners who had complained concerning trespass or destruction of property was properly admitted. The Court reasoned that settlements of related claims should not generally be admitted to show the strength or weakness of a claim, and that "when the issue is doubtful, the better practice is to exclude evidence of compromises or compromise offers," but that in this case the evidence tend to show the defendant was notified of a problem with its conduct and that the conduct was reckless. In our view, however, evidence of the complaints would have established recklessness, so the settlement evidence was unnecessary.

Offer to settle by defendant

North Am. Biologicals Inc. v. Illinois Employers Ins., 931 F.2d 839, *amended*, 938 F.2d 1265 (11th Cir. 1991): In a suit seeking indemnification from an insurer for legal fees incurred in defending a class action, the Court held that the insurer's letter after dismissal of the class action offering to pay one-tenth of the fees and to consider the action as one claim subject to a single deductible was properly excluded as an offer of settlement.

Offer to settle by plaintiff

Ward v. Allegheny Ludlum Steel Corp., 560 F.2d 579 (3d Cir. 1977): Remanding a Title VII employment discrimination case for reconsideration of the claim of religious discrimination, the Court cited Rule 408 and noted that the District Judge should not consider a settlement offer made by plaintiff one week before the trial on the issue of liability. We note that the problem in this case was that the offer came several years after the employee requested the religious accommodation, so it was not relevant to the question of what the burden was on the employer at the time the employee made the request.

Pretrial discovery

Center for Auto Safety v. Department of Justice, 576 F. Supp. 739 (D.D.C. 1983): In a Freedom of Information Act case, the Court ordered disclosure of documents relating to consent decree modification negotiations in an automobile industry antitrust case. The Court rejected the government's argument that Rule 408 authorizes a "settlement negotiation" privilege, noting that the Rule limits the use of evidence at trial and does not create a pretrial discovery privilege.

Prior settlement inadmissible to prove liability

Wyatt v. Security Inn Food & Beverage, Inc., 819 F.2d 69 (4th Cir. 1987): The Court found in a discrimination action that the Trial Judge did not err in excluding evidence concerning the settlement of two prior discrimination suits involving the defendant. See also *Fiberglass Insulators, Inc. v. Dupuy,* 856 F.2d 652 (4th Cir. 1988) (statements made by attorneys in the course of settling prior related litigation between the parties held inadmissible).

Prior settlement inadmissible to prove invalidity of claim

McInnis v. A.M.F., Inc., 765 F.2d 240 (1st Cir. 1985): The Court reversed a judgment for a motorcycle manufacturer in an action by a motorcyclist injured in a collision with a car, finding error in the admission of evidence that the plaintiff had released the driver of the car from liability prior to suing the defendant. It reasoned that

> [i]f the policies underlying Rule 408 mandate that settlements may not be admitted against a defendant who has recognized and settled a third party's claim against him, it is axiomatic that those policies likewise prohibit the admission of settlement evidence against a plaintiff who has accepted payment from a third party against whom he has a claim.

Although under Rule 408 the settlement could not be used as proof that the car, rather than the defendant's cycle, caused the plaintiff's injuries, the amount of the settlement could be deducted from any award that the jury might return.

Quad/Graphics, Inc. v. Fass, 724 F.2d 1230 (7th Cir. 1983): The Court affirmed a judgment for a plaintiff who brought a breach of contract suit. Originally, the plaintiff sued several corporations and two individual defendants, but one of the individual defendants settled with the plaintiff. The Court upheld exclusion of the settlement evidence, since it was offered to show the invalidity of the plaintiff's claim and the settling defendant was not called to testify at trial.

County of Hennepin v. AFG Indus., 726 F.2d 149 (8th Cir. 1984): The County sued a manufacturer alleging defects in insulated glass windows placed in a public building. The County also sued its insurance carrier, claiming that a storm damaged the building. After the County and the carrier reached a settlement, the manufacturer was permitted to introduce evidence of the settlement to show that the County was alleging that the storm contributed to the problems with the windows. The Court upheld admission of the settlement evidence, finding it was relevant to impeaching the County's claim that the manufacturer caused the damage to the building. We believe that the fact that the County alleged in another suit that the storm caused damage was plainly admissible under Rule 801(d)(2)(A). Admission of additional evidence concerning the settlement posed a risk of confusing the jury as to exactly what damages the settlement covered.

Special circumstances of admissibility — settlement agreement in issue

Catullo v. Metzner, 834 F.2d 1075 (1st Cir. 1987): The Court held that testimony concerning the terms of a settlement agreement was properly admitted in a suit alleging breach of fiduciary duty in contravention of the court-approved settlement.

Coakley & Williams Constr., Inc. v. Structural Concrete Equip., Inc., 973 F.2d 349 (4th Cir. 1992): The Court affirmed a summary judgment granted on ground of a previous release in a construction dispute, holding that a settlement offer was properly considered as evidence of the parties' intent when the release was given.

Cates v. Morgan Portable Bldg. Corp., 780 F.2d 683 (7th Cir. 1985): In a breach of contract case, the Court reasoned that "a settlement agreement is admissible to prove the parties' undertakings in the agreement, should it be argued that a party broke the agreement." In *Central Soya Co. v. Epstein Fisheries, Inc.,* 676 F.2d 939 (7th Cir. 1982), the Court indicated that where a settlement has been reached and a suit claims breach of the settlement agreement, nothing in Rule 408 bars admission of the agreement.

Special circumstances of admissibility — miscellaneous

Bituminous Constr., Inc. v. Rucker Enters., 816 F.2d 965 (4th Cir. 1987): The Court affirmed a judgment for a subcontractor who sued the owner of parking lots for paving work. It held that evidence of settlement negotiations was properly admitted to show that the subcontractor had made a demand for payment and to prove that the owner understood that checks were to be made jointly payable to the general contractor and to the subcontractor. In *United States v. Peed,* 714 F.2d 7 (4th Cir. 1983), the Court affirmed convictions for mail fraud and making false statements to the government, finding that recorded statements in which the defendant attempted to get a complainant to drop charges against her were not part of an offer to settle a disputed claim, but were part of an effort to obstruct a criminal investigation and were admissible.

Kritikos v. Palmer Johnson, Inc., 821 F.2d 418 (7th Cir. 1987): The Court found it was error (but harmless) to rely upon letters written by the plaintiff's representative during settlement negotiations as substantive evidence that the plaintiff was primarily the cause of the delay in the completion of a yacht. The letters had been admitted for other purposes, and the Court held that they should not have been used as substantive proof of liability. In *Breuer Elec. Mfg. Co. v. Toronado Sys.,* 687 F.2d 182 (7th Cir. 1982), the Court upheld the entry of a default judgment, finding that evidence of settlement negotiations was properly admitted to show that the defendants were on notice of the nature of the issues of which the plaintiff complained. In *Prudential Ins. Co. v. Curt Bullock Builders,* 626 F. Supp. 159 (N.D. Ill. 1985), a suit involving a creditor's claim on a promissory note and a tort counterclaim by the debtor, the Court ruled that evidence concerning meetings held in an effort to resolve the dispute between the parties would be considered, for summary judgment purposes, as potentially admissible to prove the relationship between the insurance company and another creditor, a bank.

Freidus v. First Nat'l Bank, 928 F.2d 793 (8th Cir. 1991): In an action against a bank for allegedly refusing unreasonably to consent to the sale of the plaintiff's farmland, the Court held there was no error in admitting letters exchanged during settlement negotiations to rebut testimony for the plaintiff that the bank never gave any reason for the conditions it imposed for consenting to the sale; the evidence also negatived a contention that the bank unduly delayed in acceding to the plaintiff's request. In *Vulcan Hart Corp. v. NLRB,* 718 F.2d 269 (8th Cir. 1983), an appeal from an NLRB order, the Court found no error in the admission of evidence that the company sought to make an employee's reinstatement conditional on his resignation from union office. The evidence was not offered to show a wrongful discharge, which would have been impermissible under the Rule. Rather, it was proof that the company attempted to coerce the employee into restricting his participation in organizational activities in violation of the labor statute.

Broadcort Capital Corp. v. Summa Med. Corp., 972 F.2d 1183 (10th Cir. 1992): In an action by a securities clearing firm against a corporation for refusing to transfer and register a stock certificate, the Court held there was no error in admitting evidence of settlement discussions, where they related to an entirely different claim and were not admitted to prove the validity or amount of the claim under negotiation. In *Eisenberg v. University of New Mexico*, 936 F.2d 1131 (10th Cir. 1991), the Court affirmed the imposition of Rule 11 sanctions against an attorney, holding that the attorney's statements at a settlement conference on the show cause order were not excluded by the Rule, because they were "evidence offered for another purpose." In *Weir v. Federal Ins. Co.*, 811 F.2d 1387 (10th Cir. 1987), the Court reversed a judgment for a fire insurer in a subrogation suit against a dryer manufacturer. Reviewing the exclusion of evidence concerning a settlement between the insurer and the insureds, which was offered to prove that part of the settlement involved a "voluntary" payment that could not be recovered, the Court observed that Rule 408 does not prohibit evidence of the circumstances of a settlement to prove voluntariness, but added that "many of the same concerns about prejudice and deterrence to settlements exist regardless of the purpose for which the evidence is offered." It suggested that on remand the Trial Judge should engage in an analysis of the evidence under Rule 403.

Special circumstances of admissibility — state law

Carota v. Johns-Manville Corp., 893 F.2d 448 (1st Cir.), *cert. denied*, 110 S. Ct. 3238 (1990): The defendant in an asbestosis wrongful death action concluded its case by introducing evidence that the plaintiff had received a $98,471 settlement with other defendants. The Court affirmed a judgment for the defendant, holding that the federal Court was bound to follow the governing state law, which made settlement with a joint tortfeasor admissible for consideration when assessing damages.

Statements and materials in settlement negotiations

Fiberglass Insulators, Inc. v. Dupuy, 856 F.2d 652 (4th Cir. 1988): In an antitrust suit, the Court held that statements made by attorneys in the course of settling prior related litigation between the parties were inadmissible. The prior litigation and the current case were closely related, and the Court emphasized the strong public policy favoring exclusion of settlement negotiations between the same parties litigating against each other.

Ramada Dev. Co. v. Rauch, 644 F.2d 1097 (5th Cir. 1981): One of the parties to a construction contract hired an architect to prepare a report alleging certain construction defects to be used in settlement negotiations. The Court held that the report was not admissible against the party commissioning it since the report would not have existed but for the settlement negotiations. The report was thus excluded by Rule 408, whether or not there was a pretrial understanding or agreement among the parties as to its nature.

Russell v. PPG Indus., 953 F.2d 326 (7th Cir. 1992): Affirming summary judgment for the defendant in an employee's personal injury action, the Court noted that it was improper for the plaintiff to reveal the results of a summary jury trial on appeal. Regardless of the desirability of the procedure, any potential it might have as a settlement tool would be undermined if participating parties do not adhere to the basic stricture that the results be kept confidential. In *General Leaseways, Inc. v. National Truck Leasing Ass'n,* 830 F.2d 716 (7th Cir. 1987), an antitrust case, the Court held that a telephone call was properly admitted pursuant to a finding that it was not made as a part of settlement negotiations, even though a subsequent letter offering a settlement referred to the call.

EEOC v. Gear Petroleum, Inc., 948 F.2d 1542 (10th Cir. 1991): Affirming a judgment for the defendant in an age discrimination action, the Court held that letters from the defendant to the EEOC indicating a discriminatory basis for its decision were properly excluded under the Rule because the parties were engaged in the conciliation process, even though the EEOC was still conducting an investigation at the time. Citing this Manual, the Court also rejected the argument that the letters were admissible for impeachment purposes.

Blu-J, Inc. v. Kemper C.P.A. Group, 916 F.2d 637 (11th Cir. 1990): In an action by an investor against an accounting firm for issuing allegedly erroneous and fraudulent financial statements, the Court held that materials relating to an evaluation, conducted by independent accountants pursuant to a mutual agreement of the parties as part of settlement negotiations, of whether the defendants had followed generally accepted accounting methods were properly excluded under the Rule.

Statute of frauds defense

Trebor Sportswear Co. v. The Limited Stores, Inc., 865 F.2d 506 (2d Cir. 1989): In a breach of contract action, the Court affirmed a ruling that excluded settlement documents that were offered to meet a statute of frauds defense. The Court concluded that admission of the documents for the limited purpose would undermine the policies favoring settlements. A dissenting Judge argued that the exclusionary rule should not be applied, since the documents were not offered to prove the validity or amount of a claim, but to demonstrate compliance with the statute of frauds.

Undisputed claims

In re B.D. Int'l Discount Corp., 701 F.2d 1071 (2d Cir.), *cert. denied,* 104 S. Ct. 108 (1983): Affirming a bankruptcy decision granting a creditor relief, the Court observed that the debtor's financial statements containing an entry "Payable to Bank $7,269,052" were not rendered inadmissible by Rule 408, since the entry was not made as part of settlement negotiations. Moreover, at the time of negotiations there was no dispute as to the validity or amount of the bank's claim. The debtor was simply endeavoring to get more time in which to pay. In *S. Leo Harmony v. Binks Mfg. Co.,*

597 F. Supp. 1014 (S.D.N.Y. 1984), *aff'd*, 762 F.2d 490 (2d Cir. 1985), a breach of contract action by a subcontractor against a general contractor, the Court held that a letter from the defendant's counsel to the plaintiff's informing him that the defendant was contemplating a lawsuit against a third party and inquiring whether the plaintiff wished to join was not barred by Rule 408. The Court found that there was no dispute between the plaintiff and the defendant at the time the letter was written and that it was not an attempt to compromise. Regarding another letter, written by the plaintiff's attorney to the defendant's and offering, "[i]n accordance with our prior discussions and without prejudice to our clients' respective legal positions," a summary of damages suffered by the plaintiff, the Court recognized that the "magic" phrase "without prejudice" is not dispositive of whether a statement was an offer to compromise, but reasoned that "its use may still be evidence of the intent of the speaker which we may rely upon to determine whether the statement was made "in compromise.""

United States v. Meadows, 598 F.2d 984 (5th Cir. 1979): In this case the Court assumed "the applicability of Rule 408 to govern the admission of related civil settlement negotiations in a criminal trial," but held that the statements that the defendant sought to exclude were not covered by the Rule, since they were part of an informal conversation that took place when there was no claim to compromise.

Crues v. KFC Corp., 768 F.2d 230 (8th Cir. 1985): In an action by a franchisee against a franchisor alleging fraudulent misrepresentation, the Court upheld admission of evidence that the franchisor offered to convert the franchisee's fish franchise to a chicken franchise. The offer was made before litigation arose and was relevant to the reasonableness of the franchisee's reliance on statements concerning the fish operation.

Cassino v. Reichhold Chems., Inc., 817 F.2d 1338 (9th Cir. 1987), *cert. denied,* 108 S. Ct. 785 (1988): Affirming a judgment for the plaintiff in an age discrimination case, the Court upheld admission of a settlement agreement and release that the employer offered to the plaintiff at the time of termination. The Court approved the finding that there was no disputed claim at the time the agreement was offered and added that "[w]here, as here, the employer tries to condition severance pay upon the release of potential claims, the policy behind Rule 408 does not come into play." *Cassino* was distinguished in *Mundy v. Household Fin. Corp.,* 885 F.2d 542 (9th Cir. 1989), another age discrimination case, where the Court held there was no abuse of discretion in a finding that a proposed release agreement sought in exchange of $25,000 for "outplacement services" was part of a settlement offer, since the plaintiff had already received severance pay and other benefits upon his discharge and, although he had not yet filed any claims, had already retained legal counsel.

Dallis v. Aetna Life Ins. Co., 768 F.2d 1303 (11th Cir. 1985): Affirming a widower's judgment in an action to recover the costs of his wife's cancer treatment at a Bahamian clinic, the Court held that evidence that the defendant had reimbursed another insured for similar treatment was properly admitted, since the reimbursement did not involve a settlement of a disputed claim.

Deere & Co. v. International Harvester Co., 710 F.2d 1551 (Fed. Cir. 1983): In a patent infringement action the District Court excluded evidence offered by Harvester as to a licensing arrangement between Deere and a third party and royalty offers that Deere made to Harvester concerning a license for the patented equipment. The Appellate Court held that although Deere and Harvester might have been involved in dealings that could have led to litigation, no *actual dispute* arose between them until the instant litigation, so it was error to exclude the evidence under Rule 408. The Court also reasoned, however, that the District Court did not err in excluding the evidence because it had properly determined that the evidence was of little probative value.

D. LEGISLATIVE HISTORY

Advisory Committee's Note

As a matter of general agreement, evidence of an offer to compromise a claim is not receivable in evidence as an admission of, as the case may be, the validity or invalidity of the claim. As with evidence of subsequent remedial measures, dealt with in Rule 407, exclusion may be based on two grounds. (1) The evidence is irrelevant, since the offer may be motivated by a desire for peace rather than from any concession of weakness of position. The validity of this position will vary as the amount of the offer varies in relation to the size of the claim and may also be influenced by other circumstances. (2) A more consistently impressive ground is promotion of the public policy favoring the compromise and settlement of disputes. McCormick §§ 76, 251. While the rule is ordinarily phrased in terms of offers of compromise, it is apparent that a similar attitude must be taken with respect to completed compromises when offered against a party thereto. This latter situation will not, of course, ordinarily occur except when a party to the present litigation has compromised with a third person.

The same policy underlies the provision of Rule 68 of the Federal Rules of Civil Procedure that evidence of an unaccepted offer of judgment is not admissible except in a proceeding to determine costs.

The practical value of the common law rule has been greatly diminished by its inapplicability to admissions of fact, even though made in the course of compromise negotiations, unless hypothetical, stated to be "without prejudice," or so connected with the offer as to be inseparable from it. McCormick § 251, pp. 540-41. An inevitable effect is to inhibit freedom of communication with respect to compromise, even among lawyers. Another effect is the generation of controversy over whether a given statement falls within or without the protected area. These considerations account for the expansion of the rule herewith to include evidence of conduct or statements made in compromise negotiations, as well as the offer or completed compromise itself. For similar provisions see California Evidence Code §§ 1152, 1154.

The policy considerations which underlie the rule do not come into play when the effort is to induce a creditor to settle an admittedly due amount for a lesser sum. McCormick § 251, p. 540. Hence the rule requires that the claim be disputed as to either validity or amount.

The final sentence of the rule serves to point out some limitations upon its applicability. Since the rule excludes only when the purpose is proving the validity or invalidity of the claim or its amount, an offer for another purpose is not within the rule. The illustrative situations mentioned in the rule are supported by the authorities. As to proving bias or prejudice of a witness, see Annot., 161 A.L.R. 395, contra, Fenberg v. Rosenthal, 348 Ill. App. 510, 109 N.E.2d 402 (1952), and negativing a contention of lack of due diligence in presenting a claim, 4 Wigmore § 1061. An effort to "buy off" the prosecution or a prosecuting witness in a criminal case is not within the policy of the rule of exclusion. McCormick § 251, p. 542.

For other rules of similar import, see Uniform Rules 52 and 53; California Evidence Code §§ 1152, 1154; Kansas Code of Civil Procedure §§ 60-452, 60-453; New Jersey Evidence Rules 52 and 53.

Report of the House Committee on the Judiciary

Under existing federal law evidence of conduct and statements made in compromise negotiations is admissible in subsequent litigation between the parties. The second sentence of Rule 408 as submitted by the Supreme Court proposed to reverse that doctrine in the interest of further promoting non-judicial settlement of disputes. Some agencies of government expressed the view that the Court formulation was likely to impede rather than assist efforts to achieve settlement of disputes. For one thing, it is not always easy to tell when compromise negotiations begin, and informal dealings end. Also, parties dealing with government agencies would be reluctant to furnish factual information at preliminary meetings; they would wait until "compromise negotiations" began and thus hopefully effect an immunity for themselves with respect to the evidence supplied. In light of these considerations, the Committee recast the Rule so that admissions of liability or opinions given during compromise negotiations continue inadmissible, but evidence of unqualified factual assertions is admissible. The latter aspect of the Rule is drafted, however, so as to preserve other possible objections to the introduction of such evidence. The Committee intends no modification of current law whereby a party may protect himself from future use of his statements by couching them in hypothetical conditional form.

Report of the Senate Committee on the Judiciary

This rule as reported makes evidence of settlement or attempted settlement of a disputed claim inadmissible when offered as an admission of liability or the amount of liability. The purpose of this rule is to encourage settlements which would be discouraged if such evidence were admissible.

Under present law, in most jurisdictions, statements of fact made during settlement negotiations, however, are excepted from this ban and are admissible. The only escape from admissibility of statements of fact made in a settlement negotiation is if the declarant or his representative expressly states that the statement is hypothetical in nature or is made without prejudice. Rule 408 as submitted by the Court reversed the traditional rule. It would have brought statements of fact within the ban and made them, as well as an offer of settlement, inadmissible.

The House amended the rule and would continue to make evidence of facts disclosed during compromise negotiations admissible. It thus reverted to the traditional rule. The House committee report states that the committee intends to preserve current law under which a party may protect himself by couching his statements in hypothetical form. The real impact of this amendment, however, is to deprive the rule of much of its salutary effect. The exception for factual admissions was believed by the Advisory Committee to hamper free communication between parties and thus to constitute an unjustifiable restraint upon efforts to negotiate settlements — the encouragement of which is the purpose of the rule. Further, by protecting hypothetically phrased statements, it constituted a preference for the sophisticated, and a trap for the unwary.

Three States which had adopted rules of evidence patterned after the proposed rules prescribed by the Supreme Court opted for versions of rule 408 identical with the Supreme Court draft with respect to the inadmissibility of conduct or statements made in compromise negotiations.

For these reasons, the committee has deleted the House amendment and restored the rule to the version submitted by the Supreme Court with one additional amendment. This amendment adds a sentence to insure that evidence, such as documents, is not rendered inadmissible merely because it is presented in the course of compromise negotiations if the evidence is otherwise discoverable. A party should not be able to immunize from admissibility documents otherwise discoverable merely by offering them in a compromise negotiation.

[Footnotes deleted.]

Report of the House and Senate Conferees

The House bill provides that evidence of admissions of liability or opinions given during compromise negotiations is not admissible, but that evidence of facts disclosed during compromise negotiations is not inadmissible by virtue of having been first disclosed in the compromise negotiations. The Senate amendment provides that evidence of conduct or statements made in compromise negotiations is not admissible. The Senate amendment also provides that the rule does not require the exclusion of any evidence otherwise discoverable merely because it is presented in the course of compromise negotiations.

The House bill was drafted to meet the objection of executive agencies that under the rule as proposed by the Supreme Court, a party could present a fact during compromise negotiations and thereby prevent an opposing party from offering evidence of that fact at trial even though such evidence was obtained from independent sources. The Senate amendment expressly precludes this result.

The Conference adopts the Senate amendment.

Citations to Hearings and Debates

Letter from William A. Carey to Hon. William Hungate, August 7, 1973, in Supp. to Hearings on Proposed Rules of Evidence Before the Subcomm. on Criminal Justice of the House Comm. on the Judiciary, 93rd Cong., 1st Sess., at 311-12 (1973).

Testimony of Paul F. Rothstein, June 5, 1974, Hearings on H.R. 5463 (Federal Rules of Evidence) Before the Senate Comm. on the Judiciary, 93rd Cong., 2d Sess., at 269-70 (1974).

Letter from Hon. Roszel C. Thomsen to Hon. James O. Eastland, May 22, 1974, and accompanying material, in Hearings on H.R. 5463 (Federal Rules of Evidence) Before the Senate Comm. on the Judiciary, 93rd Cong., 2d Sess., at 53-54, 58-60 (1974).

Testimony of Edward W. Cleary, June 4, 1974, Hearings on H.R. 5463 (Federal Rules of Evidence) Before the Senate Comm. on the Judiciary, 93rd Cong., 2d Sess., at 49 (1974).

RULE 409

A. OFFICIAL TEXT

Rule 409. Payment of Medical and Similar Expenses

Evidence of furnishing or offering or promising to pay medical, hospital, or similar expenses occasioned by an injury is not admissible to prove liability for the injury.

B. EDITORIAL EXPLANATORY COMMENT

Distinguished from Rule 408

This Rule provides that evidence that a party promised to pay medical, hospital, or similar expenses occasioned by an injury is not admissible to prove that party's liability for the injury. This is much like the exclusion of offers to compromise. The reason usually provided for this Rule is that it encourages people to make humane gestures and provides an incentive for the provision of necessary medical treatment. It is important to note that unlike Rule 408, this Rule does not exclude opinions or admissions of liability when made in connection with an offer to pay hospital or other expenses covered by this Rule. The Advisory Committee and the Congress apparently felt that exclusion of such statements was not necessary, because these statements need not be made in connection with the kind of offer or action covered by this Rule. They are not necessary in the same way that factual statements are necessary for the negotiations covered by Rule 408.

It would seem, however, that if offers of payment covered by this Rule are made as part of a settlement offer, Rule 408 should govern, and statements made in connection with the offers should be excluded. Also, statements that are "a part of the act" covered by the Rule may be protected, according to the second paragraph of the Advisory Committee's Note. In deciding what is part of an act, Courts may have to fall back on cases involving offers to compromise that protected, prior to enactment of Rule 408, statements inextricably bound up with settlement offers.

Unlike Rule 408, Rule 409 is not limited to offers or promises related to a disputed claim. Any offer, promise, or actual payment is inadmissible whether or not a dispute over obligation to pay had arisen at the time of the humane gesture.

Statements of remorse

It should be noted that neither Rule 408 nor Rule 409 specifically excludes statements of remorse made by someone who is involved in an accident. For example, testimony that one driver in an automobile accident states to another injured driver, "I am terribly sorry that you are injured," is not barred by any specific Rule. It is not an offer of compromise; nor is it an offer to pay medical expenses. However, in most jurisdictions, such a statement is deemed to be of very low relevance and is excluded as the kind of statement that a good Samaritan would make and one for which no one should be penalized. We would urge that the same policies that underlie Rule 409 would support exclusion of such a statement on the ground that, although it might be slightly probative of consciousness of fault, the statement's probative value is substantially outweighed by the unfairness of using such evidence against a citizen who expresses the kind of concern that a society expects of its best citizens. We recognize that Rule 409 allows into evidence statements made in connection with payment of or offers to pay medical expenses. But we view the simple statement of remorse as having close to no probative value. We recognize also that in urging this use of Rule 403, we may stretch that Rule slightly. Some may be willing to call this unfair prejudice and be satisfied with that description. The difficulty is that part of the unfairness lies in the fact that many Courts have wanted to encourage kind or humane statements, and to them it seems unfair to use such evidence against a party who has responded in a generous or caring way. *Cf.* Rule 407. Arguably, such evidence is probative enough to be admitted, however. There is a good argument that the statement is not substantially more prejudicial than probative. Our position is that it is of such little probative value that the danger that the jury could misuse it justifies exclusion. But we recognize that our argument reflects a strong feeling of unfairness that has to do more with wanting to encourage expressions of sympathy and compassion than with concern about demonstrable prejudicial effect or confusion. This may well be a type of unfairness that Rule 403 does not appear to recognize on its face. Rule 102 affords us some comfort, however. Its policies ought to be promoted by the approach we recommend. We think that it is highly unlikely that false statements of remorse will be made. And even if they are, such false statements may do as much good for the injured person as true statements and may help to reduce tension following accidents and other disruptive events. We would not recommend blind adherence to precedent, but the policy of exclusion is so well founded that it seems like a waste of scarce judicial resources to persistently relitigate a well-founded rule.

Other purposes

Like Rules 408 and 407, the Rule 409 exclusionary principle only applies if the evidence is offered for a specified purpose. If it is offered to prove anything other than liability, the Rule is inapplicable and the opponent of the evidence is left to argue for exclusion under Rule 403. For example, if the defendant in a personal injury case offers its payment of the plaintiff's medical expenses as proof of mitigation of damages, the proof will not be excluded under Rule 409.

C. ANNOTATED CASES

Savoie v. Otto Candies, Inc., 692 F.2d 363 (5th Cir. 1982): In a Jones Act case the crucial issue was whether the plaintiff was a seaman on the date of his injury. To show that the defendant regarded the plaintiff as a seaman, the plaintiff introduced letters sent by the defendant's attorney and insurance carrier revealing that the defendant had paid the plaintiff maintenance after the injury. Affirming a judgment for plaintiff, the Court found that this evidence did not violate Rule 409, since the "maintenance" payments were not shown to be expense payments of any kind and the evidence was not offered to show liability for the injury. The evidence might not have been admissible were the only issue entitlement to medical or hospital or similar expenses. Although careful instructions on the proper use of the evidence would have been desirable, none were requested. The Court declined to find that the evidence should have been excluded under Rule 403.

Williams v. Missouri Pac. R.R., 11 F.3d 132 (10th Cir. 1993): Remanding an FELA case, the Court noted that the jury should be advised that past medical expenses had been paid. Although evidence of paying past medical expenses is inadmissible to prove liability, there would be no question of liability on the retrial of damages issues only.

D. LEGISLATIVE HISTORY

Advisory Committee's Note

The considerations underlying this rule parallel those underlying Rules 407 and 408, which deal respectively with subsequent remedial measures and offers of compromise. As stated in Annot., 20 A.L.R.2d 291, 293:

> [G]enerally, evidence of payment of medical, hospital, or similar expenses of an injured party by the opposing party, is not admissible, the reason often given being that such payment or offer is usually made from humane impulses and not from an admission of liability, and that to hold otherwise would tend to discourage assistance to the injured person.

Contrary to Rule 408, dealing with offers of compromise, the present rule does not extend to conduct or statements not a part of the act of furnishing or offering or promising to pay. This difference in treatment arises from fundamental differences in nature. Communication is essential if compromises are to be effected, and consequently broad protection of statements is needed. This is not so in cases of payments or offers or promises to pay medical expenses, where factual statements may be expected to be incidental in nature.

For rules on the same subject, but phrased in terms of "humanitarian motives," see Uniform Rule 52; California Evidence Code § 1152; Kansas Code of Civil Procedure § 60-452; New Jersey Evidence Rule 52.

RULE 410

A. OFFICIAL TEXT

Rule 410. Inadmissibility of Plea Discussions, and Related Statements

Except as otherwise provided in this rule, evidence of the following is not, in any civil or criminal proceeding, admissible against the defendant who made the plea or was a participant in the plea discussions:

(1) a plea of guilty which was later withdrawn;

(2) a plea of *nolo contendere;*

(3) any statement made in the course of any proceedings under Rule 11 of the Federal Rules of Criminal Procedure or comparable state procedure regarding either of the foregoing pleas; or

(4) any statement made in the course of plea discussions with an attorney for the prosecuting authority which do not result in a plea of guilty or which result in a plea of guilty later withdrawn.

However, such a statement is admissible (i) in any proceeding wherein another statement made in the course of the same plea or plea discussions has been introduced and the statement ought in fairness to be considered contemporaneously with it, or (ii) in a criminal proceeding for perjury or false statement if the statement was made by the defendant under oath, on the record and in the presence of counsel.

B. EDITORIAL EXPLANATORY COMMENT

Amendments to the rule

Rule 410 did not take effect with the other Rules on July 1, 1975. Paragraph two provided that it should take effect thirty days later and that it would be superseded by any amendment to the Federal Rules of Criminal Procedure inconsistent with the Evidence Rule. The Rule as originally adopted by Congress read as follows:

> Except as otherwise provided by Act of Congress, evidence of a plea of guilty, later withdrawn, or a plea of *nolo contendere,* or of an offer to plead guilty or *nolo contendere* to the crime charged or any other crime, or of statements made in connection with any of the foregoing pleas or offers, is not admissible in any civil or criminal action, case, or proceeding against the person who made the plea or offer. This rule shall not apply to the introduction of voluntary and reliable statements made in court on the record in connection with any of the foregoing

pleas or offers where offered for impeachment purposes or in a subsequent prosecution of the declarant for perjury or false statement.

This rule shall not take effect until August 1, 1975, and shall be superseded by any amendment to the Federal Rules of Criminal Procedure which is inconsistent with this rule, and which takes effect after the date of the enactment of the Act establishing these Federal Rules of Evidence.

Public Law 94-64, 89 Stat. 372, enacted on July 31, 1975, did supersede Rule 410 with Rule 11(e)(6) of the Rules of Criminal Procedure as follows:

INADMISSIBILITY OF PLEAS, OFFERS OF PLEAS AND RELATED STATEMENTS. — Except as otherwise provided in this paragraph, evidence of a plea of guilty, later withdrawn, or a plea of *nolo contendere,* or of an offer to plead guilty or *nolo contendere* to the crime charged or any other crime, or of statements made in connection with, and relevant to, any of the foregoing pleas or offers, is not admissible in any civil or criminal proceeding against the person who made the plea or offer. However, evidence of a statement made in connection with, and relevant to, a plea of guilty or *nolo contendere* to the crime charged or any other crime is admissible in a criminal proceeding for perjury or false statement if the statement was made by the defendant under oath, on the record, and in the presence of counsel.

Congress thereafter, on December 12, 1975, in P.L. 94-149, copied the above Rule 11(e)(6) of the Rules of Criminal Procedure and enacted a new Evidence Rule 410 that was virtually identical to the criminal procedure rule.

The major difference between old Evidence Rule 410 and the first amended Evidence Rule 410 was found in the last sentence of the Rule. The first amended Rule permitted statements made in connection with pleas or offers to plead to be used only in a criminal proceeding for perjury or false statement if the statement was made by the defendant under oath, on the record, and in the presence of counsel. Original Rule 410 would have permitted statements made in court on the record that were "voluntary and reliable" to be used whether or not counsel was present, and to be used for impeachment purposes in a subsequent prosecution as well as to support perjury-type charges.

On December 1, 1980, yet another amended Rule 410 went into effect. It is the one set forth in the Official Text, *supra.*

Scope of the rule

Like its predecessors, the amended Rule covers withdrawn pleas, *nolo contendere* pleas, statements made in connection with withdrawn guilty pleas or *nolo* pleas, and statements made in connection with the pleas covered by the Rule. The Rule does not cover guilty pleas that have been accepted and not subsequently withdrawn; nor does it cover statements made in the course of reaching such agreements.[1] If the defendant

---

1. See, e.g., United States v. Paden, 908 F.2d 1229 (5th Cir. 1990) (Rule 410 does "not prohibit statements made during plea negotiations that lead to" an unrevoked guilty plea).

accepts an offer and pleads guilty, this fact is admissible as an admission, assuming that it passes the threshold of Rule 403.[2]

Although Rule 410 has always implicitly covered plea bargaining that does not lead to an accepted plea, the amended Rule is explicit as to such bargaining. The amended Rule also makes clear that the bargaining that is covered is that done with an attorney for the government, thus generally excluding statements to police officers from the reach of the Rule.[3] It does not matter that the police officer promises to recommend leniency, or suggests that charges may be dropped. While the police officer's statements concerning cooperation may have some bearing on the voluntariness of the confession, they have nothing to do with Rule 410, since the defendant cannot reasonably view such statements as part of an authorized plea offer.[4] On the other hand, if law enforcement officials have actually been delegated the authority to engage in plea bargaining, then Rule 410 should apply to the same extent as if the defendant were communicating directly with the prosecutor.[5]

Rule 410 provides for only two limited exceptions. First, a statement that would otherwise be excluded can be admitted if other evidence of pleas or plea discussions is introduced and the statement should in fairness be considered together with the evidence that has been introduced. This is a principle similar to that found in Rule 106. Second, a statement made under oath, on the record, and in the presence of counsel may be introduced in a subsequent perjury-type prosecution.

Seven additional points can be made concerning the scope of the Rule:

(1) The Rule now clearly covers both extrajudicial and in-court statements by defendants and their counsel.

(2) The Rule focuses only on statements by a defendant, but Courts have been reluctant to permit statements and offers by prosecutors to be used as admissions when pleas are withdrawn or never accepted. Courts have found that the policy of the Rule is to encourage the free-flow of communication and compromise from both sides.[6] Also, a plea offer from the government may signal a desire for an efficient resolution rather

---

2. See United States v. Benson, 640 F.2d 136 (8th Cir. 1981) (Rule 408 does not apply where the guilty plea is accepted and not withdrawn). Compare Rule 801(d)(2)(A) with Rule 803(22).

3. See, e.g., United States v. Greene, 995 F.2d 793 (8th Cir. 1993) (statements made to DEA agent were not covered by Rule 410, where agent had no express or apparent authority to plea bargain with the defendant).

4. See, e.g., United States v. Posey, 611 F.2d 1389 (5th Cir. 1980) (DEA agent's statement that he would bring the defendant's cooperation to the attention of the prosecutor did not trigger the protections of Rule 410, since defendant could not reasonably believe that the agent had the authority to bargain on the prosecutor's behalf). For a discussion of constitutional regulation of involuntary confessions, see S. SALTZBURG & D. CAPRA, AMERICAN CRIMINAL PROCEDURE 492-502 (4th ed. 1992).

5. See, e.g., United States v. Sitton, 968 F.2d 947 (9th Cir. 1992) (stating that conversations between accused and police officers can constitute plea bargaining where the police obtain authority from the government attorney to negotiate; no such showing on the facts of this case); Rachlin v. United States, 723 F.2d 1373 (8th Cir. 1983) (recognizing principle that Rule 410 applies if agents have authority to bargain, but finding it inapplicable to the facts).

6. See, e.g., United States v. Verdoorn, 528 F.2d 103 (8th Cir. 1976) (criminal defendant could not introduce evidence of plea bargaining by the Government to show consciousness of a weak case).

than a recognition of a weak case, and is therefore thought to have minimal probative value.[7]

(3) The Rule does not speak of pleas that are set aside on appeal or on collateral attack. Presumably, such pleas should be treated as "withdrawn" pleas.

(4) The Rule protects not only the person who utters certain words during plea bargaining or an attempt to enter a plea; it also covers anyone else who was a participant in the plea discussions at the time that the relevant statement or offer was made.

(5) The Rule only protects those who are, at the time the evidence is proffered, parties to a criminal or civil case.[8] Nothing in the Rule suggests that when a person is simply a witness he cannot be impeached with evidence of an attempted plea, an offer to plead, or statements made during plea bargaining, unless the impeachment evidence would be offered in the case of a coparticipant in the plea negotiations whom the Rule protects.[9]

(6) Unlike Rule 408, Rule 410 contains no exception for impeachment of party-witnesses. Thus, a statement by a defendant during plea discussions cannot be used to impeach his subsequent inconsistent trial testimony.[10]

(7) The Rule applies not only in an ensuing criminal prosecution, but also in any subsequent civil case in which the defendant is a party. So, for example, if a defendant pleads *nolo contendere* to a charge of vehicular homicide, the plea is not admissible in a subsequent personal injury action against the defendant arising out of the accident.[11]

Perjury exception

The House Judiciary Committee, which drafted the perjury exception, recognized that even this limited exception might discourage defendants from being completely candid and open during plea negotiations and result in deterring plea agreements. However, the Committee believed that, on balance, it is important to protect the integrity of the judicial

---

7. See, e.g., United States v. Delgado, 903 F.2d 1495 (11th Cir. 1990) (plea agreement and statements by prosecutor cannot be offered as admission by the government, since the deal may have been struck for reasons other than the government's belief in the innocence of the accused; relying upon Rule 403). Compare United States v. Biaggi, 909 F.2d 662 (2d Cir. 1990), where the defendant sought to prove his own "consciousness of innocence" by the fact that he rejected a grant of complete immunity and refused to testify because he knew nothing about the charged wrongdoing. The Court noted that a rejection of immunity under these circumstances was far more probative of an innocent state of mind than a rejection of a plea offer made by the government. The Court found it unnecessary to determine whether a plea offer by the government would be excluded under Rule 410.

8. See, e.g., United States v. Sonny Mitchell Center, 934 F.2d 77 (5th Cir. 1991) (under Rule 609, a nonparty witness may be impeached with a felony conviction based on a plea of *nolo contendere*).

9. See United States v. Mathis, 550 F.2d 180 (4th Cir. 1976), *cert. denied*, 429 U.S. 1107 (1977) (Rule 410 does not apply to impeachment of a nonparty witness, because the plea negotiations are not offered "against" the witness in this circumstance).

10. See, e.g., United States v. Acosta-Ballardo, 8 F.3d 1532 (10th Cir. 1993) (impeachment use of defendant's plea negotiations is contrary to the text and the legislative history of Rule 410).

11. See, e.g., Neuner v. Clinkenbeard, 466 F.Supp. 54 (W.D. Okla. 1978) (in diversity suit for wrongful death, defendant's *nolo contendere* plea to charges arising from the accident was not admissible due to Rule 410).

process from willful deceit and untruthfulness. We have our doubts about the wisdom of allowing any use at all of statements once a plea is withdrawn. During the bargaining process defendants do whatever must be done to secure the benefits of the plea, including saying what the Court wants to hear. Once there is a demonstration of a good reason for withdrawal of a plea, there is no reason to hold the defendant, who has abandoned the benefits of the bargain, to statements made during the bargaining process.

Counsel requirement

The counsel requirement for the perjury exception to Rule 410 may be unfortunate. It is difficult to imagine pleas or offers to plead being made in Federal Court today without appointment of counsel, except in one instance, i.e., where the defendant has elected self-representation, an election that is constitutionally protected as long as the defendant is fully informed of his right to counsel and is competent to represent himself. *Faretta v. California,* 422 U.S. 806 (1975). If there is to be a perjury exception to the Rule, then there is no good reason to treat defendants who went pro se during the plea process more favorably in subsequent perjury prosecutions than defendants represented by counsel during the plea process. Perhaps pro se defendants will be treated as having counsel present when they represent themselves and are themselves present in the courtroom.[12]

Relationship to Rule 408

The government and private citizens in some cases may bargain simultaneously with respect to civil and criminal liability. If this happens, is Rule 408 or Rule 410 applicable? Our view is the if part of the bargaining relates to criminal charges, Rule 410 should govern. This ensures that all of the protection provided by Congress will exist in practice, as well as in theory.

Nolo contendere pleas

Another difficult question not explicitly addressed by the Rule is the following: When the Judge is asked to approve a plea of *nolo contendere,* what impact, if any, should Rule 410 have on the decision? If this plea is accepted, it cannot be used in subsequent litigation, nor can any statement made in connection with it. This is not the case, of course, with a guilty plea and related statements, which are admissions and which may be used as such unless the plea is withdrawn.[13]

One of the hardest questions for a Trial Judge is what her proper role is with respect to supervision of the plea bargaining process. When should a Trial Judge intervene by refusing to accept the plea? In the environmental or antitrust area, for example, it is well known that a failure on the part of the government to obtain a plea of guilty or a

---

12. See United States v. Smith, 525 F.2d 1017 (10th Cir. 1975) (stating generally that after *Faretta,* represented defendants and pro se defendants should be treated the same for purposes of Rule 410).

13. Of course, the reason why Rule 410 excludes an accepted *nolo* plea, but not an accepted guilty plea, is that the very point of a *nolo* plea is to have no effect in subsequent litigation. If *nolo* pleas were admissible to prove fault, there would be no such thing as a *nolo* plea.

conviction may make it difficult for civil plaintiffs to win subsequent civil suits. In such cases, the Judge may be especially sensitive to the question of whether to accept a plea of *nolo contendere*.

But what about other cases? Should the Judge take into account any duty on the part of the government to take the initiative in prosecuting cases in order that potential civil litigants may benefit from a government victory? No answer is suggested here, but the point is raised so that the Judge may have an opportunity to ponder it, keeping in mind the difficult separation of powers question that lurks in the background. Whether it is desirable to require extensive factual admissions by the defendant in the context of a guilty or *nolo contendere* plea and what to do with such admissions is a question that is only now getting the attention it warrants.

State proceedings

Another question that may arise is whether statements made by a defendant in the course of negotiating a plea with Federal officials can be used against the defendant in state Courts. If the Federal Rule is to work, presumably the accused must feel confident that nothing said in the course of bargaining will later be used against him. The possibility of a state proceeding in which statements could be used might threaten the proper application of the Rule. Under the Supremacy Clause, Congress could bar state Courts from using statements of an accused covered by the Rule against him. Whether Congress intended this result in Rule 410 is open to question. One way of avoiding the problem is for federal prosecutors and investigators to zealously protect against disclosure of statements made during negotiations. If information is to be shared in a case of joint federal-state investigative procedures, the federal government should seek to ensure that state Courts will not use information falling under Rule 410 that has been shared by the federal government against those whom the Rule is drafted to protect. One must hope that state officials, who should themselves be aware of the importance of plea bargaining in the criminal justice system as it now exists, will never force the issue.

It should be noted that many states have a Rule that is substantively identical to Rule 410, so that the evidence subject to the Rule would be inadmissible even if the plea proceedings occurred in a Federal jurisdiction.[14] The conflict referred to in the preceding paragraph does not arise in these states. Similarly, the language of Federal Rule 410 referring to "comparable state procedure" means that the protections of Rule 410 are applicable to Federal litigation occuring after guilty plea negotiations in state proceedings.

Relationship to other rules

The different treatment of *nolo contendere* pleas, which are made inadmissible against the pleader by this Rule, and of convictions upon *nolo* pleas, which may be admitted under Rule 609, is discussed in the Editorial Explanatory Comment accompanying Rule 609.

---

14. See G. JOSEPH & S. SALTZBURG, EVIDENCE IN AMERICA § 20.1.

Waiver of Rule 410 protections

In *United States v. Mezzanatto,* 998 F.2d 1452 (9th Cir. 1993), the Court held that a criminal defendant could not waive the protections of Rule 410. The Supreme Court has granted certiorari in *Mezzanatto,* 114 S. Ct. 1147 (1994). The Supplement to this Manual will treat the Supreme Court's decision when it is handed down. But we think it might be helpful at this point to discuss the Ninth Circuit opinion and the possible solutions to the issues presented.

Mezzanatto was charged with a drug offense and, at his request, the government held a plea bargaining meeting with him. Before the discussions began, Mezzanatto was warned that any statements he made would be used to impeach him at a subsequent trial on the drug charges, should the case ever go that far. Mezzanatto agreed to this arrangement, and discussions began, but were fruitless. At trial, Mezzanatto testified inconsistently with statements he made during plea negotiations. Over Mezzanatto's objection, he was impeached with those prior statements, and was subsequently convicted. The Court of Appeals found that the use of the plea negotiation statements to impeach Mezzanatto was reversible error.

The Ninth Circuit began its analysis by noting the breadth of Rule 410 and that the text of the Rule provides for only two limited exceptions — where necessary for completeness and where relevant in a later prosecution for perjury. The Court also discussed the legislative history of Rule 410, which revealed that ''Congress unmistakably did not want statements made during plea negotiations to be used to impeach defendants.''

Of course, the legislative history of the Rule may well establish, as the Courts assert, that there is no *general* impeachment exception to Rule 410. But that does not address the question in *Mezzanatto,* which is whether the defendant should be allowed to *waive* the protections of Rule 410. So the Court's reliance on legislative history is inapposite to the question before it.

The *Mezzanatto* Court next focussed on the public policy supporting plea bargaining, which is the foundation for Rule 410. As the Court recognized, ''unrestrained candor promotes effective plea bargaining.'' The Court noted a strong interest in effective plea bargaining for at least two reasons: (1) plea bargaining alleviates burdens on the criminal justice system; and (2) bargaining with lower level criminals may be necessary to obtain information with which to prosecute higher level criminals. Relying on the strong policy basis behind effective plea bargaining in general, and Rule 410 in particular, the *Mezzanatto* Court held that waiver could not be permitted, because the possibility of waiver ''would have a chilling effect on the entire plea bargaining process.''

The *Mezzanatto* Court recognized the principle that most rights can be waived, including the fundamental constitutional rights to be free from self-incrimination and the right to counsel. But the Court was unpersuaded that the same principles should apply with respect to Rule 410. It analyzed this point as follows:

> To equate the waiver of these rules with that of an asserted constitutional protection is a false equality. Judicially created waivers of the latter are the result of an inescapable feature of courts interpreting the Constitution by defining the

right being asserted. To write in a waiver in a waiverless rule promulgated by the Supreme Court and Congress, on the other hand, is not an inescapable duty. It more resembles unwelcome advice.

The Court's attempt to distinguish constitutional waiver doctrine is, in our view, unpersuasive. The question is not whether to "write in a waiver in a waiverless rule." The question is whether Rule 410 is indeed a waiverless rule. Neither the language of the Rule nor its legislative history provides a definitive answer. So the Court of Appeals engaged in a question-begging analysis in rejecting the government's argument that since the defendant can waive other constitutional and statutory rights, he should be allowed to waive the protections of Rule 410 as well.

A final argument from the Court in *Mezzanatto* is that if waiver were permitted, the government could extract a heavy cost from a defendant in a weak bargaining position. For example, the government extracted the waiver from Mezzanatto not as part of a plea bargain, but as the price for entering into plea negotiations with the government. The Court concluded that "[w]ith such a high entry cost, defense attorneys will be deterred from seeking plea bargains, and this will frustrate Congressional policy."

This "high entry cost" argument has a superficial appeal, but it ignores the reality that a prosecutor may be imposing a high entry cost because she has no strong desire to entire into plea negotiations with a particular person — or at least she would not find it worthwhile to do so without the concession of a waiver of the protections of Rule 410. This would appear to be the case in *Mezzanatto,* where it was Mezzanatto who approached the prosecutor; the prosecutor only acceded to negotiations upon a condition of waiver of Rule 410 protection; and then no agreement was ever reached. The prosecutor was undoubtedly not interested in spending the time on plea negotiations with Mezzanatto, if the result would be to lead the government to believe that certain issues were not in dispute, and then at trial to discover that Mezzanatto changed his story. Such a risk was apparently not worth it to the prosecutor; the risk may have been worth it in other circumstances with other suspects, perhaps with more important information, but not with Mezzanatto.

Where the prosecutor has no strong desire, for whatever reason, to plea bargain with a particular person, it may well be that such a person *needs* an extra bargaining chip for discussions to even begin. That bargaining chip in *Mezzanatto* was the waiver of Rule 410 protection. Consequently, the majority in *Mezzanatto* has reached an anomalous result: In the guise of protecting effective plea bargaining, the Court has taken away a bargaining chip that may be necessary in order for plea negotiations even to take place.

The *Mezzanatto* Court's "high entry cost" argument might be based on a concern that a prosecutor who is allowed to get a Rule 410 waiver will always invoke that opportunity, to the detriment of defendants. But we think that this is not a realistic concern. A prosecutor who is truly interested in information or a plea is unlikely to insist on waiver from the suspect if that would impair the negotiations. We believe that the *Mezzanatto* Court has unjustifiably intruded into the market forces that are at work in plea negotiations. There is no need to regulate the "buyer" and protect the "seller" in this instance.

The *Mezzanatto* Court assumes that Congress, by specifically eliminating impeachment as one of the permissible uses of Rule 410 statements, intended to provide a virtually absolute protection for a defendant who wanted to test the plea bargaining waters, and that a prosecutor who insists on waiver as a condition of bargaining is putting a defendant in a position that Congress forbade. This argument admittedly recognizes the power that the prosecutor has to move to dismiss charges or to decline to bring certain charges, a power that has increased in importance with the adoption by Congress of mandatory minimum sentences and with guideline sentencing. But if the prosecutor would not otherwise negotiate without an impeachment concession, the result in *Mezzanatto* does nothing to help defendants. No construction of Rule 410 can make a prosecutor bargain with a suspect. The "opportunity to negotiate" ostensibly provided by a "no waiver of impeachment" rule is in reality less of an opportunity than if the suspect had the power to waive the protection of Rule 410.

Judge Wallace wrote a strong dissent in *Mezzanatto*. He thought it anomalous that Mezzanatto could have knowingly and voluntarily waived his fundamental constitutional rights, and yet, in the majority's view, could not waive the less important protections of Rule 410. He also stated that the majority, "by implicitly vaulting plea agreements to the apex of goals sought to be achieved within the criminal justice system, has exaggerated greatly the potential harm presented by waivers."

Judge Wallace argued that there is nothing wrong in allowing the defendant to freely give up "the right to lie." He also took issue with the majority's contention that waivers will have a chilling effect on plea bargains. He queried: "Given the mutual benefits achieved through plea bargaining, should we expect the government continually to require waivers if such requirements significantly reduce the number of plea agreements reached?"

C. ANNOTATED CASES

Administrative proceeding

Myers v. Secretary of Health & Human Servs., 893 F.2d 840 (6th Cir. 1990): In reviewing an administrative determination excluding the appellants from participation in the Medicare program, the Court held that the Rule did not bar evidence that they had previously been convicted on a plea of *nolo contendere* of Medicare fraud, because it does not apply to use of a conviction, nor does it prohibit use of a *nolo* plea in an administrative proceeding.

Breach of agreement by defendant

United States v. Stirling, 571 F.2d 708 (2d Cir.), *cert. denied*, 439 U.S. 824 (1978): One defendant in a securities law case had agreed to a plea bargain in which he promised to "at all times give complete, truthful and accurate information and testimony," and which provided that if he breached, he could be prosecuted and any information he provided could be used against him. The defendant testified before a grand jury pursuant to the agreement, but subsequently withdrew from the bargain and went to trial, where his grand jury testimony was admitted against him. The Court concluded that, although a literal reading of the Rule (and its counterpart, Federal Rule of Criminal Procedure 11(e)(6)) might bar use of the grand jury testimony, the policy of free and open negotiations upon which the Rule is premised did not require exclusion of statements made by a person who agreed to the use of the statements against him in the event of a breach of the plea bargain agreement. We think that the Court reached the appropriate result. The agreement between the government and the appellant could have been enforced by both sides; it made clear that the plea negotiations were over and that subsequent testimony was not a part of the already completed bargaining or relevant to future bargaining. After an enforceable agreement is made, no statement contemplated by the agreement should be deemed inadmissible under Rule 410. The Rule permits persons facing possible criminal prosecutions to bargain freely with the government without fear that their statements will be used against them, but once an enforceable bargain is made, the Rule no longer applies. Statements like those made in the instant case are not made ''in connection with'' an offer to plead guilty; they are not ''relevant to'' such an offer; nor are they are they a ''withdrawn plea,'' since no plea was entered.

Collateral estoppel in civil cases

Walker v. Schaeffer, 854 F.2d 138 (6th Cir. 1988): The Court held that Rule 410 did not bar a Court from holding that a plea of *nolo contendere* estopped a defendant from bringing a civil suit based upon a claim that the officers who arrested him lacked probable cause.

"Fruits" of plea discussions

United States v. Ware, 890 F.2d 1008 (8th Cir. 1989): Affirming drug offense convictions, the Court noted that proof that a defendant identified a potential witness to the government during plea discussions is not within the bar of Rule 410.

Impeachment

United States v. Wood, 879 F.2d 927 (D.C. Cir. 1989): In a prosecution of a drug trafficking conspiracy, the Court held that statements made during plea bargaining negotiations were inadmissible to impeach a defendant who testified. The Court vacated the defendant's conspiracy conviction, on which a concurrent sentence was imposed, without deciding whether she waived her objection by signing a letter from the prosecutor warning her that statements in the bargaining process could be used at trial to cross-examine her.

United States v. Lawson, 683 F.2d 688 (2d Cir. 1982): Reversing a bank robbery conviction, the Court held that statements falling within Rule 410 could not be used for impeachment purposes. It commented that the legislative history on the point was ''unusually clear.'' One Judge dissented on the ground that the statements had not been made in plea discussions.

United States v. Acosta-Ballardo, 8 F.3d 1532 (10th Cir. 1993): The defendant's conviction for possessing cocaine with intent to distribute was reversed because statements he made during plea discussions were introduced to impeach his inconsistent testimony at trial. Impeachment use of plea negotiations is contrary to the text and the legislative history of the Rule.

Joint defendants

United States v. Serna, 799 F.2d 842 (2d Cir. 1986), *cert. denied,* 107 S. Ct. 1887 (1987): The Court held that a codefendant's statement that the defendant was the wrong man was inadmissible in a joint trial of the two defendants for drug smuggling, since it was made in the course of plea negotiations. No limiting instruction would have been adequate to protect the codefendant. The Court also held that it was not required that the government attorney be present when a statement is made as long as the attorney is participating in the plea bargaining.

Nolo contendere pleas

Lipsky v. Commonwealth United Corp., 551 F.2d 887 (2d Cir. 1976): In an executor's action to rescind an agreement for breach of contract, the Court affirmed striking references in the complaint to a consent judgment between the SEC and the defendant, on the ground they were the equivalent of a reference to a *nolo contendere* plea. "Since it is clear that the ... consent judgment, itself, can have no possible bearing on the [instant] action, the SEC complaint which preceded the consent judgment is also immaterial...." In *Crouse-Hinds Co. v. Internorth, Inc.,* 518 F. Supp. 413 (N.D.N.Y. 1980), an action by a corporation to block a takeover as being anticompetitive, the Court decided to admit evidence that the defendant entered *nolo* pleas to antitrust charges more than twenty years earlier and that it agreed to a consent judgment in another antitrust action ten years earlier. According to the Court, the plaintiff's need for evidence of anticompetitive tendencies outweighed the social policy benefits of rules like Rule 410. In our view, Rules like Rules 410 and 408 encourage *nolo* pleas, consent judgments, and other settlements by assuring that, once accepted, they will not be used as if they were confessions. Certainly, there would be no prohibition on discovery by a plaintiff concerning earlier anticompetitive practices. This should provide useful evidence without threatening the policy of encouraging settlement.

Plea bargaining distinguished from volunteered offers of cooperation and other discussions

United States v. Penta, 898 F.2d 815 (1st Cir.), *cert. denied,* 111 S. Ct. 246 (1990): The Court held that Federal Rule of Criminal Procedure 11(e)(6) (the counterpart to Rule 410) did not exclude the defendant's statements to a government attorney and an investigator, with whom he had a number of conferences in which the prosecutor was openly trying to build a case against his associates and (in the prosecutor's unexpressed belief) the defendant was trying to avoid prosecution or a long jail sentence, because, as the defendant made no such request and the attorney made no offer, there were no plea discussions within the meaning of the Rule.

United States v. Biaggi, 909 F.2d 662 (2d Cir. 1990), *cert. denied,* 111 S. Ct. 1102 (1991): Reversing a defendant's convictions in a political corruption case on the ground that evidence was erroneously excluded that he "rejected" immunity, by denying knowledge of others' wrongdoing at a time when admitting such knowledge would have secured him immunity, the Court noted that the evidence was far more evidence of an innocent state of mind than it was a rejected plea bargain, the admissibility of which it was unnecessary to decide. In *United States v. Cunningham,* 723 F.2d 217 (2d Cir. 1983), *cert. denied,* 104 S. Ct. 2154 (1984), the Court upheld a conviction for making false statements to the IRS and members of the United States Attorney's office. It found that statements made by the defendant after he stipulated that anything he said could be used against him were not part of a plea agreement, but were an effort to convince the government that he was not guilty of a crime and should not be prosecuted.

United States v. Conaway, 11 F.3d 40 (5th Cir. 1994): The Court held that the defendant had not been engaged in plea negotiations when he turned over records to a grand jury investigating currency transaction structuring, so the records were not thereby made inadmissible. The prosecutor had given the defendant an opportunity to corroborate grand jury testimony that he had not evaded taxes by furnishing the records and had several times reminded him that they could be used against him. In *United States v. Geders,* 585 F.2d 1303 (5th Cir. 1978) (en banc), *vacating* 566 F.2d 1227 (5th Cir.), *cert. denied,* 441 U.S. 922 (1979), the Court affirmed convictions on drug charges, holding there was no error in admitting a defendant's statements made during a meeting with government agents. Because the government had stated at the outset that the defendant's case could not be discussed, the *en banc* Court, with three Judges dissenting, concluded that the record did not show that the defendant had a reasonable subjective expectation that plea negotiations were in progress when he made his statements. Although *Geders* was decided before the Rule was amended to apply only to plea negotiations with a government attorney, the Court's focus on the defendant's reasonable subjective expectations should still be applicable when there is ambiguity about whether discussions with a government attorney were plea negotiations.

United States v. Guerrero, 847 F.2d 1363 (9th Cir. 1988): The Court concluded that statements made by a defendant to the FBI and to a federal prosecutor were admissible, since they were made when the defendant admitted paying kickbacks and offered to cooperate in exchange for the prosecutor's promise to consider such cooperation in the handling of any future cases. The Court reasoned that "[a] statement was made in the course of plea discussions if: (1) the suspect exhibited an actual subjective expectation that he was negotiating a plea at the time of the discussion; and (2) the suspect's expectation was reasonable given the totality of the circumstances." It found that neither part of the test was met in this case.

Plea bargaining offered against government

United States v. Verdoorn, 528 F.2d 103 (8th Cir. 1976): Affirming convictions for conspiracy and various substantive offenses arising out of a theft of an interstate shipment of beef, the Court cited Rule 408 and and its counterpart, Federal Rule of Criminal Procedure 11(e)(6), for the proposition that criminal defendants cannot introduce evidence of plea bargaining by the government to show consciousness of a weak case. The case also serves as a reminder that a witness who pleads guilty and cooperates with the government can be impeached with evidence of the plea because the evidence tends to show bias or interest.

Relationship to Rule 404(b)

United States v. Wyatt, 762 F.2d 908 (11th Cir. 1985), *cert. denied,* 475 U.S. 1047 (1986): The Court affirmed a defendant's drug convictions, holding that evidence of other crimes was properly admitted under Rule 404(b). Although the defendant had pleaded *nolo contendere* to the other crimes, Rule 410 bars only use of the plea, but not other evidence of the underlying acts.

Sentencing proceedings

United States v. Paden, 908 F.2d 1229 (5th Cir. 1990), *cert. denied,* 111 S. Ct. 710 (1991): The Court held that statements made in plea negotiations that were unilaterally broken off by the government eight months before the defendant's ultimate guilty plea were admissible in sentencing on that plea, as the Rule looks only to the end result of the process, which is often not smooth and unbroken.

United States v. Ruminer, 786 F.2d 381 (10th Cir. 1986): Upholding drug convictions, the Court held that the Trial Judge properly considered in sentencing the fact that defendants supplied false leads to the government during plea discussions. The Court, citing Rule 1101(d)(3), observed that Rule 410 did not override the general principle that a defendant's conduct could be considered in sentencing.

Special circumstances

United States v. Roberts, 618 F.2d 530 (9th Cir. 1980): The Court reversed a conviction for attempted bombing because the prosecutor emphasized, to the point of improperly vouching for the witness, that a government witness made a deal and promised to testify truthfully.

Statements to investigators

United States v. Aponte-Suarez, 905 F.2d 483 (1st Cir.), *cert. denied,* 111 S. Ct. 531, 975 (1990): In affirming drug-importation conspiracy convictions, the Court held that statements to government investigators were properly admitted, as they were not made in the course of plea negotiations nor were they made to an attorney.

United States v. Sebetich, 776 F.2d 412 (3d Cir. 1985), *cert. denied,* 108 S. Ct. 725 (1988): The Court found that statements made by a defendant to an FBI agent could not have been within the Rule, since there was no intention of bargaining during the meeting and the defendant could not have believed the agent had any authority to bargain.

United States v. Swidan, 689 F. Supp. 726 (E.D. Mich. 1988): The Judge held that two conversations in which the defendant and a DEA agent participated were inadmissible under Rule 410. Although the agent had disclaimed any authority to plea bargain, the Judge found that the agent had promised to relay the defendant's offer to the prosecutor and that this encouraged the defendant to make his offer. Thus, the defendant had a subjective belief that he was negotiating a plea, which the Judge concluded was reasonable.

United States v. Kummer, 15 F.3d 1455 (8th Cir. 1994): The Court held in a drug prosecution that detectives' statements that they could "put in a good word for" the defendant could neither be reasonably construed to mean that their discussions were plea negotiations nor that they had express authority to enter into such negotiations, so the defendant's inculpatory statements to them were properly admitted. In *United States v. Greene,* 995 F.2d 793 (8th Cir. 1993), the Court affirmed convictions for drug offenses, holding there was no error in denying the defendant's motion to suppress statements made to a DEA agent, allegedly in plea bargaining, as the agent had no express or apparent authority from the prosecuting attorney to plea bargain with the defendant. In *Rachlin v. United States,* 723 F.2d 1373 (8th Cir. 1983), the Court affirmed a conviction for passing a counterfeit note, finding that statements made by the defendant to Secret Service agents were not barred by the Rule, since the defendant was never told that the agents had authority to plea bargain and they never offered any "deal."

United States v. Sitton, 968 F.2d 947 (9th Cir.), *cert. denied,* 113 S. Ct. 478 (1992): The Court affirmed convictions for drug charges, holding that a defendant's statements to deputy sheriffs in which he offered "a trade" were properly admitted, as the deputies were not attorneys for the prosecuting authority and the defendant did not exhibit a subjective belief, reasonable under the circumstances, that he was negotiating a plea. In *United States v. Karr,* 742 F.2d 493 (9th Cir. 1984), the Court held that a defendant's statements to an officer were not covered by the Rule, where the defendant never offered to plead guilty and never inquired into whether the officer had authority to bargain.

United States v. Ceballos, 706 F.2d 1198 (11th Cir. 1983): Affirming convictions for marijuana offenses, the Court held there was no error in admitting a letter, which one defendant gave to a Marshal for delivery to the agent in charge of the case, that expressed awareness of the details of a major smuggling operation and offered to cooperate with the government. No plea discussions were underway and the letter was not sent to an attorney for the government.

Statements to presentence officer

United States v. Perez-Franco, 873 F.2d 455 (1st Cir. 1989): In examining sentencing guidelines, the Court held that Rule 410 does not protect statements made to a presentence officer preparing a presentence report.

Waiver

United States v. Dortch, 5 F.3d 1056 (7th Cir. 1993): The Court affirmed convictions of a drug conspiracy, holding that statements made by a defendant in unsuccessful plea negotiations could be admitted to rebut testimony of a defense witness. The defendant had signed an agreement allowing the government to rebut evidence or arguments materially different from the proffered statements, and effectuating such a waiver does not jeopardize the purposes behind the Rule.

United States v. Mezzanatto, 998 F.2d 1452 (9th Cir. 1993), *cert. granted,* 114 S. Ct. 1536 (1994): Reversing a drug possession conviction, the Court held it was error to admit as impeachment evidence statements made by the defendant during a plea bargaining session, even though he had agreed that any statements could be used for impeachment at trial if a plea bargain were not made. The majority reasoned that to permit waiver of the protections of Rule 410 would undermine congressional efforts to promote the plea negotiation process. The dissenting Judge argued that waiver of rights is generally permissible, and that there is no reason to believe that prosecutors will seek waivers if by doing so they undermine their ability to enter into plea agreements.

D. LEGISLATIVE HISTORY

Advisory Committee's Notes

[The following material is the Note accompanying the Committee's draft of the latest versions of the Rule. The Rule was changed slightly after the Note was written.]

"The major objective of the amendment to rule [Fed. R. Crim. P.] 11(e)(6) [virtually identical to Rule 410] is to describe more precisely, consistent with the original purpose of the provision, what evidence relating to pleas or plea discussions is inadmissible. The present language is susceptible to interpretation which would make it applicable to a wide variety of statements made under various circumstances other than within the context of those plea discussions authorized by rule 11(e) and intended to be protected by subdivision (e)(6) of the rule. See United States v. Herman, 544 F.2d 791 (5th Cir. 1977), discussed herein.

"Fed. R. Ev. 410, as originally adopted by Pub. L. 93-595, provided in part that 'evidence of a plea of guilty, later withdrawn, or a plea of *nolo contendere* or an offer to plead guilty or *nolo contendere* to the crime charged or any other crime, or of statements made in connection with any of the foregoing pleas or offers, is not admissible in any civil or criminal action, case, or proceeding against the person who made the plea or offer.' (This rule was adopted with the proviso that it 'shall be superseded by any amendment to the Federal Rules of Criminal Procedure which is inconsistent with this rule.') As the Advisory Committee Note explained: 'Exclusion of offers to plead guilty or *nolo* has as its purpose the promotion of disposition of criminal cases by compromise.' The amendment of Fed. R. Crim. P. 11, transmitted to Congress by the Supreme Court in April 1974, contained a subdivision (e)(6) essentially identical to the rule 410 language quoted above, as a part of a substantial revision of rule 11. The most significant feature of this revision was the express recognition given to the fact that the 'attorney for the government and the attorney for the defendant or the defendant when acting *pro se* may engage in discussions with a view toward reaching' a plea agreement. Subdivision (e)(6) was intended to encourage such discussions. As noted in H.R. Rep. No. 94-247, 94th Cong., 1st Sess. 7 (1975), the purpose of subdivision (e)(6) is to not 'discourage defendants from being completely candid and open during plea negotiations.' Similarly, H.R. Rep. No. 94-414, 94th Cong., 1st Sess. 10 (1975), states that 'Rule 11(e)(6) deals with the use of statements made in connection with plea agreements.' (Rule 11(e)(6) was thereafter enacted, with the addition of the proviso allowing use of statements for purposes of impeachment and in a prosecution for perjury, and with the qualification that the inadmissible statements must also be 'relevant to' the inadmissible pleas or offers. Pub. L. 94-64; Fed. R. Ev. 410 was then amended to conform. Pub. L. 94-149.) [Note the mistake here regarding impeachment. Ed.]

"While this history shows that the purpose of Fed. R. Ev. 410 and Fed. R. Crim. P. 11(e)(6) is to permit the unrestrained candor which produces effective plea discussions between the 'attorney for the government and the attorney for the defendant or the defendant when acting pro se,' given visibility and sanction in rule 11(e), a literal reading of the language of these two rules could reasonably lead to the conclusion that a broader rule of inadmissibility obtains. That is, because 'statements' are generally inadmissible if 'made in connection with, and relevant to' an 'offer to plead guilty,' it might be thought that an otherwise voluntary admission to law enforcement officials is rendered inadmissible merely because it was made in the hope of obtaining leniency by a plea. Some decisions interpreting rule 11(e)(6) point in this direction. See United States v. Herman, 544 F.2d 791 (5th Cir. 1977) (defendant in custody of two postal inspectors during continuance of removal hearing instigated conversation with them and at some point said he would plead guilty to armed robbery if the murder charge was dropped; one inspector stated they were not 'in position' to make any deals in this regard; held, defendant's statement inadmissible under rule 11(e)(6) because the defendant 'made the statements during the course of a conversation in which he sought concessions from the government in return for a guilty plea'); United States v. Brooks, 536 F.2d 1137 (6th Cir. 1976) (defendant telephoned postal inspector and offered to plead guilty if he got 2-year maximum; statement inadmissible).

"The amendment makes inadmissible statements made 'in the course of or as a consequence of' a later withdrawn guilty plea, a plea of *nolo contendere,*' or 'plea discussions with the attorney for the government' which do not result in a plea of guilty or which result in a plea of guilty later withdrawn. It thus fully protects the plea discussion process authorized by rule 11 without attempting to deal with confrontations between suspects and law enforcement agents, which involve problems of quite different dimensions. See, e.g., ALI Model Code of Pre-Arraignment Procedure art. 140 and § 150.2(8) (Proposed Official Draft, 1975) (latter section requires exclusion if 'a law enforcement officer induces any person to make a statement by promising leniency'). This change, it must be emphasized, does not compel the conclusion that statements made to law enforcement agents, especially when the agents purport to have authority to bargain, are inevitably admissible. Rather, the point is that such cases are not covered by the *per se* rule 11(e)(6) and thus must be resolved by that body of law dealing with police interrogations.

"This amendment is fully consistent with all recent and major law reform efforts on this subject. ALI Model Code of Pre-Arraignment Procedure § 350.7 (Proposed Official Draft, 1975), and ABA Standards Relating to Pleas of Guilty § 3.4 (Approved Draft, 1968) both provide:

> Unless the defendant subsequently enters a plea of guilty or *nolo contendere* which is not withdrawn, the fact that the defendant or his counsel and the prosecuting attorney engaged in plea discussions or made a plea agreement should not be received in evidence against or in favor of the defendant in any criminal or civil action or administrative proceedings.

The Commentary to the latter states:

> The above standard is limited to discussions and agreements with the prosecuting attorney. Sometimes defendants will indicate to the police their willingness to bargain, and in such instances these statements are sometimes admitted in court against the defendant. State v. Christian, 245 S.W.2d 895 (Mo. 1952). If the police initiate this kind of discussion, this may have some bearing on the admissibility of the defendant's statement. However, the policy considerations relevant to this issue are better dealt with in the context of standards governing in-custody interrogation by the police.

Similarly, Unif. R. Crim. P. 441(d) (Approved Draft, 1974), provides that except under limited circumstances 'no discussion between the parties or statement by the defendant or his lawyer under this Rule,' i.e., the rule providing 'the parties may meet to discuss the possibility of pretrial diversion . . . or of a plea agreement,' are admissible. The amendment is likewise consistent with the typical state provision on this subject; see, e.g., Ill. S. Ct. Rule 402(f).

"The 'in the course of or as a consequence of such pleas or plea discussions' language of the amendment identifies with more precision than the present language the necessary relationship between the statements and the plea or discussion. See the dispute between the majority and concurring opinion in United States v. Herman, 544 F.2d 791 (5th Cir. 1977), concerning the meanings and effect of the phrases 'connection to' and 'relevant to' in the present rule. Moreover, by relating the statements to 'plea discussions' rather than 'an offer to plead,' the amendment ensures 'that even an attempt to open plea bargaining [is] covered under the same rule of inadmissibility.' United States v. Brooks, 536 F.2d 1137 (6th Cir. 1976).

"The last sentence of Rule 11(e)(6) is amended to provide a second exception to the general rule of nonadmissibility of the described statements. Under the amendment, such a statement is also admissible 'in any proceeding wherein statements made in the course of or as a consequence of the same plea or plea discussions have been introduced.' This change is necessary so that, when evidence of statements made in the course of or as a consequence of a certain plea or plea discussions are introduced under circumstances not prohibited by this rule (e.g., not 'against' the person who made the plea), other statements relating to the same plea or plea discussions may also be admitted when relevant to the matter at issue. For example, if a defendant upon a motion to dismiss a prosecution on some ground were able to admit certain statements made in aborted plea discussions in his favor, then other relevant statements made in the same plea discussions should be admissible against the defendant in the interest of determining the truth of the matter at issue. This change conforms to the general rule that a privilege terminates when the holder by his own act destroys the confidentiality with which it is endowed. 8 J. Wigmore, Evidence §§ 2242, 2327-2329, 2374, 2389-2390 (McNaughton rev. 1961).

"The phrase 'in any civil or criminal proceeding' has been moved from its present position, following the word 'against,' for purposes of clarity. An ambiguity presently exists because the word 'against' may be read as referring either to the kind of proceeding in which the evidence is offered or the purpose for which it is offered. The change makes it clear that the later construction is correct.

"Unlike ABA Standards Relating to Pleas of Guilty § 3.4 (Approved Draft, 1968), and ALI Model Code of Pre-Arraignment Procedure § 350.7 (Proposed Official Draft, 1975), rule 11(e)(6) does not also provide that the described evidence is inadmissible 'in favor of' the defendant. This is not intended to suggest, however, that such evidence will inevitably be admissible in the defendant's favor. Specifically, no disapproval is intended of such decisions as United States v. Verdoorn, 528 F.2d 103 (8th Cir. 1976), holding that the trial judge properly refused to permit the defendants to put into evidence at their trial the fact the prosecution had attempted to plea bargain with them, as 'meaningful dialogue between the parties would, as a practical matter, be impossible if either party had to assume the risk that plea offers would be admissible in evidence.' "

[What follows next is the Advisory Committee's Note on the original version of Rule 410.]

Withdrawn pleas of guilty were held inadmissible in federal prosecutions in Kercheval v. United States, 274 U.S. 220, 47 S. Ct. 582, 71 L. Ed. 1009 (1927). The Court pointed out that to admit the withdrawn plea would effectively set at naught the allowance of withdrawal and place the accused in a dilemma utterly inconsistent with the decision to award him a trial. The New York Court of Appeals, in People v. Spitaleri, 9 N.Y.2d 168, 212 N.Y.S.2d 53, 173 N.E.2d 35 (1961), reexamined and overturned its earlier decisions which had allowed admission. In addition to the reasons set forth in *Kercheval,* which was quoted at length, the court pointed out that the effect of admitting the plea was to compel defendant to take the stand by way of explanation and to open the way for the prosecution to call the lawyer who had represented him at the time of entering the plea. State court decisions for and against admissibility are collected in Annot., 86 A.L.R.2d 326.

Pleas of *nolo contendere* are recognized by Rule 11 of the Rules of Criminal Procedure, although the law of numerous States is to the contrary. The present rule gives effect to the principal traditional characteristic of the *nolo* plea, i.e., avoiding the admission of guilt which is inherent in pleas of guilty. This position is consistent with the construction of Section 5 of the Clayton Act, 15 U.S.C. § 16(a), recognizing the inconclusive and compromise nature of judgments based on *nolo* pleas. General Electric Co. v. City of San Antonio, 334 F.2d 480 (5th Cir. 1964); Commonwealth Edison Co. v. Allis-Chalmers Mfg. Co., 323 F.2d 412 (7th Cir. 1963), *cert. denied*, 376 U.S. 939, 84 S. Ct. 794, 11 L. Ed. 2d 659; Armco Steel Corp. v. North Dakota, 376 F.2d 206 (8th Cir. 1967); City of Burbank v. General Electric Co., 329 F.2d 825 (9th Cir. 1964). See also state court decisions in Annot., 18 A.L.R.2d 1287, 1314.

Exclusion of offers to plead guilty or *nolo* has as its purpose the promotion of disposition of criminal cases by compromise. As pointed out in McCormick § 251, p. 543, "Effective criminal law administration in many localities would hardly be possible if a large proportion of the charges were not disposed of by such compromises." See also People v. Hamilton, 60 Cal. 2d 105, 32 Cal. Rptr. 4, 383 P.2d 412 (1963), discussing legislation designed to achieve this result. As with compromise offers generally, Rule 408, free communication is needed, and security against having an offer of compromise or related statement admitted in evidence effectively encourages it.

Limiting the exclusionary rule to use against the accused is consistent with the purpose of the rule, since the possibility of use for or against other persons will not impair the effectiveness of withdrawing pleas or the freedom of discussion which the rule is designed to foster. See A.B.A. Standards Relating to Pleas of Guilty § 2.2 (1968). See also the narrower provisions of New Jersey Evidence Rule 52(2) and the unlimited exclusion provided in California Evidence Code § 1153.

House Subcommittee on Criminal Justice Notes

October 10, 1973

The Subcommittee added the phrase "Except as otherwise provided by Act of Congress" after being advised of the existence of a specific statute in the antitrust field permitting the introduction into evidence of a *nolo contendere* plea in certain circumstances. The Subcommittee did not believe that it should be the intent of the Rules to alter any such particular congressional policy judgment.

[There was no note in the June 28, 1973 draft.]

Report of the House Committee on the Judiciary

[This is the Report on the original Rule.]

The Committee added the phrase "Except as otherwise provided by Act of Congress" to Rule 410 as submitted by the Court in order to preserve particular congressional policy judgments as to the effect of a plea of guilty or of *nolo contendere*. See 15 U.S.C. § 16(a). The Committee intends that its amendment refers to both present statutes and statutes subsequently enacted.

[The House Report, No. 94-247, 94th Cong., 1st Sess., at 7, on Criminal Procedure Rule 11(e)(6), which superseded Rule 410 until it was amended, is very similar to the Conference Report on the procedure rule quoted *infra*.]

Report of the Senate Committee on the Judiciary

[This is the Report on the original Rule.]

As adopted by the House, Rule 410 would make inadmissible pleas of guilty or *nolo contendere* subsequently withdrawn as well as offers to make such pleas. Such a rule is clearly justified as a means of encouraging pleading. However, the House rule would then go on to render inadmissible for any purpose statements made in connection with these pleas or offers as well.

The committee finds this aspect of the House rule unjustified. Of course, in certain circumstances such statements should be excluded. If, for example, a plea is vitiated because of coercion, statements made in connection with the plea may also have been coerced and should be inadmissible on that basis. In other cases, however, voluntary statements of an accused made in court on the record, in connection with a plea, and determined by a court to be reliable should be admissible even though the plea is subsequently withdrawn. This is particularly true in those cases where, if the House rule were in effect, a defendant would be able to contradict his previous statements and thereby lie with impunity. To prevent such an injustice, the rule has been modified to permit the use of such statements for the limited purposes of impeachment and in subsequent perjury or false statement prosecutions.

[Footnote deleted.]

[The Senate Report, No. 94-336, 94th Cong., 1st Sess., at 10, on Criminal Procedure Rule 11(e)(6), which superseded Rule 410 until it was amended, includes the same two paragraphs as the Conference Report on the procedure rule, quoted *infra*.]

Report of the House and Senate Conferees

[This is the Report on the original Rule.]

The House bill provides that evidence of a guilty or *nolo contendere* plea, of an offer of either plea, or of statements made in connection with such pleas or offers of such pleas, is inadmissible in any civil or criminal action, case or proceeding against the person making such plea or offer. The Senate amendment makes the rule inapplicable to a voluntary and reliable statement made in court on the record where the statement is offered in a subsequent prosecution of the declarant for perjury or false statement.

The issues raised by Rule 410 are also raised by proposed Rule 11(e)(6) of the Federal Rules of Criminal Procedure presently pending before Congress. This proposed rule, which deals with the admissibility of pleas of guilty or *nolo contendere,* offers to make such pleas, and statements made in connection with such pleas, was promulgated by the Supreme Court on April 22, 1974, and in the absence of congressional action will become effective on August 1, 1975. The conferees intend to make no change in the presently-existing case law until that date, leaving the courts free to develop rules in this area on a case-by-case basis.

The Conferees further determined that the issues presented by the use of guilty and *nolo contendere* pleas, offers of such pleas, and statements made in connection with such pleas or offers, can be explored in greater detail during Congressional consideration of Rule 11(e)(6) of the Federal Rules of Criminal Procedure. The Conferees believe, therefore, that it is best to defer its effective date until August 1, 1975. The Conferees intend that Rule 410 would be superseded by any subsequent Federal Rule of Criminal Procedure or Act of Congress with which it is inconsistent, if the Federal Rule of Criminal Procedure or Act of Congress takes effect or becomes law after the date of the enactment of the act establishing the rules of evidence.

The conference adopts the Senate amendment with an amendment that expresses the above intentions.

[As explained in our Editorial Explanatory Comment, *supra,* Rule 410 was superseded by Criminal Procedure Rule 11(e)(6), until it was amended on December 12, 1975. The Conference Report on the Criminal Procedure Rule, No. 94-414, 94th Cong., 1st Sess., at page 10, contains a joint explanatory statement of the Committee of Conference, part of which is set forth below.]

Rule 11(e)(6) deals with the use of statements made in connection with plea agreements. The House version permits a limited use of pleas of guilty, later withdrawn, or *nolo contendere,* offers of such pleas, and statements made in connection with such pleas or offers. Such evidence can be used in a perjury or false statement prosecution if the plea, offer, or related statement was made

551

under oath, on the record, and in the presence of counsel. The Senate version permits evidence of voluntary and reliable statements made in court on the record to be used for the purpose of impeaching the credibility of the declarant or in a perjury or false statement prosecution.

The Conference adopts the House version with changes. The Conference agrees that neither a plea nor the offer of a plea ought to be admissible for any purpose. The Conference-adopted provision, therefore, like the Senate provision, permits only the use of statements made in connection with a plea of guilty, later withdrawn, or a plea of *nolo contendere,* or in connection with an offer of a guilty or *nolo contendere* plea.

Citations to Hearings and Debates

Prepared Statement of W. Vincent Rakestraw, June 5, 1974, in Hearings on H.R. 5463 (Federal Rules of Evidence) Before the Senate Comm. on the Judiciary, 93rd Cong., 2d Sess., at 109, 112 (1974).

Debate in the House of Representatives, 120 Cong. Rec. H12253 (daily ed. December 18, 1974).

[For debates on the amendments to the Rule see the citations that follow.]

Debate in the House of Representatives, 121 Cong. Rec. H7859-H7860, H7863-H7864 (daily ed. July 30, 1975).

Debate in the Senate, 121 Cong. Rec. S12875 (daily ed. July 17, 1975), and 121 Cong. Rec. S14031 (daily ed. July 30, 1975).

RULE 411

A. OFFICIAL TEXT

Rule 411. Liability Insurance

Evidence that a person was or was not insured against liability is not admissible upon the issue whether the person acted negligently or otherwise wrongfully. This rule does not require the exclusion of evidence of insurance against liability when offered for another purpose, such as proof of agency, ownership, or control, or bias or prejudice of a witness.

B. EDITORIAL EXPLANATORY COMMENT

The basic rule

Evidence that a person carried or failed to carry liability insurance is not admissible on the issue of whether the person acted negligently or wrongfully on a particular occasion. This Rule bars the evidence, for example, when it is offered by a plaintiff against the defendant on the theory that because the defendant was insured the defendant was probably careless. Evidence is likewise excluded when offered by the defendant to show that, because the defendant lacked adequate insurance, he had every incentive to be careful. No matter who offers the evidence of the presence or absence of insurance, if it is offered on the issue of negligence it is excluded. If it is offered for some other purpose, however, it may be admitted — subject to the Rule 403 balancing process.[1] For instance, if an insurance investigator takes the stand to testify at the trial, it is permissible to bring out the fact that he may be an interested witness because of his employer — at least where the probative value as to credibility is not substantially outweighed by the risk of prejudice and confusion.[2]

Rule 411 is based on two independent grounds. First, evidence of insurance, or the lack of it, is of minimal relevance in determining whether a person acted carelessly on

---

1. See, e.g., Palmer v. Krueger, 897 F.2d 1529 (10th Cir. 1990) (in an intrafamily suit arising out of an airplane crash that killed the father and mother, the Trial Court did not abuse its discretion in excluding the fact that the family members were squabbling over insurance proceeds; this was a "collateral issue," and the Trial Judge did not err in finding that the risk of prejudice, confusion, and delay substantially outweighed the probative value of the evidence).

2. See, e.g., Charter v. Chleborad, 551 F.2d 246 (8th Cir. 1977) (where defense witness testified that plaintiff's expert had a bad reputation for truth and veracity, it was reversible error to prevent plaintiff from showing that the defense witness was employed by the liability carrier that represented the defendant in the action; the fact of employment was "clearly admissible to show possible bias" of the defense witness under Rule 411); Pinkham v. Burgess, 933 F.2d 1066 (1st Cir. 1991) (in a legal malpractice suit, the Trial Court properly admitted evidence that the defendant-lawyer had discussed insurance issues with the plaintiff's husband; the evidence was offered not to prove wrongful conduct, but rather to prove the extent to which the defendant had become involved in the husband's business dealings).

a certain occasion. For instance, most people certainly do not view the fact that they have insurance as a license to act carelessly. More importantly, there is the concern that if the jurors hear about insurance coverage, or the lack of it, they may decide the case on the basis of the deepest pocket, rather than on the facts.[3] This is the risk of prejudice and confusion that must be taken into account by the Trial Court when evidence of insurance is offered for a purpose other than proving negligence or wrongful conduct.[4]

Prejudicial versus harmless error

Assuming that counsel manages to find a way improperly to introduce evidence of insurance, should Appellate Courts adopt a general rule that such an error is harmless on the ground that it is highly unlikely that a jury pays much attention to the question of insurance in determining liability?

The answer obviously must be "no." If the Rule is to mean anything, it must have some teeth. Many Appellate Courts seem to view such evidence as being harmless; others treat it as almost automatic grounds for reversal. Probably the best view falls somewhere in between. In any given case, it would be wise for the Appellate Court to look at the entire factual setting. It is important to keep in mind that even where the amount of the insurance is not such as to arouse most jurors, and even where an error is inadvertent, there is a danger that jurors will consider the fact of insurance, or the absence of it, and decide a close case in favor of either the plaintiff or defendant because their concern about the possibility of error is reduced or enhanced when they know that insurance does or does not exist in a particular case.

In essence, there is no reason to treat erroneous admission of evidence of insurance differently from any other evidentiary error. See Rule 103 for a discussion of harmless error.[5] In assessing whether the error is harmless, the Trial Judge should give consideration to the possibility that the jury might have assumed the existence of insurance, even if not told about it directly. This would be especially true where the defendant is a large corporation, or some other person or entity that is highly likely to carry insurance (e.g., a doctor or a lawyer).

Discovery

In order to encourage pretrial settlement, Federal Rule of Civil Procedure 26(a)(1)(D) provides that a party shall produce for inspection and copying "any insurance agreement

---

3. See, e.g., Ouachita Nat'l Bank v. Tosco Corp, 616 F.2d 485 (8th Cir. 1982) ("[I]t is generally thought that the jury's knowledge that a plaintiff is receiving insurance benefits, or that a defendant is carrying liability insurance, might serve to decrease or increase, respectively, the amount of damages awarded by the jury.").

4. See, e.g., Granberry v. O'Barr, 866 F.2d 112 (5th Cir. 1988) (no error to exclude evidence of insurance where it was only minimally probative to show bias of a witness; the witness was employed by a life insurance company, which was a separate entity from the liability carrier; any judgment against the liability carrier would not directly impact the witness' company; and the witness had given an identical account of the accident at the scene, before he could have known whether the defendant had insurance coverage or who provided it).

5. See, e.g., Reed v. General Motors Corp., 773 F.2d 660 (5th Cir. 1985) (applying Rule 103, the Court finds it was reversible error to admit evidence that a defendant had coverage in the amount of only $5,000 per person and $10,000 per accident; jury could not otherwise have known of these coverage limits).

under which any person carrying on an insurance business may be liable to satisfy part or all of a judgment which may be entered in the action or to indemnify or reimburse for payments made to satisfy the judgment.'' But the procedural rule does not make insurance information admissible at trial. If discovery of insurance takes place, it may be wise during any pretrial conference, or off the record at the outset of a trial, for the insured party to request that the Trial Judge remind counsel of Rule 411 and to indicate that violation of the Rule will not be tolerated. This will help to prevent any ''slips of the tongue'' that reveal insurance information to the jury.

The criminal case

If the first sentence of Rule 411 is read literally, it might cause a problem in a not uncommon situation. Consider, for instance, this case: One person (*A*) has property stored with another (*B*). If *A*'s business is bad and collecting on insurance would be more profitable than selling the property, *A* might ask *B* to arrange a fire. *A* also might ask *B* to first take out a big insurance policy on the stored property. This would be liability, not personal property, insurance and would be within the coverage of the Rule.

Assume also that the government charges *B* with arson and both with conspiracy. If the government's theory is that *B* burned down *A*'s property so that *A* could recover the proceeds of an insurance policy and share the money with *B*, the government traditionally has had no difficulty in offering the insurance policy as circumstantial evidence of motive. But Rule 411 suggests that evidence of liability insurance is not admissible to prove that a person acted ''wrongfully.''

We do not believe that this sentence should bar the use of the evidence in a case such as this, however. The Rule is designed to prevent the use of insurance evidence to show that someone would act more carefully or less carefully than the average person because of the absence or existence of insurance. When the evidence is not that the existence or absence of insurance tends to induce people to act in certain predictable ways, but is rather that the existence of a particular insurance policy tended to make a particular individual take a specific action in an effort to take advantage of that insurance policy, the policy of the Rule does not require exclusion of the evidence.

C. ANNOTATED CASES

Admissible for other purposes

Pinkham v. Burgess, 933 F.2d 1066 (1st Cir. 1991): Affirming a judgment for the client in an attorney malpractice action, the Court held there was no abuse of discretion in refusing to grant a mistrial after the plaintiff mentioned that the attorney had discussed liability and other insurance for lawyers with her husband, as the reference was unlikely to have been perceived by the jury as indicating there was insurance coverage in this case and it was in any event relevant to issues in the case other than negligence.

Amount of insurance

Reed v. General Motors Corp., 773 F.2d 660 (5th Cir. 1985): The Court reversed a judgment against a driver and his insurer in a personal injury case because the Trial

Judge erroneously admitted evidence of the amounts of insurance carried by the defendant. The fact that the insurer was named as a defendant did not mean that the amount of insurance was relevant, and the Court found that the error was not cured by a jury instruction not to consider the amount of the insurance in deciding the negligence of the defendant.

Bias of witness

Varlack v. SWC Caribbean, Inc., 550 F.2d 171 (3d Cir. 1977): The Court approved the mention of insurance coverage as part of laying a foundation to impeach a witness who had given a statement to an insurance investigator. Interestingly, the Court stated that "[w]e assume without deciding that the rule is applicable when the judge is the trier of fact." In our view, the policy underlying the Rule of avoiding prejudice with evidence of low probative value does not apply in a bench trial. The Trial Judge can be expected to exclude prejudice from her mind.

Ouachita Nat'l Bank v. Tosco Corp., 686 F.2d 1291 (8th Cir. 1982): Although it vacated a judgment in an automobile accident case, the Court indicated that it was either permissible or harmless error for a party planning to call an insurance adjuster as a witness to indicate to the jury that the adjuster was employed by its insurance company. This was viewed as bias evidence, and although the Court did not mention the point, it would appear that the party was attempting to bring out the impeaching fact before it was elicited by an opponent. In *Charter v. Chleborad*, 551 F.2d 246 (8th Cir.), *cert. denied*, 434 U.S. 856 (1977), a medical malpractice action, one of the plaintiff's trial witnesses as an orthopedic surgeon who was impeached by means of character testimony from an attorney who resided in the same city as the surgeon. Reversing a judgment for the defendant, the Court held it was error to preclude the plaintiff from showing the possible bias of the attorney by bringing out the fact that he was employed by the liability carrier representing the defendant in this case.

Fidelity bond

Garnac Grain Co. v. Blackley, 932 F.2d 1563 (8th Cir. 1991): In an action against an accounting firm for malpractice arising out of an employee's embezzlement, the Court held it was an abuse of discretion to deny the plaintiff's motion *in limine* to exclude evidence that the plaintiff received payment under a two-million-dollar fidelity bond. The Trial Judge concluded that receipt of the proceeds was admissible on whether the plaintiff maintained adequate internal controls, but the Court held that although the bond is not technically "insurance against liability," it is insurance that might lead the jury improperly to reduce the plaintiff's damages, the kind of prejudice the Rule was intended to eliminate.

Foundation for offer of evidence

Hunziker v. Scheidemantle, 543 F.2d 489 (3d Cir. 1976): Reversing and remanding a wrongful death action, the Court noted that Rule 411 is not a total bar to evidence of insurance, but suggested that the District Court should require the necessary foundation to be established outside the presence of the jury so that it might determine the admissibility of the evidence without prejudice to the rights of the parties.

Knowledge of trade usage

Posttape Assocs. v. Eastman Kodak Co., 537 F.2d 751 (3d Cir. 1976): The Court remanded a breach of warranty and negligence action arising out of the plaintiff's purchase of motion picture film for a new trial on the issues of limitation of liability and of damages, because the Trial Judge erroneously excluded evidence that one of the owners of the plaintiff corporation had purchased insurance indemnifying the corporation against defective film. Citing Rule 411, the Court stated that the evidence was relevant to the knowledge of the defendant of the trade usage of the words used to limit liability:

> It is doubtful that there would be any prejudice because the parties were both commercial entities, the injury was not likely to stir the emotions, and the existence of such coverage might have been so unusual that the purchase itself would have significance in the circumstances. The exclusion of this relevant evidence was far more prejudicial to the defense than its admission would have been to the plaintiffs.

Intent

B.H. Morton v. Zidell Explorations, Inc., 695 F.2d 347 (9th Cir. 1982), *cert. denied,* 460 U.S. 1039 (1983): Tugboat owners sued a shipyard for negligence after their ship was almost completely destroyed by fire while being converted into a fish-processing vessel. The defendants relied on an exculpatory clause in their agreement with the owners that provided they were to be exculpated from all risks of loss or damage. The Court held that the shipyard was properly permitted to show that the owners took out insurance on their vessel before the fire as evidence proving that the agreement that the owners signed was intended to be binding upon them.

Intercompany discussions

American Ins. Co. v. North American Co., 697 F.2d 79 (2d Cir. 1982): In an action by a primary insurer against a reinsurer for reimbursement of portions of a settlement, the Court found that evidence of the reinsurer's discussions with another company over commutation was inadmissible.

Rebuttal

Bernier v. Board of County Rd. Comm'rs, 581 F. Supp. 71 (W.D. Mich. 1983): Ruling *in limine* in a wrongful death action involving a claim that the deceased was killed because the county failed to mark an intersection properly, the Court deferred a final ruling on whether evidence that the county was insured could be admitted to respond to the defense that the county had limited funds to use to repair roadways and had to use some judgment as to which repairs were most important. It warned, however, that ''should the nature of the defendant's proofs be such that the jury might infer defendant's inability to pay a judgment, evidence that defendant has liability insurance may become admissible.''

Punitive damages

Perrin v. Anderson, 784 F.2d 1040 (10th Cir. 1986): The Court affirmed a judgment for police officers sued by the estate of a man killed when the officers attempted to obtain information about a traffic accident. Defense counsel had commented in closing argument that any judgment would be paid by the officers and not by the State or anybody else. The Court held the comments were not an impermissible mention of lack of insurance because the plaintiff requested punitive damages, so the ultimate source of payment was relevant.

D. LEGISLATIVE HISTORY

Advisory Committee's Note

The courts have with substantial unanimity rejected evidence of liability insurance for the purpose of proving fault, and absence of liability insurance as proof of lack of fault. At best the inference of fault from the fact of insurance coverage is a tenuous one, as is its converse. More important, no doubt, has been the feeling that knowledge of the presence or absence of liability insurance would induce juries to decide cases on improper grounds. McCormick § 168; Annot., 4 A.L.R.2d 761. The rule is drafted in broad terms so as to include contributory negligence or other fault of a plaintiff as well as fault of a defendant.

The second sentence points out the limits of the rule, using well established illustrations. *Id.*

For similar rules see Uniform Rule 54; California Evidence Code § 1155; Kansas Code of Civil Procedure § 60-454; New Jersey Evidence Rule 54.

[The entire Advisory Committee Note accompanying the gender-neutralizing changes effective October 1, 1987 is as follows: "The amendment is technical. No substantive change is intended."]

RULE 412

A. OFFICIAL TEXT

Rule 412. Sex Offense Cases; Relevance of Alleged Victim's Past Sexual Behavior or Alleged Sexual Predisposition

(a) EVIDENCE GENERALLY INADMISSIBLE — The following evidence is not admissible in any civil or criminal proceeding involving alleged sexual misconduct except as provided in subdivisions (b) and (c):

(1) Evidence offered to prove that any alleged victim engaged in other sexual behavior.

(2) Evidence offered to prove any alleged victim's sexual predisposition.

(b) EXCEPTIONS —

(1) In a criminal case, the following evidence is admissible, if otherwise admissible under these rules:

(A) evidence of specific instances of sexual behavior by the alleged victim offered to prove that a person other than the accused was the source of semen, injury or other physical evidence;

(B) evidence of specific instances of sexual behavior by the alleged victim with respect to the person accused of the sexual misconduct offered by the accused to prove consent or by the prosecution; and

(C) evidence the exclusion of which would violate the constitutional rights of the defendant.

(2) In a civil case, evidence offered to prove the sexual behavior or sexual predisposition of any alleged victim is admissible if it is otherwise admissible under these rules and its probative value substantially outweighs the danger of harm to any victim and of unfair prejudice to any party. Evidence of an alleged victim's reputation is admissible only if it had been placed in controversy by the alleged victim.

(c) PROCEDURE TO DETERMINE ADMISSIBILITY —

(1) A party intending to offer evidence under subdivision (b) must —

(A) file a written motion at least 14 days before trial specifically describing the evidence and stating the purpose for which it is offered unless the court, for good cause requires a different time for filing or permits filing during trial; and

(B) serve the motion on all parties and notify the alleged victim or, when appropriate, the alleged victim's guardian or representative.

(2) Before admitting evidence under this rule the court must conduct a hearing *in camera* and afford the victim and parties the right to attend and be heard. The motion, related papers, and the record of the hearing must be sealed and remain under seal unless the court orders otherwise.

B. EDITORIAL EXPLANATORY COMMENT

Background

Rule 412 was originally enacted in the last days of the Ninety-Fifth Congress, when the Privacy Protection for Rape Victims Act of 1978, Public Law 95-540, was signed into law on October 28, 1978. Most recently, it was amended by Congress as part of the Violent Crime Control and Enforcement Act of 1994. It took effect on December 1, 1994. The Rule is consistent with a point that we try to make in our Comment accompanying Rule 102: The quest for fair and just procedures is not necessarily served by the admission of all evidence that is offered by parties to litigation, even though the evidence is tangentially relevant to the issues being tried.

Rule 412 follows the lead of the states that have enacted statutes or rules of court to protect the privacy of rape victims when they testify in court.[1] It is a rule of great symbolic value, as well as one of practical significance.[2] It represents a departure from a 200-year-old view typified by Lord Chief Justice Hale, who said that rape was "an accusation easily to be made and hard to be proved, and harder to be defended by the party accused, though ever so innocent." 1 M. Hale, The History of the Pleas of the Crown at 635 (1778).

The Rule represents a Congressional judgment that it is necessary for Federal Courts to indicate clearly to sex offense victims that their self-esteem will not be unnecessarily impaired in judicial proceedings and that their privacy will be respected to the extent that such respect does not denigrate the constitutional rights of accused defendants.[3] As one Court has put it, the purposes of the Rule are "to protect rape victims from the degrading

---

1. For a discussion of state rape-shield laws, see G. JOSEPH & S. SALTZBURG, EVIDENCE IN AMERICA ch. 22.

2. For an interesting discussion on whether the rape shield laws are effective in protecting the victim, see Althouse, *Thelma and Louise and the Law: Do Rape Shield Rules Matter?*, 25 LOYOLA L.A. L. REV. 757 (1992).

3. As Representative Holtzman stated in the discussion of the proposed Rule 412:

> Too often in this country victims of rape are humiliated and harassed when they report and prosecute the rape. Bullied and cross-examined about their prior sexual experiences, many find the trial almost as degrading as the rape itself. Since rape trials become inquisitions into the victim's morality, not trials of the defendant's innocence or guilt, it is not surprising that it is the least reported crime.

124 CONG. REC. H11945 (daily ed. Oct. 10, 1978).

and embarrassing disclosure of intimate details about their private lives, to encourage reporting of sexual assaults, and to prevent wasting time on distractive collateral and irrelevant matters."[4]

As amended by Congress in 1994, Rule 412 applies in all civil and criminal cases "involving alleged sexual misconduct." This term is left undefined. Clearly it applies to cases alleging rape and sexual abuse, whether civil or criminal. But the breadth of the term "involving alleged sexual misconduct" seems also to cover such claims as for sexual harassment in employment. As such, the amended Rule is far broader that the original Rule, which was limited to criminal cases in which a sex crime was charged.[5]

There is no doubt that the Rule is well intentioned. There is also no doubt that it is part of a desirable trend to protect the privacy of rape and sexual assault victims, and to encourage the reporting and prosecution of rape crimes. However, there are good reasons to wonder about the wisdom of certain portions of this Rule. Some of the problems that may well arise under the Rule are raised in the discussion that follows. Once the Rule is described in detail, some more general comments will be offered.

The exclusionary principle and its exceptions

Rule 412(a) states that, in any case involving alleged sexual misconduct, evidence concerning the past sexual behavior or sexual disposition of an alleged victim must be excluded, with certain limited exceptions. For criminal cases, subdivision (b) provides exceptions for specific acts offered to prove the "source of the semen" or other physical evidence, and for specific acts between the defendant and the victim offered by the defendant to prove consent, or by the prosecution. There is also a "residual" exception — as if one were necessary — covering evidence of the sexual behavior or predisposition of the victim which is required by the constitution to be admitted.

For civil cases, subdivision (c) provides an exception for any type of evidence of the victim's sexual behavior (e.g., reputation, opinion and specific acts), but only so long as the probative value of the evidence substantially outweighs the danger of harm to any victim and the danger of prejudice to any party. Subdivision (c) mandates a "reverse 403" test, similar to that provided in Rule 609(b), but with one variation: harm to the victim is specifically weighed together with prejudice to a party on the exclusionary side of the scale. The balancing test set forth in subdivision (c) consequently provides for a strong presumption of exclusion, in contrast to Rule 403, which provides for a strong presumption of admissibility.

Interestingly, in a criminal case, if a specific act is offered for one of the two limited purposes provided, the act is admissible so long as it also satisfies Rule 403. That is, there is no heightened exclusionary balancing test applied. This makes sense, since if the evidence is narrow enough to fit one of the limited exceptions to subdivision (b), there is little reason to filter it further through a strict exclusionary balancing test.

---

4. United States v. Torres, 937 F.2d 1469, 1472 (9th Cir. 1991).

5. See, e.g., United States v. Galloway, 937 F.2d 542 (10th Cir. 1991) (in kidnapping prosecution, where the government alleged that the defendant's purpose for kidnapping was sexual abuse, any evidence of the victim's past sexual history was not covered by Rule 412, but rather by Rule 403).

But for Rule 412(a), the governing rule would be Rule 405(a). Rule 405(a) would have provided that when character evidence is used circumstantially, *only* reputation or opinion evidence could be admitted, not specific acts. Rule 412 takes a different approach, at least in criminal cases; it admits *only* evidence of specific instances of conduct and limits the circumstances in which even that evidence may be received.

Some may question whether the same philosophy that underlies subdivisions (a) and (b) of Rule 412 should lead to a revision of Rule 405(a). It is possible that the Congress or the Supreme Court will move to change the historic rule preferring reputation, and more recently opinion evidence, in favor of an approach that favors evidence of specific bad acts. We doubt that this move would be wise, however, in cases other than sexual assault cases. It is unlikely in other criminal cases that reputation or opinion evidence concerning a victim's pertinent character trait will unfairly prejudice the government, or that it will distort the factfinding process, or that it will traumatize the victim. What makes a sexual assault case different from most other cases is that many members of society would find it difficult to evaluate reputation and opinion evidence concerning a victim's sexual propensities, without distorting the issues in a case, and also that the victim can be especially humiliated and traumatized by this highly inflammatory evidence. These arguments bring into question why amended Rule 412 differentiates between civil and criminal cases.

Constitutional problems

We must note that there are problems with the evidentiary limitations imposed by the Rule in criminal cases. In some instances, the Rule will undeniably restrict the defendant from bringing in highly probative evidence, particularly where the defense is one of consent.

For example, since the government alleges in a sex offense case that the defendant acted intentionally, in some cases the defendant reasonably may wish to offer evidence that a victim's reputation was brought to his attention prior to a sexual encounter in order to support a claim that he either acted without knowingly using force or that he acted under a reasonable mistake of fact concerning the attitude of the victim toward the sexual encounter. In such a case, a serious constitutional question would be presented if the defendant were denied an opportunity to present a defense that, based on what he knew about the victim, he interpreted her behavior in a reasonable way.

Similarly, if the defendant was made aware of a particular act or acts between the victim and others prior to a sexual encounter, he may wish to argue that these prior acts affected his interpretation of the victim's behavior. Yet this specific act evidence is excluded under the Rule, since it would not be offered to show the source of semen or injury as to the incident charged, nor would it be a specific act between the *defendant* and the victim, offered to prove consent.

Another problem might arise in cases when the people who were involved in prior sexual activity with the alleged victim cannot be located at the time the defendant wishes to call them. The defendant, who would have been permitted under the Rule to elicit evidence from others about specific acts, might be in the position of having to offer reputation or opinion evidence or no evidence, because no better evidence is available due to the absence of the witnesses. In such a case, an absolute bar to reputation or opinion evidence might be disturbing.

The Supreme Court has held that a criminal defendant has a constitutional right to "a meaningful opportunity to present a complete defense."[6] The Court has not looked kindly upon per se rules of exclusion that prohibit a criminal defendant from introducing an entire line of evidence, without regard to how probative and reliable the evidence may be.[7] On the other hand, the constitutional right to an effective defense does not mean that a defendant can introduce whatever evidence he might desire.[8] The state clearly has an interest in excluding evidence that is not sufficiently probative or reliable enough to justify the costs of admitting the evidence — including, in the rape shield context, the costs to the victim.[9]

We suggest that the proper balance in a criminal case is as follows: Evidence concerning the victim's prior sexual activity (whether by way of opinion, reputation, or specific act) must be admitted when the defendant shows that the evidence has substantial probative value on the issue of consent or identity of the perpetrator, and where alternative evidence to prove the point is not reasonably available.[10] This proposal would protect the victim from an undifferentiated "blame the victim" defense.[11] It would also prohibit the defendant from trying to draw the unjustifiable inference that the claimant was sexually promiscuous and, thus, more likely to have consensual sex with the

---

6. California v. Trombetta, 467 U.S. 479 (1984) (noting that several clauses of the Constitution work together to provide what might be loosely called a right to an effective defense); Faretta v. California, 422 U.S. 806 (1975) (stating that the Sixth Amendment "constitutionalizes the right in an adversary criminal trial to make a defense as we know it").

7. See, e.g., Rock v. Arkansas, 483 U.S. 44 (1987) (per se rule excluding hypnotically refreshed testimony violates defendant's constitutional rights: "Restrictions on a criminal defendant's rights to confront adverse witnesses and to present evidence may not be arbitrary or disproportionate to the purposes they are designed to serve"). For an incisive discussion of *Rock* and the right to an effective defense, see Stacy, *The Search for Truth in Constitutional Criminal Procedure,* 91 COLUM. L. REV. 1369 (1991).

8. See Rock v. Arkansas, 483 U.S. 44, 55 (1987) (noting that the right to an effective defense "may, in appropriate cases, bow to accommodate other legitimate interests in the criminal justice system").

9. See, e.g., Michigan v. Lucas, 111 S. Ct. 1743, 1746 (1991) (noting that rape shield laws represent "a valid legislative determination that rape victims deserve heightened protection against surprise, harassment, and unnecessary invasions of privacy").

10. See, e.g., United States v. Bear Stops, 997 F.2d 451 (8th Cir. 1993) (constitutional error to exclude evidence relating to victim's sexual assault by other parties; this evidence was highly probative to establish an alternative explanation for why the victim exhibited behavioral manifestations of a sexually abused child; there was no other evidence reasonably available). Compare United States v. Torres, 937 F.2d 1469, 1474 (9th Cir. 1991) (evidence of child-victim's past sexual conduct was not admissible to prove an alternative source of the child's sexual sophistication; the evidence was not sufficiently probative because the victim's testimony did not demonstrate any unusual knowledge of sexual techniques or nomenclature). See also Galvin, *Shielding Rape Victims in the State and Federal Courts: A Proposal for the Second Decade,* 70 MINN. L. REV. 763 (1986), for a discussion of the balancing of interests required when a criminal defendant in a rape case proffers evidence of the victim's sexual history.

11. See, e.g., United States v. Duran, 886 F.2d 167 (8th Cir. 1989) (the fact that the victim gave birth to a child out of wedlock was properly excluded where the birth took place six months before the charged incident; defendant simply wished to reveal that the victim had been a participant in past sexual relations with another, and this was not probative of any permissible purpose).

defendant.[12] Finally, the requirement of "less onerous alternative" evidence would prevent unnecessary humiliation and harassment of the victim. At the same time, this balancing test would allow limited use of reputation, opinion, and specific act evidence of sexual behavior where necessary and meaningful to the defendant's defense.[13]

It should be noted that even when evidence of the victim's sexual behavior is highly probative and necessary, the Trial Judge has discretion under Rule 403 to redact the evidence "to a sanitized version ... sufficient to support the purpose for which it was offered."[14] For example, in *United States v. Payne,* 944 F.2d 1458, 1469 (9th Cir. 1991), Payne was charged with sexually abusing his foster child. Payne proffered evidence that the child had engaged in sexual activity with another person. He argued that the evidence was probative of bias, because Payne had disciplined the child for engaging in the sexual activity. The Trial Court permitted Payne to conduct a "sanitized cross-examination" of the child, which apprised the jury of the fact that the child had been disciplined by Payne, but did not reveal the nature of the incident that was the basis of the discipline. The Appellate Court found no error, reasoning that the "underlying facts of the incident simply were not relevant to [the victim's] purported motivation to fabricate the charges."

Of course, a sanitized version of the victim's sexual activity will not solve the constitutional problem if the version is so sanitized as to be bereft of probative value. The redaction must not be disproportionate to the purposes it is designed to serve.[15]

The Trial Court should also consider whether the evidence of sexual behavior can be proved in some way other than through the victim's own testimony, so long as these alternate sources do not substantially impair the defense. For example, in *United States v. Bear Stops,* 997 F.2d 451 (8th Cir. 1993), the defendant offered evidence that the child-victim had been sexually attacked by three boys. The purpose was to provide an alternative explanation for the victim's having exhibited signs of sexual abuse. The Trial Court restricted the evidence to such an extent that the jury was never made aware of the time and place of the attack, nor the age and sex of the perpetrators, nor the type of sexual assault that occurred. Only a few general references to the attack were made by

---

12. See, e.g., Wood v. Alaska, 957 F.2d 1544 (9th Cir. 1992) (constitutional right to an effective defense does not require admission of evidence of the victim's prior sexual activity when offered to show a propensity to have sex with the defendant; such evidence is rejected as "reflecting outdated views of women and sexuality"; the evidence "only tends to show that she was willing to have sex, not that she was willing to have sex with this particular man at this particular time").

13. See, e.g., Olden v. Kentucky, 488 U.S. 227 (1988) (finding a Sixth Amendment violation where the Trial Court excluded evidence of a rape complainant's relationship with another man, because the complainant was a crucial prosecution witness, and evidence of the relationship would have provided strong evidence of a motive to lie about being raped; the Court noted that there was no alternative evidence that would have established the motive to lie). Compare Wood v. State of Alaska, 957 F.2d 1544 (9th Cir. 1992) (holding that evidence of the victim's sexual activity was properly excluded as being more prejudicial than probative, but noting that the result might have been different if the evidence "were the only evidence Wood could present to establish a prior sexual relationship such that he would be effectively precluded from presenting his whole theory to the jury").

14. United States v. Bear Stops, 997 F.2d 451, 455 (8th Cir. 1993).

15. *Id.* (finding constitutional error because the evidence of the victim's prior sexual abuse "was so sanitized that it was insufficient to support the purpose for which it was offered").

three witnesses at trial; one witness, an expert, only considered the attack as a hypothetical. The Appellate Court found that the restriction of the evidence violated the defendant's constitutional right to an effective defense. The Court reasoned as follows:

> The district court's concerns regarding the admission of the evidence were valid. Restricting the testimony regarding the sexual assault by the three boys to only the references volunteered by the grandmother and Dr. Peterson, and the hypotheticals asked of Dr. Bean was, however, disproportionate to those concerns. Because the evidence of the incident with the three older boys was uncontroverted, the potential for jury confusion and for a distracting "mini-trial" about the event was minimal. To avoid the intrusion on [the victim's] privacy, testimony about the basic facts of the incident could have been introduced through [the victim's] mother who discovered the sexual assault by the three older boys and stopped it, or through any other witness other than [the victim] who had knowledge about it. Because of both its relevance and its uncontroverted nature, the evidence would also be a likely candidate for stipulation.

There is clearly a legitimate interest in protecting the victim from the trauma of having to relate or address prior sexual activity on the stand. But that interest is diminished, at least somewhat, if the evidence can be presented in a less invasive manner, and if that is so then there is a stronger case for admitting probative evidence of sexual behavior.

Notice requirement

Before evidence is admitted under Rule 412, the offering party must make a written motion indicating an intent to offer the evidence. This motion cannot be made later than fourteen days before the date on which the trial is scheduled to begin, unless the Court permits a "tardy" motion either before or during trial for "good cause." Any motion made prior to trial by the offering party must be served on all the other parties in the case, and the offering party must also notify the victim of the intended use.

The constitutionality of rape shield notice provisions, as applied against criminal defendants, was discussed by the Supreme Court in *Michigan v. Lucas,* 111 S. Ct. 1743 (1991). The Court rejected a constitutional attack on the notice provision of a state rape shield law. The Michigan rape shield statute requires that the defense give notice to the prosecution, within ten days of the arraignment, of the intent to present evidence of past sexual conduct with the victim. The defendant did not comply with that requirement, and the Trial Court excluded the evidence of past sexual conduct. The Supreme Court treated the case as presenting a limited question: whether the lower Appellate Court had erred in adopting a per se rule that it is always unconstitutional to exclude evidence for the defendant's failure to comply with the notice requirement of a rape shield law. The Court held that such a per se rule of unconstitutionality was overbroad. It reasoned that a notice requirement in a rape shield law serves a legitimate state purpose, and that a defendant's violation of a notice requirement could in some cases be so egregious as to warrant the sanction of preclusion.

But the Court in *Lucas* took pains to note that it was not deciding the circumstances under which the sanction of preclusion might be "arbitrary or disproportionate" to the violation of a notice requirement. Thus, the Court left room for a Federal defendant to argue that a minimal violation of the Rule 412 notice requirement should result in some remedy short of preclusion of the evidence, e.g., a continuance, and that a rigid rule of preclusion might be unconstitutional. In light of *Lucas* and as a matter of policy, we think that the "good cause" provision of the Rule 412 notice requirement should be flexibly applied in the manner of the notice requirements found in Rules 404(b), 803(24) and 804(b)(5).

In camera hearing

Subdivision (c)(2) indicates that, in connection with the motion, the Court must order an *in camera* hearing, at which time the parties may call witnesses and offer other relevant evidence. The victim has a right to be heard at the *in camera* hearing. In order to protect the victim's privacy interest, the Rule provides that the record of the hearing must be sealed and remain under seal unless the Court orders otherwise.

The 1994 amendment to the Rule deleted the provision in the old Rule which addressed the problem of conditional facts, i.e., where the relevance of the evidence proffered by the defendant depends upon the fulfillment of a condition of fact. The oldRule directed the Trial Judge at the *in camera* hearing to exclude the proffered evidence unless all necessary conditional facts were proven to the Judge's satisfaction. The Advisory Committee recognized that the previous language impinged on the defendant's right to a jury trial, because it apparently authorized the Trial Judge to exclude evidence of past sexual conduct between an alleged victim and accused simply because the Trial Judge did not believe that the acts occurred. The amended Rule 412 makes no reference to conditional facts, thus leaving the matter to standard principles of Judge and jury allocation set forth in Rule 104.

Residual provision

The residual provision states that in a criminal case, evidence pertaining to the sexual history or propensity of the victim shall be admitted when its exclusion "would violate the constitutional rights of the defendant," even if the evidence does not fit one of the narrow exceptions of subdivision (b)(1). It goes without saying that, even without such a provision, Rule 412 could not take precedence over the Constitution. The unfortunate aspect of the drafting is that this residual provision forces Trial Judges to make constitutional decisions whenever a defendant wishes to offer evidence that does not fall within one of two specified categories of subdivision (b)(1). It would have been better, we believe, if the drafters of the Rule had simply told the Trial Judges in the federal system to balance the probative value of evidence against its prejudicial effect, paying particular attention to the genuine plight of the sexual assault victim. When in doubt, evidence rules should avoid constitutional problems, not invite them. But this Rule departs from the traditional approach of avoiding constitutional issues, unwisely, we fear.

Alternative approaches

As we noted at the outset of this Comment, this Rule is of great symbolic value. But our comments suggest that we have reservations about the way that it was drafted. The truth of the matter is that sex offense prosecutions are not a large part of the federal workload. Thus, Rule 412 will not affect many trials in the Federal Courts. Adoption of the Rule for the federal system hardly was as necessary as was the adoption of rape shield laws in the states. We think that there is a good argument that under Rule 403 Federal Trial Judges would have reached results that are very similar to those reached under Rule 412 with one exception: Unless Rule 405(a) were amended, Federal Judges would not have been able to admit specific instances of conduct in lieu of reputation and opinion testimony. As we have indicated, we believe that the preference here for specific instances of conduct is generally wise, although we have doubts as to whether there should be an absolute ban on reputation and opinion testimony. It might have been better to permit the Trial Judge to have discretion under Rule 403 to make an appropriate ruling to admit the "best" evidence, if any, in an individual sex offense case. This would have avoided a host of constitutional problems such as those raised in this Comment.

The residual provision — examples

The following examples of cases in which exclusion of past sexual conduct evidence would pose constitutional problems were offered by the ACLU in Hearings on H.R. 14666 (the original draft of Old Rule 412) and Other Bills Before the Subcommittee on Criminal Justice of the House Committee on the Judiciary, 94th Cong., 2d Sess., at 64 (1976). We find these examples equally pertinent to the application of amended Rule 412 and its residual exception:

> The facts of this example are adapted from In re Ferguson, 5 Cal. 3d 525 (1971). A husband and wife allege that they were hitch-hiking and were picked up by the defendant. They state that he ordered the husband out of the car at gun point and, after driving to a secluded spot, raped the wife. The defendant states that he picked up the hitch-hiking couple and shortly thereafter a bargain was struck: he would pay a certain sum of money, and in return the husband would get out of the car and the wife would engage in sexual intercourse with him. He adds that he did drop off the husband and had consensual intercourse with the wife after driving to a secluded spot.
>
> If the defense has evidence that on several nights preceding the incident in question the complaining witnesses hitch-hiked in that area, took rides with single men, bargained for an act of sexual intercourse by the wife in exchange for money, and allowed such acts to take place after dropping off the husband and driving to a secluded spot, this evidence would be inadmissible under H.R. 14666.
>
> A woman is engaged to be married and has had sexual relations with her fiance. One evening, he believes she is acting suspiciously and he questions her as to where she has been earlier that evening and what she was doing. It develops

that she has been out with another man with whom intercourse has occurred. The woman alleges that she did not consent but was raped.

Defense counsel, in attempting to show the relationship between the complainant and her fiance as a source of potential bias — the theory being that she lied to protect her relationship — will be hampered by H.R. 14666. Any facts about that relationship will be viewed by the prosecution as intimations of her prior sexual conduct and will be the source of objections. Furthermore, the intimacy of the relationship with her fiance, the fact of their sexual intimacy, may be relevant in a particular case to demonstrate the importance of the relationship to the complaining witness, her desire to protect it at any cost, and thus her reason for lying about her sexual conduct with the accused.[16]

The defendant wished to have a police officer testify that during the past year the complaining witness has accused two other persons of rape and then later admitted that the intercourse was, in fact, consensual.

The Hearings offer the best background that is available on Rule 412, and foretell the constitutional problems attendant to the current Rule.

C. ANNOTATED CASES

Constitutionally required evidence

United States v. Saunders, 943 F.2d 388 (4th Cir. 1991), *cert. denied,* 112 S. Ct. 1199 (1992): Affirming the defendant's conviction for aggravated sexual abuse, the Court held there was no error in excluding evidence of prior sexual relations between the victim and the defendant's friend. Leaving open the question whether its decision in *Doe v. United States,* 666 F.2d 43 (4th Cir. 1981), holding that evidence of the victim's reputation could be admitted when offered solely to show the accused's state of mind, was correct, the Court held it could discern no constitutional basis requiring admission of evidence about a three-day relationship between the victim and some third person. In this case, even evidence that the defendant had sexual relations with the victim was of marginal relevance, because consent was not the basis of his defense.

United States v. Bear Stops, 997 F.2d 451 (8th Cir. 1993): The Court affirmed a defendant's conviction for sexual abuse of one victim, but reversed as to another victim. The Constitution required admission of evidence that the second victim was sexually assaulted by three boys during the approximate time period of the defendant's alleged abuse, which the defendant offered as an alternative explanation for the victim's behaviors that the government had relied upon to prove that abuse had occurred. The

---

16. See the subsequent case of Olden v. Kentucky, 488 U.S. 227 (1988), where the Court found a Sixth Amendment violation. The Trial Court excluded evidence of a rape complainant's relationship with another man. The Supreme Court found that the exclusion was constitutional error because the complainant was a crucial prosecution witness, and evidence of the relationship would have provided strong evidence of a motive to lie about being raped. The facts of *Olden* are substantively identical to those set forth in the ACLU hypothetical.

Court distinguished the constitutional basis for its decision in this case from the decision (discussed *infra*) in *United States v. Shaw,* 824 F.2d 601 (8th Cir. 1987), *cert. denied,* 108 S. Ct. 1033 (1988), where it had held that a defendant may not offer evidence of a victim's sexual past to prove emotional injuries generally.

United States v. Payne, 944 F.2d 1458 (9th Cir. 1991), *cert. denied,* 112 S. Ct. 1598 (1992): Affirming the defendant's conviction for carnal knowledge of a female under age sixteen, the Court held it was no violation of confrontation rights to exclude evidence of the victim's prior sexual conduct that was irrelevant or only tenuously probative of the claims asserted by the defendant.

Notice

United States v. Eagle Thunder, 893 F.2d 950 (8th Cir. 1990): In affirming a defendant's rape conviction, the Court held that evidence of a nonrecent tear in the victim's hymenal ring was properly excluded, as the defendant failed to file a written notice of intent to offer the evidence and, in any event, it was not relevant to the source of tears that were hours old or to impeach the victim's credibility. In *United States v. Provost,* 875 F.2d 172 (8th Cir.), *cert. denied,* 110 S. Ct. 170 (1989), the Court affirmed an aggravated assault conviction and held that a defendant was procedurally barred from offering an allegedly false statement by the victim concerning another alleged assault upon her by a cousin. The defendant had failed to give fifteen days' notice as required by the Rule at that time. (The Rule now requires notice fourteen days before trial).

Other charges by the victim

United States v. Cardinal, 782 F.2d 34 (6th Cir.), *cert. denied,* 106 S. Ct. 2282 (1986): The Court affirmed a defendant's conviction for the rape of his thirteen-year-old niece, finding there was no abuse of discretion in exclusion of other instances in which the victim reported sexual assaults by family members and withdrew the charges. Assuming that the evidence was directed at credibility, not prior sexual behavior, the Court found that the basic policy of Rule 412 supported exclusion. On the facts of the case, exclusion would appear to have been warranted in light of evidence that the charges were true and were withdrawn because of fear of retaliation from the victim's mother.

United States v. Bartlett, 856 F.2d 1071 (8th Cir. 1988): Affirming the defendant's conviction of assault with intent to commit rape, the Court concluded that it was proper to exclude evidence of a prior false accusation of rape by the victim, because the circumstances were very different from this case and the evidence of a single bad act was of marginal relevance to the victim's credibility. In *United States v. Blue Horse,* 856 F.2d 1037 (8th Cir. 1988), the Court upheld the exclusion of a sexual abuse victim's medical records. A physician testified about the nature of the victim's injuries, and the report contained prejudicial information concerning the victim's last sexual intercourse.

Prior virginity

United States v. Duncan, 855 F.2d 1528 (11th Cir. 1988), *cert. denied,* 109 S. Ct. 1161 (1989): Affirming a conviction for kidnapping, the Court held that testimony by the victim of her conversation with the defendant following an uncharged rape in which she referred to her prior virginity was properly admitted as part of a chronological reconstruction of the evening and to respond to a defense argument about her failure to escape.

Psychiatric examinations

Government of Virgin Islands v. Scuito, 623 F.2d 869 (3d Cir. 1980): The Court cited the spirit of Rule 412 as authority for upholding the Trial Judge's decision denying a rape defendant's motion for a psychiatric examination of the victim.

Relationship to other rules

United States v. One Feather, 702 F.2d 736 (8th Cir. 1983): The Court upheld a rape conviction, finding no error in precluding the defendant from asking the victim, who testified on direct examination that she was divorced and had an infant son, where her marriage and divorce took place. The defendant had been unable to find applicable records and believed that the witness had lied. Citing Rule 412 as persuasive authority, the Court found that the Trial Judge properly relied on Rule 403 to bar the questioning, since it would have suggested that the victim had an illegitimate child, which might be unfairly prejudicial against her.

Source of semen or injury

United States v. Bear Stops, 997 F.2d 451 (8th Cir. 1993): The Court affirmed a defendant's conviction for sexual abuse of one victim, but reversed as to another victim. The Constitution required admission of evidence that the second victim was sexually assaulted by three boys during the approximate time period as the defendant's alleged abuse, which the defendant offered as an alternative explanation for the victim's behaviors that the government had relied upon to prove that abuse had occurred. In *United States v. Azure,* 845 F.2d 1503 (8th Cir. 1988), the Court held that evidence that a thirteen-year-old boy had had sexual relations with the ten-year-old victim was properly excluded as irrelevant to the source of a laceration on the victim's vaginal wall, since the victim did not express discomfort at the time of the prior sexual activity and physicians testified that the laceration would have been inflicted by force and have been painful.

United States v. Torres, 937 F.2d 1469 (9th Cir. 1991), *cert. denied,* 112 S. Ct. 886 (1992): The Court, in affirming a conviction for aggravated sexual abuse, held that the Rule includes sexual behavior of the victim after the alleged incident, but that evidence of an incident involving the victim six months later was not relevant in the cross-examination of the victim or in determining the source of semen found in the victim's panties. In *United States v. Begay,* 937 F.2d 515 (10th Cir. 1991), the Court reversed a conviction for sexual abuse of a child because the defendant had been precluded from cross-examining the witness about prior sexual contacts. Particularly where there was physical evidence that the victim's conditions could have resulted from earlier conduct with another person, examination regarding the prior incidents was relevant and probative on the central issue of whether the victim's memory was clear and accurate on critical details about the charged incident as contrasted with the earlier incidents.

D. LEGISLATIVE HISTORY

Editor's Note: There is no legislative history to the original Rule 412. Nor is there legislative history to the amended Rule 412, which was passed as part of the Violent Crime Control and Law Enforcement Act of 1994. Congress did in that Act, however, adopt verbatim the version of Rule 412 recommended by the Advisory Committee. The Advisory Committee proposal had been rejected by the Supreme Court in favor of a slightly different version, but Congress chose the Advisory Committee's version over that adopted by the Supreme Court. Accordingly, we include the Advisory Committee's Note on amended Rule 412, as at least some indication of the legislative intent behind amended Rule 412:

Advisory Committee's Note

Rule 412 has been revised to diminish some of the confusion engendered by the original rule and to expand the protection afforded alleged victims of sexual misconduct. Rule 412 applies to both civil and criminal proceedings. The rule aims to safeguard the alleged victim against the invasion of privacy, potential embarrassment and sexual stereotyping that is associated with public disclosure of intimate sexual details and the infusion of sexual innuendo into the factfinding process. By affording victims protection in most instances, the rule also encourages victims of sexual misconduct to institute and to participate in legal proceedings against alleged offenders.

Rule 412 seeks to achieve these objectives by barring evidence relating to the alleged victim's sexual behavior or alleged sexual predisposition, whether offered as substantive evidence or for impeachment, except in designated circumstances in which the probative value of the evidence significantly outweighs possible harm to the victim.

The revised rule applies in all cases involving sexual misconduct without regard to whether the alleged victim or person accused is a party to the litigation. Rule 412 extends to "pattern" witnesses in both criminal and civil cases whose testimony about other instances of sexual misconduct by the person accused is otherwise admissible. When the case does not involve alleged sexual misconduct, evidence relating to a third-party witness' alleged sexual activities is not within the ambit of Rule 412. The witness will, however, be protected by other rules such as Rules 404 and 608, as well as Rule 403.

The terminology "alleged victim" is used because there will frequently be a factual dispute as to whether sexual misconduct occurred. It does not connote any requirement that the misconduct be alleged in the pleadings. Rule 412 does not, however, apply unless the person against whom the evidence is offered can reasonably be characterized as a "victim of alleged sexual misconduct." When this is not the case, as for instance in a defamation action involving statements concerning sexual misconduct in which the evidence is offered to show that the alleged defamatory statements were true or did not damage the plaintiff's reputation, neither Rule 404 nor this rule will operate to bar the evidence; Rule 401 and 403 will continue to control. Rule 412 will, however, apply in a Title VII action in which the plaintiff has alleged sexual harassment.

The reference to a person "accused" is also used in a non-technical sense. There is no requirement that there be a criminal charge pending against the person or even that the misconduct would constitute a criminal offense. Evidence offered to prove allegedly false prior claims by the victim is not barred by Rule 412. However, this evidence is subject to the requirements of Rule 404.

Subdivision (a). As amended, Rule 412 bars evidence offered to prove the victim's sexual behavior and alleged sexual predisposition. Evidence, which might otherwise be admissible under Rules 402, 404(b), 405, 607, 608, 609, or some other evidence rule, must be excluded if Rule 412 so requires. The word "other" is used to suggest some flexibility in admitting evidence "intrinsic" to the alleged sexual misconduct. *Cf.* Committee Note to 1991 amendment to Rule 404(b).

Past sexual behavior connotes all activities that involve actual physical conduct, i.e. sexual intercourse and sexual contact, or that imply sexual intercourse or sexual contact. *See, e.g., United States v. Galloway,* 937 F.2d 542 (10th Cir. 1991), *cert. denied,* 113 S. Ct. 418 (1992) (use of contraceptives inadmissible since use implies sexual activity); *United States v. One Feather,* 702 F.2d 736 (8th Cir. 1983) (birth of an illegitimate child inadmissible); *State v. Carmichael,* 727 P.2d 918, 925 (Kan. 1986) (evidence of venereal disease inadmissible). In addition, the word "behavior" should be construed to include activities of the mind, such as fantasies or dreams. *See* 23 C. Wright & K. Graham, Jr., *Federal Practice and Procedure,* § 5384 at p. 548 (1980) ("While there may be some doubt under statutes that require 'conduct,' it would seem that the language of Rule 412 is broad enough to encompass the behavior of the mind.").

The rule has been amended to also exclude all other evidence relating to an alleged victim of sexual misconduct that is offered to prove a sexual predisposition. This amendment is designed to exclude evidence that does not directly refer to sexual activities or thoughts but that the proponent believes may have a sexual connotation for the factfinder. Admission of such evidence would contravene Rule 412's objectives of shielding the alleged victim from potential embarrassment and safeguarding the victim against stereotypical thinking. Consequently, unless the (b)(2) exception is satisfied, evidence such as that relating to the alleged victim's mode of dress, speech, or life-style will not be admissible.

The introductory phrase in subdivision (a) was deleted because it lacked clarity and contained no explicit reference to the other provisions of law that were intended to be overridden. The conditional clause, "except as provided in subdivisions (b) and (c)" is intended to make clear that evidence of the types described in subdivision (a) is admissible only under the strictures of those sections.

The reason for extending the rule to all criminal cases is obvious. The strong social policy of protecting a victim's privacy and encouraging victims to come forward to report criminal acts is not confined to cases that involve a charge of sexual assault. The need to protect the victim is equally great when a defendant is charged with kidnapping, and evidence is offered, either to prove motive or as background, that the defendant sexually assaulted the victim.

The reason for extending Rule 412 to civil cases is equally obvious. The need to protect alleged victims against invasions of privacy, potential embarrassment, and unwarranted sexual stereotyping, and the wish to encourage victims to come forward when they have been sexually molested do not disappear because the context has shifted from a criminal prosecution to a claim for damages or injunctive relief. There is a strong social policy in not only punishing those who engage in sexual misconduct, but in also providing relief to the victim. Thus, Rule 412 applies in any civil case in which a person claims to be the victim of sexual misconduct, such as actions for sexual battery or sexual harassment.

Subdivision (b). Subdivision (b) spells out the specific circumstances in which some evidence may be admissible that would otherwise be barred by the general rule expressed in subdivision (a). As amended, Rule 412 will be virtually unchanged in criminal cases, but will provide protection to any person alleged to be a victim of sexual misconduct regardless of the charge actually brought against an accused. A new exception has been added for civil cases.

In a criminal case, evidence may be admitted under subdivision (b)(1) pursuant to three possible exceptions, provided the evidence also satisfies other requirements for admissibility specified in the Federal Rules of Evidence, including Rule 403. Subdivisions (b)(1)(A) and (b)(1)(B) require proof in the form of specific instances of sexual behavior in recognition of the limited probative value and dubious reliability of evidence of reputation or evidence in the form of an opinion.

Under subdivision (b)(1)(A), evidence of specific instances of sexual behavior with persons other than the person whose sexual misconduct is alleged may be admissible if it is offered to prove that another person was the source of semen, injury or other physical evidence. Where the prosecution has directly or indirectly asserted that the physical evidence originated with the accused, the defendant must be afforded an opportunity to prove that another person was responsible. *See United States v. Begay,* 937 F.2d 515, 523 n. 10 (10th Cir. 1991). Evidence offered for the specific purpose identified in this subdivision may still be excluded if it does not satisfy Rules 401 or 403. *See, e.g., United States v. Azure,* 845 F.2d 1503, 1505-06 (8th Cir. 1988) (10 year old victim's injuries indicated recent use of force; court excluded evidence of consensual sexual activities with witness who testified at in camera hearing that he had never hurt victim and failed to establish recent activities).

Under the exception in subdivision (b)(1)(B), evidence of specific instances of sexual behavior with respect to the person whose sexual misconduct is alleged is admissible if offered to prove consent, or offered by the prosecution. Admissible pursuant to this exception might be evidence of prior instances of sexual activities between the alleged victim and the accused, as well as statements in which the alleged victim expressed an intent to engage in sexual intercourse with accused, or voiced sexual fantasies involving the specific accused. In a prosecution for child sexual abuse, for example, evidence of uncharged sexual activity between the accused and the alleged victim offered by the prosecution may be admissible pursuant to Rule 404(b) to show a pattern of behavior. Evidence relating to the victim's alleged sexual predisposition is not admissible pursuant to this exception.

Under subdivision (b)(1)(C), evidence of specific instances of conduct may not be excluded if the result would be to deny a criminal defendant the protections afforded by the Constitution. For example, statements in which the victim has expressed an intent to have sex with the first person encountered on a particular occasion might not be excluded without violating the due process right of a rape defendant seeking to prove consent. Recognition of this basic principle was expressed in subdivision (b)(1) of the original rule. The United States Supreme Court has recognized that in various circumstances a defendant may have a right to introduce evidence otherwise precluded by an evidence rule under the Confrontation Clause. *See, e.g., Olden v. Kentucky,* 488 U.S. 227 (1988) (defendant in rape cases had right to inquire into alleged victim's cohabitation with another man to show bias).

Subdivision (b)(2) governs the admissibility of otherwise proscribed evidence in civil cases. It employs a balancing test rather than the specific exceptions stated in subdivision (b)(1) in recognition of the difficulty of foreseeing future developments in the law. Greater flexibility is needed to accommodate evolving causes of action such as claims for sexual harassment.

The balancing test requires the proponent of the evidence, whether plaintiff or defendant, to convince the court that the probative value of the proffered evidence "substantially outweighs the danger of harm to any victim and of unfair prejudice of any party." This test for admitting evidence offered to prove sexual behavior or sexual propensity in civil cases differs in three respects from the general rule governing admissibility set forth in Rule 403. First, it reverses the usual procedure spelled out in Rule 403 by shifting the burden to the proponent to demonstrate admissibility rather than making the opponent justify exclusion of the evidence. Second, the standard expressed in subdivision (b)(2) is more stringent than in the original rule; it raises the threshold for admission by requiring that the probative value of the evidence *substantially* outweigh the specified dangers. Finally, the Rule 412 test puts "harm to the victim" on the scale in addition to prejudice to the parties.

Evidence of reputation may be received in a civil case only if the alleged victim has put his or her reputation into controversy. The victim may do so without making a specific allegation in a pleading. *Cf.* Fed. R. Civ. P. 35(a).

Subdivision (c). Amended subdivision (c) is more concise and understandable than the subdivision it replaces. The requirement of a motion before trial is continued in the amended rule, as is the provision that a late motion may be permitted for good cause shown. In deciding whether to permit late filing, the court may take into account the conditions previously included in the rule: namely whether the evidence is newly discovered and could not have been obtained earlier through the existence of due diligence, and whether the issue to which such evidence relates has newly arisen in the case. The rule recognizes that in some instances the circumstances that justify an application to introduce evidence otherwise barred by Rule 412 will not become apparent until trial.

The amended rule provides that before admitting evidence that falls within the prohibition of Rule 412(a), the court must hold a hearing in camera at which the alleged victim and any party must be afforded the right to be present and an opportunity to be heard. All papers connected with the motion and any record of a hearing on the motion must be kept and remain under seal during the course of trial and appellate proceedings unless otherwise ordered. This is to assure that the privacy of the alleged victim is preserved in all cases in which the court rules that proffered evidence is not admissible, and in which the hearing refers to matters that are not received, or are received in another form.

The procedures set forth in subdivision (c) do not apply to discovery of a victim's past sexual conduct or predisposition in civil cases, which will be continued to be governed by Fed. R. Civ. P. 26. In order not to undermine the rationale of Rule 412, however, courts should enter appropriate orders pursuant to Fed. R. Civ. P. 26(c) to protect the victim against unwarranted inquiries and to ensure confidentiality. Courts should presumptively issue protective orders barring discovery unless the party seeking discovery makes a showing that the evidence sought to be discovered would be relevant under the facts and theories of the particular case, and cannot be obtained except through discovery. In an action for sexual harassment, for instance, while some evidence of the alleged victim's sexual behavior and/or predisposition in the workplace may perhaps be relevant, non-work place conduct will usually be irrelevant. *Cf. Burns v. McGregor Electronic Industries, Inc.,* 989 F.2d 959, 962-63 (8th Cir. 1993) (posing for a nude magazine outside work hours is irrelevant to issue of unwelcomeness of sexual advances at work). Confidentiality orders should be presumptively granted as well.

One substantive change made in subdivision (c) is the elimination of the following sentence: "Notwithstanding subdivision (b) of Rule 104, if the relevancy of the evidence which the accused seeks to offer in the trial depends upon the fulfillment of a condition of fact, the court, at the hearing in chambers or at a subsequent hearing in chambers scheduled for such purpose, shall accept evidence on the issue of whether such condition of fact is fulfilled and shall determine such issue." On its face, this language would appear to authorize a trial judge to exclude evidence of past sexual conduct between an alleged victim and an accused or a defendant in a civil case based upon the judge's belief that such past acts did not occur. Such an authorization raises questions of invasion of the right to a jury trial under the Sixth and Seventh Amendments. *See* 1 S. Saltzburg & M. Martin, *Federal Rules Of Evidence Manual,* 396-97 (5th ed. 1990).

The Advisory Committee concluded that the amended rule provided adequate protection for all persons claiming to be the victims of sexual misconduct, and that it was inadvisable to continue to include a provision in the rule that has been confusing and that raises substantial constitutional issues.

RULE 413

A. OFFICIAL TEXT

[Editor's Note: This Rule was enacted on September 13, 1994 as part of the Violent Crime Control and Enforcement Act of 1994 (P.L. 103-322). The Act gives the Judicial Conference 150 days from the date of enactment to recommend amendments to the Rule. If the Judicial Conference fails to make recommendations within the allotted time period, the Rule becomes effective 300 days after its original enactment, unless Congress provides otherwise. If the Judicial Conference makes a recommendation approving the Rule, then the Rule becomes effective 30 days after the transmittal of the Judicial Conference recommendations. If the Judicial Conference makes a recommendation inconsistent with the Rule, then the Rule becomes effective 150 days after the transmittal of the recommendation, unless Congress provides otherwise.]

Rule 413. Evidence of Similar Crimes in Sexual Assault Cases

(a) In a criminal case in which the defendant is accused of an offense of sexual assault, evidence of the defendant's commission of another offense or offenses of sexual assault is admissible, and may be considered for its bearing on any matter to which it is relevant.

(b) In a case in which the Government intends to offer evidence under this rule, the attorney for the Government shall disclose the evidence to the defendant, including statements of witnesses or a summary of the substance of any testimony that is expected to be offered, at least fifteen days before the scheduled date of trial or at such later time as the court may allow for good cause.

(c) This rule shall not be construed to limit the admission or consideration of evidence under any other rule.

(d) For purposes of this rule and Rule 415, "offense of sexual assaults" means a crime under Federal law or the law of a State (as defined in section 513 of title 18, United States Code) that involved —

(1) any conduct proscribed by chapter 109A of title 18, United States Code;

(2) contact, without consent, between any part of the defendant's body or an object and the genitals or anus of another person;

(3) contact, without consent, between the genitals or anus of the defendant and any part of another person's body;

(4) deriving sexual pleasure or gratification from the infliction of death, bodily injury, or physical pain on another person; or

(5) an attempt or conspiracy to engage in conduct described in paragraph (1)-(4).

B. EDITORIAL EXPLANATORY COMMENT

Background of the Rule

This Rule is intended to provide for more liberal admissibility in sexual assault cases where the defendant has committed a prior act or acts of sexual assault. Congress passed this Rule, together with Rules 414 and 415, as part of a general Crime Bill package, and bypassed the ordinary rulemaking process in doing so.[1] As a compromise, Congress provided for the possibility of reconsideration should the Judicial Conference make a timely objection to the new Rules. Given the fervor with which this Rule was originally passed, however, it is quite unlikely that Congress will change its mind as to the need for the Rule. There is some hope, however, that the Rule will be amended to clarify some of its ambiguities.

Scope of the Rule

The Rule applies only to sexual assault cases, and only covers evidence of the defendant's prior sexual assaults. So for example, if the defendant is charged with kidnapping, a prior sexual assault on the victim (or on any other victim, for that matter), is not covered by this Rule. Presumably the Rule is inapplicable even if the defendant kidnapped the victim with a motive of sexual assault. The Rule is limited to criminal cases "in which the defendant is accused of an offense" of sexual assault. A fair reading of the provision is that the defendant must actually be charged with a sexual assault. Likewise, if the defendant is charged with sexual assault, a previous act of kidnapping or aggravated battery is not covered by this Rule.

This is not to say the uncharged misconduct alluded to above will be inadmissible. It is simply to say that admissibility is dependent upon Rules 404(b) and 403 and, if the defendant takes the stand, Rules 608 and 609.

Rule 413 appears to be an attempt to create an exception to Rule 404(b) in sexual assault cases, where the prosecution wishes to offer a previous act of sexual assault committed by the defendant.[2] Under Rule 404(b), the prosecution would have to articulate a not-for-character purpose for a prior act of sexual assault, such as intent or motive. The prosecution would be prohibited by Rule 404(b) from offering the prior sexual assault simply to prove that the defendant has a propensity to commit sex crimes. Under Rule 413, however, it appears that the prosecution can offer a prior act of sexual

---

1. See 113 CONG. REC. H5439 (statement of Congressman Hughes), noting that the "existing rule-making process involves a minimum of six levels of scrutiny or stages of formal review. This has gone through none. This is an amendment offered on the floor of the Senate after about 20 minutes' debate, without very much thought, and it is procedurally and substantively flawed."

2. See the statement of Senator Biden in Section D, *infra*.

assault explicitly to prove the defendant's character. A limiting instruction is not required, since the jury is free to use the prior act of sexual misconduct as evidence that the defendant has a propensity to commit sex crimes.

It is an anomaly of Rule 413 that it singles out sexual assault crimes for special treatment. Assume that a defendant is being tried for a rape-murder, and has two different prior bad acts in his past — a rape and a murder. Under the Rule, the prior rape can be admitted even if it is offered solely to prove propensity, while the murder cannot be admitted without the articulation of a not-for-propensity purpose.

One justification for this differentiation, however, is that sexual assault crimes pose unique difficulties of proof. Often there is no physical evidence that ties the defendant to the charged crime; often the jury must make credibility determination between the victim and the defendant. Given these limitations, one can at least understand, if not sympathize with, Congress' desire to single out sexual assault crimes for special treatment.[3]

On the other hand, if Rule 413 is merely an exception to Rule 404, the necessity for the Rule is questionable. In the relatively few sex crime cases that have been tried in the federal Courts, prosecutors have rarely had difficulty in articulating a not-for-character purpose for a prior act of sexual assault. As discussed in the Editorial Explanatory Comment to Rule 404(b), the Courts have looked on Rule 404(b) as a rule of inclusion. So long as the prosecution can articulate any colorable not-for-propensity purpose, the Courts generally consider Rule 404(b) satisfied, and proceed to balance the probative value of the evidence against its prejudicial effect under Rule 403. Thus there is little evidence that an exception to Rule 404(b) was needed for prior sexual assault crimes.

Relationship to Rule 403

The most important question about the application of Rule 413 is whether the Rule permits the Trial Judge to invoke Rule 403 to exclude sexual assault evidence that is unduly prejudicial. It is unclear from the statutory language whether Rule 413 pre-empts Rule 403.

Some clues can be derived by comparing Rule 413 with other Federal Rules which clearly displace Rule 403. The most prominent example, Rule 609, provides that *crimen falsi* convictions (covered by Rule 609(a)(2)) "shall be admitted." In addition, special balancing tests are specifically provided for convictions offered against the accused (Rule 609 (a)(1)), and for convictions more than ten years old (Rule 609(b)). Similarly, Rule 412 sets forth an explicit balancing test for civil cases, different from that provided in Rule 403, for evidence of the victim's sexual activity.

In contrast to these two Rules, Rule 413 contains neither mandatory language nor a special balancing test. The Rule states that evidence of a prior act of sexual assault "is admissible," not that it shall be admitted. It further states that such evidence "*may* be considered for its bearing on any matter to which it is relevant." Notably, there is no

---

3. See 133 CONG. REC. H5439 (statement of Congressman Kyl): "In most rape or molestation cases, it is the word of the defendant against the word of the victim. If the defendant has committed similar acts in the past, the claims of the victim are more likely to be considered truthful if there is substantiation of other assaults."

specific balancing test for the evidence set forth in the Rule, which could arguably displace the Rule 403 test.

It should also be noted that Representative Molinari, who was responsible for inserting Rule 413 into the Violent Crime Control and Enforcement Act, had previously sponsored an identical provision. Representative Molinari stated, as to that provision, that it was not intended to pre-empt Rule 403. See 137 Cong. Rec. H3503-02 (Oct.22, 1991). While this is slender legislative history, it does support the conclusion that Rule 413 does not displace the Rule 403 balancing test.[4]

Even assuming, however, that Rule 403 remains applicable, it appears that Rule 413 mandates a change in the way Courts have traditionally balanced the probative value and prejudicial effect of prior acts of sexual assault. Rule 413 states that sexual assault evidence may be considered for its bearing on any matter to which the prior act could not be considered even though it was relevant, i.e., the defendant's propensity to commit sex crimes. In contrast, Rule 413 provides that the Trial Court is to consider the prior act as probative of the defendant's propensity to commit the crime charged. Consequently, the Rule 403 balancing test is less likely to result in the exclusion of prior acts of sexual misconduct than was the case before Rule 413 was passed. Congress has instructed the Courts to find more probative value in such evidence than the Courts were previously permitted to find.

Notice

The Rule requires the prosecution to notify the defendant of the intended use of sexual assault evidence. Notice must be provided at least fifteen days before the scheduled date of trial, unless the Court allows later notice for good cause shown.

C. ANNOTATED CASES

None.

D. LEGISLATIVE HISTORY

Rule 413 is not a product of the usual Federal Rules rulemaking process. Consequently, there is no Advisory Committee Note. We include a statement in favor of the Rule, made on the floor of the Senate, by Senator Dole, and a statement in opposition to the Rule made by Senator Biden.

Statement of Senator Dole:

[T]oo often, crucial evidentiary information is thrown out at trial because of technical evidentiary rulings. This amendment is designed to clarify the law and make clear what evidence is admissible, and what evidence is not admissible, in sex crime cases.

---

4. See also 113 CONG. REC. H5438 (1993) (statement of Congressman Kyl), stating that under the Rule, the ''judge still has total discretion to exclude the evidence if its probative value is substantially outweighed by the danger of unfair prejudice to the defendant.''

The amendment would create a new rule 413 of the Federal Rules of Evidence. This new rule would provide that in a criminal case in which the defendant is accused of assault, evidence of the defendant's commission of another offense or offenses of sexual assault is admissible, and may be considered for its bearing on any matter to which it is relevant.

....

... I think if somebody is a repeat offender, if you brought in eight or nine women, for example,... and he had one offense after another, it would be probative. If it had not happened for 10 years, it probably would not have any value.

We also provide protection for the defendant because we require the Government to disclose the evidence to the defendant, including a statement of witnesses or a summary of the substance of any testimony expected to be offered at least 15 days before the scheduled date or trial, or at such later time as the court may allow for good cause.

... [I]f we are really going to get tough, and if we are really going to try to make certain that justice is provided for the victim as well as the defendant, of course, then I think we ought to look seriously at this.

113 Cong. Rec. S15072-3.

Statement of Senator Biden

[W]hat the Republican leader is doing is changing 404(b) of the Federal Rules of Criminal Procedure [sic] .... Right now the rule in a courtroom in a Federal court is you go in and if you wish to introduce evidence of a similar crime ... you can only do it under very limited circumstances ... as proof of motive, opportunity, intent, preparation, plan, knowledge, identity, or absence of a mistake or accident. These are the only circumstances in which you can offer this as evidence.... There is a reason for that. These rules of relevancy ... it took essentially 800 years to develop the rules of evidence under our English jurisprudence system.... We found out from 800 years of experience that [evidence of prior crimes] tends to blind people [from] looking at the real facts before them and making an independent judgment, at this time, at this circumstance, at this situation, that this defendant did that thing.

113 Cong. Rec. S15072

RULE 414

A. OFFICIAL TEXT

[Editor's Note: This Rule was enacted on September 13, 1994 as part of the Violent Crime Control and Enforcement Act of 1994 (P.L. 103-322). The Act gives the Judicial Conference 150 days from the date of enactment to recommend amendments to the Rule. If the Judicial Conference fails to make recommendations within the allotted time period, the Rule becomes effective 300 days after its original enactment, unless Congress provides otherwise. If the Judicial Conference makes a recommendation approving the Rule, then the Rule becomes effective 30 days after the transmittal of the Judicial Conference recommendations. If the Judicial Conference makes a recommendation inconsistent with the Rule, then the Rule becomes effective 150 days after the transmittal of the recommendation, unless Congress provides otherwise.]

Rule 414. Evidence of Similar Crimes in Child Molestation Cases

(a) In a criminal case in which the defendant is accused of an offense of child molestation, evidence of the defendant's commission of another offense or offenses of child molestation is admissible, and may be considered for its bearing on any matter to which it is relevant.

(b) In a case in which the Government intends to offer evidence under this rule, the attorney for the Government shall disclose the evidence to the defendant, including statements of witnesses or a summary of the substance of any testimony that is expected to be offered, at least fifteen days before the scheduled date of trial or at such later time as the court may allow for good cause.

(c) This rule shall not be construed to limit the admission or consideration of evidence under any other rule.

(d) For purposes of this rule and Rule 415, "child" means a person below the age of fourteen, and "offense of child molestation" means a crime under Federal law or the law of a State (as defined in section 513 of title 18, United States Code) that involved —

(1) any conduct proscribed by chapter 109A of title 18, United States Code, that was committed in relation to a child;

(2) any conduct proscribed by chapter 110 of title 18, United States Code;

(3) contact between any part of the defendant's body or an object and the genitals or anus of a child;

(4) contact between the genitals or anus of the defendant and any part of the body of a child;

(5) deriving sexual pleasure or gratification from the infliction of death, bodily injury, or physical pain on a child; or

(6) an attempt or conspiracy to engage in conduct described in paragraph (1)-(5).

B. EDITORIAL EXPLANATORY COMMENT

Background of the Rule

This Rule is intended to provide for more liberal admissibility in criminal cases of child molestation where the defendant has committed a prior act or acts of child molestation. Congress passed this Rule, together with Rules 413 and 415, as part of a general Crime Bill package, and bypassed the ordinary rulemaking process in doing so. As a compromise, Congress provided for the possibility of reconsideration should the Judicial Conference make a timely objection to the new Rules. Given the fervor with which this Rule was originally passed, however, it is quite unlikely that Congress will change its mind as to the need for the Rule. There is some hope, however, that the Rule will be amended to clarify some of its ambiguities.

Scope of the Rule

Rule 414 is essentially identical to Rule 413, with the exception that the term "child molestation" is substituted for the term "sexual assault." As such, the questions of scope considered under Rule 413 are equally applicable to Rule 414. To summarize:

1. Rule 414 does not apply unless the defendant is charged with child molestation and the prior act offered is one of child molestation.

2. Rule 414 provides an exception to Rule 404(b). The prior act can be admitted explicitly to prove the propensity of the defendant to commit an act of child molestation.

3. It is unclear whether the Judge can use Rule 403 to exclude a prior act of child molestation on the ground that its probative value is substantially outweighed by its prejudicial effect. A fair reading of the Rule, as well as some statements by its sponsors in Congress, indicates that Rule 403 remains applicable.

4. Even if Rule 403 is applicable, the balancing test is different from that traditionally applied to uncharged misconduct evidence. The Trial Judge must consider the probative value of a prior act of child molestation in proving the defendant's propensity to commit the act charged, as well as any other probative value the evidence may have, e.g., to prove motive, intent, etc.

5. The Rule contains a notice requirement.

See the Editorial Explanatory Comment to Rule 413 for further discussion.

C. ANNOTATED CASES

None.

D. LEGISLATIVE HISTORY

Rule 414 is not a product of the usual Federal Rules rulemaking process. Consequently, there is no Advisory Committee Note. The Rule was considered by Congress together with Rules 413 and 415. A statement by Senator Dole in favor of the proposed rules, and by Senator Biden in opposition to the proposed rules, is included in the Legislative History to Rule 413.

RULE 415

A. OFFICIAL TEXT

[Editor's Note: This Rule was enacted on September 13, 1994 as part of the Violent Crime Control and Enforcement Act of 1994 (P.L. 103-322). The Act gives the Judicial Conference 150 days from the date of enactment to recommend amendments to the Rule. If the Judicial Conference fails to make recommendations within the allotted time period, the Rule becomes effective 300 days after its original enactment, unless Congress provides otherwise. If the Judicial Conference makes a recommendation approving the Rule, then the Rule becomes effective 30 days after the transmittal of the Judicial Conference recommendations. If the Judicial Conference makes a recommendation inconsistent with the Rule, then the Rule becomes effective 150 days after the transmittal of the recommendation, unless Congress provides otherwise.]

Rule 415. Evidence of Similar Acts in Civil Cases Concerning Sexual Assault or Child Molestation

(a) In a civil case in which a claim for damages or other relief is predicated on a party's alleged commission of conduct constituting an offense of sexual assault or child molestation, evidence of that party's commission of another offense or offenses of sexual assault or child molestation is admissible and may be considered as provided in Rule 413 and Rule 414 of these Rules.

(b) A party who intends to offer evidence under this Rule shall disclose the evidence to the party against whom it will be offered, including statements of witnesses or a summary of the substance of any testimony that is expected to be offered, at least fifteen days before the scheduled date of trial or at such later time as the court may allow for good cause.

(c) This rule shall not be construed to limit the admission or consideration of evidence under any other rule.

B. EDITORIAL EXPLANATORY COMMENT

Background of the Rule

This Rule is intended to provide for more liberal admissibility in civil cases concerning child molestation or sexual assault, where a party (usually the defendant) has committed a prior act or acts of child molestation or sexual assault. Congress passed this Rule, together with Rules 413 and 414, as part of a general Crime Bill package, and bypassed the ordinary rulemaking process in doing so. As a compromise, Congress provided for the possibility of reconsideration should the Judicial Conference make a timely objection to the new rules. Given the fervor with which this Rule was originally passed, however, it is quite unlikely that Congress will change its mind as to the need for the Rule.

Scope of the Rule

Rule 415 simply applies Rules 413 and 414 to civil cases involving sexual assault or child molestation. As such, the questions of scope considered under Rules 413 and 414 are equally applicable to Rule 415. To summarize:

1. Rule 415 does not apply unless relief is predicated on a party's commission of sexual assault or child molestation. It does not apply to sexual discrimination or sexual harassment that does not involve sexual assault, as that term is defined in Rule 413. Moreover, the only bad acts admitted under the Rule are those involving sexual assault or child molestation (as defined in Rules 413 and 414). Other bad acts are not covered by the Rule, even if they would be probative to prove a claim of sexual assault or child molestation.

2. Rule 415 (by way of incorporating Rules 413 and 414) provides an exception to the limitation on character evidence set forth in Rule 404(b). A prior act of sexual assault or child molestation can be admitted explicitly to prove the propensity of the party to commit the act alleged by the offering party.

3. It is unclear whether the Trial Judge can use Rule 403 to exclude a prior act of child molestation or sexual assault on the ground that its probative value is substantially outweighed by its prejudicial effect. A fair reading of the Rule, as well as some statements by its sponsors in Congress, indicates that Rule 403 remains applicable.

4. Even if Rule 403 is applicable, the balancing test is different from that traditionally applied to uncharged misconduct evidence. The Trial Judge must consider the probative value of a prior act of child molestation or sexual assault in proving the party's propensity to commit the act alleged, as well as any other probative value the evidence may have, e.g., to prove motive, intent, etc.

5. The Rule contains a notice requirement.

See the Editorial Explanatory Comment to Rule 413 for further discussion.

C. ANNOTATED CASES

None.

D. LEGISLATIVE HISTORY

Rule 415 is not a product of the rulemaking process. Consequently, there is no Advisory Committee Note. The Rule was considered by Congress together with Rules 413 and 414. A statement by Senator Dole in favor of the proposed rules, and by Senator Biden in opposition to the proposed rules, is included in the Legislative History to Rule 413.